FAILURE
FAMILY LAW REFORM AUSTRALIA

JOHN STAPLETON

Failure Family Law Reform Australia
Copyright © 2025 John Stapleton
All rights reserved.
Print ISBN: 978-0-6482933-5-4
Ebook ISBN: 978-0-6482933-4-7
Published by A Sense of Place Publishing 2025

Reviewers, editors and any interested parties may use any of the material in this book with attribution.

While the author retains copyright, it is published under a Creative Commons License, meaning the material herein is free to use. The copyright in this publication is licensed under a Creative Commons Attribution (CC BY) 4.0 International licence.

In essence, you are free to copy, communicate and adapt this presentation, as long as you attribute the work to the book Failure Family Law Reform Australia by author John Stapleton.

Cover design by Jessica Bell
Logistical support Sue Price

 A catalogue record for this book is available from the National Library of Australia

TABLE OF CONTENTS

Introduction 14
One Disaster Looming 34
Two A Little Bit of History 49
Three The Evidence Is In 76
Four Men and the Media 82
Five Dads On The Air 100
Six Jailing Parents. 117
Seven Christmas Day 136
Eight Setting the Hares Running .147
Nine Autocue: Early Days 168
Ten The Weight of Evidence: Individuals Before the Inquiry 194
Eleven Tales from the Submissions 237
Twelve Chief Justice Alastair Nicholson the Final Days. 261
Thirteen The Curious Retirement of Alastair Nicholson,
    Chief Justice of the Family Court of Australia 284
Fourteen Before the Storm 307
Fifteen The Liars the Lawyers the Bureaucrats and the Social Engineers
    Win the Day. 327
Sixteen The Twilight Zone 399
Seventeen Make No Mistake About It 430
Eighteen Worst Case Scenario 444
Nineteen The Blessed Barbara Biggs 471
Twenty Swings and Roundabouts. 491
Twenty-One The Gillard Chapter 532
Twenty-Two Pauline Hanson Gets Snowed 547
Twenty-Three Enough is Enough .560
Twenty-Four At the End of the Long March 580
Postscript 589
Acknowledgements 593
About the Author. 597

LIST OF FAMILY LAW INQUIRIES AND REPORTS

Since its inception the *Family Law Act 1975* (Family Law Act) has been amended by more than 110 separate Acts of the Commonwealth Parliament. It has grown from 57 pages to well over 700 pages.

The principal source for the following list of family law inquiries and reports is the Australian Parliamentary Library.

The *Family Law Act 1975* received Royal Assent on 12 June 1975 and commenced on 5 January 1976.

This list includes parliamentary committee reports into the provisions of family law Bills. The list does not include reports on family law inquiries conducted by state or territory governments.

The Parliamentary Library notes that while a broad scope has been adopted in compiling this list of relevant inquiries and reports, there may be some inadvertent omissions.

1974 Senate Standing Committee on Constitutional and Legal Affairs, Law and administration of divorce and related matters, and the clauses of the Family Law Bill 1974, Final Report, October 1974.

1980 Joint Select Committee on the Family Law Act, Family law in Australia, August 1980. (Volume 1 and Volume 2)

1986 P McDonald (ed), Settling up: Property and income distribution on divorce in Australia, Australian Institute of Family Studies, 1986.

1987 Australian Law Reform Commission, Matrimonial property, Report No. 39, 1987.

1987 Family Law Council, Access–some options for reform, 1987.

1988 Family Law Council, Arbitration in family law, February 1988.

1991 Joint Select Committee on Certain Aspects of the Operation and Interpretation of the Family Law Act, The retiring age of judges of the Family Court of Australia, September 1991.

1992 Family Law Council, Patterns of parenting after separation, April 1992.

1992 Family Law Council, The interaction of bankruptcy and family law, June 1992.

1992 Joint Select Committee on Certain Aspects of the Operation and Interpretation of the Family Law Act, Family Law Act 1975: Aspects of its operation and interpretation, November 1992.

1994 Australian Law Reform Commission, Equality before the law: Justice for women, Report No. 69, Part 1, 1994, Chapter 9: Violence and family law.

1994 Australian Law Reform Commission, Equality before the law: Women's equality, Report No. 69, Part 2, 1994.

1994 B Smyth (ed), Parent–child contact and post-separation parenting arrangements, Research Report No. 9, Australian Institute of Family Studies, 1994.

1994 Joint Select Committee on Certain Family Law Issues, The operation and effectiveness of the Child Support Scheme, November, 1994.

1995 Australian Law Reform Commission, For the sake of the kids: Complex contact cases and the Family Court, Report No. 73, 1995

1995 Joint Select Committee on Certain Family Law Issues, Funding and administration of the Family Court of Australia, November 1995.

1996 Family Law Council, Family law appeals and review: An evaluation of the appeal and review of family law decisions, June 1996.

1996 Family Law Council, Involving and representing children in family law, August 1996.

1996 K Funder and B Smyth, Family law evaluation project 1996: Parental responsibilities: Two national surveys: (Part one: Report), Australian Institute of Family Studies, 1996.

1997 Australian Law Reform Commission, Seen and heard: Priority for children in the legal process, Report No. 84, 1997. See: Chapters 13, 15, 16.

1998 Family Law Council, Child contact orders: Enforcement and penalties, June 1998.

1998 House of Representatives Standing Committee on Legal and Constitutional Affairs, To have and to hold: Strategies to strengthen marriage and relationships, June 1998.

2000 Family Law Council, Litigants in person, August 2000.

2001 Family Law Pathways Advisory Group, Out of the maze: Pathways to the future for families experiencing separation, AGD, Canberra, 2001.

2001 Family Law Council, Cultural-community divorce and the Family Law Act 1975: A proposal to clarify the law, August 2001.

2002 Family Law Council, Family law and child protection: Final report, September 2002.

2003 House of Representatives Standing Committee on Family and Community Affairs, Every picture tells a story: Inquiry into child custody arrangements in the event of family separation, December 2003.

2004 Family Law Council, Pathways for children: A review of children's representation in family law, August 2004.

2005 Family Law Council. Inquiry on the 'Child Paramountcy Principle' in the Family Law Act.

2006 Family Law Council, Relocation, May 2006.

2007 Family Law Council, Collaborative practice in family law, February 2007.

2007 J McIntosh and C Long, Children beyond dispute: a prospective study of outcomes from child focused and child inclusive post-separation family dispute resolution, March 2007, prepared for the Attorney General's Department.

2007 Family Law Council, Improving post-parenting order processes, October 2007.

2007 L Moloney et al, Allegations of family violence and child abuse in family law children's proceedings: A pre-reform exploratory study, Research paper No. 15, Australian Institute of Family Studies, 2007.

2007 D Higgins, Cooperation and coordination: an evaluation of the Family Court of Australia's Magellan case-management model, prepared by the Australian Institute of Family Studies for the Family Court of Australia, 2007.

2008 D Semple, Future governance options for federal family law courts in Australia: Striking the right balance, prepared for the Attorney General's Department, August 2008.

2009 J McIntosh et al, Children beyond dispute: A four year follow up study of outcomes from child focused and child inclusive post-separation family dispute resolution, April 2009, prepared for the Attorney General's Department.

2009 R Chisholm, Family courts violence review, Family Law Branch of the Commonwealth Attorney General's Department, November 2009.

2009 Family Law Council, Improving responses to family violence in the family law system: An advice on the intersection of family violence and family law issues, December 2009.

2009 R Kaspiew et al, Evaluation of the 2006 family law reforms, Australian Institute of Family Studies, December 2009.

2009 Australian Institute of Family Studies. Evaluation of the Family Law Reforms. October 2009.

2009. Australian Law Reform Commission. Family Violence Inquiry. October 2009. Separate to the Chisholm Violence Review.

2009. Professor Thea Brown. Family Violence Research Project. University of South Australia, James Cook University and Monash University. October 2009.

2010 Australian National Audit Office, Implementation of the Family Relationship Centres initiative, Performance Audit Report No. 1, 2010–11.

2010 D Bagshaw et al, Family violence and family law in Australia: the experiences and views of children and adults from families who separated post-1995 and post-2006, 2 vols, Monash University, University of South Australia, James Cook University, for the Australian Attorney General's Department, April 2010. (Volume 1 and Volume 2).

2010 J Cashmore et al, Shared care parenting arrangements since the 2006 family law reforms: Report to the Australian Government Attorney General's Department, UNSW, Social Policy Research Centre, May 2010.

2010 J McIntosh et al, Post-separation parenting arrangements and developmental outcomes for infants and children: Collected reports, prepared for the Australian Government Attorney General's Department, May 2010.

2010 Australian Law Reform Commission and NSW Law Reform Commission, Family violence–A national legal response, Report No. 114, 2 vols, November 2010. (Volume 1 and Volume 2).

2010 L Qu and R Weston, Parenting dynamics after separation: A follow-up study of parents who separated after the 2006 family law reforms, Australian Institute of Family Studies, December 2010.

2011 Family Law Branch of the Commonwealth Attorney General's Department. Family Law Amendment (Family Violence) Bill 2010 – Exposure Draft. January 2011.

2011 National Alternative Dispute Resolution Advisory Centre, Maintaining and enhancing the integrity of ADR processes, February 2011. See: Chapter 6: Family dispute resolution.

2011. Senate Legal and Constitutional Affairs Committee. Family Law Legislation (Family Violence and Other Measures) Bill 2011.

2011 Australian Law Reform Commission. Inquiry into Family Violence and the Commonwealth Laws.

2011 Senate Standing Committee on Legal and Constitutional Affairs. International Child Abduction To and From Australia.

2012 Family Law Council, Improving the family law system for Aboriginal and Torres Strait Islander clients, February 2012.

2012 Family Law Council, Improving the family law system for clients from culturally and linguistically diverse backgrounds, February 2012.

2013 R Chisholm, Information-sharing in family law & child protection: Enhancing collaboration, Attorney General's Department, Canberra, March 2013.

2013 Allen Consulting Group, Research on Family Support Program family law services: Final report to Australian Government Attorney General's Department, May 2013.

2013 Family Law Council, Report on parentage and the Family Law Act, December 2013.

2014 KPMG, Review of the performance and funding of the Federal Court of Australia, the Family Court of Australia and the Federal Circuit Court of Australia, prepared for the Attorney General's Department, March 2014. (Appendices A-C; Appendices D-G)

2014 R Chisholm, The sharing of experts' reports between the child protection system and the family law system, Attorney General's Department, Canberra, 2014.

2014 R Kaspiew et al, Independent children's lawyers study: Final report, 2nd edn, June 2014.

2014 Productivity Commission, Access to justice, Report No. 72, 2 vols, September 2014. (Volume 1 and Volume 2) Volume 2, chapter 34 deals with the family law system.

2014 L Qu et al, Post-separation parenting, property and relationship dynamics after five years (Evaluation of the 2006 Family Law reforms), Australian Institute of Family Studies, December 2014.

2015 Senate Legal and Constitutional Affairs Committee. Family Law Amendment (Financial Agreement and Other Measures) Bill 2015.

2015 Family Law Council, Families with complex needs and the intersection of the family law and child protection systems: Interim report: Terms 1 & 2, June 2015.

2015 R Kaspiew et al, Evaluation of the 2012 family violence amendments: Synthesis report, (Evaluation of the 2012 Family Violence Amendments), Australian Institute of Family Studies, October 2015.

2015 R Kaspiew et al, Responding to family violence: A survey of family law practices and experiences (Evaluation of the 2012 Family Violence Amendments), Australian Institute of Family Studies, October 2015.

2015 R Kaspiew et al, Experiences of separated parents study (Evaluation of the 2012 Family Violence Amendments), Australian Institute of Family Studies, October 2015.

2015 R Kaspiew et al, Court outcomes project (Evaluation of the 2012 Family Violence Amendments), Australian Institute of Family Studies, October 2015.

2016 KPMG, Future focus of the family law services: Final report, prepared for the Attorney General's Department, January 2016.

2016 Family Law Council, Families with complex needs and the intersection of the family law and child protection systems: Final report: Terms 3, 4 & 5, June 2016.

2017 House of Representatives Standing Committee on Social Policy and Legal Affairs, A better family law system to support and protect those affected by family violence, December.

2017 Family Law Unit, Attorney General's Department. Family Law Amendment (Family Violence and Cross-Examination of Parties) Bill 2017. Public Consultation on Cross-Examination Amendment.

2018 Senate Legal and Constitutional Affairs Committee. Family Law Amendment (Family Violence and Cross-Examination of Parties) Bill 2018.

2018 PricewaterhouseCoopers (Australia), Review of efficiency of the operation of the federal courts: Final report, April 2018.

2018 R Carson et al, Direct cross-examination in family law matters: Incidence and context of direct cross-examination involving self-represented litigants, Australian Institute of Family Studies, June 2018.

2018 R Carson et al, Children and young people in separated families: Family law system experiences and needs, Australian Institute of Family Studies, 2018.

2019 Australian Law Reform Commission, Family law for the future, Report No. 135, March.

2019 Review of the Family Law System', *Media Release*, Attorney General for Australia and Minister for Industrial Relations, the Hon Christian Porter MP, 10 April 2019.

2019 Prime Minister, the Hon. Scott Morrison MP and Attorney General for Australia and Minister for Industrial Relations, the Hon Christian Porter MP, 'Joint Parliamentary Inquiry into Family Law and Child Support', *Media Release*, 17 September 2019.

2021 Government Response to the ALRC Report 135 Family Law for the Future – an Inquiry into the Family Law System 60 Recommendations for reform.

2023 Senate Legal and Constitutional Affairs Committee Family Law Amendment (Information Sharing) Bill 2023.

2023 Senate Legal and Constitutional Affairs Committee. Family Law Amendment Bill 2023.

2024 May. Law amendments come into force. Press release. The Family Law Amendment Act 2023 and the Family Law Amendment (Information Sharing) Act 2023 comes into effect.

2024 August. Press Release. Mark Dreyfus. Announcement of the Family Law Amendment Bill 2024.

2024 31 October. Family Law Amendment 2024 Bill Committee report.

2024 Family Law Amendment Bill 2024 passes Parliament.

INTRODUCTION

It remains surprising that the ultra-woke extremist ideology which is synonymous with the Family Court of Australia evolved in the Land Down Under. For Australia, founded as a penal colony, has always been associated with anti-establishment sentiment.

In the early 1900s one of the country's most beloved poets, Henry Lawson, wrote:

> The clever scoundrels are all outside, and the moneyless mugs in gaol –
> Men do twelve months for a mad wife's lies or Life for a strumpet's tale.
> If the people knew what the warders know, and felt as the prisoners feel –
> If the people knew, they would storm their gaols as they stormed the old Bastille.
> Henry Lawson, One Hundred and Three, 1908.

The year 2025 marks the 50th anniversary of the passing of the Family Law Act, the single most impactful and destructive piece of legislation to ever pass the Australian parliament.

In that time the Family Court has been the subject of dozens of government inquiries and attempts at reform on its road to becoming the single most hated jurisdiction in the country.

Far from the helping court its founders told the public they imagined, it has become an enduring symbol of good intentions gone wrong, of the initial idealism of the left turning into a totalitarian nightmare visited upon millions of Australian families, and an enduring example of ideological extremism, political opportunism and bureaucratic refusal to take seriously the voices of those they are meant to serve. Looked at across a broader reach, an aerial view so to speak, ultimately the history of the Family Law Act demonstrates how an ideology allowed to flourish in one sacrosanct arena has metastasised across institutions to damage an entire society.

We all think we begin this journey alone. Well, I most certainly did. Like a lot of people who assume that the Australian Family Court and Australian Child Support Agency are credible, reliable and ethical institutions. Good luck with that. Once you encounter these institutions, and the phalanxes of bureaucracies and politicians which protect them, prepare to have your illusions dashed.

No one can go through the expensive rigmarole of a Family Court trial and emerge with the slightest respect for the lawyers who profit from this foul system, or the politicians who have allowed this travesty of public administration to spread its poison down the generations.

A phone call I received in the middle of the year 2000 ultimately led to the writing of this book's predecessor, an eBook called *Chaos at the Crossroad: Family Law Reform in Australia*, a poorly formatted and somewhat amateurish effort. But at least we got it out there.[1]

The caller, a former police officer called Rick Torning, wanted to know if I would be interested in contributing to a program at a community radio station in western Sydney called 2GLF. I had never heard of Rick or 2GLF. And apart from doing short radio segments on Australia's state media the ABC, promoting one story or another for the national newspaper *The Australian*, I had zero radio experience.

But what we lacked in money and experience was made up for by our fervent sense of social justice. Or perhaps more precisely, the injustice which had been done to us. And to our precious children.

As one of a small group of separated blokes who had secured some air time on a community radio station, Rick wanted to cover family law, child support and fatherhood issues. They had heard, I'm not sure how, that I was both a journalist and a separated dad.

Subsequently I met up with the initial group of what was to evolve into Dads On The Air. From those original few, I remained directly involved with the program the longest, for about ten years. As such I am sometimes referred to as "the founder" of Dads on the Air, although that is not correct and there were several of us involved in those early days, including Richard Torning aka Uncle Buck and others who for professional reasons would now rather not be named.

As of 2024 Dads on the Air is still going strong and is available to the more

---

[1] Stapleton, John, *Chaos at the Crossroads: Family Law Reform in Australia*, Dads on the Air books, 2010.

than 450 community radio stations across Australia.[2] It is a very different beast to the "bolshie" program that originally decried the many administrative and judicial travesties of both the Family Court and the Child Support Agency, but nonetheless it continues to encourage fathers who these days are more routinely decried by Australia's sad legacy media as neglectful and abusive predators rather than the protectors and providers they were traditionally seen, and biologically programmed, to be.

Rick was a domestic violence expert with the NSW Police. He mounted a number of complex legal cases attempting to demonstrate the family law system's lack of validity. His world was turned upside down when, as with so many fathers, he was falsely accused and his name dragged through the mud.

"Matt", another former policeman, was at that time a contributor to the show, before he started complaining that every time he made an appearance his child support was increased and he could no longer afford to participate. In my view this was straightforward bureaucratic abuse, if not corruption, on the part of Australia's almost universally despised Child Support Agency. Nothing was ever done about it, of course.

The CSA is one of the primary drivers of unemployment in Australia. Like many other fathers who find working while paying what they rightly perceive as draconian levels of child support pointless, "Matt" eventually gave up the job he loved and instead went to university. He has since graduated and is now a barrister.

Thanks to our family law and child support systems, there are a number of dads who have either gone back to tertiary education or pursued other dreams, such as to become an artist. Or who took the other path and are eking out their lives on welfare rather than spend them in servitude to what they saw as the system's rapacious financial demands. They might have felt differently if they thought their money was genuinely benefitting their children, but the law does not require any demonstration that this is the case.

Indeed later research showed that children were financially better off and received more money from their separated fathers before the creation of the woeful Child Support Agency.[3] The expensive scheme also failed in its objective of saving the taxpayer money, with cost estimates running between two and five times that of every dollar collected, depending on the year. But nothing stopped this stain on the Australian Public Service impacting and damaging millions of people's lives, fathers, mothers and the children it pretended to benefit.

---

2 Department of Infrastructure, Community Radio, Australian Government website, as of 2024.

3 Cost of Child Support, Property Investment Research, August, 2002.

***

Rick and Matt were particularly upset, as separated policemen tended to be. Former policemen, who comprised a disproportionate number within the atomised, disorganised and almost entirely unfunded father's and family law reform movements in Australia, were more attune to the injustices and failures of the system they had spent their lives serving and which, when they needed it most, comprehensively failed them.

Matt, one of many heartbroken men, was deeply disturbed that a one-night stand resulted in a child the mother would not let him see. His child. His son. His DNA, his genetic legacy, a biologically wired impulse many parents feel strongly. Matt's own life had been turned upside down as a result of this sorry affair, while his own parents were upset at the lack of contact with their grandson.

There were so many stories. Many of them defied belief. The system decimates the lives of ordinary, perfectly decent people. Simple as that.

The Family Court and the then Prime Minister John Howard's creation, the former Federal Magistrates Service, had always been happy to jail fathers – Dads On The Air did a story, for instance, on Desi Cochrane, a disabled pensioner jailed twice after he did not have the money to comply with magistrate Jennifer Rimmer's orders to pay $200 a week child support for his two children until they were 18 in a single lump sum.

We came to the story long after the children were adults and had left their mother behind, when the courts of the land were pursuing a disabled man to take his small home in rural Victoria, his only asset. How is this system acting "in the best interests of children"?

Jennifer Rimmer had ordered that Cochrane's humble house be sold from under him.

Rimmer resigned in disgrace in 2006 after she was caught plagiarising thousands of words of online judgements and pasting them into her own. The evil that men do lives after them. Her orders lived after her.[4]

What made Cochrane's story even more moving was that he became permanently disabled in a car accident while he was on the way to see his children on a court ordered access visit. His friend, who was driving at the time, was killed. The mother refused his desperately sad pleas to let the kids come and see him while he lay in hospital. The courts did nothing but make this man's life even worse.

Pleas by Cochrane for some sort of amnesty went unheeded.[5]

---

4 Thomas, Hedley, Plagiarising magistrate can practise, *The Australian*, 7 November, 2007.

5 Cochrane, Desi, Corruption at the highest level by Australian Government, federal, state and local departments, YouTube, 15 October, 2022.

The then Attorney General Phillip Ruddock frequently wore an Amnesty International badge, thus expressing concern for human rights abuses around the world, while sitting atop a system which routinely perpetuates these types of abuses.[6]

***

With the spread of communication technology, the Family Court's arbitrary and frequently cruel judgements were already the stuff of legends by the time we began broadcasting. One Indian immigrant was jailed for writing to his parents in English. The Court ignored his protestations that his father had two masters' degrees in English. The Court has also ordered litigants not to contact the United Nations with their concerns, not to publicise the injustices of their cases in any way and not to take their children to a doctor or raise welfare concerns.

One father was ordered not to contact his children after he allegedly carried his daughter around on his shoulders, in a crowded park. Another father who expressed a desire to see his adolescent son after the boy's suicide attempt was ridiculed from the bench while the lawyers sniggered. Yet another was jailed for sending his child a birthday card.

Similar stories of damaged lives circle the Child Support Agency. The Agency claimed to be treating fairly a young father who was losing 80 percent of his income in tax and child support and died with one of their letters in his hand.[7] Another man took more than two weeks to die when he went out to his back shed and swallowed poison following a call from a CSA officer. The CSA refused to attend the inquest despite a request from the Magistrate.[8]

We shared much in common, that first small group, most of all disgust at the rampant anti-father bias and to our minds outright corruption in Australia's family law system. We were similarly distressed at what had been so blithely done to our children, and the children of so many others, the attempted destruction of their relationship with their dads.

The pillaging of separated families is a multi-billion dollar industry. Few parents give up without a fight. They do not accept the loss of any meaningful relationship with their children. They do not shrug and say: sure, leach me for every cent you possibly can. Take my kids, take my property. In the process of

---

[6] Ackland, Richard, Suddenly, Ruddock is a human rights hero, *Sydney Morning Herald*, 9 September, 2011.

[7] Campbell, Roderick, Australian Suicide Victim "Hounded" Over Child Support, *Canberra Times*, 15 November 2000.

[8] Stapleton, John, Problem Parents Doing Time, *The Australian*, 8 April 2000.

fighting for fair reason these same parents are almost always financially fleeced by lawyers and personally crushed, the devastation wreaked upon them taking years to recover from, if they recover at all.

During those dark days, which have now returned in force, indeed are worse than ever, more than half the fathers entering the Family Court of Australia emerged to find they saw their children barely once or twice a year. All too many never saw their children again. Those who did usually got the so-called daddy pack of contact every second weekend, although there is no evidence such an arrangement is in the best interests of children. None whatsoever, despite all the false claims by Family Court apologists that their sole working rationale is "the best interests of the child".

Historically, the Family Court denied fathers contact with their children on the flimsiest of excuses or most ludicrous of accusations. Overly legalistic, enormously bureaucratic, secretive, unaccountable and extremely ideological, defying community norms of morality and propriety, it soon became one the country's most hated institutions.

***

Early in the millennium Australia was presented with an historic opportunity to address once and for all the public disquiet that child welfare and child custody had provoked. A rare confluence of political will in the shape a conservative government led by Prime Minister John Howard, who had received a bump in the polls after his original announcement of his interest in joint custody and a surprisingly sympathetic media, a widespread acknowledgement of the existing failures of the system which had coalesced around small fathers and family reform groups scattered around the country, meshed with a desire for change within the community.

The routine stripping of children from their fathers, along with much of their income and assets, arose from policy decisions made in the 1970s.

Australia adopted with alacrity the same style of family courts that had sprung up across the western world during that decade of social ferment and change. Fancying itself amongst the avant-garde on social justice issues, Australia embraced the court's anti-father anti-family ideologies under the guise of the protection and advancement of women. But with this, unfortunately, came the denigration of fathers as dangerous and unnecessary historical relics.

The playing out of these policies in the modern era and the dysfunction of the institutions which administered the nation's family law and child support policies sat poorly with a conservative pro-family government.

Established in 1975, in its early days the Family Court of Australia was widely perceived as a progressive, ground breaking institution. But within a decade the court was making headlines for all the wrong reasons, particularly its treatment of fathers. By the year 2000, when Dads On The Air first began broadcasting, the Family Court and the associated industries and bureaucracies around it, including the family law units of Legal Aid and the multi-million dollar family report writing business, were attracting widespread and significant public disquiet.

While hampered by the secrecy provisions in family law, which have worked effectively to keep the general public ignorant of the worst excesses of the court, its most farcical judgements and its repeated failure to take child protection issues seriously, particularly when those issues are raised by fathers, Dads On The Air has done its best to expose the court's practices and its many dirty little secrets.

The issues so lightly glossed over in much of the public debate represented a deep personal hurt that was disfiguring the country. MPs across the country were besieged with complaints about family law and child support; hour upon hour of their time eaten up by distressed parents whose problems were exacerbated or made intractable by their interaction with government agencies.

Modern fathers had embraced with gusto the increased involvement with and hands-on parenting of their children sparked by a feminist push to remake the family and remodel women's roles. The shopping malls of the era were full of kids crawling all over their fathers, holding hands, dribbling and drooling, while their cheerfully harassed dads struggled to do the shopping. Not to be at your child's birth was now the exception rather than the rule. The days of fathers opening up cigars and slugging down whisky with their mates while their wives bellowed their way through childbirth were a distant memory. In the contemporary urban environment in which most Australians lived, with both parents working to pay large mortgages, shared parenting was already the norm in many intact families.

But almost overnight, if his wife decided she wanted to divorce, those same fathers laughing in the sun with their children could be transformed into the now familiar sight of the lonely, sad and suicide prone separated dad virtually overnight. For most of the Family Court's history these fathers have been invisible in the public debate.

Thanks to bureaucratic, judicial and political capture, billions of dollars have been poured into funding women's and single mother's advocacy groups and championing women friendly policies, while fathers' groups receive zero or next to zero funding and have no voice in government or the formation of policy.

There was a "Sex Discrimination" Commissioner within Australia's much criticised Human Rights and Equal Opportunity Commission, a post traditionally held by high profile leftwing women such as feminist advocate and author

Anne Summers or during the family law inquiry Pru Goward, who was always insulting towards fathers. Goward's role in campaigning against joint custody while collecting a government salary was criticised by fathers groups as an inappropriate use of her office and provoked hostility nationwide.

The Justices have invariably emerged from the left. There has never been a Family Court Chief Justice who has consistently spoken up in defence of fathers and fatherhood.

Founding Chief Justice Elizabeth Evatt, who was appointed by conservative Prime Minister Malcolm Fraser, wrote about her concerns over the welfare of lesbian mothers, but not a single word of concern for fathers.[9] She presided from 1976 to 1988.

Justice Alastair Nicholson, a Labor Party loyalist who had run for parliament twice, reigned over the court as his personal fiefdom from 1988 to 2004. He was beloved by feminist lobby groups but notoriously hostile to fathers and fathers' groups. He commented freely and widely on a wide variety of social issues, invariably from a feminist perspective. A left leaning media, particularly the state media outlet the Australian Broadcasting Commission, repeated his musings as if they were sermons from on high.

Diana Bryant, who presided from 2004 to 2017, was celebrated for her promotion of women's rights and women lawyers, while ludicrously claiming the court was not biased against men. She routinely criticised the shared parenting laws. So it has gone on.

As of 2024, the current Deputy Chief Justice is Robert McClelland, who as former Attorney General from 2007 to 2011 led the Labor Party's charge against shared parenting. The Family Court always was, and as long as it remains in its current form always will be, an intensely politicised institution. Like former Chief Justice Alastair Nicholson, on the face of it McClelland's primary qualification for the appointment was his loyalty to the Labor Party. His appointment was criticised by some lawyers because he had no expertise in family law, his speciality being industrial relations.

The mistreatment of fathers and their children by state institutions was fostered by the gender politics of those in the highest reaches of the country's bureaucracy and judiciary.

***

It all began a long time ago. Most of those now in senior positions within the media and in government were in or around universities in the 1970s, during a

---

9 Lesbian Mothers' Legal Handbook, Women's Press, 1986.

period of massive expansion of tertiary education. Many have not altered their views much since then. In women's studies courses, now renamed gender studies, the traditional nuclear family was painted by academics as a patriarchal prison from which women must escape. Any desire to do otherwise was diagnosed as the internalisation of the ideology of the oppressor.

The situation improved somewhat after the introduction of the Howard government's inquiry into shared parenting and the adoption of the vague notion of "shared responsibility" into the Act, along with the notion that children should have the right to contact with both parents.

Dads on the Air was highly critical of these reforms, claiming they were too weak, too mealy mouthed and too easily overturned. Unfortunately we were proved correct. We labelled one of our shows, with characteristic chutzpah: The Liars, the Lawyers, the Bureaucrats and the Social Engineers Have Won The Day. How apt the title proved to be. The war, the battle for reason in an unreasonable world, was lost.

These reforms have not just been wound back, the situation for fathers, and thereby for the society as a whole, is now worse than ever. It should be pointed out that a Marxist feminist court such as the Family Court of Australia ostensibly protects women, but destroys the lives of many mothers, grandmothers and daughters, just as it does their male counterparts. The personal anguish and social chaos created by these Marxist feminist style courts, introduced throughout much of the Western world during the 1970s, have poisoned the social fabric. But despite the accumulated pain these institutions, now entrenched within the societies on which they feed, have changed little since their introduction.

Although its critics may well label it such, this is not a book about fathers rights. It's a book about the rights of us all, particularly our children.

Those who do not learn from history are destined to repeat it. Domestic violence allegations arose as an option for those seeking a separation first arose in the 1980s and has been curdling the public policy sphere ever since.

One of the first pieces of domestic violence legislation in Australia was the NSW Crimes (Domestic Violence Act 1982, followed by Victoria's Family Violence (Protection) Act 1987, Queensland's Domestic Violence Act 1989, South Australia's Intervention Orders (Prevention of Abuse) Act 2009, Tasmania's Family Violence Act 2004, the Northern Territory's Domestic and Family Violence Act 2007 and the Australian Capital Territory's Family Violence Act 2008.

There is little or no evidence that all this legislative activity has decreased levels of interpersonal violence in the Australian community; while in an ever escalating spiral of virtue signalling, every year Australian governments pour ever more billions of dollars into the arena.

The eruption of protest over the extreme anti-father bias of Australia's family law, child support and domestic violence industries which occurred in the early 2000s will bloom again. Nothing is more certain.

While I somewhat obsessively dedicated many hundreds of hours to Dads On The Air over the years, I am not some kind of gender warrior. As a progressive kind of guy I did a year of Women's Studies at university in the 1970s. I worked in the mainstream media, on two of Australia's leading broadsheets, for more than a quarter of a century. As a former general news reporter, a "humble hack on the highways of print", I have written thousands upon thousands of stories on a dizzying range of topics.

Family law was just one of the subjects that intrigued or outraged me over the years.

***

Groups such as Lone Fathers, Men's Confraternity, Non-Custodial Parents Party and the Men's Rights Agency had all been struggling to be heard. Dads On The Air hoped to provide them with an outlet.

At first we felt very much alone. Our bolshie broadcasts put us out on a limb. We would say what we had to say nervously, thinking that at any time the Australian Federal Police would come barging through the doors and silence us. Our fears were not unfounded. The Court, which we repeatedly referred to as The Palace Of Lies, had a long history of attempting to stifle its critics.

One man who suggested in a letter that the court belonged on a garbage tip found himself being arrested by three Federal Police at his front door.

Criticism of the court as "criminal" and "corrupt" now fly across the internet without consequence.

An extremist anti-male form of feminism captured the universities, the bureaucracies and the judiciary from the 1970s onwards. Taxpayers and the society at large have been paying for the consequences ever since.

As the years passed Dads On The Air, DOTA, as it became commonly known, was joined by other voices, both within the Australian community and internationally. There were so many stories. Fathers everywhere, often having worked in thankless jobs in order to protect and provide for their children, and then kept busy at home for the same purpose, were outraged by their mistreatment in the post-separation system they found themselves unwittingly trapped within.

When Dads On The Air began in 2000 we had no idea we were part of a worldwide trend protesting the mistreatment of fathers in separated families. As we were to discover, we were not alone. A similar bias infected family law systems throughout the western world.

Internationally, Fathers4Justice in Britain was about to climb Buckingham Palace and invade the House Of Commons. Bob Geldoff, who first rose to prominence as the lead singer of the Boomtown Rats in the 1970s, was about to speak out about "Sad Dads" and the devastating cruelties of the British Family Court system.

Their courage, and the courage of many Australian activists, helped unleash a remarkable flood; we were fortunate to find ourselves broadcasting in an era when there was no shortage of stories.

From that initial telephone call evolved Dads On The Air, which by dint of pure perseverance is now the world's longest running program dedicated to gender, family and fatherhood issues. It went on to attract a talented team of volunteers with journalistic, entertainment, legal, academic and internet experience. But back in 2000 we had no expertise, no experience in radio, and no resources. At that time we did not even have the ability to interview people on air. Convincing talent to travel out to western Sydney for an obscure radio show was difficult.

As a much touted multicultural society, immigrants from countries who come from societies which do not despise their own men are flabbergasted by the hostility they encounter the minute they cross the vestibules of Australia's family courts. For ordinary citizens, unaware of the extreme ideologies and legal madness which has overtaken these systems, walking through those doors comes as a salutary shock.

As that first small band of disgruntled dads rapidly discovered once we began broadcasting, like no other subject family law is something that cuts deep into the hearts and lives of the citizenry, a seemingly infinite well of pain.

***

Dads On The Air was in a singular position to cover and even at times to contribute to the years of government reports, committee inquiries, public debate and media coverage on reforms promoting cooperative care of children after divorce. While our politicians could take us into unwise multibillion dollar wars on the toss of a coin, or more precisely an unwise allegiance to a dangerous ally America, witness Iraq, witness Afghanistan, witness Ukraine, fixing our own internal war against fathers and fatherhood, propelled by ideologies birthed in the universities half a century ago, has proved beyond our political class.

Conservative Prime Minister John Howard mounted an inquiry into shared custody in 2003 which gathered significant public support and positive media coverage but then failed to act. Australia's politicians are frightened of the very monster they created, the literally hundreds of taxpayer funded women's legal services, advocacy groups, refuges, and an armada of feminist academics and activist judges. All this multibillion dollar army, benefiting from the demonisation of men, is arrayed against the unfunded, voluntary fathers and pro-family community groups which have not a hope of getting their voices heard.

Howard ran his government in a 1980s managerial style. Endless inquiries, commissions and reports gave an illusion of action. Nothing ever changed.

He was finally embarrassed into taking action after a pesky journalist wrote a story noting that he had initiated dozens of inquiries, and instituted not a single recommendation from any of them.

Finally, two years after the initial report the family law reform legislation was tabled in Parliament, on December 8, 2005, again at a time of year when the public, and many of the major players in Australian media, are knocking off for Christmas holidays and not paying the slightest attention to politics. Another sleight of hand.

It was very dirty politics aimed to deceive.

Howard, a lawyer by training, had already appointed a replacement for the long serving Chief Justice Alastair Nicholson who he knew perfectly well would do nothing to change the nature of the court. Her name was Diana Bryant, who would serve as Chief Justice for 2004 to 2017, and who would leave the court in just as parlous a state as her predecessors.

Then Attorney General Philip Ruddock was left holding the can. His press release stated that the Family Law Amendment (Shared Parental Responsibility) Bill 2005 reflected the "Government's determination to ensure the right of children to grow up with the love and support of both their parents".[10]

It was little better than a lie.

Insisting on calling the extremely modest amendments to the Act "the most significant reforms to the family law system in 30 years", Ruddock toured the country promoting his view of the progressive nature of the law changes. As always when he came on Dads On The Air he endured a solid grilling with good spirit.

These changes, essentially inclusions in the Objects of the Act to encourage judges to look at the notion of "shared responsibility", were finally made into law by the Australian government headed by then Prime Minister John Howard in 2006 as a bipartisan initiative.

Too little too late and too easily overturned, Dads On The Air declared. And all directed at a court notoriously resistant to change. Sadly, we were proved correct. The many thousands of volunteer hours that members of fathers and family law

---

10 Bill marks cultural shift in dealing with family breakdown, Media Release, Phillip Ruddock, 8 December, 2005.

had put into pushing for reform were ignored. And a significant social movement swept under the carpet, buried as if it had never been.

Almost immediately following the election of a left leaning Labor government headed by Prime Minister Kevin Rudd in 2007 the process of winding back even these modest reforms began in an entirely partisan way. In Australia family law amendments have never previously been introduced without bipartisan support. The debate continues to this day.

***

Dads On The Air has evolved a long way from its early years. The first programs must have been a bit of a strain on the audience, with long discussions about the impacts of family law and elaborate deconstructions of domestic violence or anti-father ideologies.

My first contribution went for 18 minutes, an eternity on radio, and contained a detailed summing up of events concerning family law around the world. We must have stretched the tolerance of our listeners. But after that first phone contribution, I began to make the weekly trek out to Liverpool in western Sydney to do the show. And after a year or so, our first amateur efforts coalesced into a dedicated radio program. The name Dads On The Air just popped into my mind one morning, and stuck.

We were fortunate to find ourselves in an era when there was plenty of material to broadcast. The early history of Dads On The Air coincided closely with the evolution of Australian groups such as Dads In Distress, the Non-Custodial Parents Equal Parenting Party and the Shared Parenting Council of Australia.

The internet proved a godsend for separated fathers, who flocked to the various internet chat lines and web sites. Their unfashionable pro-family views, their scepticism towards domestic violence legislation, family courts, child support and child protection agencies, while routinely ignored, marginalised or even ridiculed in the mainstream media, found ample room in cyberspace.

During the course of the show I met many of the various figures in the men's movement in Australia, and for a period followed several internet chat lines and news services. For a couple of years I read virtually everything published in English language media on family law in the Western world. There's a surprisingly large volume of material. The Australian system did not become as bad as it has become for lack of countervailing evidence. The invaluable work of Lindsay Jackel, a retired telecom worker in Melbourne, in collecting and redistributing gender and family law related media and academic articles on internet news services such as Manumit – which means escape from slavery – and chat lines such as Nuance convinced me there was more than enough material around to maintain a weekly radio program.

The argument over family law was essentially a "tipping point". It was simply a matter of numbers. More and more people were either directly affected or had friends and family whose lives had been adversely affected by the operations of the court.

After the establishment of the Child Support Agency in 1989, sometimes described as the "evil sister" of the Family Court, this only got worse. By 2000 the large number of fathers and their extended families had seen or experienced first hand their lives and the lives of those they loved destroyed by the conduct of the court and its sole mother style of custody orders.

The mainstream media ignored their stories, and the larger story of the decades long struggle for family law reform in Australia, not just by separated fathers, their supporters and their lobby groups, but by grandparents and other family members cut out of children's lives by the discriminatory and destructive sole-custody model purveyed by the court. But the multiple failures of Australia's mainstream media opened up channels for independent media, which back at the turn of the millennium was radio programs such as ourselves, and the then novelty of online forums.

Official Child Support Agency statistics recorded 1.1 million children and 600,000 parents were clients of the Agency and subject to orders of the Family Court of Australia.[11] With so many of the citizenry having experienced the Family Court's overly complex processes firsthand, often being burnt or becoming embittered as a result, or knowing loved ones who had, there were sufficient numbers of the disaffected to defy institutional propaganda, political gutlessness and media neglect. Or in some notable cases, the agendas of some strategically placed feminist journalists and columnists purveying year after year the ultra-feminist ideologies of their youth.

***

Through the latter half of the twentieth century, as more than half of all marriages came to end in divorce, the belief that family law in Australia was overwhelmingly tilted against fathers and that this hostility was doing massive harm to parents and children alike became an accepted truth amongst a significant section of the population, including traditional Christians and others of faith.

Equally, such claims were the subject of denial from the mandarins who administered family law and greatly benefited from its administration.

---

11 Facts and Figures, 2007-2008, Child Support Agency.

With the introduction of no fault divorce in the 1970s, the Family Court was originally created as a so-called "helping court", a progressive institution carrying out long overdue reforms.

Reforms to family law enacted in the 1970s were hailed as major steps forward in the fight for gender equality at home and in the workplace.

In reality the world's Family Courts have harmed the lives of as many women as they have men.

They have also done great damage to children under the masquerade of that great legal falsehood: "The best interests of the child".

Dads On The Air was fond of claiming it was "the most dishonestly used phrase in Australia today". Australians of the day were yet to hear the corporatist phrases "safe and effective" or "cheap and reliable".

Despite the Attorney General Lionel Murphy's vision of a "helping" court when he brought no-fault divorce to Australia in 1975, cooperative parenting after divorce was rarely encouraged. He may well have been of good motive. It didn't end that way.

As one of our guests, the greatly admired Australian historian John Hirst wrote in his compelling book *Kangaroo Court*, far from being a helping institution, as the years rolled by the Court became both feared and hated. He said: "I cannot see the way by which the Court can be rescued. Until there is fundamental change, it will continue to give offence."

Hirst became a great friend of the show, coming into the studio when he was visiting Sydney from Melbourne, and coming out to dinner with myself and my kids.

"When Family Court judges talk piously of the 'caring court', I wish they could hear the roar of pain that their piety has caused," he wrote.

In language surprising for such a stringent and well respected academic he wrote that a court which saw itself as looking after the best interests of children, instead acted as a child abuser, a gross abuser of human rights, and as a monstrosity that was not a court of justice.

He told the ABC: "It was when a student of mine was involved in a family law business and I was appointed by the court to be his official supervisor that I became aware at close quarters of the sort of experiences that the court metes out, because this young man was accused by his wife of being a danger to his children and yet I only had to be with him for half an hour when he was playing with his children to see that he was no danger at all, in fact he was a wonderful dad.

"But for six months he was sort of on trial, he had to be examined psychologically, go to a psychiatrist, have anger management, so his experience is quite a common one, that accusations are made very, very easily in this court, and then people have to prove that they're okay. And I don't think this is a good system, I think accusations are made too freely and are taken too seriously without any preliminary checking of them."[12]

The adversarial nature of family law encouraged false accusations from the earliest days of its formation. Changes which have set in since the turn of the millennium ensures there is no consequence for making false accusations, at least on the mother's part, and has simply made the situation worse.

In its playing out, in practice no fault divorce in an adversarial system simply meant all the fault was placed on dads. In a "he said she said" jurisdiction, the words of fathers were routinely depicted as the voice of the patriarchy. If they attempt to correct the record they are readily described as using the family law system to abuse their former partner. Family law became little more than a criminal assault on half the population, a justification for stripping men of their assets, their dignity and their purpose in life. The high suicide rate amongst separated men was of no concern to the perpetrators.

Almost from the minute the Family Court opened its doors it became a law unto itself, imposing sole mother custody on separating families despite the harm it caused for everyone involved, mothers, fathers and children.

It's hard to believe, as we head into 2025, that Australia's Family Law Act, the most impactful and destructive legislation to ever pass the parliament, began with such apparent optimism and goodwill.

Here is a short extract from John Hirst's *Kangaroo Court* summarising this early history: "The Family Law Act of 1975 which established the Court was a progressive social reform of the Whitlam Labor government. It was not an exclusively government measure; members on both sides were allowed a free vote and Liberals had been among those working for divorce law reform. The Act removed fault as a ground for divorce and replaced it with irretrievable breakdown, to be indicated by a one-year separation. The aim was to allow couples to part without the trauma and contrivance of one partner proving fault against the other. Marriages would be buried decently and humanely.

"The business of dividing property, arranging maintenance and determining custody of children would remain, but these were to be settled in a simple, flexible and inexpensive way. Litigation was to be discouraged and the Court was to be staffed by social workers and counsellors as well as judges. It was to be a court of an entirely new sort, a 'caring court' or a 'helping court'.

"If proceedings were to be simple, flexible and cheap, why, say the wits, were

---

12 Hirst, John, Kangaroo Divorce, ABC. 5 March, 2005.

lawyers put in charge of them? Proceedings quickly became complex, rule-bound and expensive."[13]

A caring court in the hands of lawyers? What were they thinking? They've been lying to you ever since.

***

Centre for Independent Studies scholar Barry Maley, also a former guest on DOTA, wrote in his review of the book: "You need to be a good scholar, a good writer, as well as brave, to launch a long-overdue critique of the Family Court. La Trobe University historian John Hirst fills the bill with this curial J'accuse probing the Court's injustices. The unending stream of anger directed at the Court since its inception has honed the public relations and polemical skills of its judges. So, on cue, they responded quickly to Hirst's analysis. The former Chief Justice of the Court is reported as describing the criticisms as 'emotional and unbalanced…grossly irresponsible, and just plain wrong'."

Hirst responded via the press to the usual personal attacks delivered to the court's critics, saying Nicholson had shown no evidence rebutting his central criticisms about the deficiencies of the Court and the family law it administers.

Maley credited Hirst with breaking the silence that surrounded the multiple injustices inflicted on so many of the 50,000 or more men and women who divorced each year. "It is a passionate book, but nothing more than the justified indignation of one who has seen wrongs inflicted and is driven to speak," Maley wrote.

"Hirst focuses on the perverse results of using 'the best interests of the child' as an overriding principle in guiding judgements. He says that despite attempts by the federal government and committees of inquiry to induce the Court to ensure as far as possible the full involvement of both parents in the child's life, it had not done so. The outcome is social disarray, loss of respect for the Court, more human misery than necessary, impotent rage, and sometimes suicide among its victims.

"After 30 years of the Court's operations Hirst is surely right in pressing for reform to establish that balance of legal rights and obligations, and their just enforcement, without which the institutions of a liberal society, including the family, cannot thrive."[14]

Reforms meant to promote shared parenting in 1995 actually saw the small percentage of such orders drop.

---

13 Hirst, John, *Kangaroo Court: Family Law in Australia*, Black Inc., 2005).

14 Maley, Barry, Book Review, Kangaroo Court: Family Law in Australia, Centre for Independent Studies, 11 June, 2005.

Separated fathers critical of the family law system were described as disgruntled litigants, or even as patriarchal relics unable to cope with the fact they no longer had control over their former wives or their children. These were insulting and self-serving analyses.

As many discovered firsthand, the notion that complex cases were being carefully weighed by Family Court judges according to the evidence before them and the individual circumstances of each family to reach a studied conclusion "in the best interests of the child" was simply not true. Indeed "the best interests of the child" was and remains one of the most egregious lies peddled to the Australian public.

Instead litigants are faced with a travesty of justice, indeed a travesty of common decency – a travesty for which they pay taxes. The failure of the media to investigate and expose the many problems with the Family Court ensures many unsuspecting members of the public have no idea what goes on in this troubled jurisdiction until it happens to them. Instead they are led into a trap and routinely fleeced. And left embittered, powerless, broke and heartbroken.

***

The original 2003 announcement from the then Prime Minister John Howard that his government would examine the idea of a rebuttable presumption of joint custody provoked a wave of positive media coverage and community support. His standing in the polls went up.

However the parliamentary inquiry's final report, the poorly written, intellectually sloppy and ridiculously named Every Picture Tells A Story, caused many problems. It dismissed in a single paragraph the many fathers, mothers, grandparents and children of divorced parents who gave evidence to the inquiry. It was condemned by family law reformers as a betrayal of the nation's more than one million children of separated parents and of the many tearful parents who had appeared before the inquiry.

DOTA described the report as just like a Family Court judgement, it bore no relationship to the evidence and no relationship to reality. We were spot on.

The Howard government dithered for years over the issue of family law reform, destroying the public momentum for change. Embarrassed by accusations it was influenced by men's groups, it would not be until 2006, after yet more committees and calls for submissions, that the Howard government finally passed what DOTA condemned as sadly inadequate laws promoting shared parental responsibility.

Notwithstanding DOTA's disappointment, the lengthy public debate engendered a cultural shift. After 2006 many separating parents expected to share the care of the children. But the court itself was largely hostile towards shared parenting and impatient with parliamentary interference.

In the years that followed numerous inquiries, largely the bureaucracy talking to itself through taxpayer funded groups purveying an outlandish hostility to men and to fathers, gave a thin chimaera of political action and covered or concealed the boiling discontent which continued within the community. By 2024 the most left-wing government in Australian history, headed by Prime Minister Anthony Albanese, rolled back any small advances made by fathers, throwing any notion of equity between separating parents into the garbage bin. We had all gone full circle. The genuine interests of children, who benefit from knowing both their parents, were once again ignored.

***

Apart from parking and traffic fines the most common experience Australians have with the legal system is through family law, which dramatically intrudes into people's lives while acting as the legal lynchpin for a bloated welfare system. We long maintained that no one could emerge from this system with any respect for the lawyers that profited from it, or the politicians that allowed this debacle to continue. And that it did the country no good to have such a large and disenfranchised body of citizens with such contempt or enmity towards the nation's institutions.

Its critics regard the Family Court of Australia's moniker "The Palace of Lies" to be extremely well deserved. Those whose lives have been trammelled through this abattoir of truth rarely think otherwise.

Virtually every separated father in the country knows the horror of the nation's drastically anti-male family law and child support systems.

It does Australian society no good to have such a large body of impoverished and disenfranchised men; devastated by the loss of their children, their assets, and in all too many cases their social status and standing in the broader community. No one can go near this jurisdiction and retain a modicum of respect for lawyers, or for the politicians from both sides of the aisle which have allowed this malfeasance to flourish.

Successive governments from both left and right have failed to listen to their constituents and respond to their concerns. They have resorted to vested inquiries in the hands of the mandarins and publicly funded elites whose feigned attempts to listen to the views of ordinary people have then been heavily reinterpreted. They have delayed progress through the extensive manipulation of committees or other forms of alleged inquiry. They have fed off the taxpayer funded industries as the industries have fed off them. These same governments, even when they were enacting legislative reforms, left their enforcement in the hands of institutions notoriously resistant to change. They allowed or encouraged fashionable ideology, institutional inertia and bureaucracy to triumph over common sense. Common decency was lost long ago.

In terms of human suffering, the Australian public has already paid dearly for the failure to reform outdated, badly administered and inappropriate institutions dealing with family law and child support – and for the failure of governments to take seriously the experiences and voices of the men and women most directly affected by them. The country's failure to reform family law and child support is ultimately a failure of democracy itself.

ONE
DISASTER LOOMING

WHILE APOLOGISTS for family law claim it is not systematically biased against fathers and operates "in the best interests of the child" across the last half century these claims have been widely dismissed by advocates as self-serving and demonstrably false.

The push for family law reform in the early 2000s was a long time coming, with a history of community agitation and discontent dating back to the 1970s and accelerating in the 1990s. Only very rarely was this dissatisfaction reflected in the mainstream media. In recent years, barely at all.

One exception was a story, by a Mr X, titled "Court Out: One man's battle for his kids: The awful heartbreak of families courting disaster", which was published on the front page of the weekend feature section of *The Australian* the day before Christmas in 1999.[15]

It came at a time when there was substantial criticism of the Court from several different quarters, including from the government's own legal adviser, the Australian Law Reform Commission. The strap line to the story read: "As the government tries to improve family justice, Mr X tells of his personal voyage of despair."

The story began: "Don't cry, you will lose your children for sure," your barrister says sternly; and inside all you can feel are waves of distress. For you are vulnerable through what you love the most – your children. Welcome to the Family Court of Australia. Behind the imposing facades of the courts lies the deepest hurt. Close to a million children now live away from their fathers.

"I was in the middle of an excruciating three days of being cross-examined in the Family Court of Australia, an experience that cost taxpayers many thousands of dollars. It had been an intensely difficult two-year journey getting here. I had done everything I could to protect the children, and recently everything I could

---

15 Mr X, Court Out: One Man's Battle for his Kids, *The Australian*, 24 December, 1999.

to settle the matter. I had represented myself almost all the way through. I didn't have money to pay people thousands of dollars a day to argue over my family situation."

The article went on to describe the all too common situation of an unrepresented father without the financial resources for legal representation, facing a partner fully funded by the state through the auspices of Legal Aid. The author said he faced an aggressive barrister, solicitor and legal assistant who used every destabilising tactic they could think of. None of them had met the children, or in reality could really care less what happened to them. They were locked in a legalistic and well remunerated process, nothing else.

It was through these sorts of experiences that many separated fathers came to view Legal Aid and its family law units' one sided funding of custody battles as an inappropriate use of taxpayer's money. While there were always regular news reports about the alleged underfunding of Legal Aid as reporters regurgitated press releases form various interest groups, we argued that in fact a large percentage of this money constituted back door funding to the Family Court.

Most couples not wealthy enough to fund a legal battle would likely settle their cases if one of the parties was not being driven by handsomely funded lawyers. How, Dads On The Air asked, could the government justify funding one side of a custody dispute, almost invariably the mother, thereby massively distorting the case and providing a huge advantage to one side?

Family breakdown was a multibillion dollar industry. Lawyers grew rich. Fathers grew more and more suicidal. Bureaucracies ballooned. The society grew ever more sicker. Social malaise set in.

***

The anonymous author claimed that while he had worked within easy walking distance of the Family Court's Sydney registry for most of his professional life, he was shocked to find out what was going on behind its expensive marble facade: the leisurely pace of the judges, the bizarre complexity of its procedures, the contempt with which lone litigants were treated – and most of all, the behaviour and professional misconduct of the court's family report writers, whose practices family law reformers had done their best to expose.

Way back in 1999 the author Mr X went on to expound his own conclusions: "It is in the family reports that the alchemy of truth characteristic of the court occurs: where black can be turned into white, junkie mums into sober paragons of maternal virtue and men into violent sub-Neanderthals. It is here where the accusations of women, no matter how implausible, can be reported as fact."

Can, and often are. Those family report writers know perfectly well that if they began writing pro-father reports their lucrative stream of work would dry up overnight. There's always someone low enough to take the work.

The report writers, often enough the same corrupt and dishonest psychiatrists or psychologists utilised by child protection departments, are virtually immune from any oversight of their conduct. Complaints made to the Federal Attorney General are met with a lecture on the separation of power between court and state. Complaints to state based Health Care Complaints Commissions are given short shrift and referred back to the Family Court as the most appropriate place for such complaints.

But the Court, of course, is the last place to make a complaint about the conduct of their experts, because they have relied for years on these very reports to justify their style of custody order. The circular nature of the complaints system has failed the consumers of these services. It is a hermetically sealed evidentiary loop; no truth need enter.

The psychs have grown rich. Sad dads have increased in number. The experts themselves, with their well established legal networks, are highly litigious. Because it requires the confrontation of much propagandised feminist orthodoxy and a massive legal and bureaucratic cash cow, requires hard work and investigative skill and is thereby expensive, no newspaper in Australia has made a serious attempt to expose their practices.

Most decisions which do not settle prior to trial were and still are made on the basis of reports from a coterie of Family Court report writers, at one time largely the court's own in-house counsellors and now likely to be one of a small network of psychiatrists who get this lucrative work.

From its inception Dads On The Air claimed that there were significant problems with these reports.

Custody decisions, when not made at interim hearings on little evidence but the affidavits of feuding parents, are almost invariably made at trial on the recommendations of a family report writer who has rarely seen the parties involved for more than an hour each, if they are lucky. Departure from their recommendations can offer grounds for appeal.

***

There is no proof that an hour long interview under such conditions provides anything but a brief glimpse of parents in stress. Putting aside the frequent complaints about the bias and extremely poor quality of the reports, such interviews are simply insufficient to determine the appropriate future for a child. They are certainly insufficient to justify the removal of a child from one parent or the other.

It appeared to DOTA self-evident that the "experts" and family report writers used by the court were chosen over time for their preparedness to perpetuate its agenda. The judicial requirement for what were known as 30A Reports provided a cash cow for psychologists and counsellors prepared to do the court's bidding. While expert witnesses are a problem throughout the Australian legal system, their routine abuse is particularly evident in family law. The "experts" charge thousands of dollars for reports based on little if anything more than brief interviews with each parent accompanied by their children, combined with their subjective impressions or prejudices.

Dads On The Air consistently argued that these reports constituted the core of the corruption within the Australian family law system. They formed the evidentiary bedrock of Australian family law. Expert witnesses were a problem throughout the Australian judicial system, but in family law their extreme anti-father bias reached the point of absurdity.

In the DOTA submission to the 2003 parliamentary inquiry into family law we wrote: "The systemic abuse of psychiatric evidence within the court is at the heart of its discredited practices. It is self-evident that the court uses those psychiatrists and family report writers which comply with its agenda.

"The conduct of this comparatively small clique of report writers should be the subject of a Royal Commission or similar inquiry. Michael Green QC, author of *Fathers After Divorce*, described the reports on which decisions are often based almost exclusively as 'very very poor and entirely suspect'. That's being polite. The poor quality, extreme bias and often farcical nature of these reports will ultimately be exposed as corrupt practice. We suggest that any objective investigation into their conduct would provide enough evidence for them to be de-registered, if not charged. Any reform of family law and the introduction of shared parenting or joint custody cannot proceed effectively while these practices continue."[16]

The entire troubled, dysfunctional arena of family law and child support is clearly a case where government intervention has had little or no benefit, and on balance the entire Australian population would be better off if the government stayed out of the private sphere altogether. The handing of power to the outmoded "all men are rapists", "all marriage is oppression", ideological feminists

---

16 Submission to Inquiry into the Family Law Amendment Bill 2003, available at Dads On The Air website, dated 19 January, 2004.

who pervade the court and its flanking bureaucracies creates an entirely inappropriate and destructive gender war for the 2020s. The perverse motives over money and property fuels false accusations of domestic abuse, consuming vast amounts of police time and trivialising the societal role of law enforcement.

***

The author Mr X went on to record his experiences in the witness box across three days: "In all those days of cross-examination I was never asked about my relationship with the children or attitudes to parenting. Past relationships were referred to snidely as sexual difficulties, things that happened 20 years ago flung in my face. I can't pretend to have been the cleanest of skins throughout my life, but as I said in the court: I might have a history, but I also have a present. I get up, I go to work, I pay my taxes and I have every right to expect that the mechanisms in this society which are supposed to protect children will also protect my children."

While women are natural networkers and often well prepared when they enter the family law arena, like most dads Mr X claimed he was entirely ignorant of the system, assuming it would work in a fair and reasonable manner. "While some may naively expect consistent honesty, accuracy and decency in our public institutions when it comes to children, many mothers and fathers ultimately find nothing of the kind."

Fathers damaged by family law and child support are all too easy to find. Next time you're in a taxi drop the subject and you are just as likely to find a separated dad who slept in his taxi for months after his court case, or who is being hounded by the Child Support Agency, or who has gone back to live with his parents and misses his children badly. These are the same people so arrogantly dismissed as nothing but disgruntled litigants.

Many fathers, often legally unrepresented and unprepared intellectually or emotionally to deal with the complexities of a Family Court case, blame themselves for not succeeding. They think: if only I had done this, if only I had done that. It is only slowly they realise there is no sanity in the system from top to bottom, and that no number of legal appeals or appeals to reason can win the day. For months after their cases end they replay the circumstances in their minds, involuntarily shouting out in their sleep at the family report writer, telling him or her what a liar they were, rehearsing what they would say to the children's lawyer who had done such a disgraceful job if they ever met him or her in the street, dreaming that when the judgement was handed down they should have stood up and shouted "Bastard", but didn't.

One day, in desperation in the early months after separation, having rung around domestic violence refuges and other places looking for support and discovering, like so many before me and so many since, that if you're a man no support is available, I rang Sue Price from the Men's Rights Agency. She listened to my distress, offered comfort.

"One day you might write about all this," she said. "Never," I sobbed. "I couldn't."

She was right of course. Over the years I came to respect her. It's all too easy when you're government funded and spruiking a fashionable piece of victimology to speak out publicly while being comforted by a committee. To do as she has done and speak out boldly on behalf of unfashionable victims, fathers, while facing derision for having allegedly betrayed her own gender, requires genuine courage.

Price said at a parliamentary forum in Canberra organised by family law reform proponent Ken Ticehurst in 2002: "I'm frequently asked, What's a woman doing in a Men's Rights organisation. It's easy to answer when one has an understanding and appreciation that men are an essential part of our lives, and vice versa. We complement each other in so many ways.

"There should not be a gender war, but unfortunately the need for the Men's Rights Agency has come about as a result of the bias that has escalated beyond all reason against men and boys, affecting all facets of their life. Most of which has occurred because of oppressive affirmative action legislation, the introduction and misuse of domestic violence laws, and family law perceptions that favour maternal preference.

"Boys' educational disadvantage is just the start of the problem, jobs for men are disappearing, whilst more are created for women, little money is spent on improving men's health, yet men die earlier, the bias even extends to sentencing for criminal offences. Women will undoubtedly receive a lesser sentence for a similar crime.

"If we continue to raise our children in an atmosphere where boys' masculinity is suppressed as if it is a disorder, men are told they need to be deconstructed and reconstructed, where girls are told they can do anything without reminders that with rights come responsibilities, our next generations are facing a bleak future, and even greater family dysfunction.

"If the Australian people knew the full extent of the unfair treatment dished out to loving, caring parents and their children on a daily basis they would be horrified, but this treatment will not be uncovered until Section 121 of the

Family Law Act is repealed. The secrecy clause just cloaks the abuse against the family that is allowed to flourish in the Family Court on a daily basis.

"After an appearance in family court, fathers repeatedly tell me they feel as if they are being treated like criminals."[17]

***

Men typically do not cooperate well with each other, and do not network in the same way as women. They are embarrassed to protest. They are, as we sometimes described them on Dads On The Air, like bulls all in their separate paddocks. They all want to get out, but they'll be buggered if they're going to cooperate to do so. One woman's pain is an Oprah Winfrey show, one man's pain is a public embarrassment.

Without the same massive public funding available to women's groups and women's causes, the family law reform movement in Australia was atomised and uncoordinated, made up of people burnt by the system or incensed by its manifest injustices.

Only a few fathers stay around to fight the good fight on behalf of their brothers. After the custody dispute is over and they have got whatever help they need from the various groups, most dads crawl off under a rock to lick their wounds or drink themselves to death, or simply return to their everyday lives, never to be heard of again.

They will tell you in private, for hours sometimes, how disgusted they are by the state of family law in Australia and the government's complicity in it and what a pack of bastards the Child Support Agency are. But for most, particularly those who can no longer see their children, campaigning for the rights of fathers and children to maintain a relationship after divorce is nothing but salt in an unhealable wound. Even if they do become active after being burnt by divorce or separation, they rarely stay around for more than a few years, burning out quickly.

One day such a person, David, who had been phoning me at work and keeping me abreast of the more outrageous cases he came across, insisted that I come down and watch his own case. He had been extremely wound up during the lengthy process of preparing for trial, and desperately concerned over the welfare of his adolescent son, who the mother was preventing him from seeing and who had recently attempted suicide. From what I understood, the boy was not even going to school anymore, just staying at home with his mother.

---

17 Men's Rights Agency presentation to the Parliamentary Forum arranged by Ken Ticehurst MP held in Canberra on 12th November, 2002. Available on the Australian Parliament website.

David was insistent that the judge and the court's behaviour defied belief. Fearing that I might be being used as a prop, but also understanding how difficult sitting in the witness box being cross examined over your own children for days on end really was and wishing to lend some support, I attended, sitting quietly up the back of the courtroom with a reporter's pad clearly in hand.

A reporter's pad was not enough to stop that judge. By mid-morning he was going hammer and tongs, provoking snickers from the work experience girl hanging behind the bench. The fact that David had been critical of family law in recent months in numerous online forums no doubt did not help his case.

Obviously dissatisfied with the barrister's cross examination, the judge took over.

"What do you mean, Mr G, what do you mean when you say in your statement that you wanted to be there after your son attempted suicide?" he demanded from the bench.

"I merely meant that after his suicide attempt, which must have been very distressing, it would have been nice to be able to see him, comfort him," David answered.

"That's not what you meant at all, is it?" the judge demanded. "You wanted to be there to watch, didn't you? Didn't you?"

Shocked at the accusation, David continued to protest from the witness box. "All I wanted to do was to be able to talk to my son after his suicide attempt, to comfort him, talk to him."

"You wanted to be there to watch, didn't you? Didn't you?" the judge continued.

"I meant nothing of the kind," David answered.

"You wanted to be there to watch, didn't you, didn't you?" the judge thundered.

I couldn't believe this bullying, disgraceful behaviour from a judge of one of the country's so-called "superior" courts. A man paid hundreds of thousands of dollars a year to sit where he was sitting, to supposedly serve the public. But I had begun to realise that these cases, far from being unusual, were the norm. In a secretive jurisdiction fathers were routinely treated with hostility and disdain, the most ludicrous accusations made against them treated as fact. The words of a court appointed counsellor or psych, who the litigants often believed had deliberately misinterpreted everything they said, were taken as gospel.

The court itself, as was evidenced by these cases, had developed its own strange psychopathology.

***

Mr X recorded recent research showing the average lone litigant spent 42 days preparing for trial. The family matters basket on his computer had 273 files in it; submissions, affidavits, solicitors' letters, complaints. As he described it: "The process is like climbing Mount Everest a dozen times in a state of emotional distress."

It is no wonder your average truck driver or tradie gets rolled in the Family Court. What was originally meant to be a simple, user friendly, caring jurisdiction evolved into one where the processes are so complex they exclude ordinary people; and few people can afford to pay lawyers hundreds of dollars an hour to squabble over their private affairs.

A newspaper graphic recorded that the costs in a contested action can range from $10,000 to $100,000 plus for each party. The median annual income of people attending the court is $25,000 to $30,000. Some parents spend two to three times their annual income on legal fees. In the quarter of a century since then, those figures have increased significantly.

This was at the turn of the millennium. Costs have soared ever since.

The author wrote that it was just after Father's Day when the judgement was finally handed down: "My time with the children was to be progressively decreased over the next three years. I went home to a house still full of banners from the children: 'We Love You Dad', 'You're the Best Dad'.

"The judgement did not get my age or the hearing date correct, falsely claimed that I had an AVO against me and that the mother was the primary carer. The judgement ignored four days of evidence and regurgitated the report of a 'specialist' who had never been cross examined because I didn't have $1500 to pay for his court appearance. It was as if the trial had never happened. I had seen the specialist with the children for perhaps six minutes.

"The judge went out of his way to say how helpful the reports were. But I knew they were patently biased and inaccurate."

***

This was one man's story, but at Dads On The Air we heard of too many cases to think this one was unique. It was common to find stories of courts ordering children back into the hands of violent, abusive, drunken, drug-addicted mothers when there was a perfectly good home for them with their fathers, of men being stitched up by biased and inaccurate reports. No one listened to the grief and injury of men falsely accused of sexually abusing children, of being violent and neglectful fathers when nothing of the sort was true; of their disgust at an industry thriving on false claims, the pain of a system which left them impoverished and their children's lives wrecked.

There is a widespread belief amongst separated fathers that far from assessing the facts before them to determine the "best interests of the child", the Family Court judges, indoctrinated with an old-style 1970s and 1980s "all men are rapists" feminism and who would not have achieved the positions they had if they were not prepared to peddle these antiquated ideologies, were more likely to follow those precepts set out in the book *Feminist Jurisprudence* – facts are nothing but weapons that men use to batter women and perpetuate the system. Desperate fathers would if they could spend hundreds of thousands of dollars to get a reasonable outcome from the court but almost never succeeded. For the simple reason that truth had nothing to do with any of it.

Mr X stated in his windup that despite almost two decades as a journalist and a comparatively colourful life, he had never met a more dishonest group of people than some of those he encountered while fighting a custody battle.

"I have formed the view that like any institution neither transparent nor accountable, the culture of the Family Court is corrupt; that ideology has replaced decency and the ones suffering the most are children, mine and many others."

***

The newspaper received more letters than the Saturday features editor at the time, well known Sydney journalist Ean Higgins, had received on any other topic. Most were supportive.

One wrote giving his hearty thanks for publishing the story. "From personal experience I know without any doubt that everything Mr X wrote is true, because he did no more than describe how the Family Court industry operates. There are many fathers quietly battling 'the system'. In my own case, even though I have committed no crime, and want more than anything else to be a good father, I have had my little son taken away from me via the court process and, of course, my little son has lost his father."

Another wrote: "The Family Court specialises in first removing parenthood, then property, possessions and pride from any loving father through any means available to them, and any woman even considering a change in lifestyle without the father of her children being involved knows full well the power that she has at her disposal through the threatened use of this court."

Another declared that similar stories could fill page after page of our newspapers if any journalist bothered to hunt out the men churned through this system. "I am one of those stories, but I am forbidden to publicly give that story, by a piece of Family Law legislation known as s121, that is designed to protect the children, but in fact does far more to protect our judges and their decisions from any close scrutiny."[18]

***

The then Chief Justice of the Family Court Alastair Nicholson, however, was singularly displeased. Nicholson had long been a thorn in the side of successive governments, regarding it as part of his duties to comment on many of the social issues of the day. Nor did he hesitate to personally attack his critics within the journalistic, legal, academic and community realms. He would routinely condemn the work of anyone who dared to question the dysfunctional Court he had presided over for much of its life as doing them "no credit".

Somehow none of the normal constraints on judge's making public comments or attempting to dictate public policy applied to Nicholson. He regularly harangued the government about lack of funding for his already handsomely resourced Court – as well as the lack of Legal Aid funding.

Nicholson complained the paper had given an anonymous individual, apparently a journalist, the opportunity to personalise his version of a Family Court dispute in a highly dramatic manner to a national audience.

He wrote: "In publishing this sensational account *The Australian* has managed to send a poisonous Christmas message to the many families for whom Christmas is already a difficult time because of family breakdown. It also succeeds in undermining faith in the judicial system in a most irresponsible manner, and in unfairly criticising dedicated legal and other professionals who work in one of the most difficult and stressful areas of the law.

"The Family Court cannot respond properly to this scurrilous story because of restrictions on the publication of details of Family Court proceedings, nor can it verify or check the accuracy of the allegations made because of their anonymous nature."

It was commonly understood by family law reform activists that the Family Court issued or approved more surveillance orders than any other institution in the country.

None of us who worked on Dads On The Air were in any doubt that we attracted some level of surveillance. They had the low down on all their critics. As well, officers from the Australian Federal Police were used, or misused, as props in court cases where there were accusations of violence. Their attendance only dramatised many situations which should never have gone before a court in the first place, and wasted yet more public resources. There is little doubt Nicholson knew exactly who the author was.

---

18 Letters to the Editor, *The Australian*, 30 December, 1999.

"In publishing one side of what is inevitably a complex story, *The Australian* has shown a complete abdication of its responsibility to the public and to the concept of balanced journalism. Long experience in family law shows that many people are unable to be objective about their involvement in such proceedings and when such accounts are examined from both points of view, the real story is often very different.

"It is all too easy to blame the Family Court for failing to solve the consequences of relationship breakdown but perhaps it is time to ask as to why the author and people like him were unable to do so themselves.

"Your story has done much to encourage those who bring a sense of not only irresponsibility but violence to family relationships and may well have put at risk women and children involved in family law matters during the tense festive period."[19]

It was typical of the Court's culture that its numerous problems and poor reputation were being blamed on litigants for failing to resolve their own cases, despite the Court regularly making those cases worse and despite the Court's many suspect practices and unhelpful processes. And despite the fact that many fathers, caught in a system they quickly learnt to despise, were there by no choice of their own and had little option but to fight if they wanted to see their children at all.

As well, it is little appreciated that many parents have no alternative but to go to the court at least in the first instance as such orders are a contingent part of receiving welfare benefits post separation. It is at this point that custody decisions, usually the standard "daddy pack" of alternative weekends, are made on minimal evidence. As the status quo sets in, these original orders become almost impossible to overturn.

The unfortunate connection with the social welfare department Centrelink, which demands that separated parents have orders so that they can claim various tax benefits and welfare payments such as the sole parent's pension and child support payments, is a major factor in forcing parents into conflict most would prefer to avoid. There are numerous stories of separated parents who got on reasonably well until they were dragged through the excruciating processes of the court and the battle lines of child support.

Nicholson's claim that the story promoted violence against women and children was insulting nonsense. The claim that the paper was hiding behind anonymity was also nonsense. The paper, by law, could not publish the name of the author. The secrecy provisions of the legislation protecting the court, the notorious

---

19 Nicholson, Alastair, Letters, *The Australian*, 28 December, 1999.

Section 121, have significantly hampered any proper journalistic inquiry into its operations for decades. Legislation which is supposed to protect children in custody disputes has simply hidden its worst excesses behind a cloak of secrecy, doing the nation's children far more harm than if the occasional child of divorce underwent the discomfort of having their parents squabble become public.

***

DOTA editorialised that there were many scandals associated with the court which had never been publicly aired because secrecy provisions inappropriately protected an institution long overdue for reform. Corrupt processes thrive behind a wall of secrecy, no matter what the justification or jurisdiction. Negative experiences in the court were far from a rarity. The only difference in this case was that a journalist felt compelled to write about what he had seen and experienced. Originally written in the third person as a generalised feature, its personalised tone was as a result of a direct request from the paper's editor.

Nicholson's letter, published four days after the story itself, showed the court ignored the pain and stress its procedures imposed on fathers over extended periods of time during custody disputes. Sheltered by magnificent salaries and regarding themselves as champions of women, they appeared blind to the hurt of the litigants before them. Heroic and expensive appeals to the full bench of the court are almost entirely pointless.

On the same day there was a letter from a Dr Vincent Patrick of Western Australia proposing a solution the government would later adopt in some measure: "Although a happily married man, I am aware of the poor treatment meted out to fathers in the name of family law, and the irrational doctrines which allow it to happen. Much of the problem would be solved with changes to the law to provide default equal parenting on separation, with variations from this requiring agreement by both partners."[20]

The Family Court judge involved in Mr X's case retired in 2005. The same judge where unfortunate litigants cautioned each other it could take a good two years or more to recover from his judgements, the same judge who couldn't even get simple things like trial dates correct, was given a full ceremonial sitting of the court upon his retirement after a "long and distinguished career". It was presided over by the then fairly new Family Court Chief Justice Diana Bryant.

He was also lauded by the then Attorney General himself Phillip Ruddock. Others to attend included the Chairman of the Family Law Section of the Law Council of Australia Ian Kennedy; President of the NSW Bar Association Michael Slattery and President of the Law Society of NSW John McIntyre.

---

20 Patrick, Vincent, Letters, *The Australian*, 28 December, 1999.

The sitting was held at Goulburn Street in the centre of Sydney, site one of the country's grandest Family Court registries. In later years Dads On The Air would play a song called Goulburn Street Hall by the band Horizon Shine and my good friend Ian Purdie.

> Innocent families, lambs to the slaughter,
> They separate brother and mother and daughter,
> The corridors echo with silent screams,
> Agony etched into every ream,
> Of paperwork piled from wall to wall,
> Lost in the horror of Goulburn Street Hall
>
> Goulburn Street Hall where love has to crawl,
> Down comes the gavel, the winner takes all,
> Goulburn Street Hall my heart is appalled,
> At the calm, casual, carnage behind every door.
>
> Pillars of marble, wood panels, horse hair,
> The symbols of conflict, dead love and despair,
> Institutionalised horror all day,
> Haunting sad hearts that can't run away,
> All for nothing and nothing for all,
> Lives slip through fingers in Goulburn Street Hall.
> A modern torture chamber, disguised as a court,
> Processing daily, an endless onslaught,
> Of pain and dysfunction, of lies and deceit,
> While lawyers circle round like spaniels on heat,
> Nobody knows how far they can fall,
> Until they have been to the seventh floor.
>
> Goulburn Street Hall where love has to crawl,
> Down comes the gavel, the winner takes all,
> Goulburn Street Hall my heart is appalled,
> At the calm, casual, carnage behind every door.

Apart from giving the long list of senior roles the judge had held within the court, the notice alerting the media of the ceremonial sitting carried a warning of the reporting restrictions which had protected the court's functioning from public scrutiny over so many years: "Filming, photography and interviews are restricted by section 121 of the Family Law Act 1975. People who are involved in family law cases – litigants, lawyers, witnesses and the like – must not be identified or be identifiable."

Within months of the publication of the Mr X story the Australian Law Reform Commission handed down the final results of its extended inquiry into the federal justice system, including the most extensive inquiry ever conducted into the Family Court.[21] The review had been initiated by the Howard government. It found a secretive, beleaguered and defensive institution immune to positive criticism. It also found overwhelming disquiet from both litigants and the solicitors with the court and its processes.

"Practitioners deplored and regretted the poor relationship they had with the court." It recommended an external review, the first step towards abolition, if changes were not implemented. No changes took place. No independent review was ever initiated.

---

21 Australian Law Reform Commission, Managing Justice: A Review of the Federal Civil Justice System (ALRC Report 89), 17 February, 2000.

TWO
A LITTLE BIT OF HISTORY

ON THE 5th of January 1976 the Family Law Act 1975 came into effect. It was passed into law by just one vote. This marked a controversial and historically significant turning point for Australian family life. Making contentious changes to the law relating to marriage, Australia had introduced no fault divorce. For the first time, married couples could seek a divorce by demonstrating a separation of 12 months duration.

The single ground of irreconcilable breakdown was controversial in the early 1970s and much of the lengthy parliamentary debates were dedicated to the abandonment of fault in divorce proceedings. Traditionalists saw it as an assault on the institution of marriage.

The Family Law Act of 1975 also created the Family Court of Australia to interpret and apply that law and with the stated aim of ensuring matters of family breakdown, separation and divorce were managed in a more family friendly manner. It would prove to be one of the most hotly debated and often despised pieces of legislation in Australian history.

The Family Court has jurisdiction over all marriage-related cases in all states and territories of Australia, except Western Australia which has its own family court. Its jurisdiction covers applications for declarations of the validity or nullity of marriages, divorces, residence, contact, maintenance, child support and property issues. It also has jurisdiction over de facto couples and parents who have never lived together.

The only avenue of appeal for the Court's often arbitrary decision making was to a Full Bench of the Court, an extremely expensive, complex and more than likely pointless exercise.

Conciliation and counselling services were originally designed into the Family Court's structure to assist the dissolution of marriages in a less hostile manner than previously. This service quickly fell foul to accusations it was little better than a lesbian or feminist cabal. Whatever the case, many fathers reported extreme dissatisfaction. Those same counsellors, originally intended to be so helpful, were later to become the subject of much hostility from fathers' groups for their frequently alleged bias.

Children's custody matters were to be determined with "the best interests of the child" as the paramount consideration and all matters coming before the Court were to receive individual attention specific to the parties' unique circumstances. As previously stated, "the best interests of the child" was a nebulous legal term which could mean more or less anything, depending on the bias of the beholder.

A government media release described the initiative as "sweeping away the laws and procedures of the past and providing a new era of calmness and rationality, presided over by specialist judges assisted by experts and which would introduce speedy, less expensive and less formal procedures."

Seen through the lens of half a century of fraught litigation, devastated parents, a ballooning welfare budget and the close involvement of Australia's legal and political establishment in the debacle, these assurances appear utterly naive.

***

The original intention of the Family Court of Australia was, allegedly, to improve the manner in which separation and marriage dissolution had been previously managed.

Underlying the vision of the Family Law Act, its architect, the late Senator Lionel Murphy, claimed the court would operate on principles supporting humanitarian values. The Court was to be a 'helping' court. The need for improved access to justice was also identified as an aim.

The Court's processes were to be less formal, services were to be provided to remote areas and child-care was to be provided for parents using the Court's services.

In a speech to the Federal Parliament in March 1973, Senator Lionel Murphy said, "When a family is broken up, when there is a divorce, at least let us enable those people involved to solve their differences in a decent human and dignified way, and without their being subjected to this kind of expense."[22]

As it evolved, the court, with its extensive delays and elaborately complex and overly legalistic procedures, was light years from this aim.

Hansard's record of the debates surrounding the Family Law Bill demonstrated the intention of the parliament to establish a child custody regime which would see the care and upbringing of children equitably shared between

---

22 Murphy, Lionel, Senator, Address to Australian Parliament, 28 March, 1973.

separating parents. In a parliamentary debate in October 1974, the late Senator Alan Missen explained that the Family Law regime would "create the concept of joint custody under the law".[23]

Original lofty intentions were rapidly lost. Appeals to the High Court case forced the Family Court to act like a normal court and emphasised the importance of traditional legal practice rather than "palm tree justice", thus locking the adversarial trial system into place.

Parliament's intention that the Family Court would operate with less formal processes and as a "helping court" collapsed, leaving two of the original presumptions of Parliament in passing the legislation undelivered.

Instead separating couples had to slog it out in front of a judge, often creating an enduring bitterness. False accusations of domestic violence, for which the court became infamous, fuelled the fire and helped destroy the morale of the nation's police.

Nor was the notion of joint custody proposed by the original proponents of the legislation ever realised, with the feminist orientation of its early personnel leading to sole mother custody as the standard.

The appropriateness of adversarial trials was the subject of debate throughout the life of the court. The sight of separating couples locked in protracted battles they could seemingly not escape became all too common. Critics argued that the wild claims separated couples were encouraged to pitch against each other and the high conflict it generated between parents meant adversarial trials themselves were against the best interests of children.

The Shared Parenting Council's submission to the 2003 inquiry summed it up thus: "Every year or so, a Family Law Amendment Bill is passed by the Federal Parliament – each one seeking to rectify problems identified in previous inquiries. Without exception, there has been a Legislative failure of Family Law Amendments to achieve outcomes that resemble the system originally planned and designed by the Late Senator Lionel Murphy and introduced by the Whitlam Labor Government in 1975.

"The majority of Australians have determined that the Family Law Courts are biased, unfair, expensive, incapable of dealing with family matters in a timely and orderly manner, and of more concern, expose children to risk of abuse or harm.

"Similarly, we have an overwhelming majority of Child Support Agency 'clients' bitterly complaining that the Agency has destroyed their Lives.

"How is it possible that review after review, amendment after amendment, reform after reform, have so clearly failed to achieve a system of fairness, justice,

---

23 Missen, Senator Alan, Australian Parliament, Hansard, 29 October, 1974.

and equity in Family Breakdown situations. It is fair to say that the Family Law Act and the Family Court are a failure of public policy, a failure of legislative intent and a failure of the implementation of the will of Parliament."[24]

***

At the turn of the millennium when I first became interested, difficulties with the application and interpretation of the Family Law Act were evident. Families engaging the Family Court had become more ready to agitate their concerns. Constituent pressure for reform was building in Parliamentary Members and Senators offices around the country.

The Family Court was controversial from the minute it opened its doors. One common thread in the history of Australian family law has been the multiple amendments to the Act and numerous changes to procedures.

Rather than improving the quality of service delivery, multiple inquiries into family law from various government bodies has allowed ideological capture and successive governments to cherry pick recommendations, almost invariably with an ever increasing hostility to fathers.

Politicians themselves became trapped in an ever escalating feminist fuelled derision of the role of fathers in family life by the very monster they themselves created and funded – the literally thousands of personnel in taxpayer funded women's legal services, feminist advocacy groups and gender studies courses, many of whom had no hesitation in publicly criticising any politician who deviated from their doctrinaire line of women as victims, men as perpetrators and the nuclear family as dangerous. No politician wanted to take the risk of being described as anti-woman.

As early as 1978 a Parliamentary Joint Select Committee was asked to review the Family Law Act and whether there should be additional grounds for divorce. The report did not recommend a reconsideration of no-fault divorce, but several Committee members expressed concern.

In 1980, the Fraser Coalition Government set out to hold the first comprehensive inquiry into the operations of the Family Law Act, only four years after the court began operating. Many concerns of individual MPs had been canvassed during this period, including proposals to lower the retirement age of Family Court Judges to age 65 to keep them more closely in touch with changing social mores. This was a matter strongly supported by former Prime Minister and then Fraser Government Minister, John Howard. What at the time might have seemed an obscure legal point became of great interest in future years.

---

[24] Shared Parenting Council of Australia submission, House of Representatives Standing Committee on Family and Community Affairs, received 15 August, 2003.

In 1987, the Advisory Committee on the Australian Judicial System received numerous submissions on the position and role of the Family Court in the federal judicial structure.

***

By 1990, there was clear unrest in the electoral offices of Members of Parliament in relation to the operation of family law.

An area of concern, particularly in rural areas, was that with family breakdown escalating farmers were losing their generational farming properties, with a significant number of people being forced to sell because of the property division orders of the Family Court.

Economic circumstances in the early 1990's were difficult for farming families, and the country towns that relied on the income from surrounding farmlands for their survival were also under stress. Drought, escalating interest rates, high debt and pending economic recession were taking their toll throughout rural and regional Australia.

At the federal election held in March 1990, the Liberal National Party Coalition committed to a review of the operation of family law if elected.

After the election, NSW National Party Senator David Brownhill sought assistance from other Senators for a parliamentary inquiry into the operation and outcomes of family law. Because the conservatives in Australia, the somewhat oxymoronically named Liberal Party and the National Party, the big end of town and the rural areas, are in Coalition in Australia, the Nationals held significant sway in the early discussions on the impacts of family law.

Senator Brownhill, himself a farmer and grazier, held the view that the family law system was significantly contributing to the devastation of rural family life.

Many of his constituent's were watching their livelihoods evaporate in the struggle to maintain their farming operations. They were confronted with further devastation through the loss of their marriages under the economic strains of high debt and rising interest rates. Suicide was on the increase, and country towns were being economically savaged by the exodus of broken families fleeing to the cities.

Increasing numbers of rural constituents faced the final blow to any hope of recovery dished out in the shape of Family Court judgements. The most significant complaint made by these rural families was the devastation faced by having to sell farm and grazing property to satisfy Family Court orders. For the first time established family farms that had been passed down through families for generations, were being sold.

John Stapleton

***

Senator Brownhill continued his push and by March 1991 had secured the numbers in the Senate to establish an inquiry in that chamber. He hoped to convince a reluctant Labor Government headed by Bob Hawke, a Prime Minister who portrayed himself as a friend of the working man throughout his career, to expand the inquiry to the House of Representatives to examine custody, property determinations, access and the cost of family law matters, all of which were causing difficulties within the community.

In March, after Brownhill and Leader of the Opposition in the Senate Robert Hill reached agreement with other Opposition parties, including the Democrats, the government agreed to a select joint committee. Brownhill noted the problems besetting family law. There had been 21 separate amendments to the original Act since 1980 when the last parliamentary inquiry was undertaken into a review of the original 1975 Act.[25]

The Report of the Joint Select Committee on Certain Aspects of the Operation and Interpretation of the Family Law Act was tabled in January 1993. It agreed with Senator Brownhill's concerns in relation to family farms and advised that the Act be amended to distinguish farming properties from other matrimonial property so that the Family Court was able to consider whether the farming property was brought into the marriage by one or other party and the necessity for the retention of a farming property as an income producing unit for the future needs of the separating family.

While accepting most of the 120 recommendations of the Joint Select Committee, the Family Law Council was opposed on the vexed issue of farming property. The impact of family law in rural areas remained an issue. The Court's favouring of sole mother custody and its rewarding of mothers, often enough school teachers who had only been in the rural district for a short time, with up to 90 per cent of assets on separation mitigated against any cooperative parenting after divorce and destroyed farming operations built up over generations.

The Committee recommended there be no change to the terminology of the Act in relation to custody and access, until there was clear evidence that a change would be advantageous to the settlement of custody and access disputes. The Family Law Council did not agree and stated they would "continue to monitor this situation with a view to ensuring that changes in terminology are implemented at an appropriate time".

---

25 Select Committee on Certain Aspects of the Operation and Interpretation of the Family Law Act, *The Family Law Act 1975: Aspects of its operation and interpretation*, tabled 26 November, 1992.

The Family Law Council's 1992 report Patterns of Parenting After Separation, attempted to soften the distinction between one parent, usually the mother, being seen as the "real" parent, while the other, usually the father, was seen as a visitor. The terms "custody" and "access" were thought to suggest both a proprietorial and a gendered attitude to parenting. The report emphasised cooperative parenting after separation, resolution of disputes through mediation and the use of parenting plans rather than traditionally formulated court orders.[26]

The issue of reforming family law terminology became a part of the debate over family law reform. A Shared Parenting Council submission observed that the influence of the Family Law Council within the Attorney General's Department and the Hawke and Keating Labor Governments was unparalleled.

Ultimately, the Family Law Council successfully had Family Law terminology changed in the 1995 Family Law Reform Act despite the 1992 Joint Select Committee's opposition.

Having effectively ignored the parliamentary committee findings, the terms "custody" and "access" were replaced by the terms "residence" and "contact" in 1996.

Almost universally, critics of the Family Court and simultaneously, academics, and even the Chief Justice realised the terminology change had been a resounding failure, and many family law reform organisations identified it as a "smoke and mirrors" trick to convince the hundreds of thousands of dissatisfied litigants, predominantly, but not exclusively fathers, that their minimal contact award was much better for them, because it was now called contact instead of access.

***

The raft of amendments in the Family Law Reform Act of 1995 emphasised that, except when contrary to a child's best interests, children should have the right to know and be cared for by both their parents, regardless of whether their parents are married, separated, have never married or have never lived together; children had a right of contact, on a regular basis, with both their parents and with other people significant to their care, welfare and development; parents should share duties and responsibilities concerning the care, welfare and development of their children; and parents should agree about the future parenting of their children.

In the lead up to the passing of the legislation, in 1995 Yuri Joakimidis of the Joint Parenting Association and several other children's rights advocates met with

---

26 Family Law Council, Patterns of Parenting After Separation, 1 April, 1992.

Parliamentary Secretary Peter Duncan. At the meeting the Minister stated his government would introduce presumptive joint custody legislation.

The Family Court got it wrong was the message from Peter Duncan when he moved the Keating Labor government's 1995 amendments. His words made clear that, in the view of the Parliament the Family Court had handled child custody matters inappropriately.

"The original intention of the late Senator Murphy was that the Family Law Act would create a rebuttable presumption of shared parenting, but over the years the Family Court has chosen to ignore that. It is hoped that these reforms will now call for much closer attention to this presumption and that the Family Court will give full and proper effect to the intention of Parliament."[27]

Despite the Duncan speech however, the legislated changes omitted the above statutory instruction.

The changes, which came into effect in 1996, were associated with an increase in the number of men making applications to the court for a greater role in the lives of their children post-separation.

Many fathers attempted to gain more contact through contravention applications, which were at that time one of the few litigation remedies available to parents seeking to restore or increase their parenting time.

The number of contravention applications by fathers almost doubled in the year following the legislation's enactment. Large numbers of the applications were dismissed.

The 1995 legislation aimed at encouraging fathers into their children's lives post separation was ignored by the Family Court. Shared parenting orders are variously estimated to have subsequently halved, from 5 per cent to 2.5 per cent.

***

Warnings that there were serious problems with the court came early.

In 1985, only a decade after the court's establishment, Australia's proud old weekly *The Bulletin* ran a story on its front cover: "The Devastation Of Divorce: Why Men Hurt The Most". It was written by Bettina Arndt, for many years virtually the only columnist in the Australian media to show any sympathy or understanding of men's issues.[28]

In an era when media was transfixed by latter-day feminism and masculinity was out of vogue, Arndt stood out for her courage to be different. Ridiculed by

---

27 Duncan, Peter Duncan MP, Parliamentary Secretary to the Attorney General, House of Representatives, Hansard, 21 November 1995, p3303.

28 Arndt, Bettina, The Devastation Of Divorce, *The Bulletin*, 1985.

her liberal critics as an old fashioned right winger, she was a hero to separated men around the country.

On one occasion, almost 20 years after her *Bulletin* article, she gave me a lift out to western Sydney for a public meeting. When we alighted from the vehicle she was surrounded by men saying how much they appreciated her work. Sad, she commented, that I have become a celebrity to these people just for showing a bit of sympathy.

Her *Bulletin* article began with a series of quotes: "Total devastation"; "like being hit on the head by a piece of four by two"; "falling apart"; "shattered".

Arndt went on to disclose the details of research by Family Court counsellor Peter Jordan showing the crippling effects of divorce and separation on men's emotional and physical health. It contained the first published Australian research focusing on male reaction to divorce and confirmed overseas evidence of men's vulnerability in the breakdown of a marriage.

In a world where men were characterised as controlled, unemotional decision makers the research held a number of surprises, including that only 19 percent of divorces were initiated by men, contradicting the image of unfaithful, feckless men. The report also showed that upon separation most men experienced emotional and physical symptoms normally associated with extreme grief, including crying and sleeplessness, and also had difficulty concentrating at work. They often suffered loneliness and social isolation.

While more than half of the men surveyed attempted reconciliation after separation, only seven percent of women bothered trying. Up to two years after divorce most men still felt they had been dumped, a third felt the divorce was a horrible mistake and a third still felt they would never get over the breakup.

Peter Jordan decided to conduct research into the effects of divorce on men after counselling his first 21 males involved in separation proceedings and discovering that 20 of them were bewildered, angry and often in tears.

"I was surprised because I expected the women to be the ones who were distressed," he said. "Here were these men desperately wanting the marriage to continue, pleading, crying, offering anything, promising anything to persuade their wives to come back. I thought: 'What is going on here?' and went looking for research on male reactions to divorce and found very little had been done."

***

The research involving 168 men between one and two years after separation who were contacted through the Brisbane registry of the Family Court. Most were in their late 20s or 30s.

One respondent said: "I always considered myself a pretty independent guy. I have a staff of six under me at work and they know I'm boss. I never realised how much I miss my kids and my old house and even the arguments with my wife. I feel like I'm falling apart."

Another said: "The turmoil made me sick. The self-hate ruined my appetite and sleep. The ghost of the relationship lived on in the inanimate objects around me. I wanted to run away but felt trapped... I wanted to be alone but felt lonely. The same rotten unanswerable questions kept coming up over and over. Was I really that bad to live with? What was wrong with me or was it her?"

Arndt wrote that it was only when the marriage ended many men realised the extent and intensity of their attachments to the marriage, their wife and their children. The man was often confused to discover the depth of his feelings and searched blindly for an explanation.

Jordan's research found men experienced a range of problems in coping after separation, from difficulties at work, financial and domestic problems – house cleaning, washing, shopping and so on. And most of all, social isolation – difficulties in making new friends, developing and maintaining new relationships, finding people to talk with and feel close to.

There would be no policy response from the Australian government.

Parliament paid no heed whatsoever to the mounting evidence of the family law system's consequences on fathers. The stories of fathers' treatment by the Family Court and concern over the impacts on children of losing the male parent from their daily lives were ignored.

***

As the *Bulletin* story demonstrated so well, knowledge of the harm being done to fathers, and consequently to their children and to the community at large by the Family Court of Australia through its religious adherence to sole-mother custody and mistreatment of fathers had been well known for decades.

Yet politicians and political parties ignored their pain. How different this country would be if politicians took the same oath as medical practitioners – "do no harm".

Back in 1985, 21 years before the Howard government chose to act, or pretend to act, on child custody, Arndt recorded that many men felt unfairly treated by the court system.

"Men often resent decisions made about property and alimony, are frustrated at their inability to prevent an unwanted divorce and are particularly bitter about that most difficult of issue – care and responsibility for their children."

Far from the image of distant and uncaring fathers painted by feminist lobby groups, Jordan found 98 percent claimed strong feelings for them and 91 percent did not want to be separated from them.

Interestingly, Arndt quoted novelist Al Alvarez, who I had interviewed in London during the 1980s. He was a lovely writer, author of that classic of my youth, *The Savage God*, a study of suicide and Sylvia Plath. As he wrote so perceptively in his early 1980s book *Life After Marriage*: "To leave a husband or a wife whom one no longer loves may be sane and natural but there is no easy way to divorce a child and, until shared custody becomes the standard practice, no marriage counselling or social reform or enlightened legislation will cure the breaking of the heart."

***

The problems with family law and the widening gulf between the government and the court were increasingly evident as the 20th century came to a close. A recent murder-suicide in Western Australia, involving a father and his children following a custody case had provoked criticism of Family Court delays.

A war of words over legal aid funding erupted between the then Attorney General Daryl Williams and Chief Justice Nicholson. "I just don't feel he has a great understanding of family law," said Nicholson.

Williams countered he hoped they were progressing to a stage where there was a smaller role for courts, judges and litigation.

There were reports that dismantling the Family Court was one option under serious consideration by the government. The argument between Nicholson and Williams reached a peak when the pair "took their battle" to the national family law conference in Tasmania that October, where genteel fur was said to have flown between the pair, allegedly "appalling" international visitors.

Nicholson suggested Williams had made the debate personal. Williams responded in kind by rejecting Nicholson's allegations of government cuts.

One conference guest recorded: "I was in the audience in Hobart and I was sort of ducking and weaving for the skin and bone flying – it was all very genteel but in the context of the Chief Justice of the Family Court and the Attorney General of the Commonwealth, it was pretty heavy stuff in terms of vitriol."

According to guests, the mood of the 600 invitees was substantially behind Nicholson. Central to the debate were ideology and economics. Nicholson wanted to expand the Family Court's role while Williams did not support its social functions.

"The core function of a court is to hear cases, not to run a social service," Williams said.

Defenders accused the Attorney General of removing control of the counselling service from the Family Court "and once that happens it won't be too far before the whole thing is dismantled."[29]

While critics saw the lack of independence and objectivity of the court's counsellors as a major issue and the pro-mother anti-father bias of their reports well established, Nicholson did not. For any father who had been the subject of one of these reports and found themselves losing contact with their children on the recommendations of a Family Court counsellor, this was a significant dispute.[30]

***

Throughout the late 1990s the Court remained in the news.

In 1998 then legal affairs reporter for *The Australian* Janet Fife-Yeomans reported that the Family Court was to investigate whether mothers or fathers were more likely to win custody of their children as its Chief Justice, Alastair Nicholson, defended his court against unprecedented claims of bias from men.

Justice Nicholson rejected claims that men were being "taken to the cleaners" in decisions by the court. He said he was concerned that there was a perception of bias, but when the court produced figures to counter that perception "some people don't want to believe them".

Fife-Yeomans reported that the court, which was then dealing with 24,930 custody applications a year compared with 9286 in 1977, had come under attack from large numbers of men and men's groups lining up as candidates in the federal election with the Family Court as their target.

One candidate in John Howard's seat of Bennelong called himself Prime Minister John Piss The Family Court and Legal Aid.[31]

Another candidate faced contempt proceedings in the Family Court in Melbourne after using a loud hailer and handing out allegedly offensive leaflets outside court.

"One of the problems about it is that making a lot of noise often gives people the impression there is a problem where there isn't," Justice Nicholson said.

"I reject the claim that people are biased against men in this court. It is a fairly

---

29 Merritt, Chris, Williams takes Family Court to task, *Australian Financial Review*, 23 October, 1998.

30 Lane, Bernard, Court Out, Trial Separation, *The Australian*, 24 December, 1999.

31 EMILY's list and angry white men: Gender wars in the nineties, *Journal of Australian Studies*, 1999.

extraordinary proposition when you look at the gender make-up of the court where two-thirds of the judges are men. Why a male-dominated judiciary would either collectively or individually set off on a campaign of bias against men is hard to understand."

Money. Ideology. Institutional capture. Status. Power. Applause. The answers were simple.

***

In the fight over the counselling service, the government was to get support from an unusual source, a Family Court judge. Justice Alwynne Rowlands warned that having an in-house counselling service put the independence of the court at risk and went beyond the primary role of the court to hear and decide cases.

"Given its umpiring role, should a court employ and control these social science experts?" he asked in the NSW Law Society Journal. "And does democracy, the division of powers, really allow in-house witnesses?

"After interviewing family members, court counsellors often give evidence in cases that involve children. A disgruntled party might believe judges give extra weight to these witnesses because they are court officers."

Removing the court's "internationally acclaimed" in-house counselling would be "disastrous", Chief Justice Nicholson claimed, dismissing Rowlands' views as unrepresentative of the majority of judges.

"Rowlands' statement that counselling and mediation should be conducted outside the court system reflects an outmoded view of modern courts," he said. "Most of our main courts now have mediation services; it is difficult to see why only the Family Court should be excluded.

"His reported views would indicate resistance to best practice developments and an inability to understand the role of a continually evolving counselling and mediation service that puts a premium on quick, cheap, user-friendly solutions to family disputes."

Justice Rowlands also backed the conservative Liberal National Coalition government on other issues, expressing support for a new Federal Magistracy in family law, kept separate from the Family Court, so magistrates did not "ape" the more formal, lengthy and costly ways of judges on superior courts.

"Prompt and affordable justice is the best kind," he said.[32]

---

[32] Forbes, John, Judicial Tidy-Up or Takeover?, Samuel Griffith Society Proceedings, contains a backgrounder to the dispute between Justices Rowlands and Nicholson.

Control of the proposed magistracy had developed into a major source of tension between Justice Nicholson and then Attorney General Daryl Williams.

Rowlands' article was evidence that Family Court judges were as divided about the future of the court as was the community and the industry. Nicholson had a vision for a "one-stop shop" for family services while the Government's view was that much of the non-judicial work should be done outside the court.

Rather than increasing the Family Court's power, influence and funding, the Attorney General wanted the Family Court pared back by diverting less complex and interim cases to a new cheaper Federal Magistracy, independent of the Family and Federal courts.

The proposed Federal Magistrates Court would be more flexible and help remove cases from the "panoply" of the Family Court's set-up, the AG said. In essence it was the government's way of circumventing the Family Court's manifest failures.

Nicholson said he first proposed a Magistracy in 1994 and "common sense" meant it should come under the Family Court's umbrella.

"To have to negotiate with some outside body in relation to that would make something of an administrative nightmare," he said.

In late 1999 Daryl Williams stepped up his feud with Nicholson over the future of the court by taking a swipe in parliament at him and other judges over extensive delays. It could take months and even years to hear a case.

Williams said the problem deserved "better attention than it's been getting from some of those involved in the system". "It now takes, for an average children's matter – and the issues concerned there are simply what is the residence of the child, which parent, and what contact the other parent had – it takes an average 3.3 days for that in the final hearing before a judge," Williams said. "If you can knock one day off that you'd have 50 percent more judge-time available. I think the legal practitioners and the judges who are dealing with those cases need to have a look at that."

The conflict between the Attorney General and the Chief Justice was well known. At this time the hostility between the Howard government and the Family Court was running on several different fronts: levels of legal aid funding, in-house counsellors, extensive delays, the lack of new judges and sharpest of all, the shape and function of a proposed new Federal Magistrates Court.[33]

---

[33] Alexander, Harriet, How the Family Court failed to live up to its promise, Sydney Morning Herald, 6 January, 2021.

***

In a feature published by *The Australian*, Chief Justice Nicholson wrote that the differences he had with the Attorney General about the Government's proposal for a federal magistracy have been misconstrued.

"In fact, the idea emanated in large part from the Family Court. For years I have been urging successive attorneys-general to accept there is a need in the family law area for a method of summarily resolving certain types of disputes."

He argued that "because of procrastination by the Government and increasing delays in trials, the judges of the court have endorsed a proposal to delegate the power to make interim parenting orders to a specially selected group of experienced family lawyers to be employed by the court. Because of constitutional difficulties, judges are unable to delegate the power to make final orders in cases that could otherwise be determined summarily.

"My proposal to the Government, which was rejected, was that these people should be appointed as magistrates and so have the power to make final orders. This could have been achieved within the court's existing budget or at minimal extra cost.

"Instead, the Attorney General intends to set up a separate magistrates' court, with all the bureaucratic panoply that this involves, presumably at considerable additional cost. One of the problems about this approach is that family law cases are not readily divisible between different courts because the complexity of a case is often not initially apparent.

"It is difficult to see how a new Federal Court exercising jurisdiction under the Family Law Act, dealing with the same families, could as efficiently case manage disputes as does the Family Court, with its established procedures, centralised computer systems and other mechanisms to track matters filed all around the nation.

"Opportunities for duplication of activities, difficulties in transferring orders between the two courts, misplaced files and other mishaps multiply with the addition of another court. It is difficult to see what advantages there could be for families in adding another forum."

Nicholson compared Australia's Family Court with its 56 judges to New Zealand, where there were more than 30 for a population less than a quarter of Australia's. "In New Zealand, you can get a final hearing of a children's matter in four months," he said.

In the absence of a Magistracy, Nicholson wanted the immediate appointment of nine extra judges. The Chief Justice claimed government cuts meant that in 35 percent of contested cases, at least one party now had no lawyer – thereby prolonging cases and compounding delays. Williams denied there had been any cuts.

The policy of Legal Aid to only fund one side of a dispute, usually but not always the mother, meant the struggle over self representation and the cost of lawyers would continue to bedevil fathers.

Nicholson said he had no regrets his spat with the government had spilled into the public arena. "I feel it's my duty when I'm faced with a situation where the court is not being given proper support by government, to draw attention to that fact," he said.

He claimed his relationship with Williams was "perfectly civil" and he remained "hopeful" their differences could be resolved. "We can disagree in public and negotiate and agree in private," he said.

***

On April Fool's day 1999, the same day Justice Rowland's countervailing views on in-house counsellors were published, *The Australian* ran a lengthy editorial about the competing visions for the Family Court over the future of a "sometimes troubled institution".

"Few would disagree that the court has its problems – delays, complaints of inefficiency, and doubts about public confidence. But too often the argument about the court has been heated, personal and uninformative."

Nicholson dreamt of a "one-stop shop" for a wide range of family services, including the in-house counselling of which he was proud. There was little wrong with the court that more judges and Legal Aid funds would not put right.

The contrary view, articulated by Attorney General Daryl Williams, was that judges should be restricted to the core task of hearing and deciding those cases that must go to trial. A new, cheaper and more flexible magistracy would do much of the simpler work now preoccupying the judges. Those magistrates would be insulated from the Family Court culture.

None of these people thought about keeping the government out of people's lives.

The paper concluded that by implication the government's reform proposals suggested the Family Court had failed to fulfil its promise to be a user-friendly alternative to the adversarial system and instead had been "overtaken by judicial formality and lacklustre administration."[34]

Later in the same month the Family Court announced a pre-emptive strike to halt the decline in its public standing. Chief Justice Alastair Nicholson launched

---

34 Editorial, *The Australian*, 1 April, 1999.

a reform plan for the court, Future Directions, reflecting "first-hand feedback" from meetings between court personnel and 100 litigants, family lawyers and welfare groups. He said the Family Court would bring a more human touch to its work after a round of face-to-face encounters between judges and people involved in family disputes.

He said litigants wanted the court to treat them "as individuals, not units to be processed in what some described as a sausage machine-like manner".

Criticism that emerged from the focus groups was different from the "second-hand" feedback of men's groups and the media. Cost, delay and anti-male bias did not figure as primary concerns, Nicholson claimed. Men's groups were not represented in the encounter groups but litigants were not screened, apart from security vetting. Those who used the court were asked to nominate positive and negative aspects.

"After all, the court is there for them," Justice Nicholson wrote in an article headed "A People's Court for Families".

"In a manner unprecedented in Australian courts, judges have sat down in groups with past litigants, who have had the opportunity to tell them candidly what they think of our services and how to improve them. I suggest such initiatives are hardly indicative of a court that has been overtaken by judicial formality and lacklustre administration. Rather, it is evidence of a progressive court that puts children and families first."

One prominent Family Court judge, Sally Brown, said: "It was a challenging experience to listen to litigants' perceptions of the court process, lawyers and judges and to do so in silence."

Journalist with *The Australian* Bernard Lane reported the clearest message to emerge was that litigants wanted respectful, personal service, not a timetable dictated by the convenience of judges and lawyers.

Nicholson said: "I'm still reasonably optimistic we can revamp our activities in a way that will make a difference."

He ordered changes to the court's case management system, allegedly to make it more user-friendly. He said better use of computers would give litigants improved access to information and free up counter staff for more individualised service. Whether any of these announced reforms made the slightest shred of difference in practice is a moot point.

***

Not exactly helping the reputation of fathers, In May of 1999 a man was convicted for murdering his wife outside the Family Court in Melbourne.

During a lunchtime adjournment of a 1997 hearing, Robert Clive Parsons stabbed his wife, Angela Parsons, 48 times in front of stunned witnesses.

As he killed her, he cried out: "It's over, bitch, it's over." The Supreme Court heard Parsons had buried $400,000 in his backyard to prevent his wife gaining access to his money. She had cut off his access to the couple's children after Parsons refused to increase maintenance payments.[35]

In later years an intermediary approached me to publish a book Parsons had written in jail about the whole affair. I didn't have the resources to proceed with such a legally contentious document, but it was an interesting work nonetheless. Parsons had been pushed to breaking point by one fraught and complex legal proceeding after another, and he broke. As politically incorrect as it may be, I left the text with the thought that it's a wonder more didn't break, the hell that so many litigants, both men and women, are forced to endure in this utterly broken system. Lawyers grow richer. Litigants are more and more devastated. And still, after all these years, this same brutal and inhumane system continues to destroy lives.

***

Also In 1999 the Australian Law Reform Commission, the government's chief legal adviser, handed down a draft report which found the Family Court to be a "beleaguered and defensive institution" with a history of failed reform and hostility to constructive criticism. The Commission urged an external review of the court, claiming lawyers who used the court had little confidence in its ability for internal reform.[36]

The detailed report, conducted as part of an overarching review of the federal court system, contained many criticisms of the Court's operations. Solicitors interviewed agreed that demonstrating a risk of "serious violence" at an interim hearing was "dependent on your affidavit drafting ability".

One judge indicated his dissatisfaction with these hearings by saying, "What we do in interim matters is highly artificial. We present it as a judicial exercise but it's more artful dodging."

Too true.

Amongst other observations, the Law Council noted "the perception of over servicing" derived from "the number of interlocutory processes and the degree of case management".

---

35 R v PARSONS, Supreme Court of Victoria, 23 February, 2000.

36 Australian Law Reform Commission, Managing Justice: A Review of the Federal Civil Justice System, ALRC Reports, 1999.

The Council noted the dilemma that once proceedings were filed, apart from the streaming into the direct track, standard track and complex track, there was no ongoing analysis of the nature of the proceedings. All cases were managed as if they would proceed to a hearing rather than as is the current position ninety five percent of matters settled.

"Now the Court must be involved at every stage and this has made the process less flexible. It seems the matters are fitted to the Court and not the Court to the matters."

Another solicitor observed: "Procedures are very bureaucratic. Even in urgent cases, to get an ex parte order you have to get past the filing clerk and the duty registrar, who sits at 2 pm. To get through the screening process I write on the form: I insist on seeing a judge."

Yet another solicitor observed that requiring a party to go to an information session, first directions hearing, conciliation conferences for financial matters, counselling for children's matters, a pre-hearing conference and so on caused enormous inconvenience and cost.

"Simple solutions are ignored by the court," observed one solicitor. "For example, why isn't an information session video available for parties to watch? Most parties take a day off work to attend court. Most are now saying that they will lose their jobs if they take more time off."

***

The Australian Law Reform Commission noted a major issue raised by many practitioners and parties was the lack of continuity in the management of cases. Parties encountered a number of different Court officers presiding at successive appearances. Litigants and lawyers frequently spoke of their frustration that the Court provided repeated opportunities for all other processes, except the one they wanted – determination by a judge.

The Commission observed: "Interim or procedural hearings are held to resolve matters arising during the case. Compliance conferences are held shortly before a hearing where one or both parties has not complied with directions. Comments made to the Commission indicated that some of these events are ineffective at narrowing or resolving issues.

"Many of the problems relating to case management in the Family Court arise from the lack of consistent overview of cases, and the related lack of attention to the particular needs and circumstances of the case. A minority of cases experience repeat case events and take significant time to be resolved. Because there is no continuity in the counsellor or registrar assigned to a particular case, some parties are required to explain their circumstances a number of times to different court officers."

***

One litigant observed: "We have had the same judge a couple of times, but most of the time we have a different judge or magistrate, or registrar. If I had a judge who knew the history and knew what the girls had been through for the last three years and what I had been through for the last three years and all the rest of it, maybe it would have been easier for me to get final orders."

Another complaint was that the person on the bench did not read the material which has been presented in the case. "This fragmentation rankles many litigants," a solicitor observed. "Surely a person can expect a matter to proceed and all evidence be heard with continuity, which does not currently occur."

Practitioners and parties complained the court did not effectively or consistently enforce compliance with its own complex rules and directions.

One litigant complained: "I was advised by my lawyer that in order to prevent a paper war only three affidavits were allowed. However, each time we had a scheduled hearing I would be given new affidavits, minutes prior to the hearing, necessitating a new hearing and contributing to escalating legal costs, for both parties. To date my legal bills have amounted to $29,000.

"The value of the property settlement was $120,000, and the amount of my former wife's legal bills must be at least $30,000. Where are the interests and welfare of the children in such a waste of money?"

The difficulties experienced by unrepresented parties was also an issue. One practitioner commented: "People don't realise they will get virtually no assistance from the Court with solving their problem. People need advice that is addressed to their specific situation."

One litigant said: "I found it very difficult in even finding out which forms to obtain, which direction to follow and what was expected from me. This was from counter staff or duty solicitor. When conducting my own case, the judge was not the slightest bit interested in my situation."

***

A person subpoenaed in Family Court litigation, in the following extract from a radio broadcast, said: "The lawyer, and then the barrister, admitted they had seen no documents, they had followed no line of research, so the judge said, 'Well you don't expect me to do your homework for you?' That day cost me $5,000 for ten minutes in court."

Another litigant reported: "We went back and we arrived at 10 o'clock and the judge said 'Come back at half past twelve'. We went back at half past twelve and one of the plaintiffs lobbed some more ad hoc affidavits onto his Bench. He said 'I'll have to read these. Come back at 2 o'clock'.

"We got back at 2 o'clock, and we were on edge on our side. We were taken at half past three, and he said, 'Oh, I'll have to read these. I haven't had time, I have had other matters to attend to. Come back in a fortnight'. That's cost me another $5,000."

***

The Family Court never took criticism well and condemned the research, conclusions and reform proposals in the Australian Law Reform Commission paper, styling them as "facile, insensitive, ill thought out, misguided, poorly researched and impractical", "largely based on the remarks of persons who have no expertise in case management" and as "failing to appreciate the Court's true workload and the constraints on resources available to it".

Chief Justice Alistair Nicholson characterised the Commission as "wandering the countryside talking to Uncle Tom Cobley" instead of the people in charge of case management in the court", and stated "the contradictions, and at times facile observations, contained in the paper give little credit to the challenges that face separating families and those in the Court that support them".

Nicholson claimed the ALRC had been "snowed" by self-interested lawyers, had relied on outdated complaints and misinterpreted data, and had not given enough weight to the special nature of the Court's work, its achievements and reforms.

His press release on the subject was also critical of "selective and gratuitous report of comment of anonymous persons cloaked in the guise of 'research'."

"It is extremely disappointing that the Commission has chosen to include such gratuitous, ill-informed and wrong comments about a court whose task is perhaps the most sensitive and difficult in the country."

Nicholson, once again in spirited defence of his court, claimed the proposal for a separate magistracy, with virtually the same jurisdiction as the court, was "a bit like saying we don't like the Supreme Court so we'll open another Supreme Court. It's a deliberate attempt to downgrade the importance of family law."[37]

---

[37] Lane, Bernard, Report puts Family Court in the dock, *The Australian*, 20 August, 1999.

The Attorney General on the other hand seized on the report as vindicating his proposal for family law magistrates to work independently of the Family Court.

Daryl Williams said the finding that Family Court procedures were not tailored to a range of cases was "particularly significant, given the Government's determination that the new separate federal magistrates service should be flexible and innovative".

By the end of 1999 the Federal Magistrate's Court had been established. Its jurisdiction covered the dissolution of marriage, property disputes, parenting orders and the residence of children.

Attorney General Daryl Williams made it clear he wanted the Magistrate's Court to take up most of the running on family law. He described the Family Court as inflexible, over-formalised, fragmented, uncoordinated, unplanned and gave insufficient attention to the needs of children.

The following year the Family Law Amendment Bill 2000 was passed. The amendments sought to remedy one of the most contentious areas of family law: the enforcement of parenting orders. They aimed to do this via a three-stage process, in which the Court informed parents of their obligations under a parenting order and advised them of the services available to assist them, should they encounter any difficulties. If the order was not complied with, parents could be directed by the Court to attend a relationship program designed to resolve parental conflict. Should non-compliance continue, the Court would be able to impose a variety of sanctions, including imprisonment.

***

In September of 2000 Dads On The Air began broadcasting. We were in place to document the latest dramas in the push to reform the family law in Australia.

They weren't long in coming.

In July 2001 the Family Law Pathways Advisory Group handed up its report Out Of The Maze: Pathways to the future for families experiencing separation.[38] The Group, originally formed in May of the previous year, was one of the Howard government's first fumbling attempts to reform family law. It was the subject of much speculation and at times optimism from reformers. DOTA criticised the makeup of the Group and the appointment of a senior bureaucrat, Des Semple, former head of the strife torn NSW Department of Community Services, as inappropriate in a push for genuine reform.

---

38 Out Of The Maze: Pathways to the future for families experiencing separation, Family Law Pathways Advisory Group, July, 2001. Available from the National Library of Australia.

The Liberal government's move to consult "key stakeholders" in the form of the Family Pathways Advisory Group did not have a single father's group on it despite ample representation from heftily funded feminist advocacy groups, academics and institutional heavyweights. The makeup of the group ensured that no real action, change or reform would result. Members included Chief Executive Officer of the Family Court Richard Foster, General Manager of the Child Support Agency Catherine Argall, Justice Linda Dessau of the Family Court of Australia, Professor John Dewar of Griffith University, Scott Mitchell, a NSW Local Court Magistrate dealing with family matters, Secretary of the Women's Action Alliance Pauline Smit and Winsome Matthews, Project Development Officer for Indigenous Women's Unit of the Women's Legal Resource Centre. Not one of these people represented the interests of fathers and not one had expressed any genuine desire to reform of Australia's family law system.

John Dewar's faculty had just received $500,000 in funding and he was on record suggesting the broad push to shared parenting was detrimental to women's interests.

President of Lone Father's Barry Williams said the failure to include fathers on the Family Pathways group was blatant discrimination. "If this government was listening to the people who are hurting they would abolish the Family Court," he said. "It hasn't changed in a quarter of a century, it seems to be a protected species. It has to be replaced. The court is bringing the entire legal profession into disrepute. We get 22,000 calls a year. People are committing suicide as a result of court decisions."

Semple noted in his letter of transmittal that the inquiry canvassed "complex and diverse issues relating both to the family law system in all its parts and the experiences of families dealing with separation." Its activities had included inviting submissions from the public, consultations with consumers and service providers in every State and Territory, targeted consultations with interest groups, a literature review and commissioned research.

While still in its early days, DOTA was no great fan of the multi-million dollar Out Of The Maze report. Perhaps the lack of specificity in its Terms of Reference was part of the problem: "Vision: An integrated family law system that is flexible and builds individual and community capacity to achieve the best possible outcomes for families."

The bureaucratic nature of the language was also a problem, such as the purpose of the inquiry being to "provide pathways that are effective and appropriate". The Terms of Reference suggested the group should "consult appropriately", examine existing barriers to accessing services, including cultural and linguistic barriers, customer service issues and "best practice".

It was all a very long way from the raw anger existing in the community and DOTA editorialised it was an attempt to dilute or divert public outrage.

Out Of The Maze began: "It is always difficult when families split up." Oh you don't say.

The Executive Summary noted community concerns over the family law system taking too long, as well as being too hard and too expensive.

"The Advisory Group envisages an integrated family law system in which family members experiencing separation can easily and quickly identify and access help when needed. The system's primary focus would be to support family decision making and family nurturing. Such a system would be responsive and coordinated. It would provide appropriate assistance to family members as early as possible. It would treat all comers fairly. All those in the system would, above all, promote the interests of children and attempt to meet the needs of children."

The Advisory Group considered that a family law system should be one that acknowledged the value of family relationships and sought to provide families with a range of support services and information at various points in the family life cycle and valued and supported the ongoing capacity in families, whether intact or separated, to provide nurturing parenting to their children.

The Group recommended "that the family law system, in whole and in all its parts, be designed to maximise the potential for families to function cooperatively in the interests of children after separation. In doing so, it would ensure fair and equitable treatment for all, with particular attention to the ongoing parenting roles and support needs of both parents. Wherever possible, family decision making would be encouraged, with parents making their own decisions about their complementary roles, with appropriate support from the family law system."

The Advisory Group heard that "a number of people are frustrated and discontented about how the family law system currently operates. Men, in particular, feel angry and frustrated, and believe that the system is biased against them."

It recommended helping all family members quickly, fairly, appropriately and without bias.

The government's response was also bureaucratic. It assured anyone who could be bothered paying attention that the government already provided a number of services to separating families, including Centrelink, the Child Support Agency, Legal Aid Commissions and the Family Court.

None of these organisations served the needs of fathers.

***

The Liberal government's move to consult "key stakeholders", the Family Pathways Advisory Group, became the Royal Commission that never was.

The Group did not have a single fathers' group on it despite ample representation from heftily funded feminist advocacy groups, academics and institutional heavyweights. The "Group", set up in the wake of an Australian Law Reform Commission report which found overwhelming disquiet with the Family Court and its processes, comes at a time when there are mounting questions over the level of public confidence in the court. One of its founders, Gough Whitlam, has declined the opportunity to defend the contemporary court.

Yet virtually no one in the group was even remotely critical of the Family Court. One of its members, Cathy Argall, publicly denied the Child Support Agency's role in the 20 suicides a week committed by men after separation.

Academic John Dewar, who's faculty received $500,000 in funding, suggested the broad push to shared parenting was detrimental to women's interests. Despite their importance and the millions of dollars of funding flowing to organisations such as the Australian Institute of Family Studies and the Family Law Council, there had never been an audit or academic study of family reports. Both the government and the Australian Institute of Family Studies refused to offer an explanation.

National President of WhistleBlowers Australia Dr Jean Lennane, who I knew personally, said the same misuse of psychiatry occurs in the Family Court as other courts, but its secrecy meant it was less well documented and led to "some very bad miscarriages of justice towards children who are deprived of access to one or other parent on the basis of ... very dubious psychiatric evidence. They are relying on spurious reports and misinformation. The secrecy has allowed enormous abuses of process to develop."

She was a hero. And she was hated by those defending the corrupt practices within legal aid, family law and child protection.

***

President of Lone Father's Barry Williams said the failure to include fathers on the Family Pathways group was blatant discrimination. "If this government was listening to the people who are hurting they would abolish the Family Court," he said. "It hasn't changed in a quarter of a century, it seems to be a protected species. It has to be replaced by a Tribunal.

"The court is bringing the entire legal profession into disrepute. We get 22,000 calls a year. People are committing suicide as a result of court decisions."

Mr Williams said fathers could lose any relationship with their children based on "very biased" reports by court counsellors made up of "innuendo or make believe" which they may not even be permitted to see.

"When a man wants to see his children they say he is trying to control the woman. It is not true at all. They want to see their kids because they are part of their life.

"The reports are ill written, foolish and irresponsible."

***

In launching the Out Of The Maze report Attorney General Daryl Williams and Minister for Family and Community Services Senator Amanda Vanstone said it demonstrated that the effects of family separation were far-reaching, costly and, when families experienced a lot of conflict, children could suffer long term effects.[39]

The Attorney General said of key concern to the Howard Government was the finding that lack of coordination in the system made things worse for family members already struggling to manage emotionally and financially difficult issues.

Family members often found themselves on a slippery slope, with disputes about issues such as parenting arrangements and child support getting out of hand. They faced costs they could not afford, because they did not know their choices or understand the consequences of advice given to them.

"It is also clear from the report that a number of people feel they are treated with disdain, disrespect or bias as they attempt to sort out their separation issues," Wiliams said.

The report also recommended increasing access to services for men to help them effectively co-parent their children after separation.

In a supportive release the Joint Parenting Association of Australia said the report acknowledged the destruction caused by the current system of family breakdown administration.

Association Secretary Dr Shane Kelly said: "While extra family and support services, especially for men and fathers, are long overdue, unless these initiatives are coupled with a statutory regime of a rebuttable presumption in favour of joint residence orders, it will be a cruel hoax perpetrated upon the children of divorce and their parents.

---

[39] Joint Media Release, Attorney General and Minister for Family and Community Services, Family Law Pathways Advisory Group Report Released Today, copy available on the Men's Rights website, July, 2001.

"The sole custody model has been shown to place children at an unacceptable risk of losing important familial relationships. The latest research evidence shows that children raised in fatherless homes are significantly more likely than average to have problems in school, run away from home, become delinquent, develop mental illness and drug dependency, commit suicide and experience other serious problems.

"In marked contrast the American Psychological Association has reported that following parental separation children in joint residence fare better in all areas of child well being. United States surveys also indicate that joint parenting laws have had the effect of lowering the divorce rate by up to a factor of eight, lowering litigation and increasing child support compliance to around 95 percent."

The Joint Parenting Association encouraged the Government to provide an early response which included "legislative change to enshrine in law a child's fundamental human right to an equal relationship with both their parents following separation or divorce."

The Family Law Pathways Advisory Group's Out Of The Maze report sank with barely a trace. Two years later the Howard government would embark on yet another attempt to reform family law. Perhaps having learnt its lesion, this time around it ignored the family law industry and the so-called experts to whom it had previously turned.

THREE
THE EVIDENCE IS IN

Although by 2000 I needed no further convincing of the desperate need for the reform of family law, such proof was to come anyway. I was assigned to a story which involved the longest running case in The Family Court of Australia's history. That trial was spread across 25 days. To my mind this story demonstrates clearly that the Family Court is the last place on earth one should trust to take care of the welfare of children, putting the lie to all the claims the court must be given the legal power and the funds to act quickly to protect women and children if there was any evidence of domestic violence.

It also demonstrated that campaigns against shared parenting laws ignored repeated statistical findings that biological fathers are the least likely to abuse their children and that pathological campaigns painting them as dangerous to their children are ideologically, not factually based.

The story was published under the heading "Battered By The System" with the strap "Nobody believed 'Frank' when he tried to protect his son from bureaucratic bungling…nearly 20 years on, Frank has been proved right, even though he lost in court."[40]

This was the second time Frank, as we were obliged to call him, had made himself known to *The Australian*. The first time round, he had wandered in off the street demanding to speak to a journalist, claiming he had a story worth telling about his experiences in the Family Court and its failure to protect his child. Of course most members of the public wandering into newspaper offices are quickly and politely dismissed as either suffering from mental health issues or having no understanding of what is required for a news story.

That first time, back in 1991, the journalist, James Morrison got a front page story out of the Family Court's failure to protect a child headlined: "Why it took

---

40 Stapleton, John, Battered by the System, *The Australian*, 3 June, 2000.

years for Frank to save his son."[41] It illustrated one of the most under reported and under discussed crimes in Australia: physical and sexual abuse of children by women.

Now, years after that first front pager, it was my turn to deal with the strange, determined man we called Frank. What made him exceptional was that as a tireless litigator he had obsessively kept every shred of documentation to do with his case.

I still remember vividly, although it is now almost a quarter of a century ago, choosing to work in the office in the wee hours of the morning when it was easier to concentrate. To make sure I understood the sequences correctly, I would line up all the documents to do with the case in a long string on the floor of the office, stretching more than 30 metres in a straight line. Sometimes I had to dodge the cleaners, who I got to know well for a few weeks there.

The story began: "The boy was eight weeks old when his father called welfare authorities and pleaded with them to take his son into foster care. He alleged that the mother was being violent towards the child, throwing him against walls and trying to smother him. The authorities ignored him, as they did for years to come, but the father persevered.

"Twenty years, 550 days in court and tens of millions of dollars of public funds later, the matter which has run across the civil, criminal and family law jurisdictions, reached its final chapter this week.

"Last year the Office of the Director of Public Prosecutions, satisfied there was a prima facie case, laid charges against the mother for tying her son in a cot with a rope, striking him in the face, throwing him against a wall and 'causing him actual bodily harm', events alleged to have occurred in 1981-82."

But in a judgement critical of earlier police inaction, Sydney's Downing Centre Local Court issued a permanent stay on proceedings, primarily due to the time that had elapsed since the alleged offences occurred.

***

Magistrate Hugh Dillon said the disappearance of police records raised the suspicion of a cover-up. But he said the treatment the Police Service meted out to the father did not detract from the issue of the mother facing a possible abuse of process because of the 20-year delay.

One of the sad ironies of the case was that, although the father did not see it that way, in many ways his claims of judicial, police and political inaction as well

---

41 Morrison, James, Why it took years for Frank to save his son, *The Weekend Australian*, 6 April, 1991.

as inappropriate behaviour by the NSW Department of Community Services had been vindicated in a series of court judgments. But nobody was ever found guilty, no compensation was ever paid.

Magistrate Dillon wrote: "There is no explanation before the court as to why or how the investigation stopped once the father had set it in train. No one has ever explained to the father what happened during the investigation or what decisions, if any, were made by those originally in charge of it. The fact that police records, which would, presumably, explain these things, have disappeared raises a suspicion that police officers have been involved in covering up their own negligence or the negligence of colleagues. Beyond this, we can merely speculate.

"I feel considerable sympathy for the father. It is appalling that it has taken him almost 20 years to get the Police Service to take action on evidence it has had for most of that time.

"A reasonable and right-minded person might have his or her confidence in the justice system undermined because the father has been treated so badly.

"Yet is it now just ... to continue the proceedings because the father was unjustly or unreasonably treated ... for many years? This is ... one of those rare or exceptional cases where the delay in proceedings has been so excessive that the proceedings constitute an abuse of process.

"These proceedings are permanently stayed."

I was particularly interested in the Family Court's involvement in the case. As the father was to tell me in heartbreaking detail, he had been repeatedly refused by the court the right to see or care for his son.

Amongst the judicial figures involved in the case who ruled against the father was Justice Elizabeth Evatt, the court's first Chief Justice. At the time she was a member of the UN Human Rights Committee.

The obsessive campaign for justice by the father touched many of Australia's best known people and it had been mentioned in parliament 14 times. The dozens of politicians whom the father approached for help included one of the left's leading lights, former Prime Minister Paul Keating, Prime Minister and Neville Wran, former NSW Premier.

***

The long history of the case offered a time-tunnel view of the behaviour of bureaucracies in the face of a determined and persistent litigant. An expert on female abuse of children, Dr. Malcolm George of St Bartholomew's Hospital in London, said it was "par for the course", where the mother is the alleged abuser, for institutions to spend large amounts of money defending their decisions, based on an ideology that "denies that women can be violent and abusive".

Although Australian and international research clearly indicated that children were most at risk from their mother, followed by their step father and live-in boyfriends, crimes of this type remain significantly underreported and under researched for the simple reason that it doesn't fix the mother as noble victim narrative peddled by government ideologues.[42]

With the ceaseless taxpayer funded campaign to portray fathers as a threat to their children it is perhaps worth repeating the statistics I found for that story:

"The US Government's 1997 report Child Maltreatment found 62.3 percent of perpetrators were women. The Heritage Foundation Study, The Child Abuse Crisis, found that of the approximately 2000 children killed each year, 55 per cent were killed by mothers, 25.7 per cent by live-in boyfriends, 12.5 per cent by stepfathers, and 6.8 per cent by biological fathers.

"The 1995 report US National Incidence of Child Abuse and Neglect found that where maltreatment led to death, 78 per cent of perpetrators were female. Boys were four times more likely to be fatally abused and 24 per cent more likely to be seriously abused than girls.

"The book *Broken Homes and Battered Children* reports that the child of a biological mother cohabiting with a man other than the natural father is 33 times more likely to suffer serious abuse than a child living with their married biological parents."

During the child's early years, Frank made hundreds of calls and applications to police, welfare organisations, the NSW Department of Community Services, parliamentarians and the Family Court. But it was not until 1984, when the child was four years old, that at least some members of DOCS began taking the accusations seriously.

A report by a clinical psychologist independent of the courts gave a graphic account of James attempting to have oral sex with her – behaviour considered to have been acquired from a woman. A departmental psychologist and a child protection worker then interviewed the mother and the child. They concluded that the child, "James", was an "emotionally deprived little boy who has been sexually abused and has been exposed to adult sexual behaviour".

***

For almost two years from this date, the father was prevented from seeing his son through Family Court orders, actions by departmental officers and recommendations by Sydney psychiatrist Dr Brent Waters, who for many years had been a favourite of DOCS, the Family Court, Legal Aid and at times journalists seeking a quick quote on just about anything.

---

42 A list of the current research was contained in the MRA Newsletter, May, 2003.

Waters recommended custody be with the mother and that the father be denied access. James, 20 when I interviewed him, was on medication and rarely left his father's house. Court documents showed that he consistently maintained over several years that he remembers psychiatrist Waters saying: "Don't tell anyone about the naughty things mummy's doing."

Waters refused to comment on the case, but later attempted to sue the paper over the story. Despite the legal threats, *The Australian* did not cave. In the end Mr Waters, back then a darling of Sydney's legal fraternity and a favourite of the family law child protection systems, did not proceed.

Repeated attempts by the father Frank in the early 1980s to gain custody failed.

Only after the boy was found wandering a street of one of Sydney's suburbs after being bashed with a cricket bat in 1986 did Frank finally get to care for his kid.

The alleged perpetrator of the cricket bat incident was never questioned. A Children's Hospital report from the time reported evidence of a recent severe beating "suggesting he had been held on the face and struck". The report noted "extensive bruising ... blue black in colour" and recorded the six-year-old's long association with the hospital for similar problems.

The father finally gained full custody of his son by locating the home of the then Federal Attorney General Lionel Bowen. Braving dogs, Frank knocked on the door. Bowen was not at home but his wife answered the door and listened to Frank's story. The boy, we called him James, has not seen his mother since.

***

The Ten network's footage of the child when he was 11 shows a quiet, well-mannered boy asking: "Why was it me, why was it me that got hurt?" He said his mother "should be put in jail for life, I just hate her". When I interviewed him there was no artifice in the way the story emerged.

"I was so young, the main things that come across now – I get flashbacks: a smell, an idea can trigger them," he said. "It is more a sense of fear. I used to dream a lot, nightmares ... about my mother. I was extremely scared of her. I remember certain episodes and events... when her husband beat me with a cricket bat ... I felt anger, but more than anything, now I feel pity."

The father may very well have not helped his case through the years by calling everyone who would not help him, including judges, politicians and police, "evil, disgusting, protectors of pedophilia". Transcripts from the NSW Supreme Court show much legal huffing and puffing over the man's "scurrilous" attacks.

After failing in a Supreme Court action to expose the Department of Community workers involved in the case which briefly preceded his action before Magistrate Dillon, the father came to believe that the judiciary and politicians generally had acted to protect the interconnecting webs of Legal Aid, DOCS and the Family Court. He claimed the entire system was "immoral, inhuman"; and had acted to protect the very people who were abusing his son and the very institutions which had placed him in harm's way.

His hope that his actions would help other fathers battling the system was unrealised as a multibillion dollar government funded industry invested in portraying men as abusers swept all reason before it.

Whistleblowers Australia's national president Dr Jean Lennane, an extremely admirable and accomplished woman with whom I became friendly, concurred. She told me, for the record, that DOCS, Legal Aid and the Family court all had very close connections, "incestuous you might say".

But litigation is rarely satisfying, and the father's hope that his case would help stop other children being abused and provide a comfortable future for his son were in ashes. The story concluded with Frank's claim there were other fathers doing, as he did, everything they could to protect their children and being constantly frustrated in the process.

"There is no doubt it is still happening today," he said.

Unfortunately, that claim is just as true or even more true now as when he first made it a quarter of a century ago.

FOUR
MEN AND THE MEDIA

IN TERMS of the media's treatment of men and fathers' issues, the more things stayed the same, the worse things got. Masculinity became unfashionable, at least in the eyes of Australia's shallow media pond. The non-stop derogatory treatment of men, of fathers, of traditional family values, all of it stemming or originating from tertiary institutions and government departments, had the advantage of novelty to begin with. In the long term, all those efforts to reshape society into a more tolerant place embracing "diversity" led instead into a monoculture where no one dared to speak out.

We were looking at the parking lot at the end of the Long March, half a century of Marxist inspired rhetoric against fathers and families leading to nothing but desolation in an aspic glue of male bashing which had metastasised across the nation's institutions.

The rainbow warriors poured scorn upon traditional masculinity, toughness, hard work, mateship, and the drive to universal tolerance was itself driven on a wave of intolerance. The woke scorned the unwoke, media dignified minorities and demeaned the muddling middle, and the country was in no way better for any of it.

Australia's mainstream media is entirely manipulated by the so-called Deep State, or in this context the existing bureaucracies and their agendas, with the rippling changes of parliamentarians from one election cycle to another barely touching their entrenched interests.

Decades of anti-male propaganda and an education system embracing the new so-called enlightenment made the general population immune to the obvious sexism of their ideologically saturated media. The result: more and more defeated, disaffected and disillusioned became Australia's men. The more broken the nation's families. The more disrespected the nation's legal system. The more taxpayers were leached for billions of dollars over an extremely dishonest narrative. And the more fragmented and dysfunctional the society as a whole became. Throughout history unappreciated and undervalued men have been the base resource for revolutionary ferment. And so, as these trends became not passing fads but entrenched down the generations, Australia became increasingly divided, and turned upon itself.

Outrageous outcomes and flights of malfeasance rarely surfaced into the mainstream discourse. And the disaffected mumbled defeat in their tortured dreams. Try losing your children at the behest of the state and see how well you sleep.

Way back in the year 2000 I wrote a feature for the Media Section of *The Australian* newspaper where I worked called Men and the Media. After a considerable amount of umming and ahhing the editors simply refused to run it. So instead it was published on the Dads On The Air website.

The Australian is often described as a conservative, even right wing publication. Certainly it is the part of Australia's media spectrum which you would assume would not buy into the loopy left anti-male anti-father anti-family rhetoric spewing out of the nation's feminised bureaucracies and the captive media. No such luck. First, second and third wave feminism, wherever you sat, had commandeered the high moral ground, the universities, and the media. Nobody wanted to be seen as reactionary or anti-woman. The worst offender of all was and still is the extravagantly funded Australian Broadcasting Corporation. Pro-father commentators are even rarer on Australia's state funded media than climate change sceptics.

These people did not fight in an open paddock. Their ideas could not stand the light of scrutiny. While some journalists outdid each other in painting their own gender as victims and men as violent patriarchs, for a journalist, displaying sympathy towards men's issues could prove a career ending moment, leaving the perpetrator to be defined as anti-feminist, misogynistic or far right, as infamously happened to Irish journalist John Waters, who fought and won a custody battle with singer Sinead O'Connor.

***

What is remarkable, if anything is remarkable in this dead cat bounce realm where so little makes sense, where rationality and reason have long since fled, where original ideas go to die, is that in the quarter of a century after Men and the Media was first written so little has changed in Australia's media landscape. In their abandonment of any social responsibility, the situation on the ground has simply got worse, the Family Court has become more dysfunctional, and outcomes for so many Australian citizens have got worse.

Very few constituents' concerns over the conduct of Family Court judges, legal aid lawyers or child support officers ever made it from the desks of politicians into parliament house or onto journalists' desks and thereby onto the public record.

The disorganised voices of protest from separated fathers were drowned out by well funded women's lobby groups and their media sympathisers. Nor were fathers themselves, often poor, angry, heart broken, frustrated and disempowered, always their own best advocates.

The media was slow to report the public's discontent; flummoxed by the he said she said nature of the stories. Secrecy provisions in the Family Law Act, ostensibly designed to protect the identity and welfare of children, made it almost impossible to cover the high-profile cases which might have brought attention to their farcical nature. While of intense interest to those who had been through the Family Court or the Child Support Agency, news editors tended to view the issues as of minority concern.

As well there was a reluctance to attack what were still largely seen as feminist icons. While women were once a rarity on newsroom floors, by the beginning of the 21st century they constituted about 70% of all new recruits, according to the journalists union The Arts, Media and Entertainment Alliance. Social welfare rounds were almost invariably assigned to women. Many of them used these positions to promote what they saw as social justice causes, most often the agendas of women's groups. On the rare occasion when a male did become a social affairs reporter, they were usually men sympathetic to women's causes who largely ignored the concerns of their own gender.

The role of fathers as parents, nurturers, protectors and advisers was written out of the public discourse. Every fathers' group in the country complained that they could not get their concerns heard. Their own naivety and lack of experience in dealing with the media, the unfashionability or even conservatism of some of their views and the lack of funds to employ dedicated media officers all no doubt played a part.

The ideologically driven state and taxpayer funded creation of the single mother household, spawned and indeed enforced as the normal family pattern post-separation, created a multi-billion dollar industry. Enormous slabs of the country's $80 billion welfare tab were taken up catering for the welfare of single parents, primarily mothers; with a slew of benefits flowing on from obtaining custody of children. These included family and child payments, child support, housing or rental assistance, and reduced medicine and transport costs. Any attempt to reform family law was a threat to this empire.

Even back then at the turn of the millennium the Australian public had already endured decades of anti-male bile, since male bashing became fashionable in the public discourse and feminism became the sole party of gender politics in the universities. Dismissing the concerns of fathers became de rigeur; they were just poor losers being justly cremated on the bonfire of progress. Indeed the more vicious the male bashing the better some female journalists did, their entire oeuvre easily summed up in a single sentence: "All men are bastards."

No editor, or certainly very few in Australia's mainstream media, felt any compulsion to run a countervailing view. It was an era when everybody wanted to be seen as "progressive", where the prevailing feminist orthodoxies of the day had seized the moral high ground, and those who showed an interest in men's issues were dismissed as reactionary, right wing, misogynistic bigots, historic relics who could not embrace the bright future of equal rights and female empowerment.

Yes, well… You could waste your breath forever pointing out that equal rights actually does mean equal rights. The herd holds their government manufactured prejudices close. The truth lies elsewhere. We've seen it so often, on race, on gender, on climate, on the virtues of strip mining the middle class to build multi-billion dollar windfarms which benefit only the oligarchs and corporatists. As the Covid era demonstrated in roaring technicolour, the Australian population are easily manipulated. And dissidents banished to the far reaches of the internet.

***

A quarter of a century ago I wrote that *The Sunday Tasmanian* had nowhere near the clout or the distribution of mainland papers like *The Age* in Melbourne, *The Sydney Morning Herald* or *The Australian*. Yet it was the only newspaper in the country which reported that the male suicide rate in Australia was then at its highest since the Great Depression.[43]

The paper puffed the story on its front page under the headline "If Men Were Whales" and a full front page picture of a group of men marooned on a sand bank.

It began: "More than 40 Australian men commit suicide each week. If men were whales, this would cause community outcry and public mourning."

The accompanying inside story, one of the best compilation of male suicide statistics published in Australia at the time, showed that more men suicided in the previous decade than died in World War II, and the male suicide rate in a single year was four times that of the total number killed in the Vietnam conflict.

---

43 Stapleton, John, Men and the Media, Dads On The Air, 2000.

"The entire mainland press was creamed on what is a fundamentally important social story. Why? It's not a lack of interest."

Reporter Simon Bevilacqua noted: "We had an amazing amount of feedback from people working in the industry, like nothing else, from left, right and centre, from the federal government to people in the industry. There were a lot of people pleased the issue was raised."

Managing Director of media monitors Rehame Australia Peter Maher said there was a distinct increase in the reporting of men's issues and the Family Court throughout 2000. He said "huggy stories" about men wanting to spend more time with their children ran all year with coverage of family law reform peaking in December after the proposed introduction of new jailing provisions into the family law – yet another insulting rabbit hole in the history of the appalling political mismanagement of family breakdown.

***

The government's big push for men that year was the Men and Relationships Conference, organised by the Office of the Status of Women.

Not one newspaper in the country seemed to think it odd that millions of dollars of public funds was spent flying 300 public servants and so-called "domestic violence experts" from around the country to a very comfortable hotel in Sydney for a two-day male bashing exercise of the "all men are violent" type.

Not one newspaper raised the point that numerous reputable domestic violence studies show both men and women are equally guilty of domestic violence, or that the Office of the Status of Women had been previously caught out making exaggerated claims about domestic violence. Nor did anyone seem to think it odd that there had been no invitations to a men's conference issued to anyone from the broad spectrum of men's groups to speak and which clearly failed to address any issues that actually concern men.

Indeed Adele Horin of *The Sydney Morning Herald* told a million or so readers: "Hardly a single 'angry dad' could be sighted at the Men and Relationships conference the Federal Government put on in Sydney this week. It was a civilised, hand-picked gathering. New Age men. New Age women. About 300 in all hopping from workshops on domestic violence, to workshops on men's post-separation services. It was a festival of enlightenment… those incendiary words 'Family Court' and 'child support' were barely uttered."[44]

---

44 Horin, Adele, Calculating the Cost of a Father Figure, *The Sydney Morning Herald*, 25 November, 2000.

Why should the disenfranchisement of men's concerns be such a source of delight? In reality this was a "festival of enlightenment" which many of the nation's men would have preferred these public service fat cats held on their own time and at their own expense.

***

That the left and right of Australian politics were equally as bad as each other in this conflict ridden domain, just as hostage to bureaucratic agendas and just as contemptuous of pro-father pro-family advocates, is obvious to anyone who looks back across the history of family law reform in Australia.

The Coalition's major effort to review the troubled family law domain also ignored half of the population.

The hapless conservative Attorney General of the day, West Australian Daryl Williams, initiated an inquiry into family law chaired by a former head of the notoriously dysfunctional New South Wales Department of Community Services, consisted almost entirely of feminist advocacy groups, feminist academics or industry insiders. There was not a single representative from any of the nation's men's groups.[45]

That any findings by such an unrepresentative group would lack public legitimacy did not appear to bother the government a jot.

The government's response to criticisms of the make-up of the group was that the Attorney General had confidence in its members. He might. Half the population had zero reason to trust anything they said.

No newspaper commented on any of this.

The outcome of the inquiry, the Out of the Maze report, launched by the Attorney General and Liberal Party loyalist the Minister for Family and Community Services Senator Amanda Vanstone, found the effects of family separation were far-reaching, costly and, when families experience a lot of conflict, children could suffer long term effects.[46]

The report also found a number of people felt they were treated with disdain, disrespect or bias as they attempted to sort out their separation issues.

No shit Sherlock! I could have told you that for free.

The report recommended that Federal and State government and community agencies streamline services and focus on helping all family members quickly, fairly, appropriately and without bias.

---

45 Williams, Daryl, Jocelyn Newman, Family Law Pathways Advisory Group established, Joint Media Release, 17 May, 2000.

46 Williams, Daryl, Vanstone, Amanda, Family Law Pathways Advisory Group report released today, Joint Media Release, 29 August, 2001.

Needless to say, none of it happened. The bureaucrats got paid. Another report got shelved. The taxpayers got fleeced. And on the ground separated families continued to suffer the outrageous imposts and complexities of the system.

Aware of the foment in their conservative base against the multiple lunacies of the family law and child support systems, the government of then Prime Minister John Howard passed legislation jailing parents who defy Family Court orders. It was an absolutely bizarre response to such an infamously troubled jurisdiction.

***

Two of the nation's leading broadsheets at the time, *The Sydney Morning Herald* and *The Australian*, incorrectly reported that men's groups supported the legislation.

In fact, jailing was opposed by most men's and women's groups, none of whom were consulted. Men's groups in particular were opposed, seeing the jailing of former wives as inappropriate and fearing the laws would be unjustly used only to jail fathers. As turned out to be the case. In some of the most egregious cases, the Court simply refused to jail mothers while feeling no such compunction or sympathy for fathers.

There had been a number of appalling stories in the international media at the turn of the millennium on the consequences of these types of laws: a man in the US jailed for three months for ringing his daughter on Monday and not Sunday suicided within hours of being released; a bus conductor in Britain was jailed for waving at his children out the window of a bus.

In Australia a man was jailed for sending his daughter a birthday card.[47]

No mainstream interest.

Also in Australia an Indian man was jailed for writing to his parents in English, not Hindi. The Family Court was not satisfied he was attempting to comply with their orders. His efforts to point out that his father had two masters degrees in English fell on deaf ears. The story received extensive coverage in the ethnic press, but not a word in the mainstream. I could not interest the paper where I worked to run it.

So much for Australia as a multicultural paradise. Australians of English heritage might have shrugged it all off more easily, knowing, from their convict heritage, that the authorities are bastards. But being from India, being jailed was a social disgrace he struggled for a long time to come to terms with. This man kept good records, and I had all the documentation for this case.

No mainstream interest.

---

[47] Nowell, Laurie, Fury at ruling in custody battle, Sunday Herald Sun, 10 January, 2010.

The Family Court had ordered outraged litigants not to contact the United Nations over their concerns about the court's conduct.

No mainstream interest.

***

It all began a long time ago. Most of those then in senior positions within the media and in government were in or around universities and the burgeoning of secondary education in the late sixties and early seventies. Many hadn't altered their views since Germaine Greer published her bestseller *The Female Eunuch* in 1970.[48] Women's Studies, which morphed into Gender Studies, same thing, were in their foundation years.

The Marxist feminist style of Family Courts which were birthed in the academic corridors of America's universities in the 1970s spread rapidly across the Western world, and were adopted with alacrity by Australia's legal fraternity, its phalanx of bureaucrats and legions of toady academics, all happy to suck up the money being hoisted around on the latest intellectual fad.

What was once the cutting edge, widely supported by many men, became in its playing out in family courts, social welfare departments, armadas of domestic violence advocates and all the hundreds of millions of dollars worth of supporting bureaucracies, a shock to many of its original male supporters.

One of my childhood ambitions, God bless my younger self, was to understand everything. Thus I ended up studying philosophy at one of Sydney's redbrick universities. Fortunately for me, it was the philosophy of the Philosophy Department that everything was valid, and so I struggled through.

Each year one of our lazier professors would set an essay for Shulamith Firestone's *The Dialects of Sex: The Case for Feminist Revolution*, also first published in 1970.[49] The basic tenet of the book was that for true liberation all traces of the patriarchy needed to be excised from women's lives.

Firestone described the biological family as "tyranny", her particular innovation being to include gender in traditional Marxist analysis of social power structures.

In the opening paragraphs of *The Dialectics of Sex*, Firestone wrote: "If there were another word more all-embracing than revolution we would use it. To so heighten one's sensitivity to sexism presents problems far worse than the black militant's new awareness of racism: feminists have to question, not just all of

---

48 Greer, Germaine, The Female Eunuch, MacGibbon & Kee, 1970.

49 Firestone, Shulamith, *The Dialects of Sex: The Case for Feminist Revolution*, William Morrow and Company, 1970.

Western culture, but the organisation of culture itself, and further, even the very organisation of nature. Many women give up in despair. Others continue strengthening and enlarging the movement, their painful sensitivity to female oppression existing for a purpose: eventually to eliminate it."

Fast forward 50 years, to the 2020s, and Firestone might as well have been the Prime Minister of Australia, her beliefs having lurched out of the academy to become all pervasive in the nation's institutions.

Raised on a diet of this sort of rhetoric and now in senior and powerful positions in the bureaucracy, graduates of the 1970s saw themselves as righting historical wrongs.

Despite the level of concern in the community, the mistreatment of separated families had traditionally been protected by an unofficial bipartisan veil drawn across family law. Both major political groupings in Australia, the "conservative" Liberal National Party coalition and the "leftwing" Labor Party, knew there was little to be gained by bashing each other up over the issue, and much to be risked in openly attacking another wing of government, the courts. Any such action undermined the public's confidence in the judicial system and opened a "can of worms". For every Family Court decision which defied community norms, there was another right behind it.

***

As a progressive kind of guy who had even done a year of Women's Studies at university I never seriously questioned any of it. Until confronted with it myself and witnessed firsthand the extreme bias and the truly astonishing levels of dishonesty rampant in Australia's family law system.

It was an eye opening experience for many men. And so it proved for me. I worked within a 10 minute walk of the marbled halls of the Sydney Registry of the Family Court of Australia and had always assumed it functioned as a normal court. Like most people, I had no idea what went on behind its marble facades.

By the time I became interested in the issues, fathers had been consistently demonised for more than 20 years with relentless anti-male propaganda. In classic Marxist language interactions between the genders was boiled down to power relations while the nuclear family was painted as patriarchal nests of violence and abuse.

The founding Chief Justice of the Family Court, Elizabeth Evatt, was an outspoken advocate for women's rights. There is no public record of her having ever said anything positive about fathers. If anyone can disprove this statement, I am happy to correct the record. Activist judges have plagued the court and destroyed its reputation ever since.

Studies which consistently showed children to be better off in intact families or with a substantive relationship with their fathers were studiously ignored.

In the universities where it all began, the bias against men both in terms of courses and behaviour was evident wherever you looked.

At the turn of the millennium a proposal for a men's issue of the University of NSW's pioneering student paper Tharunka was squashed by the Guild Council It condemned "any proposal to produce a men's edition or white heterosexual male edition of Tharunka.

"Accordingly, Guild Council directs the media directors/Tharunka editors not to produce any such editions or publish material which contravenes general guild policy or anti-discrimination legislation or which undermines the purpose of women's, lesbian/gay, indigenous or ethnic students departments."[50]

At the same time the Guild passed a proposal for a women's only edition.

***

Australia was not the only country struggling with its family law system. There was often scathing media attention focused on family courts around the world throughout 2000, the year Dads On The Air was born.

The then well regarded British broadsheet *The Observer* completed a three month expose into the British Family Court, concluding that custody evaluation procedures were utterly flawed. They found "a shocking culture producing routine misery on a vast scale for both children and parents". The paper continued: "We have found wide ranging inadequacies in the legal system, ill-trained professionals, badly prepared judges and decision making which is often a lottery."[51]

These conclusions could have equally been written about the Family Court of Australia, but no newspaper in the country has had the guts to do it.

The series opened with a quote from a father: "It makes more sense to forget I ever had a child."

Journalist Dina Rabinovitch, who died in 2007 of breast cancer at the age of 45, wrote that family law was a world of uninformed decision-making, impatient judges and rigid court orders.[52] She could easily have been writing about Australia.

"In family law, judges have the widest discretion and are least restrained by precedent. The thinking is that there can only be loose guidelines within family law, no strict rules, to allow for the 'uniqueness' of each family. But this results in a 'complete lottery', says one barrister specialising in family law. 'With family

---

50 Korogiannis, Michael, "Are some more equal than others?", Tharunka, November, 2000.

51 Rabinovitch, Dina, It makes more sense to forget I ever had a child, *The Observer*, 2 July, 2000.

52 Dina Rabinovitch, *The Telegraph*, 15 November, 2007.

cases – and this is different from any other area of law – the judge is given this excuse to be inconsistent, quite maverick in approach, or even outrageous.'"

Rabinovitch said she began taking an interest in family law following her own and friends' divorces, witnessing the reckless decisions being taken about families' lives. "At first, I couldn't believe what I was seeing. Some of the characters within family courts seem to come straight from the pages of Charles Dickens.

"Those going through the system are often rendered passive by it. They can see the problems but don't want their whole lives affected, so they choose to 'get on with things' rather than fight back. Or worse, they do fight back, and become manic, angered by the intricate injustices which, in turn, might result in them being seen as the problem.

"So much of what is going on in the family courts is secret. If family court hearings were open, bad practice could be exposed much earlier. We would also all have at least the chance of a clearer idea of what constitutes family law and what fashions are being followed at any time.

"In the early 1990s the Lord Chancellor's Department carried out a consultation about whether family justice should come out from behind closed doors, but the outcome itself was never published – a muffling of the secrecy inquiry worthy of a Blackadder script. But while the political shenanigans continue, parents – and children – carry on suffering."

***

For many years and to this day the blurring, if not total lack of separation, between women's affairs rounds and social affairs rounds on newspapers, radio and television has meant that the concerns of women's groups are put forward as newsworthy while the concerns of men and fathers are simply ignored or dismissed as reactionary.

Many but not all of these reporters are women.

American author of *The Myth of Male Power* Warren Farrell, wrote extensively about the media's silence on men's issues and what he called "the lace curtain".[53] He wrote: "Gender issues are regularly covered by feminists whose gender reinforces their political ideology. Feminism achieved power informally, by becoming the one party system of gender politics: creating a new arena of study, defining the terms, generating the data and becoming the only acceptable source of interpretation."

In many of the opinion pages of Australian newspapers the words of the Women's Electoral Lobby or other activist feminist groups sympathisers were

---

[53] Farrell, Warren, *The Myth of Male Power*, Simon and Schuster, 1993.

paraded as the cutting edge of social commentary. The opposite view was almost never put forward.

The so-called "sinister men's groups", to quote the Chief Justice of the Family Court Alastair Nicholson, in reality nothing more than rather informal collections of fathers who wanted to see more of their kids, had long complained of the media bias against them.

Lone Fathers, Dads, Fathers Against Family Equity, Men's Rights Agency and many other smaller groups all struggled to get their views across against what they perceived as overwhelming odds. Outfunded more than 1000:1, they were no match for the public relations expertise of the women's groups. The media rarely bothered to include their views on any of the issues affecting families or single parents.

Over the years many family law reform campaigners viewed the wall of silence arrayed against them as some kind of leftwing conspiracy. Indeed, as professional surveys have shown, journalists tend to be left leaning partly by the nature of their work and the impulses which drove them to it.[54] Like most people, they tended to want to leave the world a better place, and for some this meant making a strike for the disadvantaged.

Women's groups have managed to define themselves as victims and to draft the entire debate of divorce and the position of single mothers into a left/right, progressive/conservative dichotomy. They also commandeered the much abused phrase "the best interests of children". The concerns of men and fathers were dismissed or categorised as gun toting four wheel driving "send them back to kitchen" Neanderthals. But in the new millennium, when most men supported their wives in their career choices, it was by no means clear that separated mothers were any more disadvantaged than separated fathers.

The media has never seriously tackled one of the most impactful examples of censorship in the country, Section 121 of the Family Law Act, which prohibits the identification of parties to a Family Court case. It makes coverage of family law issues impossible for television. People expressing their views on radio have been taken to court purely on voice recognition. To my knowledge this censorship has never been tested in the High Court.

The secrecy laws have effectively shielded the Court and its decision making from any detailed public scrutiny. This protection spills over into the operations of children's courts, welfare departments such as the Department of Community Services in New South Wales and Human Services in Victoria as well as the family law units of Legal Aid.

---

54 Ketchell, Misha, Whose views skew the news? Media chiefs ready to vote out Labor while reporters lean left, *The Conversation*, 20 May, 2013.

The legislation meant that the agencies that intrude most into the private lives of individuals have evolved in secrecy. These agencies impact on the lives of millions of Australian adults and children, and will impact them for generations to come. And yet no one questions or exposes the behaviour of lawyers in any of these jurisdictions, their agendas or their use of psychiatric evidence. It's just not politically correct to do so.

Journalists also rarely question the conduct of the protecting bureaucracies and handsomely funded academics circling family law. The dictums of the Australian Institute of Family Studies, founded under the same legislation as the Family Court, are repeated as fact. Academics know better than anyone which side their grants are buttered on.

The Institute has spent far more money on studies of social capital, an academic discourse devoted almost entirely to attempting to define itself, than it ever has in investigating the position of fathers after divorce. It has never properly investigated the high suicide rates of fathers and the linkages to family law. But there were signs of change, we so naively hoped, back then at the turn of the millennium.

***

Significantly, *The Australian* ran a number of stories and editorials critical of the Family Court. These were written by then High Court writer Bernard Lane, who relied closely on Australia Law Reform Commission's reports which had found overwhelming disquiet with the court and its processes.

"The Family Court is a beleaguered and defensive institution with a history of failed reform and hostility to constructive criticism, the federal Government's chief law reform advisers have reported," Lane wrote. "The Australian Law Reform Commission yesterday urged yet another external review of the court, saying lawyers who used the court had little confidence in internal reform."[55]

The questioning of senate committee member and former barrister Senator Mason, who asked a string of parliamentary questions on the travel budgets of senior judges, delays in the court and even the extravagant cost of the china in their tea rooms. The Court refused to answer a number of the questions.

An editorial in *The Australian* in August 2000, written by the paper's High Court writer Bernard Lane, who had followed the Mason investigation closely and used the Senator's investigative talent as a major source for news stories, declared: "The Family Court is the last court that should be resisting public accountability. Its work can have profound personal and social consequences for Australians.

---

55 Lane, Bernard, Reformers return fire at Family Court, *The Australian*, 18 February, 2000.

"Chief Justice Nicholson...is wrong to resist an attempt by the Senate to scrutinise the efficiency of the court under his management.

"Not so long ago, Coalition MPs and Justice Nicholson rarely rose above mutual recrimination. But the argument about the court was transformed last February when the Australian Law Reform Commission published a report on federal justice. It gave detailed evidence of basic failures of management. Taken together, these suggested a dysfunctional culture at the highest levels of the court – for which the Chief Justice must take ultimate responsibility.

"The culture appeared to be inward-looking, defensive and hostile to constructive criticism. Its priorities seemed distorted. It encouraged judges engaged in bureaucracy and committee work, while giving less attention to the core business of a court: the hearing and deciding of cases."[56]

But while the Family Court remained a sacred cow for most of the media, the same is not true of the Child Support Agency, which received more hostile or mixed coverage in that period than ever before.

The exception to all this goodwill was Sydney's mass circulation tabloid *The Daily Telegraph*, which ran a series kicking off with a screaming headline "Child Cheaters" and a photograph of a father with a Porsche evading child support. It would have been just as easy to find a woman living high on the hog on income from the government, the ex, the latest boyfriend and her own business, but that was not to be.

But even the Tele felt obliged to run a range of views in its followup stories and letters to the editor. At the same time at the more serious end of the spectrum *The Canberra Times* broke a string of excellent stories on child support; including running on its front page twice in the same week a story on the inquest into a 28-year-old man with three children who suicided with a Child Support Agency letter in his hand. He was losing 80 percent of his pay in tax and child support. The Agency claimed it was treating him fairly.[57]

The Brisbane Courier Mail also ran a three part series on child support throwing up a range of moving stories. As well, *The Adelaide Advertiser* ran an excellent piece called Fathers Fighting Back.

Men and the Media concluded: "With the government having just thrown jailing into the present toxic mix of family breakdown, media interest is unlikely to die off. The day when we have a National Council for Single Fathers as well as one for mothers, the day when shared parenting is the norm after separation,

---

56 Editorial, Family Court must accept more scrutiny, *The Australian*, 28 August, 2000.

57 Campbell, Roderick, Suicide victim hounded over Child Support, *The Canberra Times*, 15 November, 2000.

when destructive custody battles are a thing of the past and family courts are a long forgotten institution, is the day when we will be able to say we have truly made progress towards equality in all areas."

***

Spill down the years and the one-sided pile on against men has simply grown worse.

The Sydney Morning Herald back then was the Bible of the chattering classes, and as its Social Affairs Reporter Adele Horin was its resident and much celebrated feminist. She was also a scourge to the burgeoning fatherhood movement of the day.

In a 2009 column titled "Four crafty women teach a deadbeat to mend his ways" Horin celebrated a group of women who had superglued an unfaithful husband's penis to his stomach, a macabre story which fed and bled straight into the extreme male bashing of the era. It's hard to believe this kind of extreme sexism would get published, much less rewarded, but that was the fashion. And we all pay a price for this both historic and continuing insanity.[58]

In terms of media, Dads on the Air was just about the only antidote in the country to this madness.

Of the "crafty women" piece Greg Andresen, at the time the Research and Media Liaison Men's Health Australia and a valued contributor to DOTA, compiled a list of comments from famous feminists of the day contradicting Adele Horin's claim that "middle-class feminists" weren't man haters.

It's worth repeating a few of them just to give the temperature of the times.

"I feel that 'man-hating' is an honourable and viable political act." Robin Morgan, Ms. Magazine Editor.

"I feel what they feel: man-hating, that volatile admixture of pity, contempt, disgust, envy, alienation, fear, and rage at men." Judith Levine, author and journalist.

"All men are rapists and that's all they are." Marilyn French, author of *The Women's Room*.

"I want to see a man beaten to a bloody pulp with a high-heel shoved in his mouth, like an apple in the mouth of a pig." Andrea Dworkin, author and activist.

---

58 Horin, Adele, This is a stick-up: four crafty women teach a deadbeat to mend his ways, *The Sydney Morning Herald*, 8 August, 2009.

"The nuclear family must be destroyed. Whatever its ultimate meaning, the break-up of families now is an objectively revolutionary process." Linda Gordon, leading Second Wave feminist author.

"No aspect of society being at all relevant to women, there remains to civic-minded, responsible, thrill-seeking females only to overthrow the government, eliminate the money system and destroy the male sex. Valerie Solanas, author of The SCUM Manifesto – SCUM meaning "Society for Cutting Up Men."

"Since marriage constitutes slavery for women, it is clear that the women's movement must concentrate on attacking this institution. Freedom for women cannot be won without the abolition of marriage." Sheila Cronin, leader of America's National Organisation for Women.

Australia's media charlatans lapped it all up. Academics thought it was all so clever. Bureaucrats built their empires.

Andresen asked: "If the majority of feminists love the male of the species, why have we not heard a peep from them about these sorry statistics:

- 50% more Australian women than men now graduate from our universities
- twice as many men as women are victims of violence every year and one-in-three victims of sexual assault are male but there are no "stop violence against men" campaigns or councils
- men die more often than women from all major causes of death but there is as-yet no men's health policy
- four men commit suicide for every woman that kills herself.

"And why, if Ms Horin truly loves men, does she paint loving fathers who have had their children forcefully removed from their lives as 'all those angry men'."[59]

***

Soar across the intervening years and nobody, well certainly nobody in Australia's diminished mainstream media, and this freakish anti-male rhetoric has become an accepted part of public discourse, the purveyors of this misandry amply rewarded.

In October 2015, one of Australia's most prominent feminists Clementine Ford tweeted "'kill all men" after a woman suggested on Twitter her "blind hatred of males" made it hypocritical of her to be an advocate of equal rights. She became synonymous with the hashtag #killallmen.

The author of *Fight Like A Girl* had also previously tweeted "I bathe in male tears". She wrote "Have you killed any men today? And if not, why not?" in a book signing for a fan. Another of her charming tweets read: "All men must die."

---

[59] Andresen, Greg, It's Not OK to Bash Men, Dads On The Air, 9 August, 2009.

In 2018 suicide prevention group Lifeline, a highly valued Australian service, cancelled a domestic violence forum featuring Clementine Ford after a petition against her appearance attracted almost 14,000 signatures.[60]

Protestors questioned how Lifeline could give her a platform, considering many men with mental health problems relied on the service.

In 2019 Clementine, after seven long years as a columnist with the Fairfax newspapers *The Sydney Morning Herald* and *The Age*, was finally removed from her position after an expletive filled rant against unpopular Prime Minister Scott Morrison.[61] The Nine group, which by then had assumed ownership of the papers, had close ties to the conservatives.

In 2020 the same darling of the left was pictured giggling with Australia's first female Prime Minister Julia Gillard, who did a podcast with Clementine Ford at the end of the year: "We speak about her honest and uncompromising approach to feminism; misogyny; and the pressures placed on young women," Gillard said.[62]

In that same year Clementine Ford had tweeted: "Honestly, the corona virus isn't killing men fast enough." She then blamed the backlash on "male fragility".

In 2023 Our Dearest Clementine published a book *I Don't: The Case Against Marriage*, joining the river of Marxist inspired anti-nuclear family rhetoric which had wormed its way into the mainstream.

The febrile atmosphere created by all this male bashing enabled the most leftwing government in Australian history, led by Labor's Anthony Albanese in the 2020s, to ramrod changes to family law, taking the entire system back to the dark ages when many men entering the Family Court rarely if ever saw their children again.

***

The false allegations which were the bread and butter of the parasitic lawyers feasting on the misery inflicted by the nation's dysfunctional family law and child support systems were allowed to flourish, with domestic violence accusations becoming the standard tactic at the beginning of any custody battle. Fathers were

---

60 Johnson, Stephen, Hardline feminist Clementine Ford's Lifeline speech is CANCELLED, Daily Mail, 15 May, 2018.

61 Clementine Ford quits Nine newspaper column, ABC, 31 January, 2019.

62 Barraclough, Corrine, Clementine and Gillard? Together? Am I dreaming of a blight Christmas? *Spectator Australia*, 18 December, 2020.

inevitably assumed guilty, stripped of their homes, their assets and frequently their jobs, while acres of police time were consumed by battling couples claiming abuse by the other party.

It's not worth anybody's while to buck the system, certainly not for a police officer, and so one after another fathers were carted off to a homeless misery of the state's making.

All men were deemed guilty by dint of their very nature, their gender, the social and personal cost of this debacle brought to you by the taxpayer.

That small flurry of positive stories about the need for change in Australia's family law, child support, child protection and domestic violence systems way back in the early 2000s, which at the time seemed like barely a crack in the dam wall, a small and long overdue acknowledgement of a desperately bad dysfunction, are now not just a distant memory, but almost feel like a golden age.

Protest has been fully relegated to the margins.

Most of the activists of the day burnt out long ago.

The multibillion taxpayer funded industry demonising men is in full stride. Those who suffer are silenced, ridiculed or ignored. The universities and bureaucracies remain entirely captured by these antiquated ideologies. The heartbreak of men, children, extended families and the women who love the men in their lives, brothers, sons, grandsons, are ignored. Australia's legacy media becomes increasingly discredited and irrelevant. Truth, always a scarce commodity in this realm, has vanished altogether.

And with the mainstream having so thoroughly discredited itself, independent media, outside the control of government, now inspires a new generation.

FIVE
DADS ON THE AIR

Dads On The Air, which established itself in 2000, was born not just out of a sense of injustice, but out of frustration with the mainstream media's failure to take men's issues seriously, or in most cases to even report on them.

DOTA was proud to broadcast a range of voices little heard in the mainstream, as well as having politicians, authors and academics whose voices, at least on these subjects, were routinely ignored by gender study courses and journalists alike.

The studio where we broadcast from was located at the offices of 2GLF in Liverpool in western Sydney, an area which even back then was seeing massive population growth. The station, one of the oldest community radio stations in Australia, was amongst the first tranche of four community radio stations that were established by Gough Whitlam during the 1970s, a time of great social ferment and optimism in Australia.

From the establishment of the first four there are now more than 450 community radio stations around Australia, a unique opportunity for local people to have their say and in international terms a rare instance of genuine democracy at work.

Depending on the quality of your radio we could be heard from the mountains in the west to the coast in the east. While they were not all listening, indeed the numbers were probably not all that impressive, it had a footprint of more than two million people across the demographic heart of Australia's then most populous city, Sydney.

Technology had rapidly changed the father's movement by enabling the almost instantaneous spread of information, news stories, research and developments worldwide. Once separated fathers had been socially isolated and largely withdrawn. Now they realised they were not alone, that their cases were far from unique. The internet facilitated the rapid "wising up" of separated fathers. In the previous five years there had been a rapid expansion of internet chat-lines and on-line communities which meant anyone struggling to understand court processes or to handle the emotional fallout of divorce or separation could benefit from other's experience. All they had to do was put out a simple request about forms or procedures and they would be deluged with advice.

Dads On The Air was itself a prime example of the way revolutions in computer science were transforming social debate. The technology which made it possible for a small group in western Sydney to create a 90 minute weekly program that could be downloaded in Mongolia and attract the country's and the world's leading political, academic and social commentators on fathers issues simply hadn't existed five years before.

***

We made mistakes. At first we tried to fill three hours a week with dads' related material. Then the station management suggested not so subtly that it might be easier on their listeners to condense our separated father focused material into a shorter time span. For a while the program was 60 minutes long. We finally settled on a 90 minute format. In its contemporary, less politicised format it is around half an hour.

In the early years we ran an often lively public forum. But we found that while the forums were valuable in spreading information and displaying the grief and despair of fathers for all to see, they were also easily abused. A few used the forums as a way of recruiting people to their legal adventurism, dispensing poor advice for money distressed dads could ill afford. And a drunken and obsessive disenfranchised father with a head full of conspiracy theories can be an unlovely beast at 2am. With some repeat offenders, no amount of reasoning could convince them to temper their online and therefore very public conduct.

We also found that because of the volatility of the subject matter the forums sometimes associated us with positions and attitudes which did not reflect our own views. Intemperate comments on the forums were easily used against us by our critics; yet we had not authored them. We were faced with many hours of work to clean up the forums or on occasion to comply with police requests to remove material. Finally we abandoned them altogether.

The show played a pivotal role in the debate over family law reform in Australia during the first decade of the new millennium, acting as a conduit for groups and individuals whose voices were rarely if ever heard in the mainstream media.

The program today is very different to what it once was, including being less political, more professional and probably considerably more entertaining. As the show evolved we continued to follow Australian family law, child support and fatherhood issues more closely than any other media outlet, but also pursued broader debates, from men's health to early childhood development to parental alienation. As the years passed, Dads On The Air widened its focus to promote a positive view of men, boys, fathers and to explore social issues around gender and fatherhood.

***

As mentioned before, Australia's unique network of community radio stations, established by Gough Whitlam in the early 1970s, was one of the main reasons the show arose in Australia. Ironically it was also Whitlam who established the Family Court of Australia, following a similar trend towards secretive Marxist feminist style family courts in other Western countries. While internationally there was widespread discontent amongst men over the operations of family law, child support, child protection and other gender related issues, there has so far been nothing else quite like Dads On The Air anywhere in the world. As a result we regularly interviewed international guests and our archives contained interviews with many of the major figures in fatherhood politics around the world.

The show followed more closely than any other media outlet in Australia the struggle for reform of family law in the early 2000s. Ultimately, through its programs and early forums, it provided the most complete record available of the long, difficult and passionate struggle for reform of what separated fathers regarded as the extreme anti-male anti-father bias of Australia's family law system. As we were to discover, we were not alone. A similar bias infected family law systems throughout the western world.

Dads On The Air was in a unique position to cover and even at times to contribute to the years of reports, committee inquiries and debate on reforms promoting cooperative care of children after divorce. Watered down and ultimately ineffective changes were finally made into law by the Australian government headed by then Prime Minister John Howard in 2006 as a bipartisan initiative.

So many people worked so hard over so many years to bring sanity to Australia's family law, child support and child protection system, yet there is now little to show for their heroic, herculean efforts.

But there is nothing like a burning sense of injustice to drive action.

***

We were up against it from the very start, without resources or funding of any kind, heavily disturbed by our bruising encounters with the nation's reviled family law and child support agencies, without, except for myself, any media experience and justifiably fearful of retribution.

We were determined to bring these stories to light, all those advocates who laboured without public funding to fight off the tsunami of government funded anti-father propaganda; and to all those dads, stepmothers, grandparents and extended families who fought so valiantly to see, to know and to help their children and grandchildren, and to make the society better as a whole.

Dads On The Air was born on the cusp of gathering outrage around the globe about family law and child support systems, the latter in effect an onerous additional tax imposed almost solely on separated dads, the former arbitrary, capricious, secretive and unaccountable. This international outrage reached its most colourful apogee early in the millennium with the antics of the British group Fathers4Justice. Their stunts included climbing Buckingham Palace in London and invading Parliament House at Westminster, where purple powder was thrown at the politicians, purple being the adopted colour for justice. Bridges across Britain were climbed, traffic brought to a standstill.

While there was much talk at various times, and even at one point the creation of a Fathers4Justice Australia group, such overt acts of civil disobedience never came down under, perhaps because of our smaller population, perhaps because Australian men are less inclined to showy displays. Whatever the reason, at least questions were beginning to be asked over the routine demonisation of men and the ideological shift away from the nuclear family and the role fathers had traditionally played as protectors and providers. The most concrete demonstration of these ideological shifts could be found in the operation of the Family Court.

Amongst the community leaders we welcomed onto the show were researchers from the University of Western Sydney Michael Woods and John MacDonald, activists including Matt O'Connor, Ray Barry, and Jolly Stansby from Fathers4Justice, Sue Price from the Men's Rights Agency, Warwick Marsh from the Fatherhood Foundation, John Flanagan from the Non-Custodial Parents Party, Barry Williams from Lone Fathers, Yuri Joakimidis from the Joint Parenting Association, family law maverick Simon Hunt and Mark Bourne from the Richard Hillman Foundation.

Michael Green, when we first began broadcasting, was best known as the author of Fathers After Divorce, a practical guide to coping with custody disputes and their aftermath, including the loss of children, assets and income. As a senior legal figure who had nonetheless been brutalised by the system just like so many others, in the early days his moderate and educated tone was important in giving credibility to our own often more strident criticisms of the court.

Later Michael Green was to co-author a second book, in conjunction with psychologist Jill Burrett titled *Shared Parenting: Raising Your Child Cooperatively After Divorce*.[63] Of course we were to interview him once again. Over time he became one of the most learned and reasonable of the voices calling for reform as we ourselves became increasingly critical of the judgements, the secrecy and the conduct of the Court. As a lawyer himself, Green was far more polite than we would ever be. Later he became closely involved with the drafting of the Howard government's legislative reforms.

Green argued that when people thought of separation they thought of lawyers and all too easily ran off to find out what their rights were. The true question separating couples should ask themselves was not what were their rights and responsibilities but what were the best arrangements they could put in place for the parents and for the children.

***

Far from being concerned about "the best interests of the child", as we were often to say on radio one of the most dishonestly used phrases in Australia today, its social aim appeared to us to be the marginalisation of perfectly decent dads and the creation of that noble victim, the single mother, the linchpin and justification for billions of dollars of social welfare spending, complex administrations, thousands of jobs and a welter of supporting programs.

The Family Court at the turn of the millennium had been very slow to adjust to changing social mores which once again increasingly valued the role of fathers. Or to take note of the new generations of fathers closely involved in the day to day care of their children.

There were many issues impacting on separated fathers, most dominantly the long battle for joint custody or shared parenting, but many other factors impinged on their lives as men and fathers. In our early days at DOTA we were keen to cover them all.

One topic of particular concern to separated fathers but probably of little interest to anyone else was child support. Despite every father's group in the country claiming that child support is directly linked to the high death rate amongst separated men, no government inquiry has ever addressed this scandal. Almost no politician ever speaks up. And no mainstream media outlet has ever tackled the story in depth.

The rigidities and complexities of the child support formula and its poor interaction with the real world of separating couples, whose lives are often in flux, has created distress and frustration from clients and child support workers alike.

---

63 Greene, Michael and Burrett, Jill, *Shared Parenting*, Celestial Arts, 2009.

Despite the bureaucratic propaganda demonising "deadbeat dads" and boasting about the millions collected, at great expense and allegedly in the best interests of children, the case for the abolition of the Child Support Agency is as strong today as when we first began broadcasting. Based on information obtained under Freedom of Information laws, we estimated that as of 2010 more than 13,000 clients of the Agency had died since Labor came to power in late 1997. This was significantly higher than would be expected in a similarly aged group of non-child support payers.

Along with bread and butter stories of changing government policy and institutional and legal reform, many often wrenching individual tales came to the attention of Dads On The Air. We broadcast or brought attention to as many of them as we could; the fathers jailed for sending birthday cards to their children, or who have had their homes or businesses destroyed because of the claims of their former wives and the viciousness of court decisions. The rural families who lost family operations built up over generations. The fathers falsely accused of sexual crimes against their children, simply in order to gain advantage in a custody battle.

The fathers who spend the rest of their lives grieving for the children they have lost and who are so often and so painfully turned against them. While some dads hope and pray their children will eventually return to them when they are old enough to make their own decisions, in practice many of these often damaged kids are indoctrinated for life. Many painful stories remain untold, non-existent in the public conscience.

***

Other guests on the show included Senior Researcher for Kids Help Line Ian Thomas, former and current heads of the Shared Parenting Council of Australia Geoffrey Greene, Ed Dabrowski and Warwick Marsh, and head of the for a time hugely successful self help group Dads In Distress Tony Miller. A regular guest was a Director of Social Policy Programmes at the Centre for Independent Studies, Peter Saunders, whose books include *Poverty In Australia*, *The Government Giveth and the Government Taketh Away* and *Australia's Welfare Habit*.

Yet others included father Terry Hicks, whose son David was accused of terrorist activities and left to rot by the Australian government in Guantanamo Bay, despite his case being more a matter of a naive suburban lad dreaming of a life as a soldier of fortune getting caught in the wrong place at the wrong time rather than being any terror mastermind. Just as his successors also exploited the terror threat for electoral gain, the Prime Minister of the day John Howard was in no hurry to rescue David Hicks from his situation.

We also interviewed 2006 Australian Father of the Year Ron Delezio, whose daughter Sophie Delezio was severely burnt and injured after a car ran into a childcare centre. The two-year-old toddler spent six months in hospital and suffered burns to 85 percent of her body. She lost both her feet, a hand and her right ear. Less than three years after her first devastating accident she was run over on a pedestrian crossing as she was being walked home from school and had a heart attack, broke her jaw and shoulder and fractured her ribs.

I had covered the story for the mainstream press from various angles before interviewing Ron on community radio.

Then there was Cheryl King, wife of Liam Magill, who ran a famous Australian case against the Child Support Agency after discovering the children he was paying child support for were not biologically his. The story fascinated many separated fathers, with the Family Court of the day opposed to DNA testing of children without the mother's consent amid much talk of "social fatherhood". Social enough to pay, that is, without any guarantee of contact.

Still others included Di Underwood from Grandparents Rights, Terry Melvin from Mensline, Teri Stoddard from the US organisation Shared Parenting Works, all with their own powerful stories, and much loved activist Lionel Richards, whose insomnia meant he always seemed to be awake in the crisis hours of the early morning when suicide prone fathers most needed help.

***

A number of people created original music for the show, including Peter van de Voorde, who showed up with an album of music he had just released called Our Stolen Children.

He stayed to pour a massive amount of time and energy into the project, becoming a co-presenter, administrator, researcher and music programmer.

His entertainment career included writing and recording a top-10 hit single, TV appearances and a seven month tour of Southeast Asia entertaining troops during the Vietnam War. Could he come in and play his album?

For sure.

He did huge amounts of volunteer work for Dads On The Air in the subsequent years, including arranging interviews, writing editorials, managing the website, editing and uploading the shows each week.

"It was a full time job," he recalls. "It was a five hour drive from my farm at Gum Scrub to the studio. I was dedicated. Bloody mad, mate. Obsessive.

"But I'm glad to have done it, it was part of the journey and life's adventure. I learnt so much. People like Greg Andresen, another volunteer on the show, taught me all the technical stuff. John Stapleton used to send me up because when I first met him, I didn't know the difference between an email and a website. I've come a long way."

Peter always argued that we should call ourselves Families on the Air, not Dads on the Air. To be more inclusive. Back then we saw it as appeasement.

Later, with some assistance, Peter set up a small lobby group, Family Briefing, which aimed to take the fight on child protection to the perpetrators of the country's rotten-to-the-core systems.

"I had so much information running around in my head and had gathered so much evidence I didn't know what to do with it all," van de Voorde recalls. I produced a one hour audio documentary recording many of the voices of those affected as children and intertwined them with the voices of our political leadership apologising for the pain inflicted by their predecessors, for the babies stolen from their mothers at birth and for the children transported to the colonies as child migrants. And for the so-called Stolen Generation – the indigenous children routinely removed from their parents.

"It clearly illustrated the hypocrisy of those apologies, since they were in the process of inflicting the very same pain on their own constituents of which they were accusing their predecessors."

***

Peter van de Voorde later went on to write a book *Children of the State: Stolen for Profit*, which he hoped would unravel the entire legal morass which had strangled and destroyed so many of the nation's citizens.[64]

Peter argued in the book: "Today, every Australian child is at risk of being deprived of the protection of their biological family, because we have collectively failed to recognise the supreme guardianship powers of the State. Perceived legal rights to the protection of their own family, something everybody assumes parents and children are entitled to, are in fact non-existent. This has resulted in the creation of a multi-billion-dollar child-removal industry, engaged in the redistribution of stolen children for profit, across the Western world.

"Cumulatively impacting more than six million Australians and currently draining our annual taxpayer funded budgets to the tune of $53 billion, without rights or anyone to turn to, the overwhelming socioeconomic consequences of misguided family and child protection policies reach deep into every community."

---

64 Van de Voorde, Peter, *Children of the State: Stolen for Profit*, Family Briefing, 2018.

Twelve years in the making, *Children of the State: Stolen for Profit* set out a devastating compilation of statistics and analyses of failed family and child protection systems. It provided a detailed account of morally indefensible international family and child protection laws and practices, which combine to provide legitimacy to the involuntary removal of millions of children from their biological families.

Peter wrote: "Impacting more than 25% of the Western world's population, with most countries pouring more of their taxpayer funded budgets into waging war against their own constituents then they spend on national defence against external threats, that this issue is not at the top of national agendas places a huge question mark over the quality of our collective conscience and vigilance.

"Without rights or anyone to turn to, the overwhelming socioeconomic consequences of misguided family and child protection policies reach deep into every community. It's where our families, friends and neighbours, struggle in silence each day with the effects of their imposed loss of family protection."

An author for the first time in his life, Peter van de Voorde described the process of producing *Children of the State* thus: "I had never written a book and will never write another. It was momentous. It took two years of my life. It was the hardest thing I've ever undertaken."[65]

***

Search For Your Family

> If you are a child, in a one parent home
> The thoughts that you think, may not be your own
> When you're old enough, independent of thought
> Search for your lost parent, challenge what you were taught
> You may have a family, who is loving and kind
> Who through lies and deception, have been wiped from your mind
> It's not your fault this injustice occurred
> So, search for your family and don't be deterred
> Kept as a hostage, to the truth you were blind
> So try and make contact, for your own peace of mind
> Grandparents and other family, have all disappeared

---

65 Stapleton, John, Classics of the Fatherhood Movement. Children of the State: Stolen for Profit by Peter van de Voorde, A Sense of Place Magazine, 3 October, 2024.

They've all been prevented, from becoming endeared
You have the right, to discover for yourself
That half of your family, who were stolen by stealth
One day you may, have children of your own
They'll ask about that family, the one you should have known
It's not your fault this injustice occurred
So, search for your family and don't be deterred
Kept as a hostage, to the truth you were blind
So, try and make contact, for your own peace of mind

Peter van de Voorde.

***

As well musician Ian Purdie, who styles himself as a "DJ Impersonator", came to the program in March 2006 after we interviewed him about his book *The Daddy Split Guide*.

Ian Purdie, who had been playing around the pubs of Sydney for decades, also showed up out of the blue after having penned a work heavily criticising the Family Court and the entire destructive system Australia had so sadly embraced.

We noted that there was a genre of men's literature developing with everything from the angst and anger of separation to practical guides to the many problems life throws up. "Ian Purdie's *The Daddy's Split Guide* is a bit of both; not always the most politically correct tract you'll ever read; but it has its moments; enormously entertaining, angry and occasionally wise."

Ian Purdie was quick to point out that research showed most divorces were initiated by women. "The blokes are just getting up and going to work, putting one foot in front of the other, fulfilling their time honoured role as protector and provider," he said.

"They are completely taken aback when they are hit not just by the fact that their wife wants to leave them, but that an entire government funded industry backs her decision and treats him with contempt.

"Most men have no idea what to do when they are first hit by aggressive legal letters outlining the fact that they are unlikely to see their children again, or at best will be reduced to having limited fortnightly contact. Most of them basically act like wounded animals, crawling into their 'caves', embarrassed and ashamed. Most have let their wives or partners organise their social lives, and they just don't know where to turn. The silence of men is one reason why they have been almost invisible in the public debate. That just wasn't me. I've spent much of my working life in rock bands and I'm just not the silent type."

His central thesis was: "It's time for the fathers of the world to stand up and say "ENOUGH!" As fathers our primary duty is to protect our children so that they can lead happy productive lives. This goal becomes less realistic every day as we continue to ignore the damage we are doing to our planet, our political and legal systems.

"At one point you loved each other and created a child or children. Even though your paths have changed, you once possessed the love necessary to bring a young child into this world and that love still exists in that child. You may have separated from your partner but the children still deserve every ounce of your love. No matter how hard it is for you and your ex to relate to each other, the children that you both created deserve that effort from you both.

"Sadly, many separated couples these days choose to use their children as bargaining chips or as weapons to damage each other emotionally. The impact of this upon children is incalculable. It really screws them up.

"The adversarial court system automatically favours the mother above the father and merely facilitates this emotional abuse of children. Lawyers encourage it.

"You must under every circumstance put your children's needs above your bitterness and hatred. They need your love, whether you are their mother or their father. They need you both in their lives, cherishing them as the precious miracles that every child is."

A born entertainer who was never, and I mean never, short of a word, Ian Purdie was invaluable for radio. There's no greater sin on radio than "dead air", and while a lot of broken dads could be more or less monosyllabic in front of a microphone, Ian was happy to tell everyone what he thought.

***

This is not to say that we were only interviewing community spokespeople.

In the early 2000s, when there was a political will to address the problems within the family law jurisdiction causing so much anger and distress in the community, we had many of the leading figures of the day. We were seen as the principal conduit to a difficult to access group of fathers and disenfranchised parents, people who weren't easily influenced by the government propaganda messaged through the mainstream media.

Many prominent political figures came onto the show over the years, including Phillip Ruddock, Attorney General for four years from 2003, who displayed sympathy towards fathers and the need for reform while elegantly defensive of the good intentions of those in his Department. A lawyer's lawyer, one could say.

Member for the rural seat of Riverina, Kay Hull, was appointed head of the 2003 government inquiry into child custody announced by Prime Minister John Howard in the House of Representatives in June. She came on the show a number of times and was expansive in her enthusiasm for change and spoke widely across the Australian media about the destructive nature of the system as she encouraged the public to express their concerns to the inquiry.

Highly regarded in her rural electorate, and with three sons herself, she had at least initially, before it all fell into ruins, appeared to have been a good pick to be the public face of the government backed push for change.

"As every Member of Parliament would know from the amount of inquiries to their offices, this subject is both important and highly emotional," she declared in her press release announcing the inquiry.[66] It was conducted under the auspices of the Family and Community Affairs Committee rather than the Legal Affairs Committee as an attempt to extricate it from the sticky fingers and self-serving obfuscations of government lawyers.

Fast forward to the 2020s, and it's hard to imagine any senior politician appearing on a community radio program critical of the Family Court.

***

Mark Latham was also happy to come on the show. A western Sydney politician close to his electorate and at the time Labor Party leader, he stood every chance of becoming the future Prime Minister in a race against the then Prime Minister John Howard. His seat of Werriwa encompassed the Liverpool studios from where we were broadcasting, he had once been the Mayor of Liverpool, and was happy to come into the studios. We didn't have to explain to him where they were.

He wasn't so friendly after I was forced by work to stake out his house day after day, along with a mob of other journalists, in the dying days of his Labor Party leadership.

But back in the early 2000s relations were good. He put his boots up on the studio desk and rattled on about how he had only one testicle due to cancer and urged blokes to be aware of such issues.

His kids were only young back then, he was a devoted and enormously proud dad, and he was happy to expound on all things related, very different to some of the other wings of his party.

---

66 Hull, Kay, Inquiry into Child Custody Arrangements, House Family and Community Affairs Committee, Press Release, 3 July, 2003.

***

Another of Australia's colourful politicians, Alby Schultz, was a welcome interview subject. A popular rural Member of Parliament, he won six different elections beginning in 1988 and retiring in 2013. He lost an eye in an accident in 2003.

One of the only Australian politicians with the guts or the integrity to publicly criticise the Child Support Agency and to not follow the party line, we interviewed him when he put out a booklet titled Child Support in Australia – A Heartfelt War of Relationships, Families and Money, the Battle for Balance.[67] The aim was to highlight the "massive social problems" being created by the government itself.

"It's been compiled from the extensive database that I've collected over the last two years in particular, which contains thousands and thousands of case examples of how the Child Support Agency, and indeed to a lesser degree the Family Court, has created massive problems of a financial, social and emotional type to different family groups.

"In terms of the Family Court, participants reported anger and resentment associated with the costs and the ability of residential parents to exploit the system for financial gain, and it was also suggested that the legal system was unable to enforce orders relating to access.

"In relation to the Child Support Scheme, two sub-themes emerged, administrative fairness and fairness in terms of policy and legislation. They had been completely financially stripped and emotionally devastated."

Alby said it looked like 6.1 percent of all cases terminated due to the death of a party, amounting to about 12 deaths a day.

"There is a huge body of thought that would suggest that the CSA is very closely related to the high death rates among separated men.

"The Child Support Agency has been allowed by successive governments to practise unheard of powerful procedures which is creating enormous problems for people."

***

There was so much more evidence of the massive harm these institutions were creating and the massive harm they were doing to so many parents, and consequently to the nation's children.

---

67 Interview with Australian Politician Alby Schultz on his booklet Child Support in Australia – A Heartfelt War of Relationships, Families and Money, the Battle for Balance, Dads On The Air, 14 August, 2006.

But one government after another ignored the outrage and pain from the constituents they were meant to serve.

In 2005 the freshly appointed Chief Justice of the Family Court of Australia Diana Bryant, no doubt eager to see her court shrug off the odium of the past, came on the show.

Chief Justice Bryant replaced the longest serving CJ in the Court's history, Alastair Nicholson, who had reigned over the Court since 1988. He was beloved by the nation's feminist and single mother's groups and utterly despised by the fatherhood movement. His peculiar psychopathology and merciless hostility towards fathers was seen as a key determining factor in the appalling destruction of fathers and families around the country.

Well aware, of course, that the conservatives then in power were advocating a populist push for shared parenting, Bryant gave everyone hope that change was afoot, and that she represented a new broom through this troubled jurisdiction.

Hope rapidly evaporated. When it came to the welfare of fathers and the rampant institutional bias against them, Diana Bryant proved just as bad as her predecessors.

In 2006, on the day before Christmas, the single most emotional and distressing time of the year for separated fathers who would not be seeing their children as a result of the Court's decisions, Bryant was quoted in *The Age* newspaper in Melbourne: "One of the things that frustrates me most is people saying that the court is biased – or that there is a systemic bias against fathers."[68]

The timing of the claims showed an extraordinary level of insensitivity, if not outright cruelty.

By the time Chief Justice Bryant retired in 2017 there were three year delays on hearings and the legal quagmire separating parents faced was as bad as ever.[69] Handsome salaries, prestigious positions, zero action. That was the nature of the beast we faced.

***

There was no money, zero funding, in promoting men's issues and Dads On The Air was literally up against a multi-billion dollar taxpayer funded industry of relentless one-eyed feminist advocacy.

As small, as under-resourced and as professionally inexperienced as we were, we also attracted many of the leading father or gender oriented authors of the day.

---

68 Porter, Liz, Family Court fights back over bias claims, *The Age*, 24 December, 2006.

69 Powell, Robin, Family Court underfunded, letting people down, Chief Justice says, ABC News, 30 April, 2017.

They included Stephen Baskerville, the legendary author of *Taken Into Custody: The War Against Fathers, Marriage, and the Family*.[70]

Baskerville argued "the long march" through the institutions was almost complete in the Western world.

While writing of the situation in America, his comments were equally valid in Australia. He wrote that families have been systematically portrayed as dangerous places for women and children and men propagandised as violent, abusive patriarchs or historical relics. He argued the divorce industry was a serious perpetrator of human and constitutional rights violations.

On the program we read out the following extract from *Taken Into Custody*: "The divorce regime is the most totalitarian institution ever to arise in the United States. Its operatives in the family courts and the social service agencies recognise no private sphere of life.

"The divorce regime is responsible for much more than 'ugly divorces,' 'nasty custody battles,' and other clichés. It is the most serious perpetrator of human and constitutional rights violations in America today. Because it strikes at the most basic institution of any civilization – the family – the divorce regime is a threat not only to social order but to civil freedom. It is also almost completely unopposed.

"No political party and no politicians question it. No journalists investigate it in any depth. A few attorneys have spoken out, but they are eventually suspended or disbarred. Some academics have written about it, but they soon stop. No human rights or civil liberties groups challenge it, and some positively support it. Very few 'pro-family' lobbies question it. This is because the divorce regime operates through money, political power, and fear.

"The divorce regime is much more serious than simply 'unfairness' or 'gender bias' against fathers in custody proceedings. It is the government's machine for destroying the principal check on its power – the family – and criminalising its main rival: fathers. The most basic human and constitutional rights are routinely violated in America's family courts. The lives of children and parents are in serious danger once they are, as the phrase goes, taken into 'custody.' Systemic conflicts of interest among government and private officials charged with child custody, child support, child protection, and connected matters have created a witch hunt against plainly innocent citizens.

"The terror of the divorce regime is not a future possibility; it is a present reality."

---

70 Baskerville, Stephen, *Taken into Custody*, Cumberland House, 2007.

Failure Family Law Reform Australia

***

At the time of writing, after decades of ferment and change, procrastination and failed reform, the Australian Labor government has chosen to ignore history and further empower the truly dysfunctional institutions tasked with handling family separation. Family Law Amendment Bills introduced in 2023 and 2024 were some of the most totalitarian pieces of legislation ever seen in Australian history, even including the disposition of pets. The nation as a whole, its children, and countless numbers of parents, suffer as a result.

Other writers included Sanford Braver, author of *Separated Dads: Shattering the Myths*, Mark Harris, author of *Family Court Hell*, Steve Biddullph world renowned Australian author of *Manhood* and *Raising Boys* along with Drs Paul Nathanson and Dr. Katherine Young, authors of *Spreading Misandry: The Teaching of Contempt for Men in Popular Culture* and *Legalising Misandry: From Public Shame to Systemic Discrimination Against Men*.

Christina Hoff Summers, author of *Who Stole Feminism?* and *The War Against Boys*, regarded essentially as underground classics, was also a great interview.

All this effort produced zero discernible change in the prevailing hatred of men spewing out of Australia's universities, bureaucracies and media outlets.

None of these well credentialed authors ever made it into the gender studies courses churning out generations of outraged women who seized, as they moved through the bureaucracies, any chance they could to instigate the cultural changes they had been taught were so vital to society's betterment.

A classic example of the wilful blindness of the academy was Warren Farrell, whose first book, *The Liberated Man*, was written from a feminist perspective. His 1988 book *Why Men Are the Way They Are* became a bestseller after America's leading talk show host Oprah Winfrey threw her weight behind it.

As he observed, going against the prevailing western orthodoxies and putting father's and men's side of the debate in the single party arena of gender politics produced neither sales nor applause.

In 1993, with an astute eye for feminist hypocrisy and the cant of the academy, Farrell penned *The Myth of Male Power: why men are the disposable sex.* and copped all the predictable flack for daring to question the feminist narrative.

Farrell's other books included the *Father and child reunion: how to bring the dads we need to the children we love* and *The Boy Crisis: Why Our Boys Are Struggling*.

When Farrell came to Australia on a speaking tour Uncle Buck and myself interviewed him in an inner-city pub we found quietly mannered and charming, hardly the strident figure some of his enemies had painted him.

Farrell's efforts to negotiate the thicket of the Western world's numerous gender studies programs and get at least some fatherhood material onto the syllabus lists failed.

Even his book published by Oxford University Press, *Does Feminism Discriminate Against Men*, targeted at the massive tertiary education and gender studies market, failed to become a standard text or achieve significant sales. The book presented a debate between Farrell and philosopher and feminist advocate James Sterba.

Truth, or even just neutrality, could not be found in this heated domain. There was zero chance of changing the academy or the courts, their enabling bureaucracies and their apologist politicians.

Revolutions are made on the ground. But in the end no revolution ever came. We paddle around in a land of defeat.

Was it all in vain? All that arranging of interviews, all that posting of material online, all the unpaid contributions and voluntary hours so many put in to make the show, all the surveillance, harassment and disdain we received, the long trek out to that community radio station in western Sydney each week?

Each of us can only do the best we can by the time we have.

And remember the words of Margaret Mead, one of history's most renowned sociologists: "Never underestimate the power of a small group of committed people to change the world. In fact, it is the only thing that ever has."

SIX
JAILING PARENTS

IN APRIL 2000, before Dads On The Air began broadcasting and before I was blocked from writing about family law after persistent complaints from the then Family Court's Chief Justice Alastair Nicholson, *The Australian* published a double page feature under the heading: Problem Parents Doing Time. It explored the Coalition governments' first haphazard attempts at family law reform with its Family Law Amendment Bill 1999. The article was introduced with the words: "Attorney General Daryl Williams wants to jail more mums and dads who defy family law. But critics say it is the system that is at fault."[71]

The scene was set with the story of a former professional sportsman, now disabled and unable to work, who was being hounded by the Child Support Agency after his marriage broke down in 1987, more than a decade before.

Once upon a time, Frank played professional sport and was married with two young sons. In 1987, his marriage broke down. He lost his children, his house, his furniture, all of which he left with his former wife because he thought it was the best thing to do. "I walked out with my bags," he recalls.

Orders for maintenance were made by the Family court at separation and these were collected through the Child Support Agency. Partially disabled by two accidents and unable to work since, Frank's only source of income is a parenting payment for his stepdaughter.

In 2000, shortly before the article appeared, he lost his Family Court case to have the claims dismissed. Under the proposed new laws, if found guilty of "willfully" refusing to pay he would face up to 12 months in jail. The definition of willful was to be left to the Family Court.

"I couldn't understand why", he told me. "It is not as if she never got anything out of me. She got everything. They have no compassion."

---

71 Stapleton, John, Problem Parents Doing Time, *The Australian*, 8 April, 2000.

The Government's push to jail parents who defied court orders included provisions to jail those who refused to comply with parenting orders on a "three strikes and you're in" basis.

After Nicholson's complaints, the paper, which normally trusted its senior journalists, the editors insisted on seeing every last piece of documentation.

The point of all this being, there are so many stories, and so much readily available well documented evidence that there really is no excuse for the nation's media not to have inquired more closely. Ideological blinkers blinded not just the perpetrators in the media, but the public at large. Instead the anguish of those most affected, those who have suicided or been hounded into an early grave, remain to this day largely unrecorded.

***

A significant part of the work for Problem Parents Doing Time story was compiling case studies of people trammelled by the system, some of which I remember vividly almost a quarter of a century on.[72]

The worst case, or the one that haunted me the most, was labelled Case Study: Death by Poison. I remember to this day the anguish of the man's sister who told me in graphic detail the entire story of her brother's death, only a fraction of which made it onto the printed page.

Their names were changed for publication.

The story began: "Katherine always cries when she talks about her brother Joseph, who committed suicide at the age of 34 after a call from the Child Support Agency. He had four children between three and 12, who were living with his ex-wife.

"He was a very naive person, gentle, kind, caring person, never pushy," Katherine recalled.

"He had been depressed because he had no money, he had absolutely nothing. Mum fed him, his sisters bought clothes. That day he went to the doctor. The doctor said he was happier than he had normally been.

"We left the house to pick up a daughter; I said, Joseph, your dinner is in the fridge."

The coroner's report records how the Agency phoned Joseph on the evening of his suicide attempt, telling him that because he had overpaid by $800, he had to write a letter so his former partner could get the money – otherwise, it would go into administrative costs. He was told he could not have it back.

---

72 Ibid.

Joseph went out to the back shed behind the family home and drank a poison known as Lethabarb. It is an excruciating way to die, as it eats out the lining of your stomach.

It took him 19 days to die.

The coroner's report records that an attempt was made to identify the relevant agency officer for the purposes of the inquest and to have him or her called as a witness.

However, the coroner recorded that "secrecy provisions" meant the Agency was not required to disclose any information. Agency representatives did not attend the inquest.

In the years that followed the Agency has consistently refused to attend coronial inquests. Yes, we pay taxes for a garbage administration that can't even be bothered to investigate the deaths of its own clients.

"Eight hundred dollars, that money would have eased things so much, made such a difference to his life," Joseph's sister said.

A month after his funeral the CSA wrote wanting to know why he wasn't paying his child support.

"How are we supposed to teach our children not to run people into the ground, humiliate and degrade them, just for your own benefit?" Katherine asked.

Yes, indeed.

***

In 1989 the Hawke Labor government launched the Child Support Agency with accompanying legislation, based on the motherhood argument that parents should support their children post separation and amidst exaggerated claims separated dads were not supporting their children after divorce.

It was introduced following Bob Hawke's much ridiculed claim that by 1990 no Australian child will be living in poverty.[73]

Despite all the evidence that the Agency achieved none of its stated goals, it did not improve the financial situation of children post separation nor did it save the government money, and the evidence of its dire impacts on parents, including its close association with the high suicide rates of paying parents, the CSA remains intact.

Overseeing the introduction was Social Security minister Brian Howe, a member of Labor's Socialist Left faction and sometimes referred to as the most leftwing of Hawke's ministers.

---

73 Koziel, Michael, No child will live in poverty? 30 years on, Bob Hawke's promise remains an elusive goal, *Sydney Morning Herald*, 22 June, 2017.

Father's representatives of the era were not consulted or involved in its creation.

As DOTA had noted, we had all been paying for Bob Hawke's stupid electoral comment that no child would live in poverty ever since.

Many separated dads struggled with the large imposts imposed upon them, the bureaucratic inflexibility of the Agency and the overt hostility of its staff towards fathers. Fathers regularly complained truth appeared to be of no importance to child support officers, who regularly took the word of the mother over anything the father said, just as did the Family Court.

Many disgruntled fathers who have dealt with the Child Support Agency have noted its intrusive and communistic nature. It was no accident. The first child support agencies were introduced by the Bolsheviks in Russia to prop up their fight against the nuclear family, which they saw as the major barrier against true socialist reform.

Identical or remarkably similar rates of payment operate in Australia's child support system as operated in the Russian system more than a century ago.

Blind Freddy should have been able to predict that imposing an onerous level of additional taxation on separated parent's way in excess of Australia's already heavy tax levels would cause nothing but trouble. And that placing the state dead bang in the middle of separating couples would exacerbate conflict. But no one paid any heed to what fathers thought, or showed any concern for their welfare. They were invisible in the public debate.

***

The Child Support Agency has been one of the great failures of Australian public policy, its maladministration and inept procedures legion. Stories abound. One father received seven different letters in one week, all detailing different amounts owed.

Richard Cruickshank, a well regarded researcher and director of the consultancy firm Property Investment Research, did a study in 2002 on the financial impacts of the child support scheme as part of a community project by his company. We were pleased to have him on Dads On The Air.[74]

Incensed by the conduct of the Agency and the government coverup of its negative impacts Cruikshank paid for the research himself.

Rather than saving the taxpayer money, Cruickshank estimated that the Child Support Agency had cost the Australian $28 billion dollars since its inception in 1989 – that is $2700 for every taxpayer – when welfare payments and lost tax

---

74 The Child Support Agency, with Richard Cruikshank, Dads on the Air, 31 March, 2003.

income was calculated. He estimated that the direct cost of child support welfare payments was in the order of $1.74 billion per year. This cost was spiralling. He estimated the scheme would cost the community a further $40 billion over the next decade.

"There is no doubt the schemes promote welfare dependency from both the mother and the father," Cruickshank declared during a Dads On The Air interview.

"The unemployment rate for paying fathers, at 39%, is more than six times the national average. Male payers make up 76% of the unemployed nationwide. The unemployment rate amongst recipients is also extremely high. Payers are more than 92% male, a figure that is rising, not falling, putting the lie to the claims that more men are gaining custody of their children.

"The CSA has refused to release the percentage of female payers who are in default of their payments, believed to be close to 100%."

Cruickshank said the Agency, at that time a $200 million plus bureaucracy with more than 2800 staff, had clearly failed in its objective. The average take per child at that time was $26; less than the average take in the mid-1980s of $35 per child.

He said the latest figures available suggested that 41% of child support payers did not lodge a tax return. The percentage of males on welfare or extremely low incomes was 45%.

Cruickshank calculated that for every dollar transferred between parents – $1.4 billion for the financial year 2000/2001 – it costs $2.80. He estimated the indirect cost of child support, including loss of tax revenue if payers were employed, was $3.7 billion for the same year.

Cruickshank described co-operation from the CSA while conducting his research as "non-existent". That should surprise no one who has ever dealt with them. Just as the Family Court was a law unto itself, so too the Child Support Agency.

He said it took months for the Australian Tax Office to provide the figure on the number of payers not lodging tax returns. Centrelink were also unhelpful. As a result of the lack of cooperation he filed a formal complaint to the Australian National Audit Office.

"The Child Support Scheme was primarily introduced by women's groups and passed through parliament without any broad community support from fathers, or even many thousands of women who have since partnered these fathers into second families. It is therefore not seen by most men as providing necessary support for children, but more as never ending vindictive action by women against former partners.

"To add insult to injury the men have no choice as to the level of ever increasing mandatory child support and the continuous scrutiny into their financial affairs provided to the other party, who has no accountability for money or access. The Act provides for no privacy or any rights for payers, including mandatory disclosure of financial affairs, garnishees, seizure from bank accounts, seizure of tax returns, child support debts that endure bankruptcy, even restricted travel rights are just a few of the undemocratic examples of the tactics frequently used by the CSA.

"The review process is primarily utilised by payees. It is mandatory and judgmental, it is free to payees and based on one public servant's subjective evaluation of income earning capacity and assumed ownership of assets.

"The appeal process via the Family Court, already perceived as biased against men, is expensive and beyond the resources of most payers. It is common knowledge right across the nation that many thousands of men have been forced to resort to unemployment as their only defence against the excessive demands of the CSA. Yet the CSA adamantly denies the problem exists and at the same time refuses point blank to obtain independent research.

"The number one driver of unemployment is the Government's own Child Support Agency. The disincentives to work enshrined in the Child Support Scheme need urgent review."

DOTA continued to argue that the Agency was harming thousands of parents, destroying businesses and fathers motivation to work.

***

In the late 1990s, when I first came to all of this, yet another attempt to appease the enormous disquiet in the community over the actions and orders of the court was in play. And the truly bizarre solution from the conservatives, headed by the Attorney General Daryl Williams and Prime Minister John Howard, was to jail people who did not comply with the court's orders.

This was a jurisdiction which had never built trust with the Australian community. There was no faith in its justices, and no faith in its orders. Horror stories abounded.

That it was now jailing parents not for crimes but for breaching its often capricious if not downright ludicrous orders was, for many, a step too far.

The Government's push to jail parents who defied court orders included provisions to jail those who refuse to comply with parenting orders on a "three strikes and you're in" basis. The child support provisions would mostly affect men while the penalties for parenting orders will mostly affect women.

The new legislation, Family Law Amendment Bill 1999, by increasing punitive powers, was an attempt to overcome the biggest problem with Family Court orders – they are virtually unenforceable.

Both men's and women's lobby groups and some family law observers argued that the proposals would prove dangerously counterproductive, saying the proposed laws were a draconian way of avoiding the real problem, which lay in the nature of family law in Australia and the institutions that administered it.

A common criticism was that the Child Support Agency, in making "quasi-judicial" decisions which were virtually impossible to appeal and often had the effect of putting parents into debt unfairly. Many of those who could be jailed would be placed in this predicament not because they did not want to pay but because the imposts were entirely unreasonable and outside their ability to pay.

The Labor Party supported the jailing of those who failed to pay maintenance, mostly fathers, but not those who refused to comply with parenting orders, mostly mothers.

That these moves were being introduced not by the totalitarian left but by the nation's so-called pro-family conservatives added to the piquancy of a steadily building revolt.

In matters of family law reform, it was a red flag for the nascent fatherhood movement and for all those who, without public protest, had suffered enormous personal damage but had sunk quietly into the humus, so to speak, of the social dysfunction thus engendered.

But once a movement begins, it gathers strength. Crowds and power, to reference an old title on the behaviour of large groups of people.

***

Oddly, it was a politician who mounted one of the most lucid and vehement attacks on Australia's family law system, Peter Lewis, who served for a time as the Speaker for the South Australian Parliament. He articulated well the reputation of the court in the broader community.[75]

The claims were made in the context of yet another inquiry and report but indicate very well, in plain language, the reputation of the court.

"The Family Court system and the publicly paid servants in the processes which hang off it are racist, sexist, abusive, biased, crook and often criminal in their impact on too many parents who have to go through it.

- They are racist because too often, they assume Anglo Saxon cultural mores.
- They are sexist because too often, they assume that a woman will be a better parent than a man.

---

[75] Lewis, Peter, Business as Usual, Media Release, 31 December, 2003.

- They are abusive because too often, they assume that a man should earn the money and support the children, after the former wife has lied about and vilified him and obstructs his lawful access to children.
- They are biased because too often, they assume children don't need their father.
- They are crook because too often, they allow perjury without penalty in their processes and actions.
- Finally, the Family Court system covers up criminal conduct by allowing too many publicly paid servants in the processes associated with its actions to ignore the public duty of the Court to uphold the law, including its own Orders."[76]

***

Conservative Attorney General Daryl Williams, in introducing the Family Law Amendment Bill 1999, reopened a broader debate. The dysfunctions of family law highlighted by the jailing initiatives reignited calls for a non-adversarial tribunal system to replace the Family Court and focused attention on the Child Support Agency, five years on from an exhaustive 580 page Joint Select Committee report that made history for the number of submissions to its drafting.[77]

The report said there were many complaints about the CSA, including "inconsistent advice, administrative errors and refusal to verify data. The inaction or lack of service is inexcusable. The end result is an often appalling client service delivery."

Many of the report's 163 recommendations – including an external review of the CSA "as a matter of priority", close study of its social impacts, its impacts on subsequent families, disincentives to working and a re-assessment of the child support formula were never carried out.

Commentator on public sector ethics at Central Queensland University Professor Robert Kelso, a regular on Dads On The Air, said jailing could exacerbate the high suicide rates among parents separated from their children.

He said the Child Support Agency was a self-contained bureaucracy whose clients have "no way out to the normal legal system". The 1994 Inquiry, read in conjunction with the Hansard of the time, clearly identified systemic corruption by public servants whose objective was to minimise the cost to the Commonwealth of supporting single parents by maximising revenue from their non-custodial former spouses.

---

76 Also referenced in Stapleton, John, Collusion and Corruption in Family Law, Dads On The Air, 19 January, 2004.

77 Child Support Scheme, An inquiry into The operation and effectiveness of the scheme, Joint Select Committee on Certain Family Law Issues, November, 1994.

"Neither the Labor government nor its Liberal successor have been interested in examining the behaviour of these public servants," Kelso said.

The fact that later work by researcher Richard Cruikshank showed the cost was more than double that returned to the Commonwealth, and that children of separated parents received less after its formation than before, were never enough justification to abolish the CSA, to have the tentacles of this poisonous bureaucracy removed from parents' lives. It remains a stain on the Australian Public Service to this day.

Kelso said there was ample evidence the CSA was acting against the public interest, creating false debt by exaggerating incomes of fathers and ignoring social security and taxation fraud when it favoured the custodial parent, usually the mother. He said it was thereby failing in its duty to the Crimes Act and, in its complicity in fraud, was breaching the Public Service Act.

"It is in this context we are talking about sending parents to jail," he said. "The Government is exacerbating an already poisoned environment by introducing jailing penalties. Government agencies and welfare industries have studiously avoided the wide-ranging research into the failure of the scheme. What is needed is a royal commission with the widest possible powers. In this climate, in the hands of the CSA and the Family Court, the last thing we need to be doing is introducing jailing penalties."[78]

***

The jailing furore cast a shadow over the Attorney General's well-intentioned attempts to reform family law. The Federal Government was already encouraging separating couples to avoid, where possible, the Family Court in favour of mediation and counselling, and discouraged litigation by cutting Legal Aid, always a vector for backdoor funding of the Court.

The Attorney General's overall idea was simple: create a streamlined federal magistracy service, with a hefty start-up budget of $30 million, to begin operations midyear, to partially sideline the Family Court; then make orders enforceable so children would not be denied either money or a relationship with their non-custodial parent, the two biggest beefs on either side of the custodial divide.

Designed to appease everyone, the proposed new laws pleased no one.

Williams said the new enforcement regime was "to better protect the interests of children".

"The threat of imprisonment is being reserved for the most serious cases," he said. "It is entirely appropriate that the court had available to it, alongside the range of sanctions that already existed, the sanction of imprisonment."

---

78 Stapleton John, Problem Parents Doing Time, *The Australian*, 8 April, 2000.

The Family Court already had provisions for jailing and imposition of fines, and the CSA could already seize assets, impose penalties, sweep bank accounts and initiate prosecutions with a six-month jail penalty. The new legislation added to the arsenal by providing a more direct avenue to jail parents who disobey court orders, and stiffer penalties.

The Attorney General refused to answer questions on the legality or constitutionality of the legislation. He also declined to say how children would be ensured a continued relationship with their jailed parents and why he was handing more power to the judges of the Family Court.

Williams also declined to say whether jailed parents would be placed on suicide watch.

***

If, as research from leading suicide expert Pierre Baume and others suggest, 70 percent of suicides of adult males aged 20 to 60 were related to relationship breakdown, based on the most recent Australian Bureau of Statistics figures at least 20 men a week were killing themselves after separation. this was five times the rate of youth and female suicides, which attracted all the funding and media attention.[79]

Dads On The Air pursued the question of how many clients of the Agency die each day, the most basic indicator of its impacts, as hard as we could with our limited resources. While under questioning the Agency acknowledged that like other government bodies it had a duty of care to its clients, a succession of ministers and chief executives have refused or failed to answer the question on how many clients of the Agency are dying.

As DOTA editorialised, somewhat sarcastically, it appeared to us that one of the most basic aspects of a duty of care is to know whether your clients are dead or alive.

Bundled in with other legislation and with no public debate, the Howard government repealed a section of the law requiring the Agency to act "in the best interests of children".

The move was very telling.

Exasperated by the government's repeated refusal to provide the figures on the numbers of deaths of its clients, and claims by the Agency itself that it did not keep such statistics, Dads On The Air finally put a death toll counter on the front page of its website, calculating that 12 clients of the Child Support Agency died

---

79 Baume, P. J. M., Cantor, C. H., & McTaggart, P. G. (1998). Suicides in Queensland: a comprehensive study; 1990-1995, Australian Institute for Suicide Research and Prevention, 1988.

every day. In 2010 this translated to more than 13,000 deaths since the Labor government came to power in 2007. No other institution could produce these kinds of outcomes and continue to operate with impunity.

Concerning this issue, Dads On The Air spelt out on air that we were a community radio station with all the usual obligations which that entails, and declared we would happily publish the correct figure if the Agency provided it. There was never any word, certainly no denial, and no cease and desist notice despite their arsenal of lawyers.

The rate was calculated on information provided by the Agency from freedom of information requests which showed that 6.1 per cent of all cases had terminated due to the death of a party since its formation. The figures are now well out of date and have probably worsened, but at the time around 75,000 cases were terminating each year. This, using Institute of Health and Welfare figures on death rates in the community, resulted in a figure of around three times what you would expect in a similarly aged group in the broader community. We argued that this death toll was largely due to the poor treatment dished out to separated dads by the Family Court, the Child Support Agency; and all their supporting bureaucracies; including Centrelink.

If our estimates of the numbers of deaths of child support clients were correct – and DOTA has argued they could well be an underestimate – this represented a major public administration scandal.

Every fathers' group in the country maintained that the high death rate amongst separated men was directly linked to their mistreatment at the hand of government bodies. There are numerous desperately sad stories to back up the argument.

Griffith University research psychologist Susie Sweeper, an expert on separation, said there were high levels of stress associated with the Family Court and CSA.

"The accumulation of stress from not seeing the children, low finances, litigation, and low levels of social support can lead to psychopathology such as suicide," she said. "Some parents are very angry. That is certainly expressed."

"By putting these people in jail, you would increase their stress levels further. This would not assist children."[80]

***

With paying parents unable to specify how their payments were spent, CSA research suggested that half of all payers did not believe their money was benefiting their children.

---
80 Stapleton, John, Problem Parents Doing Time, *The Australian*, 8 April, 2000.

CSA policy director Sheila Bird said Australians had much to be proud of, with 90 percent of all liabilities having been paid since the agency's inception. She claimed this was the world's best.

She disputed doubts raised by men's groups over the honesty of the agency's review officers and disputed claims made by many paying parents that the formulas used by the CSA were inflexible and failed to take into account individual circumstances.

Bird said that where a parent refused to pay, it was appropriate for the CSA to take court action.

"If parliament gave the court the authority to jail a person for an offence, then the court determined whether that was appropriate," she said.

Bird said she did not know the suicide rate among paying parents.

Really, a government agency which had "Helping parents manage their responsibilities" as their slogan couldn't tell you how many of their own clients were dying!!! It was beyond disgraceful. The Agency always has been, and remains, one of the worst examples of government maladministration in Australia.

The chairman of the 1994 joint select committee on the child support scheme, Roger Price, who we would have had on the show multiple times, said no one should think the CSA was set up to benefit children.[81] He said its sole rationale was to save taxpayer money by clawing back social security payments, as each dollar paid by a parent reduced the amount of social security paid to the recipient. "It is not about the best interests of children and never has been," he said.

He was angry that the effort that went into the 1994 inquiry had been wasted, with the Government "cherry-picking" the punitive measures suggested in the report to further enforce money collection.

Price, one of the most high-profile advocates of a non-adversarial tribunal to replace the Family Court, said there had to be a better method than jailing people.

"We have to find a less battering, bruising, and financially crippling system," he said. "The Family Court and Child Support were a nightmare legal maze. Jailing was most definitely the wrong way to go.

"What frightened me while doing the report was the level of frustration I found. People had spent all their money on legal cases, borrowed from credit cards, borrowed from parents, and were seething with anger. I was frightened to see that level of frustration and anger. This continues to this day, absolutely.

---

81 Joint Select Committee on Certain Family Law Issues, The operation and effectiveness of the Child Support Scheme, November, 1994.

"Back in 1994, when I said people were committing suicide in major part because of family law matters, people were disbelieving. No one disbelieves it anymore."

Despite the 1994 findings of a Joint Select Committee that illegal activities were occurring within the CSA, the government had done nothing to correct problems which amounted to systemic corruption.[82]

These activities included the CSA deliberately not adhering to accurate record keeping, deliberately not taking or ignoring information, and advising in favour of Payee clients for the purposes of aiding and abetting Payee clients in false receipt of funds.

The report concluded "Equitable change to Child Support legislation is paramount in the minds of thousands of Australians. The community is looking for a Government who will not only acknowledge the inequities and failures of the current legislation and Scheme. In a country that prides itself on democracy and equity, it is a disgrace that Governments have not been willing to significantly address this highly discriminatory legislation."

***

The greatest paradox of the jailing debate was that both men's and women's groups, two groups which saw eye to eye on virtually nothing, were united in their opposition.

Sole Parents Union president Kathleen Swinbourne, normally a relentless critic of fathers, said: "Children do not benefit from seeing either of their parents dragged off by the police and put in jail."[83]

Sarah Maddison from the Women's Electoral Lobby said the general response across women's groups had been one of horror at the suggestions that parents could be jailed for failing to comply with Family Court orders of any description.

"Child Support is not working for either parent at the end of the day," she said. "Both sides feel ripped off."

The men's groups, whose members would be most affected by the jailing provisions, were vociferous in their opposition.

Barry Williams of Lone Fathers, another frequent online presence at Dads On The Air, said: "I do not trust the Family Court to make fair decisions."

---

82 Child Support Scheme, An examination of the operation and effectiveness of the scheme, Joint Select Committee Inquiry into Certain Aspects of Family, November, 1994.

83 Allum, Margaret, Women main targets of family law amendments, Green Left Weekly, 29 March, 2000.

Malcolm Mathias of Fathers for Family Equity, yet another person who dedicated many hundreds of hours in attempting to bring fairness to the system, described the proposals to jail parents as "extreme, unwarranted, ill-conceived and draconian".

"Many non-custodial men are forced to live in cheap accommodation, are compelled to leave paid employment, forced into bankruptcy, lose contact with their children, lose any prospect of a comfortable retirement and a growing number ultimately commit suicide," he said.[84]

Sue Price of the Men's Right's Agency said the jailing furore highlighted the need to look at the financial and social cost of the style of custodial orders made by the Family Court since its formation a quarter of a century ago.

"It is a harsh regime when people are having more than one third of their income garnisheed, yet have no say on where the money goes and are not sharing in the joys of raising their children," she said.

The jailing, the rampant injustices of this despoiled system, continue to this day, travesties stretching across time, spilling down the years, and harming everyone in the families involved. While the over indulged judges who passed these orders, immune from prosecution, pocketed their handsome salaries and travelled the world on luxurious junkets to international conferences where the words "the best interests of the child" were bandied about as if they meant it.

No wonder the public was sickened by the whole sorry mess.

***

I did multiple case studies for the Problem Parents Doing Time story, only a few of which saw the light of day. One of those was James, who had four children aged 10 to 15 whom he sees more than 40 percent of the time.

I remember to this day the outrage and upset in his voice as he detailed the story to me. The paper, as I said, insisted on seeing all the documentation first hand.

"I have done the right thing by the children," he told me. "When my wife left me she said I was too much of a family man.

"The impact the CSA has had on my children's lives has been pathetic. It has to be held accountable. I believe the time will come when children will take the CSA to court."

James, like so many other parents, had accumulated a back debt of $40,000. The CSA was notorious in imposing insurmountable debts on beleaguered parents. About $27,000 of that alleged debt was a penalty for late payment. He

---

84 Stapleton, John, Problem Parents Doing Time, *The Australian*, 8 April, 2000.

claimed this was a false debt because it accrued when he had lost an $80,000-a-year job but a review from the agency kept him on that salary.

That was a totally standard Agency tactic, ignoring the reality of a parent's income and manufacturing another, sometimes, like this one, based on a former job they had lost, or on a made up notion of "earning capacity".

All imposed on parents doing their best under difficult circumstances.

And they wondered why they were so truly hated.

The previous year the Agency snaffled his $4500 tax refund, just as they routinely did for thousands of others.

Then on Christmas Eve he received a letter informing him that his bank accounts had been swept, the money seized.

One of the accounts was money in trust for the children – $2000 – which James said took the children five years to save. He was so outraged, it became a mini cause celebre in the local media. There was heartbreak in his voice as he told me all the things he and the children had done together to raise that money, including lawn mowing and collecting bottles.

"The CSA's response was they didn't know where the money went but that it probably went to the custodial parent," he said. "The kids have asked about it and she denies knowing anything about it. What really gets under my skin is the injustice."

Join the queue. From our experience at Dads On The Air, the Child Support Agency really was one of the most hated agencies in Australian history.

***

The Attorney General responsible for this fiasco, Daryl Williams, had been a barrister since 1968 and everything about him signalled privilege and cloistered success in the upper realms of the legal profession. He was appointed by John Howard, another lawyer turned politician.

Williams was certainly from the available evidence out of touch with the citizens he supposedly served, and uncomprehending of the experiences of ordinary people in the charnel house that was the Family Court of Australia. And for which he now bore legislative responsibility.

My enduring image of Attorney General Daryl Williams was when I was sent down by *The Australian* to report on a conference he was addressing at Sydney University.

At the end of the speech, which I found meandering, dull and certainly for a journalist difficult to generate a story from, but that's the life of a general news reporter, Williams stepped down from the podium.

And appeared totally lost, unable to find his seat or shortly thereafter the exit, an early antipodean version of Joe Biden. I had the distinct impression he didn't know where he was, and from the speech, which had no doubt been written for him, what he was talking about.

But perhaps that is unkind.

About as unkind as jailing parents for failing to comply with the orders of the nation's most reviled court.

***

By the time I came to write the story Problem Parents Doing Time the paper was being regularly criticised by the Chief Justice of the Family Court Alastair Nicholson for its coverage of family law, specifically for the work of the paper's High Court writer Bernard Lane, and myself, one of the paper's most experienced general news reporters.

Nicholson thought he knew better than a lower form of life such as a journalist, or that's the way he came across to me, as supremely arrogant. Traditionally fawned upon by Australia's left leaning outlets, particularly the Australia's state media the Australian Broadcasting Corporation, the reality, of course, was that the Court had a great deal to hide, and was not the least bit open to journalistic inquiry. A pity. The jurisdiction would never have degenerated to the point it has if there had been proper investigation into its notorious administrative dysfunction, complexity and delays, its suspect practices including the use of family report writers, its mistreatment of litigants and the often outlandish judgements emanating from its judges.

Once again, after the publication of Problem Parents Doing Time the Family Court's Chief Justice Alastair Nicholson went on the attack, claiming the article was riddled with errors, although he did not point out what they were. He also claimed the article was one-sided, although I had gone to considerable lengths to quote both men's and women's groups, which were in rare accord.

In his published letter Nicholson wrote: "The article 'Problem' parents doing time reflects little credit upon your newspaper and its journalistic standards. It is riddled with inaccuracies and contains unsourced personal accounts. It gives undue prominence to the views of well-known critics of the family law system without providing any balance.

"The article asserts that Family Court orders are virtually unenforceable. Yet the vast majority of orders are complied with and are enforced when they are not complied with. The fact that difficulties are experienced with the enforcement of orders in a small minority of cases has more to do with the people involved and their attitude to the orders than it does to the issue of enforcement."

Nicholson continued: "A caption to a photograph asserts that the welfare of second families is not taken into account by the Family Court. Child support legislation does limit what the court can do on appeal from assessments, but this is hardly the fault of the court. The article speaks as though the current federal Government invented the encouragement of dispute resolution to avoid litigation. The first thing that the Family Court does when approached by separating couples is to refer them to its counselling and mediation services. Approximately 70 percent of proceedings that commence in the court are resolved within four months and only 5 per cent ever require a judicial determination."[85]

***

Elspeth McInnes from the National Council of Single Mothers also appeared on the letter pages: "The article rightly stated: The maintenance provisions will mainly affect men while the penalties for parenting orders will mainly affect women" and then goes on to canvass only the maintenance order issues. While building sympathy for parents who won't pay, the poverty of children living without child support was not presented. The article gives mainly men's perspectives on men's problems.

"The public needs to be aware also of the implications of a mandatory sentencing regime proposed for parents who don't comply with parenting orders. Parents jailed under mandatory sentencing will not necessarily even have the benefit of legal representation. From the perspectives of children and women and men after separation there is no advance in justice in the jailing of parents."

Another letter, name and address supplied, read in part: "Having been placed in a similar situation to that reported has made me realise that I am not alone. I lost my home, my family, contact with my children and more recently my 20-year job. I feel that the persecution and sheer bloody-mindedness of the CSA drives many good parents to despair. The persecution is even extended to second families, where any children born from this relationship are treated with disdain and blatant discrimination by the CSA."

Another name and addressed supplied thanked the paper for drawing attention to the excesses, irrationality and peculiar mismanagement of the Child Support Agency. "For 12 months I struggled to meet my payments. I was given to understand by my legal adviser that I had to maintain mortgage repayments, private medical health cover, rates on investment land, ambulance ... all commitments in place at the time of separation.

---

85 Letters, *The Australian*, 14 April, 2000.

"I went broke, then into child support arrears, while I still had a full-time job from which support was garnisheed monthly. Except for the kindness and support of my siblings, who kept lending me money, I could well have been one of CSA's delinquent payers, and a jail candidate. How dare the Government consider legislation allowing the jailing of non-custodial parents at the subjective behest of such an irrational, autonomous mediocrity as the CSA."[86]

***

In a supportive letter Alison Pearce from the group Partners of Paying Parents wrote that children in second families were treated inequitably and non-residential parents were left with little money to cover the basic necessities of survival for himself and his second family.

"The law needs to be changed so that all children with the same father will benefit equally. Children from the second relationship are discriminated against by the formula used by the CSA."

Partners of Paying Parents would go on to produce a devastating critique of the operations of the Child Support Agency in their working paper "Discrimination against Paying Parents and their Second Families" disseminated in September 2001.

In brief it declared that paying parents and their second families were suffering critical financial and relationship breakdown due to the inequities of child support and family law.

The group objected to the CSA's practice of refusing to refund monies falsely paid, complained the Review Officers were not held accountable and found that prosecutable practices by the CSA needed to be addressed.

The institutional mistreatment of fathers and their children led by extension to the mistreatment of their new partners and often enough of the second wife's children from a previous relationship. It was a common enough refrain on DOTA that there was more likely to be government action and change of policy as a result of the conflict between the rights of one group of women with another than because of the numerous cries of upset from fathers.

Discontent over the issues led to the creation of groups such as the Second Wives Association, Partners of Paying Parents and the StepFamilies Association of Australia and in America the powerful National Association of Non-Custodial Mothers, all of whom were happy to feature on the show.

In Australia the mistreatment of non-custodial mothers was swept under the carpet, an embarrassment to women's lobby groups focused on working for single mothers in the scrabble for the welfare dollar.

---

[86] Letters, *The Australian*, 11 April, 2000.

***

In what rapidly turned into a public relations disaster, the Child Support Agency started holding Community Information Nights around the country.

In those I attended as part of my work for the program it was notable that there were just as many aggrieved women as there were men, frustrated by the Agency's bureaucracy and delays, and its devastating impacts on their new partners and their children.

No one should think this is simply a gendered issue concerning only aggrieved and damaged fathers.

Just as many women as men are negatively impacted by this disastrous agency.

Here, to close, is another case study, this one from a mother. And yes, another classic case of bureaucratic insanity rewarding bad behaviour while destroying the lives of the nation's citizens.

Leandra's two youngest children, four and seven, live with her; she is bringing them up in the most expensive city in the country. Her former husband lives on a pension in a Queensland coastal town. Her eldest son, 10, lives with his father.

"Because I am working, I have to pay him $150 per week," she told me. "He is not working and is on a full time sole parent pension, although he does work for cash in a boat yard.

"Even though I have made this fact quite clear, no one wishes to look into it. They say until he lodges a tax return, it is on their records that his only income is a pension.

"He is getting $700 a fortnight, $300 from me, plus his cash income, plus the child is living with his grandparents at least four nights out of the seven.

"I doubt very much if my child sees that $600 a month, or the grandparents. There are lots of extras I could buy my children for the $600 a month. And the only time I get to see my son is when I fly up or pay to fly him down.

"The CSA is bound by ridiculous policies, it is definitely encouraging welfare dependency."

Whistleblowers from the Agency who contacted me said the phone would not stop ringing from the minute they logged on until close of day, a wall of complaint and misery which made their working lives unbearable. In the quarter of a century since I wrote Paying Parents Doing Time, the situation has simply grown worse. And one government after another has done nothing about it.

SEVEN
CHRISTMAS DAY

CHRISTMAS DAY. A police station car park. Malcolm has not seen his nine year old son and six year old daughter for more than a month.

The children don't get out of the car. Their father pushes presents at them through the car window, and tries to talk to them. After five minutes, the children are driven off. Malcolm has only seen his son in sessions with a Family Court appointed psychologist since.

Malcolm is one of an estimated 326 Australians, primarily fathers, accused of sexually abusing their children each week – the atomic bomb of custody disputes. Like thousands of other fathers; his life has imploded into an expensive nightmare of litigation and conflicting experts.

A senior public servant with special security clearance, he can be trusted with the country's secrets, but not with his own children. While a female child protection worker found no evidence of abuse and condemned the mother's behaviour; it is a crucial family report by the court appointed psychologist, who recommended the father have minimum contact, that Malcolm will have most difficulty overcoming.

Despite their notoriety amongst father's groups for their bias, inaccuracy and unchanging nature over a quarter of a century the Federal government has refused to acknowledge any community concern over their veracity.

These reports, the evidentiary bedrock of Australian family law, are written by court counsellors or court appointed psychiatrists and psychologists, who normally interview each of the parties for an hour each. Research shows judges rely almost totally on them to make their judgements. Many of these "experts" spend longer in the witness box, in itself a lucrative or costly exercise depending on whether you're the well heeled expert or the desperate dad, than they ever do interviewing the families involved, yet there is no scientific evidence to suggest that interviewing people is the best way to determine a custody issue.

The widespread hopes held by many community groups that the Liberal government would move promptly to reform family law, and the family reports on which it is based, had already been dashed.

The divorce industry was then worth an estimated $5 billion a year, an industry as big as beef, sheep or horse racing. A quarter of a century later estimates for the industry ranged over $13 billion. That didn't even include the bureaucratic megaliths for which the Court operated as a legal lynchpin, including welfare departments and a plethora of feminist advocacy groups.

That the then Attorney General, Daryl Williams, had no intention of seriously tackling this cash cow for his fellow lawyers was evidenced by his choosing personnel from deep within the industry for his new Federal Magistracy and for the so-called Family Pathways Advisory Group.

The dirty little secret, the secret that these lawyers had no intention of blowing the whistle on, is that this industry rests on spurious, often blatantly dishonest reports from Family Court Counsellors, psychiatrists and psychologists. This was perjury on a grand scale – and the legal profession was entirely complicit in it.[87]

***

The $26 million Federal Magistrates Service, created in 1999, got up and running around the country in 2000, showed no signs of differentiating itself from the Family Court. It turned for magistrates to people who had a long professional association with the much reviled family report writers and whose biases if not outright corrupt conduct were for the main part well known.

The government did not deny that the magistrates had all received the approval of the Family Court.

One newly appointed magistrate, Judith Ryan, former head of the notoriously one eyed Family Law unit of New South Wales Legal Aid and yet another senior legal figure not known to have ever said a positive word about fathers, was responsible for the repeated use of Sydney's "big three" Doctors Peter Champion, Brent Waters and Chris Rikard-Bell, all favourites of the NSW Department of Community Services as well as the Family Court.

With their reputations and their lucrative practices to protect, they were also known as highly litigious, brooking no criticism of their practice. It would take a major newspaper with determination, resources and talented journalists to crack this nut, and, unfortunately, no such newspaper existed.

It was left to our under-resourced little radio program Dads On The Air to untie this Geordian knot, and we simply didn't have the backing or the deep pockets required.

---

87 Stapleton, John, Christmas Day, Dads On The Air, 2000.

Let's leave it at that.

Magistrate Judith Ryan took it upon herself to seek the silencing of one of the most outspoken family law critics after he appeared on a radio show Life Matters on Radio National.

She requested one of her employees to listen to a tape of Radio National in which National President of Dads Against Discrimination Peter Vlug highlighted the issue of false sexual abuse allegations in the Family Court. That Legal Aid employee was then requested to write an affidavit claiming she recognised the voice of Mr Vlug. He regards the actions taken against him by Legal Aid as a blatant abuse of public funds.

"I was asked to go on the program," he said. "False allegations occupy a considerable amount of the court's time and therefore taxpayers money. It was a matter of public interest."

***

Malcolm's case came at a time when there was scathing media attention on family courts throughout the English speaking world. Prominent feminists in the US have come out recently supporting father's groups ' position that shared parenting liberated everyone involved, adding a twist to the ideologically driven vortex. In Australia the totally antiquated notion of mothers as primary carers trapped generations of single mothers into welfare dependency and produced very poor social outcomes for both parents, children and the society as a whole. Not to mention the cost to the taxpayer.

The quarter of a century which had passed since the establishment of the Family Court of Australia was characterised by a potent mix of feminism, psychology, psychiatry and the law.

But at the time there was hope that it might all unravel.

The European Human Rights Court had recently awarded a father $40,000 in compensation for breach of his human rights after the father was denied access to his child in the German courts.

Equally in Australia there had been much talk of a class action. The now defunct Fathers for Family Equity commenced a project to initiate a wide-ranging class action against the government and the Family Court over bias, discrimination, injustice, abuse of power and damage to children, pushing it as far as they could with the resources they had.

With more than 20 men a week killing themselves post-separation, simple arithmetic shows such an action could cost taxpayers tens of billions of dollars.

In a landmark case, Blue Mountains solicitor Hal Ginges was awarded an undisclosed sum and a public apology from the Department of Community Services over false allegations of sexual abuse of his children involving DOCS officers.

Illustrating their close connections, the investigation by DOCS led to orders in the Family Court that the father's contact with his children be restricted and supervised. "Ultimately the children found their own way back," Mr Ginges said, who practises in the Children's Court and the Family Court.

"Things haven't changed. Fathers are still being falsely accused and under trained officers of DOCS are still taking children away and relying on untested allegations."

***

Former President of the NSW Family Law Reform Association Max King, yet another father to produce a book and make major submissions to various inquiries in an effort to bring about change to the jurisdiction, had recently begun a $1.4 million dollar compensation test case in the New South Wales Supreme Court, naming Chief Justice of the Family Court Alistair Nicholson as a defendant in his role as administrator of the Court.

There was a hope at the time amongst activists that class or civil actions against the Court would become a common part of the legal landscape. Nicholson himself enjoyed lifelong immunity from civil suit that was enjoyed by all judges of superior courts in Australia. He had no immunity from the processes of the criminal law for acts done in the exercise of his judicial functions.

Max King had hoped the case would expose the practices of the Family Court, including the nature of the family reports, to public scrutiny. Those who attempted to bring light into the firmament of this dark quagmire were often exposed to harassment, surveillance or other forms of abuse. He said that as a whistleblower himself he had experienced similar treatment.

"Fathers soon discovered there was no such thing as free speech in Australia," he said. "There was an enormous fear generated by the court, with trumped up criminal charges levelled against fathers, and the constant threat they would never see their children again.

"In the Association meetings shell shocked fathers would arrive unable to believe what had happened to them and their children.

"The story was always the same: the false allegations, of violence, the false child abuse allegations, the loss and alienation of their children. It is no wonder so many thousands of fathers have committed suicide."[88]

---

[88] Background. Silvester, John, Milton's death notice highlights family breakdown, *The Age*, 1 April, 2004.

King, who I also knew personally, would frequently recall Association meetings where he would ask the assembled crowd where he would ask if there were any fathers in the room who had been falsely accused of abusing their children. Most of the crowd would raise their hands.

Through the case, in which he invested hundreds of hours of preparatory work, he had hoped not just to expose the Court, but to pave the way for numerous similar actions in the coming years as "the true history of the Family Court becomes apparent".

King's legal action was dismissed on technical grounds.

Lawyers always protect their own.

No matter how good the evidence, how outrageous the conduct, a lay litigant stands no chance.

And the Family Court of Australia, a relic from the extreme feminism of the 1970s, continues to line the pockets of lawyers while laying havoc through people's lives, to this very day.

***

Any discussion of the role of psychiatric evidence in the Family Court leads straight to the question of false sexual abuse allegations.

For Malcolm, caught up in a maze of conflicting affidavits and legalistic complexities, it was a personal and legal nightmare. An affidavit from a babysitter, who notified the police, reported the mother dropping off the children, claiming they had been sexually abused, and then promptly going out on a date.

Malcolm was never charged or found guilty of anything, but like many many thousands of other fathers, if the matter ever went to trial the war of contradictory experts would in all likelihood obfuscate the truth. Many of these so-called experts spent more time in the witness box than they ever did interviewing the family, but their evidence, even without a single shred of medical evidence, might well be enough, for a judge to entertain "lingering doubts" sufficient to deny him any contact at all with his children until they turn 18.

Needless to say, this abusive sleight of hand did not impact on women before the court.

Very few of those accused of sexual abuse of children are ever convicted; but the allegations prompt a cascade of events from *The Child Abuse Industry*, to quote the title of a 1980s American book warning that the self referencing and ideologically driven child protection bureaucracy was out of control.

As forensic psychologist Yolande Lucinde wrote in a paper presented to the Australian Academy of Forensic Sciences, the child abuse epidemic "has all the characteristics of mass hysteria, now called moral panic...driven by hysterical beliefs, unvalidated and untrue".

Dr Lucire said that in terms of the numbers of people and resources involved we were in the greatest moral panic since the Salem witch-hunts.

She regarded the "so-called substantiation" recorded by welfare departments as nothing more than assertions and notes that in reality child sexual abuse is "very very rare", and only found amongst "very disordered people in disordered families".

"It is quite improbable," she said. "The allegations arise in the context of custody battles. Some studies indicate 80% of the accusing parents have massive personality disorders... probability analysis indicates that any one report is many times more likely to be false than true.

"The terror that an innocent person might be found guilty, which has traditionally and rightly been the foundation of our justice system, has been replaced by the terror that a guilty man might go free. In a moral panic, hysterical beliefs short-circuit reasoning and an illusory paradigm governs perception. Judges, juries, social workers and doctors fear offending against the newly imposed values, and suppress their own common sense."

***

With the most draconian secrecy legislation in the country centred on The Family Court and closely linked welfare departments, the richest sources of information on the operation of the court and the nature of the reports came from whistleblowers. One former Family Court officer, who worked in the Sydney Registry for 14 years, Bill Sheridan, said: "Whoever pays the piper calls the tune. Some of these reports are almost in the word processor, it is a matter of changing the names around.

"One will describe every parent that comes before them as a 'dysfunctional personality', others will have different quirks. If you went to six different psychiatrists or psychologists you would get six different views.

"By the time they get over their lengthy CVs you will probably find the reports are all on the same lines. From my personal experience watching the 'experts' being cross-examined, I did not think these reports were a good method of determining custody issues.

"The report writers can't help themselves but to twist things, and they get the information supplied to them wrong. They will misinterpret.

"It is verballing. They do it for the money. There are great financial rewards for their behaviour, in the millions of dollars per year.

"Any false allegation by either parent can be reported as fact. Without any testing at all to gather the truth they will embark on some campaign, such as that the father is oppressive or abusive.

"They will twist and manipulate the facts. They embellish the evidence.

"The family reports are not expert evidence, simply opinion. They are doing nothing to assist anyone in any shape or form."

***

Another retired court officer, so distressed by what he witnessed, wrote a book, *Child Sexual Abuse Allegations in Australia*, which was placed on an international web site outside Australian jurisdictions.

He noted that the death of the premise of "innocent until proven guilty" had been replaced by "groundless suspicion, ad hoc accusations, arbitrary judgements and premature condemnation".

"It is my opinion that, in the past 15 years, the insidious invasion of a child's suggestibility by inept child sexual abuse interviewers has been instrumental in more children becoming victims of manufactured 'sexual abuse' than actual instances of this abuse," he wrote. "A witch-hunt mentality emerged in earnest during the mid-80s as Australia literally became a Little America overnight – a nation of accusers and litigants – adding to the coffers of the legal profession, while depleting the self esteem of thousands of innocent children and adults.

"Too ready access to Legal Aid and the lure of victim's compensation further smoothed the way for this litigious onslaught, aimed mainly against males, as the spectre of child sexual abuse appeared ad nauseam in the media. The dissemination of child protection misinformation by misguided child protection zealots resulted in chaos and confusion, as parents started notifying thousands of alleged cases of child sexual abuse in all States.

"The reluctance of courts to enforce harsher disciplinary action against inept welfare workers is unconscionable…"

The former court officer, who spent much of his final months as a court employee at the photocopy machine, in his chapter Child Sexual Abuse and the Family Court, broke down in detail the original "M&M" and "B&B" cases which led to the notion of "lingering doubt" and the "capricious" judicial reasoning that went on behind them.

Under this tenet, to deny a child any contact with their father after the allegation of sexual abuse has been made, it is not necessary to prove that the child has been sexually abused or that the child may be at risk if access were granted. All that is required is for a trial judge to have "lingering doubts" as to whether access would or would not expose the child to an unacceptable risk.

As the author said, in the family reports, many of which sit on the fence when such allegations are raised, it can be not what is said so much as what is not said that leaves the father damned and the children without a male parent.

Exploring the situation in NSW, he looked at the estimated 35,000 cases of allegedly "confirmed" child sexual abuse in the last decade and asks why not one investigative reporter had asked the obvious question: "Why is it that, of the thousands of alleged cases classified 'Actual - Confirmed Child Sexual Abuse', less than 3% result in convictions."

He said that after many years in the court room he had formed the view that the treatment of sexual abuse allegations had created a "kangaroo-court mentality" that was a blatant denial of natural justice which left thousands of children the subject of interrogation and unwarranted sexual abuse therapies.

He was left in despair at a system which had so seriously degenerated "at the expense of vulnerable children and innocent adults". He noted as proof that most sexual abuse allegations coming before the court were mischievous the fact that the alleged abuse is never claimed as the reason for the breakup of the marriage.

***

Fed up with what they perceived as outrageous behaviour by the Family Court and family report writers, increasing numbers of men were posting virtually everything about their cases to the internet.

One senior academic, accused of molesting his children over a decade before, had already been threatened with jail for publicising his case. Along with other outraged litigants he was ordered by the Family Court not to contact the United Nations with his concerns. He posted his entire case on the internet.

Although denied access to his three children, the academic was never found guilty of anything.

A family report criticised the father for becoming obsessed with clearing his name, quoting approvingly another report criticising him for his "lack of appreciation, if not disregard" of his former wife's feelings and the emotional consequence the father's persistent publication of his plight might have on her.

As in so many other cases, the counsellor concluded that there was "considerable potential for emotional risk" if the children were to see their father and "regardless of the veracity of the sexual abuse allegations...one questions the benefit to the children of resuming any form of contact with their father."

Transcripts of court proceedings also posted to the internet showed the father in a verbal stoush struggling with "Her Honour", finally pointing out to the judge the irony that if he had actually been found guilty of sexually abusing his children the effect would be the same: denial of any relationship with their father for more than ten years. There was no apology forthcoming from the court. Ordered to stand back from the bench, the father's final words: "It just seems so unfair."

***

Campaigner against the abuse of psychiatry in courts Stewart Dean recommended that anyone being interviewed by a court appointed expert should take a support person such as himself to act as independent witness.

"The biggest use of these reports is when the mother wants custody and she alleges paedophilia against the husband. They got away with it for a long time. The women's groups have been coaching women in the steps to take. In that way they were more or less assured to get custody of their children. The cliches are the same. That has been the biggest misuse in the Family Court.

"Psychiatrists in general have overplayed their hand and have come in for such criticism they are not carrying the same weight.

"Lawyers and psychiatrists feed off each other. The lawyers more than anyone know how crook the psychiatrists are, but they use them to win or create cases. Cases should not be judged by psychiatrists, but by evidence."

The close indeed incestuous relationship between psychiatrists, psychologists and the legal profession was clearly illustrated by the judgement of the Psychologists Registration Board of Victoria which deregistered cocaine addicted psychologist and Family Court favourite Timothy Watson-Munroe.[89]

The Board received more complaints over Family Court reports than any other matter, and as they were largely prevented from investigation by secrecy provisions, had written to the Court over the matter.

In the sad footnote to a 44 page judgement on Watson-Munroe by the Board, newspapers reported a man taking the psychologist to the Board after he was denied any contact with his son as a result of orders made by the Family Court on recommendations by Watson-Munroe.

Five QCs went as character witnesses for the disgraced family report writer. He procured his cocaine from a solicitor who gave him briefs. Some of the evidence showed him watching videos of police interviews for the purpose of writing court reports while snorting cocaine and dealing with drug-dependent clients while under the influence.

Police tapes recorded him, referring to lines of cocaine saying: "There's nothing like the joy of waking up and realising that contrary to…every urge in your body not to leave one, you have in fact left a small one for the morning."

---

89 Disgraced psychologist loses new bid to practise, *The Age*, 19 April, 2002.

One father, who consulted a string of psychiatrists and psychologists in his battle to rescue his child from an allegedly abusive situation, only got one good report – from the disbarred Watson-Munroe. Another father lost any chance of custody when Watson-Munroe misinterpreted the father's plans for accommodation of his young son. There was no retraction, no apology.

The lobby group Men's Rights have called on the government to fund a review of all custody orders made as a result of recommendations by Watson-Munroe and urged all fathers who lost their children as a result to consider seeking compensation.

Attempts to have judgements made on Watson-Munroe's "evidence" overthrown reversed all failed.

***

In one report a famous Sydney DOCS and Family Court favourite, psychiatrist Brent Waters, stated that the most disturbing thing was that the parents couldn't see that there was anything wrong with them. They lost all four of their children. In another the mother, who hated the welfare authorities and was admittedly no saint, was described by Peter Champion, another favourite of DOCS and the Family Court, as being arrogant and unable to admit that she was wrong. She lost her two children.

The Citizens Commission on Human Rights, which made its name in Australia campaigning for the deep-sleep Chelmsford Inquiry, released a guide to dealing with psychiatric and psychological testimony in the Family Court and social welfare departments. CCHR advised that no one should submit to such an interview without an accompanying witness, without the interview being videotaped and without clear legal advice on their rights.

National President Lyn Cottee said the inaction of professional bodies, medical boards and health care complaints commissions actively protected corrupt psychiatrists and psychologists. The protection of psychiatrists in the Family Court spilled over into other arenas such as DOCS in NSW, Human Services in Victoria and Family Services in Queensland.

"Psychiatrists and psychologists are employed in particular jurisdictions because they produce the answers that are desired or that fit into the prevailing ideology of the court," said then President Lyn Cottee of the Citizens Commission on Human Rights, a group which campaigns against psychiatric abuses.

"They have become a new power elite. Everything they say is taken as gospel no matter in some cases how preposterous.

"In the case of the Family Court, psychiatrists often become the determiner of fact rather than the judge. Character flaws of the preferred parent are overlooked in favour of magnifying and sometimes even fabricating the flaws in the other parent. These unscientific, biased, opinion-based pronouncements are often sufficient for parents to lose any contact with their children."

It was well recognised amongst social scientists that interviewing people was an unreliable form of evaluation, one of the ironies of family reports and the enormous weight placed upon them. There was no evidence to indicate it was an appropriate way to determine custody arrangements.

Sanford Braver, author of *Divorced Dads: Shattering the Myths*, wrote: "There is no evidence that there is a scientific valid way for a custody evaluator to choose the best primary parent. Instead there is convincing evidence that their recommendations merely follow the evaluator's own gender biases."

In the US, Margaret Hagan, author of *Whores of the Court: The Fraud of Psychiatric Testimony*, noted in her chapter "In the best interests of the Child" the shock the contributions of the "psycho-experts" often gave to parents.[90] She said a psychological professional who had never met the children could hold their future in his or her hands. One mother lost custody of her children because the judge determined that by refusing to be assessed she had shirked her duty to have her parental fitness assessed by a psychologist.

"It is no step at all to turn...personal value judgements into professional opinions to support the case of a parent making claims," Ms Hagan wrote.

One father lost any contact with his child after a report from a women's health centre, Gunedoo in the Blue Mountains, suggested that the son had no worthwhile relationship with the father, who was never interviewed. Another accused the father of harassing his son at school, without any evidence at all. Another suggested the father should not be granted shared parenting because it might give him hope of reconciling with the mother. Another psychiatric report stated he couldn't understand why the father was putting the mother through the stress of a trial he could not win.

Along with the contradicting experts, Malcolm and his ex-wife's affidavits also contradict each other. Amidst the sad horrific battle of contradictory experts, one of the father's affidavits reports the child saying: "Mummy said that you touched my fanny, but you didn't, did you Daddy?"

For him and for his children, as for hundreds of thousands of others, the agony of Australian family law will never be over.

---

90 Hagan, Barbara, *Whores of the Court: The Fraud of Psychiatric Testimony and the Rape of American Justice*, HarperCollins, 1997.

EIGHT
SETTING THE HARES RUNNING

PUBLIC DEBATE had shifted and the suffering of separated families was on the political radar. With public and media sympathy running in favour of change, the government was in a position to alter for the better the destiny of the country's one million children from separated families; and the many children who would follow them.

The sight of emotional couples at war with each other, burning through thousands and even hundreds of thousands of dollars of their own and taxpayer's money in bitter and chaotic fights over property and the custody of their children, often accompanied by a blizzard of false or exaggerated claims, could have been relegated to history.

The Prime Minister of Australia John Winston Howard set the hares running in mid-June of 2003 when he told his Coalition MPs, the parliament and thereby the country, that it might well be worth re-looking at the issue of joint-custody. The story ran all week, and then just kept on running, on talkback, on television and in print.

It was classic Howard. As a newspaper reporter you never paid any attention to what he said. You watched what he did. Howard was just testing the water, and as a lawyer playing both sides of the fence, in this case in the fraught realm of gender politics and the army of taxpayer funded women's groups against a community upswell focused around fathers. Howard had touched a raw nerve. He barely said anything, committed nothing but ignited a chain of events which sparked public debate and led to the formation of committees and inquiries, providing an illusion of action while keeping his powder dry.

Howard also got a bounce in the polls. He received instant support across political divides. The general public, tired of the angry, sad and chaotic stories emanating from family law and the chronic welfare dependency that it promoted, backed him immediately.

This was an issue whose time had come. In a rare confluence of opinion, the public, the media and numerous politicians all supported change. The mind-boggling bureaucracy of the Child Support Agency and its staff's overt hostility towards separated fathers rubbed salt into wounds from dysfunctional Family Court cases. In the padded surrounds and heavy security of their plush offices judges continued to make judgements "in the best interests of the child" while out in the real world politicians, counsellors, refuges and ambulance officers were left to pick up the mess.

***

Like every other politician in the country, the Prime Minister knew that this so-called "sleeper" issue was asleep no more. The devastating personal and social consequences of the family law and child support systems in Australia were clearly evident to all but the industry itself.

Howard, always one to sniff the political wind, knew that a large number of voters were looking to him as a conservative purportedly pro-family Prime Minister to fix the lunacy of Australia's Family Court and the Child Support Agency, both creations of the country's Labor Party during its many years in power throughout the 70s and 80s.

The most effectively political operator of the era, Howard promoted himself as a suburban solicitor who supported traditional family values, and many assumed that the Prime Minister could not have personally condoned the travesties of decency and the extreme anti-father bias of these institutions, their arbitrary decision making processes, or indeed what many saw as blatant corruption in the rigging of evidence and procedures. For many Australians one of their only interactions with the legal system during their lifetimes is the Family Court. They never left impressed.

There was also considerable discontent within the legal profession at the time, with the shoddy quality and outride corruption inherent in the family reports known to everybody.

Many of the country's lawyers regarded the court as an embarrassment, a haven for social justice dreamers, but not for "real" lawyers.

While some newspaper editorials hedged their bets, the networks of groups including legal, women's, domestic violence, academics, the judiciary and the bureaucracy, which benefited from the sole custody regime of the Family Court of Australia, were yet to rally their forces.

Howard received frequent praise, particularly on talkback radio, for raising a subject that appeared to ignite an egalitarian spirit in the Australian psyche.

The Prime Minister told his Coalition colleagues he was "interested in the broad concept" of rebuttable joint custody – where the court presumes a child should spend roughly equal time or large amounts of time living with each parent unless there were strong reasons against it.

He said he would not commit his government to it.

"It may on further examination turn out to be prejudicial to the child, unworkable, but we should be willing to have another look at it," he said.[91]

The flagging of potential custody reforms provoked a tidal wave of coverage and commentary on radio, television and especially talkback and the Shared Parenting Council of Australia, a loose association of 28 fathers and family law reform groups whose organisers were closely linked to the government, took on a profile they probably never dreamed possible.

Many of the talkback gurus and much of the reporting of the issue was, in the first instance, positive. Fathers groups were exuberant at the Prime Minister's comments, but a great deal of support came from women. Talkback radio hummed with tale after tale of child custody fiascos. The story of the government's willingness to look at reforming family law and child support ran all week, and then just kept on running; on talkback, on television and in print.

***

On the 17th of June, 2003, the story ran prominently in a number of newspapers around Australia, including the *Adelaide Advertiser*, *The Australian*, the *Brisbane Courier Mail*, the *Melbourne Herald Sun* and the *Townsville Bulletin*.

The papers reported that the Prime Minister had been lobbied heavily by members of his backbench, who had raised repeatedly family support and custody issues at party meetings in the preceding months – and that Liberal MPs, including Ken Ticehurst, Barry Haase, Jeannie Ferris and Margaret May, had led the charge.

A subsequent rewriting of history saw feminist critics repeatedly claim that the push for a more reasonable family law system during the Howard era came from fathers' groups to which he was overly influenced. It was a straight out lie.

Ferris, who passed away in 2007 from cancer at the age of 66, was a significant supporter of family law reform. As the mother of three adult sons and a proud grandmother in one of the many rural areas badly affected by family law, she could hardly have failed to understand the depth of hostility in the community

---

91 PM Transcripts, John Howard, Interview with Jeremy Cordeaux, Radio 5DN, 19 June, 2003.

over the family law and child support industry.

A senior member of the Liberal Party, she was elected as the Government Whip in the Senate in 2002 and had a professional background as a journalist and political lobbyist.

Senator Ferris said the group had been working with advisers from the Prime Minister's office since the middle of 2002 on a review of child support payments and custody issues and had begun working on the terms of reference for the inquiry three months before.

In an interview with Dads On The Air she said: "Every child has a fundamental human right to an equal relationship with both their mother and father following parental separation or divorce. My interest in child access has been ongoing for many years. Working for a Federal and State Member of Parliament before I became a Senator showed me just how important this issue is to so many families. Custody issues can take up to 25% of work for members of Parliament and it is a highly emotive issue for everyone involved.

"One of the major issues in child custody agreements is the ability for grandparents to have regular access to the child. Under the current system, grandparents have no legal recourse in the arrangements and important bonds between grandparents and their grandchildren can often be destroyed by a system that does not consider them in custody arrangements.

"Only 16 percent of divorced couples have their children living with each parent for more than 30 percent of the time. The inquiry into child access will look into ways that we can raise this figure considerably.

"I believe that if we start from the basis that both parents are jointly responsible for the child and then try to work through from there how the living arrangements will apply, better access could be established for parents and children.

"Recently I travelled overseas and spoke to several joint parenting organisations to look closer at the changes that have been made overseas. During my trip I was also fortunate to meet a Canadian Senator, Anne Cools, who has dedicated much of her time in public office to progress joint custody access. It has always been her strong belief that children benefit from joint parenting and a society that accepts this presumption will work better for everyone involved in such painful circumstances.

"Children are not prizes in a competition and a parent should not try to prevent access to the other parent for reasons such as power or money. The focus of custody arrangements needs to examine more of the benefits for children from equal parenting to educate people that amicable arrangements can be made and their children can continue from loving relationships – no matter where their parents live."

The Sydney Morning Herald followed up on the weekend with a largely sympathetic front-page story using the example of a couple in a shared parenting arrangement who found they loved their kids more than they disliked each other. For the bible of the chattering classes, it was a significant story. They also reported various views for and against, noting the flood of phone calls into the offices of Members of Parliament on the issues.

The Herald Sun also reported that Family Court custody battles faced an unprecedented overhaul under plans to slash costs and defuse bitter court hearings. The large circulation Melbourne paper quoted Matilda Bawden, president of the Shared Parenting Council of Australia, saying shared parenting would force warring parents to get along by taking litigation out of the family breakdown picture to the greatest extent possible and encouraging parents to work it out themselves. At the same it would also benefit other family members, including grandparents, aunts and uncles, who may not see children after a divorce.

"Get the lawyers, get the judges, the psychologists and social workers out of the picture and families might stand a chance of working things out," she declared.

Prominent social commentator Bettina Arndt wrote an opinion piece for *The Sydney Morning Herald* and *The Age* headlined Fathers May Get Justice At Last.[92] She argued that joint custody was usually better for children and that it was the type of arrangement that most children wanted.

Arndt wrote: "John Howard made a crucial decision this week to support a new look at child custody. By doing this, he is acknowledging the festering community discontent over the failure of the family law system to effectively handle this most emotional issue.

"Next week, federal cabinet will meet to approve terms of reference for an inquiry into child custody issues by the House of Representatives family and community affairs committee. These seem set to include not only a presumption favouring joint custody but also, amazingly, the question of whether the Child Support Act is fair to both parents, as well as changes in child support to cover costs of contact. These are all highly controversial issues.

"Very few Australian children experience the type of care they would prefer after divorce – namely equal care by both parents. Our adversarial family law system, and a long history of the Family Court awarding 'custody' to mothers, has meant that most children of divorced parents are brought up with their fathers cast in a visiting dad role, and contact with the child often at the whim

---

92 Arndt, Bettina, Fathers may get justice at last, *The Age*, 20 June 2003.

of the mother."

She said that while women's groups would no doubt play the usual "violence card", joint custody was the type of care preferred by most children. While previous pushes for even small reforms have been torpedoed by leftwing parties firmly in the sole parent camp, "this time the push for change has the backing of a powerful, popular Prime Minister with a record of supporting fatherhood".

***

In what was little more than a dream come true for family law reformers, at the end of the week "Give Dads A Go" was the front page headline of the mass circulation Sydney tabloid *The Daily Telegraph*, a newspaper any Australian politician ignored at their peril.[93]

The paper wrote: "Young boys need a male role model in their lives, Prime Minister John Howard said yesterday, paving the way for broad-ranging changes to child custody laws.

"Mr Howard yesterday singled out young boys as the group most likely to be affected when their parents separated or divorced.

"He said this was exacerbated where there were no close uncles or relatives because there were now fewer male teachers.

"It is a view that has led him to consider allowing immediate joint-custody to divorced dads and mums."

***

Having tested the waters so successfully, the next week, on 25 June 2003 the Prime Minister announced an inquiry into custody issues, including a brief to examine the notion of rebuttable joint custody or shared parenting, whether or not the child support scheme was fair and issues over contact with grandparents.[94]

The inquiry was to unleash a remarkable flood of material.

Prime Minister John Howard, himself a lawyer turned politician, told parliament that he was aware, along with members from both sides of the house, that "within the Australian community there is a level of concern and unhappiness with the operation of matters relating to the custody of children following marriage breakdown and a measure of unhappiness with the operation of the

---

93 Cazzulino, Michelle, Kamper, Angela, Give Dads A Go, *The Daily Telegraph*, 20 June, 2003.

94 PM orders inquiry on joint custody, *The Age*, 25 June, 2003.

Child Support Agency.

"The government wants to respond to that concern because we believe that these are issues that go to the heart of personal happiness for millions of Australians."

***

The Prime Minister's comments on the Child Support Agency were an understatement.

Politicians were being bombarded with complaints about the child support system and the CSA, with claims that staff discriminated against non-custodial parents, most often fathers.

As if to reiterate the point about child support and the problems being experienced in separated families, in case anyone had missed it, that weekend *The Australian* ran a story on some of the multiple dysfunctions of the Child Support Agency. It was written by its Freedom of Information editor Michael McKinnon, journalist Christine Jackman and myself.[95]

That story kicked off: "Hundreds of threats of assault, murder and suicide by angry parents have been mishandled or ignored by the Child Support Agency.

"Federal Children and Youth Affairs Minister Larry Anthony yesterday ordered the Agency to explain itself after it was revealed he had been misled by a CSA briefing on its safety procedures."

Documents obtained under Freedom of Information laws had revealed that the Minister was told any "possible murder or suicide" threat from CSA clients would be referred to police. The Agency claimed staff were trained to refer on to qualified counsellors the "distraught" parents who "occasionally" contacted them.

"A few of these threaten to harm themselves or others," the CSA brief noted.

Minister Anthony admitted writing on the CSA's briefing paper that it was "an understatement" for the agency to claim distressed parents "occasionally" contacted the service.

Internal documents obtained during a six-month investigation by *The Weekend Australian* showed the CSA fielded hundreds of threats to harm ex-partners and children, use bombs or commit suicide each year.

The Agency received 184 suicide threats, 320 client-to-client threats, 48 bomb threats, with four bomb incidents, and 453 harassment calls between 1996-97 and 2001-02. But security incident reports revealed the police were called in fewer than half a dozen of these cases.

---

95 McKinnon, Michael, Jackman, Christine, Stapleton, John, Child Agency Ignored Threats, *The Weekend Australian*, 28 June, 2003.

A CSA spokeswoman said no records had been kept of police referrals before July 2001. In the financial year to June 25, 2003, the CSA had received 111 suicide threats, 81 client-to-client threats, 74 threats to staff and seven bomb threats. In the two years since July 2001, 59 client-to-client threats and 46 suicide threats were referred to police.

The article spilled to page two, where it was accompanied by a story I wrote about CSA payers being pushed to the brink.

It recounted the case of Jack, a senior public servant, who slashed his wrists after receiving 36 letters from the Child Support Agency in one day.

"I am being pushed against the wall emotionally, financially and in every other way. The best analysis: you get stuck in a dark tunnel, you keep walking down the tunnel, there is no light at the end, so why keep walking?"

Two years before he had rung the CSA: "I was losing control, I was thinking of chucking it all in and said I might as well go the whole hog. I made it very clear to them that I was contemplating suicide."

Jack was not provided with professional counselling and did not receive any expression of sympathy. To his knowledge the police were not informed.

He handed over 27 per cent of his pay in child support payments while also supporting his second family, which included two teenagers.

"You ring up the CSA and tell them your situation. They don't care."

In a separate background piece Christine Jackman wrote that the suicide and assault threats were only a miniscule part of the Agency's clientele, but it would be folly to assume the remaining 99.95 per cent of the agency's clients are satisfied with the system.

"On the contrary, grim anecdotal evidence from the fraught frontline of family breakdown suggests the agency's incident reports are the mere tip of a much larger iceberg threatening the child-support system."

***

As a result of the CSA stories an employee turned whistleblower contacted the paper and penned a piece about his own experiences. He said he was fearful he was breaking the Public Service code of conduct after threats from management that speaking out about Agency matters could land staff in jail.

He told me the Prime Minister's acknowledgement there was "unhappiness" in the Australian community with the Child Support Agency and the coverage documenting the Agency's failure to properly deal with suicide threats from clients was only the tip of the iceberg in an Agency characterised by high staff turnover and deeply flawed management practices.

"The unending stuff-ups and the caller discontent and hatred are dispiriting for staff," he said. "At 8.31am the phones start ringing. You'll be answering near constant calls in a four hour block, often taking call after call from unhappy, resentful, fed-up and disbelieving mothers and fathers.

"We get a lot of calls where the blokes are at the end of their tether. They say things like 'I might as well not go on'. None of these types of calls are reported as suicide threats. But when a payer calls and the threat is for real and you find out the police were involved and the client has gone to hospital or worse it makes you feel like you want to quit.

"While the staff cop much of the abuse from disgruntled clients, the faults of the staff are very much to do with their lack of time to follow up on work or undertake decent training.

"The phone staff at the CSA really do what they can – but the work culture is so damaging it is difficult to see outside the 'madhouse' of the Agency. I hope to have a different job soon."

***

Of course it wasn't just the Child Support Agency which was upsetting separated families, with the operations of the Family Court square in their sights.

In his address to Parliament announcing the historic inquiry Prime Minister Howard said: "We all aspire to an ideal but an ideal is never realised in an overwhelming majority of cases, and the obligation of society when a marriage breaks down is to have arrangements which are in the best interests of children but which also have proper regard to the interests of the parents of those children."

Howard said he would be asking the House of Representatives Standing Committee on Family and Community Affairs to examine "whether there should be a presumption that children will spend equal time with each parent and, if so, in what circumstances such a presumption could be rebutted.

"The committee will also be asked to investigate in what circumstances a court should order that children of separated parents have contact with other persons, including their grandparents.

"We will also be asking the committee to examine whether the existing child support formula works fairly for both parents in relation to their care of, and contact with, their children, because…there are many non-custodial parents in Australia who are profoundly unhappy with the existing formula used by the Child Support Agency and wish that matter to be examined.

"We are asking the committee to report to the parliament by 31 December. There is no point giving it two or three years. I think that six months, given the intensity and amount of public interest in this matter, is an appropriate period of time.

"I encourage the committee not to see its remit as a licence to recommend large increases in the expenditure of taxpayers' money but rather to look at the structure of these arrangements.

"I cannot think of anything that is more important to millions of Australians than current custody arrangements. This issue is properly the concern of the national parliament, and I hope it brings forth the genuine bipartisan involvement of the opposition."

***

Radio, television and newspapers once again all ran the story prominently, just as they had the previous week, much of it positive to the notion of shared parenting. Talkback once again ran strongly in favour, with callers split equally between men and women. It appeared in the first flush to be a clear vote winner. Howard's poll numbers went up.

Some of the toughest women journalists in the country penned passionate pieces in support.

On the 24th of June, under the headline Dad's The Other Word, *The Courier Mail* ran a piece by well known journalist Madonna King. She wrote: "This year, more than 1000 fathers will commit suicide, many such deaths blamed on family law issues. This weekend fathers across Australia will travel to pick up children for an access visit to find their children missing. And today, hundreds of mothers will seek help after their former partner refuses to pay child maintenance.

"And they say family law works. It doesn't and it's about time it was overhauled.

"For 20 years, we've told our fathers, our husbands and our sons to play a bigger role in their families, to spend fewer hours at work and to take a bigger role in their children's future. And they have.

"Then, when a relationship breaks down, reports suggest only three percent of fathers are awarded equal joint custody.

"It's about time that changed and Prime Minister John Howard should be applauded for flagging his family law review."

***

Well versed in media campaigns and well funded by the taxpayer, the National Council for Single Mothers spokeswoman Elspeth McInnes shot off a response to King demanding "in the interests of balanced and informed journalism" there be equal column space given to opposing arguments.

"The claim that 'women's groups have controlled the debate for decades' is not supported by any evidence. Your claim that women's groups don't want fathers to have a role in their children's lives after separation is wrong."

McInnes, long one of the country's most virulent anti-father campaigners, argued for a rebuttable presumption of no contact where there were allegations of violence established "on the balance of probabilities".

"Persons found on the basis of civil proof to have used violence would have to show why they were safe before contact was allowed," she said.

"On the balance of probabilities" was a legal nicety which in the heated realm of feuding couples, money grubbing lawyers and a dysfunctional court meant in practice "without any concrete evidence whatsoever". So much for the old legal principle of "beyond reasonable doubt".

Fathers often complained that the solid evidence they did present to the court was routinely ignored.

How could cutting dads out of children's lives possibly be in their best interests, Dads On The Air regularly asked.

***

One of *The Sydney Morning Herald*'s most senior and experienced reporters, Paola Totaro penned an opinion piece calling the decision to re-look at joint custody as humane and long overdue. She said it was a win not just for "angry dads" but "for the thousands of silent women and men who choose to put their children not bitterness and anger first."

She derided another of the paper's prominent feminist columnists Adele Horin for suggesting that while divorced fathers may have a point about wanting more time with their kids, seeking equal time was veering into "dangerous territory".

"Angry dads"? "Dangerous territory" for men to want to have equal time with their children?

"As a woman, divorced mother and now a remarried step mom too, these arguments strike me as the worst kind of sexism. How can we, as a civilised society, continue to suggest that capable men do not have the same rights to bring up their children, post-divorce, as their female partners?

"And how can we women who quite rightly expect and enjoy an equitable arrangement both in parenting and in the domestic environment inside marriage then argue that post-divorce, only motherhood is sacrosanct?"[96]

The Adelaide Advertiser also gave the story a good run, with a feature titled Question of Balance.

---

96 Totaro, Paola, Family Law: A Question of Balance, The Sydney Morning Herald, 30 June, 2003.

The paper quoted Michael Green QC, author of *Fathers After Divorce*, extensively. He said: "When people think of separation they think of lawyers, and all too easily run off to find out what their rights are. The true question separating couples should ask themselves is not what are our rights and responsibilities now but what are the best arrangements we can make for this family."

The Advertiser editorialised: "It is a message being heard in MPs' offices around the nation, where staff are often snowed under with traumatised parents and grandparents denied the right to see their children. But it is a message MPs have seemingly failed to act on – until now."

The paper went on to detail the commitment of a number of MPs to the issue. It reported that among Liberal MPs pushing for change was Parliamentary Secretary Jackie Kelly, who advised the Prime Minister on women's issues. She reportedly spent hours in her Sydney electorate office trying to help parents gain access to their children.

"Access is the killer and access is the tragedy," she said. "The enforcement of it is a joke. It really must be about acting in the children's interests. Children really need both parents. We are really chopping off whole extended families – the grandparents, the aunts and the uncles.

"I believe we will be paying as a Federal Government for that social injustice 20 or 30 years down the track."[97]

***

On the weekend *The West Australian* editorialised: "The review of child custody laws promised by Prime Minister John Howard will be contentious but necessary. Mr Howard identified an increasingly worrying social trend when he said too many boys grow up without male role models after their parents divorced.[98]

"He has been criticised often for his conservatism and apparent attachment to the past – the so-called white picket fence view of the world. But he is right this time.

"Ideally, children should be brought up by both parents. Loving mothers and fathers, in cooperation, both have vital contributions to make in caring for children."

The paper went on to say: "There is a significant body of opinion that men endure systematic discrimination under the present arrangements. It is not surprising that coalition MPs have raised concerns about what they say are unfair

---

97 A Question of Balance, *Adelaide Advertiser*, 21 June, 2003.

98 Editorial, *West Australian*, 21 June, 2003.

access arrangements and child-support payments.

"There are many furious men who assert – sometimes in concert with new wives or partners – that they have been dudded by their former wives and denied justice by the court. This chorus seems to be getting louder.

"Proposals for reform might be driven by disaffected fathers, but the main issue has to be the effects on children of the current arrangements. Mr Howard's review is timely and should be supported by everybody with the best interests of children at heart."[99]

At the weekend *The Sun Herald* also covered the story: "They live next door, across the road and in every classroom in the country. Sometimes they're even in our own homes. They're the children of what are called 'dissolved partnerships'."

The paper went on to say that "children are the silent sufferers in angry confrontations between warring parents. They often are used as weapons of retribution. The world has moved on since the Family Law Act was introduced in 1975.

"Even though the Family Law courts must place the children's best interests first, only three percent of orders made are for joint custody."

The editorial concluded that behind the statistics of more than 50,000 children being affected each year "lie the stories of great tragedy, revealed only in the secrecy of the Family Court or the anguish of mediation conferences. We await with great interest the establishment of the committee, its terms of reference and its deliberations."

***

Also on the weekend *The Age* ran an oddly conspiratorial story on its front page suggesting that a group of disgruntled Adelaide dads had laid the groundwork for custody reform. It was all part of a campaign, with full cooperation from elements of the media, to paint fathers groups as some sort of far right Klu Klux Klan style movement.

The paper suggested the moves were originally floated by One Nation, a much demonised splinter conservative party which was enjoying some solid electoral popularity at the time. *The Age* suggested that one John Abbott, whose only previous claim to fame was as cousin of a bank robber known as the "Postcard Bandit", had laid the groundwork for the move to joint custody with two other Adelaide denizens scarred by Family Court battles, Geoff Greene of the Shared Parenting Council and Joint Parenting Association president Yuri Joakimidis.

It was an absurd story. Geoffrey Greene, was a senior backroom Liberal party operative and one of the figures behind John Howard's enduring electoral success,

---

99 *The West Australian*, Editorial, 2003.

while Yuri Joakimidis was a prolific and well regarded supporter of fathers. His thorough research added credibility to the push for shared parenting and he was a frequent contributor to Dads On The Air.

Reaction to the story suggested John Howard, as the wiliest and most successful conservative politician of his generation, was more than capable of recognising a hot button issue in the electorate all on his own.

DOTA commented that it seemed unlikely such a small group could dictate or initiate such a major policy debate in isolation. Fathers who had met with him all reported him sympathetic.

Greene denied any linkage between the proposals and One Nation, saying it was his lobbying for the Joakimidis extensively researched and well documented proposals for joint custody contained in publications such as Back To The Best Interests Of The Child, that finally brought it to the Prime Minister's attention, first through the auspices of South Australian MP Christopher Pyne; and then through SA Senator Jeannie Ferris and later NSW MP Ken Ticehurst.

Greene was also quick to credit the behind the scenes work of SA Senator Nick Minchin, who was then Finance Minister in the Howard government.

Greene declared with a certain characteristic pugnacity: "Once the Prime Minister is on your side it's easier to get your story heard. Cabinet sets policy and Attorney General's will do what it's told. I think it's possible we'll have legislation before Christmas. I think we have very good odds of success."

The forecast, as it turned out, was way too optimistic.

***

A number of family law reform groups issued press releases in support of the inquiry. The Shared Parenting Council of Australia put out a congratulatory release heaping praise not just on the Prime Minister but "the numerous back-bench Coalition Members and Senators who have supported this review".

The formation of the Shared Parenting Council of Australia the previous year, a representative body of various children's, father's and church groups around Australia, was one of the many crystallising forces leading up to the inquiry and lent a coherence to atomised groups calling for reform.

The statement read: "The current 'one size fits all' model of sole custody orders of the Family Court has clearly failed children and the wider Australian society and must be reformed.

"Children of separating or divorcing parents are the real victims of current failed Family Law policies. Under the sole custody regime, children are automatically deprived of a continuing and meaningful relationship with both their parents, and the social outcomes for children as a result of this loss is a national disgrace.

"Only by recognising and upholding the fundamental rights of children to maintain an equal relationship and opportunity with both their mother and father will society reduce the impact of family breakdown on children of divorce".

The West Australian group Reliable Parents also congratulated John Howard, going on to say that the introduction of a presumption of shared parenting would represent a shift from sole parent possession of children to an arrangement that recognised the needs and responsibilities of all involved.

"At present many families reach an agreement on parenting based on the impediments to equitable arrangements brought about by obstacles put before the non-resident parent. These include lack of legal assistance and family court pressures to accept lesser contact in order to avoid the high costs associated with court appearances."

Spokesman for the group Tony Borger said the sole parent model showed little regard for the best interests of the children. He went on to state that children shared equally in the lives of their parents prior to divorce and every means should be explored to ensure this continues, where practical, after divorce.

"After all it is the parents that are divorcing, not the children," he said.

***

Men's Confraternity, established in 1985, a particularly active and outspoken group, also from Western Australia, was jubilant.

"Finally Australia has a Prime Minister who has the courage to tackle this immensely difficult issue, in the hope of creating a system that no longer discriminates against children and fathers," their release read.

"The current adversarial system of winner takes all, has contributed to the escalating divorce rate being initiated predominately by females, and lead to the appalling level of suicide amongst divorced and separated men.

"Contrary to the misandrist ravings of many women's organisations, men truly love and care for their children, and the current Family Court system, which actively seeks to alienate them from their children, has resulted in a shocking loss of life.

"Research both within Australia and internationally, strongly supports the irreplaceable role that fathers play in the development and growth of children.

"The sole parent regime purported by the Family Court and its Chief Justice Alastair Nicholson to be in the child's best interest, is a complete failure."

Most papers published a scattering of letters in support of shared parenting.

The West Australian ran a letter from Lionel Richards, who ran the OzyDads internet chatline, linking fatherlessness to the recent spate of juvenile crime in the west. He wrote: "The problem with delinquent youths in the streets at night is that they are living in fatherless homes with many suffering very low self-esteem as a result of parental alienation and denigration of the absent father.

"As well as the obvious drop in the abhorrent suicide rate of disfranchised dads, the Federal Government's announcement of shared parenting presumption as the default position in family breakdown will go a long way to remedying the problem of our youths on the streets at night."

***

At first it appeared that family law reformers were fortunate in the constitution of the Committee, all of whom laid claim to understanding of the issues from their work as parliamentarians.

There was some argument over whether the Inquiry should have gone to the Legal and Constitutional Committee rather than the Standing Committee on Family and Community Affairs, which would have produced an entirely different inquiry – lawyers talking to lawyers with a result something along the lines of the previously failed Family Law Pathways Advisory Group's report Out of the Maze from the previous year.

That inquiry had also stirred hope and confusion in equal measure and became a class study in bureaucratic frustration of reform.

The Standing Committee was one of 13 general-purpose investigatory committees established by the House of Representatives of the Parliament of Australia.

The committee Chairwoman was the popular Mrs Kay Hull, the National Party member for Riverina. Known as the "pocket dynamo" for her size and energy. She brought to the job a great deal of intelligence and personal charm. She quickly established a distinguished and authoritative hold over the Committee's proceedings.

Ms Hull said early on in the piece that the problems with family law and child support had been evident for some time. She continued to make public statements questioning the status quo and suggesting significant change was appropriate.

Another member, Roger Price, MP for the western Sydney electorate of Campbelltown, had been chairman of the 1994 Joint Select Committee Inquiry into the Child Support Scheme. This far reaching investigation had received a flood of complaints about the Agency a mere five years after its creation.

Price had previously expressed anger at the failure of the government to implement most of the recommendations of the inquiry, with the bureaucracy only cherry picking the most punitive of the recommendations and ignoring others, such as a study of the social impacts of the scheme.

He was forceful in his questioning of some witnesses as to why a 50/50 presumption would not work. He has previously said the stories of the hurt and individual pain that so many experienced had only made him more radical on the issue since he chaired the inquiry.

He described the level of anger in the community as frightening.

***

Liberal Member of Parliament Chris Pearce, also on the committee, penned a piece in *The Herald Sun* in early November titled "Sharing parents for life" which said the Family Law Act of 1975 had sought to deal with separating families in a fair and sensitive manner but "with the benefit of 30 years experience, the overwhelming evidence from children, parents and professionals reveals significant flaws in the system."[100]

He wrote that although it may be challenging at times, shared parenting had many advantages. "It would allow both parents to be active and ongoing role models for their children. It would provide greater equality between the parental roles of the mother and father, which is often a source of conflict. This greater equality would mean that separated parents would be less likely to become overwhelmed by the burden of sole parenting or largely cut out of a child's life."

Also on the committee were Deputy Chair Mrs Julia Irwin, of the Australian Labor Party, Alan Cadman, Trish Draper, Cameron Thompson and Peter Dutton from the Liberal Party, a former policeman whose line of inquiry during the hearings indicated a clear disgust for the present system. Twenty years further down the track and Dutton would assume the leadership of the Opposition, and be an election away from becoming the Prime Minister.

There was also Jennie George, the well known former President of the Australian Council of Trade Unions and the ever volatile Harry Quick, both of the Australian Labor Party. The latter's derisive comments towards the judiciary and the "industry" during the progress of the public hearings did much to enliven the inquiry.

***

Kay Hull was going into Question Time in the House of Representatives in Canberra when she heard news of the inquiry.

"I thought to myself, that is an amazing job for someone and one that would

---

100 Pearce, Chris, Sharing Parents for Life, *Herald Sun*, 8 November, 2003.

be very difficult and I was rendered a little speechless when it turned out we would be doing it. I was quite gobsmacked. I picked myself up off the floor and said: here we are, we are going to be very busy."[101]

The committee set about hiring extra staff and organising an itinerary. A date for receipt of submissions of Friday 8 August 2003 was set. The tight deadline was designed to focus attention in an emotive and divisive area and to avoid prolonged campaigning and manoeuvring by various interest groups.

However the committee continued to accept all submissions after this date and repeatedly said they were prepared to accept any material right up to the end.

***

At the same time as the inquiry was being established the country's leading research facility dealing with fathers, the Men's Health and Information Resource Centre at the University of Western Sydney, released a report urging general practitioners to be more aware of the poor health and high suicide rates of separated men.[102]

The most recent Australian Bureau of Statistics report revealed that in the prime divorce age bracket – of 25 to 44 years – suicides remain stubbornly high, or were increasing. This age group of men accounted for almost 50 percent of all suicides.

Co-director of the Centre, Professor John MacDonald said doctors, along with other professionals, were well equipped to help play an important role.

"The sources of stress belong in the social domain and often in the legal domain," he said. "But if the doctor has a list of relevant agencies that can help, some legal agencies rather than medical, for example, then such a GP would be bringing a holistic service to his clients. That would be the doctor acknowledging what we call the 'social determinants of health'."

MacDonald said statistics showed separated men were up to six times more likely to suicide than separated women, although this depended on the age group. He said several doctors were now asking what they could do to make their services more accessible to men.

"Even when doctors are referring men on to counsellors or other agencies, it is important that such services are male-positive," he said.

MacDonald pointed out that many community health services don't deal with men at all unless they are in crisis, for example for drug and alcohol problems.

"Most of the medical profession would accept that there are very few services

---

101 Hull, Crispin, Hull's shock at family law role, *The Canberra Times*, 23 July, 2003.

102 General Practitioners and Separated Men's Health, Men's Health and Information Resource Centre, University of Western Sydney, 2003.

directed at men," he said. "We would definitely like to see."

Director of the Shared Parenting Council Geoffrey Greene said general practitioners were usually the first place where fathers suffering the process of separation presented.

"Losing your children is one of the single most distressing experiences any person can go through," he said. "Doctors need to be aware that if their patients are experiencing separation or divorce they are at high risk of suicide. Even if they are not suicidal they can present with stress disorders."

***

At the time the government funded Mensline was managing to answer only one-in-four of the deluge of the calls to its emergency service.

"Clearly from our experience, men dealing with family and relationship breakdown deal with a range of physical and mental health issues," Mensline manager Terry Melvin said. "We find callers on the line with high levels of anxiety and stress, depression, and risk of suicide or self-harming behaviour. Six percent of our callers are men who are either threatening suicide or where the suicide is actually in progress."[103]

Melvin said there was a spillover effect from separation into men's working lives. Mensline research showed high absenteeism, conflict with their peers, inability to concentrate and the potential for industrial accidents.

"There is often a high use of drugs and alcohol as men struggle to cope with the loss of daily contact with their children and the loss of the relationship. The level of stress increases when they have to deal with the legal system."

Board member of Suicide Prevention Australia Julian Krieg said many separated men were "falling through the cracks" of the health system. "There are support mechanisms for the wife and kids, but the blokes are expected to carry on, doing the provider thing. There is no approach that recognises these blokes are, in reality, heart broken. The blokes are saying, 'it's over. I've failed at my job, my life, my marriage.'

"The reality is that the man is stressed out of his brain. When people are going through a divorce there are critical things going on. The whole spectrum of care needs to recognise that separation and divorce is a time of risk."

***

At first the slowness of submissions going up online caused some disquiet. Most

---

[103] The Crisis Amongst Men, Terry Melvin, Director of Mensline, Dads On The Air, 24 March, 2003.

of the first fifty or so submissions placed on line in the first few weeks were from various segments of the divorce industry, and all against shared parenting, seemingly at odds with an inquiry into joint custody.

To begin with the only groups in favour with submissions up on line were The Shared Parenting Council of Australia, the Lone Fathers Association, Tasmanian Men's Health Well Being Association, The Joint Parenting Association and the Australian Family Support Services Association.

Already the women's legal and domestic violence groups, all taxpayer funded, were well represented; including the Women's Information and Referral Exchange, the National Welfare Rights network, the Domestic Violence and Incest Resource Centre, Relationships Australia, the Law Council of Australia, the Human Rights and Equal Opportunity Commission, National Legal Aid, and the Governments of Tasmania and South Australia.

But what followed was a flood of many hundreds of submissions, more than 1700 in the end, where in combination with the Hansard transcripts of the public inquiry, the individual stories of people's lives mangled by the family law industry stood out in contrast to the bland assurances of experts.

***

At the same time as the inquiry was proceeding the politics and personnel in the upper echelons of the Family Court and the Attorney General's Department were in flux.

The entire shared parenting or joint custody debate was made more piquant by the fact that these were the final days and months of the reign of Chief Justice of the Family Court of Australia Alastair Nicholson, who had been in position since 1988, only the second Chief Justice in its more than quarter of a century history.

Nicholson had been the dominating figure on family law in Australia for the entire modern era, either fawned upon by his supporters or regarded with reptilian fascination by his critics. He was leaving behind an institution engulfed in controversy and the subject of the most far reaching and transparent inquiry ever conducted into it.

Nicholson had been appointed by the Hawke government in 1988 to the age of 65, which came to pass in 2003. DOTA described him as perhaps the most hated figure in Australian judicial history. Certainly the fatherhood movement saw it that way.

During the inquiry there was also a change of Attorney Generals, from the mild mannered Daryl Williams, who family law reformers regarded as totally useless, to the more politically savvy Philip Ruddock.

Daryl Williams was the Attorney General who infamously claimed to an international conference of visiting judges that Australia had a world class family law system, a claim met with widespread derision from fathers and family law reform groups.

There was, to the very end, a total disconnect between the community experience exemplified by compelling stories of grief, dysfunction and difficulty with family law and child support issues and the snivelling self-serving assurances of the industry's experts and the grandiosity of its princelings.

The nation was about to embark on a journey through this same disconnect between the reality on the ground and the industry's mandarins.

NINE
AUTOCUE: EARLY DAYS

AFTER THE remarkable wave of largely supportive media following the Prime Minister John Howard's June, 2003 announcement of an inquiry into joint custody, child support and related matters media interest began to wane.

But still, with submissions open and the public phase of the inquiry about to begin, there was a steady spattering of positive and negative attention in a number of major newspapers, on radio and on television.[104]

The most prominent opponents of a rebuttable notion of joint custody were Chief Justice of the Family Court Alastair Nicholson, Elspeth McInnes of the National Council of Single Mothers and Their Children and the extremely outspoken Pru Goward, Sex Discrimination Commissioner, whose extreme hostility towards men appeared to her critics to border on the pathological.

Ms Goward played a spoiler role throughout the inquiry, culminating in claims outside a public hearing in Wyong on the New South Wales Central Coast that fathers needed an autocue in order to remember the names of their own children.

This staggering style of abusive insult led to considerable backlash, but also marked, in a sense, Australia's descent where this type of conduct from a public official became acceptable. In later years Australia would become a world laughing stock for its lame embrace of all things woke, transforming from a larrikin culture to a place where a Minister for Men's Behaviour Change, I kid you not, became perfectly acceptable.

The Human Rights and Equal Opportunity Commission, always a significant

---

104 Almost all the material referenced in this section can be found on the Australian Parliament House website for the House Standing Committee Family and Community Affairs report Every Picture Tells A Story: Inquiry into child custody arrangements in the event of family separation, including transcripts of the public hearings, tabled on 29 December, 2003.

burden on the taxpayer, put in a submission to the inquiry arguing against joint custody, adopting almost identical positions to the women's groups and claiming that the Child Support formula was "fair".

The formula operating in Australia was almost identical to that adopted by the Bolsheviks in their war against the family almost a century before, and to make such a claim at a time of heightened condemnation of the Child Support Agency and at a time when the ludicrous imposts of the scheme and the suffering it was causing were well known, was in itself remarkable for a taxpayer funded body.

Sex Discrimination Commissioner Pru Goward, herself a single mother who the media had always found easy to report because of her strident outbursts, was fresh from a failed bid to convince the government to implement a paid maternity leave scheme. She had run a taxpayer funded campaign which in the end damaged the very government from which she sought support.

Once close to the Prime Minister, the relationship between John Howard and Pru Goward was rumoured to have cooled.

Right from the beginning Goward was hostile to the joint custody inquiry, making numerous put-down remarks about fathers. If the genders had been reversed she would have been widely condemned.

On the 16th of July 2003 *The Sydney Morning Herald* reported her as saying: "Equal parenting is not the 16 minutes of child play a day that is the average amount of time men spend with their children." By the time of divorce "one parent by then has invested so much more time and energy in the relationship with the children".[105]

At a speech Goward made to a women's employment conference, she complained about the "unattractive face" of the men's movement focusing on rights rather than responsibilities.

"There are men working very long hours, apparently by choice, not accessing family-friendly provisions, but then concerned that their sons have no role models.

"In theory there is nothing stopping men from accessing part-time working arrangements or flexible work hours. In reality, we do not live in a society which tolerates or venerates men who do part-time work or leave work early to pick up a sick child from school."

***

Only fat cat bureaucrats and well remunerated public servants think working long hours to provide for their family is a matter of personal choice.

---

105 Melvin, Terry, Equal Parenting, *The Sydney Morning Herald*, 16 July, 2003.

One letter writer, Colin Smith in *The Daily Telegraph*, responded: "The reason most men have to work long hours is because their wives or partners do not wish to do so. They would much rather be home with the children and not have to travel, put in long hours and put up with the daily pressures of work. A survey a few years ago indicated that more than 60 percent of women did not even wish to work part time if they had a choice. Why? Because they would rather be home, thanks very much."[106]

Not just a single mother herself, the estrangement between Pru Goward and her daughter, the model Kate Fischer, who later changed her name to Tziporah Malkah, was an infamous piece of Sydney gossip.

Back in the days when she was Kate, she was well known in various of Sydney's inner city circles. Kate, an extremely successful model in her earlier years, had the type of rare beauty and personal charm that made most men soggy in the brain when they were in her presence, as I had witnessed firsthand.

But that's all an aside. Women in glass houses.

***

In this game of political correctness, the forerunners of today's sad and unthinking ultra wokeness, it was impolite to raise Goward's personal circumstances. The bitterness of failed relationships should never be allowed to dictate political advocacy or public policy. But of course it did.

And nothing stopped Pru Goward, who declared that the parliamentary inquiry into joint custody should explore the question of whether "men should have to put in equal parenting time while the marriage is intact" if they want to be more involved after separation, suggesting there might be fewer divorces if they did.

Goward said the men's movement wanted 50/50 care arrangements post divorce, "without any suggestion that men will have to put in equal parenting time while the marriage is intact, or that they will need to rearrange their lives if they want to be more involved after separation."

Despite all the feminist advocacy, studies are clear that men and women contribute more or less equal hours in maintaining and running a household, simply contributing in different ways.

The Sydney Morning Herald reported Goward as warning of a possible new gender war unless men shared more of the burden of child rearing, and more of the career sacrifices needed to raise a family.

"Shared caring has to start before the divorce," she said. "It could drive exactly

---

106 Letters, *The Daily Telegraph*, 16 July, 2003.

the change that the women's movement wants if it's done wisely. Equality between men and women has hit a brick wall, and only the engagement of men in the struggle for work and family balance will move equality closer."[107]

A *Herald* letter writer, Colin Anderson, wrote in response: "A child who thrives on the presumption that her father is an equal part of her life before marriage breakdown, whatever the work-family balance, is entitled to the same presumption after marriage breakdown."

Each time Pru Goward spoke out during the course of the inquiry she attracted negative responses. Sydney's leading talkback station 2GB reported a "meltdown" over her comments.

In *The Daily Telegraph*'s feedback one respondent in July asked: "How many fathers have to go to court just to see their kids? Most men work hard and long hours. This is for the family."

Another, Brett Kessner, described her as a "hypocrite" and said "we live in a society that does not value fatherhood".

Another, Wayne Smith, wrote: "Pru Goward has not walked in my shoes, I have three children 2x11yrs 1x10yrs and have paid maintenance for many years. It's about time that men had equal rights. So Pru Goward, there's only one attitude that needs changing, yours."

One woman wrote in support of joint custody, saying the father leaving created even more problems for the child and just because society expected men to be the breadwinner didn't mean they should be punished by the courts.

Shane said he thought it was amazing that the Sex Discrimination Commissioner continually groups all men into a single stereotype and offers her sagely advice. "Could you imagine what she would say if any man grouped all women into a single stereotype, then proceeded to explain why they are ALL not up to the standard of the other?"

Luc van Uffelen wrote: "Prior to divorce as a father whilst being on shift work I contributed enormously to the children's welfare. After divorce the Family Law Court deems that I now can see the children every weekend. I have lost that role as a parent by not being there for them. Divorced fathers are certainly being DISCRIMINATED against The upcoming changes being reviewed in Parliament hopefully will give equality back to fathers that so rightly deserve it."

But it was Goward's "autocue" comments that provoked the most outrage.

***

The Sydney Morning Herald reported her as saying she believed introducing a presumption that child-sharing arrangements should be 50-50 would "make no

---

107 Goward warns of new gender war, *The Sydney Morning Herald*, 16 July, 2003.

difference at all" to the outcome of custody disputes, because "in the end a guy who is working 60 hours a week does not want the kids. He just can't. He sees his primary responsibility as earning money. You will not be able to impose this."[108]

Goward said it was unrealistic to expect a father to step into an equal custody arrangement when he might not have been fulfilling such a role prior to separation. "You can't expect a person to step into that role when the child's ten, having never seen them before, needing an autocue to remember their name."

But at that Wyong hearing, as at many others, there were moving tales of Family Court disasters to counterbalance what was becoming to seem very much like feminist inspired extremism.

One non-custodial woman told the five hour hearing that she had spent $230,000 in legal fees and had still not been able to gain reasonable access to her children.

The committee and other politicians were quick to seize on the evidence of non-custodial mothers, whose issues were in many ways identical to non-custodial fathers.

Local Federal member Ken Ticehurst, a significant proponent for change, said: "It proves the case that this is not just an issue for fathers, which is the public perception at the moment."

But despite the mounting body of evidence, it was once again the extreme misandry of the Sex Discrimination Commissioner which got all the mainstream media coverage, and thereby all the reaction.

In a letter to *The Sydney Morning Herald* Ian Tuit wrote that Goward's office should be renamed the Sexist Discrimination Commissioner.

"At a time when people in Australia are working harder and longer than at any other time in our history, it is a very poor effort by the Commissioner not to support and encourage fathers trying to balance work and family commitments.

"The Commissioner's remark that working fathers need an autocue to remember their children's name is ludicrous and sexist beyond belief.

"Her statement that separated fathers don't want the kids is patronising and ignores recent research by the Australian Institute of Family Studies, which shows that 74 percent of non-resident fathers would like to have more contact with their children and 41 percent of resident mothers reported that they would also like to see more contact between fathers and their children.

"How can anyone make these kind of statements and remain Sex Discrimination Commissioner?"[109]

The Shared Parenting Council of Australia put out a press release saying: "The

---

108 Goward on 50/50 Custody, The Sydney Morning Herald, 16 July, 2003.

109 Letters, *Sydney Morning Herald*, 18 July, 2003.

evidence given by Ms Goward, in reference to the true wishes of men and fathers in Australia, is unsupported by any research and describes the complete opposite position of those fathers who put submissions forward to the current inquiry.

"Every father's group, church group and grandparent organisations have clearly and unequivocally said that they want to share the care of their children – regardless of the implications to future work patterns.

"Many family law 'experts' and feminist contributors to the current custody inquiry have universally opposed the introduction of shared parenting in family law matters, with spurious and weak arguments against its operation, yet when confronted with the appalling outcomes of the current system, they have failed to provide any guidance or solutions that will alleviate the waste, despair and destruction caused by the Family Court's handling of child custody matters in family breakdown situations."

Waste, despair and destruction. Exactly right. That was the Legacy of the Family Court of Australia. And remains so half a century after its formation.

***

The public hearing phase of the inquiry began on 28 August in the Centenary Hall in Greater City of Geelong, an industrial but often scenic regional hub west of Melbourne.

The hearings ran for three hours from 8.30 am and later that same day the committee would move on to Melbourne.

At first no one knew what to expect. Fathers groups remained sceptical from long experience.

The guest list for the first public hearing did not bode for fathers and family law reformers, kicking off with the Women's Information and Referral Exchange, followed by Family Law Working Party, Federation of Community Legal Centres and the Domestic Violence and Incest Resource Centre, No To Violence and the Male Family Violence Prevention Association.

Critics said it was hard to believe that the committee could not find a single fathers group or family law reform advocate in the whole of Geelong.

This disparity however was balanced to some fair degree by previously selected witnesses and community witnesses chosen on the day. In the end, as the inquiry progressed, there was a significant body of evidence from both sides of the fence.

The generously funded National Council for Single Mothers and their children was one of the most vociferous complainers over their treatment at the inquiry.

Kathleen Swinbourne of the Sole Parents Union was also off to a frosty start.

Fathers and family law reform groups who appeared as witnesses before the inquiry were generally positive about the experience, saying they were treated with respect, asked intelligent questions and given the opportunity to put across their views.

***

In her first opening remarks Chairwoman of the Inquiry Mrs Kay Hull, who was already gaining respect for the intelligence, compassion and authority she brought to the Inquiry said: "I declare open this first public hearing of the House of Representatives Standing Committee on Family and Community Affairs inquiry into child custody arrangements in the event of family separation.

"This inquiry addresses a very important issue which touches the lives of all Australians. To date the committee has received over 1,500 submissions. This is a record number for an inquiry by this committee and amongst the highest ever for a House of Representatives committee. We are grateful for the community's response.

"This is one important way in which the community can express its views.

"From the outset of this inquiry I want to stress that the committee does not have preconceived views on the outcomes of the inquiry. Accordingly, throughout the inquiry we will be seeking to hear a wide rage of views on the terms of reference.

"While at any one public hearing we may hear more from one set of views than another set – for example, more from men than from women – by the end of the inquiry we will have heard from a diverse group and thus received a balance over the range of views.

"The public hearings the committee is undertaking are focused on regional locations rather than just capital cities. At these regional hearings the focus will be on hearing from individuals and locally based organisations.

"Later in the inquiry we will hear from the larger organisations, such as the Family Court and Child Support Agency, in Canberra or via videoconferencing."

Outlining the process that would be the basic format for more than 20 public hearings right around the country, in both rural and metropolitan locations, Kay Hull said: "I remind everyone appearing as a witness today that the comments you make are on the public record. You should be cautious in what you say to ensure that you do not identify individuals and do not refer to cases before the court. Aside from that, you should feel free to speak without any fear of reprisal or intimidation.

"About two hours has been set aside for the public hearing. This will be followed by about an hour for community statements of about three minutes duration each so that we can give as many people as possible the opportunity to speak. I ask that each individual speaking in the community statement segment keep their comments to three minutes."

***

Although the inquiry became more focussed and more searching as it went along, many of the themes were established or hinted at on that first day, in the morning in Geelong and in the afternoon in Melbourne.

The domestic violence industry, which had ballooned over the previous 15 years, was to play a significant role in the inquiry and was amply represented.

Some of the groups making submissions included Women's Legal Service Victoria, Women's Information and Referral Exchange, Centre Against Sexual Assault, Hornsby Women's Domestic Violence Court Assistance Program, Armidale Domestic Violence Steering Committee, Australian Coalition of Women Against Violence, Taree Women's Domestic Violence Court Assistant Scheme, Albury Wodonga Women's Refuge, Tweed Shire Women' Service Inc, Hume Domestic Violence Network, Domestic Violence Advocacy Service, Victorian Women's Refuges and Association Domestic Violence Services Inc., and so on.

All argued against joint custody. All were taxpayer funded.

There was no countervailing tax payer funded industry representing the other half of the equation, the views, sentiments and desires of fathers.

Yet with the newly discovered wonders of the world wide web, any disaffected bloke could get on the internet and in five minutes find ample research to indicate that domestic violence was an equal opportunity employer being shamelessly exploited by partisans.

Internationally there were numerous voices, in newspapers and without, raising concerns about the operation of the domestic violence industry.

Pity the Australian government paid no attention, and ultimately became hostage to the very voices it funded.

Alternative, more authentic voices were derided or excised, and a one-eyed view became the only view being peddled in the social discourse of the time. In the decades to follow, the social discourse would only become more curdled. Gender politics truly was a one party form of politics.

***

In *Human Events*, a US public policy newspaper, Dr Stephen Baskerville wrote: "Men's groups are beginning to fight back, pointing out decades of unchallenged research establishing that domestic violence is perpetrated as much by women as men. Most of the domestic violence hysteria is generated for one purpose: to gain advantage in custody battles."[110]

In Australia the size of the domestic violence networks and funding apparatus was on parade throughout the inquiry. The groups mounted very similar arguments. Essentially that shared parenting is not a good idea because it exposes women and children to the greater risk of violence.

There was no evidence that the hundreds of millions, indeed billions of dollars poured into the area had led to a decline in interpersonal violence.

Each year the claims of an epidemic of domestic violence grew, and each year the clamour for yet more public money became ever louder.

That's called failing upwards.

First up at the Inquiry was Ms Louise Mitchell, Development Coordinator with the Women's Information Referral Exchange.

She took little time to get to her point: "Each year we hear the stories of thousands of Victorian women. From our own experiences in working with women, WIRE contends that joint residency is the optimum outcome for separating families but is not universally achievable.

"We further contend that a presumption of joint residency will expose children and women to violence and abuse.

"The Family Court is currently given discretion to make orders for the residence and contact of children, looking at the situation of each family with reference to a number of factors. It therefore deals with each case that comes before it on its individual merits. WIRE believes that this is the correct approach. It is important to note that it is entirely possible for separating couples to negotiate joint residency under the current Family Law Act.

"Less than five percent of couples currently enter such arrangements voluntarily. We believe that this small proportion, as well as the likelihood of women being awarded custody, stems from women still doing the vast majority of caring for children during relationships and prior to separation and structuring their lives around their children by not working or working only part time, for example.

"The evidence available does not support the idea that men do not fairly obtain access to their children, as the majority of child custody matters are settled independently with the consent of both the mother and the father. Of the cases that are referred to the Family Court, only five per cent are decided by a judge."

There it was, minutes into the inquiry and some of the greatest furphies of the debate had already been floated.

---

110 Baskerville, Stephen, The Real Domestic Violence, *Human Events*, 10 October, 2003.

The Committee including the Chairwoman Kay Hull became progressively clearer in their public rejection of the claim, made repeatedly by apologists for the status quo, that 95 percent of separated parents settled their differences amicably.

"We haven't bought that one," Hull told one media outlet.

Within minutes of the claim it was also under attack from committee member Roger Price; who knew from his previous roles in advocating for reform of family law and from his own electorate that the claim was preposterous; that most matters settled unhappily in the shadow of the law, or at the doors of the court, as the colloquial saying went, with interim orders soon becoming permanent as people gave up in frustration.

Ms Mitchell was soon taking a question on notice about this issue as well.

The violence card was played for all it was worth; it would not be the last time.

Ms Mitchell said: "One, if the presumption is of joint residency, children may be forced to live with a violent or abusive parent while the rebuttal proceedings are underway."

Never mind the reality that the Court routinely awards custody to violent, abusive, drug addicted women all the time.

"Two," Ms Mitchell said, "it puts the onus on women to prove domestic violence exists despite the underreporting of domestic violence as a crime, particularly non-physical forms of violence or abuse. If a woman has not made reports of domestic violence to the police or other agencies, she may not be able to prove her claims that domestic violence is occurring.

"Three, women earn disproportionately lower incomes than men and tend to be worse off financially than men following separation. Given that the vast majority of victims of domestic violence are women, we have grave concerns as to whether women will be able to finance the legal proceedings around rebuttal and that this inability will result in women and children being exposed to violence.

"WIRE believes that it is in the best interests of children that there is a presumption of no contact with a parent where there is any evidence of domestic violence or child abuse until a thorough risk assessment has been undertaken and it is shown in the individual case that that child is safe from abuse and that contact truly is in their best interests."

Ms Mitchell appeared flabbergasted when Committee member Harry Quick appeared to brush aside her speech and immediately asked what she meant when she said the inquiry itself had arisen over a misconception from men that they do not fairly obtain access to their children.

"I think there is a perception in the community that Family Court proceedings are unfair to men and that men are disproportionately denied access to children," she said. "We do not believe this is supported by the evidence."

But she soon became lost for words. Harry Quick asked her about the ability of families to afford two separate households that are completely set up for their children and the impact this might have on second relationships and second families.

Right from the start there appeared little doubt in which direction the Committee was heading. Mr Quick proceeded to say: "We have this concept of equal time and shared custody. There is an expectation, I guess, that you have two separate households so the children go one week to one and one week to another and that both houses are set up as ideal homes. That is assuming there is not a second relationship and a second family being introduced.

"The idea of two identical houses excludes any concept of another relationship and another family. Do you have any views on that?"

To which Ms Mitchell replied: "I do not have any particular views on that."

Committee member Julia Irwin followed up: "Could you comment on how we manage shared parenting or equal time? What strategies does your organisation feel are needed to assist parents who are in an ongoing conflict to manage shared parenting or equal time?"

To which Ms Mitchell replied: "I think it is very difficult for families that do feature a higher degree of conflict to enter into genuine joint residency arrangements."

The gravel voiced Jenny George asked: "Have you thought about ways in which all of this process might be taken out of the litigious area and having some kind of mediating process before parents avail themselves of the court process?"

The reply: "WIRE is not an expert on family law proceedings."

And so it went.

***

Next up were Ms Belinda Lo and Ms Helen Yandell, both members of the Federation of Community Legal Centres.

Ms Yandell also took little time to get to her point, noting that there were some concerns that the terms of reference themselves were in contravention of Article 31 of the Convention on the Rights of the Child, which required that the best interests of the child be taken into consideration at all times.

"Because the terms of reference of this inquiry refer to a rebuttable presumption, it is that presumption that is actually contrary to the best interests of the child and the best interests of the child would need to be looked at in each case in detail.

"We believe that each child's circumstances are unique and each family's circumstances are unique, and that is what needs to be taken into consideration when there is family breakdown. In 95 percent of cases, family breakdowns are sorted out amicably by agreement between the parties and we believe that right of families to make that determination needs to be maintained. The presumption of shared care of children would remove the right of families to make that determination and we believe that would not be in the best interests of children."

Ms Lo backed her colleague: "It is in the children's best interests that they be provided with stability and security in an otherwise traumatic situation that occurs upon relationship breakdown. In order to ascertain what is in the children's best interests in terms of security and stability, normally the court looks at what the parents' relationship was and roles were prior to the breakdown.

"Because of the way that society is at the moment, mothers generally are considered the primary caregivers. I again reiterate Helen's point that only five percent of marriage breakdowns go to the Family Court and these situations are such that the parties are so conflicted and so divisive that the only way that they can have decisions made in relation to the children is to have a third party's intervention, that being the Family Court."

***

The Committee was hot on the trail of the 95 percent myth almost immediately; with Roger Price asking: "You seem to place a great deal of weight on the Family Court's much touted five percent success rate conforming to international standards of best practice for family courts. As a community legal centre, do you get approached by women – and men, for that matter – who believe they have matters they wish to pursue in the court but for which you do not get funding and have to decline? Is that very many? How does that get caught up in the five percent?"

Then came the following exchange with the future leader of the Liberal Party Peter Dutton and very possibly the future Prime Minister of Australia. Throughout this period Dutton appeared to be knowledgeable of the chaos and duplicity which characterised Australia's family law. His party's subsequent behaviour made this apparent empathy even more perplexing.

Dutton: Can I take you back to a statement that you made – I think I am quoting you correctly – when you said 95 percent of cases were resolved amicably?

Yandell: Yes.

Dutton: Where is the evidence of that, or how do you base that statement? Would it be fair to say, though, that there is a vast number of people, and it could be men or women – I am sure five per cent of people would not be adequate to cover them – who opt out of the legal process because it can go on for up to two years in the Family Court.

Yandell: But that is those five percent.

Dutton: Let me finish. It can cost tens of thousands of dollars and sometimes people believe it is best to quit not whilst they are ahead but before they get any further behind and they really accept a position that they would not otherwise accept, and it is anything but an amicable situation.

Yandell: I would agree with that within that five percent.

Even ultimate Labor loyalist Jenny George weighed in: "I want to query on what basis you make the assumption that, if you do not end up in court, it is all sorted out and things have moved on. I deal with a lot of people where the animosity and the non-resolution of the parents' responsibilities are still very entrenched."

There was however one note of accord. All parties appeared to agree that the adversarial system was an inappropriate way to deal with children.

Ms Lo said: "We are talking about an extremely emotional situation. We are talking – no matter what – about there being no winners or losers; children will be suffering at all times.

"Unfortunately, there are going to be situations where parties are not able to agree, where parties are not able to come to any type of arrangement for the children without the intervention of a third party. That is why, unfortunately, it seems we have the adversarial system for a situation which is probably quite unsuitable for an adversarial system."

***

In Australia much of the conflict post separation is created by the government itself due to the interaction of Family Court orders with the social welfare system. You cannot claim a single parent's pension or payment without Family Court orders, and as a simple matter of financial incentive in a winner takes all system the fight is on. There is zero motive to reach an amicable resolution, and a financial incentive not to do so.

Next up were Ms Alice Bailey, who ran Training, Development and Consultancy for Domestic Violence and Incest Resource Centre and Mr Anthony Kelly, who represented the Men's Referral Service, No to Violence, funded as always by the taxpayer.

If these organisations didn't peddle the government line on violent men they didn't get funding, simple as that. It's a lucrative game they play.

In what was already becoming an established pattern, Ms Bailey said: "In cases of family violence, we are concerned about a presumption of shared residency because children should never have residence with a violent parent and because victims of violence are not in a position to equally negotiate with a violent ex-partner about parenting arrangements."

Amidst frequent, and what critics saw as exaggerated claims of the extent of domestic violence in the community, Ms Bailey went on to say: "Research also shows that perpetrators of violence do use children as tools in the legal process as a means of continuing control over families post separation.

"Litigation as a form of abuse is not only unaffordable for mothers but also very costly to the community.

"All of these issues that impact negatively on children we believe would be exacerbated by a rebuttable presumption of joint residence. This is because a rebuttable presumption creates a climate of acrimony. It will force parents into an adversarial position and therefore place children at a greater risk of violence and abuse."

***

The first of the individual witnesses ended up giving evidence in camera, as his matter was before the courts. Kay Hull said: "I am not prepared to muddy the waters for you, so in the interests of fairness we should not make anything difficult for you or for anyone else."

Both the Family Court and the Child Support Agency made extremely adverse findings against critics of their systems during the course of the inquiry. While the Chair had assured witnesses that they could speak freely, there was no parliamentary protection from decisions of the bodies that were most under investigation.

The issue of vindictive judgements against litigants providing evidence to the Inquiry was raised by the Shared Parenting Council but received little play in the media.

In previous years debate had often been characterised by a prevailing fear of criticising the Family Court for dread of what vindictive action it could take. The fears were well founded, with an established record of the court serving up hostile judgements to its critics. During the course of the inquiry one prominent advocate received a stinging judgement from the court which removed his children from a shared parenting arrangement which had been in place for a number of years and gave custody to the mother – causing enormous distress to the family involved.

The judgement was little more than a sustained character assassination. Around the same period the same judge made a number of attacks on litigants for their involvement in fathers groups.

The Shared Parenting Council of Australia called for immediate legislative action to protect Family Court litigants giving evidence to the House of Representatives Child Custody Inquiry.

"There is a widespread perception that critics of the Family Court, many of whom are publicly giving evidence in the current parliamentary inquiry, have been targeted by the Court in unreasonable custody decisions made against them," President of the SPCA Matilda Bawden said.

"In the Adelaide registry alone, there are numerous court transcripts where repeatedly the fact that a father may have sought help or assistance from a men's information and resource organisation or men's group, is directly being used as a tactic against the father's case and his fitness to continue parenting their children. The Family Court's reaction against litigants, particularly fathers that may have any association or membership of men's or father's help groups, is an appalling application of bias.

"Arguably, litigants before the Court could be frightened to speak out or give evidence to the inquiry for fear of consequence on their children."

***

The very first voice to be raised in support of fathers was Witness Two, whose evidence was significant because it illustrated a shared parenting arrangement where there was no love lost between the parties.

One of the most common arguments against joint custody was that it would not work without cooperation between the parties. Witness Two was to appear in the mainstream press more than two and a half months later in a sensational story in the leading Melbourne tabloid *The Herald Sun* under the headline Divorced Dads Pay To See Their Kids.

The paper reported that a Geelong father gave his ex-wife $10,000 to ensure she signed a court order giving him five days a fortnight with their child.

"Other frustrated dads are paying between $40 and $80 a fortnight in exchange for the honouring of court-ordered contact visits. The money these dads pay is on top of compulsory child support payments.

Family Court Chief Justice Alastair Nicholson described this 'cash for kids' as appalling. "One party should not have to pay the other to make children available," he said.

Witness Two told the inquiry his daughter benefited in a "huge way" by the shared parenting arrangements that were in place: "You were talking before about how children could be transferred in situations that are not amicable. My situation is not amicable. It has not been for a year, but it works very well.

"I have good clear orders and the transfers, in my case, are at the school of my daughter. So she is transferred on a school day. My ex-partner will drop her off and I will pick her up. So we do not have to have detailed or involved contact. As a result, that works very well.

"We both still have the best interests of our daughter at heart. But it is very easy to be coerced when you are stressed and upset into going down a legal path that is detrimental to any future relationship or anything from that point on.

"In my environment, I have realised now that to have five days in my case of time with my daughter is extremely unusual in a shared care environment. It is extremely unusual. I cannot believe that, because to me it works fantastically.

"It is in the best interests of my daughter because she gets time with both parents. She settles in very well. There is less contact. There is less friction, if you like. We do not have any issues. If there were, we could have grandparents who are more than happy to take time with their granddaughter in terms of transfer and things like that.

"It is very distressing to see some parents having very limited time with their children. The grandparents really get very little at all, either, because they are reluctant to take time with their grandchild away from their own son or daughter."

After questioning he reiterated he had residence of the child five nights a fortnight. He said: "It is classified as shared care under the law. To me to have such a block of time in a row – not a night here and a night there – makes the biggest difference.

"I can get involved with her school, with her friends, with her teachers and with what is going on – dropping her off at school, picking her up from school. Doing that with your child means everything to a child. It is routine. You are involved in their day-to-day life as opposed to being just a weekend parent. Although you can provide a lot in a weekend, you can provide a lot more when you can be involved and grandparents and others and family and friends can be involved with school.

"What is the alternative? To have a home where you spend only two days? From my point of view, surely a child sleeping at your house for them is reassuring and for them is part of the day-to-day routine. They get up and who do they see? That parent. It is all about being involved. Most of the people who I have talked to, those who are older as well, tend to say that it is about time. You do not necessarily even have to be totally involved all of the time.

"Kids just love the fact that you are there sometimes. But of course being part of the routine makes it even more beneficial.

"In my case, I would argue with the figure mentioned before in that five percent go to court. I mean, 95 per cent are not successful and are not agreeable even. Many people drop their cases prior to going to court because it just takes too long. That can impact children in a massive way. In my case, I basically paid for more time.

"I would have loved to go to counselling or some sort of agreement where there are practical and realistic means with which to proceed. I did not have that."

***

The third witness, a particularly lucid man, said he appeared as a "father of a wonderful 10-year-old son and as a man who carries with him all of the hopes and dreams that accompany parenthood. Sadly, my expectation of occupying a meaningful place in my son's life has been shattered by the outcome imposed upon my son and me by the Family Court.

"The normal order of the court whereby a non-resident parent is afforded two days contact with their children out of every 14 offers meagre opportunities for that parent to fulfil their crucial role in ensuring that their children develop as happy, healthy and confident members of the community.

"The unique and valuable contribution of grandparents, extended family, friends and significant others also falls victim to the court's normal order. Obviously, it is the group of people surrounding the non-resident parent of whom the children are largely deprived of the benefit.

"The precedent in the Family Court that the resident parent has primacy all too often results in a situation where that parent can dominate aspects of the lives of other family members, often for base motives. Absolute power corrupts absolutely, as they say, and the Family Court seems too ready to vest almost absolute power in the hands of just one of the parents.

"In producing the outcomes that it does, the court frequently cites the need to reduce the deleterious effects of conflict upon children. Whilst not denying the negative impact of that conflict, I believe the court is wrong-headed in its approach, because it can encourage some parents to create an environment of conflict in order to secure an outcome favourable to them.

"The court is thereby fuelling conflict, not lessening it, and this is the fatal flaw in its philosophy."

The witness said he was desperate to have more of a role in the caring of his son and was particularly offended by this concept of a primary carer, a notion invariably used against fathers in the court.

"I do not see that we should be put in boxes, as it were; that one parent should be encouraged to have more of the responsibility for the hands-on care of the child. That certainly is consistent with what my son has said right from a very early stage, that he craves and aches for both of us to look after him, but that has been frustrated to no end in my case."

Repeating the complaints of countless other fathers, he said he was very critical of the Family Court counselling service which he thought was "particularly bad" in respect of the process that was used most recently in his case to produce a family report. The systemic abuse of psychiatric "evidence" by the court is endemic.

"I am, I would have to say, disgusted at the way that took place. It was a very selective report that was produced. It ignored large, prominent parts of my response to the mother's application that was brought before the court. That was pivotal in the outcome. The trial judge placed a lot of emphasis on that family report and I was very disappointed at the selective nature of that report."

Committee member Jenny George asked what reason had been provided to him to deny him extended contact hours so he could take his boy to school on Monday mornings after having moved to be closer to his son.

"On the face of it, I would think that is a terrible thing for the Family Court to do in terms of the principles they are supposed to operate under," Ms George said.

"I was staggered," the father replied.

He also relayed his negative experiences with community legal centres, where he said the women had been more interested in talking him out of taking out a contravention order on his ex-wife rather than listening to him or helping.

***

Then came the community segment where witnesses were encouraged to put their case in a brief three minutes.

First cab off the rank was a family law barrister and mother of three Anna who seemed at odds with the idea of rebuttable joint custody, but at the same time was involved in a shared parenting arrangement herself.

"We do have equal time," she said. "But the basis of our shared parenting befits the nature of our jobs. I am able to work very hard in the week I do not have the children and then devote my sharing and parenting role to the children to a very high degree in the weeks that I do have them. Not many jobs allow you to do that. Things have got to be considered in relation to the practicalities of shared residence.

"I have a certain socioeconomic status. My children have two sets of school uniforms and two sets of casual clothes. We do not have the trauma of packing up the car with everyone's bags. The changeover for my children is extremely clean cut. It is about going to 'our other home'."

Another woman Kerry, who had been a family law solicitor for 15 years, said she understood the frustrations of many people in the court system and had "long felt that it is very unfair, particularly to fathers of children, and I have represented both men and women in the Family Court and the Federal Magistrates Service."

While she raised doubts about rebuttable joint custody she was in a position "where my husband is the primary carer of our five year old and four-month-old baby. When things have been rough in my marriage, I have been more than aware of the situation that I have put myself into as far as I would hate to be in a situation where I was reduced to seeing my children two days out of 14 because I have taken that responsibility for financially supporting my family.

"My husband can parent just as well as I can, if not better. Hopefully we will not ever separate, but I am sure that if we do we would work something out where I spend as much time with my children as I do now and it would not be two days a fortnight."

***

Representative of the many people who were dissatisfied with the operations of the Family Court and the Child Support Agency, Barry said the present presumption was the fathers would get every second weekend and described himself as "a typical example of how the system has been operating for far too long. Personally I have witnessed and resemble what this process creates for families involved and the community in general.

"The children, in particular young boys – and it is well documented – are not getting sufficient male role modelling or bonding whether from the father or even the father's extended family such as uncles, grandparents, cousins and other long-term male role models. How can these brief periods of contact adequately establish and maintain important relationships?"

Max, the father of three children, told the inquiry that at the time of separation his solicitor had told him: "Don't go to the Family Court because you won't get custody of your children. It's just a waste of time. Thankfully I had a truthful solicitor for a change.

"He said, 'It'll cost you about $10,000 to $30,000 to go to the Family Court but you won't get custody so don't bother about it.' I thought that that could not be right and I then attended a Family Court counsellor who basically told me exactly the same thing – it is virtually impossible for a man to get custody of his children. I believe that had we had shared custody in the first place things would have been much easier for us."

He also raised concerns over the way domestic violence issues were being discussed, asking: "Is this just an avenue to get custody of the children?"

Another father, Graham, said he was just one of the thousands, maybe millions, who had been negatively impacted. "I feel that the present presumption in law is a horrible case and it does not help the children. Ask a child and a child will say, 'Half with you; half with mum.' I always had a positive view of the legal system. I thought it was about safety. These days I am extremely disillusioned by it.

"All my ex-wife had to do was just resist and throw a few stories into an affidavit. I am still scratching my head a few years down the track as to why my children just cannot have quality time – just a shared time, for me to be a father.

"We seem to negate the whole purpose of fatherhood. People do not seem to know what a father is today, what the role of a father is. How did we get ourselves into this rotten mess in the first place?"

***

Another father, and another supporter of shared custody, Greg, said he had just spent the previous year in litigation in the Federal Magistrates Court over his five-year-old son, which he had found very expensive and frustrating.

"The welfare report strongly supported my application and heavily criticised the mother. We went to court on that. It was in Geelong with the Federal Magistrates Court. They only come down four times a year and sit for one week. The system is very clogged up. It took me a year to get to court.

"In the end, just back at the beginning of August, they had 100 cases listed for a week. So we asked the magistrate to give us her thoughts on the case, like a preamble so we can negotiate. Because with 100 cases listed there was little chance of us getting to court again. The magistrate, after reading the welfare report which strongly supported my case, said that, no, it would be too disruptive to the child to pick him up on a Thursday night and take him back on a Monday morning. So we ended up with a compromise.

"I cannot see any reason why I cannot spend more time with my son rather than him being in family day care. We live only half an hour apart. All the allegations she made in her affidavits were disproved. I have come to the end of my tether. I do not know where to turn next to obtain more time with my son."

***

With the government industry, with all its solicitors, judges, bureaucrats, academics and domestic violence propagandists giving evidence to the inquiry, all opposed to joint custody, it was the individual tales of devastated fathers which helped balance the equation.

Christos, a single dad, said: "There are no winners here. When things go wrong between two people and there is a child involved, there are no winners, the Family Court cannot help us. The rebuttable joint custody idea I think is a good one because it will take away the slanderous affidavits that so-called once lovers throw at each other. They are mostly lies and hurt the kid – the one we both should really focus on. I do not think we can be helped here.

"I went through the odyssey – like the rest of us. I urge everybody to be kind to each other for that child's sake. The Family Court cannot help you."

A woman known only as Individual A, said she believed the Family Court, Centrelink and child support needed a major overhaul and she sympathised with the fathers who had spoken because "what happened to them happened to me, only I am female".

She said she had been fighting in Family Court and had lost custody of her children. She was particularly upset that she was ordered not to take her children to the doctor except in an emergency, an order commonly made against fathers.

"The joke is that I am living in a country where we are creating a very poor society with poor relationships with our children. They need their mother and they need their father."

It was tales such as this, the same tales these same politicians had heard in their own electoral offices, which had led them to look seriously at gutting the child custody functions of the Family Court. With the cumulative weight of exactly these stories, that was leading inexorably to the conclusion that the Family Court could not be allowed to continue to devastate the lives of parents and children alike.

A second wife and stepmother Jackie spoke movingly of her situation and how it impacted on her and the children. She said the Family Court needed to realise that 50/50 could work and that men "just become resigned to the fact that that is the way that the courts are, that is the way life is and there is not much else they are going to get."

There were other contributions for and against. Many raised issues of child support. Already there had been a kaleidoscope of issues and emotions. And this was just the first hearing on the first day.

***

The House of Representatives Family and Community Affairs Committee then travelled to Melbourne, an hour's drive away, for another public hearing that same afternoon.

It was held at the Hungarian Community Centre in Wantirna, illustrating a deliberate attempt to hold hearings in working class suburbs.

Once again the Committee heard from three organisations, the Youth Affairs Council of Victoria, Australian Family Support Services Association and Australians Against Child Abuse, along with two individuals and an hour of community statements.

Both Ms Georgie Ferrari, Executive Officer and Ms Paula Grogan, Policy Officer spoke on behalf of Youth Affairs Council of Victoria, the peak body for youth issues across the state.

In line with so many other government funded Ms Grogan said: "While we certainly believe that it is preferable for all children and young people to have frequent and positive contact with both parents after separation if that is appropriate, we do recognise that that is sometimes very difficult, given the often acrimonious situations that arise from relationship breakdowns. For this reason we do not support the presumption of joint residence.

"Such a presumption we believe offers a simplistic one size fits all model, and you certainly cannot impose a one size fits all model on the difficult relationship issues that we are talking about here today."

The group got a good grilling from Committee member Cameron Thompson: "You are the Youth Affairs Council of Victoria and you are talking about what is in the best interest of the child. What numbers and what proportion of children are telling you that they do not want to spend 50 per cent of the time with either parent? You are the Youth Affairs Council. How important is this issue to children?

"I am putting to you that if it is that important shouldn't you be able to tell us more emphatically just what children themselves are thinking? Shouldn't it be part of your responsibility to tap into that?"

They were not having an easy time of it.

Committee Member Peter Dutton weighed in: "I understood your evidence to say, at least in part, that we do not need a rebuttable presumption because already in the Act we speak about shared parenting, and that is one of the desires; therefore, we do not need the presumption that we are speaking about.

"For whatever reason, that part of the Act is not working, either because of the costs of court or people saying, 'I'm fed up with this process and I'm opting out' – and I suspect that they are a large proportion of the 95 percent that we were speaking about before. We are saying that, even though it is there in legislation, we acknowledge it is there and you have said that it is there as part of your evidence, it is not coming through in some of the outcomes or the decisions that the court makes."

***

Next up was Mr Joseph Tucci, Chief Executive Officer for Australians Against Child Abuse. This led to the following exchanges between him and Committee Member Roger Price.

Price: With regard to your earlier comments about the Family Court, isn't it a disgrace that it takes so long in the court to get those cases heard? Without wanting to lead you, isn't it the case that at your level both in the Family Court and in the departments we are spread so thinly across so many children and that we need to spend a lot more money on the severe cases?

Tucci: It is disgraceful that children in cases that involve child abuse and family violence have to wait for long periods. It is not unusual for children in those situations to wait four, five or six months, in our experience."

Price: I take issue with one aspect of your submission. You say that a presumption of equal time focuses on parents' rights, rather than on the best interests of the children. As a general proposition, isn't there a presumption that children are going to benefit from both parents? Let us put aside an abusive situation. Why can't equal time be the starting point for those considerations? It does not have to be the template with which you force all situations through, but what is wrong with that as a starting point?

Tucci: The way you have put it, there is nothing wrong with it. You want to leave aside the issue of child abuse and family violence.

***

The first witness in support of shared parenting was Geoffrey Brayshaw of the Australian Family Support Services Association who said the point of his organisation was to give men, in particular, the tools to network and meet other people in similar situations and to work with them through their processes.

"We believe that joint parenting or shared care – whatever you want to call it these days – should be the starting point. As we have heard, there are obviously times when this is not necessarily the right way to go, but the feedback we get from fathers, grandparents and second families, in particular, is that if we start at the middle, with shared care, we can then go either way."

Brayshaw argued particularly strongly against the costs of litigation in the

Family Court, saying: "We heard that only five percent of all marriage breakdowns actually go to litigation. Well, I can tell you that 95 percent of them would love to go to litigation.

"However, they do not have the spare $30,000 in their pockets to do it – and that is both parties."

He was also, like so many others, critical of the child support system and argued for the encouragement of flexible working hours to facilitate shared parenting.

During the community session in Melbourne that late winter day a number of women spoke strongly against a notion of rebuttable joint custody. But just like the fathers who addressed the Committee, they were almost universally unhappy with the operations of the Family Court and the Child Support Agency.

Witness Two, a single mother with a five-year-old boy, was one of the many women who would appear before the inquiry who expressed their utter frustration with "the Family Court thing".

"It is my experience at this point in time that child custody and contact time with both parents are not handled very efficiently, not very effectively, nor truly in the child's best interest," she said.

"It was my belief that the Family Court was set up as a fair and economical way of settling contact issues, and this has not been my experience at all. It has been my experience that this process has been horribly expensive and that lawyers, solicitors and barristers are the only ones to gain from this process.

"I hope that separated parents can learn to replace the hatred, the accusations and the allegations with communication. This is what is missing from the system. The lawyers – the solicitors and the barristers – should not be speaking on our behalf.

"We need to get more mediation and, considering the number of people we are talking about, perhaps a bit of education so that we can get some good old-fashioned values back, starting with communication between the two parents no matter what the ill-feeling is. That is my hope."

***

Fathers also spoke strongly in support of shared parenting and against the present system. Lindsay described himself as a deserted single working father with shared parenting that has been working for six years quite successfully with school transfer Friday nights with before and after care, which a lot of mothers avail themselves of.

"That has given me the opportunity to have a great deal of input into the relationship with my daughter," he said "A lot of sharing, caring, teaching, shepherding, listening, being an advocate when things go wrong at school, spending time together, doing activities together, sharing experiences, laughing together."

Richard, a father of four boys, three from his first marriage and the one from his second marriage just three weeks old, began by saying he wanted to apologise if he sounded venomous. "But I have been distilled through the system and the system creates venom and it creates a lot of heartache and pain, so I do apologise if I come across strongly," he said.

"I am a father who lives in a house 600 metres away from my children. I have flexible work arrangements. I was very involved in bringing up my children. When they were crying at nights, when they were sick, when they needed food, I was the one who got up and still worked a 12-hour day.

"My children have been neglected. They have been to doctors who have said, 'I have never seen medical conditions this bad before.' This is a mother who supposedly loves her children.

"Today's children will be termed the stolen generation of Australia in years to come. My three boys say to me, 'Daddy, why have I been taken away from you? You have put me in jail.' They are in an emotional jail, these children.

"I have three sons – eight, 11 and 13 – and they cannot understand why the system has done this to them when both their parents supposedly loved each other and were good enough at one stage to be parents.

"I am also the victim of unproven claims of physical abuse of my children. They have not been proven. I am a police-checked member of the Scouting Association; I take children away on scout camps. I am a Sunday school teacher. I have never ever physically abused a child. Yet every time some move is made to get more access or to change the access rules this is thrown in my face on a regular basis.

"Sadly, it does not only happen to me; it happens to many, many fathers – not just physical abuse allegations, but sexual abuse too."

The hearing was adjourned at 5.04 pm. It had been a long day. It would be the first of many.

***

The debate was still running strong in the media. Both *The Sydney Morning Herald* and *The Age* in Melbourne ran a feature by Bettina Arndt respectively titled "If courts won't change custody parents should" and "After divorce, kids need both parents".

Arndt, as previously noted, was virtually the only mainstream Australian journalist and commentator who had been consistently supportive of fathers over many years. She had served on the previous Family Law Pathways Advisory Group, and was known to have despaired at the lack of progress from the group's multi-million dollar Out of the Maze report.

She wrote that the chance of shifting attitudes in the Family Court on these matters was slim and a better strategy "is to encourage couples to rethink their own approach to post-divorce parenting.

"Parents should be encouraged to start a different conversation – without ever going near the court – a conversation that might sometimes lead to shared custody or at least children maintaining close relationships with not only their fathers but other key people such as grandparents."

She concluded that the present system resulted in distressed children, particularly young children, missing out on the comfort of attachments vital to their sense of security. She wrote: "We have to find a better way."

TEN
THE WEIGHT OF EVIDENCE: INDIVIDUALS BEFORE THE INQUIRY

It was always going to be an emotion drenched inquiry. The point of all this being that in the 50 years of the Family Law Act the voices, the cries of anguish, the despair, the destruction of individual lives and the consequences for children, are virtually interchangeable. If anything, it has grown worse over time. There is no shame in having a problem. The shame is knowing there is a solution and doing nothing about it. That shame adheres to Australia's politicians, who have done nothing to quench the grief of hundreds of thousands of Australians crushed by this out of control system.

While the government funded domestic violence industry, along with the entire bureaucratic and judicial edifice, all united in their opposition to shared parenting, were very well represented in that historic 2003 inquiry and the media coverage, there was also a solid body of evidence taken from fathers, grandmothers and non-custodial mothers to indicate the sweeping sense of pain and enormous private distress that existed in the community around family breakdown and separation issues. These are the voices either ignored or deliberately suppressed.[111]

The poor reputations of both the Family Court of Australia and the Child Support Agency were clearly on display. The government inquiry, the most

---

[111] All the material referenced in this section can be found on the Australian Parliament House website for the House Standing Committee Family and Community Affairs report Every Picture Tells A Story: Inquiry into child custody arrangements in the event of family separation, including transcripts of the public hearings, tabled on 29 December, 2003.

publicly open and comprehensive of the many inquiries held into family law, heard numerous tales, in some ways similar in some ways very different, right across the country.

The Committee kept up a cracking pace. From the first day in Geelong and then Melbourne it travelled to Launceston in Tasmania and in the following week moved several thousand miles up the east coast, taking in Wollongong, Sydney, the Gold Coast, Brisbane and Cairns. In a second dash mid-way through the inquiry it took in Adelaide, Darwin and Perth and in the final stages of the inquiry it took in three regional locations, Wyong, Coffs Harbour and Gunnedah.

From the beginning there had been an apparent determination to implement change.

In the Launceston hearing, in an exchange with the Tasmanian branch of Relationships Australia, committee member Chris Pearce said: "We have had quite a lot of evidence, and our own practical experience demonstrates to us as members of parliament, that in fact the system is not working very well overall. It is quite clear, in my experience anyway, that we need to make some significant changes."

Committee Member Harry Quick, himself a Tasmanian, chimed in: "We are hearing from the fathers. We are hearing from the mothers. We are hearing from Relationships Australia. I want to see the judges come before us so we can ask them some really important questions because they are, in my mind, one of the contributors to this stupid foul-up."

To which Witness One responded: "From my point of view, I will hold you to that because time is running out with my children. They are growing up and I would like to spend quality time with them, so I will hold you to that."

The emotional swings and roundabouts of the inquiry were also there from the beginning.

Ian Hickman from the Tasmanian Men's Health and Wellbeing Association was particularly intense: "On my way up here today from Hobart, I was just overcome by the emotion of the whole thing. I was thinking, 'I want to say this. I want to tell them that story.' I want them to feel the pain of the children, and of the fathers and the mothers too.

"My contact has been mostly with the fathers. I want them to know that this is an issue right now. No more research. The research is out there. This is an issue right now that needs to be dealt with before we lose too many lives or wreck too many more lives because too many people have already gone under."

Chairwoman Kay Hull concluded that part of the morning with the words: "We really do understand that it is a very difficult and emotional issue."

There would be plenty more tears.

***

One of the first individual witnesses in Tasmania, a school teacher, was cogent in his condemnation of the system: "Even though the law of this nation allows and permits males through the Law – men who have the capacity, I might add, to care equally as well as Mothers – to have dual custody rights, a judge or magistrate in the Family Court, if this decision has to be made by such a person, will not allow dual custody to be a reality for fathers.

"If you are part of that five percent, you often come away badly. But that is unless the father can afford the most expensive lawyer or can prove beyond a shadow of a doubt, and then some, that the mother is an unfit person. This second option only helps to undermine future mother-father and family relationships.

"The adversarial nature of the Family Court is the wrong way to settle such personal disputes. This common knowledge is not just privy to this room. All separated mothers, greedy lawyers, Family Court registrars and Family Court counsellors are also aware of it, thus forcing less well off separating fathers to settle for far less contact than what they or their children would have wished.

"After being a teacher in a low socioeconomic area high school, I can definitely attest to witnessing the problems that teenagers of separated families have. This is especially evident for boys, who suffer from a lack of contact or regular contact with their fathers."

He said of changes ordered in his case by the Family Court: "I cannot tell you the distress it caused to our situation. I could not – you know how I feel, you can see that.

"This caused considerable emotional distress to them, and the adversarial nature of the court caused irreparable damage to myself and the boys' mother. We are three years hence and it still exists.

"The conclusion I came up with as a citizen, a father, a businessman, a teacher, is that I am expected to have and demonstrate an equitable moral point of view to participate in the modern world and especially within Australia. I am just asking this Committee to recommend to the Federal Parliament that this equity point of view be legislated into the Family Court structure. As a male, I feel that I am not equal.

"In the words of my sons, 'Dad, we want to see you and mum fairly.'"

"A clearly moved Julia Irwin said: "I hope that there can be changes made and I am sure when your beautiful boys grow up and you keep a copy of this Hansard, you can say to them, 'Well, kids, I tried to make a difference.'"

Kay Hull wound up by saying it was a difficult hearing for the Committee because each and every one of them had a role as a parent and as a grandparent.

"I think the issues we are confronting are daunting and difficult, and a lot of times it is not made easier by the very difficult circumstances that we hear people are in."

***

The next witness was equally as strong, intelligent and articulate.

She spoke from the perspective of having been the spouse of a weekend contact father for the past five and a half years. In her submission, which related to both the Family Court and the Child Support Agency, she said she talked of the huge financial burden imposed on parents who use the Family Court system.

"In our case, we had no choice but to either give up on contact or fight through the court. Costs and the long delays, which also add to costs, mean the current system of resolving disputes over custody or contact between parents is not proving effective and nor is it available to those people disadvantaged financially or socially...that the current system is inequitable in its treatment of fathers' custody rights and that the court system creates further animosity between parents where they cannot agree by making parents adversarial rather than encouraging negotiation and mediation from the outset.

"If I had not agreed to assist him to pay the legal fees and assist with providing for his child he would not even be able to have contact now.

"Legal Aid was not a possibility as means tests factored my wage into the equation. Our first bill for initial contact arrangements from 1999 to 2001 we have only just paid off, at the rate of $100 a fortnight. I raised the issue of the huge financial burden this has placed on us. We are about to receive a bill for the period going forward from 2001. I encouraged my husband to pursue, perhaps naively at the time, what I saw as his right and his child's right to have a relationship going down the track. At the time I encouraged him I had no idea of the effect this would have on our ability to have a different sort of lifestyle or even to consider a child within our own marriage.

"For many people who do not have this financial or emotional support, to even contemplate court is not an option due to the prohibitive costs. The Child Support Agency does not factor in legal fees as a valid cost associated with contact in its current formulas, and this is a further deterrent for parents choosing the Family Court route."

She said gender inequality was evident in the system and for any father to get beyond the standard contact arrangements to a dual parenting situation required costly litigation for fathers "to prove themselves worthy or, worse, the mothers need to be proved unworthy, causing parents to come into further conflict over the issue of custody contact, rather than there being an expectation of continued dual parenting of the child or children beyond divorce."

Her submission also gave extensive details of the poor administrative processes, errors and poor computer systems of the Child Support Agency, with long delays in getting action, which she said in her case had created confusion and immense distress.

She called for reforms to address these imbalances and to ensure all the structures – the Child Support Agency, the Family Court and all the support mechanisms – were in line with current community values and norms. Hers was important evidence because it demonstrated that many women, often highly articulate in their denunciations, were extremely upset with the status quo. But all the platitudinous rhetoric emanating from the court and its apologists focused on the court as protecting and benefiting women. That was the official line. It wasn't true. For every woman supposedly advantaged by the court, others were damaged. Not to mention that the welfare dependency the Court created in its ideologically nonsensical one-eyed glorification of single mothers was also extremely damaging within itself. A lifetime on welfare in a depressed neighbourhood is no life at all, not for mothers, not for children, not for fathers, not for anyone.

Committee member Jenny George said that as a feminist herself she was interested in how the system was promoting the model of the primary caregiver as a stay at home mum.

To which "Witness Two" replied: "Certainly in our case the presumption all the way through, both in the courts and with the Child Support Agency, has been of the mother as the primary caregiver at home. The reality was that my husband's former wife worked and she earned a lot more money than my husband – three times his salary. That just did not fit into any of the equations where the CSA was coming from and where the court was coming from."

***

First of the community witnesses, confined to three minutes each, was an impassioned father Justin who told the committee he believed every parent had the obligation to care for their children 50 percent of the time, as they were 50 percent parents, which fitted in with what "you guys" were proposing.

He said: "I do not believe that any legal process is needed, unless there is molestation and everything else going on. Why do we need lawyers to figure out the shared proportion of a parent's obligation to care for the child? For me, child support is a punishment on a parent."

Many grandparents across the country spoke passionately to the inquiry. Thus the quip: it's a brave government that ignores the grannies of Australia!

In Launceston Maria said: "I have a question. We have been everywhere, to lawyers and all, trying to get some kind of legal advice on behalf of the grandchild. The girl ran off with him two years ago. We have not seen him since. My son cannot get any help. I do not know who to turn to. We do not know where to turn to. Nobody really gives us any advice. How can we get in contact with him? My son is paying the child support, but he does not know if his son is alive or dead. I really do not know what to do about it."

The previous day in Melbourne a string of grandmothers also gave evidence, already establishing one of the significant themes of the inquiry.

Grandmother and member of Grans Victoria Margaret Moder said: "I can see where grandparents and other family members could be a part of helping this new system to work. We could be there as a backup to both parents. As somebody pointed out, there are four grandparents in most cases.

"We would like to be able to see this system work. I think it would work in being more equitable in the costs involved in rearing children. I think it would reduce a lot of the costs and the need for government personnel to police infrastructures like the CSA to try and retrieve money. I think it would reduce the waiting list times for family law court hearings, because parents would then have to accept the responsibility of the care of their children. That covers all aspects of their care."

The spreading communist inspired restructuring of Australian society and the war on the nuclear family of which the Family Court was such a major player always downplayed or belittled extended families, which were ready, willing and able to help when marriages broke down but almost invariably became collateral damage in the government and lawyer inspired battles for custody which almost inevitable ensued.

What, with a little good will, could have been a negotiated settlement turned into a war zone.

Motivated by money and bitterness, the custodial parent walked away with the family home, income and the kids, the glorified role model of the single mother. It was a disaster. The state makes a very poor parent. And an even poorer guardian.

And being a single parent is not glorious. It's damned hard work. It's ludicrous, this Marxist fuelled war on traditional families so eagerly embraced by the Australian government.

Another grandmother who spoke to the Inquiry, Ann, had two divorced children, including a son who rarely even got to see his kid on Fathers Day. Now that's hurtful.

"Children in marriage and partnerships are the emotional and financial responsibility of both parents," she said. "Both parents should have joint input into their children's lives. Both parents are responsible for their children's care, wellbeing, education, health and upbringing. Both parents have the need and emotion to give their love, affection and time to their children.

"Children need this love, affection, contact, discipline and time from each parent equally. If joint parenting was mandatory at divorce or separation, in most cases all these needs would be met and a huge disruption in lives, as experienced in the current family law custody orders, would hopefully be minimal."

***

The following week in Cairns, thousands of miles to the north, yet another grandmother, known as Witness Three, said: "We have a grandson who is three and a half years old. We love him dearly and he loves us, but we are not allowed by the mother to see him, speak to him on the phone or have any contact with him whatsoever.

"Up until eight months ago we played a very big role in this little boy's life, even up to the point where the mother left him in our care for five days while she went on a trip to Bali. Then one day the mother decided she had had enough of the lifestyle she was living in Cairns and took our grandson away.

"He was taken away from his father – our son. It has taken our son six months to access some rights through the legal system to enable him to see his son. But these rights do not make any allowances for us, as grandparents, to see our grandson. It is quite the contrary. If the mother knew that we were seeing our grandson at the times that his father had access, she would undoubtedly put greater restrictions on the father's access."

Another heartbroken grandmother in Cairns told the story of her son: "Last month he had occasion to take the truck down to Gympie with some horses for somebody that we had sold them to and he was to have two days of access. He had not had access since January or February because of the hospitalisation of the child.

"In the agreement that they have stamped by the court he cannot have him a month either side of major surgery, so he had not had any access. But there is no catch-up mechanism in that for him to make up for the access he lost in the first six months of the year and he begged her for a second lot of two days, giving the child two days rest in between, and she refused.

"She said if he kept pestering her she would bring a domestic violence order against him."

***

In Darwin, midway through the inquiry, a grandfather said: "First of all let me say that, while most people seem to think the Family Court functions very well, it does not function at all.

"Firstly, people tell lies and, while the magistrate says such things as 'If the wife is proven to be telling lies, she will be severely punished', the wife can be proven to be telling lies but there seems to be no punishment for perjury.

"They say to us, 'We would like mummy and daddy back together.' This is not practical, but they would like to see more of daddy."

Weeks later, at Coffs Harbour, Bev Pattenden, co-founder of a group called Grandparents in Distress at Grafton and another activist to appear on Dads On The Air, said her organisation had been founded "after we realised that we were not alone in our anguish over our grandchildren being separated from us and from one of their parents, usually the father – our sons. We felt we were powerless to make changes unless we formed a group.

"We found that we were just part of a system where members of a family had lost their rights and that lawyers, psychologists and the court had taken over the role, causing suffering, hardship, dismay and suicide. We found that mothers now had all the rights and fathers had none until such time as the court decided otherwise, that in most cases the fathers had been pushed aside as being irrelevant and unworthy of fathering their children and that it could cost thousands of dollars to prove their worthiness to be included in the child's life.

"The child support system was enough to cause the non-custodial parent to sometimes live in desperate poverty. We found that the word 'violence' had been twisted to mean even an angry word. After much anguish and research, we found that we were fighting a powerful and secret government authority that had been instigated in the days of the federal Labor government and had not been changed in the days of the Coalition."

She said many grandparents would not speak out for fear of creating further problems.

"As you will have gathered by now, this is a worldwide problem in Western societies and so it is no use trying to correct the problem unless we know how it started, who the actual enemy is and why it continues to this day," she concluded.

"Unless we realise that it is part of social engineering, based on the socialist-communist manifesto to destroy the family unit and religion, we are wasting our time and will bring even further anguish and sorrow upon our society."

***

The evidence of non-custodial parents was also often gut wrenching.

Back in Launceston, where the tapestry of pain continued to gather an undeniable force, one father, Brett, said: "Only recently my little boy came up to me and he said, 'Dad, why didn't you ever want me?'

"I said, 'What do you mean?' He said, 'I've always wanted to come and spend more time with you than every second weekend.'

"I said, 'That's true, and I wanted to spend more time with you.'

He said, 'But now I think it's just good to leave it the way it is.'

I said, 'Why do you think it's good to leave it the way it is?'

He said, 'Because mummy showed me some court orders with your signature on it to say that you never wanted me.'"

A non-custodial mother Jo, amongst the first of a number of powerful speeches by non-custodial mothers, told the committee she let her son's father acquire full custody to allow him a stable life and to avoid bickering, arguing and fighting.

She said of the father: "He has avoided any sort of allowance for me to have contact with him over the years. At every stage he has travelled the country extensively with our child and created for himself a status quo that will allow him to be able to continue to do this throughout the course of our child's adolescent life.

"Currently I have to somehow find the funds just to correct the wrongs. The injustice is that he has 100 percent custody. My child is now 12 years old. Again, as one other person said, he believes that I abandoned him."

Before spending the afternoon taking in camera evidence the Chair Kay Hull thanked the audience and witnesses and described the morning as "an awakening".

"Certainly every day we hear further and further evidence which means that we can perhaps look to having a bipartisan outcome that perhaps can make the position better for the children and for the adults in the children's lives," she said.

***

With a short break for the weekend the Committee resumed the following Monday morning in the traditionally industrial city of Wollongong south of Sydney, Committee member Jenny George's seat.

In the afternoon they travelled to Blacktown in Western Sydney, another working class area.

Once again it was the community statements which provided some of the strongest evidence to the Inquiry of the dysfunctional nature of the system and its destructive impacts on people's lives.

One father, Stephen, reported: "I came to a conclusion with my ex-wife only after we lost a house in legal costs fighting it in the Family Court and then, after four years, they decided to start back at square one and we were both broke. Then we had a mediation session and we sorted it out. I now am a non-custodial parent under the Family Court Act and under the decision of that court, but I am a shared parent: I have two children; my ex-wife has two children. We have alternative weekends. And this was sorted out after we lost everything, after we sat down.

"I was not the one – my ex was told by her lawyer she would get everything. So for four years I fought her to prove that she was not going to get everything. That was between us. Our children suffered. Now our children are better adjusted."

Another father, Dennis, described the Child Support Agency as "harsh and unfair" while John said: "There is a financial inducement because of the amount of support that I have to pay which prevents me from seeing my son on some occasions. I find it absolutely abhorrent that the system is set up in such a way that it can be used to prevent fathers from being able to have contact with their children."

In something of a rarity one father Robert didn't use up his full three minutes. All he said was: "I would like to spend more time with my daughter. Meanwhile, she is stuck in day care because the mother is worried about her pension being reduced and her family payments being reduced. To go through all this she has wasted taxpayers' money through Legal Aid and day care."

One separated mother Barbara, whose ex was a Qantas pilot with an irregular routine, spoke strongly in support of the shared arrangement they had evolved, saying children were very adaptable.

Shelley, who was engaged to a father who paid child support, said they had been in court for a year and a half and spent $30,000 on court and legal fees. She described the process as drawn out and expensive.

"Without the presumption of shared parenting, there is the presumption that both parents are not equally important and not equally capable, which I think is not fair," she said.

The hearing in Wollongong ended with Andrew Thompson, secretary of the Non Custodial Parents Party, saying: "Please, it is very important for our children that we do something about the system. In relation to lawyers, it is a disgrace. Why do we spend $120 million per annum on the Family Court?

"Why do we spend millions of dollars on the Child Support Agency when they do not do their job? I am sure you know that they are not efficient. I have had my wages garnisheed and I have had my tax return taken from me. I have a second family now with three children under eight years of age so I know what it is like from both sides. I have not seen my first two children for the last nine years.

"My oldest boy is 21 and my daughter is 14 and I do not even know what they look like.

"I have done nothing wrong. I have got no criminal convictions whatsoever. I was led astray by my own solicitor and barrister. I took them on as well. You have got lawyers investigating lawyers. You have got barristers investigating barristers. It is an absolute joke.

"I lost $50,000 to $60,000 of money which I did not have. I had to get a mortgage to pay for it. I lost my property outright at the court hearing. I was told to pay for her costs as well. I have done nothing wrong. I am just here for justice for all of us, and we have to do something. Please do something."

To which Kay Hull, in closing, responded: "This is a hugely emotional issue, not just for yourselves but actually for the Committee members as well. We are hearing some significantly difficult issues that we need to come to terms with and be able to understand completely so that we can, hopefully, put forth recommendations that will try and redress the problems that are out there at the moment."

***

By 3pm the Committee was once again facing a crowded room, this time at the Blacktown Civic Centre deep in Sydney's west; once again a working class area where the problems of family law and child support impacted significantly on people's lives.

The first of the individual witnesses was an Aboriginal woman who spoke about domestic violence and read the committee a poem: "If a child lives with acceptance and friendship, He learns to find love in the world."

Witness Two, a registered nurse, argued for mediation and said: "Sometimes ordinary people can strive to do extraordinary things."

Witness Three was a psychologist and researcher at the University of Western Sydney with an academic interest in the area. He said his own shared parenting arrangement had worked well for his children but he was concerned about the lack of shared parenting in Australia, given the social changes of the past 30 years.

He said his own ex partner, also a psychologist, only agreed to a trial run of shared parenting 12 years ago because he was threatening to drag the matter through the courts.

"At the end of that year she was satisfied that it was good for her, too. She was also interested in her career. That was one of the things, during that year, which really helped her to realise, 'Hey, wait a minute. I've got some freedom.

"I can look after my career interests now, too. I don't have to try to juggle everything. I've got someone I can call on if I am sick, when I have special times or when I have to go to meetings.' All those things became clear for her in that intervening year of the trial and at the end of that year she said, 'Fine.'"

He said if separating couples were obliged to enter shared parenting trials for a year "a lot of them would realise that it is not only for the benefit of their children but for their own benefit to do that."

"The experience of fathering for me has been very powerful in my life," he said. "If I had been deprived of that experience it would have been a terrible loss. I only know about it because I have been through it. I would never have known about it otherwise.

"Looking back, 12 years ago, if I had gone to the Family Court I would have lost. I would not have had my kids; that is very clear. I know too many dads – and they were good dads – who did end up in the Family Court and did lose; they lost the opportunity to have the sort of input into their children's lives that I was lucky enough to have."

***

Fathers were particularly strongly represented among the community witnesses at Blacktown. These parts of the hearings were inevitably intense.

One father, Ryan, said he was the primary carer of his daughter before she was abducted to the United States by her mother more than two years before and pleaded with the committee to introduce not just a rebuttable presumption of joint custody but to ensure that such abductions could not take place.

"I have slept little since my daughter's abduction. I have not been to bed since, waiting every night for the phone to ring. I do not know anything about my daughter. I do not know whether she is well. I do not even know what she looks like. I spent over two years fighting to get this matter into the Family Court of Australia, whilst my now ex-wife is allowed to frustrate the process. The Hague Convention does not work."

Dr Monaem, who had two daughters aged ten and six years old, said as a Muslim man and an ethnic person he was fearful of the court system. He said since his wife left three months previously he had been allowed to see the children for only a couple of hours a week.

"My problem is, as an ethnic father, should I go to the Court? As I have heard from so many people around here, I am very sceptical about family courts – whether I can get a proper hearing. Coming from an ethnic background and also as a Muslim person, I am more sceptical. In a way, I am very scared of the current political situation: how will my case be heard in the court?

"I understand from various sources that my wife is preparing something for court so that I can be demonised as a bad Muslim, as a violent Muslim man. That really scares me to go to the court. Before the separation, I calculated that I spent about 60 percent of the kids' time going to the school, piano lessons, swimming lessons – all of this – but now I can only see them for a few hours a week."

One divorced father, Mr B, condemned the court as an adversarial environment without "the best interests of the children at heart" while another from the Lone Fathers Association in Newcastle said he went through "a very nasty, savage and brutal hearing" to get access to his three daughters aged eight, six and four. He said after a spate of false accusations he had not seen them for two years, "so the four-year-old will not remember me".

Another father, Robert, said his strong attachment to his children was ignored by the Court. "I found that the words 'the best interests of the children' were mentioned in nearly every single page in my hearing, whereas nothing whatsoever in the hearing was to do with the best interests of my children."

***

Not for the first time, and certainly not the last, one of the most powerful speakers was a grandmother Rhonda, whose son, a high profile advocate of joint custody, had, during the course of the inquiry, just had an extremely negative judgement in the Family Court, losing the shared parenting arrangement that had been in place for three years.

The government had done nothing to protect the children and parents from the institutions they were criticising during the Inquiry.

She said after her two grandchildren had been abducted into a cult by their mother it had taken a great deal of money and effort to try and get some normality for the two children involved, costing more than $50,000 to get a shared parenting arrangement in place.

"I had to sell my house as my son could not afford litigation," she said. "This resulted in a shared parenting order for my grandchildren, which was working well for the children for about three years.

"Unhappy with lack of control of the children and her ex partner – my son – the mother filed a further application for sole residency. At the directions hearing my son was refused to allow bringing evidence of the mother's previous conduct of abducting the children and her involvement in the cult. Subsequently the court went ahead with no evidence of material harm to the children by the current shared care arrangement.

"The Family Court subsequently sided with the mother and criticised my son for his desire to stay at home and parent his children. All evidence brought by my son was completely ignored, notwithstanding the children were thriving under the current arrangement.

"Last Friday the Family Court in Adelaide took the children from my son and they have now exposed my grandchildren to further psychological and emotional harm by disrupting a well-established, equal and fair residential arrangement.

"The Family Court takes little or no consideration of the permanent harm caused to children by having their relationship with one of their parents terminated. The Family Court has demonstrated, in my son's case, its absolute opposition to shared parenting."

The hearings adjourned at 6.25 pm. It had been another long day.

***

The next day *The Illawarra Mercury* carried the story on page eight with the headline "Parents plea for custody fairness".

The paper quoted Committee Chair Kay Hull as saying: "Primarily what we're seeing is a cross-section of issues – dads who are paying child support and who don't appear to be getting contact with their children, and mums who are in the same position. There is strong concern that the cost of family law and the cost of fighting for your rights is just so almost insurmountable that they don't have a choice."

The Daily Telegraph also reported Hull saying they wanted to remove the law and adversarial focus from the process as much as possible. She floated the idea of children having their own legal representation. The idea ignored the very poor if not appalling reputation of those already practising this craft.

By Thursday of the same week the Committee would travel to Queensland, first to the Gold Coast and then on to Brisbane.

Witness One, a divorced father of two, said the whole point about 50-50 contact is that it is fair: "It is fair for the father, the mother, the children and the extended family. The public – those who are not involved in divorce or have not been touched by it – do believe that the present system is fair. Only when they enter a divorce or are touched by this do they realise how unfair the present system is.

"The Australian ethos is based on fair play. This is what the public expect and this is what they want. It will empower him to be more financially responsible. It will also allow him to be practically involved in the day-to-day care and upbringing of the children. The education system is continually crying out for more male influence in the system. This will also encourage him to be included and valued in and throughout the schooling life of the children. This sort of parenting will also allow a balance of religious views to be imparted to the children from both the mother and father.

"The mother will also benefit from a 50-50 parenting arrangement as she will be given more time to better establish herself in the workforce. She will also be allowed to share the pressures of single parenthood with the father."

Committee member Julia Irwin stated: "For that to work you would have to be close to their schools and their sporting activities, for example."

To which he replied: "Bring it on. I am living here. I am staying close. I am doing everything I possibly can to be close. I am stopping promotion. I am not moving back to Sydney. I am doing everything I possibly can to be there. We want to make those decisions. We want to live close.

"We want to deny ourselves climbing the corporate ladder to be with our family and kids. That is what we want.

"I spent $100,000 to get every second weekend. I could have walked in off the street, put my hand up and said, 'I am the father,' and I would have got every second weekend."

**

Witness two, a father of four children aged 24, 14, 12 and 10 said: "All the wake-up calls that have been given to anybody have never been taken notice of by any political party, by any committee or by anyone in the Family Court. You people have the chance to make a very fundamental statement – not for the next few years, not as an experiment. You have to look at the principle involved here, and that principle has to be enshrined so that it will stand the test of time, forever.

"The Family Court, with respect, have failed in their application of the Act of the 70s. There is no performance criterion that can be used that says they have been successful.

"They have failed and you have got to accept that. If you do not accept that, the solution that is going to come out of this will not be a good one for the future of our children. You have got to attack that legislation and ask, 'What is right for the children?' What is right for the children is an equal right of parenting for those kids by the mother, the father or whomever – an equal right to both of the parents for the children. How that is worked out and drafted I do not know…but I know it was not drafted properly in the first place."

Witness Two said he had avoided the Family Court "because it was a fruitless, pointless, prescribed route".

In response to questioning he said he believed the Court should be opened up to greater public scrutiny. "You need only to go into that temple in Brisbane to see that it is not a family court – that is a shrine of intimidation. It is a venue that is not family orientated. It is not user-friendly. It is a very frightening experience to go into those so-called hallowed chambers and people are not friendly – everybody. It is not a family court. I find it to be misnamed.

"I agree that they have to open it up. It has to be made accountable; it has to be open and transparent."

It was here that committee member and future Opposition leader Peter Dutton gave the clearest exposition yet of the idea of a tribunal to replace the Family Court, a window into the evolving thinking of the committee.

It was an idea that once understood by the media would go on to make repeated headlines.

"One of the suggestions that has been made is that we should take this whole matter out of the Family Court, that we should exclude lawyers from the process and that we should have people speaking to each other through mediation. One of the suggestions, as I say, that has been made is that we set up a tribunal where we have, say, a three person panel that people deal with – it might be a child psychologist, somebody who is a trained mediator and somebody who might have a legal background."

At one point the Chair asked of one of the apologists for the status quo: "My question is: if people legitimately believed that the odds were not stacked against them – for various reasons the perception certainly is that the odds are stacked against people in the family law courts – and they knew they did not have to go through the huge cost and the trauma of going there, don't you think that would take some of the angst, anger and aggression out of the whole debate?"

***

As always, in Queensland the community statements provided some of the strongest material. One of the novelties of this inquiry was that the material was all available on the internet within days.

John said: "I am here today because I feel that my role as a father has been trivialised and nebulised by the current laws and the family courts. I feel that both boys and girls need a father in their lives. From birth to the age of two, I was denied contact with my daughter by her mother.

"After paying to go to the family courts, they said I could have contact for four hours a week under supervision of the mother, because she was bonded with her mother. How she was supposed to bond with me if I had not seen her, I am not sure.

"For two years, I had contact with my daughter on the driveway in fine weather and in a rubbish bin enclosure when it rained. When I asked for a cuddle from my daughter she said, 'Mummy said no.'"

One working mother, Jennifer, whose former husband did not work, had waged a long legal battle for shared care. "I was forced back to work because my husband lost his job and as I have no other way of supporting my son and myself," she said. "If I had thrown myself on the mercy of the social welfare system, my position in the family law court would have been entirely different.

"Working parents, whether they are mothers or fathers, are extremely disadvantaged under the current Family Law Act."

Too true. Australia's family law system encourages welfare dependency and provides the legal lynchpin and moral justification for a bureaucratic monolith supporting single parents. All done at the expense of people who do get up and go to work, one of the many inequities built into and now entrenched within Australian society.

Echoing the concerns of many fathers, Jennifer said: "No mother can establish a relationship with her child, particularly with one as young as my son, every second weekend. This would not allow me to be a mother to him, to play with him, to bath him or to have any sort of meaningful input into his life."

She said fortunately her family had provided sufficient financial support to obtain an interim order for shared care, which her husband continued to resist, and the next round in the Family Court was expected to cost in excess of $20,000.

"While it is clear that shared care will not work in every case, it is the best starting point to negotiate a fair and equitable outcome for children," she said. "Currently family law court mediators do not even consider shared care as an option."

***

The evidence continued to mount.

In Cairns, a week after the Committee had begun its sweep up the eastern seaboard, Witness One declared: "In my situation I worked the hours and made the money by mutual agreement and my ex-wife stayed home. When it came to the separation and the court proceedings, I was told that I had no chance of even going for custody of the children because she spent most of the time with the children. Therefore, she was most likely going to get the children. That is what happened in my case.

"If we have joint custody, I believe that this will certainly ease the pain of children upon separation. It certainly will ease the pain of the parents and grandparents. Hopefully, it might even make people try to work their marriage out a little bit better before they do separate. I believe that it will decrease any suicidal risks or suicidal thoughts that pop into people's heads upon separation.

"Grandparents play a big part in the children's lives before separation so I believe they should play a great part post separation, and that is on both sides of the family."

Witness Four was one of a number of concerned citizens without a personal grievance who made representation to the committee. He was expressing concern over a workmate: "I have seen what it has done to him and how it has affected his health. He is absolutely financially destitute and he is on the verge of selling his house. The Family Court does not care – it says, 'Sell your car as well, as long as she is getting her payment'.

"I have seen what it is doing to his life and what a mess it is making of him. His health has suffered and he has got to the stage where he is passing blood. He is just a nervous wreck. Something has to be done. He does not know where to turn for help."

Mr Pearson, 26, said he was about to go to court to fight for access to his son, "but the thing that pushes me away is that it is going to cost me thousands. I am going to send myself bankrupt in order to see my child."

James said emotional and spiritual support were difficult for a non-residential parent to offer "when courts, agencies, society in general and ex-spouses, male or female, insist on using children as pawns in a game of revenge, which is never conducive to helping the child achieve their full potential.

"Emotional support is difficult to offer when these external influences insist on depleting the non-residential parent's finances – and, ultimately, their esteem and chances of recovering and bettering themselves.

"Often when separation occurs, to avoid rocking the boat, non-residential parents will forgo their legal status and rights with regard to contact. Finances are often settled to their detriment, they are emotionally distraught from loss of contact with their beloved offspring and they have few avenues open to them to address the trauma and grief. The emotional issues are compounded by the insistent pressures of financial stress.

"Without any doubt in my mind, the ultimate twin losses are the non-residential parent's inability to live their own life properly, prosperously and fully and the children's lack of much-needed and desired stable emotional support from the non-residential parent."

Another father, Mr A, described his expensive court proceedings as absolute madness and the results devastating.

"At my son's first birthday, I would get 12 hours contact per week and, at 18 months of age, I would get 16 hours per week. In January 2004, when my son is two, he will get his first night with dad. At two and a half years of age he will get alternate weekends with his dad and at five years of age he will spend half the school holidays with me. At no stage is shared residency implemented.

"The mother immediately swore, 'You will never have him overnight and I will gather as much evidence as is necessary and spend every last cent to ensure that.'"

The Cairns session ended on yet another highly emotional note with a father of an eight-year-old girl presently in a 50/50 shared parenting situation speaking of his fears of the situation breaking down and having to go to a court he could not afford.

"To date I have spent about $15,000. Where I am going to find the money for the rest of it, if I have to go to court, I don't know. I don't know if I will be able to. If I can't find the money, I guess I will just have to walk away. The only way I can get her mother to budge is to do it through the Court with the order of a judge.

"They talk about a child's best interest. We have a little girl here, who is eight years old, who wants to see her mum and her dad. In a lot of ways it appears that no-one is really listening to what she wants. I just hope at the end of the day we end up with a system that is more workable, that makes things more equitable for all members of the family – not just one person.

"If you did put some sort of arbitration system in place, it could achieve more results, rather than put families through a mediation system that often does not work or through a family court system that no-one can afford and where the money spent could better be spent in the interests of the child."

***

After a hiatus of ten days the "industry" in the form of the Attorney General's Department, followed by the Department of Family and Community Services and the Child Support Agency, faced their first grillings at a committee room in Parliament House in the heart of the nation's capital, a room the bureaucrats no doubt learnt to dread. The role of these agencies in the present debacle was under intense scrutiny.

The starting time of 8.30am was indicative of a committee which meant business.

Nine days later the Committee was once again clocking up thousands of miles of air travel as it moved in successive days from Adelaide to Darwin to Perth.

As with other locations, some of the most powerful and damning evidence the committee took was from individuals.

In Adelaide the atmosphere was already heightened with the appearance of a bristly Elspeth McInnes from the National Council of Single Mothers and their ideological opposites, the Joint Parenting Organisation and the Shared Parenting Council of Australia. While most people were arguing for a rebuttable presumption of joint custody, McInnes was arguing for a rebuttable presumption of no contact in cases of domestic violence.

Once again, too, it was the volatile Tasmanian Labor man Harry Quick who provided some lively exchanges. In grilling yet another representative from the domestic violence industry Quick commented: "The 'best interests of the children' is bandied about at will. How do you do that in an adversarial setting where Family Court lawyers are reaping in money hand over fist and not having anything to do with the interests of the child – just their own self-interest?"

He went on to declare "This whole issue of separation, family payments and child support and the Family Court is a bit like cancer or AIDS – if it does not affect you, you do not want to know about it."

In Darwin Quick compared the system to a sausage machine where "the lawyers are reaping untold wealth and there is this adversarial, dog-eat-dog situation."

It was also here that Quick quizzed "Witness Two" as follows: "We hear 'in the best interests of the child' bandied about ad nauseam. If we got your son here and said to him, 'How do you feel about the shared care arrangement?' what do you think he would say?

"Witness Two – I asked him that question and he said, 'It's good.' He likes it as it is and he said that – in his words – he gets to go fishing twice as much."

It was here, too, that the notion of a tribunal was once more enunciated: "Some of us are of the view that before it gets to that, before you start spending some money, there ought to be some sort of tribunal where parenting plans are put forward and all the people involved in the children's best interests are somehow coerced or forced to sit down and work out a parenting plan in the best interests of the children."

It was also in Darwin, in yet another exchange with the domestic violence industry, that Chair Kay Hull quizzed a representative as to why a father that had been prepared to spend $180,000 in the Family Court should not be allowed to share the care of his child.

To the by now familiar arguments from the industry that there would need to be good communication between the parties Hull pointed out that "the majority of individuals who have come before us who have shared care have basically no relationship – they are unable to get on with each other as individuals – but they still have a successful shared care relationship. That has been the norm in the individuals who have come before us who have shared care."

***

Back in Adelaide, the torrent began with Witness One: "At no time has the system taken into account the care I have given to my child or the relationship I have with my child... I am of the view that the current system has developed a culture where it encourages further disharmony between parties, in particular where children are involved, from lawyers who inflame already emotional situations – I believe so that they can earn more fees – to the Family Court itself.

"All I ever wanted to know was that my child was going to have the best upbringing that she could receive and that I would play a part in it. I am of the opinion that the system fails to ensure that this happens.

"Everyone who has been involved with the Family Court or the Child Support Agency has had a painful experience. The system simply must change, as it does not work."

Like many another, Witness Two condemned the Child Support Agency.

"I work a lot of hours and it is very annoying on a Sunday when you know you are only getting 24 cents of your dollar," he said before the following exchange between him and committee member Chris Pearce.

"Do you think that your former wife would say to you that that is too much?"

"She has said it. She laughs about it."

"She laughs about it?"

"Yes."

***

Later in the day another father, Martin, said men were killing themselves daily and if it had been women there would have been an inquiry years ago. He said the Child Support Agency "does drive you nuts." I pay 80 percent gross income, I pay for their sports, full doctors and medication, full rent, rego and movies, but nothing is taken into account by the CSA.

"All the while my ex-wife is sitting home, having a beer, watching Foxtel with her pension card with all discounted, subsidised fees."

In Perth one of the major witnesses spoke passionately against the CSA. He was particularly incensed by the word "their" in the organisation's logo "Helping Parents Manage Their Responsibilities".

"It is only to be wondered at, what sort of person works for the CSA? Everyone

– all the despots in the world – needs someone to back them up in order to support their regimes. How can this exist in Australia in 2003?

"I have a stack of letters to the editor there, with people complaining about it. Everyone can read these things, including Labor politicians, but what has been done about it? Isn't that the reason we are here, so that something is done?"

Like others, penalty payments were imposed the moment a person falls behind, also incensed him.

"I have a friend in Kalgoorlie whom I spoke to just yesterday. He owes $1,000 in penalty payments. Where do these go to? How come we cannot find out? It seems to have little consequence that the child is not being looked after, as long as this person pays that penalty first.

"Why is it that I cannot find out whether my child exists? Why is it my responsibility to find this out at my expense? Why is there no-one to turn to in this country?"

In finishing up, Kay Hull asked Witness Four: "So primarily it would be a distance factor that would prevent you from seeking to go to court to get some contact with your daughter?"

To which he replied, "I am reluctant to do that. Why should you have to go to court to have access to your flesh and blood? Why should this be?"

***

In Adelaide one child of divorce, Chantel, described the consequences of sole custody after her mother made false allegations of abuse against both her father and her paternal grandparents. As a consequence she did not see them for 10 years.

She said although the accusations of abuse were proved to be false "when my mum went to court for sole custody, she still won due to the fact that she accused my father of being abusive. Little did I know that it was shown in court that my mum was the abusive one and he was just defending himself and me.

"Part of the reason the court said to my father and his family that he could not see me was because I said so, but little did they know that the reason I said the things I did was because of my mother and what was going on behind closed doors.

"For the 10 years that I was living with my mother, I do not recall one week that my mother did not pressure me into talking to her and listening to my so-called sexual abuse story.

"I have lived 10 years of hell and have been deprived of a childhood with a family that loves me – which I now know – and had to live a life full of lies and pain. If it had not been for my father keeping the papers in the hope that I would one day return, I would never have known the truth and would not have had the chance to finally be with my family. My case was also the longest Family Court case in South Australia, to my knowledge.

"It went for 54 days; not to mention the amount of taxpayers' money that was spent on my case, money that could have been spent on a case based on truth rather than on a case full of lies; not to mention the money that my family spent fighting for me – money which they needed to survive.

"Once the case was over, that was it. No-one checked up whether I was okay. Nothing ever happened. I was just alone with my mum for 10 years."

***

Amplifying the theme of false sexual abuse allegations, in the Adelaide community session Stephen said: "I would like to tell you that in no way, in no arena – whether it is the Family Court or the child welfare agencies or the Youth Court – dealing with the best interests of the child, is there any way in which a person accused of any type of child abuse, particularly sex abuse, can demonstrate their innocence.

"In my case, my children were removed and my case went from the Family Court to the Youth Court, because my children were then in foster care. I had to represent myself but all other parties had their representation paid for by the state government."

He recorded that on the first day of the trial "the barrister supposedly representing the children stood up and said, 'I object to the return of any child to this man on the grounds that he's never admitted to anything he's been accused of'.

"I have not seen my son now for two years and I have not seen my daughter for three years."

Other witnesses came forward. Mark said he went to jail for 42 days after false domestic violence accusations were made against him.

He said his cellmate was known as the Samurai sword killer and other inmates were laughing at him for simply being there on a domestic violence order.

"There were people in there wanting to go over and get my wife fixed up," he said. "Can you tell me how jail helped anybody in any way in that case?

"I have been the subject of several police raids. They have raided me for drugs, which they have never found; they have raided my parents' house for drugs, which they have never found. They even raided their own police force up at Aldinga looking for drugs that they never found, all on the accusations of my ex-wife."

Mark said he was charged with 37 different domestic violence orders and found guilty on two. "Those two were me writing a love letter and the other one a poem. The gist of the matter is now that I have not seen my children in two and a half years; my wife has a $400,000 house on the esplanade at Silver Sands; she has my grandfather's stamp collection and my stamp collection.

"Everything I have ever owned since I was a child, she has. She had no house, she had no car, she had nothing when we entered the relationship, yet she moved away with everything. I was left with a 1992 Honda and $8,500 after 14 years.

"Where has the Family Court helped me in any way, shape or form as a male? It is not necessarily male against female, but I have not seen my children in those two and a half years. What about their rights to see me? They have no rights. You have a woman making up any bullshit under the sun and getting away with it.

"She had me locked up, with no evidence, no proof, nothing at all and I spent 42 days in Yatala. I had to spend 42 days covering my rear end. That was the most horrible thing about that place. I doubt whether any of you have ever been in that situation."

***

Pauline, a grandmother who says she was falsely charged with sexual abuse of her granddaughter, said there was no evidence to support the claim but the child had suffered enormously through repeated interviews and internal examinations while she and her husband had been targeted at work.

"There was no checking up," she said. "There was no communication between the Family Court and the criminal courts. Hearsay evidence was taken as being true evidence.

"Hearsay evidence from the mother was quoted as being from the child. Perjury and collusion were also involved; perjury with the mother saying that I had committed these offences and collusion when friends of hers said the same thing.

"Witnesses were never told at the end of the trial that we were cleared by the judge in the Family Court. They still believe that we are sexual abusers. My mother and my brother have not spoken to me for 13 years, because they believe I am a sexual abuser."

In Wyong another grandmother, Rosemary, said they had been subject to Apprehended Violence Orders being handed out willy-nilly.

"Our son has had it done to him," she said. "It is a horrible thing, isn't it? It is a horrible thing to have put on you when it is absolutely false. She pleaded with the committee to "get to the bottom of all these matters, because there is a terrible lot of injustice. Men are just as loving as women. There are some loving men out here, and grandparents as well."

In Perth yet another father said the current situation in the Family Court was that an allegation was almost as good as a conviction.

"Allegations are made at a very strategic point during proceedings," he said. "It is never investigated, it is never disproved and it immediately works.

"Many people, once they are issued with a restraining order, wonder: 'What's happened? I've been a responsible citizen. I've never been in trouble with the law. Suddenly, a restraining order presumes that I am guilty.'

"The restraining order is heard ex parte. The husband does not know about the proceedings until he is served with a restraining order. He is immediately judged guilty until he can prove himself innocent – if he can. It is a reversed onus of proof, and it may be three or four months before the ex parte restraining order is heard in court."

He said there was a very high level of strategic use of restraining orders within the context of family law proceedings.

"The reason that restraining orders are so successful is that they need to alienate contact with one parent," he said. "It bumps up the property percentage. That, to my mind, is the saddest condemnation of our family law system as it stands."

The words corrupt, criminal and hypocritical were used to describe the family law system on a number of occasions.

And rightly so.

***

One father, Dennis, said: "As far as I am concerned, based on my experiences over the years with the Family Law Act and the people involved – including politicians, certainly the police force and others – I regard it as a corrupt faggot-ridden system and it has been that way for a very long time."

Not very politically correct, but there you have it. No journalist has ever pursued the frequent accusation that the Family Court is essentially a gay cabal, an impolite explanation for its perceived anti-family ethos, a conspiracy theory if you will.

In Darwin the next day a Mr Kennedy talked of the "corrupted role taken by the Family Court of Australia".

"I know of a father who had 42 percent contact with his child after separation. They had a private agreement. The mother was sleeping over with the boyfriend and sandwiching the other child in with his children, and he did not like that.

It does not sound satisfactory. One of the days of the week she was putting the kid in a creche. He went to the court to ask if he could have that extra day and the extra night.

"The Federal Magistrate, without argument from the other side, said, 'You're going to get the fathers package,' and he was cut back to 19 per cent.

"So the child spends another day and God knows how many more nights sardined in with other kids.

"To me that is absolutely corrupt. They say it in the child's best interests; that is not in the child's best interests."

He said the court, by routinely placing the child in the statistically most dangerous environment of single mother households, was "corrupt and hypocritical".

***

In Adelaide a string of aggrieved fathers told of their disgust and horror at the present system.

Witness "Peter 1" described a common scenario of coming home to find his wife had left and taken their young children, leaving a note to say they had been taken away.

"She played hide and seek with the children for several weeks, denying me contact. I sought legal advice. Her lawyer never got back to us, prevaricated and it was only in the week before it finally got to court for an interim hearing that I was granted two hours access to my children.

"I say to the Committee that the experience of having one's children taken and kept away from you and being legally unable to do anything about it is extremely distressing. I would not wish that upon anyone and I can understand why there is a high suicide rate in these situations."

Reflecting broad dissatisfaction with the court processes, he said: "When it finally got to court the system seemed to rely a lot on affidavits. It appears to me that one can write anything they like in an affidavit, sign their name to it and it is considered to be fact.

"The judge or magistrate, who had supposedly read these lengthy documents, did not even know the basic details of the children's names and ages. He struggled to do some very basic calculations determining my capacity to pay child support and spousal maintenance. His opening statement to my solicitor when he was responding to my wife's offer of one night per week was, 'Well, that's a pretty reasonable offer, isn't it?'"

He was left paying $554 per week in child support plus $60 spousal maintenance and got to keep about 20c in every dollar that he earnt after tax and payments.

"I was successful in my work. I have now lost most of my possessions. I am back home, living with my family like a monk.

"My experience of the system has left me quite appalled by how it operates and I would urge you very strongly to do something to give fathers a fair go."

***

Roy, an RAAF officer and one of a number of servicemen and women who feel poorly served by the system, recorded: "I have been in the system for four years. There are a lot of familiar faces here. It is a tragic venue to make acquaintances. I have paid $80,000 over this divorce and subsequent custody issues. It is not just about the legal fees; there is so much more involved there. I pay $900 a month for my daughter, who I never get to see because the court has allowed her to go to Canada on orders that they cannot enforce.

"I fought to keep my daughter in Australia so that we could see each other because it is beneficial for her and both parents. The judge basically said, 'You're wasting my time. You'll lose. She goes to Canada. I'm loading you with $5,000 for the court costs because you're wasting my time,' and he would not allow me to see my daughter who was leaving the following week.

"The court system rewards the best storyteller regardless of truth or lies, as we have heard here today. I reiterate that. By lying in the court the custodial parent ensures that they are going to get financial benefits in most cases and definitely access to the child more than the non-custodial parent.

"Clearly I have to say divorce is not a crime. There is no way in hell I should have been treated like a criminal. The punishment obviously is the loss of my daughter. Nothing I say here today is going to get my daughter back into the country, so I have no obligation to be here. I am doing this because I do not want to see anybody else suffer."

In Darwin another serviceman father, Brett, said he was paying for two children he loved dearly, one of whom was not biologically his, but his ex-wife "stops me from seeing my children at whatever opportunity she can, even telephone contact. I have my court orders here, which is the 80-20 that I am really happy with – not! So it is a bit of a farce.

"There are that many loopholes in the court orders that she gets away with, and she knows that I cannot take her back to court because of the money that I am earning. I cannot do it by myself."

Another witness, Tony 1, said he ran a children's program in Palmerston for children between the ages of five and 15. "Particularly in Palmerston, one of the things we do during the program is ask the children, 'What would you like to pray for?' Week after week the children's hands would leap up and they would almost dislocate their arms to say, 'We want daddy back. We want daddy back.'"

"The problems we see in our youth come back to the family. I guarantee you that if this fifty-fifty comes in there will be a lot of happy children and they will not be saying, 'We want daddy back,' because they will have daddy back. That is half the problem: the children are angry, hurt and bitter inside.

"They know the lying that has gone on; they know who is abusing whom and they are carrying a lot of hurtful secrets in their hearts. That is what is happening, and if you can bring this fifty-fifty in, it will relieve an enormous amount of pressure in the children."

***

Fathers groups, with the existence of Men's Confraternity, Reliable Parents, Dads Landing Pad, Ozy Dads and others, had always been a strong and lively outpost of the fathers movement.

Brett, a representative of one fathers' group, said the current system did not work.

"In our experience, we have found that the majority of the people that approach come to us having approached lawyers and sought legal advice.

"They have been told that seeking shared parenting is a fruitless exercise. They have been told that the only way they can achieve any reasonable amount of contact with their children is to show that the other parent is somehow deficient. This is the crux of the problem with the current system. It makes the system adversarial and it makes it so that the parties must fight each other – and the problem with this is that the children are the ones that lose."

He was also upset over the use of the man's breadwinner status.

"I think it is disastrous that the honourable sacrifice that a man makes in choosing to go out and work to provide for his partner and children can then be used against him in the event of separation so that he cannot continue to have a proper relationship with his children," he said.

There was a string of grievances over the court processes. Also in Darwin, Kevin said: "In the time that I have been representing myself, I have noticed there are more and more men representing themselves. The women have lawyers, because they get Legal Aid as they do not work. The men have jobs – most of the time – or have assets, so they do not get Legal Aid. So we are behind the eight ball right from the start."

***

Just as the internet had transformed the fatherhood debate around the world, it was clear at points in the inquiry that a number of the witnesses determined to give evidence in the community sections were well up to date with recent research and trends.

Dave noted that it was soon to be the internationally promoted Equal Parents Week, and dismissed the opposition to joint custody of the Family Law Practitioners Association and the Family Law Foundation as commercially based. He said: "There are irrefutable reasons demonstrating the need for rebuttable presumption of shared parenting and a complete modernisation in family law reform.

"Statistical research confirms an incredibly baneful social trend for children who have a biological parent absent through separation and divorce.

"However, by far the greatest negligence of today's Family Court is the failure to address the insidious incidents of parental alienation – a prominent and destructive form of domestic violence. The non-residential parent and their families are continually obstructed, denied and quite often ostracised from their children because of the former spouse's selfish intentions.

"I have been denied access from my only child for over three and a half years. It is because of nothing other than malicious intentions. I have found the courts not to be accessible. It is very restrictive for the greater majority of society, and it pains me each time I watch reports or read editor's comments that take for granted that the courts will be there to resolve these issues. That is far from the truth."

***

One father of two sons spoke strongly in support of shared parenting and his travails with the Child Support Agency.

"I feel that I would be better off in jail, locked away from the society which I can only view as I walk past, with my wallet never having any spare cash. Living like this I am on the edge of suicide. There is constant stress in not having enough money and not feeling or being able to start over again.

"The erosion for me of a fair society is such that while my ethics and morals do not allow me to become involved in illegal activity they are slowly being eroded as this goes on. That is my personal story and it upsets me."

One father, who had driven hundreds of miles to be at the inquiry, said he had only achieved shared parenting by spending $150,000.

Bruce, a divorced dad with two children seven and five years old, described the situation as a Pandora's box and the use of the "best interests" of the child phrasing as a complete cop-out.

"As people, we have only two parents – a mum and a dad. Nobody will ever love us to the depths that they do, and I find it astonishing to suggest that it is in the child's best interests to remove them from access to the love of one parent. It is such an absurd piece of logic. The thought that a judge who will never know, never meet, never even see my children and only be aware of their existence for one day can decide that it is in my children's best interests not to see me to the degree that they do not is quite astonishing.

"That is myth No.1 – that best interests are actually being addressed right now."

***

The next month was hearing free after a bank of industry interrogations in the middle of October. But as October ended the committee took a sweep through three rural locations; Wyong, Coffs Harbour and Gunnedah. These hearings received sympathetic local media coverage, including the front page of the *Coffs Harbour Advocate*, and were, just as they had been a month before, emotion drenched.

There was compelling evidence from non-custodial mothers on this wing of the inquiry. At Wyong these women's voices made an odd contrast to Sex Discrimination Commissioner Pru Goward's strident anti-father comments, which had culminated in the claim that fathers would need an autocue to remember the names of their children.

But it was some of these non-custodial mothers that reflected very strongly the sentiments of non-custodial fathers.

Witness One at Wyong said that as a result of her children living with their father she was not able to adequately share the parenting.

"This has arisen for a number of reasons. One is the constant breaking of court orders for which I believe there is no adequate enforcement, other than my returning to court to try to represent myself. This has been a costly exercise.

"Over the last five to six years that I have been involved in this, it has cost me in excess of $200,000 with the legal profession to have orders put in place, then to go back to court to get orders reinforced, only to find at the end of the day that certainly the access orders are not adhered to.

"This occurs with physical access and telephone access – for instance, on a stated day when I was to speak to my children, the fax machine was usually on. The children do not come up to visit me very often, because in our orders I should go down to the South Coast to collect them and the father should come to our area to return them. But he insists that, if the children wish to see me, they have to be placed on the train – which of course is a disincentive for them."

Her complaints against the Child Support Agency mirrored almost exactly the complaints of many fathers.

"Within a week of my children moving to the South Coast, my ex-husband put in an application against me to the Child Support Agency for child support," she recalled. "He refused to come to an agreement with me on the day of the court hearing for payment in an ongoing way. Therefore, I was left to be assessed by the Child Support Agency at a cap income because of my profession.

"But he had not put in his tax return for four years, so he submitted to the Child Support Agency that he was in fact earning only $35,000 per annum. Therefore, the Child Support Agency assessed him as having no child support income, and my child support income was assessed at the cap, which meant that I would have been paying $36,000 after tax in that year."

She further complained, as so many men had done, that the onus was on her, the other parent, to provide all the relevant information to the agency. "The custodial parent does not have to reply if they do not wish to, let alone provide documentary evidence," she said.

She also spoke of the enormous distress the Family Court and its processes had caused. She said in the final judgement, the judge suggested that he would 'give' the father her eldest son so that he would not be seen to be a resounding loser in the case and 'anyway the child would grow up to see through the antics of the father'.

"I am very concerned that if we have children in the sole custody of one parent, particularly at young ages, it will be extremely damaging to the relationship with the other parent. For the children, it means that for many years they are often estranged from the families of the other parent and are unable to get a good understanding and a feel."

There were clearly issues around the psychiatrist who had recommended she relinquish custody of all of her children. "His comment was: 'Even though I'm asking you to give these children to him, he doesn't love them, you know.'

"That was very distressing for me. He added: 'Other than the fact that he wants to be able to say, "This my son, the doctor," or "This is my daughter, the whatever." He said: 'He cares about them, but he doesn't have the capacity to act in a way that is good for them.' I think that, if you are dealing with those problems, the only way you can deal with them is to legislate. Those people are not going to have the insight."

Chairwoman Kay Hull said: "More and more throughout this inquiry we have seen women in your position who are non-custodial parents. There is a feeling in the community that non-custodial parents are all men, not women. The fact that this is taking place more often, as you have indicated, with women as well as men is constantly within the submissions and before us.

"It is really not a gender issue, it is about the children."

On questioning from Kay Hull Witness One confirmed, on that Sunday late in October, that shared parenting had never at any time been encouraged by the Family Court.

"One of the greatest griefs for me is that it feels like a death. I feel like each child has died. There is no relationship because I do not know their friends, I do not know their interests, I do not know their clothes size and I do not know their latest music. The way this is occurring for the non-custodial parents at the moment is incredibly damaging to relationships and also for the children, I might add."

Speaking of her now 14-year-old girl, she said: "Every time we see each other there is inappropriate time to educate ourselves mutually about what has happened in that intervening period. In other words, she has started to menstruate so she wanted to tell me about all these things and then tried to ask me what my experiences had been. She has looked to a girlfriend – excuse the frankness of this – to teach her how to put in tampons because her mother was not available, she was not going to ask her father and the relationship with her de facto mother is not all that great.

"There needs to be a lot more contact and a lot more legislation so that, irrespective of the agendas of either parent, for the sake of the child it happens.

"She told me recently that her life was – excuse the expression – shit, and she said, 'Oh well, I suppose you're just getting on with your life, are you?' looking to me.

"I said, 'Darling, I miss you every day and I think of you every day.' But because of this win-lose situation – because we are told, 'You can have the children and you can be the accessing parent' – in my view the children are suffering."

***

Witness 2, another non-custodial mother, was equally as strong and equally as powerful in her condemnation of the system.

It was unfortunate that the shallow, callous mainstream media of the day chose to ignore this testimony, and instead to focus on the easy copy provided by Sex Discrimination Commissioner Pru Goward's inflammatory statements.

Witness 2 told the following story of the destruction wrecked in her own life and that of her children: "Over a 13-year period, access to my child has been continually denied me by the custodial father. Over that time, due to lack of contact, I have been unable to explain the reasons behind my absence to my child.

"Consequently I no longer have what could be described as a good relationship with my child, who is now 15 years of age. Over the last 13 years, every effort I have made to have those original court orders enforced has been thwarted by the very court that instigated them in the first place.

"In these years, the father has received a social security pension and remains unemployed. I am at his mercy as he uses this situation to maximise his financial status through the welfare system. As a result of his actions, I have been ordered by the court to furnish all my financial and personal details, including bank account numbers.

"This is not only unfair; it is also dangerous. I have not adhered to these orders as that would allow this man to have access to my personal documents. Therefore, I am liable for prosecution. Also bear in mind that this man receives Legal Aid at the expense of the taxpayer.

"I also have four other small children and I receive minimum wages. I am trying to keep my home business afloat to be around my family. I now have to work the graveyard shift while my children sleep as the financial burden for us is too much. On top of that, I cannot apply for Legal Aid and cannot afford a solicitor – I represent myself.

"I believe the Family Court system is a destructive system and is contrary to fostering a good relationship between a non-custodial parent and their child. It works to keep them apart by supporting a parent who prefers to use the child as a weapon.

"The current legal system offers no motivation for custodial parents to take some responsibilities for themselves and promotes welfare dependency with the assistance from the non-custodial parent through child support payments.

"How can I get on with my life when I have to face a family law system that actually promotes vindictive behaviour due to the biased way it supports the custodial parent in the quest for revenge through welfare dependency and the denial of access for the other parent? As a non-custodial mother, I believe in the child's rights to have equal contact with both parents as well as with grandparents."

Witness 2 also said she had also been through the Family Court system in relation to another child and another ex-partner which had made both their lives miserable until they settled on a shared care arrangement.

"The Family Court officers were of no help whatsoever," she said. "It was not until a year or two later – when both of us grew up as adults – that we put what our child wanted first, instead of what we wanted. We now share everything. We share his life, his schooling, his grandparents.

"When he is in his father's care, what he decides is up to him; when he is in my care, what I decide is up to me.

"We come half way between and that is only for him. We have had to do that so he could have a good life and a good future. But while we were in the Family Court system, it was horrible, especially for him. It does work but the parents have to grow up and be adults about what they want for their children – not what they want for each other – and it will work."

***

Provoked by Witness 2, once again we were to witness an enunciation of the evolving thinking of the committee in the words of the Chairwoman Kay Hull: "The reason why we have spoken at length about tribunals is that, in our observation – after listening to all the witnesses who have come before us and certainly after reading over 1,600 submissions, most of which I have read, and I am sure most of which the committee have read – it has been indicated to us that the family law process, the adversarial process, creates animosity between partners.

"It can break down a fairly good relationship, rather than establish a better relationship. Once solicitors become involved in the issue of contact and residency orders, it tends to deteriorate significantly.

"As you have said, you can go through a family law court process, pay squillions of dollars, not get on at all and be unable to come to an agreement, and then come to some sort of sense after a lot of pain, expense and emotional trauma. You then sit down, grow up, and do the right thing and come to an agreement about your child."

***

In her interaction with Pru Goward that same day Kay Hull was providing even clear indications of the committee's thinking: "There are a lot of unhappy people out there. We are not just responding, as it has been put to us, to an aggrieved male audience who do not want to pay child support and who want to manipulate things.

"We do have a major problem: the children are unhappy because they want to see more of their individual parents; the women are unhappy because they want their children at times to be seeing more of their ex-partner; and the men are unhappy because they want to see more of their children. We have all these tools available to us. Why isn't that happening?

"There are people who are currently in shared parenting arrangements who are unhappy about the amount of time and the cost that it took to get there. They are unhappy with the Family Court system. There are people who have been outside the Family Court system and who have come to arrangements where they do not get on at all, they do not even speak to one other, but their shared parenting arrangement works very well because they have the interests of the children at heart.

"It works very well, even though they do not get on and they do not share a lot of things. We have also heard people, whether it be the female or the male non-resident, complaining that contact is denied them. They turn up to collect their children, the children are not there and the child has been told that daddy or mummy did not come. It is manipulated dreadfully.

"There has been concern and criticism about the Family Court, the adversarial process and the legal profession – that once they are involved it seems to go downhill and people move further and further apart. It is only when they leave that process that people finally come together. It is difficult not to say, 'Why did you go down that pathway?' "

***

While non-custodial mothers got a lot of attention during this final swing through regional areas, once again there was a string of strong statements from fathers during the community statements in Wyong, Coffs Harbour and Gunnedah.

Alex, the father of one adult son and two girls aged 10 and 11, said his contact had been continuously sabotaged for eight years.

"To go to the court and show contempt of the court orders costs a fortune and is just impractical. I feel that it is in the best interests of the children that two parents look after them and physically spend time with them.

"The money which the mother receives through the Child Support Agency does not go directly to the children. More often than not it just goes to support her lifestyle rather than the children's interests. Of course, the lawyers also have a vested interest, because they like their revenue to be maintained – not the children's but their own revenue.

"During this inquiry I had a conversation with my eldest daughter, who is 11. My daughter said, 'Hey Dad, why don't you go and talk to Mum and agree? Why don't we make an arrangement so we will be one month with you and one month with mum and so on, and that would continue through the year? We would go to the same school and have the same friends and the same lifestyle, but we would just avoid all that continuous uncertainty and pushing from one place to another.'

"So that is the children's wish. And never go through the Family Court – if you go to the Family Court it will go through a very corrupt process and the outcome will be anti-father and anti-children.

"Find a way to actually get feedback from actual children and hear their voices and what they think. I think most of the children would say, 'We would like to see Mum and we would like to see Dad.' "

***

Gary, a non-custodial parent, said orders for access to his young daughter had been breached some 47 times. He said he was reluctantly about to go through the court process but was unable to get Legal Aid. Nor could he afford a solicitor and had to represent himself in court.

"This is very unfair because the court system is very complex and affects normal people in a way that they should not be affected," he said.

He said due to his commitments and child support payments he was living on the breadline and he felt penalised by the Child Support Agency, which he regarded as very unfair.

"I think the system in its current form encourages non-custodial parents who are overcommitted in a lot of areas to go on the dole, to be dishonest and to work for cash, which they do not pay tax on. The system in its current form is letting a lot of people down – both parents and children – and it sets the wrong example for everybody in the community."

He said "if there was a fairer system available to everybody involved, you would find more men back in the workforce, fewer people on the dole and more men facing up to their commitment of paying their child support and looking after their kids' needs. A fairer system would make it better for everybody involved. It might even stop some of the bitterness that the courts and the child support system produce."

A custodial father, Craig, said the Child Support Agency had made his life very difficult after his ex-wife's visitation had gone over the 109 day a year threshold.

"I am bringing the kids up at home, trying to keep everything going, and she is getting child support for her visitation rights. It just makes it unbelievably hard. She has got on with her life, which is good. She has a partner and is getting married to him. He has his own business and there is no shortage of money for her to live off. It is getting to the point where my mortgage and support for the kids is getting near impossible, and the Child Support Agency cannot do anything about it.

"I have sent them all my expenses, telling them what is left at the end of the month and they say, 'Sorry, that is the formula. See you later.'"

***

The next morning, further up the east coast at Coffs Harbour, a tourist, fishing and commercial centre on the picturesque mid-north coast of NSW, saw yet another emotional roller coaster of a day begin, this time with a doctor with 20 years experience who was also a separated father with three children.

He said he had seen many people going in and out of the family law system.

"One thing is for sure: the current system is not working," he said. "There is a lot of pain and suffering that surrounds any form of involvement in the current family law system. In fact, some of the suffering is horrendous. Children are being told they cannot ever see their father again in some cases, and men are being accused of the most horrendous crimes against their own children, purely as a part of the Family Court system.

"Lawyers are using these techniques to win cases. There is often a callous disregard for the welfare of the families involved, in an effort to win a case in the Family Court.

"Currently there is too much that is unknown in the family law system, and it is causing absolute chaos. I think very few people who have gone through the system are happy with it."

He described the abuse of Apprehended Violence Orders as "horrendous". "Here would be a father who loves his child, used to love his wife, has never done a thing wrong in his life, who is suddenly landed with some legal criminal accusation. It is appalling. All these violence organisations and so on are drumming it up; they have hijacked the family law system.

"Parents generally love their children; parents generally are good. You have got to get all these organisations away from them. That is criminal law – put it aside and leave it for the criminals."

***

Witness 3, another non-custodial mother, said the fact that she worked while her husband did not and that she had been the one to leave the house had all been used against her. She said she lived near her 10 and 11-year-old but was only allowed to see them every second weekend. She disputed the assumption that someone who worked full time could not also be the primary carer of their children. She said that as the residential parent her husband held "all the cards".

But even she said she had no doubt a 50/50 split arrangement could work. "Certainly my children believe it would work. They see their friends living in shared arrangements and moving between houses, and they do not see any reason why it would not work for us.

"The other thing that astounds me is that, on the two occasions I have appeared before the deputy registrar, the children have not been mentioned. The first time I was absolutely astounded. I thought that finally somebody will ask whether my children are safe and well. All they said was, 'You'd better get a valuation of property. You'd better get a valuation on that. What's this amount here? Better go and look at that.' I was just dumbfounded. I wrote a letter of complaint.

"The person who handled it did not look at me. They had their head down. I was in there waiting for my children's names to be mentioned and the person I was appearing before did not even make eye contact with me or with my husband."

An exasperated Chairwoman said the situation "always inflames my intestines because the Family Court process has continually indicated that all areas are always looked at for and on behalf of the children and that you go through all these processes first in looking at the parenting responsibility"; but while even the previous day taxpayer funded bodies had been declaring that no parent was disadvantaged in family law and the child's best interests were paramount, there hadn't been a single individual case before the inquiry where that had proved to be the case.

Kay Hull said she had not come across a single instance where "the Family Law Act works as it is written".

Witness 3 said she had been assuming that once they got before a judge then the children's interests and needs would be heard.

To which Kay Hull replied: "I am probably becoming sceptical, but do not hold your breath!"

Sadly, Witness 3 described how she had to sneak around to have contact with her children and how they called her behind their father's back.

"I go there every day," she said. "I am allowed to sit outside the house and spend time with the children. They sneak away to see me. I take my children to doctors and dentists but, again, by subterfuge. If I ask permission, it is denied.

So I am doing everything that I can to be actively involved and to influence choices."

***

Once again the fathers statements from the community section were also very strong.

David, a separated father, said: "My children were taken from me the day my ex-wife left our marriage. Since that day, nearly three years ago, I have been fighting her and the whole system for regular contact with my children. This is a system that has armed my ex-wife with money and the children, who she uses against me as weapons and human shields.

"This is a system that makes my children cry in anguish because they cannot see me. It makes me cry in anguish because I cannot see them.

"This is a form of child abuse, I think, and a form of domestic violence and I think it should be seen as that. This is a system that depletes so much of my salary in child support that I literally struggle to survive. I walk around with painful teeth, I avoid medical treatment, I have to sleep in cars at times, I drive unsafe vehicles and I shop at St Vincent de Paul. There is no light at the end of this tunnel. I will be 52 years old when I finish paying child support and before I can start saving again.

"This is a system that pretends that Family Court consent orders are working. They should be called blackmail consent orders or 'sign here or I'll take you to court' orders. I signed on the dotted line knowing that it was not in the best interests of my children. I had no choice, because I had no money.

"This is a system that pretends there is justice in the so-called Family Court. My experience so far is that this is not a Family Court. It should be renamed 'men's and children's discrimination court'. I feel that I am teetering on the edge at times. I struggle to keep fighting."

He said any decision by the Committee short of shared parenting would not help his situation.

"Please do not be misled by the fear campaign that men are a risk to children. I am here to tell you that I have been beaten numerous times by an angry woman. My child alleges that he has been physically and emotionally abused by a woman. My understanding and experience is that children are at just as much risk from their mothers as their fathers. But we never hear this.

"There are already numerous services protecting children at risk out there – I have used them. As a health care worker I am mandated to screen women for domestic violence but not men. No-one is counting these abused men."

Another father, Michael, said he had four children in his care and was still forced to pay child support for one child that was with his ex-wife, said: "We should understand that the child is brought into this world in a partnership which is 50 percent woman, 50 percent man. That partnership endures past the separation. To see it as a 50 percent partnership is the correct way. To see it as one partner having to battle to get the field level before they can have a normal arrangement with their children is wrong.

"To be able to have normal access to your child is a human right that is not available to most, unfortunately, after a family breakdown."

Yet another father, Matthew, said the majority of children wanted to spend time with both parents but his children had been denied that.

"I think it is ridiculous that I have not seen my children since January," he said. "If I am lucky, I will see them again next January."

He said he had been forced to cash in his superannuation, sell furniture and disconnect his phone in order to keep up child support payments.

"I know that my children are suffering now, and that is grossly unfair on them," he said. "I would love to have my children with me 24 hours a day, but that would not be fair on my children, because I know that they need their mother.

"It would also not be fair on their mother, because I would not want her to go through what I currently go through. I would not want to inflict that upon her.

"Please let me have 50 percent of the time with my children. Please let me be a father to my children."

***

One woman, Harriet, said she had always been encouraged to be proud of being a woman, but "lately I have been ashamed of the behaviour of some women in Australia who are causing much unnecessary grief."

"I, like most of my friends and family, have been oblivious to the unhappiness that is going on right in our own communities. Since I have become the partner of a divorced man with children, I have seen and felt his pain and his children's pain when the children are kept away from their father. I have seen and heard of the manipulation of many children which stops them spending precious time with their fathers, whom they love dearly.

"I have heard many stories highlighting the same patterns of behaviour, and all I can think of is: why on earth is this happening? What can make a woman stop the children whom she loves from spending a reasonable amount of time with the other parent? Once a fortnight, if it happens, is not enough time to continue a close relationship with a child. People in jail have more time with their families than my partner does with his daughters.

"It is critical that the government urgently stops encouraging and supporting parents to separate and use their children as a means to ensure their own financial security. Fathers are capable carers – I have seen it with my own eyes – and they want to be part of the day-to-day lives of their children. If anyone bothers to listen to children, they want their fathers to be there for them.

"This inquiry has the capacity to help the next generation of children in separated families, and it is not too late to help the current cohort of children who are suffering."

She said while feminism had produced many positives, "when separation occurs, all the outdated clichés about men's role as the main breadwinner are resurrected to justify women being able to take away everything from the marriage, including the house and the children. No wonder men in this situation have absolutely nothing to live for.

"Men need representation and their rights recovered. Currently, separated men have a very poor standard of living. This inquiry has the capacity to help Australian men have a fair go. I hope that these men and their children will see positive changes in their lives soon."

***

Later the same day, in the agricultural centre of Gunnedah, the Inquiry was to hear from the last of the individual witnesses. Once again the evidence was emotional and compelling; and it was these very voices which provided more than enough evidence for the government to act.

Witness One was concerned that the announcement of Inquiry it being "broadcast that the government would be looking to have more husbands getting custody" appeared to have influenced the judge in her own case.

Chairwoman Kay Hull, by now clearly frustrated by the family law industry, said: "I do not know that the Family Court judges take any notice of governments, let me tell you. They do not demonstrate it in some of the things that they deliver. There is a clear intent in legislation and a clear intent in law but that does not appear to be what is out there, so I would relieve your mind of that."

With the individual contributions to the public hearings winding up in Gunnedah, fathers remained strongly represented.

Witness Three said there was absolutely no reason why joint custody would not work in his case and in the case of many other parents in similar situations.

"My son lives three kilometres away from me. He would attend the same school, his friends would stay the same and he would live in a house that he is very familiar with. Nothing would really change in his life. I see my son every day from a distance. I pass him on the way home from school and I wave to him. His grandparents pick him up – my ex-wife's parents. I am not allowed to speak to him. The only time I can see him is on my allotted weekends each fortnight. I think that is extremely unfair. My son and I were always extremely close; we still are. He wants to spend more time with me.

"I have to return him home at 5 o'clock on Sunday afternoon or all hell breaks loose. I have often said, 'We'll come home a little bit later. It'll be alright,' and he says, 'We can't do that; Mum will blow her head.' So I get him home.

"He constantly emphasises to me that he wants to be with me more. He still loves his mother and he wants to be with his mum but he wants to be with his dad too."

***

Wayne said: "I am a loving and committed dad who, after separation, simply wants to share in and carry on with the upbringing, welfare and schooling of my little boy, now aged four and a half. I separated in October 2001 and, from the first day of separation, the mother maintained an absolutely cruel and vindictive campaign of a zero contact regime.

"The mother simply deemed that no contact would be in order, and that position has been supported in the last two years that I have been involved in the Family Court. The mother filed for sole residence orders in the Family Court. After huge amounts of exchange between our solicitors, still my son did not get much contact with his father.

"Not a single shred of evidence supporting the current sole custody model has been presented to this parliamentary inquiry by the array of family law industry participants. The reason for this is simply that none exists."

Ben said he was a recently separated father of two young children he loved dearly. "I want the opportunity to be there as a good role model to my children and a positive influence in their lives without robbing my children's mother of the same opportunity, and to have a situation where we accept that our rights and responsibility are shared equally, where we both work together to further the interests of our children, putting aside our own differences.

"The reason I want this is because I genuinely believe that it is in the best interests in the long term of our children. It enables them to maintain strong relationships and bonds with both parents and overcomes the need for parents to be adversaries in court over the kids, greatly increasing the likelihood that they will remain on speaking terms."

Rex, father of an eight-year-old boy, said he had been to the Family Court. "I have no contact on Christmas Day, no contact on his birthday, no contact on Father's Day, and no contact on my birthday because the court has granted the mother discretion on those occasions. I do love my children. I want to see more of them.

"Who has been to Family Court? It is not tennis; it is like football: the parents are the captains of the team and the child's best interest is the football. Hopefully, when you go to Family Court, the playing field is level – you think it is going to be. You hope that you can score a few tries that you think are worth trying for, for the child; you hope the goalposts are not too far away.

"And, by the way, whatever you do, never argue with the ref and put on a good public show."

There were many other voices, both in the public hearings and in the submissions, which added powerfully to the volume of evidence before the government.

Chairwoman Kay Hull, who had by this stage already admitted to the emotional strain and intensity of the inquiry, nonetheless wound up the Gunnedah hearing on that mid-Spring afternoon of 27th October 2003 by saying the public hearings had been a very valuable process.

"It is important that everybody is exposed to other people's experiences," she said. "I think that this is why the public hearing process is good. If you think that you are the only person with a problem or the only person who is experiencing a certain issue, you start to understand that other people are experiencing them as well.

"If you think that men are the only ones who experience this problem, it is also very good for you to recognise and hear that there are women who are experiencing the same problem.

"In the last 24 hours we have had people come in and say, 'When I came in this morning I was just coming to be abusive and disruptive. I wanted to scream at you and tell you that you didn't understand. Having sat and listened through the whole day, now I want to come up and say that, because of everything that everyone has said here today and the questions that you sometimes asked, I feel confident that you do understand.'

"That lady also indicated that she had not realised that there were others in her position. Some of the gentlemen came up and said, 'I didn't realise that there were women non-residential parents as well. We thought it was all us blokes.'"

One reason we have recorded these stories so extensively here is that they were essentially wiped from the record. In the end all these witnesses were dismissed in the final report Every Picture Tells A Story in a single short paragraph which suggested those who appeared before the Inquiry appeared more concerned with their own problems than with the welfare of their children.

It was offensive, insulting, untrue and remarkably dishonest. The Inquiry was an amazing waste of public money. The bureaucrat who oversaw the writing of the final report was immediately transferred to another department in order to shield her from any backlash. And all those parents, grandparents and concerned citizens who shed tears and poured forth their anguish and concern to Kay Hull and the other Committee members wasted their time.

ELEVEN
TALES FROM
THE SUBMISSIONS

NOTHING HAS changed. If anything, the situation in the Family Court and the poor outcomes for parents and children since these events have grown profoundly worse. These are not historic justices. They continue to the present day.

Combined with the people who appeared before the 2003 inquiry, the volume of submissions from individuals, a record for the Family and Community Services Committee, showed the level of angst on the subject.

The inquiry, far more public an exercise than its predecessors and made more so by the internet, provided a chance for those outside the taxpayer funded cliques to put their views and describe their experiences.

All the material going up online was immediately available from the Committee's website. This was in stark contrast to the comparatively secretive public meetings of the government's previous inquiry culminating in the Out of the Maze report, where the input of witnesses was heavily interpreted and the will to do nothing to reform the system apparent to many suspicious participants.

There was a battery of hundreds of government funded bodies, bureaucrats, the judiciary, the numerous representatives from the domestic violence industry, the academics, the women's groups, all making representations on child custody and almost all opposed to shared parenting or joint custody.

On the other hand volunteers in the various unfunded groups spent countless hours preparing submissions in favour of shared parenting.

In the blizzard there were also many hundreds of submissions from individuals. Some women and even a few men argued against shared parenting, but the majority of mothers, fathers, grandparents and sympathisers were in favour. A number of politicians made private submissions. And many other professionals, including doctors and teachers, wrote in passionate support.

Some of the submissions, naïve in tone, were little more than pledges of support for shared parenting or joint custody.

Elvira Martin of Toowoomba in Queensland wrote: "I know a father in this type of situation, that was going through a Family Court matter, in trying to get some visitation to see his daughter. And for a number of times the mother has breached the order. It is very heartbreaking to see this guy, in the state he's in.

"There is not a day goes by when he says to me that he wishes that he can see his daughter more often and to even have her stay with him just on the weekends. I feel that fathers should spend more time with their children no matter what the case may be, as children need a father as well as a mother."

***

Glen Gordon of Bellbird in NSW said the proposal for joint residency arrangements for children in separated families was long overdue and there was no incentive in current family law practice for cooperation between parents. He said in his own experience his legal advice was basically "forget it, you are the father and the courts will always side with the mother".

"I thought that this was an appalling approach giving no consideration for the past relationships and bonds that I had forged with my children. I look forward to the development of a family law system that recognises the importance of fathers in their children's lives."

Others were bitter in their condemnation of the system.

Dennis Brown of Calala said there should be an inquiry or Royal Commission into the Family Court and "that to ostracise me in an illegal separation from my own flesh and blood and I will always believe the family law court is a very high profile criminal activity and whether right or wrong it would seem that child abuse and drugs, prostitution, street kids all stem from it."

Errol Hunt of Manly in Sydney wrote that since he had first contacted the government on the issue "the male suicide rate has accelerated due in no small part to the utter helplessness felt by the dispossessed party, as I prefer to call the poor male who inevitably loses his children to the occasional contact offered.

"He is required to pay the bulk of the monies he earns to the ex-wife, save for that obligation to the tax department of 50 percent. This woman now inevitably has another 'partner' in tow. He also has no idea as to how his funds are even spent, if such monies are indeed spent on his children. The ex-wife's income does not seem to be taken into consideration, nor the live-in-lover's finances.

"The courts are a graveyard for hopes of equity in an inequitable situation. Costs of action to attempt a modicum of fairness are prohibitive. The result is utter hopelessness, depression and often suicide."

***

Evan Carson, from the fishing village of Ulladulla on the NSW south coast, said he would have loved to have equal care of his children but was strongly advised by his solicitor that there was no point in going for anything but every second weekend and half the school holidays and if he did he could be up for costs.

"This news was fairly devastating as I was not in a financial position to go to court and all local anecdotal evidence suggested that my solicitor was correct," he wrote.

"The Family Court should be removed from making as many decisions as possible. Bearing in mind that almost 50 percent of marriages end in divorce, local institutions need to be established that look at a fair and prompt closure to the most complex of decisions. All relevant information can be heard in the local environment and air decisions made.

"It has been apparent that the Family Court has never been able to make fair decisions regarding custodial arrangements of children. When the Family Court is forced to make decisions, the mother almost always wins custody. Mothers know this. Fathers know this. Solicitors know this. This understanding does not make that decision correct. What it does is to keep many people out of the court system because decisions are costly, time consuming and predetermined."

Mr Carson said he had remarried but as a second family they were struggling to cope with the imposts of the system, particularly with the combined operation of the Department of Social Security and the Child Support Agency.

"This means that we can hardly afford to live together on what remains of my salary after my own child support payment is made. The laws at present and the anomalous regulations of both Departments concerned contrive to make our lives extremely difficult and are unfair and inequitable.

"It is hardly surprising that so many second marriages fail when you weigh the negative financial situation against the stressful dynamics involved with establishing a new family. The desire for success in a new family situation can easily succumb to financial stresses despite the best efforts of all concerned."

Carson, like so many others, was highly critical of the administration of the Child Support Agency, saying information received from them is frequently incorrect or misleading, and that one frequently has to make several phone calls to find someone who can provide support and more importantly, correct information. "I feel that I am burdened with an emotional and financial cost that I have no option but to pay."

He said throughout Australia people were battling with what appears to be a raft of unjust and inequitable regulations that are the cause of much desperation.

He concluded: "It is no surprise that teachers spend a large part of their day addressing social issues, many the result of baggage brought to school by children from broken homes. It is no surprise that many men feel that current laws are biased in favour of the mother and these laws have created a large body of angry and distressed men.

"It is no surprise that so many mothers walk out on marriages when they know that current laws support them in regard to child access and support. It is no surprise that in anger, distress and confusion so many men create further problems for themselves by the non-payment of child support or violence towards an ex partner. It is no surprise that there has been a dramatic rise in male suicides."

***

Other contributions, as with the public hearings, also condemned the Child Support Agency. Harold Craig of Bellambi said the existing child support formula "does not work and is in fact preventing non-custodial parents in many cases from being able to practise and enjoy access to their children. It is far too rigid with little or no consideration of extenuating circumstances. It is unfair that two children of the same parents can have very vastly different opportunities in life... It is my personal experience that the children are nothing more than a source of income and opportunity to most custodial parents and a very spiteful way to destroy the other parent."

A number of politicians made personal submissions to the inquiry, some in camera.

Government Whip Joanna Gash, member for Gilmore centred around Nowra on the New South Wales South Coast, said amongst the issues being raised in her office by fathers included paying child support children and not being given access ordered by the Family Court.

Paul Neville, the Federal Member for the rural seat of Hinkler around Bundaberg in Queensland and National Party Whip, said he saw a constant pattern of abuse, especially on the part of the custodial parent.

"Frequently, vindictive custodial parents will place as many hurdles as possible in the path of the children having contact with the non-custodial parent," he said. "For example, 'the child is in the grand finals and shouldn't miss their chance', 'I can't afford the warm clothes needed for your climate' or 'the child is sick'.

"I see many non-custodial parents, deprived of contact with their children, becoming extraordinarily stressed. In many instances they cannot afford legal redress and the custodial parent, for want of a better expression, 'gets away with it'.

"When eventually some 9, 12 or 15 months later the non-custodial parent obtains Legal Aid (most infrequent), or raises the money for a legal action, the custodial parent is invariably given a caution or rap on the knuckles."

***

Ken Ticehurst, Federal Member for the NSW Central Coast seat of Dobell, also a guest on Dads On The Air, was one of the figures who had for months been urging the Howard Government to acknowledge the outcry around the country relating to laws governing child access rights and our family law system.

In his submission he said that in the previous year, after having many mothers, fathers, grandparents, aunts and uncles approach him with their painful experiences of the current family law system, he formed a discussion group of politicians to address the need for family law reform.

He described the inquiry as good news for many people in the Central Coast region who had expressed to him their frustration with the Family Law and Child Support Acts and their administration. He said he had been bombarded with congratulatory messages since the inquiry was announced.

Ticehurst detailed common themes brought to him:
- Lack of enforcement of Family Court rulings with respect to access, further legal action by non-custodial parent is too expensive
- More support to encourage self-representing litigants
- Perceived bias toward custodial parent in the Family Court
- Not enough emphasis on mediation
- Family Court delays in interim access orders
- Calculation of Child Support Agency payments far too onerous, formula is unsuitable
- Non-custodial parents' living arrangements not fully considered when determining child support payments
- Non-custodial parents' children not considered in child support assessments
- Child support payments made to custodial parent while children in care of non-custodial parent
- No progressive review of custodial arrangement as child grows
- Grandparents and great-grandparents not recognised formally in custodial arrangements.

A significant number of professionals made well argued contributions. Dr Brian Ronthal, a doctor in a country general practice with experience in managing families going through separation, divorce and custody battles, wrote: "A retrospective law allowing equal custody needs to be made for the thousands of children who currently already have court orders restricting access with their fathers to fortnightly or less.

"These children cannot be left out. Existing court orders restricting paternal access to fortnightly visits needs to be annulled without having to go through a court case. This ought to be achieved by filling out an application form.

"The presumption of equal custody needs to be achieved without court judgments... The extreme adversarial nature of the Family Court adds dramatically to family conflict with children being the ultimate casualties.

"Families which manage separation with minimal Family Court interaction fare best. Equal custody needs to be presumed with as little Family Court interaction as possible. The 50/50 custody arrangements between both parents need to be made law by default without requiring Family Court assessment first because there is little chance of changing the current mindset of the experienced professionals already running the system.

"Adversarial Family Court proceedings have a severe impact on the developmental psyche of children, which cannot be blamed on the parents but rather on the system itself."

***

In one of the best argued of all the submissions Angela Dreibergs from Katherine in the Northern Territory said she was writing as a woman, teacher and someone who considers child custody to be one of the most important issues of our time. She said as a primary school teacher she had come across many instances of children who have no contact with their fathers.

"This has not been as the result of a Family Law Court ruling but has been something decided upon by the mother," she wrote. "This failure to allow contact is often accompanied by snide comments about their father and general put-downs regarding his character. I have seen first hand the doubt and confusion in the hearts of these children who for one reason or another wonder about their fathers and think that the father doesn't care about them because they are not around.

"I have a boy in my class who lives with his father as his mother is an alcoholic and abandoned her son. The father does very well with his sons' care and is a proud parent. Another boy will be going to live with his father at the end of the year. He has difficulties with his stepfather and his older brother is already living with his father. The boy is incredibly excited and pleased by this.

"I am definitely in favour of custody to be shared equally with both parents. This would give the children a sense of belonging and to have the opportunity to actually know who their parents are and where they themselves have come from. There would be balance for the child. It would also be a fair and equitable system for both parents as they should both be able to see their children grow and develop.

"Many women decide, for whatever reason: jealousy, nastiness, power, revenge etc that they will make the lives of their ex-partner difficult by refusing any access to the child. This is not because of any direct order from the Family Court. It is something that these women implement as a result of manipulative behaviours.

"Over 41 percent of all fathers have been denied access to their children in this way. As a woman and a teacher I find it reprehensible that a child can be used like this."

***

Amid the wide variety of material there were even some stabs at black humour.

Matt Shields of Armadale in Western Australia had given much thought to the idea of shared parenting and decided it should be prohibited entirely.

"Non-custodial parents have parental responsibilities, specifically to pay child support to their former partner; but these responsibilities do not extend to include any further contributions to the lives of their former children whatsoever.

"The relatively few shared parenting decisions made in court is proof that we just don't need it. In the future those judges who attempt to make shared parenting decisions should be horsewhipped for their stupidity and then sacked.

"The Chief Justice of the Family Court has made it clear that the concept of shared parenting would make the whole process of family law unworkable. This makes sense because the notion of shared parenting is alien to the spirit of the Family Law Act. We should take the advice of the Chief Justice and ban shared parenting right now. In fact anyone who attempts this obscene practice should be fined, incarcerated and perhaps horsewhipped with the errant judicial officers as mentioned above.

"Many people have suggested that shared parenting has the potential to cast children into harm's way. I don't know who these people are, but they are obviously right. Anyone with half an eye can see that those persons who struggle to get contact with their kids are really desperate individuals who only want to cause their kids a serious physical injury.

"Children who are denied contact with the non-custodial parent become emotionally enmeshed with the custodial parent and this is good because it makes the custodial parent feel important.

"Denying a kid contact with the other parent is obviously good for the kid. Ban shared parenting!"

***

Others were more learned in tone.

Paul Johnston, a 31 year old computer software engineer in Canberra, said: "The time that a father forsakes with his children so that he may provide as best he can for the family he is supporting is grossly undervalued by society at large. Indeed, father finds separation a particularly galling experience for the following reasons: "The time a father spends with his children is reduced to being negligible, because of the roles he and his wife assumed during the marriage, as the courts, and legal profession in general, assume the mother will retain residency, and persuade the father that the idea of "fortnightly fathers" is a fair compromise.

"The father retains as little as 20 percent of the matrimonial property, because he has a demonstrated earning capacity that the courts expect to be met indefinitely.

"The father is compelled to work to continue to support his child and his wife to within his demonstrated earning capacity.

"I argue that by working, at the expense of time with children, particularly young children, the father is indeed caring for the child, and indeed for the mother of the child, in the most practical way, but at great personal and emotional cost.

"The sacrifices of the father has made in working at the expense of time with his family are not ignored by courts, but rather used against him to ensure that those sacrifices continue into the longer term."

***

A number of academics arguing on both sides of the fence put in submissions independent of their institutions.

Family law provided a study in the power of the distribution of grant money to academics and researchers to define the debate and for the ability of academics to confirm and validate agendas; often enough to the backdrop of fine wine and late night oceans and yet another international conference in luxury surrounds. There were rich pickings to be had.

The Counsel of Perfection, a 1996 book on the history of the Family Court of Australia, seriously, you couldn't make this stuff up, received ample funds from the taxpayer to bring it to fruition. Author Leonie Star did not think it appropriate to talk to litigants who had survived the experience.

The book was a part of a long tradition in Australian academic life of totally ignoring or dismissing the country's entire fathers and family law reform movement as unworthy of study.

Academic discourse is dictated by grants, and there was no money in men's issues.

The blurb read in part: "*Counsel of Perfection* examines the dominant personalities who have shaped the Family Lionel Murphy himself, Justice Elizabeth Evatt, and the second and present Chief Justice of the Family Court, Alistair Nicholson, who, she argues, has moved the Family Court away from Murphy and Evatt's more informal, non-confrontational model, introducing greater formality and a new managerial regime, and spending more money on the Court itself."[112]

***

The Family Court repeatedly funded academic projects with sympathetic feminist researchers and used the results to justify its own conduct. One of their favourites, Professor of Law at Sydney University Regina Graycar, had been a determined critic of fathers' groups. Her investigation into shared" parenting, along with other academics, was used by the Court to support its stance.

She told columnist Catherine Lumby in the now defunct news magazine *The Bulletin* that fathers' rights groups had been tremendously successful at gaining the ear of senior politicians but their major claims had no empirical support.

Lumby, who I worked with at *The Sydney Morning Herald*, before she went on to become a professor at Sydney University, was never one to miss the ideology in a point. She wrote: "But is greater parenting equality really what this proposal is all about? Scratch beneath the surface of Howard's rhetoric, and much of what is said by fathers' rights groups, and it becomes clear that the real agenda is about reasserting a patriarchal model of the family, not replacing it with a contemporary one.

"Uppermost in Howard's mind, as he told parliament, is the concern that 'far too many boys are growing up without proper male role models'. It's a concern which distinctly echoes the rationale behind Howard's opposition to lesbians and single women accessing fertility services. The only 'proper' family in Howard's view is a heterosexual nuclear one."[113]

Academic apologists helped provide the intellectual props justifying the present

---

112 Star, Leonie, Counsel of Perfection: The Family Court of Australia, Oxford University Press, 1996.

113 Lumby, Catherine, *The Bulletin*, 2003.

family law regime. That much of the population suffered deeply as a result of family law and child support was of no concern to them.

The government, or at least politicians, embraced them because of a neat mind trick. Academics could absolve them for the private and social disasters they had legislated into being. Like the Family Court itself, some academics blamed the social phenomenon of rising divorce rates and the poor conduct and unrealistic expectations of the battling litigants for the community's intense unhappiness with the system the politicians had created. In the end no one was responsible, or prepared to take responsibility.

The heroic and expensive legal battles of fathers trying to do the best by their children led them to be denigrated for their inability to reach agreement with their often Legal Aid funded ex-wife.

***

One of Dads On The Air's favourites, Dr Robert Kelso from Central Queensland University, wrote that it was 28 years since the creation of the Family Law Act and 13 years for Child Support legislation.

"The deleterious effects upon Australian families and children and the economic destruction associated with those pieces of legislation and practices are increasing at an exponential rate.

"Despite the damning evidence presented to two parliamentary inquiries and numerous reviews, and the overwhelming rejection of the legislation by ordinary Australians, the reaction to date by the legislators, judiciary and bureaucrats has been to strengthen the punitive and regulatory mechanisms in the hope that crude force will prevail over morality and common sense.

"The greatest immediate losers in this process have been children and fathers; the long-term destructive effects upon Australian society have been evident for more than a decade and the time for the parliament to either radically overhaul or abolish those institutions is long overdue.

"Current government policy approaches to marriage and divorce have been driven by ideology rather than the best interests of children. Recent attempts by the parliament to improve the situation have been worse than ineffectual, in many cases they have contributed to or exacerbated the very problems which they were designed to prevent."[114]

Kelso had taken a particular interest in the operations of the Child Support

---

114 Kelso, Robert, The Curse of the Law: A History of the Legal Profession in Australia, University of Queensland Press, 1994.

Agency from the standpoint of public sector ethics. It was established in 1988 after Prime Minister Bob Hawke claimed that by 1990 "no Australian child will be living in poverty". In the early years it was managed by his most leftwing minister, Brian Howe, Minister for Community Services.

Kelso said administrative decisions by child support officers were in effect final determinations and there was no proper appeal mechanism, for example where public servants deem an individual's income. He said the courts refused to charge the CSA Registrar with contempt when the Registrar or a delegate blatantly ignored court orders.

"Child Support officers also know that despite overwhelming evidence of illegal activity presented to the Joint Select Committee which reported in 1994, that the parliament refused to refer that criminal activity by public servants to the Director of Public Prosecutions or Federal Police.

"That refusal to address illegal activity by CSA officers has legitimated the contempt for payees' legal rights and entrenched a culture of systemic corruption within the Agency. Any doubt about these issues can be easily dispelled by asking front counter staff in parliamentary offices about the complaints received.

"It is this blatant contempt for the parliament's intentions in legislation and the rights of payees and their children which lead to more than 20 years of complaints and charges of bias and corruption against the Family Court and Child Support Agency. Until now it has been the Federal Government's practice to ignore those obvious breaches of the laws in the hope that the money collected will balance the evil it has perpetrated.

"It is obvious now that the strategy is both morally corrupt and economically bankrupt. All we ask is that the government have the courage to confront the vested interests which have constructed the current systems, and that you act in the best interests of children and their families, assert your moral authority and remove this evil source from our children's future."

He recommended that all deaths of "clients" subject to the Child Support Agency be recorded on those institutions' respective files and reported to the relevant ministers and the number be published in the Hansard each year.

***

Dr Kelso told Dads On The Air unemployment was one of the few safe havens for fathers, with up to 40 percent of CSA clients unemployed. "The loss of productivity and diversion of welfare dollars to what should otherwise be a productive individual is significant. These practices and outcomes are not in the best interests of children; they are not in the best interests of the nation.

"In order to restrict the Australian public's access to the complete data and the effect of their practices, the Family Court and Child Support Agency resort to secrecy, official misinformation (lies) and refusing to collect critical information on the number of suicides.

"Section 121 secrecy provisions, jailing CSA defaulters and measures to increase the collection rate from struggling non-custodial parents are signs of a system in crisis.

"The root cause of that crisis is a lack of legitimacy, the most obvious manifestation is the systemic corruption of administrative systems and legal procedures designed to manufacture consent...manufactured by coercion and exhaustion, emotional, physical and economic. Tearful consent and the subsequent denial of contact with their children in many cases ends in suicide and violence.

"Every day across Australia men suicide as a result of their treatment by the CSA or the Family Court and neither of those institutions will acknowledge their part in the process. The Family Court separates children from their parents. A new stolen generation of children is being created. Civil libertarians who would normally be allies in the fight against injustice are more concerned with fathers and children in detention centres or in overseas countries but are deaf to their neighbours' cries."[115]

Chairwoman of the inquiry Kay Hull said the suspected death rate of child support payers showed that the difficulties with the CSA go well beyond the hot topic of the suicide rate of paying fathers.

"Without doubt the Agency is causing many personal and social problems and that was reflected in the evidence we took," she said. ``In many cases there was a very poor attitude within the Child Support Agency.

"The issue we wanted to deal with is how to do we stop not only suicides but mental health issues, emotional breakdown, physical incapacities. It is not just the suicide rate."

***

Malcolm Mathias, former President of the Victorian Branch of Lone Fathers and later President of the defunct Fathers For Family Equity, was another who toiled nobly in the field over many years trying to provide an articulate voice at a time when fathers groups were routinely parodied as right wing rednecks who could not accept the empowerment of women.

In 2000 Mathias, a school principal with responsibility for hundreds of children during the day but who the Family Court had decreed could not be

---

115 The Kelso Interview - Family Court and Child Support Agency, Dads On The Air, 17 November, 2004.

trusted with his own children, produced a detailed report Family Breakdown In Australia. Using material from the Australian Bureau of Statistics and the CSA it attempted to provide a statistical analysis of what was happening to separated families. The report demonstrated that many child support payers were not being left with enough money to survive, thereby making work pointless.

An articulate professional, unfortunately by the time of the 2003 Inquiry he had given up his activism and writing. He told me by phone he felt completely broken by his own situation and that of so many others. And that the government knew perfectly well what was being perpetrated against its own citizens, they just chose to ignore it.

In Family Breakdown Mathias wrote: "The feeling of isolation which the non-custodial parent feels after the forced separation from the children is intensified by the apparent lack of statistical data, and the lack of community concern. The non-custodial parent often feels forced to fight a lone battle against the Family Court, the Child Support Agency, the Child Support Review Office, Federal politicians and an ignorant community.

"However, far from being alone, the number of non-custodial parents caught in this trap is increasing rapidly, but the Family Court, the Child Support Agency, and the Federal Government attempt to keep the magnitude of the problem a secret. The non-disclosure provision in the Family Law Act (Section 121) denies the 'media democracy' which is available to other community issues, thereby maintaining community ignorance of details about the magnitude of, and factors contributing to, family breakdown."

***

The suicide rate of child support payers was a topic raised by numerous witnesses and fathers groups. But at the end of an inquiry, which was supposed to determine amongst other things the fairness of the child support system, we were no closer to being able to answer one simple question: how many child support payers die each day?

In its submission Dads On The Air wrote that the issue of the death rate of child support payers would not go away.

"These schemes are being associated with high death rates amongst separated men wherever they operate in the Western world," DOTA's submission read.

"Family law reform groups around the country have all claimed that it is likely that around three clients of the Agency suicide each day. The official suicide statistics do not rule out the feasibility of the claim. The government has acknowledged that there is no documentary evidence to contradict the claim.

Others suggest that the death rate is likely to be higher than the mere suicide rate suggests because of the poor health outcomes for separated men, exacerbated by poverty, depression and loss of children.

"The government through the Minister Larry Anthony has acknowledged that it does not know how many clients die each day. This is an extraordinary admission. The government needs to take immediate action to monitor the death rate of child support payers so that it can be compared with the general population. It needs to immediately release the figures on how many clients are dying. This is a fundamentally significant indicator of the health of family law in Australia.

"The Child Support Agency needs to be either totally reformed or abolished. It is a clear case of good intentions gone savagely wrong. The take per child is now less than when it was created. The CSA is one of the most deeply hated of all government institutions. There are numerous very well-documented tales of the CSA's destructive impacts on people's lives, including on second families.

"The Agency creates massive conflict between separated couples and between itself and its clients. It acts to discourage co-operative parenting after separation. It promotes welfare dependence and is the driving force behind the extremely high unemployment rates of separated fathers. It needs to be reformed or abolished to encourage productive and cooperative joint custody arrangements to become the norm."

The submission from the team at Dads On The Air pointed out that for there to be a genuine and effective introduction of joint custody there needed to be fundamental and sweeping reform of the institutions responsible for the welfare of separated families.

"We are aware of a number of scandals circling the operations of family law and child support in Australia which have the potential to seriously embarrass the government," the submission said. "It is unlikely that the mainstream media's traditional reluctance to broach these issues will continue. We believe if the government does not take action it will ultimately be propelled to do so.

"The disenchantments with the operations of the Family Court are broad and profound and extend to the operations of the family law units of Legal Aid.

"We believe a proper external audit of the court would reveal much utterly inappropriate conduct by the judges of the Family Court and there is much anecdotal and documentary evidence to support this claim."[116]

***

---

116 Submission to Inquiry into the Family Law Amendment Bill 2003, Submission from the Dads On The Air Team 19 January 2004, available on the Dads On The Air website.

Throughout the inquiry the government, or more precisely the public service bureaucracy, dodged the issue of how many child support payers were dying.

Here is the Hansard transcript when the question was finally popped to the head of the Child Support Agency Cathy Argall and the head of the Department Mark Sullivan.

Chair: Do you keep records and statistics on deaths of child support payers?

Ms Argall: On individual records, we would record information that became available to us about the death of either parent or the children.

Chair: I ask that question because it has been raised, as you might note, in submissions, particularly from the Lone Fathers Association, that indicate that there is a significant proportion of male payers who suicide over the issue of child support and contact and I understand that child support is not associated with contact and that that is not your issue.

"But it has been raised time and time again in these submissions that there is a significant amount of despair happening, particularly in male payers, in relation to child support, when they cannot particularly afford it or they cannot see a light at the end of the tunnel with respect to their financial circumstances and maybe if they are in a new relationship.

"If there have been deaths or suicides, can the Child Support Agency extract this type of information? I do not how we can refute the claim that is constantly being made. Is there an ability to extract that sort of information?

Mr Sullivan: "There is no doubt there is an issue of increased suicide rates amongst separated males. There is no doubt that separation, and everything that goes with separation, does influence suicide rates in males. One of those factors is child support. It does not provide evidence for or against those who assert that the child support aspects of separation are the issue that drives men to suicide."[117]

If the claim by fathers groups that at least three payees died each day was true, then the government had a very serious problem. This was a crude but fundamental indicator of the health of family law and child support in Australia today.

That a government body could care so little for and have so little duty of care towards its clients that it could not implement recommendations in the Price report that there be an inquiry into the social consequences of the scheme showed a pretty damned atrocious level of irresponsibility. That it could not answer a simple, straightforward question about how many of its clients died each day was

---

117 Australian Parliament House website for the House Standing Committee Family and Community Affairs report Every Picture Tells A Story: Inquiry into child custody arrangements in the event of family separation, transcripts of the public hearings, tabled on 29 December, 2003.

simply appalling. The death rate of child support clients is a crude but fundamental indicator of the health of family law and child support in Australia today. It should be public knowledge.

The bureaucrats involved in this debacle continued to defend the indefensible. And there was never any public inquiry.

***

With family law and child support issues running hot, Dads On The Air attended a number of government run information nights where it was obvious that both men and women were incensed by the injustices and trauma associated with the child support scheme.

A second wife lamented that her husband had been stressed out of his mind and had a brain tumour.

We asked if the cancer had made the Child Support Agency lay off.

"Are you joking!?" she exclaimed.

It made good radio. It didn't make for a good society.

***

In its submission to the inquiry the Shared Parenting Council recommended: "That the Family Law Act be amended to require parents to jointly and equitably share the rights, duties and responsibilities of parenthood.

"That the Family Law Act be amended to include a statement acknowledging the fundamental rights of children to maintain frequent and continuing contact with both their mother and father following parental separation or divorce and to experience and enjoy the love, guidance and companionship of both their parents in an equal and shared manner.

"That the Family Law Act be amended to establish a rebuttable presumption in favour of both shared residence and shared parenting responsibility with the burden of proof to rebut the presumption being placed upon the party seeking to impinge upon the rights of the child, a parent or other significant person, in specified circumstances where there is a clear and imminent risk of harm to the child.

"That the burden of proof that a shared parenting order ought not be granted falls upon the party requesting alternative custodial arrangements."

There was no tradition or history of easy cooperation between the various fathers' groups, despite the fact they were largely campaigning for exactly the same things. Previous attempts to make Lone Fathers the peak body had failed. Keeping them together in even loose alliances was like herding cats.

The creation in February 2003 of the Shared Parenting Council of Australia, with close to 30 affiliated members, was an important step forward in the campaign for family law reform. It gave the media an easy moniker to hang an idea around. As Federal Director Geoffrey Greene, a single father of two with close ties to the Liberal Party, brought to an often politically and media-naïve movement a new and articulate voice due to his experience both as a lobbyist and Liberal Party staffer.

Its formation was always a political operation and had involved some of the conservatives most senior "backroom boys", most particularly Nick Minchin, Howard's Finance Minister at the time and who, as it so happened, I had been friends with at school many years before.

Greene was tasked with the job of uniting the groups into a coherent voice. He may have been a political operative, but he was also a highly effective advocate and the SPCA gave the media an easy reference point.

He argued that any rearguard attempt to save the Family Court was doomed: "There is no place in Australian society for an institution that operates in the way the Family Court operates. What an indictment it is of the court that the vast majority of Australians want to take it apart."

***

The fathers' groups, which had virtually no funding or resources of any kind, functioned purely on the good will of volunteers and were borne largely out of personal grief, rarely put out press releases and rarely had members with even the most rudimentary experience of the media.

As a result they always had problems establishing a media profile and were easily vilified by the pack mentality which had set in with the armada of lobby groups arrayed against them. The veteran of them all, Barry Williams of the Lone Fathers Association, did not, despite all his good heart, present as the most articulate or well educated advocate. He was easily snowed by Canberra's femocracy.

While barrister Michael Green QC, author of *Fathers After Divorce*, was a reasoned and educated voice, he had not until recent times shared the same profile as Williams.

With the confusing array of groups and their vilification over the years, the Shared Parenting Council gave the media someone else beside Barry Williams they could turn to for a quick quote, a detailed backgrounder or a bit of gossip. Many other groups operated only part time and their volunteers were people who had never written a media release or been on radio or television in their life and who were caught up with their own jobs and lives and children. Often it came down to the simple fact that Greene was readily available when the media needed him.

The unity of the SPCA in putting a respectable mantle onto a disparate group of family law reformers and fathers groups had been a significant factor in breaking down the demonisation of fathers groups. This demonisation had picked up pace since the appearance of a fringe group the Black Shirts in Melbourne in 2002, a group whose paramilitary style outfits and extreme tactics led them promptly to court accompanied by lurid headlines; none painting a redeeming picture of separated fathers. In the rearview mirror it looked like some kind of counter intelligence operation.

With a cosy fit between left wing journalists, a predominantly female work force in the nation's newsrooms and feminist ideology pumping from numerous taxpayer funded bodies, getting journalists to look beyond stereotypes or to bother ringing anyone besides Barry Williams had long been difficult.

In their submission the Shared Parenting Council suggested the imposition of the will of the parliament to promote joint custody and reduce the level of animosity generated by the court proceedings had been ignored by the Family Court and the Family Law Council. This refusal to take heed of parliament's wishes had led to a hardened backlash by backbench members and senators to the family law industry.

An example of this distrust and parliament's avoidance of seeking advice from the Family Court of Australia and the Family Law Council could be seen by the Federal Parliament's 2003 Inquiry into Child Custody, in which the entire review was referred to the Family and Community Affairs Committee, chaired by Kay Hull, and which bypassed all traditional aspects of the family law Industry and its administration.

The inquiry was established without any reference to the Attorney General's department, the Family Court of Australia, the Family Law Council, or the Australian Institute for Family Studies. The disappointment for this complete sidelining of the gatekeepers to the Family Law industry was reflected by the Chair of the Family Law Council, Professor John Dewar, when in a television interview he was asked if had been consulted prior to the Prime Minister's announcement of the pending inquiry. Professor Dewar replied somewhat acidly, "No we have not".

***

The Shared Parenting Council's submission read in part: "There are numerous research studies available that specifically look at the issues of child adjustment following parental separation or divorce. There is no valid empirical research available that justifies the current Family Law policy of making sole-custody orders in the ordinary everyday case coming before the Family Court in Australia.

"It is therefore surprising that the Family Court itself has failed to improve its 'client' outcomes by facilitating 'shared parenting' orders for families, and accordingly it has now become necessary for the Parliament to act to rectify the escalating problems experienced by children of divorce.

"In a recent 'meta-analytic' review by Robert Bauserman, published in the American Psychological Association's Journal of Family Psychology, Bauserman assessed that: 'Children in joint physical or legal custody were better adjusted than children in sole-custody settings, but no different from those in intact families. More positive adjustment of joint-custody children held for separate comparisons of general adjustment, family relationships, self-esteem, emotional and behavioural adjustment, and divorce-specific adjustment. Joint-custody parents reported less current and past conflict than did sole-custody parents, but this did not explain the better adjustment of joint-custody children.

The results are consistent with the hypothesis that joint custody can be advantageous for children in some cases, possibly by facilitating ongoing positive involvement with both parents.'

"Research evidence demonstrates that children from divorced families are not as well adjusted as those from intact families. However when looking at all the custody options available at the time of parental separation or divorce, the option that is most likely to result in emotional harm and increased maladjustment of children is the sole-custody model currently practised by Australia's Family Court.

"There is no doubt that the available research indicates that joint physical custody (Shared Parenting) outcomes after parental separation or divorce has the least harmful impact on children, and provides the best child adjustment outcome when compared to the intact family."

***

In their submission The Lone Fathers Association's noted there had been a large increase in children growing up in fatherless families over the previous 30 years, very few children were receiving the type of care they would prefer, that is equal time with both parents and boys were growing up without appropriate male role models while girls suffered without appropriate adult male figures which would be important to them in later life.

"Empirical evidence clearly indicates that children raised by a divorced single parent are significantly more likely than average to have problems in school, run away from home, develop drug dependency, and/or experience other serious problems.

"Prima facie, the community should, in the interests of children, avoid having them living in sole custody arrangements wherever practicable. In a large proportion of cases the alternative of joint physical custody would be practicable, if it were not discouraged by the legislature and/or judicial authorities. The greater cooperation between parents which necessarily occurs under a shared parenting model improves parental attitudes, in many cases out of sight, and results in great benefits to the children.

"The adversarial model, by causing both parents to fear that they will lose the children, effectively compels many parents to fight hard, where they can, through the legal system. This then tends to give the judicial authorities the appearance of parents in sharp conflict – although this conflict would usually subside when the more natural arrangement of shared parenting was granted.

"There is also a serious problem in the philosophy and approach of the Family Court of Australia, which has the main responsibility for dealing with these matters. The Family Court effectively encourages and implements a model of sole parenting. This creates a win/lose mentality on the part of parents.

"The loser often becomes a mere transient in the lives of his/her children, and this is almost invariably bad for the children."

Lone Fathers went on to note that the Family Law Act stipulated that children have the right to know and be cared for by both their parents. "The Family Court could make shared parenting orders even without parental consent now. But it has largely ignored this opportunity. The Court has, in fact, gone in the reverse direction, as the proportion of shared parenting orders granted has steadily declined over time. There have also been major problems with the accuracy of advice given to the Government on shared parenting by the Family Court and the Family Law Council."

***

The submission from the Men's Rights Agency noted: "Since the Prime Minister expressed interest in the concept of rebuttable joint custody – where the court presumes a child should spend equal time living with each parent unless there are strong reasons against it – there has been an incredibly positive reaction from the Australian public. Three media polls, albeit straw polls, indicated substantial support for change and for the proposal in particular."

News Corporation asked its readers, Do you think joint custody should automatically be awarded when parents break up? 62.6 percent answered Yes.

Melbourne's *Herald Sun* asked, Should Australia's custody laws be overhauled? 86.9 per cent said Yes.

The Sunday program on Channel 9 asked, Should divorced parents be given equal shared custody of their children? 82 per cent answered Yes.

"Perhaps the removal of 'fault' has failed because of the nature of the court system needing to find a winner and therefore a loser; perhaps it became easier to award custody of children to the mother, together with inequitable amounts of family assets when believing the father to be a scoundrel, despite any allegations of domestic violence or child abuse being unproven and unlikely.

"The benefits to be gained by Australian families and society in general from the introduction of legislation that will reduce the loss of fathers from family life will be untold."

***

The Joint Parenting Association, particularly utilising the work of Juri Joakimidis, had produced an impressive volume of material on the subject of shared parenting, including the monograph Back To The Best Interests Of The Child: Towards A Rebuttable Presumption of Joint Residence.

This was used as the organisation's submission.

The paper argued that "current family law pathways seem to be wrong with only limited attention given to the emotional, social, and financial well being of all members of the defunct family system. Even a cursory look at the evidence documents that children are victimised by sole custody decisions in at least three ways: emotional victimisation, economic victimisation, and increased risk for child abuse.

"Research results on joint custody have changed and consensus has emerged in the psychological literature, which suggests joint custody should be a rebuttable presumption of the Family Court. The available literature also supports the following conclusions:

- Children adjust much better to divorce in joint custody compared to sole custody
- Children's attachment bonds to both parents are essential for healthy development, and those bonds should be protected by the Family Court
- Non–custodial parents are often intentionally victimised through contact denial, and children are hurt when the relationship with either parent is broken in that manner;
- Joint custody leads to much higher compliance with financial child support;
- Mothers are much better adjusted and supported more in joint custody situations;
- Fathers are much better adjusted in joint custody arrangements;
- Litigation and re–litigation is lower in joint custody situations;

- Divorce rates are much lower in jurisdictions which have a presumption for joint custody;
- Joint custody is the preferred option in high conflict situations, because it helps reduce parental conflict over time—and that is in the best interests of children;
- The current winner–loser system is irrational. The typical custody dispute involves two fit and loving parents who each want to avoid being cast out of the role of parent and into the role of visitor."

The Joint Parenting Association submission recorded that it did not believe that government officials should delay legislative action in anticipation of future research findings.

"To do so would jeopardise the well–being of at least 50,000 children who experience either divorce or unwed motherhood each year, as well as countless others who are currently struggling to cope with the confusion and adversity foisted on them by misguided adults. We now have had the advantage of approximately 25 years of research studies to inform our legislative decisions. It is time to act on this accumulated wisdom."

***

The currents running against the Family Court of Australia were ably assisted by developments internationally, where there had been a number of exposes of the ad hoc decision making of Family Courts creating "routine misery on a massive scale", to quote one UK piece. These essentially Marxist feminist courts, creations of the 1960s and 1970s, were in savage disrepute wherever they operated.

In Britan *The Spectator*, in a cover story The Rape of Justice, described the "spurious" if not "incomprehensible" reasons for father's losing contact with their children.

"There was the father whose overnight contact with his five-year-old was stopped because 'the child had many mile-stones ahead of him'; another who was denied contact because he 'had to prove his commitment'; another because 'this is the mother's first child'; another because he was 'over-enthusiastic'; yet another because 'the child fell asleep in his car on the way home'. And so on and so, appallingly, on."[118]

A similar litany of disaster and denial of relationships with fathers or less commonly mothers is true of Australia. A father's close relationship with a son is described as "unhealthy"; another parent is described as having a psychiatric

---

118 Frederic Raphael, The Rape of Justice, *The Spectator*, 1999.

condition of unknown name immutable to treatment, another as having a controlling and intensive intelligence, another as being too involved with his children's schooling.

The intervention of public figures such as Sir Bob Geldof, along with public intellectuals like Dr Sanford Braver, author of *The Myths of Separated Fathers*, and author of *Father and Child Reunion* Dr Warren Farrell, who visited Australia, also helped transform the debate at a time when dissemination of information had never been easier.

Only the month before Chief Justice Alastair Nicholson's appearance before the 2003 Inquiry, British rock singer Sir Bob Geldof had made another impassioned plea for fathers to be given equal access to their children.

He had been attending the launch of *Children and Their Families*, a collection of academic essays to which he had contributed. The rockstar had fought a custody battle with his former wife Paula Yates and claimed he had been treated unfairly during the process.

Geldof declared: "The judiciary finds it almost impossible to take on the notion I should be with my children 50 per cent of the time. This law ridiculed me. Its implementer humiliated and belittled me and would not accept I was as capable of bringing up my children as a woman. I want to be recognised as the father of my children and I want to bring them up equal to their mother."

The previous year Geldof had declared that at the heart of family law was a grotesque injustice: all women were angels, all men were ogres. "At Day One I was handed this piece of paper saying 'You may see your children on this day and every second weekend'.

"Why? What had I done? I saw them every day. I took them to school. I bathed them. I fed them. I cooked for them. I read their stories. I cuddled them before going to bed. I listened to them in sleep.

"Why now was the state and all its instruments of justice – but in this case I call it discrimination - why were they all aimed at me?

"As I was just about to enter court and was very nervous and trying to look neat, a well-meaning person came up to me and said: 'One tip Bob - whatever you do don't say you love your children'.

"I said 'Why?'

"The answer was as shocking as it is illustrative. He said: 'Because the courts will deem it unhealthily extreme if a man articulates his love for his children and they'll vote you down'.

"I waited for a long while and I got tired of hearing how much Paula loved her children – which she did – she did endlessly – as did I. And I eventually said: 'I have to say this – I have been advised not to, but your honour I am here – I am bankrupting myself – because I love my children. And all I want to do is to be their dad'.

"The law does the very opposite of what it intends to do. When it denies that the love of a man for his child – which is the real love that dare not speak its name – the love of a man for his child – a father for his child – is equal to the love of a mother for her child. It is precisely equal. It could be expressed in different ways but it is equal, and the law will not recognise that and therefore it is discriminatory and unjust and should be scrapped."[119]

Geldof's comments were widely circulated. We at Dads On The Air were happy to spread them to our audience.

Hard to believe with the passing of time, but in the early years of the millennium the rapid spread of information through the internet was still regarded with a sense of wonder, as an historical novelty and as the heralding of a new era of freedom of expression. And hope for those whose lives were being damaged by governmental and judicial systems outside of their control.

---

119 Geldof, Bob. Transcript. 17 June, 2002. Available on the Shared Parenting Information Group's website.

TWELVE
CHIEF JUSTICE ALASTAIR NICHOLSON THE FINAL DAYS

THE APPEARANCE of Chief Justice of the Family Court of Australia Alastair Nicholson at the government's 2003 inquiry was cheered on by his supporters and watched with a horrified fascination by his many critics, particularly those in the fatherhood movement.

There had been some specifically hated and feared judicial figures in the early days of the Colony, but Nicholson eclipsed them all for the pure vitriol he attracted.

Nicholson was the unsuccessful Labor candidate for the seat of Chisholm in Victoria in both 1972 and 1974. But for the man who was to become the face of such a divisive jurisdiction, and who 15 years later was about to leave it in disarray with its public reputation in tatters, there was little beyond being a loyal Labor man in his background to justify his elevation to Chief Justice. There was nothing DOTA could find to suggest any prior interest in family law.

Nicholson graduated in 1960, became a QC in 1979 and during the early 1980s acted as Chairman of the Town Planning Appeal Tribunal and Land Valuation Board of Review in Victoria. He was a Judge Marshall with the RAAF just prior to his appointment to the Family Court, and a Judge Advocate General with the Australia Defence Forces right up until 1992. None of these fitted very well with his later façade as darling of the left, alleged champion of the oppressed and disadvantaged.

From enlightened progressive to brutal Stalinist, the views circling Nicholson and his court had hardened as he aged.

On the other hand, to his supporters within the family law industry Nicholson's impending, although utterly confused, departure into retirement was a matter of consternation. The appointment of a Family Court Chief Justice would be in the hands of a conservative government. Just as former Prime Minister Bob Hawke's appointment of Nicholson fifteen years before was one of his most significant, so Prime Minister John Howard now had the chance to remake the Family Court; and thereby considerably alter the country's social agenda.

Once again he was to blow the once in a generation opportunity. While not seeking the same profile, Nicholson's successor Chief Justice Diana Bryant did nothing to differentiate herself from her predecessor or to reform the court and its practices.

Howard must have known when he appointed her that she was a vocal opponent of shared parenting and would not reform the jurisdiction. At the same time his acolytes continued to push Howard and the Liberal Party as sympathetic to fathers and families. It was a bitter hypocrisy and an example of why some people argued that lawyers should be barred from becoming politicians. They choose the interests of the legal profession over the interests of the public.

***

While it is open to any visiting dignitary to enter Parliament House in Canberra via the underground car parks, and thereby avoid any unwanted media attention, Nicholson chose to enter via the front door, and was talking to his favourite media outlets, including *The Age* and the taxpayer funded Australian Broadcasting Corporation virtually to the doors of the inquiry.

Nicholson's appearance at the inquiry on the 10th October, 2003, was accompanied by a spate of media stories reporting his opposition to joint custody.

It was classic Nicholson. He released his submission to media outlets, including *The Age*, the day before, ensuring he got maximum media coverage.

On the face of it Nicholson's behaviour would appear to be a clear breach of one of the founding principles of Australian governance, the doctrine of the separation of powers which divides the institutions of government into three branches: legislative, executive and judicial. The legislature makes the laws; the executive puts the laws into operation; and the judiciary interprets the laws.

While dating back to antiquity, in the modern context the separation of powers was adopted from the British system. The House of Commons Library records its purpose was to "safeguard liberties and guard against tyranny".

In practice senior legal figures in Australia are expected to stay out of politics and the daily fray of policy making. The man who had done more to shape

Australian family law than any other individual felt no such compunction. Nicholson had always courted the nation's left leaning media.

On that day *The Age* newspaper in Melbourne ran a front page story headlined: "Family judge warns MPs on custody."[120]

The paper suggested the Family Court would sound a strong warning against the introduction of formal joint custody arrangements between separating parents, saying it could lead to an increase in both violence and litigation.

The story quoted the Court's submission, signed by Nicholson, at length: "If separated parents are expected to share their children equally…the legislation will create a normative standard which will be unattainable in practice for many, and which may jeopardise the best interests of the child.

"A parent who has been living in a violent or oppressive relationship may be persuaded to 'agree' to a shared care relationship in inappropriate circumstances. Counsellors and judges are also aware that increased contact may provide some parents with opportunities to control and harass their children and former partners."

The paper also recorded that in a personal note concluding the submission Nicholson cautioned the committee to beware of the submissions made by interest groups. "The court's experience is that there are usually two sides to the story in family law matters and the situation is rarely black and white, but rather various shades of grey."

The Family Court submission also suggested that the inquiry itself was creating problems. "The raised expectations which accompany inquiries and the amendment process inevitably produce a groundswell of hostility towards the court and the Parliament, because in many cases the expectations cannot be met."

***

Barry Williams, the founder of Lone Fathers and one of the country's most long term campaigners, was one of those family law reformers who had long had a hostile relationship with Nicholson. He told *The Age* he didn't think Nicholson should be allowed to give evidence.

"I think it's a breach of the separation of powers," he said. "He is a judge, not a law-maker and he had made it quite clear in the past that he does not believe men to be capable of looking after their children."

But since the 1980s, nothing had ever stopped Nicholson speaking out on his numerous hobby horses.

---

120 Farouque, Farah, Family judge warns MPs on custody, *The Age*, 10 October, 2003.

In the year or so before the inquiry began Nicholson had created a series of stirs; one of them by calling for the removal of the common-law defence of reasonable chastisement.

He supported the call for laws banning physical punishment of children so that smacking would become "socially unacceptable".

Next, he declared, after a retrial of an unrepresented woman in a case where there were accusations of domestic violence, that the lack of Legal Aid appeared "to infringe the practical enjoyment of rights" under international conventions. Never mind the numerous self represented men who struggled every day to get a fair hearing in the court.

Yet more debate was stirred when he suggested decision making about asylum seekers "ought to be properly understood as an aspect of family law."

And on DNA testing, an increasingly hot topic amongst men, he argued against discrete testing without court orders, saying: "I think there's a considerable element of invasion of privacy involved in one person unilaterally going off and getting a DNA test for a child."

In other words, a father was not entitled to take a hair off his son or daughter's head and discretely have it tested to prove whether or not the child was biologically his. The issue was a live one because a significant number of fathers feared they were paying crippling amounts of child support for children that were not theirs.

***

Appointed as only the second chief justice of the Family Court of Australia, Nicholson had been in power since 1988.

Approaching retirement, there were many signs he was trying to establish his legacy. With a clear eye to the future, Nicholson had overseen a string of appeal judgements in the preceding years, the impacts of which defined family law and which critics said would take legislators years to undo.

Some of the precedents the Shared Parenting Council described as counterproductive and discriminatory included: The fact that children might wish to live with their fathers is not sufficient reason to let them do so, property settlements could be made 90 percent to the wife and financial hardship of the father deemed unimportant, shared parenting or joint custody was not encouraged, litigants concerns over the efficacy of family reports should be dismissed, a judge need only have "lingering doubt" over abuse allegations to deny fathers contact with their children and stepfathers were liable along with biological fathers for child support.

The inquiry, which was examining the fundamental philosophies and practices of the court, was a threat to all that Nicholson was trying to leave behind.

In attacking the notion of joint custody Nicholson had from the beginning been the nation's leading critic, repeatedly claiming that joint custody or shared parenting was unworkable for most families.

***

Nicholson had long reigned as some kind of mystical saviour of children, fawned on by left wing journalists, feminist academics and some sections of the legal industry. The views of Nicholson often jelled with the views of the feminist oriented journalists interviewing him.

The taxpayer funded Australian Broadcasting Commission, studiously ignoring community outrage, had displayed extraordinary sycophancy towards Nicholson throughout his career, while he has also had numerous apologists in the mainstream media. But personnel in the mainstream media were not immune to the ravages of the system. The turning of the tide of public debate was assisted by the increasing number of separated men with raw experiences of the system who were working in newspapers, radio and television.

Draconian censorship built into the Family Law Act, the notorious Section 121, which prevented the naming of litigants in a Family Court case without the consent of the Court, had also played a significant role in protecting the Court and Nicholson from full journalistic scrutiny.

In Sydney's *The Sunday Telegraph*, under the headline "Disorder in the courts", Sarah Harris wrote that the Family Court had consistently pursued its critics by instigating contempt charges. But lately these citizens had been beating their powerful foe.

"We can't show you his face or tell you his real name. Yet, ironically, he recently won a major victory for free speech."[121]

Harris went on to report the man's win came when a charge of 'contempt' for scandalising the Family Court was dismissed and a judgement for costs made.

The man's alleged crime had been to stand on the footpath outside the court handing out leaflets and hollering through a megaphone his protest about the court's handling of his children's custody arrangements.

Harris noted that as one of a group dubbed the "Family Court Four" he faced an unlimited fine or jail term under an arcane 18th century law of "scandalising the court".

This was a David versus Goliath case, a group of poorly resourced litigants against all the might of the Family Court. But as the losers the Family Court faced a legal bill estimated to be upwards of $100,000.

---

121 Harris, Sarah, Disorder in the courts, *The Sunday Telegraph*, 19 October, 2003.

***

Court research showed up to 40 percent of cases now involved an unrepresented litigant.

The Chief Justice himself claimed that the lack of Legal Aid could be "killing people" – while at the same time, as the ALRC had revealed, the Court refused to provide detailed accounting which might prove his case.

"There is a serious problem in family law involving violence between the parties," Nicholson claimed. "If you increase the frustration and parties don't have the benefit of legal advice you increase the chance of violence being perpetrated."

Harris noted: "For a senior officer of the court to then criminally charge these very same frustrated and disadvantaged parties – who, left with little other avenue, took to the streets in protest – seems a somewhat inflammatory response."

Ultimately the bills incurred by the court in retaining at least two senior silks to prosecute the charges of "scandalising the court" would be picked up by the taxpayer.

It was the second such case the Family Court had lost that year. In March 2000, a man who spent two years stridently voicing his frustrations at being denied contact with his two children outside the Family Court building in Melbourne had contempt charges against him thrown out. Actions against another man were dropped as the

Family Court beat a tactical retreat.

To lawyer Gabriel Kuek – whose firm represented the first three of the four defendants either privately or under the limited provision of Legal Aid, the issue was clear-cut.

"As we have said again and again, Australia is a free, democratic society which ought to be able to withstand robust debate and criticism by people against the arms of government," he said. "The Family Court is part of the judiciary which, under the Westminster system, is one of the arms of government."

The Sunday Telegraph also observed that Justice Nicholson had previously categorised the courts most vocal critics as dysfunctional misogynists who regarded women and children as objects who have no rights.

"The most strident critics of the court emanate from groups of men who regard themselves as having been badly treated by the family court system," he told a national conference in 1998. "There is a more sinister element at work. I have absolutely no doubt that there are many persons associated with men's groups in particular who have an agenda to change the law to the disadvantage of women.

"Many demonstrate in strident terms outside the court. Some even stand for Parliament, with signal lack of success."

Federal Labor MP Roger Price from Western Sydney doubted the wisdom of painting the court's critics as mad, bad and dangerous. "Is it impossible, for example to conceive that some of them may have been driven to extremes and wrongly penalised because of false accusation made by no less bitter partners?" Price asked.

***

Disgruntled clients, journalists and fatherhood activists were in the company of the Australian Law Reform Commission when it came to being targets of withering scorn from Nicholson.

Unable by law to show identifying photographs, use names or even identify occupations meant media accounts were restricted to describing the participants as "anonymous persons", a practice to which the Chief Justice objected.

But under Section 121 of the Family Law Act, it is an offence to publish or disseminate anything which may identify any party to the proceedings in the court.

The only exemptions to this could be made by the Family Court itself, which allowed publication of cases complete with names on the Internet in the interests of the legal profession or for propaganda purposes.

The anonymity blanketing the Family Court may or may not protect the privacy of children. But it also encouraged the feuding parties to make outrageous claims without fear of defamation or the requirement of proof.

Roger Price, now a member of the committee interrogating Nicholson, argued that suppression of reporting about the Family Court had given rise to suspicion and distrust. He had proposed in a private member's bill to lift reporting constraints and vowed to continue his crusade to open up the court to greater public scrutiny.

"My proposals are not about tilting the Family Court in favour of men, or women or children," he said. "They are about accountability."[122]

In his crusade for greater openness Price found a surprising ally in Ian McCall – the former Chief Justice of the Family Court of Western Australia.

Harris recorded that the Attorney General Daryl Williams asked McCall to re-examine section 121 after *The Sunday Telegraph* first revealed the Family Court had breached its own rules of publication by allowing judgments to be posted on the Internet.

---

122 Farouque, Farah, Family judge warns MPs on custody, *The Age*, 10 October, 2003.

McCall found the stringent rules on reporting had a negative impact on the court. McCall quoted the famous words of British legal scholar Jeremy Bentham: "Publicity is the very soul of justice. It is the keenest spur to exertion and surest of all guards against probity. It keeps the judge himself, while trying, under trial."

Also quoted was Lord Kenneth Diplock's words: "If the way that courts behave cannot be hidden from the public ear and eye, this provides a safeguard against judicial arbitrariness or idiosyncrasy and maintains the public confidence in the administration of justice."

***

The Attorney General Daryl Williams initially embraced the report, saying it gave "compelling reasons" to drop the Family Court ban on naming people.

His views were echoed by others who believed it would counteract flourishing conspiracy theories about the court.

But, in the end, a gutless Howard Government backed away from the reforms recommended in the McCall report.

After a considerable number of submissions from community and welfare groups the Federal Government decided in August 1999 not to amend the infamous secrecy clause known as Section 121 of the Family Law Act.

"It was felt on balance that the potential risks to children outweighed the benefits," a spokeswoman for Williams said.

Critics argued that this was yet one more failure of courage by the Howard government when presented with an historic opportunity for reform.

***

The Nicholson who presented himself to the parliamentary inquiry, far from being the enlightened intellect once so admired by the country's intelligentsia, had made many enemies. His performance at the inquiry was watched with a kind of reptilian interest.[123]

The 25th anniversary celebrations for the Family Court of Australia in 2000, where Nicholson played a prominent part, garnered virtually no positive media coverage, a significant shift in public sentiment. That was Nicholson's legacy, as much as his judgments.

The days of fawning over Nicholson were ending, except perhaps at the national and international conferences of which he was such an inveterate attendee.

---

123 Almost all the material referenced in this section can be found on the Australian Parliament House website for the House Standing Committee Family and Community Affairs report Every Picture Tells A Story: Inquiry into child custody arrangements in the event of family separation, including transcripts of the public hearings, tabled on 29 December, 2003.

Shared Parenting President Matilda Bawden said she doubted if there was one individual in any of the family law reform groups who would argue that Nicholson was a fair or just judge.

"The mere fact that there has been such a large explosion of anti-Family Court lobby groups which have sprung up in the last few years should be sounding alarm bells," she said. "The Family Court is perceived by many as a secretive court that is an impenetrable quagmire of corruption. It is truly hated.

"Nicholson has made it absolutely clear throughout his reign of terror that he hates fathers. What else can you say?

"How can he oversee the Family Court when he has such a myopic view of family life? Under Nicholson, the Family Court has become an example of everything a court, and we as a community, should never be.

"The Family Court has ignored or subverted the progressive legislative reforms to the Family Law Act enacted in the mid-1990s which promoted joint or shared parenting after divorce, the outcome ample research clearly shows produces the best outcomes for children of separated families."

As such, said Bawden, the court was failing to comply with the legislation requiring it to act "in the best interests of the child" and ignoring the will of parliament.

***

Fathers and their supporters were far from the only critics.

Lawyers who use the court complained that it is "overloaded with bureaucrats" and Mason examined the complex structures which had been allowed to evolve, including various committees and a bureaucracy of judges within its bureaucracy of administrators.

In recent years the persistent questioning of a recalcitrant Court by former barrister Senator Brett Mason through the Senate Estimates Judicial Committee had already exposed numerous issues of public concern, including a profligate level of extravagance.

The persistent questioning of a recalcitrant Court by former barrister, Liberal Senator Brett Mason, through the Senate Estimates Judicial Committee, was the most detailed examination it had ever undergone. Mason exposed extensive and needless delays and the low number of sitting days for many judges, including the Chief Justice himself, who sat around 45 days a year.

It also exposed the practice of providing numerous grants ranging up to the hundreds of thousands of dollars to various consultants with little apparent benefit. "Specialised and unique expert knowledge" was often provided as the reason for the projects not going to tender. Grants of substantial sums to favourites of the court for their "intellectual" contribution, with no explanation as to what the contribution actually was, should have been exposed to the public.

The Court's first Deputy Chief Justice the Honourable Alan Barblett, reportedly a close friend of the Chief Justice, received two such grants in one year for a total of more than $70,000 following his retirement in 1998.

Being chauffeur driven was all part of the aggrandisement of the Court's senior judges, and questions were also raised over the use of Commonwealth cars.

Nicholson, an inveterate conference goer, was a "devout member of the international judicial jet set", as Janet Albrechtson at *The Australian* described him.[124]

While Nicholson never ceased complaining about the government's tight fisted conduct in allegedly starving his court of funds and slashing legal aid, all of this rhetoric clashed with the truth of the Court's extravagant travel budgets.

But his questioning also exposed the limits and flaws of Australian democracy. There were many questions about the Family Court's profligacy and poor administration since previous governments had allowed it to become self administering with control over its own budgets. The Court's refusal to cooperate or answer many of the questions about areas of its operations demonstrated its ultimate lack of accountability to the parliament and to the people it allegedly served.

As a small sample of his travel expenses, Chief Justice Alastair Nicholson was forced to report that he and an adviser spent $24,753 on a May 1999 "work trip" to South Africa, while a "work trip" to Hong Kong and Canada with his wife in May and June 1999 cost $19,842.

Nicholson's "consultative council" of judges and managers spent $158,403 on travel and accommodation in less than two years.

But the court claimed it was "not appropriate" to give details of travel budgets for the so-called "judge administrators" and refused to do so.

Nicholson had been well known since the 1980s for spending much of each year attending overseas conferences. To his critics it was self-evident that this luxurious first class lifestyle was of no benefit whatsoever to the taxpayers footing the bill.

In the previous 18 months before his appearance at the Inquiry Nicholson had attended conferences in England, Hawaii, South Africa, Scandinavia, Port Moresby, the Great Barrier Reef, the Gold Coast, Sydney, Perth, even his home town Melbourne. There was no publicly available list of all these conferences or of their cost.

Where is the evidence that this kind of behaviour does not continue to this day?

---

124 Albrechtsen, Janet, The Inquisition: How Just Is Our Family Law?, *The Australian*, 24 September, 2003.

***

Nor was it just a case of the Court's generally appalling public reputation. With more than a $100 million budget, Nicholson had a great deal of largesse at hand to build an empire of sycophants. He was surrounded by his closest allies, all of whom held prestigious positions within the court and frequently accompanied him on his international jaunts.

Senator Brett Mason said complaints about the administration of the Family Court came from many quarters.

"It was widely acknowledged within the court itself and in the legal community that some Family Court judges were not pulling their weight," he said. "With the Chief Justice seemingly unable to address this issue the Court's morale was affected."

In refusing to answer a number of questions posed by the Senate, Nicholson claimed that the independence of the judiciary was being attacked.

Nicholson refused to tell Senator Mason and the Senate Estimates Committee the salaries of his personal staff, whether any judgements had been written by persons other than judges or which specific judges sat on cases or had leave.

In 2000 Nicholson had refused to reveal the names of judges responsible for long overdue judgments and warned that their "public shaming" would only increase the stress they suffered.

The Court acknowledged that as of June, 53 trial and appeal judgments had been outstanding for more than three months and a further 24 outstanding for more than six months.

The Court's own time standard was a maximum of three months. "It's very unfortunate for the litigants and the reputation of the court," Mason commented.

In a letter to then Attorney General Daryl Williams, Justice Nicholson he would not name names because it would "draw personal information about judges into the public domain".

He said stress was "a very real factor" for judges with outstanding judgments and if they were "publicly shamed", it would only increase the pressure on them.

Try the stress of being one of the families being churned through his court.

"This is an organisation with a 25-year tradition of secrecy and minimal accountability," Mason said. "The parliament has finally lost patience with it."[125]

But in Australia's battered democracy there were many examples of institutions which survived public odium and lingered long past their use by date.

---

125 Lane, Bernard, *The Australian*, 27 October, 2003.

"Despite the Chief Justice's protestations, the Family Court must be accountable," said Senator Mason. "Judges are paid by the public and are accountable to the people's representatives – that is the Parliament – it is pompous posturing to say that parliamentary scrutiny of the Family Court has amounted to an attack on judicial independence."

***

Lecturer in public sector ethics Dr Robert Kelso, editor of the academic journal on family issues Nuance, said, the report clearly showed the court's failings, not just in the eyes of the general community but also for influential sections of the legal community. He was never a man shy of putting forward his numerous views on human rights and the best interests of children. But to his many critics in government, the legal profession and the community, Nicholson's legacy was a destructive, dysfunctional and discredited court.

"Nicholson leaves the court in a very vulnerable state," he said. "It has been politicised and has become utterly dysfunctional.

"The Family Court's philosophies have never reflected general community understandings of family or of probity in public life. It is secretive and resistant to change. It is one of those social experiments that has diminished the rule of law, not improved it. It has diminished the understanding of courts as places where justice is dispensed in the best interests of the country.

"The effects of the Court on second wives and their children have been particularly harsh. These are the people the Family Court, the government and the legal system refuse to recognise in an equitable way.

"Rising suicide levels among excluded parents and extremely poor outcomes for children has created broad antipathy within those sections of the community which have been adversely affected by the Family Court and related government agencies.

"Nicholson's very public approach to judicial activism has led him to imagine he has a duty to change community standards on a whole range of issues, on everything from DNA testing to social parenting and the importance, or as he sees it unimportance, of biological fatherhood, even if that means confronting the parliament and the legislation in ways which clearly overstep the separation of powers."[126]

***

---

126 Dads On The Air, Chaos at the Crossroads, 2004. Available on Australian Parliament House website, Inquiry into the Family Law Amendment Bill 2003.

Since the pomp and circumstance of his appointment in 1988 the world had changed around Nicholson.

Once widely revered, outside the cloistered realms of public service hangers-on he was now far more likely to be reviled.

He was, figuratively and more or less literally, considering the power and largesse he held in his hands, an ailing, failing king despised by his own people who were now in revolt. Everyone knew he had feet of clay, that his frequent claims of representing the best interests of children were questionable at best. His extreme grandiosity jarred in an essentially egalitarian culture.

Nicholson was appointed in an era before the internet had transformed debate on family law by allowing the rapid transmission of information and the formation of geographically isolated men with similar experiences into ad hoc groups. The net proved all over again the old adage that knowledge is power, turning once secretive courts on their head and transforming the father's movement into an outraged and for a time savvy force, empowering individuals with legal know how and survival strategies but also allowing scattered groups more cohesion through chat lines and a more immediate means of communication.

The Nicholson who appeared before the 2003 inquiry was a diminished figure in an argument to which he had been relegated to a bit player. He was offside with the government, his peers and many in the community.

Numerous scandals circled the court. A once sycophantic media was proving far less compliant. The wails of discontent which had been relegated to the early morning hours on talkback radio were now running prime time.

Australia's number one talkback host Alan Jones received more than 6,000 emails when he raised the issue of child support and the treatment of non-custodial parents, more than he had ever received on any subject.

Chief Justice Nicholson had spent much of the previous 15 years immersed in the radical feminist analysis of power as the sole explanation for social construction. He was now forced to watch as his own power ebbed inexorably away.[127]

***

In his public statements Nicholson rarely expressed the slightest respect for fathers or their role. True or not, there was considerable speculation amongst his critics that these attitudes were a psychopathology stemming from his own unusual upbringing and lack of a normal childhood; first being brought up with his mother in New Guinea and then later spending his school years as a boarder.

---

[127] Stapleton, John, *The Final Days of Alastair Nicholson, Chief Justice of the Family Court of Australia*, 2013.

Nicholson dismissed out of hand one of the greatest grievances expressed by fathers and their representatives against the court – the failure to enforce its own orders in regards to access to children.

Many of these men had paid large sums of money to obtain orders which could be ignored with impunity.

Nicholson, as he did so often, blamed the litigants for the Court's failings, suggesting it was the fathers' fault they could not get the mothers to follow the orders.

Nicholson declared: "I think very often the marriage, or their approach to a marriage, may have been conditioned by older ideas.

"And I think there is very much a power factor comes into this. And I think the loss of that power that stems from the breakdown of the marriage is something that some men just cannot cope with. They in fact expected to control their wives, they expected to control their children, and they expected that they would do what they were told by them. And once that ceases to happen, I think they find that almost unbearable from the point of view of their ego.

"The ones that I've observed, anyhow, that seem to have the greatest problem, are the ones who are in access situations where they are, for one reason or other, unable to get their former partner or the children to comply with the access orders that have been made. And they then come to the court and expect the court to solve the problem for them. And the court can't always solve that problem for them."

His critics regarded all this as patent, insulting rubbish. Just like that, a father's unconditional love for his children and his desire to see, care for and have contact with them were dismissed by the Family Court's Chief Justice with a gendered and outdated theory on the dynamics of interpersonal power.

Hundreds of thousands of dads pining to see their children were as nothing.

***

Three years before *The Australian* had declared in an editorial that Nicholson was the wrong man to lead the court into the new millennium and he should step aside. This was an unprecedented stance for a national broadsheet to take on a superior court judge; and the calls went unheeded.

But each passing day proved the paper's original judgement correct.

While even during the inquiry the Court continued to comment adversely in judgements on fathers who were politically active, largely gone were the days when the Family Court of Australia was not just hated but feared; when fathers frightened to speak out or become politically active for fear of the consequences for their children.

Nicholson frequently attempted to suppress criticism of his court by denigrating those who dared suggest the Family Court had major problems – including the country's national daily *The Australian*, the country's primary legal adviser to government The Australian Law Reform Commission and one of the nation's most distinguished academic historians John Hirst.

In response to Hirst's book *Kangaroo Court,* one of the best books ever written in the sparse literature on the subject, Chief Justice Nicholson replied in correspondence to the *Quarterly Essay*: "It is so riddled with factual inaccuracies, misunderstandings of the law and the Australian court system, and so affected by actual bias and prejudice, that it is not worthy of a detailed reply. I consider that Hirst does a grave disservice to Australians and particularly to Australian women and children. The attacks made are emotional, far from child-focused and contain a surprising degree of misogyny. It is more than time that the family law debate was returned to objective ground where arguments are based upon evidence rather than myth."[128]

The Court under Nicholson had long been in the habit of bringing contempt charges against its critics. It was one of the reasons we at Dads On The Air had been so nervous when we first began.

On 14 June 1990 father Charles Jensen was arrested and charged by a posse of three Australian Federal Police after he sent four letters of complaint, three of them addressed to the "Chief Justice of the Anti-Family Court of Australia Mr Nicholson".

The letters suggested the Court should be located at the Eastern Creek dump "considering the garbage that issues from the present building".

Mr Jensen was convicted for sending offensive material through the post. Now, from the learned to the profane, far worse terms of abuse and allegations of corruption than a mere suggestion the court belongs in a rubbish tip flash across the net everyday. Fathers regularly share their disgust over the perceived bias and extremism of judges and family report writers and plotted ways around them.

Times had changed.

In one celebrated case PT, a 49-year-old pensioner, was charged with scandalising the court, a somewhat arcane piece of legislation. It was alleged PT had handed out leaflets titled "Killers!" and "Blood on who's [sic] hands?" accusing the court of anti-male bias and responsibility for deaths.

Perhaps immodestly, PT told The Australian's High Court reporter Bernard

---

[128] Nicholson, Alastair, Correspondence, Issue 17, Kangaroo Court, *Quarterly Essay*.

Lane: "My job is to close down the Family Court. I'm not a lunatic, I'm a loving father. And I'm not a woman-hater – that's how I got myself into trouble, because I love women."

In well-publicised remarks, the Chief Justice spoke of a "sinister element" among the critics. "I have absolutely no doubt that there are many persons associated with men's groups, in particular who have an agenda to change the law to the disadvantage of women," he said. "A feature of their rhetoric is a complete absence of concern for children other than as objects of their right and entitlements. Many demonstrate, in strident terms, outside the court."

Half an hour after his case was dismissed PT was back outside the Family Court building in Melbourne, proffering pamphlets and crying out, "Read the facts about the Family Court".[129]

***

The 2003 government inquiry had itself posted submissions on the web which labelled the court as "criminal" and referred to the "hated" Nicholson.

Nicholson had made many enemies.

He had dominated the nature, style and substance of family law in Australia since he was appointed in 1988 by then Prime Minister Bob Hawke, who positioned himself as a champion of working people. Yet no institution, and indeed no man, had done more harm to the working class Hawke purported to champion.

In the more than a quarter of a century since its founding no Chief Justice of the Family Court, neither its founding head Elizabeth Evatt nor her successor Justice Nicholson, had ever, that we at Dads On The Air could find, said a positive public word about fathers or fatherhood.

To fathers and family law reform groups Nicholson was Public Enemy Number One.

For them, his reign had seemed interminable, as if he was the beginning and the end of everything that was wrong with Australian family law; and to his increasingly vociferous critics on the country's ballooning men's internet news and chat lines he was the focus of blame for everything that had gone wrong in their lives.

Nicholson's high profile meant his numerous widely publicised pronouncements were followed with a kind of lurid distaste.

Chief Justice Alastair Bothwick Nicholson appeared before the House of

---

129 Lane, Bernard, Street protester beats judges at own game, *The Australian*, 8 March, 2000.

Representatives Family and Community Affairs Committee inquiry into child custody matters in the company of Justice Richard Chisholm, Chief Executive Richard Foster, Principal Mediator James Cotta and General Manager of Client Services Jennifer Cooke.

***

The Committee took the unusual step of releasing a summary of the Family Court's submission, which explained the major provisions, philosophy and effect of the changes made to the Family Law Act in 1995.

"In particular it notes that the change of language (removing terms implying children as property) in that legislation has changed neither behaviour nor language in the community. It also is critical of the lack of clarity around the terms in the legislation and submits that this has exacerbated disputes between parents.

"The submission provides information on several previous parliamentary considerations of the issues before the committee since the Family Law Act was first enacted, and discusses the diversity of clients who seek assistance from the Court and how this would relate to a 50/50 presumption in the best interest of the child.

"The submission explains the Court's approach to case management and resolution of disputes, interim applications, the voices of children and enforcement, including how the Court's non-judicial processes encourage on-going involvement of parents.

"The Court itself is questioning the impact of the traditional adversarial model of litigation in disputes over children. It takes the position that the problem with the current family law system does not lie in the legislation but in the procedure. The submission refers to the possibility of increases in litigation from the proposed amendment (based on the experience of the impact of the 1995 reforms) and the need to manage disappointment when expectations are not met because of the complexity of family situations which do not fit the 50/50 template.

"The Court will be providing information from a statistical survey of court files in order to provide the committee with more detailed information on outcomes, which is not generally available."

***

Nicholson, with all the pomposity for which he was renowned, opened with these remarks: "Chair, as a matter of form, I would like to indicate the way in which both Justice Chisholm and I are here, and I do so simply for the record. As you know, judges are not normally summoned to parliamentary committees but both Justice Chisholm and I took the view that we wanted to be of assistance to the committee and felt it appropriate that we should attend.

"The first time I appeared before such a committee, I took advice from the then Chief Justice of the High Court, who was of the view that that was an appropriate course. I mention that simply for the record."

Throughout the day Nicholson showed no self doubt. He had no answers for the court's numerous problems. But plenty of questions went unasked. The spurious decision making processes, the systemic abuse of psychiatric evidence, the massive volume of complaints from the litigants themselves, the connection between family law, child support and welfare payments, and the poor outcomes for all involved, all these questions went unasked.

As far as family law reform groups were concerned, the moniker The Palace of Lies was well deserved. One of the first questions Nicholson did face was on the issue of perjury in the court.

Committee member Julia Irwin noted that the Committee had heard complaints, particularly from men's groups, about perjury in family law proceedings and that the courts did nothing about that.

"This is most often raised in the discussion of false allegations of violence or child abuse, as you would be aware," Ms Irwin said. "Given that perjury is a criminal offence that requires police action and a decision to prosecute, what can the Family Court do to address this problem?"

Chief Justice Nicholson responded that "allegations of perjury are thrown around very freely in family law matters, and understandably because two people often have two very different views about sets of facts.

"Undoubtedly, there are some people who do tell lies in court – there always have been. The Court is not an investigative agency. If a judge feels that there are particular concerns about the evidence of a witness all they can do is refer that matter to the Attorney General's Department.

"They cannot really refer it to the Director of Public Prosecutions. My experience of having done that is that nothing happens. Very rarely someone might refer it to the Australian Federal Police and they go round and make some investigations, but that is quite uncommon."

This response attracted an almost instant denial from the Attorney General's Department. *The Age* on the next day, a Saturday, reported that the Family Court Chief Justice had accused bureaucrats of failing to act against those who lie in court during custody disputes. It said a spokesman for the Attorney General's

Department rejected the claims, saying the department received "no more than three or four referrals a year" of alleged perjury from the Family Court, and the Department took the claims very seriously.

That the Department no longer appeared to be protecting Nicholson was perhaps indicative of the change in Attorney Generals, from the mild mannered Daryl Williams to Philip Ruddock, who had appeared interested in reforming the jurisdiction.

***

On the question of introducing a rebuttable notion of joint custody Nicholson said there was evidence that judges "sometimes get a bit lazy in relation to a presumption like that and tend to find it easier to apply it than to not apply it. I would hope that would not happen here, but I think the effect would be less there."

Following further questioning he said: "I do not think it is a workable proposition in the Australian community. I do not think that is going to fit very many families. We are dealing not just with middle class families who are involved in a split; we have serial families. There might be three children of three different fathers in one family – there are constellations in those families.

"To start imposing this kind of concept of equal sharing is so inappropriate to most Australian families that it is just not going to work. I think it is so inappropriate to most Australian children to say, 'There is a presumption that you have to spend equal time with your father and mother.'

"You are not talking about quality time, you are talking about equal time. It seems to me that quality is the important thing about the relationship between parents and children, not the measure of time. Try to tell a 14-year-old that they have to go to dad's next week because that is the rule. That kid is going to say, 'I have this on and that on and I have to see my friends.' It just does not seem to me to be a realistic concept."

Nicholson denied that the court had an "80-20" presumption where fathers were given a standard "daddy pack" of every second weekend and half of school holidays for fathers.

"From my point of view as a judge – and, I am sure, for all my colleagues – the most horrible decision we ever have to take is to say that someone should have no contact with a child. That is something that is extraordinarily stressful and very difficult to have to do – and it is very rarely done. We try and produce the best contract arrangements that we can. It is not a question of just simply applying a formula."

Committee member Labor MP Jenny George asked: "So is it just coincidental that, in the statistics that you give us, contact agreed to in consent applications is 40-odd per cent in that 51 to 108 days, contact agreed to in settled applicants as high as 50 per cent and in judicially determined matters around the 70 per cent mark?

"Is there a mind-set that the system has perpetuated that we need to understand or try and break?"

To which Justice Nicholson replied: "I do not believe so."

***

What the Committee failed to note in its frequent affirmation of this so-called 80-20 presumption mention was that this was "if you're lucky" and if the custodial parent complied with the Court's orders; for which there was almost no realistic method of enforcement.

Or that prior to reforms in 1995/96 one in four fathers had no contact with their children after leaving the Court; and almost 50 percent of fathers continued to lose almost all contact with their children within two years of separation, often because of the enormous road blocks put in their way by the Court and the mother.

Nicholson said: "I think that what is happening here when you talk about 80-20 is that the court is being blamed in effect for what is a societal expectation in relation to young children. The court does not have any 80-20 rule, for the reasons I have been explaining. It deals with matters on the face of them as they happen.

"I do not sit there, count it up and say, 'Who's this way and who's that way?' You have got to realise that quite often there is no issue when we are talking 80-20.

"There are a lot of cases where there is absolutely no issue – that is, the father does not want the children on terms other than those being discussed.

"As I said, there are occasions when our counsellors have to actively persuade the father that they ought to see the children. There are many cases where the father does not turn up when such an arrangement is made.

"So it is not a presumption. If you have a proper case on residence to place before the court, there is absolutely no presumption against you at all and you are dealt with in the same way as any other litigant: you have either got a case or you have not.

"The interests of the children are what we are concerned about, not the interest of the person. It seems to me that the presumption has this problem: you are saying that there is a legislative expectation that the children will be shared equally, and that just is not the reality of Australian homes. That just is not the reality of life at the moment; you just do not have people who can comply with that sort of a presumption. I think it will cause a lot of difficulty."

***

The reluctance of the court to alter its practices or admit fault was evident when Committee member Pearce asked what would, given that the Court already had discretion to make shared parenting orders, actually change if the legislation was shifted to a rebuttable presumption of joint residency.

Nicholson responded that "If you are talking about actual hearings before judges, the effect would be much less than would be the situation prior to that time because, as you correctly say, the issues would all be before the judge and it is subject to a best interest test anyway. The judge would, I expect, proceed to examine the evidence and probably come to a decision in much the same way as they now do.

"The real effect comes at the earlier stage because we know it is an expensive business to go to court, we know how difficult it is to go to court without representation and we have got a situation where the legislature is saying there is a presumption of fifty-fifty. Parents may be more inclined to simply give in on that without regard to the fact that it might have a detrimental effect on their children.

"There is plenty of evidence already, with the Legal Aid difficulties, of people not being prepared to pursue litigation simply because they cannot. I am not prepared, as a matter of principle, to say that in general it is better to have an equal sharing of time of children between parents; I think each family has to be looked at in its context.

"I get concerned when we start to say that, for people who are in conflict, there is a presumption that they ought to share their children equally. I just have great concerns about it. I have great concerns when I look at the differing ages of children and their development, too. One thing might be good for a three-year-old.

"It is a sort of one-size-fits-all suggestion that does not take into account the effects on individual children. I am concerned that it will be forced on people. Also, I am concerned about aspects of violence in relation to it. When there has been, for example, a history of violence in the family I am concerned that a controlling type person may well say, 'I want my half share' and the other party may well not be able to withstand that."

***

While Chief Justice Nicholson did not get the grilling that some family law reformers would have liked to see, the Committee appeared at the time to be fairly sceptical of many of Nicholson's pronouncements.

Committee Chair Kay Hull queried Nicholson's assertions that there could be a significant increase in litigation if rebuttable joint custody; saying she thought the presumption of joint custody could mean fewer cases going through the Family Court "simply because we will have put in an intervention pathway".

Committee member Chris Pearce said of the Court: "We have heard time and time again that it is just a toothless tiger, particularly in relation to contact. That is the classic, I would think; dad has shown up to pick up the children on Friday afternoon and mum has done every single thing possible to stop the contact – for example, she has gone away for the weekend. It happens time and time again and the court does nothing in relation to enforcement."

To which Nicholson responded: "I had one of those cases before me recently. I said to the father, 'You've proved all these breaches and I gave her the complete dressing down; what do you want me to do? Do you want her to go to jail? I'm prepared to send her to jail if you want me to.'

"That was a bad one. He said no. So what is the next step? It is not as simple as saying the court should get tough. Quite often the parents do not want that sort of result either."

***

Asked over the question of the possibility of juries in Family Court cases, in order to eradicate the bias of a single judge, Nicholson said it was "an appalling suggestion" which would constitute a "leap back in time" because it would encourage cases being conducted "on quite irrelevant issues about sexual mores and all sorts of matters that would normally now not form part of family law proceedings."

Committee member Pearce noted in the Family Court's submission the statement: "A well planned family law system does not exist in this country and has never done so. Why hasn't it ever existed? What has the Family Court of Australia tried to do to establish a family system that does work?"

To which Nicholson once again repeated his dream of a unified Family Court system that dealt with everything to do with children with professionals working in a "holistic way".

"So far as the Family Court is concerned, if I were asked about our difficulties, I would say that our primary difficulty is the ability to provide swift and reasonably inexpensive justice to people.

"I think that is one of the areas that we still need to work on. We are working on it, as I have indicated, but there are problems. You have to have the resources to do that – and resources have been and remain a problem. I suppose that applies to any institution but, nevertheless, it is a significant problem. There are areas of Australia, for example, that I do not believe we can service as well as I would like to service them or as well as they should be serviced."

Nicholson also suggested that joint custody imposed major difficulties in cases where children were conceived through IVF using donor sperm or eggs or through rape.

The next day a significant number of outlets ran with the Chief Justice's stance on joint custody. *The Sydney Morning Herald* headlined theirs: "Family Court chief at odds with PM."

The wire service AAP ran a story, picked up the next day by a number of newspapers, which began: "The head of the Family Court has lambasted the Prime Minister's proposal for shared custody of children from broken homes, saying it would never work. Chief Justice Alastair Nicholson was scornful of any suggestion the Family Law Act be changed to presume divorced parents received equal access to their children."

Chief Justice Alastair Nicholson was back in the news a mere four days later, once again espousing a single court to preside over all child matters when he delivered the John Barry Memorial Lecture at Melbourne University. Quixotic, perhaps, considering the number of critics of his court, Nicholson said reform of the Family Court system was overdue, saying the current system was compromising the welfare of vulnerable young people.

He argued for a unified or single Family Court which would have jurisdiction over juvenile crime, child abuse, adoption, child support, guardianship, divorce and paternity. He said one court handling all child matters would provide a unified response to the families.

The concentration and aggregation of yet further power into the Family Court sphere as championed by Nicholson met with zero enthusiasm.

THIRTEEN
THE CURIOUS RETIREMENT OF ALASTAIR NICHOLSON, CHIEF JUSTICE OF THE FAMILY COURT OF AUSTRALIA

Word spread, I guess, that there was a journalist on the nation's national newspaper *The Australian* interested in exposing the practices of the Family Court.

One day a former judge of the court rang me at work and suggested we meet. In the Australian context there aren't too many judges who contact journalists and are prepared to become whistleblowers.

I readily agreed to meet, and so we did shortly afterwards, at a cafe in the trendy Inner West suburb of Balmain.

The man was charming, and as I soon realised, still practising as a senior figure in the New South Wales judiciary after having retired from the Family Court.

In a wide ranging conversation all about his years in the Family Court, and his steady path into disillusion, we talked about the court's present dismal reputation.

"I started off as a fan of Nicholson, but he has turned the court into a disaster," he said of the present.

We laughed about the gossip of the court's senior judges as a coterie of top shelf drunks on five star jaunts around the world, gossip which was already widely known within the legal profession.

And we talked about the media's abject failure to cover the many issues arising out of the Family Court. He lamented about how he had handed over two boxes of damming files on the court to investigative journalist Chris Masters at the ABC who not only didn't return the files but never did the story.

The story he had to tell was a complicated one, involving how in his mind most of the judges in the Family Court had breached the Australian Constitution by resigning their commissions and then accepting their recommissions, all in secret, so as to extend their retirement ages.

Only a very few of the judges resigned in protest at what they saw as a flagrant and illegal breach. He was one of them.

***

Nicholson had been appointed by the Hawke Labor government until the age of 65; August 19th, 2003; slap bang in the middle of the parliamentary inquiry.

Family law reformers saw the Chief Justice as the single biggest impediment to reform. If there was to be proper implementation of joint custody they believed it would be impossible without a clean broom through the Family Court. His retirement was greatly anticipated by family law reformers.

In July 2002 Nicholson announced via a media release and on the Family Court website that while he had greatly enjoyed his time as Chief Justice he would cease hearing cases on 1 February 2003 and take accrued leave until March, 2004. As it turned out, these statements were false. His initial statements that he would take a year's accumulated leave were rescinded and he continued to carry out what he saw as his duties.

The announcement of Nicholson's departure led to headlines ranging from "dark legacy" to "the man who loved children", after a literary classic by Australian author Christina Stead of the same title, and illustrated the divisive nature of the opinions held about him.

Writing in *The Age* longtime social commentator Bettina Arndt observed, under the headline Nicholson's Dark Legacy: A court that failed Men, that in choosing his replacement "The Howard Government should be mindful of Nicholson's greatest failure – his refusal to acknowledge any substance to the widespread perception that his court has been biased against men. Not only has Nicholson persistently dismissed the problem, but he has inflamed resentment with a series of public relations disasters showing contempt for these genuine grievances.

"During Nicholson's tenure, the Family Court has been subject to numerous inquiries that have found evidence of inequitable treatment by the court. Among the issues causing resentment have been the failure of the court to enforce child contact orders, false allegations of sexual abuse and violence resulting in men being denied contact with their children, men's lack of access to legal aid, and prejudicial treatment by counsellors and judges."[130]

A fortnight before he was due to stop hearing cases, Nicholson announced he

---

[130] Arndt, Bettina, Nicholson's dark legacy: a court that failed men, *The Age*, 17 July, 2002.

now "took the view it wasn't fair" to step aside and didn't "want to let anyone down". He blamed in part the Federal Government's tardiness in appointing new judges for being forced to soldier on.

Dads On The Air suggested that this was rich coming from a man who, as exposed by Senator Brett Mason in hearings of Senate Estimates Committees, sat less than 45 days a year and headed a court where some judges sat even less than that.

August the 19th, 2003, came and went and Nicholson did not retire.

There had never been any public announcement of any kind to suggest that he would serve beyond the date of his appointment.

Why, fathers and family law groups around the country asked, was he not retiring?

There was no explanation coming from either the government or the Family Court to explain the mysterious vagaries of the retirement schedule of Nicholson. There was no public acknowledgement that the judges of the Family Court had, with a few principled exceptions, en masse and in secret, previously resigned their commissions and then been reappointed.

***

Critics argued that Nicholson's failure to retire on schedule raised issues of conflict with the Australian Constitution. Working off material that I passed on to them as part of my work at Dads On The Air, both the Shared Parenting Council and the Men's Rights Agency put out detailed statements on the issue.

When the Family Law Act was created in 1975 there was no set retirement age for judges, who were appointed for life.

Following a referendum in 1977 a retirement age of 70 was set for most judges; while subsequent changes set the retirement age of Family Court judges at 65.

Later the same year, 1977, an amendment to the Family Law Act 1975 was introduced by Prime Minister John Howard, then a senior figure in the government of Malcolm Fraser, to lower the retirement age for the judges of the Family Court to 65 years of age.

His argument detailed in the political transcripts of Hansard suggested that: "It is generally conceded that in family law, more than in most other areas of law, judges adjudicating over disputes should be aware of and keep abreast of current social values and attitudes. For this reason, and also because of the demanding and arduous nature of at least some of the disputes – notably, defended custody disputes – there seems to be good reasons for requiring judges of the Family Court to retire at least by the age recognised as the maximum retiring age for most other occupations in the community."

The Parliament accepted this bill and the Family Law Amendment Act 1977 was assented to and commenced on 11 October 1977.

In 1977, after the referendum, the Australian Constitution was changed to read in part: "The appointment of a Justice of a court created by the Parliament shall be for a term expiring upon his attaining the age that is, at the time of his appointment, the maximum age for Justices of that court and a person shall not be appointed as a Justice of such a court if he has attained the age that is for the time being the maximum age for Justices of that court.

"Subject to this section, the maximum age for Justices of any court created by the Parliament is seventy years. The Parliament may make a law fixing an age that is less than seventy years as the maximum age for Justices of a court created by the Parliament and may at any time repeal or amend such a law, but any such repeal or amendment does not affect the term of office of a Justice under an appointment made before the repeal or amendment."[131]

There it was. Clear as a bell. Justice Nicholson should be retiring on schedule. If not, why not?

**

No more changes to the retirement age for judges of the Family Court were made or suggested until the first report of the Joint Select Committee on Certain Aspects of the Operation and Interpretation of the Family Law Act in 1991.

The Report recommended that the Family Law Act be amended to fix a maximum retirement age of 70 years for Family Court judges in line with other courts.

That legislation was enacted and commenced on 25 October 1991.

When the Chief Justice of the Family Court Alastair Nicholson expressed his views to the Joint Select Committee on Certain Aspects of the Operation and Interpretation of the Family Law Act in 1991 he still wielded considerable influence. The Committee recommended the retirement age for Family Court judges be extended to 70 years.

MP Ian Wilson in his second reading speech, said: "I note the views of the Chief Justice of the Family Court, the Honourable Justice Nicholson, who queries whether the job of a Family Court judge is necessarily more stressful than that of a judge in any other court or the jobs of many other people who are aged between 65 and 70."

Wilson quoted from Justice Nicholson's submission to the Committee from

---

[131] Constitution Alteration (Retirement of Judges) 1977, Australian Constitution, Section 72. The amendment was enacted on 29 July 1977.

whose recommendations the Bill emanated. His Honour said: "The work of Judges in all such Courts is stressful. There is little to choose between the emotional strain of conducting a criminal trial and arriving at an appropriate sentence, for example, then there is in conducting a trial of a custody or access issue.

"Matrimonial property disputes frequently require judges to display the same skills and learning as is required of a Court of Equity."[132]

On the face of it, Nicholson appeared to be one of those who should, according to any straightforward reading of the Constitution, retire at 65.

Certainly that was the view of the former Family Court judge who had alerted me to the story. He himself had refused to accept the later retirement date, believing it to be unconstitutional, and I attempted to speak to every last one of the small coterie of judges who had followed suit. Later to become a senior legal figure in NSW, the whistle blowing judge described his years in the court as the worst of his professional life. He leaked the story in an attempt to expose Nicholson's conduct.

To others, as well, it appeared clear that Chief Justice Nicholson should retire.

***

The Shared Parenting Council of Australia put out a statement that in accordance with Section 72 of the Constitution of Australia, the Chief Justice, having reached age 65, must retire from the bench, and leave the Court, contrary to his own decision to stay until February 2004.

The SPCA statement read: "The Family Law Act, at the time of Alastair Nicholson's appointment, was unambiguous about the retirement age of a judge appointed to that Court – and they must retire once attaining the age of 65 years. The Constitution is also unambiguous."

Rod Hardwick, President of Dads Australia, also lent his support to the calls for Nicholson to retire on schedule.

"Family law is in complete disarray in this country," he said. "That is in no small part the responsibility of the present Chief Justice, Alastair Nicholson.

"The massive harm that the Family Court has done to hundreds of thousands of families and to the community at large cannot be underestimated in financial, emotional or legal terms. The government should take the opportunity of his retiring to completely reform or abolish this institution. That the Court is failing to comply with its legislative obligations to act in the best interests of children is self-evident to every objective observer of the court.

---

132 Second reading speech by Ian Wilson, Hansard, Australian Parliament House, 1991.

"Nicholson's claims that the court is not biased against fathers are simply preposterous.

"How can fathers possibly have faith in a court where the judges cannot even retire when they are supposed to?"[133]

***

Without fanfare or any public announcement, but clearly prepared for potential controversy over the issue, the Attorney General Daryl Williams' office placed a statement on their web site which raised as many questions as it answered.

Here is the statement in full.

"Talking points by the Attorney General for the media in response to a news release by the Shared Parenting Council of Australia:

"Consistent with the relevant provisions of the Family Law Act when he was appointed to the Family Court in 1988, Chief Justice Nicholson was originally appointed until he turned 65.

"In 1991, a Parliamentary Committee recommended that the Family Law Act be amended to increase the retirement age for Family Court judges from 65 to 70.

"Legislation to give effect to this recommendation was passed by the Parliament and came into effect in late 1991.

"Subsequently, Chief Justice Nicholson and all other Family Court judges who had been appointed until age 65 were offered the opportunity to be appointed until age 70.

"On 28 October 1993, Chief Justice Nicholson and a number of his colleagues were each appointed until they attained 70 years of age.

"Any suggestion that Chief Justice Nicholson's appointment is unconstitutional is misconceived."

But just exactly how the claims were misconceived was never explained.

The statement was useful in several ways:
- It was the first public admission that Family Court judges had, in apparent secrecy, resigned their commissions and been recommissioned to extend their retirement ages.
- It sheeted home blame to the former Keating government.
- It failed to offer any legal argument or any legal explanation to rebut the claims by the Shared Parenting Council and others over Nicholson's retirement.

---

133 Dads On The Air, Chaos at the Crossroads, submission 2003. Available on the Australian Parliament website.

***

The Shared Parenting Council of Australia requested from both the Family Court and the Attorney General's Department the full list of judges involved in the resignations and re-commissions, the resignation letters of the judges to the Governor General of the day, Bill Hayden, and copies of the Government Gazette Notices and Media Releases of the AG and FCA that advised the public of these re-appointments.

The SPCA put out a statement suggesting that the groups they represented awaited the information with interest.

"The Question that now remains is: What possible reason was there for a number of judges resigning and being reappointed other than to defeat Section 72 of the Constitution?

"Where are the Gazettes and the Media Releases of the Attorney General and the Family Court of Australia from October 1993 that proves this to be the case?

"The basic principle of law, arising from the English Law and inherited into Australia, is that a Court cannot do indirectly, what it cannot do directly. In other words, if the parliament cannot alter the terms of office of a judge directly, it cannot do it indirectly – by a contrived resignation and reappointment.

"The next legal question is – how can this appointment be upheld as constitutional if the purpose and only purpose of the resignation and re-commissioning is to defeat Section 72 of the constitution?"[134]

The government refused to provide any evidence that the re-commissions were conducted through the Governor General in Council, as required by law. They also refused to provide the legal advice the Governor General and the Attorney General's offices relied on to determine that the resignations and re-commissions were not a breach of the Constitution, the names and number of judges who took part, the legal advice arguing that the moves were illegal circulated by a dissenting judge within the court, our whistleblower, the resignation letters of the judges, or indeed any documentation at all.

Nothing to hide?

***

The Attorney General Daryl Williams invoked the 30 year cabinet secrecy rule to explain why he would not release any documentation to demonstrate that Nicholson's secretive resignation and re-commissioning in 1993 was legal.

Here's the exact wording of his rejection of the request for such documentation:

---

134 Ibid.

"Chief Justice Nicholson's October 1993 appointment would have been considered in Cabinet by the Keating Government. Subject to the 30-year rule, Cabinet documents are not available to governments other than those which created them.

"Under the Archives Act 1983 Cabinet documents are generally open to public access only after thirty years."[135]

Dads Australia, attempting to turn up the heat, said the Criminal Code of 1995 is applicable to the judiciary as well as each and every member of the public.

Dads Australia called for an inquiry into the resignations and re-commissioning of the Family Court Judges. "If their re-commissioning and/or term of office past the age of 65, is found to be unconstitutional we demand that appropriate criminal proceedings be commenced. This is potentially the greatest constitutional crisis in Australia since the 1975 sacking of the Whitlam Government by the then Governor General Sir John Kerr."

But nothing happened.

Nicholson continued to hear cases, he continued to give speeches and he continued to write and make public pronouncements against joint custody.

***

Appointed by then Prime Minister Bob Hawke, Nicholson's primary qualification for becoming the Family Court's Chief Justice was his loyalty to the Labor Party. He had twice run for election in the Victorian seat of Chisholm as a member of the Labor Party, failing in both 1972 and 1974.

Bob Hawke painted himself as the great hero of Australia's working class. Yet there was no group more affected, or destroyed, by the operations of the Child Support Agency he initiated or the family law he had failed to reform than the nation's workers.

Through his office I questioned him whether, considering the multiple controversies now surrounding the court, he had any regrets over the appointment.

Hawke said he believed Nicholson had done an excellent job.

Go Bob.

No one is accountable. No one expresses regret. No one apologies. And the trainwreck rolls on. There is no final destination, only destitution for some, desolation for others. And a gleeful gaggle of lawyers rubbing their hands as billions of dollars flow their way.

---

135 Correspondence with the author. Some of the correspondence between Dads On The Air and Attorney General Daryl Williams' office on this issue can be seen at Questions and Answers from the Attorney General Daryl Williams, Dads On The Air, 1 July, 2002.

To jump out of the timeline, some two decades or so later there was a very curious footnote to the sorry tale of the secret resignations and recommissions of the Family Court's judges and the difficulties I had getting it published in the mainstream press.

The 2021 story was titled The Hanging of Christian Porter, and was about the then Attorney General. It also showed some of the social and cultural consequences of the abject failure of the nation's elite media to stand up to the Family Court behemoth and its feminist lackeys.[136]

While chronological order is almost always the best way to tell a story, we live in a time where it feels as if time is collapsing in on itself, and so I reproduce the story here.

It reads as follows, bearing in mind we are talking about the year 2021: The devolved state of journalism at the $1.2 billion Australian Broadcasting Corporation is now on full display.

The current witch hunt of the nation's Attorney General over entirely unsubstantiated claims of an alleged rape 33 years ago, when he was a teenager, is a classic case in point.

What amazes old-timers like myself is that any of it even went to air.

The national broadcaster's narrow range of left wing obsessions, gender politics, refugees, climate change, indigenous disadvantage and multiculturalism, entirely ignore the lived experience of mainstream Australians and are the primary reason for their declining influence and poor audience numbers.

Now they've taken it all to a whole new level.

The hunt for Australia's chief law officer began in November last year with a broadcast portentously titled Inside the Canberra Bubble. It featured "investigative journalist", the ABC's Princess of Woke Louise Milligan, as presenter and leader of the charge.

The program's central claim was that Parliament House had a culture toxic to women, and featured an array of well known, and yes, taxpayer funded, gender warriors, including former NSW Premier Kristina Keneally. Her blockbuster claim was that some men hit upon her, that is flirted with her, perhaps clumsily, at a function she attended without her husband.

Really!!! How truly appalling!!! Honestly, get a grip. No woman has ever flirted with someone at a function in the absence of her husband??? Grow up you dismal excuses.

---

136 Stapleton, John, The Hanging of Christian Porter, A Sense of Place Magazine, 28 December, 2021.

***

Every last person appearing on Inside the Canberra Bubble had an axe to grind, not least the heavily featured former Prime Minister Malcolm Turnbull, who proved as vindictive in defeat as he was self-aggrandising in office.

Turnbull reportedly despised Attorney General Christian Porter and was willing to throw him under a bus perhaps because of the role Porter played in Turnbull's overthrow in an internal party coup in 2018.

Ever politically correct when it suited him, Turnbull has appointed himself the saviour of Australian women, claiming amid lingering shots of Canberra watering holes and entwining feet, that the governing culture shows a "lack of respect for women".

Turnbull was frequently quoted, never contradicted, and there was no attempt to put his manipulative spite into context.

Christian Porter was the target of that first broadcast, and now, four months later, has been brought down by a howling media mob.

It was another scalp for the Australian Broadcasting Corporation's star reporter Louise Milligan, fresh from her Cardinal George Pell debacle, during which she led a three year "investigation" of child sex abuse, again based on entirely unsubstantiated allegations.

"Without a doubt this is the toughest story I have ever done," Milligan claimed of the Pell story. "This is a person who had immense political and cultural power so taking that on is enormous and very, very stressful. Being at the centre of this storm, it doesn't get any harder than that as a journalist."

Pell went to jail, only to be fully exonerated in a unanimous decision by the High Court of Australia.

But by that stage much of the nation, convinced of his guilt as a child molester thanks to the work of one ABC journalist, would have happily seen him hang. Milligan never apologised.

She moved on to the Attorney General.

A handsome man from a patrician background, Porter's main crimes as displayed in that first broadcast were to have been a bit of a lad at university, to have been partial to a party throughout much of his life and to have a liking for the company of women.

Shoot me now.

Parliament House is haunted by a new and truly insane puritanism, one where men are always guilty.

***

Inside the Canberra Bubble was so prejudicial and so poorly based it should never have seen the light of day.

The sight of two of the country's most privileged women, Sarah Hanson-Young of the Greens and Louise Milligan of the ABC, discussing on film how a third woman may have felt "trapped" by an affair with a cabinet minister has to be seen to be believed and epitomises all that is wrong with the public broadcaster.

Human lives are often messy. Not everyone thinks monogamy is a human ideal. So damn what?

The unsubstantiated accusations that Porter may have been involved in raping a fellow student when he was a teenager began circulating in December of 2020 after the broadcast of Inside the Canberra Bubble. Journalists were alerted to the story through an anonymous letter.

The accusations were made by a reportedly gifted but mentally ill woman who never made a formal complaint and had attempted to kill herself several times. The quasi-journalism that turned those accusations into a national issue and a major threat to the government, encased in the solemnity of theme music and lingering, atmospheric shots of parliamentary corridors, have become tantamount to fact.

Any journalist working on a mainstream outlet encounters mentally ill people on a regular basis. "They're following me everywhere. You have to do a story." And any normal journalist without an agenda shows them kindness but pays them no heed.

Christian Porter, in an unwise move, outed himself as the subject of the anonymous letter at an extremely emotional press conference, allowing the media to go straight into a shark attack frenzy while providing the fodder for women's marches around the country.

The allegations against Attorney General Christian Porter prompted more than 100,000 women to march in Canberra, Sydney, Melbourne and Brisbane.

And allowed Louise Milligan to produce a followup program, Bursting the Canberra Bubble, which was just as execrable as Inside the Canberra Bubble.

Her old employer, *The Australian*, described her latest efforts on Christian Porter as plumbing "the depths of unprofessionalism". Other conservative leaning news sites were equally vitriolic.

***

Adding to making Porter's demise so pivotal and his media sledging so consequential was that he was regularly touted as a future Prime Minister at a time of increasing discontent over the leadership of incumbent Scott Morrison.

But there was strong speculation that the timing and framing of the stories targeting Christian Porter, their nature of contextualising slurs and the febrile atmosphere from which they are birthed, are related to Christian Porter's abolition of the Family Court of Australia and its merger with the Federal Court.

I sat next to Louise Milligan for some two years when I worked as a general news reporter at *The Australian*. I am familiar with her work.

Almost 20 years ago I wrote the story detailed above involving the mass resignation and recommissioning of Family Court judges in secret in order to extend their retirement ages.

The story took weeks to write and was done in close consultation with both the paper's Editor-in-Chief and the informant. Great effort went into ensuring it was 100 percent watertight.

Hours before scheduled publication the paper decided to get Louise Milligan, who has a law degree, to check over and rewrite the story. The thinking being that as a separated father I might be biased on the issue.

But a staunch feminist dealing with a story on that great feminist icon the Family Court, she wouldn't be biased?

The entirely eviscerated result, published on page two the following day, barely made any sense. I had to continue sitting next to Milligan for several more months. I didn't dislike Milligan as a person. But I certainly disliked her style of journalism.

I later apologised to the informant judge when I ran into him at a function. "I knew it wasn't you, John," he replied.

***

Details of the scandal were passed to One Nation leader Pauline Hanson, who co-chaired a 2019 inquiry into family law. They were also believed to have been passed on to Christian Porter.

After decades of expensive and completely useless government inquiries, hundreds of thousands of damaged children and even greater numbers of destroyed or embittered litigants, not always fathers, Christian Porter is the first politician to have stood up to powerful interests invested in this debacle.

The Turnbull menace behind Porter's framing was in plain sight.

With very little fanfare, legislation passed through parliament in February to merge the Family Court with the Federal Court, effectively abolishing it. Whether the long hidden story of the judge's mass resignations and recommissionings fed into the abolition of the court we may never know. Certainly some people close to the story thought so.

To this day I believe it is a story that should not have been killed off.

***

West Australian Law Reform Commissioner and Law Professor Augusto Zimmermann said the Family Court had been a dark stain on the nation's legal, social and political history.

"There is speculation that the hunting of Christian Porter is simply a bit of Canberra femocracy payback for the destruction of their beloved Family Court," Professor Zimmerman told A Sense of Place Magazine. "At the very least the timing is uncanny. There is an old saying: 'There is no such thing as coincidence.'"

Certainly the travails of the Attorney General, who subsequently sued the ABC and Louise Milligan, met with little or no sympathy from separated fathers, many of whom have lost contact with their children on the basis of false and entirely unsubstantiated claims of domestic violence or sexual abuse.

As one Facebook group calling itself Domestic Violence Awareness Australia put it: "The Attorney General now understands how damaging allegations of sexual abuse and/or domestic violence are when made against a man by a woman, no matter how powerful his position or standing. Now perhaps, and especially if you are actually not guilty of the allegations raised against you now, you might finally understand how it feels."

***

Once upon a time journalists told stories. Other people's stories. The nation's stories.

The turbulence of daily life, the dishonesty of councils, courts, corporations and an ever colourful parade of ne'er-do-wells were all grist to the daily news cycle.

Now we are seeing, on open ground, the full consequences of the sad devolution of journalism away from its original story telling functions.

The extreme bias of the Australian Broadcasting Corporation lay not only in the stories themselves, but in the stories they didn't run.

The ABC's incessant feminist advocacy and complete failure to investigate the scandals circling the Family Court of Australia, including the many questions over legitimacy raised by the secret resignations and recommissioning of its judges to circumvent the Constitution, has real life consequences.

While endlessly pursuing stories on minorities and victim groups the ABC ignored the declining fortunes of Australia's working classes and the almost complete collapse of its now ice riddled underclass, events which will prove to have profound effects on the nation's future.

Given the circumstances, the Australian Attorney General should have the last word.

At his press conference a highly stressed Christian Porter, in words that many Australian fathers could sympathise with, said: "I have been subject to the most wild, unrestrained, intense series of accusations I can remember in modern Australian politics. Maybe that is the new normal. I hope for everyone's sake it is not."

***

In April 2004, Dads On The Air noted that at long last Chief Justice of the Family Court Alastair Nicholson had retired after 15 years in the position.

At a ceremonial sitting on 2 April 2004 his service to the law and the people of Australia was honoured by judges, members of the legal profession, politicians and other citizens.

DOTA provided a link to the Family Court publication Courtside, which carried a lengthy interview with Nicholson. But we also pointed out that less flattering views were not hard to find.

One of Nicholson's last actions before retiring was to release one of his judgments allowing a 13-year-old girl to begin gender reassignment therapy to become a boy. It was an Australian first and attracted worldwide attention. Critics said the judgement demonstrated everything that was wrong with the court. Given the disrepute into which gender reassignment surgery would later fall, it was a fitting epitaph.

At a ceremonial sitting on 2 April 2004 his service to the law and the people of Australia was honoured by judges, members of the legal profession, politicians and other citizens.

In an interview published in the legal newsletter CCH Nicholson said that unfortunately the Family Court did not get good press and when he came to it in the 1980s morale was low.

"The thing that struck me before I came to the Court was that everyone was prepared to throw mud at the Court and no one was doing much about defending it. I determined then that I wasn't going to take that sort of attack and as far as the Court was concerned I was going to be pretty noisy, and quick to defend it from public attacks.

"I was also trying to get on the front foot to an extent to get some reasonable media coverage of what we did do right. Certainly, I've never regretted having spoken out on the Court's behalf. People know if they do have a go at the Court they're going to get a strong response.

"Another belief that I hold strongly is that judges and particularly chief justices have not only a right but also a duty to speak out on human rights issues or those that detrimentally affect people using the court system.

"Accordingly, I have made public comment on indigenous issues, issues affecting the rights of children, and issues such as the reduction in legal aid for family law litigants. I have no regrets about having done so."

Nicholson said their strategic plan Future Directions published in July 2000 "was the first time we were really looking at a client focus. The consultant interviewed clients as well as us. We listened to these interviews and got rather a nasty shock when we heard what clients were saying.

"We'd regularly consulted with representative organisations but I think they tend to tell you what they think the users' concerns ought to be. It's very different and, in a sense, quite raw information when you hear it direct from real people.

"This is something we have to guard against – getting filtered information. Actually, that leads me to comment on another notable change. When I first came to the Court the women's groups were more strident in their approach to things than now. Men's groups have become more so and I am very concerned that the men's lobby, which is not just confined to Australia, is going to really affect the position of women to their detriment in family law proceedings.

"That's something we've got to be very careful about. This is in no way to denigrate the role of fathers in families. That is and remains very important and, contrary to popular belief, fathers are often successful in contested proceedings."

***

There were a number of high profile tributes.

Principal Family Court Judge of New Zealand Judge Patrick Mahony said Chief Justice Nicholson was one of the great international figures in family law. "In an era which will be remembered for the development of children's rights, he has been a powerful advocate for children in fearless public statements and in his contribution to a developing jurisprudence building on the United Nations Convention on the Rights of the Child.

"He has been closely associated with three World Congresses on Children's Rights. He has been an outstanding leader in his own Court in Australia, generously sharing educational opportunities through conferences and seminars with judicial colleagues from New Zealand, United States of America, Canada, United Kingdom, Pakistan, Japan, Singapore and several Pacific countries.

"Behind this profile is a man of imposing stature, benign and kindly, generous and outgoing, even-handed, loyal and protective but with a powerful intellect, strong willed and always the courage of his convictions."

Len Glare, Chief Executive Officer of the Family Court of Australia between 1990 and 2000, said: "For about six years we 'suffered' the attentions of various Parliamentary Committees enquiring into the Court's administration. This was a great distraction from our work and a serious diversion of scarce resources. The Court generally, and Alastair particularly, had to deal with strong attacks from a wide variety of critics.

"However, he remained fiercely protective of the Court and fought battles on many Parliamentary and media fronts. I think he did it well and the critics had relatively few successes."[137]

***

Justifying a number of overseas trips, Justice Nicholson served as President of the Association of Family and Conciliation Courts AFCC's first President from outside North America in 1997/98.

Justice George Czutrin, then serving as President of the Association of Family and Conciliation Courts and a judge of the Family Court in Ontario, Canada, said few leaders of the AFCC have had as profound an impact as Chief Justice Alastair Nicholson.

"While I am limited by the words allotted to me, it seems that there are nowhere near enough words to adequately do justice to Justice Nicholson's contributions."

Describing Nicholson's accomplishments as extraordinary, Czutrin said in 1998 Nicholson presided over the largest ever AFCC Annual conference, in Washington, DC.

"His participation influenced the way family courts are run in North America, as he introduced the work of the Family Court of Australia to AFCC members," Czutrin said.

At a special function in Melbourne a portrait of Nicholson by the award winning artist Robert Hannaford was unveiled. The portrait hangs in the judicial chambers of the Melbourne Registry.

Hannaford observed: "Alastair was a delightful sitter and most importantly, I found him a wonderful man. I developed a deep sense of someone who is a very balanced person, someone who has great convictions about his responsibilities and concerns for families, especially for children and for Indigenous people, and also someone who has many and varied other interests."

***

---

137 Stapleton, John, The Final Days of Alastair Nicholson, 2013.

The forums on Dads On The Air, as one might expect, were less positive.

"Fab" wrote: "Yeah right...Nicholson go and tell your pathetic story to all the children that long for their dad that you and your evil court have ripped away from them. Go and tell all the men that have been physically abused by their wives that all men are violent.

"Go and explain to all these people in jail now that come from fatherless homes. Go and tell the men that have been falsely accused and the penalty of being involved with a greedy lying bitch is the loss of their children thanks to your loony courts that allow perjury to be freely practised in them."

Another, signing himself as a "Caring and Loving Father", wrote: "I no longer have contact with my children because of Nicholson's Family Court and because of the Labor Party agenda of social engineering. For me, a one-time Labor supporter, I will never vote for the Australian Labor Party again because they caused me to be separated from my children."

***

On 15 April 2004 High Court Justice Michael Kirby, the first openly gay High Court judge and a hero to the Australian left, gave a valedictory address to the University of Melbourne's Faculty of Law.[138]

Kirby said: "The retirement of most judges passes without notice, outside the cloistered world of the legal profession. This cannot be said of Alastair Nicholson, a distinguished alumnus of this Law School. An insightful essay on his long service observed: 'Nicholson has been a spectacular judge; perhaps appearing more extraordinary as the society around him has grown increasingly conservative.'

"In person, Nicholson is genial, and quick to talk about issues. He is a journalist's dream in one sense — never failing to answer a question directly and with a candour unusual in public life. But he is slow to delve into the personal, and seems almost puzzled when asked about the effect on him of his work — all the pain, love and hate he has seen pass through his Court.

"It is fitting that I should be called on to honour him. In a dark moment, his was a rare judicial voice publicly lifted to defend me and the independent courts when so many other voices fell silent. Such conduct was typical of the man. Brave, forthright and valiant..."

Kirby was referring to the scandal that engulfed him in 2002 after Senator Bill

---

138 Kirby, Michael, Chief Justice Nicholson — A Valedictory Address, Melbourne Journal of International Law, 2004.

Heffernan, on a crusade against child abuse, made claims the High Court judge had used Commonwealth cars for inappropriate purposes, that is, picking up young men.

As a general news reporter I had to go and knock on his door at his beautifully located harbourside home on several occasions, only to be given fairly short shrift by his longtime boyfriend. Some time later, at some function or other, I apologised to him personally for the invasion of privacy. "We all have to do our jobs," he said, brushing it off.

Kirby never hid the fact that he was gay but denied the allegations, which turned on reports and documentation by a Commonwealth driver which were subsequently demonstrated to be false.

Kirby continued: "Alastair Nicholson has known from an early age that to endure, great institutions must be defended but also must change and adapt. From the start, his court because of the nature of its duties was a target for criticism and calumny, most of it undeserved.

"He could have ignored the attacks and the personal affronts. Yet that was alien to his upbringing and character as a child of the Enlightenment. He wanted to engage with critics and supporters and with the Australian community whom he served. Not for him to preside over a court sailing in a sea of dispirited morale.

"He led from the front, for that was his nature. This made him controversial in some circles. He was more candid and forthright than most judges. This brought him into difficulties with successive governments, ministers, legal personalities, media pundits and civic groups."

Kirby reported observations that Nicholson wore his battles with successive Attorneys-General as a "badge of honour".

"The law and liberty in Australia will lose a devoted judicial servant at the head of a great national judicial institution."

***

As part of the numerous events marking Nicholson's departure from the Family Court, a scholarship to acknowledge the academic achievement of an indigenous law student was established at Melbourne University. It is known as the Alastair Nicholson Law Scholarship.

In a piece expanding on his speech and published in the Australian Journal of Family Law, Justice Kirby concluded that different writers would emphasise different aspects of Chief Justice Nicholson's contributions to the Commonwealth.

"His engagement with the media. His attention to the better administration of his large, national court. His loyal support of the judges of the Family Court as they performed their difficult, stressful work under great pressure. His acceptance of large burdens in participation in judicial tasks at home and abroad. His engagement with the practising profession from which he had come.

"His outreach to global organisations concerned with the universal issues of family law and the law relating to children. His determination to fulfil a full working load as a sitting judge: not for him management by remote control. As a human being, a lawyer, a judge, a chief justice and an officer of the Commonwealth, Alastair Nicholson served the Australian people with admirable fidelity."

***

Not everyone thought the same.

Brian Taylor from the group Reliable Parents said Nicholson's constant deferments of his retirement date, culminating in his announcement that he would sacrifice his own holidays to continue sitting through till March 2004 had dismayed groups seeking reform of the Family Court.

He said Nicholson was widely seen by opponents of current Family Law structures as having institutionalised a bias against men in the Family Court.

"As Chief Justice for the last fifteen years, he has been in a position to make and influence judgments which form the basis for interpreting laws that give judges and magistrates wide-ranging discretion," Taylor said. "The Full Court, under Justice Nicholson has also defined the intent of the legislators who framed the laws, an exercise that some claim as judicial activism."

Taylor said Nicholson never made any positive comments about men in all his time at the court and had recently lambasted fathers who sought private paternity tests and claimed that men only sought increased contact with their children in order to lower their Child Support costs.

"With statistics linking juvenile crime and drug taking with a lack of contact with fathers, the entire area of family breakdown and support needs urgent review," Taylor said. "If this is the legacy that Alastair Nicholson is leaving the country, then many would applaud his departure."

***

There had never been any doubt about the former Chief Justice Alastair Nicholson's partisanship and open hostility to the conservative Howard government.

But if further proof was needed it came in June 2007, when, in his latest taxpayer funded role as a Honorary Professorial Research Fellow at the University of Melbourne, Nicholson wrote an article titled "Human Rights Under The Howard Government".

In the lead up to the election later in the year Nicholson wrote that "history would come to regard the rule of the Howard Government over this country as one of the darker periods of the country's history.

"It will do so not because of any economic failures of the Government, or of any particular incompetency on its part, but rather because of its destruction of the accepted structures of our community and its almost complete disregard of the human rights of not only Australians, but of so many other people, both within and outside Australia.

"Fortunately it appears that the innate good sense of the Australian people may be recognising this and it may be that we are embarking upon the last few months of its rule. However, the ill effects of this regime will be felt for years to come.

"Under Howard, every public office holder whether judicial or administrative, has had to undergo rigid screening for political correctness along conservative lines. Many highly talented people have been overlooked for office as a result and many drones have been appointed instead."

Nicholson also went on to complain that the Howard government had stacked the ABC board with conservative appointees; as he had done with countless other Boards including the Family Law Council.

"It will be many years before this malign influence is eradicated."

***

Nicholson also went on to complain about the Howard government's "inhuman interpretations of the immigration laws to justify the holding of large groups of men women and children who had committed no offence in detention centres for periods of many years.

It succeeded in doing so with the apparent approval of the Australian people by demonising these unfortunate people as "queue jumpers" and potential terrorists."

Nicholson also condemned the Howard government's treatment of indigenous people, particularly the "Intervention" in the Northern Territory which involved the use of the Army and the suspension of the Racial Discrimination Act. The highly politicised "Intervention" was justified by the chaotic state of indigenous communities, including low life expectancy, chronic petrol sniffing amongst the young, high rates of sexually transmitted diseases amongst children and low life expectancies; amongst other factors.

But Nicholson had always been a thorn in the side of both sides of politics. He later attacked the Rudd government's failure to keep their promises to reinstate the Racial Discrimination Act by introducing legislation which continued income management policies, mandatory child health testing and alcohol free zones in the remote parts of northern Australia. Suggesting he was saddened to see a Labor government acting in such a way, he declared: "It is quite clear that this legislation is inconsistent with the UN Declaration on the Rights of Indigenous Peoples which the Government has indicated that it supports.

"It also ignores the rights of Aboriginal peoples and their leaders to participate in and consent to policy and service developments which directly impact upon their lives."

***

In 2010 Nicholson was speaking out on family law yet again, this time in support of his successor Chief Justice Diana Bryant's assertion that admissions or claims made to mediators or counsellors should be admissible in court.

It is standard legal practice that matters arising out of mediation are not admissible in court.

In *The Age* Nicholson wrote: "Common law has long recognised that it is in the public interest that discussions between litigants, with a view to settling litigation, are to be regarded as privileged.

"This does not mean that mediation is sacrosanct. In family disputes, children are involved. Their best interests must be protected. The question is whether and at what point the competing public interest in protecting children should take priority over confidentiality of mediation.

"Children do not usually participate in mediation. They are usually the people most affected by it. The Family Law Act and the UN Convention on the Rights of the Child recognise that their best interests are paramount.

"Our law does not recognise this principle, because it says that anything disclosed or said in mediation cannot be used as evidence in any court."

***

In mid-2012 Nicholson was in the news once again, this time declaring victims of bullying should be able to make parents of their tormentors pay for their pain. And schools should be made legally responsible for student bullying that takes place off campus and outside school hours.

Nicholson argued that tougher laws could be crucial in the fight against bullying.

In late 2012, then well into his 70s, Alastair Nicholson continued to make the news. when he spoke out about the debate over the sterilisation of children with disabilities. He argued that the Family Court needed to be directly involved in the decision making and should not be left in the hands of the parents. He argued that an "independent assessment with the child's best interests in mind" needed to be involved in such emotionally charged decisions.

In the same month he was also speaking out in his role as the chairman of Australian-based group Children's Rights International, declaring that "children were the future of Cambodia". He focused particularly on the appropriate development of child welfare infrastructures and evolution of the court system to deal with and rehabilitate juvenile offenders. That any Asian country had anything to learn from Australia in this field was laughable.

Also in October 2012, his views that accusations of child abuse should be heard in a separate court to the Family Court were once again being aired in the national newspaper by one of his supporters.

Many of his critics personally blamed Nicholson for the loss of any meaningful contact with their children and their hatred of him ran deep. But Nicholson proved as indomitable in retirement as he was in public office.

Whether you agreed with him or not – and many do not – Alastair Nicholson remained as energetically outspoken and as peripatetic in his interests as ever. And to this day, he has never shown any regret at the role he played for so many years as the Family Court of Australia's Chief Justice.

***

Many of Alastair Nicholson's critics within the Australian fatherhood movement were hopeful that once he retired in 2004 they would never have to hear his name again – that the dominant influence he had held in national debates over so many years would disappear. His critics have been sorely disappointed.

Far from sinking into an uncomfortable retirement as some of his critics had hoped, Nicholson has continued to speak out in the years following his departure from the Family Court on a range of issues, was still lionised by the Australian left, and appeared as comfortable with his own determined views as ever.

He last made the newspapers in 2020.

Madonna King wrote in *The Sydney Morning Herald*: "Former Chief Justice of the Family Court Alistair Nicholson has called for coercive control or 'intimate terrorism' to be criminalised in all Australian states, in a bid to help curb domestic violence.

"His comments, made on the eve of White Ribbon Day, add weight to campaigns being waged to make coercive control, or non-physical domestic violence, a specific offence in mainland Australian states, as it is in Tasmania and some overseas jurisdictions.

"Mr Nicholson, who served as chief justice from 1988 until his retirement in 2004, said police also needed to be taught to look for covert emotional and non-physical violence when investigating cases of domestic abuse."

The former Chief Justice, one of the most influential people in the formation of Australia's ultra-feminised anti-male trending to totalitarian culture, said: "Certainly I think the pattern of shutting someone off from their friends and relatives is a very common feature of that sort of behaviour. And I think it's one of the more frightening ones because victims become too scared to seek help. Police need a lot more training in the dangers of that. They're inclined to dismiss it unless something overt has happened; unless there's been some incident to cause the problem."

Four years on, and at the time of writing Alastair Nicholson is now 86 years old. He appears, at last, to have lapsed into silence.

FOURTEEN
BEFORE THE STORM

AFTER THE House of Representatives Family and Community Services Committee wound up its public hearings on 3 November 2003 coverage of the inquiry into joint child custody and other matters lapsed into silence for a good fortnight.

The evidence was in. There was nowhere to go.

Amongst family law reformers there was a strange disquiet; was it all another hoax? Would anything really change?

In a moment of surreal and in retrospect naive optimism Dads On The Air expressed surprise that one of the most vexed issues of the era, child custody and the appropriateness of the sole custody model, along with the operation of child support, could be about to be solved. The silence did not last.

Later in November controversy began to pick up once again with a string of stories from Melbourne's *Herald Sun*, the first kicking off with the headline "Divorced Dads pay to see their kids". The story provoked another eddy of talkback.

"Desperate dads are secretly paying former partners to buy time with their children," the paper reported. "A Geelong father gave his ex-wife $10,000 to ensure she signed a court order giving him five days a fortnight with their child."

The paper went on to say that frustrated dads "are paying between $40 and $80 a fortnight in exchange for the honouring of court-ordered contact visits. The money these dads pay is on top of compulsory child support payments."

The soon to retire Family Court Chief Justice Alastair Nicholson described the case as appalling and told the paper: "One party should not have to pay the other to make the children available."

Surely that was exactly what many court cases were about?

The paper's Paula Beauchamp followed up with several strong stories, including "Desperate dad pleads to see kids", about a man whose children were taken overseas: "The thing I loved the most was stolen from my life."

And "Second Wives Worse Off" which began: "Child support number crunching is tearing second families apart, family law specialists say. And some second wives are better off leaving their husbands."

***

Next up in the media sparring was the appearance of Geoffrey Greene of the Shared Parenting Council of Australia on the ABC's Lateline debating Kathleen Swinbourne from the Council for Single Mothers and their Children.

It was strikingly unusual for Australia's state media to have any pro-father advocate on air or on screen.

Geoffrey Greene said: "The first principle is that it's about recognising that every child has a fundamental human right to equal opportunity and relationship with both their mother and father when they separate. And the second principle about this inquiry is that it's about establishing responsible parenthood and for Australia to say to the people or to parents or prospective parents, that we expect you both, jointly, to raise your children and to share the care, the duties and responsibilities of the upbringing of those children.

"Our view is that we believe that we need a system or a structure in Australia to cope with family breakdowns that in the very first instance upholds that child's fundamental right to that relationship with their mother and father and to act in the best interests of the child, which all sides of this debate believe is crucial, we say that you need to uphold that right first.

"And once you've done that, once you've protected that right, and these are children who can't protect themselves, once that's acknowledged, then it's about looking at each individual circumstance of each family and coming to an arrangement that suits the parents and children."

In Sweden joint custody is automatic after separation. Really, how difficult is it?

***

The weekend edition of the *The Sydney Morning Herald* carried as its front page story "Parents face custody overhaul" framed around a photograph of father Greg Cairns with his three daughters. It was maximum coverage. The piece was run across five columns and pointed to the front page of their News Review Section, which also ran across its entire front page a long feature by Lauren Martin called "Middle Ground", spilling to stories on "How father shares the care", "Robbed by the System", on grandparents, and "The Children: What it is like to be Shared".

In *Sydney Morning Herald* terms, back in those days when newspapers were regarded as a credible source of information and played a dominant role in the public discourse, it was impossible to get more prominent coverage.

Flagging the gutting or removal of child custody matters from the Family Court, the paper's Lauren Martin wrote: "All separating couples with children would have to lodge 'parenting plans' before a new tribunal under proposals to reduce the trauma of custody disputes.

"Unless violence or abuse was at issue, custody disputes would be removed from the Family Court and dealt with by tribunals or even an administrative Agency."

Inquiry Chairwoman Kay Hull said she was "very keenly" examining the idea, but could not confirm that it would be recommended in the report.

Committee Member Peter Dutton said a compulsory tribunal could comprise a child psychologist, a mediator and a family law expert who would be able to draft the conditions of any binding agreements.

It was an odd recommendation, considering that child psychologists, mediators and so-called "family law experts" were amongst the most compromised of all the parasites making a living off the destruction of fathers' roles in their children's lives.

***

The Family Court remained in the news with a report from the Law Institute of Victoria that delays between the time proceedings were initiated and the time cases were heard now stretched beyond two years.

The Institute's family law section painted a grim picture in a submission to the Australian National Audit Office. Average delays Australia-wide were up to 23 months to complete the Family Court process. In Melbourne the delay could be up to 27 months.

The Law Institute of Victoria found that: "Despite the best efforts of judges and administration...the court is in a 'parlous' state, causing enormous stress to litigants and children. Neither the Family Court nor the Federal Magistrates Court are fulfilling their charters."

Institute president Bill O'Shea said he wanted the Federal Government to halt the crisis by providing more funding to both courts.

Pleas for more money were not likely to be met with much enthusiasm from the Howard government, long critical of the court's overly legalistic pomp and circumstance and its' excruciatingly complex, expensive and time consuming procedures.

***

On the 25th of November *The Australian* ran a story titled "Prison and fines to enforce family law" by Patricia Karvelas, following a leak of a section of the draft report from within the Committee.

Leaking an internal parliamentary document was notionally an offence punishable by imprisonment. No one paid a price. It was all strategic. It was all politics. One rumour was that the leak had come from the Labor side in order to help ensure that Howard did not get credit for the reform of family law.

"A three-strikes plan, which uses the threat of fines and jail to force parents to meet their parental obligations after divorce, could be introduced under a draft proposal from the parliamentary committee charged with reviewing the Family Law Act," Karvelas reported.

"Non-custodial parents, mainly fathers, who for example fail to pick up their children at the time dictated by Family Court orders would face 'reasonable but minimum financial penalties' the first and second time they breach conditions. If the parent breaches the conditions for a third time and shows a 'pattern of deliberate defiance', then all access rights could be withdrawn.

"The parent could also face imprisonment if consistently continuing to breach court orders."

Like her or not, there was nothing wrong with Patricia Karvella's reporting skills. She went on to have a stellar career at the national broadcaster. I sat next to her for a couple of years at *The Australian*. Even as a young reporter she had an excellent ability to break stories, and most appealing, or galling depending on whether or not you were the target, she knew no fear.

The news about further potential for jailing parents was met with incomprehension by family law reformers. Was the government really going to jail the same parents who had just appeared before the Inquiry, some shedding distressed tears as they told of the tale of the destruction that the Family Court and the Child Support Agency had wreaked in their lives and with their children?

Why weren't they going to prosecute those who had created and protected this fiasco: the entirely suspect if not outright corrupt psychiatrists and family report writers, the child support review officers who routinely ignored the evidence in front of them and instead took the mother's fantasies as fact, the judicial officers who allowed ideology to rule as the clients and their children were brutalised, the public servants continuing to ignore the death rate of child support payers and the scheme's disastrous social impacts?

***

The story was picked up on the national broadcaster the ABC. Continuing their traditionally abysmal coverage of family law issues, The World Today's reporter Peta Donald claimed the Shared Parenting Council and other lobby groups supported the three strikes and you're in idea contained in the leaked draft: a range of penalties including losing access, being fined and being imprisoned. That was not correct.

The SPCA said they were misinterpreted. In a difficult interview, and amidst claims that the committee would not recommend a rebuttable joint parenting, Geoffrey Greene said: "We do believe that that right to that equal opportunity and relationship must be a starting point for any custody determinations coming out of these reforms."

The leaks reportedly created consternation in the Committee but were not to stop there.

By the time the report was handed down virtually all the major recommendations of the report had been leaked, culminating in *The Daily Telegraph*'s front page "Access Denied" – a bitter follow up to the campaigning "Give Dads A Go" headline only months before.

The media leaks were all accurate, adding in the end to the impression of chaos, confusion and lack of professionalism which was now adhering to the Committee.

The hope that shared parenting offered to so many separated parents and the heightened sensitivities surrounding Christmas, boosted by positive media coverage, all took a great lurch backwards.

So many witnesses had appeared before the inquiry in tears. So many people had worked so hard on so many submissions; and in making sure they were heard at public hearings. The committee had appeared to understand.

It was a brutal slap in the face.

***

The chaos surrounding the leaks was in contrast to the conduct of the public hearings, where many participants reported positive experiences. Witnesses left feeling not only that they had been listened to, but that by baring their souls and their personal struggles with the Family Court of Australia and the Child Support Agency to the Committee they had helped to bring about fundamental and desperately needed reform.

The public hearings, held at a cracking pace from one end of the country to the other, had been well run by the Chairwoman Kay Hull, with certainty and compassion. She gave numerous interviews suggesting significant reform was on the way. The Committee had shown every indication of understanding the issues.

***

The day before the launch of the report and the Canberra press conference Labor Party's Opposition spokesman on Family and Community Affairs Wayne Swan came out declaring his party would adopt all of the report's recommendations. That Australia's leftwing party, with a long long history of pandering to women's groups and demonising fathers, was happy with the report told family law reformers all they needed to know. Labor's delight at having such a difficult issue for their party apparently neutralised was clear.

For a conservative government to inflame the sentiments of the fathers groups right around the country in an election year was clear political insanity. There had been a 12 percent swing to the Coalition amongst males over the past three elections. They were about to spit on them.

But whichever way the eddies and currents of coverage, rumour, distrust and hope went each day, there was no doubt of one thing; the media thought significant change was on the way.

For every negative story came a positive one.

On the ABC's Law Report that week Michael Green QC, the Sydney-based barrister, a divorced dad and author of the book *Fathers After Divorce* who, as mentioned before, was a regular on Dads On The Air, described shared parenting as "a necessary revolution, because we know and all professionals and all people in this area, apart probably from some judges and lawyers, believe that the present system is simply not good for children and parents, and it's not working and it's not giving children an adequate opportunity or a very good opportunity to bond with both parents in a realistic way.

"Certainly not with the separated father, because of the shortness of time that he has with his children, it's very difficult for him to develop a meaningful relationship with the children, one that will be for their good and welfare and development. And on the other hand, for the mother, places an unnecessary burden of the responsibilities of raising these children, economically, socially, developmentally, and that's not a good thing either. So what we need is a revolution, and the joint rebuttable presumption I believe is the only way that we'll obtain that revolution."

***

In a front page story by Chris Griffith in Brisbane's *Courier Mail* headlined "Top judge hits family law plan" the paper reported that Chief Justice of the Family Court had berated Prime Minister John Howard's plan for reforming family law in a major attack on government policy.

Nicholson had been speaking to a forum by the Domestic Violence and Incest Resource Centre in Melbourne, his natural hunting ground.

He described Mr Howard's plan for automatic 50-50 child custody after divorce as "unworkable" and detrimental to the interests of children: "It is far too simplistic to change the law and expect parental behaviour to change as a consequence," he said.

Nicholson went on to say separated families needed more information and services, not legislative reform "which is more adult than child-focused and which puts unnecessary pressure on parents and children alike to rely on a one size fits all' arrangement. Our experience strongly suggests that a proposal of equal time would be detrimental to the best interests of children and would increase disputation and litigation."

Chief Justice Nicholson also poured scorn on the idea that men are often victims of domestic violence, a claim supported by ample research around the globe.

In a cartoon which was immediately offensive to male victims of domestic violence, well known cartoonist Tandberg portrayed a man being attended to by a doctor.

"Your knuckles are badly damaged," the doctor said. Needless to say, ridiculing female victims of domestic violence would have got the cartoonist sacked.

Nicholson said the mythology that portrayed men as victims was driving debate over domestic violence, child custody and child support issues. He said there was a common view that men were victimised by the Child Support Scheme, and the myth was at its most extreme with claims that men were as often victims of family violence as they were the perpetrators of it.

But in the days of broadband internet and the miracles of Google, it can take less than a minute for anyone to find references to a substantial body of research to contradict the Chief Justice's claims.

The Age reported Nicholson saying a renewed emphasis on men's rights was fostering, at all costs, an environment of encouraging paternal contact after separation. He went on to detail a case of alleged sexual abuse where the experts had encouraged contact but he had refused to order it.

Justice Nicholson said he favoured children having contact with both parents, but the proposal for a presumption of equal joint custody of children after family break-ups, now being considered by a federal parliamentary committee, would lock couples into maintaining relationships that had ended often because of violence.

"The violence card", as this style of accusation in the midst of a custody dispute became known.

The next day, Thursday the 27th November, *The Courier Mail* followed with another front page story, this time by their national political correspondent Malcolm Cole, reporting that the Family Court could be stripped of its powers to decide child custody arrangements for separated parents.

The paper went on to say a new mediation tribunal would instead make determinations on how child custody should be shared between the parents.

"Lawyers would be removed from the child-custody process, potentially saving tens of thousands of dollars for parties involved," the paper reported.

In spectacular fashion, *The Courier Mail* detailed government members of the committee returning fire on Justice Nicholson, accusing him of being out of touch with widespread community concern over the operation of his court. It was unprecedented. Dickson MP Peter Dutton said the committee had taken evidence from thousands of Australians who were unhappy with the current process.

"There are obvious problems with the Family Court and the way it deals with matters surrounding children at the time of their parents' separation," Mr Dutton said. "My view is that Justice Nicholson's comments have been completely unhelpful and I see Justice Nicholson as part of the problem, not the solution."

Cameron Thompson, the Member for Blair, said Justice Nicholson was "kidding himself" if he believed the system worked properly. "If there was some hypothesis out there that the Family Law Court and the current system was out of touch, then Alastair Nicholson has proven it," he said.

Thompson said Justice Nicholson was "probably starting, after years of insulation, to feel the winds of change that are blowing through the community over this issue. He's probably getting very defensive, and with very good reason."

Two wings of government were at each other's throats in what turned out to be an entirely phoney war.

The Courier's front page story spilled to another headlined: "Many boys don't see their separated dads"; yet another story compounding the problems for the court and escalating demands for reform.

"A quarter of boys whose parents have separated have no contact with their father," the paper began. "And even those who do see their fathers are less likely to seek help and emotional support when they needed it, according to a survey by Kids Help Line."

***

The first day of summer, and the kitchen just got hotter.

"Judge should go, says MP" was the headline in the *Herald Sun* on 1 December 2003. The paper reported the "bold call" for "the resignation of controversial Family Court Chief Justice Alastair Nicholson" by Victorian Liberal MP Chris Pearce, who claimed the judge had tried to interfere in the outcome of a Parliamentary inquiry into child custody.

"It is Justice Nicholson's role to administer the law, not make it," Mr Pearce said.

The Shared Parenting Council of Australia rushed out a supportive press release overnight and by the morning the story was on the AAP wire service, going to every significant radio, television and newspaper in the country.

The Age newspaper reported: "Chris Pearce, Liberal MP for the eastern Melbourne seat of Aston and a member of the parliamentary committee examining reforms to joint custody law, said yesterday Chief Justice Alastair Nicholson should step down because he had unduly tried to influence the committee. A prominent parenting lobby group, the Shared Parenting Council of Australia, joined the call for Justice Nicholson's resignation."

But Justice Nicholson told *The Age* via a spokeswoman he had no intention of resigning. 'I view calls for my resignation by the Victorian MP Chris Pearce and the Shared Parenting Council of Australia as an attempt to intimidate me in the carrying out of my duties,' he said. The outspoken Justice Nicholson has attacked suggestions that the Family Court should be stripped of the power to adjudicate in child custody battles."[139]

Citing undue influence and inappropriate public comment on the current Federal Parliamentary Inquiry into Child Custody matters, the Chief Justice had brought an entire judicial institution and arm of government into disrepute, Geoffrey Greene, Federal Director of the Shared Parenting Council of Australia said.

"We support the claim made by Federal Member for Aston, Chris Pearce, in the *Herald Sun* today, that the Chief Justice has attempted to pervert the course of a Federal Parliamentary Inquiry through his constant attacks upon the committee, its reference and its members," he said.

"Clearly the Family Court under the stewardship of Alastair Nicholson, has now degenerated into a failed institution with little or no respect from the general public, in either its administration of justice or in its capacity to hear matters before it – without bias or prejudice.

"The public attacks upon the parliamentary inquiry, and his direct opposition

---

[139] Judge claims intimidation in row over child custody, *The Age*, 1 December, 2003.

to the rights of children of separated parents to continue their relationship with both their mother and father has effectively prevented any party seeking a shared parenting Order in the Family Court from ever receiving a fair trial.

"This is an intolerable situation that the Chief Justice has created and leaves the Attorney General and the Federal Parliament with little choice but to act immediately, to restore some faith to a judicial arm of government."

***

The fathers groups, growing progressively more media savvy, chimed in with supporting releases. In an open letter to the Prime Minister, Men's Confraternity in Western Australia wrote claiming the Chief Justice had attempted to pervert the course of this parliamentary inquiry through his constant attacks upon the committee, its reference and its members.

Reliable Parents also joined the fray, describing the calls for Nicholson's resignation as "not without foundation". The group said the Family Court system was unworkable and the Chief Justice had bought the Family Court into disrepute. He had undermined public confidence in the court's ability to administer the will of the Parliament, and in doing so, also the will of the people.

Chairman of Reliable Parents Tony Borger stated that "the ingrained bias that exists within the Family Court and its agencies has clearly influenced the Chief Justice and rendered the entire Family Court system unworkable. The Parliamentary inquiry and the steadfast determination of its Chairperson, Kate Hull can be credited with having brought to public light the extent to which fathers and their children have been callously disregarded".

Even Fathers4Justice International weighed in with another open letter to the Australian Prime Minister claiming the Family Court had the worst reputation of any court in the country.

The next day the national daily *The Australian* ran a story across the top of page two which amplified Pearce's comments, recording him as saying Nicholson's attacks showed a "total lack of regard and respect for the parliamentary process and the parliament's role in developing and legislating the laws of Australia.

"There are clear and distinct roles for the parliament and for the judiciary. It is important that both parliamentarians and members of the judiciary respect that distinction.

"Justice Nicholson's comments demonstrate a clear and worrying failure to respect this important principle."[140]

Not surprisingly Justice Nicholson was unimpressed.

---

140 Lane, Bernard, Judge's comments 'disrespectful' to Parliament, *The Australian*, 2 December, 2003.

"I have no intention of resigning over comments I made during a speech at a family violence forum on the needs of vulnerable and abused children," he told the paper. "I view calls for my resignation by the Victorian MP Chris Pearce, and the Shared Parenting Council of Australia, as an attempt to intimidate me in the carrying out of my duties."[141]

***

On Friday the 12th of December *The Australian* ran a story that the minimum $5 a week child support payment extracted from the unemployed would be doubled as part of recommendations from inquiry.

It didn't go down well with those most affected.

There were a quarter of a million fathers in this situation. This was $20 a fortnight these poor bastards could be spending on their kids, the last shred of dignity.

Oddly even the National Council of Single Mothers criticised the move, referring to the "groundswell of opposition to child support" and saying it would trigger disputes between parents.

But with the December 31st deadline rapidly approaching, the pettiness and blind bureaucratic insanity of it all acted as a neat counterpoint to the well of misery that family law and child support represented.

The froth on choppy seas was to cause further infighting and shadow boxing in an always disparate and geographically scattered family law reform movement filled with strong and often obsessive characters whose healthy egos and personal encounters with the system led to sometimes difficult and almost always pointless division.

In the end: so close and yet so far. All this work, all this strategising, all this good intent. All this political astuteness. All to fall over at the last hurdle.

***

As the deadline grew ever closer, almost, it seemed, as part of the pre-report nerves, an unfortunate squabble broke out in the Shared Parenting Council over the question of whether a Tribunal should replace the Family Court, a spat which led to the departure of the Men's Rights Agency.

While there was some support for the abolition of the Family Court and the creation of a Tribunal in its place, Sue Price, co-founder of the MRA, put out a public notice on their website saying they did not see the tribunal as a workable solution and claiming that the issue would divert attention from the crux of the matter.

---

141 Lane, Bernard, Nicholson: I won't resign over custody comments, *The Australian* 3 December, 2003.

She claimed that debate on the issue had been stifled within the SPCA and that the same people who worked at the Family Court would simply make the dash across the road to the Tribunal. In the minds of some it was a fair enough call; and perhaps a good example of the intractable issues anyone trying to reform the family law arena faces, not least all the entrenched interests.

She wrote: "The problem is so much greater than just bringing in a new quasi-legal level of adjudication. The solution lies in ensuring the rebuttable presumption of joint custody 50/50 (shared and equal parenting) becomes the accepted norm.

"Once that is in place we can then start to introduce programs to elevate the status of fathers to ensure all those with a misandrist outlook come to understand the importance of both parents raising their children."

"The SPCA Executive had not even discussed the Family and Community Affairs Committee latest recommendation to introduce a tribunal system to replace the Family Court's handling of children's issues, yet the Federal Director Geoff Greene was obviously promoting this concept without the authority of the Executive. Not only did he attempt to stifle debate, but tried to silence criticism of the proposal for fear of upsetting the Committee."

She claimed that "it felt like we belonged to a branch office of the Liberal Party. We do applaud the Government's initiatives, but we feel we must remain non-political in our approach to achieving a better result for parents and their children if their relationships fail."

Greene denied the claims. While the arguments created some consternation or exasperation on the various men's chatlines, the rupture did not receive mainstream media coverage. In the end, after much debate, the tribunal never got off the ground anyway and was criticised by some strategists for diverting attention away from simpler solutions.

***

Politicians and lobbyists were on holidays for Christmas but the media retained its interest in the shared parenting legislation.

The strongest piece appeared in Queensland's high circulation *Sunday Mail* on 21st of December, when emotions surrounding children were already high. It was titled "Children Caught in the Crossfire".[142] Like other pieces now beginning to appear, it was written with the assumption that the Family Court was about to be substantially demolished.

---

142 English, David, Children Caught in the Crossfire, *Sunday Mail*, 21 December, 2003.

Reporter David English began: "Christmas is looming and millions of divorced Aussie dads are dreading it. It's not creeping credit card debt or even monster hangovers that loom large in their minds. It is the stark realisation that time with their children will be brief and in many cases non-existent.

"The animosity between the Family Court and the 10-member committee over possible change is palpable as anyone knows who has followed the exchanges of fire in the media between Family Court Chief Justice Alastair Nicholson and committee members in recent weeks."

English went on to say the Committee had been told loudly and clearly that lawyers and judges should have nothing whatever to do with the process of separation and that "most certainly the Family Court should be stripped of all its powers over custody considerations. It has also been given ample evidence that justice in Australia comes at a very high price, usually $100,000 to $150,000 for a case to go through court and even then a final decision may not be made."

Liberal committee member Peter Dutton said: "The overwhelming message is a need for change. We have had it put to us that the system does not work."

To the end the women's groups were defensive of the court which had for so long reflected their ideology. Yvonne Parry of the National Council for Single Mothers said: "We think the court does a wonderful job in very trying circumstances."

She dismissed the push for change as coming from "a vocal minority who've been pressing the backbenchers for change". She said she saw some of that minority as pretty nasty.

"We've had death threats here since the inquiry was announced. People have sent emails saying they hope we die and they hope our kids die and stuff like that. It's not nice."

***

Significantly in terms of the Australian push for reform, there were also major breakthroughs in the international campaign for equity in family law. These events demonstrated that the push for shared parenting from Australian fathers was by no means an isolated event.

One of the world's most powerful newspapers, the downmarket tabloid *The Sun* in Britain, launched a national campaign in mid-December for 50/50 child custody after separation.

While it might not win on intellectual clout, with its multi-million circulation and brash attitude *The Sun* was one of the few newspapers that could single-handedly influence election outcomes and public attitudes.

Declaring that more than one million children in Britain would not see their fathers for Christmas, *The Sun* called for dads to be given equal rights and announced that it was backing rock star and father-of-four Sir Bob Geldof, who had branded the country's family law system as "grotesque" for its failure to maintain links between children and their parents.[143]

Writing for the paper to coincide with the launch of the campaign Sir Bob said: "For those divorced men with children, Christmas is a travesty, a repulsive contradiction of a family holiday, of a loving celebration, of a special children's time.

"These are the men who will be forced to be alone without their babies, who will commit suicide most frequently at this time of year in an age when male suicides are already 300 percent greater than women's. These are men who, in the eyes of what is sickeningly called Family Law, committed the greatest crime – of being divorced. Men who are guilty of the worst sin – of being fathers – because dads, to the great dismay of the secret elite who sit in secret judgement in these secret courts are, shockingly, ALL men!

"This Christmas Eve…there will be many fathers forbidden by the savagery of our laws to be with their children, standing broken, as I have, outside their old homes, the keys still in their pockets, weeping and whispering goodnight as they watch each child's bedroom light switch off before turning away, maddened with grief, to the pointlessness of a lonely Christmas Day.

"What have we become? In whose name is this brutality done? Who are they who do this and why do they not account to us, the people? What unthinking fools perpetrated these unlawful laws?"[144]

***

Also in the days before Christmas a Sydney University study "Adolescents' Views on the Fairness of Parenting and Financial Arrangements After Separation" by Judy Cashmore, Patrick Parkinson and Judi Single from the faculty of law, added weight to suggestions children were better off spending equal time with both parents after divorce.

The study was one of the first in Australia to look at how children feel about spending time with their parents and canvassed the views of 60 teenagers.

When asked how parents should care for children after divorce, the most common answer was "equal" or "half and half". Half also said they wanted more time with their non-residential parents.

Professor Parkinson said the results were striking. "It suggests that adolescents

---

143 Dads' Rights for XMAS, *The Sun*, 24 December, 2003.

144 Geldof, Bob, *The Sun*, December 24, 2003.

are willing to move between homes, at least in principle," he said, adding that the research suggested the 1970s custody model in which children saw one parent "every second weekend and school holidays" was outdated. The study also found children had an acute sense of fairness in money matters. They did not like it if one parent appeared to have a better standard of living, or if the children from another relationship received bigger Christmas presents.

Parkinson had previously said, "In the past 30 years, we have sown the wind in the revolution in attitudes to sex, procreation and marriage. We are now reaping the whirlwind. The societal problems which this has caused are problems that no law can resolve."

**

The mix of Christmas and the impending conclusion of the inquiry propelled *The Australian*'s conservative columnist Janet Albrechtsen into the debate. Sometimes reading her was like taking a cold shower, her astringent style bracing. I was still working as a general news reporter, and I remember well her ringing me one day, before she became so famous and so closely linked to the paper, asking my advice on how she could get some of her writing into *The Australian*. Bettina Arndt had recommended she give me a call. I put her on to the opinion page editor, and she was soon well outstripping me in terms of pay and influence. She's still there, all these years later.

Legally trained and with a sharply critical brain, the left hated her. To her eternal credit Albrechsten had long been an outspoken critic of the Family Court and its Chief Justice. She condemned the court as ideologically driven and as having overseen the bastardisation of the best interests of the child test.

Despite the legislative reforms of 1995 intended to promote shared parenting, fathers were continuing to be stripped of a genuine relationship with their children, "all in the name of ideology".

She had previously written: "Sadly the Family Court is caught downwind of the more illogical parts of feminist thinking that sanctifies the womb as soon as a marriage is over. The real victims are children, who may miss out on the best custody outcome because there is no level playing field."[145]

Nicholson's views on virtually everything, from domestic violence to shared parenting to the disciplining of children were on the record and she condemned his ceaseless public statements and his obvious desire to change the law to match his own views. His behaviour frequently raised the question of how any applicant applying, for instance, for a shared parenting order, could get a fair trial.

---

145 Albrechtsen, Janet, Children, the real victims of this ideological battle, *The Australian*, 2 May, 2003.

Under the headline "Fathers given raw custody deal" Albrechtsen wrote: "Tomorrow, thousands of children will celebrate Christmas away from their fathers. Next week the Standing Committee on Family and Community Affairs will deliver its report on child custody.

"The juxtaposition of these two facts is a stark reminder that restoring fatherhood could be John Howard's finest legacy to us. But it will require a very clear, very loud message to the proverbial men in white coats – the judges of the Family Court – to end the experiment, to start over, to welcome fathers back into the lives of children.

"The social experiment began with the best of intentions. The Family Court, established in 1976, promised a revolutionary system for dealing with family breakdown - one that sought outcomes in 'the best interests of the child'.

"But the 1970s were feminism's heyday. And so that message - the best interests of the child – was filtered through a feminist prism where the denigration of men refracted into the belittling of fathers."[146]

She said the statistics showing the court making a paltry number of shared parenting orders, 329 out of a total 13,000 orders in the financial year 2000-01 for example, "translated into thousands of fatherless children and childless fathers.

"One million children live with only one parent, usually their mother. Less than half of these children see their other parent, usually their father, at least fortnightly. More than a third see them rarely - once a year or less. Less than half of the fathers have their children stay overnight. And yet 72 percent of non-resident fathers want more contact and most children want to spend more time with their fathers."

Albrechtsen said Nicholson was claiming shared parenting to be unworkable where there is parental conflict yet he knew the legal process based on the victor and the vanquished promoted the very conflict to which to which he pointed.

"There is now too much evidence to ignore the positive outcomes for children who maintain genuine loving relationships with their fathers," she wrote.

"There is another reason for restoring fatherhood. Every young boy needs to know he is important and that society treats fathers with respect. If fatherhood matters, every young boy matters. A simple message that we ignore at our peril."

***

After so much hard work that so many fathers had put in to fighting for reform, including contributing to the inquiry, confronting perhaps the saddest and most private element of the lives and the consequences on their own children of what

---

146 Albrechtsen, Janet, Fathers given raw custody deal, *The Australian*, 24 December, 2003.

had happened, some felt sick to the stomach over what could or could not be about to happen.

How many fathers dreamed that next Christmas, unlike this one, they would be spending with their children after the government changed the law and gave them their children back?

The eddies of hope, the heightened sensitivities at Christmas, boosted by positive media coverage, all took a great lurch downwards with the publication of a front page story on the Saturday edition of the *Daily Telegraph* with the brutal headline: "Access Denied".

So many witnesses had appeared before the inquiry in tears. So many people had worked so hard on so many submissions; and in making sure they were heard at public hearings. The committee had appeared to understand.

The story by Tory Maguire, which was published in many other News Limited publications around the country, increased the despair levels of just about every family law reformer in the country.

It began: "Separated parents are unlikely to get automatic 50/50 joint custody of their children as a House of Representatives committee prepares to reject the proposal…the committee, which hands down its report on Monday, is likely to unanimously reject ordering that a child's time be automatically split evenly between separated parents."[147]

Maguire went on to say "the rejection of 50/50 joint custody will disappoint fathers' advocates, who have argued that the present system is stacked against them." It was a massive understatement.

He went on to suggest the inquiry would propose "significant changes" to the Family Law Act, which could include the introduction of a special tribunal to decide custody outside the courts. "There will be other suggestions for involving both parents in a child's upbringing, including radical overhauls of the way child maintenance is paid and the consideration of grandparents in parenting plans. The possible tribunal to decide custody would include child psychologists and legal experts, and parties would not require legal representation."

But of course it was the "legal experts" who had contributed to the present unholy mess; and the systemically corrupt conduct of child psychologists in family law was one of its major problems, as more than one submission to the inquiry had pointed out.

DOTA's editorial stance reflected singular unhappiness with these developments, and we opined that it was "the same unworkable platitudinous rubbish

---

147 Maguire, Tory, Access Denied, *Daily Telegraph*, 15 December, 2003.

everyone had seen before. It means, in cold blood, that without a rebuttable notion of shared parenting nothing will really change. The government has just spent millions of dollars stirring up passions over child custody and child support, encouraging countless thousands of fathers who did not get to see their children to hope that things would change, and were not only not going to do anything to improve the lot of them and their children, but was about to make things worse."

Lone Fathers' Association president Barry Williams said he would be "very unhappy" with anything less than "shared parenting". Others were in equal dismay. "I don't think anything but compulsory shared parenting is acceptable."

**

And so Monday 29th December 2003 rolled on. Unusually for a committee report, the report was released at 10.30am exactly, with a press conference called for one hour later. It was to be a day of judgement and despair.

What so many had hoped would be an historic day when the nation's children were given back their fathers turned out to be bureaucratic and political obfuscation at its very worst.

To put it into Australian parlance: "It was an absolute dog act." Done for purely political purposes. An idiotic miscalculation which would backfire.

Both sides of politics are guilty of protecting and perpetuating the chaos of family law in this country. But at this point in time the nation's conservatives were front and centre of an historic sleight of hand which killed not just any hope of genuine reform in this jurisdiction but would impact on millions of Australians for years to come.

The hundreds of thousands of hours put into pressuring the government by volunteers calling for change had been wasted. In the end they were shown nothing but contempt.

The timing of the announcement should have been the dead giveaway. In Australia the Christmas New Year period is the height of summer. Essentially the entire country goes to the beach. Nobody is paying any attention to politics. Governments only make announcements at this time of year unless they're trying to conceal something.

The report was released at a media conference in the nation's capital Canberra and gained widespread coverage. The report may have been front page news but coverage dried up rapidly. Long term family law campaigners were visceral in their contempt for the report.

Some said Every Picture Tells A Story itself resembled a Family Court judgement, it bore no relationship to the evidence and no relationship to reality.

Allegedly charged by the Prime Minister to fix the problem "once and for all", at the end of the day the inquiry's report killed any chance of that happening.

***

The committee's rejection of the rebuttable presumption of joint custody, with no logical explanation whatsoever and clearly for misguided political purpose, created far more problems than it solved. But despite the disappointment, Dads On The Air argued the inquiry in itself would come to be seen as a watershed in family law reform. It brought to public view the many failures of the sole mother custody model and the compelling arguments for reform. And it brought to public attention the impassioned stories of fathers, mothers, non-custodial mothers, second wives, grandparents and children.

The weight of these stories, both in the public hearings and in submissions, made for a significant body of evidence. The dysfunction of the family law and child support systems in Australia were clearly illustrated. The repeated evidence of the mismanagement of people's lives should have left any responsible government with little choice but to act.

Despite all the momentum, the public debate and the media supporting change, the Howard government baulked at the last fence. Instead of joint custody Australia ended with "joint parental responsibility". Instead of shared parenting centres dotted across the country helping parents to come up with sensible plans for the care of their children after separation there are Relationship Centres, producing mixed results and run by the same people who had been mismanaging Relationships Australia.

Dads On The Air was always critical that the reforms did not go far enough and was suspicious of the many compromises made. We predicted that in five years time there would be another round of inquiries as the government tried once more to take the lid off the pressure cooker; the wall of discontent that would once more be impossible to ignore.

And that there would be a replay of the inquiry just completed: "At these same community consultations an armada of heftily funded women's and domestic violence groups will present submissions prepared by paid staff and will relay horror stories of the mistreatment of women at the hands of men. And at these same meetings unfunded fathers groups relying on volunteers will sometimes inexpertly present their point of view.

"The politicians chairing the events will once more express sympathy to tearful individuals, men and women, and will promise faithfully that the government is looking closely into their issues."[148]

---

148 Community Consultations: A Tale of Two Perspectives, Dads On The Air, 22 October, 2003.

Conservative icon Prime Minister John Howard had the rarest of historical opportunities to fix the situation once and for all. He blew it. He was tossed from office in 2007, becoming only the second Prime Minister in Australian history to lose his own seat. From being his most ardent supporters, many fathers and family law reformers would have happily pissed on his political grave.

In the pubs and the public narrative, amongst those who did not follow the ins and outs of this debate, there was a general perception that the situation had improved. Many approaching separation operated under the illusion that the system was fairer. They were soon enough to find themselves heartbroken and suffering the rapacious demands of the system.

They were the years of Australia's headlong rush into the Iraq War, becoming its second largest Western contributor after America. Howard rode high on the so-called War on Terror.

In the end he did nothing for the terror people experienced in their own lives, stripped of children, assets and dignity by the legal caste to which he was so closely aligned.

The political operatives behind the faux push for reform of family law were amply rewarded. Nick Minchen went off to the plum post of Australian Consul in New York. Geoffrey Greene went on to be the Director of the Queensland Liberal Party. Joe Hockey, the man declaring he would chase child support payers to their grave, became Australia's ambassador to the United States.

The party suffers to the present day as a result of the confusion, obfuscation and mixed messaging on family matters and for, to put it bluntly, being so utterly gutless.

A conservative party which can't stand up for conservative values and its pro-family constituency, that rolls over in the face of the anti-family bias of the nation's bureaucratic elites, is no conservative party at all. A government which does not serve the people's interest first reaches in its tools of armament against a restive population to authoritarianism, but ultimately cannot survive.

FIFTEEN
THE LIARS THE LAWYERS THE BUREAUCRATS AND THE SOCIAL ENGINEERS WIN THE DAY

ONE OF the sickest jokes of the whole fiasco of the government inquiry into child custody which reported on December 29th of 2003 was the sight of the Family and Community Services Committee members warning the Chief Justice of the Family Court Alastair Nicholson to accept the report.

The Dads On The Air show and accompanying article immediately after the Christmas period was labelled "Collusion and Corruption in Family Law". It garnered over 29,000 comments.

It read in part: ""In the end Nicholson was one of its only supporters, that fact alone ensured the hostility of fathers.

"It took a few hours, sometimes days, for fathers and family law reform advocates to realise how thoroughly they had been deceived.

"But realise they did."[149]

Lone Fathers described the rejection of a rebuttable notion of joint custody as silly and said they would appeal directly to the Prime Minister.

Dads Australia called it a betrayal of the million Australian children of separated parents.

The Men's Rights Agency, which did numerous interviews on the subject right around the country, dismissed it as the greatest betrayal by any Australian government in the nation's history.

---

149 Stapleton, John, Collusion and Corruption in Family Law, Dads On The Air, 19 January, 2004.

The politicians all knew how crucial this issue was to the many fathers who were denied contact with their children. They raised their hopes in what in the end was little more than a cruel hoax.

***

While fathers and family law reformers were visceral in their contempt, in the end Chief Justice Nicholson, the living embodiment of everything wrong with family law, was one of the report's only supporters.

And why wouldn't he embrace the report?

It set out with what was on the face of it clear collusion between the major political parties to protect the appalling legacy of the hated Family Court of Australia and the rampant corruption in the family law and child support systems.

Perhaps a deal was done between the parties to reject a rebuttable joint 50/50 custody after separation in return for bi-partisan support. And to protect the profession and the government itself from claims of malpractice, and thereby civil suit. As anyone who had been anywhere near the system knew, such claims were entirely credible.

It was open to the committee, on the evidence before it, to adopt shared parenting or joint custody as government policy. Its rejection of joint custody relied on an extremely selective choice of arguments. It would have been much easier to make a cogent argument in favour. If Sweden can do it, with extremely positive results, why can't Australia?

Because there's too much money in family breakdown, for the lawyers in private practice, for the armies of bureaucrats in government departments, and for the nation's ballooning social welfare sector.

The report ignored the personal and social consequences of the conduct of Family Court judges. It ignored the massive bias in the system. It ignored the many moving tales of distress from fathers, second wives, grandparents and non-custodial mothers.

It failed to recommend exposure of the biased and dishonest conduct of family law experts. It failed to recommend a scrapping of the Family Court as a failed social experiment. The report did not recommend the abolition of the secrecy clauses of the Family Law Act, the notorious Section 121, and it failed to even recommend the counting of the death toll of the Child Support Agency, believed to be more than three a day.

The intellectually sloppy report did not even bother to give a logical explanation for its rejection of a rebuttable presumption of joint custody. With its lack of depth or coherent argument and the punitive nature of many of its recommendations, Every Picture Tells A Story pleased almost no-one but the high priests of the industry.

***

Deeply disappointed by the results of the inquiry, which had appeared to hold so much hope in resolving what had been an intractable problem in Australian society for so long, the tone at Dads On The Air turned cold towards the Howard government.

The show's editorial on the subject read: "Every last attack on fathers will be met with a vociferous campaign from the fathers' groups. Traditionally fragmented and disorganised, they have been united in their campaign for reform. While there will never be across the board co-operation between the groups, dominated as they are by strong personalities, most are aiming for much the same things.

"While still lacking in the millions of dollars of public funds that flow to the women's groups and women's advocacy organisations, including the domestic violence industry, the fathers and family law reform groups are now better coordinated and better organised than ever before.

"The focus of the inquiry has consolidated the belief that the only way for parents to protect their children's interests after separation is to remain fully involved in their upbringing in joint custody arrangements.

"This government committee, by first inviting fathers to be heard and then completely ignoring everything they said, has created its own worst nightmare, inflaming sentiment and outraging reform advocates.

"The report is clear political insanity on the part of the Howard government."

The government was only eight seats away from losing control of parliament, and was characteristically, and deceptively, playing both sides of the fence.

"The Prime Minister John Howard raised the hopes of millions of people affected by family law and child support in Australia and led them to believe that long overdue reform was on the way. And then he sided with the Chief Justice of the Family Court, one of the most reviled and discredited judicial figures in Australian history."[150]

DOTA declared that the report essentially spat in the face of the hundreds of thousands of pro-family men and women, many of them more naturally aligned to the Labor party than to the conservatives, who had drifted to the Coalition in the hope that they would reform family law.

---

150 The Great Betrayal, Dads On The Air, 13 March, 2004.

There are very few vote changing issues. Family law is one of them.

The report not only told the hundreds of thousands of people currently adversely affected by family law and child support that it would be pointless for them to do anything to improve their situation, it told fathers then and into the future that they were second class parents who did not deserve to be treated equally. This contempt for fathers would ultimately metastasise through the nation's institutions, and is alive and well more than two decades later.

The report, which not only used completely spurious non-arguments to reject the proposal of joint custody, a popular and common sense idea, but made numerous recommendations, such as the taking away of driver's licences, which would criminalise fathers yet further and clearly make their lives worse.

Not to mention that for many people their driver's licences were essential for their employment, and by taking these absurd and vindictive actions propelled by an already dysfunctional court system, would simply further impoverish families and drive yet more separated parents on to the welfare rolls.

Without a rebuttable notion of joint custody, which was so clearly supported by many in the community, the committee's recommendations for a tribunal to try and take the heat out of the adversarial system of Family Law, fell more than flat.

The idea that the Committee would recommend a tribunal with a child psychologist and family law experts on it, when every man and his dog in the country knew how utterly dreadful the experts infesting family law are, was simply preposterous.

Dads On The Air argued: "Without a rebuttable notion of joint custody such a tribunal would not be helping separating couples to achieve cooperative parenting arrangements after divorce. Instead it would be replicating the same practices that exist now; but making things even less accountable than at present. Does the country really need another secretive, corrupt and ideologically driven tribunal mucking with people's private lives?

"While we rarely agree with Kathleen Swinbourne of the Sole Parents Union, she got it exactly right when she said the recommendations of the report would make little difference in practice and that fathers having their children taken off them would hate a tribunal just as much as they hate the court."[151]

It was a disgusting report, a sleazy sleight of hand on the part of the perpetrators of this debacle. No wonder the government chose to release it during the holiday period, when the broader public was not paying attention.

---

151 The Need for Rebuttable Presumption of Joint Custody, Dads On The Air, 29 October, 2004.

***

One of the more coherent attacks on the committee report came from the eccentric speaker for the SA parliament Peter Lewis, who released a statement slamming the House of Representatives' Standing Committee on Family and Community Affairs, Inquiry into Shared Parenting (HORISP), Report into Child Custody Arrangements.

"Of course, the existing 'Industry' would say the kind of complimentary things they have said about this report!

"It's business as usual for them, with a cursory slap on the wrist for the crook, abusive, sexist, racist, biased, criminal things they have been doing, all still permissible under the new regime recommended by HORISP.

"At present, a vindictive parent of a broken marriage can still go into 'the system' and lie their heads off under oath, thereby destroying the reputation of their innocent ex-spouse and get away with it! AND WORSE still these liars (perjurers) will most likely get custody/residency of the children, &/or at least prevent the other parent from reasonable (or any) access.

"Taxpayers will continue to foot the bill for many more years for all the problems which caused the Family Court's rotten reputation to come under the Parliamentary Committee's spotlight in the first instance; namely, anti-father bias and false allegations, including perjury, accusing one or other of the parents of violence and abuse.

"Their Number One recommendation should have been to make perjury (telling lies under Oath) in the Family Court processes a criminal offence. Such a recommendation would then have allowed an additional criminal charge of Criminal Defamation to be brought against the liar. They don't address this major problem anywhere in the Report.

"However, in their No 1 recommendation HORISP talks about "shared parental responsibility" which is what the current practice in the Family Court jurisdiction now claims to deliver.

"At present, the Court awards 'shared responsibility' by giving one parent responsibility' for residency/custody - whilst giving (compelling) the other parent 'responsibility' for the supply of the money, called 'support', without satisfactory (or any) access, i.e. one gets the kids and the other pays the bills under the 'shared responsibility' model at present. HORISP has not recommended any change to the definition of 'shared responsibility'.

"Yet in recommendation No 2, HORISP want "a clear presumption against shared parental responsibility ... (where there are allegations about)... entrenched conflict, family violence, substance abuse or established child abuse, including sexual abuse".

"Under current case law this recommendation will aid, abet and encourage liars and cheats to an even worse degree than the current practice of the Family Court allows. They seem to me to be shamelessly stupid, or insensitive, or ignorant, or all three.

"The report fails to recommend an abolition of the Family Court case law and precedents flowing from it, which it created. This will continue to affect and determine its future deliberations unless it is abolished by Statute. Any new system which is going to be built on the foundations of the old, will be destined to failure.

"The only people who will view this Report as progressive will be those who weren't around at the time of the 1992 and 1995 inquiries, and those who depend on the existing injustices of the system to make their living.

"I am angry that this will do nothing to reduce the suicide rate and mental illness which has arisen in consequence of the practices in the Family Court system, until now.

"The Family Court system and the publicly paid servants in the processes which hang off it are racist, sexist, abusive, biased, crook and often criminal in their impact on too many parents who have to go through it. HORISP has missed the need to recommend changes to the law which would change these things.

"The only significant change has been a recommendation to replace part of the work of the existing Family Court with a Tribunal. Yet the Tribunal will not require people appearing before it to tell the truth nor do HORISP's recommendations compel the Tribunal to try and discover the truth before making its Orders. This will make things worse, not better. Moreover, it is probably unonstitutional anyway.

"It seems the Committee (HORISP) has attempted to avoid offending the Family Court, the publicly paid people who work in the industry and the entrenched structured, leftist views and injustices of the politically correct ninnies who gave evidence to it.

"The Honourable Speaker is concerned that Legal Aid will continue to be used to prop up more litigation against too many fathers, who in most cases will have no access to any fair and comparable representation in court.

"The Committee has wimped out in its duty. The basic reason for its establishment was to discover the causes and eliminate the injustices of the current Family Court system. It was told by the Prime Minister to work out the changes to the Family Law Act to fix the problems with the Family Court system. It has not done that.

"The major parties were represented on this Committee and have had their chance to get it right but failed. They have even recommended things which will compound the felony of the system and which are probably unconstitutional. The Prime Minister must now kick butt and fix the problem himself."[152]

Dads On The Air couldn't have said it better.

**

What so many had hoped would be an historic day when the nation's children were given back their fathers turned out to be a day of bureaucratic and political obfuscation at its worst.

Optimistically, just before the release of the report, Dads On The Air had labelled their shows The Family Court Faces Dismissal, Fundamental Reform Coming Your Way, The Weight of Evidence and just before the report's release, Fathers In Waiting: History In The Making.

How naive we were. The headlines were all misguided. The campaigning role the program had played was to no avail. The lawyers, liars, bureaucrats and social engineers had won the day.

The idiotically named report Every Picture Tells A Story did not recommend a rebuttable presumption of joint custody but instead creating "a clear presumption, that can be rebutted, in favour of equal shared parental responsibility, as the first tier in post separation decision making."

The Report suggested a clear presumption against shared parental responsibility with respect to cases where there is entrenched conflict, family violence, substance abuse or established child abuse, including sexual abuse.

In the Palace of Lies!!??

The Committee defined shared parenting responsibility as involving a requirement that parents consult with one another before making decisions about major issues relevant to the care, welfare and development of children, including but not confined to their education, religious and cultural upbringing, health, as well as changes of surname and usual place of residence. This should be in the form of a parenting plan.

Under questioning, even the then Attorney General Philip Ruddock appeared uncertain of how this would play out between feuding, emotionally distressed parents.

Chair Kay Hull said the Committee was unanimous that each separated parent should start with an expectation of equal care and responsibility, and substantially shared parenting time. But children should not be put in any circumstance where their safety and wellbeing were at risk.

"The goal for the majority of families should be one of equality of care and responsibility, along with substantially shared parenting time," she said.

---

[152] The Family Court's Unchanged Ways, Dads On The Air, 27 March, 2004.

"The Committee agrees that, all things considered, each parent should have an equal say on where the child or children reside. Wherever possible, an equal amount of parenting time should be the standard objective, taking into account individual circumstances.

"However, the committee does not support forcing this outcome in potentially inappropriate circumstances by legislating a presumption – rebuttable or not – that children spend equal time with each parent."[153]

Weasel words. The court had no intention of changing its ways. And never did.

***

Many if not most accusations of domestic violence come in the context of attempting to gain advantage in family law proceedings, and all this report did was to encourage the practice to continue. Lucrative for lawyers, devastating for litigants, ruinous for children.

The point of a shared parenting presumption was to take the minutiae of family life out of the hands of lawyers and judicial officers and into the hands of separated parents so arrangements could fit their work commitments and other circumstances.

The community forums on Dads On The Air's old website went ballistic.

Dads Australia's public statements read in part: "DADs Australia condemns the recommendations of the Parliamentary Committee into Shared Parenting as a blatant act of betrayal against separated fathers, grandparents but most importantly, the one million children from separated families. The committee caved into pressure from small, self-interested letterhead groups. The Prime Minister should step in to implement the equal-time parenting proposal to stop the suffering of fathers and their children."[154]

The post garnered 6,111 comments. We were usually lucky to get five or ten comments on any particular subject.

The recommendations contained in the report Every Picture Tells A Story, to which DOTA posted a link, garnered an extra 2,631 comments, almost universally hostile.

Dads On The Air was the only media outlet to broadcast the morning's press conference live.

---

153 Lane, Bernard, Family Law Inquiry Recommends Shared Parenting but with Caution, The Australian, March 8, 2004.

154 Dads Australia Slams Parliamentary Committee's Shared Parenting Recommendations, Dads On The Air, 17 March, 2004.

Our editorial, headlined Betrayal, began: "Dads On The Air has been a significant supporter of the government inquiry into child custody which reported today. Our support was clearly misguided and we apologise to our listeners."

The editorial garnered 3,717 comments.

***

After all the alleged hostility between himself and the Howard government, in the end Family Court Chief Justice Alastair Nicholson was one of the few supporters of the Committee's report.

He declared the plan for equal time shared care was always doomed to failure, said many of their recommendations "had merit" and congratulated the members of the Committee on their courage and foresight.

"I think the Report is a very good one," he said. "You can't have a one-size-fits-all arrangement because children and families are too different. It just did not seem to me to have any sense about it."

Writing for the nation's second largest newspaper group Fairfax, Nicholson said: "Thankfully, the committee has resisted the simplistic argument that a presumption that children spend equal time with both parents would ensure better outcomes. Such an approach was always more likely to benefit parents than children.

"The report also sensibly suggests that shared parenting is inappropriate in situations of high conflict and where there are serious concerns about violence, substance abuse and child abuse, including sexual abuse.

"These cases will remain with the courts. Such cases already form the bulk of children's cases that go to trial so in this regard the committee's recommendations are unlikely to reduce the workload of the court. This is as it should be."[155]

Chief Justice Alastair Nicholson, who himself had always resented the interference of parliament, declared that nothing had changed. The court would consider anything that parliament proffered but it would decide matters according to its own view.

"Despite all the changes to the law, if the Court's view remains that in a standard case a child is better off seeing dad only every second weekend it can still so rule."

"The court has always been compelled to consider a situation that's in the best interests of the child," Nicholson claimed. He described joint custody as a mathematical division of time, "but the real problem is that it presumes that that is an ideal situation, whereas in most cases it's not for all sorts of reasons.

---

155 Ackland, Richard, Family Court Chief Justice Backs Committee Report on Shared Parenting, *Sydney Morning Herald*, 11 March, 2004.

"I think that's more or less an attempt to, if you like, pander to the strong pressure that's been put on the Government by various militant fathers' groups."

That was a slur Nicholson's many critics saw as based on a falsehood, dirty politics perpetrated by a senior judicial officer.

***

Also backing Nicholson were the elements of the family law industry the Howard government had in the first instance judiciously attempted to bypass. The acting chairman of the Family Law section of the Law Council of Australia, Martin Bartfeld, said the report was an attack on the Family Court and the justice system. "The tribunal is going to have some sort of investigative arm and they are going to conduct some sort of inquisition," he said.

"Why should children be the ones on whom this experiment is conducted when we have a system that has been around and developed over a very long period of time? It's hard to imagine the Government will have the money to set up this new system. The Family Court is not excluded. It is just put to one side temporarily."[156]

Another officer from the Law Council Shanna Quinn said that even the committee's view about equal shared parenting responsibility was "naive". Not all parents might be able to, or want to, participate in their children's upbringing. "That is predicated on the assumption that both parents are equally capable, competent and willing to take on that responsibility," she said. "It also is predicated on the assumption that neither parent is a threat to the other."

Nicholson's overall praise for Every Picture Tells A Story guaranteed that it would receive no acceptance amongst fathers' groups and advocates for reform.

***

June 2004 saw the arrival of a new Family Court Chief Justice in the shape of Diana Bryant. Appointed by Prime Minister John Howard, who knew perfectly well from her time on the Federal Magistrates Service the type of custody orders she would make and that the war on fathers, the very fathers whose vote he had been flirting with, would not end under her reign. In the many years that would follow, hundreds of thousands of Australian families churned through the abattoir of decency that was the Family Court of Australia discovered that Bryant was no better no better than her predecessor Alastair Nicholson.

---

156 Donovan, Samantha, Family Law Section Criticizes New Tribunal Proposal, *The Age*, 15 March, 2004.

She did, however, in her relatively few public appearances, come across as more personally charming than Nicholson. Nor did she make the mistake of her predecessor of feeling compelled to comment on all the major social issues of the day, and was more than happy to keep herself and her court out of the headlines.

Or operate in the dark. At least to operate away from public scrutiny or even a whiff of journalistic inquiry. An old government strategy. Wait them out. Without funding they'll die off eventually.

***

By March of 2004 tempers had cooled a little. Our editorial for a show titled We Stood At The Turning Point noted: "The Howard cabinet is likely to look at the child custody inquiry in the coming days. There is a massive schizophrenia in the debate; with rekindled mainstream media interest. Comments coming from politicians have been stronger on the need for family law reform in preceding days, but exactly how that will progress is a matter of much consternation. It seems churlish to mention that the report, while it had some moments of reason, was on the whole a shocker when there is so much apparent good will and determination to enact reform."[157]

This was followed by a show Tough Choices In Tough Times, in which we interviewed the Minister for Children and Youth Affairs Larry Anthony over the release of a survival guide for separated men in conjunction with Mensline and Relationships Australia. Once again the issue of the death rate amongst separated fathers; and therefore amongst child support payers, was dodged.

In March 2004, under the headline Never Again Never Ever, we noted that newspapers around the country had reported that the cabinet would be considering changes to child custody laws, with particular focus on a Families Tribunal. The issue of the Tribunal not only preoccupied various people in government with views for and against, it also took up a lot of attention on various chat lines and separated dad networks.

Despite initial opposition to a new body from senior ministers including Treasurer Peter Costello, Attorney General Philip Ruddock was believed to be making a last-minute bid for the tribunal.

An article in the *Sydney Morning Herald* later in April reported that a new Tribunal would encourage separating parents to agree to joint custody of their children under a two-year trial endorsed by the federal cabinet.

"The tribunal, which aims to reduce the adversarial dimensions of the Family Court, will comprise child experts, psychologists and a judge or senior lawyer.

---

157 We Stood at the Turning Point, Dads On The Air, 22 March, 2004.

During the two-year pilot study, it will complement the Family Court. If found to be successful, it could ease much of the court's workload.

"Cabinet has been considering for two months plans to encourage shared custody after Government MPs were inundated by claims from aggrieved fathers that the current system discriminates against them."[158]

Some cabinet ministers doubted the Tribunal would work, but cabinet had authorised the Attorney General, Philip Ruddock, to consult backbenchers on the trial.

"But the pilot may face resistance from some Government backbenchers who believe the tribunal does not go far enough. Many of them want to throw lawyers out of the divorce process and replace them with a shopfront – within Medicare or Centrelink offices – where separating parents could get advice, paperwork and referrals to mediation if they could not agree on arrangements for the children. Only after all these measures failed would they go to a Families Tribunal."

Indicative of the confusion following the custody report, and vindicating DOTA's editorial line that Every Picture Tells A Story created more problems than it solved, four months later Cabinet had still not fully debated its recommendations.

Ms Hull met with the Attorney General Mr Ruddock in early 2004 but said no one had contacted her Committee about a pilot scheme. "'I'd be asking them to explain," she said. "There is an absolute commitment to this. We are not going to lie down."[159]

Ms Hull said keeping separating parents from going straight to a lawyer was critical to avoiding the acrimony that had such devastating effects on children. She said if the Family Court administered a pilot of the Families Tribunal, "that's a total duplication".

The proposed Tribunal would be informal, with little documentation and no lawyers.

The paper reported that lawyers have lobbied against the tribunal scheme, arguing it will leave people vulnerable without legal representation – and that it was outside the committee's terms of reference.

In the end, despite all the talk, the Tribunal never got off the ground. In the DOTA forum it was noted: "Without the abolition of the precedents in Family Law, the corrupt psychologists and the corrupt lawyers that infest family law we

---

158 Ackland, Richard, New Tribunal to Encourage Joint Custody in Family Law Trial, *The Sydney Morning Herald* on April 28, 2004.

159 Lane, Bernard, Hull Meets Ruddock Over Shared Custody Pilot Scheme, The Australian, 2 April, 2004.

simply do not see how a Tribunal will work. Nothing in the disgraceful report by the inquiry suggested that it will be anything but another scandal ridden department in the style of NSW DOCS. We're happy to be proven wrong."[160]

But with cabinet split on the Tribunal and other solutions such as the shop front and mediation and the government gearing for a re-election fight later in the year, family law reform was left in limbo. Nor was there any immediate action on plans to fix child support.

***

With heightened sentiments within the fatherhood movement throughout 2004, there was at this time a brief flirtation with an Australian branch of Fathers4Justice, the British group which had been so successful in attracting attention to the plight of fathers. We carried an interview in April with Trevor Arthurson, the Australian coordinator, who had organised demonstrations outside Perth, Brisbane and Melbourne Family Courts with the theme of decontamination.

With a lot of good will towards the government having evaporated as promised reforms failed to eventuate, later in April 2004 we interviewed Tony Miller of Dads In Distress under a program titled Thousands Die Government Does Nothing. We editorialised on a theme we persistently pursued: "Fathers and family law groups around the country have long claimed there is a direct link between the high death rates amongst separated fathers, with male suicide now at century high levels, and the operations of the child support and family law systems.

"If, as they claim, some three clients of the Child Support Agency suicide every day; that makes some eight thousand payers since John Howard came to office as Prime Minister of Australia.

"We don't know if the claim is true. Official suicide statistics suggest it is well within reason. What we do need out of this government is a direct and published audit of the death rate of child support payers. Anything less is an abrogation of their moral obligations to govern in the best interests of the people and borders on criminal negligence."[161]

The titles of subsequent shows all signalled a high level of disenchantment: Calumny and Hope, Reform Failure, Missed Opportunity, Howard Duds Dads and The Failure of Parliament.

---

160 Dads On The Air forums, Shared Custody Tribunal - A Non-Starter? 15 November, 2004.

161 Thousands Die Government Does Nothing, Interview with Tony Miller, Dads On The Air, 27 April, 2004.

Forum guest Matthew's comments were fairly typical: "I have recently been the victim of a malicious and vindictive woman's attempt to not only leave me but take the children along with her. She is now using the LAW to hide behind and achieve her objectives. The NET losers are the Children and I (Ten year old Daughter and THREE year old son). They are so innocent as to see how they are being USED... To REMOVE only the Father from the children is CRUEL. In an age where FEMINISM and EQUALITY is the order of the day, why is it then that MALES who are otherwise contributing in all aspects of family life, being EXCLUDED only in the event of a separation?

"The Government and the Judicial system must HELP!!! Healthy children are the lifeblood of social continuity and for our country this is a paramount issue as we prepare to engage and shine in the 21st Century economy."[162]

***

In the lead up to the election later in the year the Howard government promised everything from lifestyle support payments for Centrelink clients, mostly women, a domestic violence campaign which supporters claimed the government had delayed implementing and which critics condemned as vilifying men, lying about the nature and extent of DV in the community and promoting public hysteria. Against the wishes of many of its own socially conservative constituency Howard also announced a $1.5 billion maternity payment in the May budget, beginning at $3,000 and rising to $5,000. Critics claimed the money encouraged unmarried teenage mothers to have children outside of a stable relationship and choose a lifetime on welfare as a single parent.

To DOTA it appeared obvious that the Howard government was embarrassed by claims of being influenced by men's groups during the family law inquiry and was bending over backwards to sell itself as attune to women's concerns. Treasurer Peter Costello declared he wanted to make Australia the best country in the world for women to live in.[163]

Not, DOTA noted, the best country in the world for all its citizens.

The Shared Parenting Council claimed the maternity payment demonstrated that the Howard Government had completely ignored the cry of fathers to have their existence recognised in law.

"The Howard Government is intent on rewarding only one gender for having babies," spokesman Ed Dabrowski said. "It had failed the simple test of fairness by not matching paid maternity leave with paid paternity leave.

---

162 Fathers' Rights and Family Law: Personal Experiences, Dads On The Air, 12 April, 2004.

163 Costello Aims to Make Australia Best for Women, *The Age*, 13 March, 2004.

"Moreover, the Government was showing its' contempt for fathers and their dignified role in nurturing their children by ignoring urgently needed Family Law reform to put noncustodial fathers back into the lives of their children.

"It is astounding that after all the rhetoric of family friendly and inclusive language the Howard Government has espoused over recent years, they have engaged in an act that is only likely to further support irresponsible parenthood.

"The Howard Government has ignored the plights of fathers and in particular the needs of children to have two parents in their lives, by compounding and developing a further bias supporting motherhood over the recognition of children's and fathers' rights."[164]

***

In the same month three condoms filled with purple powder hit the British Prime Minister Tony Blair in the House of Commons, and if they didn't already the world then knew about Fathers For Justice. It was clear the issues facing Australian fathers were very similar to those of their British cousins.

We interviewed F4J founder Matthew O'Connor over his escalating campaign of civil disobedience. The group's spectacular series of superhero stunts and protests, targeting courts and solicitor's offices in particular, had attracted sympathetic and often searching coverage.

June 2004 saw the arrival of a new Family Court Chief Justice in the shape of Diana Bryant.

The appointment was generally welcomed and she was praised for being "a brilliant lawyer, unpretentious, with an innate sense of justice and fairness".

Bryant had headed the Federal Magistrates Court since 2000. While it was regularly criticised for failing to differentiate itself from the culture of the Family Court in terms of personnel, procedures and attitudes towards fathers and shared parenting, it was also regarded as on the whole delivering simpler, faster and fairer judgements.

Bryant had left her mark on the Federal Magistrates Court, which began as a controversial initiative to simplify, demystify, speed up and lessen the expense of procedures for family law litigants, many of them unrepresented.

It became the preferred court of many lawyers and the majority of family law cases were now filed there.

Sue Price at the Men's Rights Agency said Bryant had to be an improvement on Nicholson and at least she appeared to have a good grasp of the problems presented by the Child Support Agency.

---

164 Shared Parenting Council Criticizes Howard Government's Maternity Payment, Dads On The Air, 12 April, 2004.

"Hopefully, she might bring some realism to this situation," Ms Price said. "She is by no means the worst possible appointment."[165]

The Age newspaper commented: "The new Chief Justice will need to maintain internal morale in the face of external attacks, funding vagaries and fast-changing family dynamics. Lawyers say Ms Bryant is the ideal person for the task.

"The outgoing Chief Justice, Alastair Nicholson, has spent much of his 16 years at the court publicly defending it against litigants, lawyers, men's rights groups, conservative family groups and politicians.

"Ms Bryant has made no notable public comments as Chief Magistrate and is not expected to be outspoken like Chief Justice Nicholson.

"She is apolitical really, not someone like Alastair Nicholson, say, with a sharply delineated social justice agenda."[166]

Subsequently Bryant said she was uncomfortable with the notion she might have some influence on shaping society. "I don't think that is the role of Chief Justice to the extent of the decisions of an individual court or the Full Court," she said. "I interpret legislation. I suppose that's influence, but we have a lot of legislation and Parliament itself takes a much more active role in shaping how they want things to be than in the past. As for my own place in history, it's too early to tell."[167]

***

On 29 July 2004 Prime Minister Howard, as part of his electioneering, released a discussion paper outlining proposed changes to the family court system in Australia. The government rejected proposals for a Tribunal and the calls for fathers to be given equal time with their children.

"Every Australian in different ways is touched by, whether directly or indirectly, by family or relationship breakdown, the impact it can often have of a very serious kind on young children and an impact that can last with them for the rest of their lives," Howard said. "I think most people regard the present system as too adversarial and too costly and increasingly unreceptive to the warmth and the interests of many people who are touched by these breakdowns."[168]

---

165 Men's Rights Agency Reacts to New Family Court Chief Justice, Dads On The Air, 27 June, 2004.

166 Donovan, Samantha, New Family Court Chief Justice Faces Challenges, *The Age*, 28 June, 2004.

167 Lane, Bernard, Bryant on Role and Influence as Chief Justice, *The Australian*, 14 October, 2004.

168 Ackland, Richard, Howard Proposes Changes to Family Court System, *The Sydney Morning Herald*, 30 July, 2004.

Howard announced the introduction of a nationwide network of family relationship centres that would act as a first shock absorber when people's relationships broke down. "And it's designed further to cement the concept that the natural parents of children have, each of them, the mother and the father, an inalienable right to be involved in the raising of their children, to have a say in their future. This is a government that is not only interested in economics and the benefits that flow from good economic prospects, it is a government that is interested in the long term social health of our nation."

On the same day Attorney General Philip Ruddock said one of the key changes would be an amendment to the Family Law Act to entrench equal-shared parental responsibility as the starting point in disputes.

"We will be amending the law as the committee recommended to accept that the starting point in relation to any matter involving children is equal-shared parental responsibility ... and that parents should share the key decisions in relation to the child's life regardless of how much time the child spends with each parent," he said.

"So we will be amending the Family Law Act to refer to the need of both parents to have a meaningful involvement in their children's lives and the children have a right to spend time on a regular basis with both of them."

He said most cases would be handled by the national network of 65 family relationship centres to be operated by churches and community organisations, but the option remained open for trickier matters to go to court.

"The centres will offer assistance to all separating couples whether or not they've commenced any legal proceedings," Mr Ruddock said. "It will be focused on providing practical assistance and it will help those couples resolve those disputes promptly and before, hopefully, relationships deteriorate and conflict becomes entrenched.

"We see it as a very substantial change and a very beneficial change."[169]

***

The Age newspaper asked its readers what they thought, garnishing a range of responses from God help us to JB's: "The Family Law Act is a joke. The best interests of the children are never considered. The woman uses the system to get her own way and uses the children for financial gain. The father is nothing more than a sperm donor and bank account. The Child Support Agency is nothing more than another form of revenge for women.

---

169 Lane, Bernard, Ruddock Announces Family Law Act Amendments, *The Australian*, 30 July, 2004.

"The law should state, if a woman intends to claim child support she should have a job herself, instead of expecting the x to support her while she claims a taxpayer funded pension. DNA testing should be made compulsory at the time of an application for child support. Child support shouldn't be based on taxable income either, some men are paying over $300 per week in support, yet the mothers claim pensions and are not required to work, how unfair. No wonder so many men are angry."[170]

Also, following recommendations from the parliamentary inquiry, the government announced that a Child Support Task Force would report on possible changes to the child support payment system by March the following year. The Committee had made a number of recommendations in relation to the child support scheme, including a comprehensive re-evaluation of the scheme focusing on contemporary work, parenting and family structures as well as the income profiles of child support payers and payees.

Having lost patience, in August, on a show titled Mounting Outrage, DOTA editorialised: "There's barely a separated father or fair minded person in the country who isn't frustrated by the Howard government's callow, shallow and completely pathetic response to family law and child support reform after eight years of government and a trail of wrecked lives a mile long. Anyone who is going to vote for Prime Minister John Howard thinking he will reform child support and family law is living in pixie land."[171]

Discontent with the Child Support Agency remained a live issue. Commentary on the DOTA forum suggested that one of the central themes running in father's groups is the lack of penalty upon payees who withhold contact in order to blackmail payers into paying exorbitant child support.

"CSA are an accomplice in this process for they garnishee payers wages regardless of contact issues. The Constitution is meant to protect citizens from abuse of power by the State but CSA and the Family Courts are in clear breach of this duty. It has become apparent that the State is actively engaged in manufacturing consent of child support payers in order to implement the State approved solution. This is an abuse of power and is wrong, very very wrong."[172]

***

---

[170] Readers React to Proposed Family Law Changes, *The Age*, 1 August, 2004.

[171] Mounting Outrage, Dads On The Air, 15 August, 2004.

[172] Discontent with the Child Support Agency, Dads On The Air, Forum, 22 August, 2004.

In August 2004 the then Minister for Children and Youth Affairs Larry Anthony announced the Terms of Reference for a child support inquiry, reiterating the aims of the scheme.

Beyond the litany of complaints about its "Gestapo like" tactics and insatiable demands, the Agency had clearly failed in areas such as ensuring incentives for both parents to participate in the workforce were not impaired; and ensuring "overall arrangements are simple, flexible and efficient".

Previous programs on Dads On The Air highlighting the child support fiasco were under unsubtle headlines such as "Child Support Agency to cost taxpayers $40 billion" and "Child Support Agency a National Financial Disaster".

DOTA editorialised: "The justification for the CSA was based on very poor research and followed the American fad at the time of introducing similar schemes – with elaborate justifications from left-wing academics.

"The first child support schemes were created by the Bolsheviks after the Russian revolution as a way of providing for children outside the nuclear family. They were a way to fund the Bolsheviks' war on the traditional family, which they saw as the major stumbling block to social reform.

"Just as the Bolsheviks introduced them as a way of protecting children while dissolving the nuclear family, in the west they were sold to governments as a way of funding sole mother custody and the style of orders normally made by the Family Court. They were introduced as a way of protecting the taxpayer from the cost of the spiralling number of single parent families.

"Similar child support formulas as operate in Australia persist to this day in the Russian Family Code. They are believed to have been a major factor in the once massive Russian black economy. But just as in Russia the schemes have backfired. In Australia they are now being attributed as a major cause of unemployment and welfare dependency."[173]

The Child Support Task Force was charged with paying particular attention to the Government intention to support the involvement of both parents after separation when examining the costs of raising children and relooking at the formula.

Patrick Parkinson, professor at the Faculty of Law at the University of Sydney and Chairman of the Family Law Council was appointed Chairman of the Inquiry.

For once there were several father-friendly figures on the Task Force. They included Michael Green, author of Shared Parenting, Tony Miller, founder of Dads in Distress, Barry Williams, founder of the Lone Fathers' Association of Australia and Bettina Arndt, social commentator.

---

173 The Origins and Justifications of the CSA, Dads On The Air, 5 September, 2004.

Minister Anthony observed in his media release that there were now more than 1.3 million parents registered with the Child Support Agency involving 1.1 million children. In 2003-04, $2.19 billion in child support was transferred between parents "for the benefit of their children".

The claim was spurious because there was no guarantee how any of the money was spent. Its main rationale from a government's point of view had been social security claw back, mitigating the cost of separated parents on the taxpayer.

"The paramount concern of the Government is to ensure that the child support scheme operates in the best interests of the children of separated parents," Anthony said.[174]

***

Finally, after the Howard government was returned to office in October 2004 and a year after the inquiry into shared parenting finished taking evidence, there was something that resembled action. The Attorney General Philip Ruddock and Community Services Minister Kay Patterson issued a discussion paper titled A New Approach to the Family Law System on 10 November 2004. The paper suggested that three hours of mediation could be provided free of charge through the new Relationship Centres for people trying to sort out their situation upon separation.

The Government sought comments from the public with submissions closing on the 14th of January, 2005.

DOTA editorialised in a program featuring the Attorney General: "This is your last chance to have any direct input into what the government is calling the most significant changes to the family law system since 1975 after a long period of inquiry, delay and uncertainty.

"In this interview the Attorney General of Australia Philip Ruddock appears well aware of community discontent around the issues of family law and child support. He has called on community input into a discussion paper which promotes wide-ranging reforms to the family law system to be introduced by the middle of next year.

"Our editorial position is that the reforms will fail unless there is a more determined approach to entrench shared parenting and joint custody as the most common outcome post separation, accompanied by bureaucratic, institutional

---

174 Minister Larry Anthony's Media Release, Child Support Agency Statistics and Government Commitment, October 19, 2004.

and judicial reform. For the sake of children, who need both parents, this needs to be accompanied by a sustained community education program on the benefits of cooperation after separation and fundamental changes to the welfare, child support and child protection cultures."[175]

***

While Dads On The Air did not usually make written submissions to inquiries, seeing our role as simply reported the actions of others, in this case we felt compelled to contribute: "We do not believe the current proposals by the government go anywhere near far enough to solve the quagmire of family law and child support which is causing so much harm in this country, both in financial and human terms.

"Family law is every Australians' most common experience with lawyers. The experience leaves virtually all of them with contempt for the law and for the government which allows this farce to continue.

"The government has been slow to come to the issue of family law reform and while it should be congratulated on finally responding to the level of community concern over family law and child support issues and the high level of public support for shared parenting, and congratulated on the aspects of the proposed changes which encourage shared parenting, we believe the government is wrong to have rejected the idea of joint custody.

"We believe the government should immediately legislate for 'shared care and responsibility' and all arms of government should work to entrench joint custody and shared parenting after divorce as the result in all but the most extreme of cases.

"We believe this would genuinely comply with the government's determination to act in the best interests of children. While the move might be all too simple for the family law experts who have made such a spectacular hash of the present situation, conveniently for the government it would also be popular amongst voters.

"At present the judiciary, the welfare bureaucracy, the legal profession and politicians all work in cohesion to achieve the opposite end and to prop up the discredited sole mother custody model.

"Much of the verbal and written evidence gathered by the House of Representatives Committee inquiry into child custody was a compelling argument for

---

175 Last Chance for Input on Family Law Reforms, Interview with Attorney General Philip Ruddock, Dads On The Air, 26 October, 2004.

change and provided emotionally charged and again compelling evidence of the massive harm being done to parents and children alike by the present system.

"The government was in our view correct to ignore the recommendation for a Tribunal, which would in all likelihood have turned into a bureaucratic nightmare within nanoseconds.

"Every Picture Tells A Story arbitrarily rejected the notion of joint custody without any proper examination of the evidence. It was poorly written and poorly argued and should be re-examined.

"The notion of 'shared responsibility' is at best dangerously vague and at worst means absolutely nothing. It allows far too much room for disputation between separating couples and far too much room for the parasitic multi-billion dollar industry that surrounds separation to continue on its disastrous way."[176]

***

DOTA reiterated its scepticism over the Relationship Centres but argued that they could help establish shared parenting arrangements immediately after separation.

"The family law changes need to be accompanied by welfare reform which, rather than encouraging the chronically high level of welfare dependence amongst separated mothers and fathers, spreads the benefits equally and encourages both parents to be self supporting and actively employed.

"We also believe that the government should introduce a new charge of administrative manslaughter so that those child support and child protection bureaucrats knowingly administering policies which lead to high death tolls of fathers and children can be brought to account. Such a move would prevent such disasters as the present child support and family law developing again in the future.

"The conduct of the Family Court has not changed since the Howard government came to power more than eight years ago. During that period hundreds of thousands of children have been arbitrarily ripped off their fathers.

"With the advent of the internet, the debate over the conduct of the Family Court and its judges has changed dramatically. Few fathers entering the court now expect to be treated in a fair and reasonable way for the sake of their children.

***

In a press release John Flanagan from the Non-Custodial Parents (Equal Parenting) Party referred to the Government's new Family Relationship Centres.

---

[176] Dads On The Air Submission on Family Law Reform, Dads On The Air, 1 November, 2004.

He said that if the family law and child support system were equitable in the first instance, less than three hours of the free counselling being proposed by the government would be required.

However as the system is now, 300 hours of counselling would not be enough! The Party, later to add the words "Equal Parenting" to their title, was another organisation which shared a largely concurrent history with DOTA. Formed in 1998 it had fielded candidates in every Federal election since, increasing its votes each time.

"Real reform needs to be first considered by the Government. This all requires legislative change on the part of the Government. The Family Court needs to be re- structured into mediation centres. At the same time, a rebuttable presumption of 50:50 shared parenting has to be introduced through legislation as a starting point after separation. Children are not the personal property of any one parent.

"Any reform needs to be looked at as a complete package. In that respect, the Government's Child Support Agency has to be abolished. Both parents have to be put back into control of supporting their children after separation. Property settlements and superannuation splitting need to be made fairer and equitable after separation. What is brought into the marriage should be taken out of the marriage.

"These necessary reforms would have the added benefit of reducing the divorce rate. There will be no monetary benefit for one parent to seek a divorce or a separation as it is now.

"The present family system was created by people and can be changed by people. Success will come with vision, hope and determination. There are many separated parents throughout Australia seeking the path of social and legislative reform."[177]

***

In one of our final shows for 2004 we once again interviewed Michael Green, emphasising his description of shared parenting as "the necessary revolution".

We concluded the year with the following editorial: "It began with great hope that Australia would finally be seeing genuine reform of family law and child support; followed by great disappointment. But in a strange way, the reform and the broad community push for shared parenting to become the norm post-separation just

---

177 Flanagan, John, Media Release, Non-Custodial Parents Party, 11 November, 2004. Found at Fathers – The Family Anchor, newsletter, 22 November, 2004.

kept on moving despite all the bureaucrats, lawyers, so-called experts and politicians who stood in the way. For the distress over these issues has reached critical mass. And of course the spectacular progress of F4J in England – who could forget Buckingham Palace and Tony Blair's purple condoms for instance – added a new dramatic edge to the debate."

In January 2005 the new Family Court Chief Justice Diana Bryant came on to Dads On The Air in a show we titled "The Future of the Family Court". She denied any problems with family report writers or any systematic bias in her court. In the interview she appeared to be in favour of shared parenting as a common sense outcome for separating couples.[178]

In March, under the heading Old Soldiers, we interviewed Barry Williams, reiterating the general discontent: "Family law and child support is an unmitigated mess in this country, doing massive harm to parents, children and families alike. Yet the Howard government, after almost nine years in office, has been prepared to watch and do nothing as hundreds of thousands of people's lives are damaged by the dysfunctional and discredited family law industry.

"While the scene has changed dramatically in recent times, for many years the media treated Barry Williams as if he was the only separated father in the country. He was the sole voice for destroyed dads."[179]

In the hiatus between the 2003 inquiry and the enactment of any legislation, there were many other signs of ferment and disquiet. While the government, well over a year after the parliamentary inquiry ended, had yet to formulate any response, community agitation continued.

In the lead up to a planned march on parliament house in Canberra mid-year, in early April 2005 an enterprising couple Michael and Tanya from the Hunter Valley in NSW organised a picnic day at Sydney's historic Domain for people interested in family law and child support reform. Their signs of protest were odd in the otherwise idyllic scene. It attracted about a hundred of the disenchanted and like minded, some waving banners. Their own dreams of happy family picnics had been shattered long ago.

***

In April, too, there were a number of leaks from the impending Child Support Task Force report. There were reports that single mothers would get to keep

---

[178] The Future of the Family Court, Interview with Chief Justice Dyana Bryant, Dads On The Air, January, 2005.

[179] Old Soldiers, Interview with Barry Williams, Lone Fathers President, Dads On The Air, March, 2005.

more of their welfare payments in exchange for fathers paying less child support. The Child Support Taskforce was also considering allowing divorced fathers who looked after their children for at least one night a week to pay less maintenance.

Under this plan, the taxpayer would foot the bill for the reduction in income that single mothers would face as a result of the lower maintenance payments.

In a press release, John Flanagan from the group Fairness in Child Support attempted to explain why it was all a bad idea. At least he managed to demonstrate how complex the whole system was.

He said: "The link between child support and Family Tax Benefit payment is being used as a de-facto child support registration system for separated parents. At the same time, it is also being used to contribute to the ever-increasing size of our government bureaucracy".

After family separation, the custodial parent normally registers with the Family Assistance Office for Family Tax Benefit Part A payments. According to the Child Support Agency this occurs after 93 per cent of all separations.

"The Family Assistance Office has to then decide whether reasonable action has been taken. This is before more than the minimum Family Tax Benefit Part A payment is approved. This simply means determining whether or not a custodial parent has registered for child support.

"No one explains to the custodial parent that once they have registered for child support and receive more than the minimum Family Tax Benefit Part A payment, they then lose some of these benefits back to the Government," Flanagan said. "That is, once the amount of $1,149.75 is received in child support by the custodial parent, 50 cents in the dollar is then deducted from the Family Tax Benefit Part A payments."

This deduction adds up to hundreds of millions of dollars each year. These deducted funds are then used to totally finance the running of the Child Support Scheme – $470 million in 2008-2009.

The Family Tax Benefit payment was originally called child endowment. It was brought in by the then NSW Premier Jack Lang in the Depression years of the 1930s. Bob Menzies made it a national payment in the early 1940s.

Flanagan concluded: "The child endowment payments were meant to be for the kids. Neither Jack Lang nor Bob Menzies would have foreseen that these payments would have been syphoned off to provide employment for Government bureaucrats. This has occurred since the Child Support Scheme commenced in Australia in 1989."

***

Maverick Liberal MP for Hume Alby Schultz, one of the few members of parliament with the guts to consistently speak out about the Child Support Agency and a guest on Dads On The Air on a number of occasions, said while media coverage had hinted at some coming changes "simply decreasing a parent's liability based on the amount of time they spend with their child and increasing the payment for people on welfare is not going to solve this problem.

"The evidence quite clearly identifies blatant misuse of the legislation, bullying and standover tactics and bias against one party over the other.

"Just this week a mother of two has written to me because the Child Support Agency recently froze her ex-partner's bank account in an attempt to re-claim arrears owed to the other woman. This has left him with no money to fulfil his obligations to his other two children! When she contacted the Child Support Agency to complain she was told in no uncertain terms that they were not worried about her or her children because they were not clients of the Child Support Agency."

In addition Mr Schultz said he remained concerned about the Child Support Agency's ability to secretly intrude into the lives of third parties associated with non-custodial parents. Earlier the same month the *West Australian* newspaper had highlighted that the "embattled" Agency had been secretly accessing the bank accounts of people not on its books in a bid to track down parents who refused to pay child maintenance. The CSA has for years had the right to glean information from bank accounts held by people who were not its clients, providing it was for the purpose of chasing child support.

"This legislated power given to the Child Support Agency to spy on people's financial affairs – people who owe no debt to anyone – is simply wrong and a blatant invasion of privacy. I can fully understand the Child Support Agency wanting to re-claim monies owed but this is not a police state, and people's basic right to privacy should be protected.

"Allowing a police state mentality to permeate government agencies such as the Child Support Agency is irresponsible, undemocratic and un-Australian."

In his valedictory speech to the Australian Parliament in 2013, before he passed away from cancer in 2015, Alby Schultz recorded: "Marginal seat politics, party-political point scoring, failure to act on serious social issues and irresponsible waste of taxpayers' resources are both frustrating and morally wrong. As an example, in 2005 I produced a booklet based on three years of hard research about the Child Support Agency and its relentless, unjustifiable anti-male culture, which culminated in the suicide of a number of my young constituents. Confronting the very serious issue of male suicide caused by the gender biased CSA was treated as a politically sensitive no-go area by many politicians, which

I embraced as a challenge on behalf of 4,000 families and individuals across the country.

"That culture, despite some cosmetic changes, is still endemic in the CSA today. The increase in male suicides are due in no small part to the unrelenting anti-male culture of the CSA. The Lone Fathers Association, led by Barry Williams— the man is a saint – is taking 70,000 calls per annum from depressed males, many of whom are desperately trying to deal with CSA pressure. Were it not for him, the suicide rate would be even higher.

"The incoming government would be doing a great service to oppressed payers facing criminal activity, such as entrapment and denial of natural justice – which is the modus operandi of the CSA today – and to the nation as a whole, if it introduced a parliamentary inquiry which would allow people to give evidence of the covering up of male suicides caused by the Child Support Agency. More importantly, it will give those living under threat of legal action by the CSA – if they release any part of taped conversations which prove intimidation, false information, abuse of civil rights and denial of natural justice — an opportunity to expose these issues under parliamentary protection."[180]

***

In June, after a month's delay, the Parkinson report The Best Interests of Children – Reforming The Child Support Scheme, was made public.[181] It began: "To a considerable extent, the Child Support Scheme has achieved the objectives that successive governments have given for it. The Scheme has also been successful in promoting community acceptance of the idea of child support obligations. However, much has changed in the circumstances of Australian families since 1988.

"There is now a greatly increased emphasis on shared parental responsibility, and the importance of both parents remaining actively involved in their children's lives after separation has gained much greater recognition. Child support policy can no longer just be concerned with enforcing the financial obligations of reluctant non-resident parents."

How, DOTA wanted to know, could the report claim the CSA had fulfilled the objectives of successive governments? Had they really requested the level of conflict, anger and angst that the scheme generated, the constant accusations of maladministration and outright illegality?

---

180 Schultz, Alby, Valedictory Speech, House of Representatives, 25 June, 2013.

181 Parkinson, Patrick. In the Best Interests of Children – Reforming The Child Support Scheme. Report of the Ministerial Taskforce on Child Support, Australian Government Department of Family and Community Services, 2006.

As could be expected in Australia's parallel bureaucratic universe, no examination of the social consequences of the Scheme was recommended or undertaken.

Apparently immune to the hardship and disastrous personal and social outcomes produced by the Agency and so easily evident, the Howard government, keen perhaps not to be perceived as pandering to the fathers groups, announced that a hundred thousand fathers who had not lodged tax returns for the previous five years, allegedly to avoid paying child maintenance, would be targeted.

Senior Howard Government figures said "heavy compliance" to target maintenance dodgers was essential to ensure the Task Force proposals did not end up as a one-sided attack on mothers. They said "only" 500 men a year were currently investigated by the Child Support Agency because the CSA did not have the resources to investigate more."

Every year handsomely paid politicians preened themselves as they announced yet another crackdown on separated dads – almost all of whom were on low incomes and many of them in debt to the Agency purely because of its bizarre accounting methods, relentless greed and excessive compounding penalties. All the punitive measures accumulated over the years had led to nothing but chaos. But here the government was at it all over again. And the Agency would not even count its own dead.

The report showed a system in crisis. Almost 40 percent of parents paid less than a quarter of their child support payments, with previously unpublished data from the CSA showing only 13.5 percent of people paid the correct amount in full and on time. Nearly half of the non-custodial parents paying less than a quarter of their child support payments had annual incomes of less than $25,000, substantially below average earnings.

High-income earners were also failing to meet the Agency's demands, with 20 percent of those with incomes of more than $85,000 found to be in arrears.

The Task Force's first amongst 30 recommendations was that both parent's incomes be taken into account: "The existing formula for the assessment of child support should be replaced by a new formula based upon the principle of shared parental responsibility for the costs of children. The new basic formula should involve first working out the costs of children by reference to the combined incomes of the parents, and then distributing those costs in accordance with the parents' respective capacities to meet those costs, taking into account their share of the care of the children."

Never simple, child support was about to become more complicated. The often tumultuous lives of the parents they were dealing with, particularly around the time of separation, made it all the more complex. And potentially more damaging.

The issue of how to reform the scheme attracted substantial coverage. Research released concurrently by the Australian Institute of Family Studies found more than 62 percent of non-resident fathers and 45 percent of resident mothers thought the system did not work well. Of non-resident fathers 74 percent thought the system unfair. Mothers were evenly divided.

Taskforce chairman Patrick Parkinson said the perception that child support payments were more about the lifestyles of the parents than about looking after the children was the reason the issue had become so inflammatory, "The parents paying a lot are saying, 'I just don't think kids cost that much.' They want child support to be based on a reasonable estimate of what they cost."[182]

***

One man's submission to the child support inquiry read: "It is my personal experience that children are nothing more than a source of income and opportunity to most custodial parents and a very spiteful way to destroy the other parent."

Judging by the DOTA forum this was not an isolated view.

Another father said custody arrangements had left men such as himself as "little more than visitors in their children's lives while still being expected to meet much of the financial burden". He said: "I have watched what was once a close relationship with my children gradually being eroded until the only contact I now have is when I visit them during their school lunch break."[183]

Non-custodial fathers who felt they were paying too much inundated the committee and were matched by mothers who felt their former partners were trying to punish them by paying too little.

The *Sydney Morning Herald* observed that "the old arrangement was simple – and in a lot of cases, simply unfair. Its blanket provisions took no account of individual circumstances and life changes. Non-resident parents rebelled against its provisions and often refused to pay. Instituted in the late 1980s, it took no account of recent tax changes which now mean in effect that for many single-parent families, the taxpayer largely supports the children."

Under the previous system non-custodial parents paid 18 percent of their gross income taken out of their net pay for one child, 27 percent for two, 32 percent for three, 34 per cent for four children and 36 percent for five or more. Under the new plans, child- support payments were to be calculated on the basis of both parents' incomes and the time each parent spent caring for the children.

---

182 Metherell, Mark, Many fathers to pay less child support, *The Sydney Morning Herald*, 14 June, 2006.

183 Ibid.

Among the recommendations was a formula that would set higher payments for teenagers; the exemption of overtime and second jobs from the assessment of a father's income for five years after separation; a discount in the amount fathers owed if their children stay with them at least one night a week; and a change that would see custodial parents, mostly women, keep all of the family tax benefits, unless a father has the child more than 35 percent of the time.

The Task Force claimed the changes would result in an estimated 60 percent of non- custodial parents – typically fathers – paying less child support.

***

President of the Lone Fathers Association, Barry Williams, predicted the changes would mean child support would no longer be about "socking non-custodial parents for money for their kids" and would benefit non-custodial parents and their children.

"We never dreamt we would get so much," he said. "It couldn't have been fairer to men if they tried."

Tony Miller from Dads In Distress said: "The Taskforce has heard our complaints. Fathers will certainly be paying less than they are paying now." But the sweeping recommendations of the ministerial taskforce on child support will take time to understand, both men said. The proposed changes were complex and the amount of child support would depend on parents' income, the number of children, their ages and how much time children spent with the non-resident parent.

Elspeth McInnes of the Council for Single Mothers and their Children said overall less child support would be paid and many children would be worse off if the Government accepted the recommendations.

"The Taskforce did their job with goodwill but the social policy problem was seen as 'poor dads' rather than outcomes for children of separated parents," she said. "The evidence we have is that child support, when it was paid, was effective in relieving and reducing poverty in single-parent households. If you reduce the amount of child support payable, there's a risk that poverty will increase."

Parkinson insisted that children would not be worse off as a result of lower payments because the resident parent would also be able to claim all the family tax benefits.

"Child support has to be about the kids. It can't be about welfare, it can't be about maintaining the resident parent's living standards," he said. "That's what the Government does, that's what getting back into work does. Some of those payments will go down and some will go up. The majority will probably go down, but many, many resident parents will be receiving more as a result of our recommendations. We've tried to be fair to both parents and, above all, fair to the kids."

***

An appearance by Dads In Distress founder and Task Force member Tony Miller, along with a group of dads on the ABC's Four Corners current affairs program, provoked an avalanche of emails and personal stories. Miller wrote: "Our website has exploded with hits and our phone system at our base has been unable to cope with the demand. This isn't a boast but a sad indictment of our times. Far too many are suffering across the country from a flawed system."

One father wrote: "I am a wage earner and have not missed any payments over the past seven years. So unfortunately I am a loser. I have been fortunate enough to remarry and have a lovely supporting wife. We have just been through a year long court battle that cost us our house and almost our marriage because the ex wouldn't let me see my son, funnily enough after the CSA ruled against one of her endless re-assessments. I now have access.

"The family reporter found that my ex had 'not given emotional permission' for my son to have a relationship with me and also that she had 'deeply influenced his decision not to see me'.

"So here we are. The experts say I am to have access. She is now playing the denial game again. My lawyer said I could go contempt of court but it was unlikely much would happen – and they say child support is not linked to access – she has me up before the CSA again because my son needs braces. I would love to help but we now live hand to mouth.

"She took out an intervention order because I wrote and advised her of my change of address and didn't go through the Mediator. I have lodged an intervention order against her because I am sick of her constant harassment of my family – telling my employer I am rorting the system. I simply can't afford a lawyer and am sick of lying in the darkness listening to my wife crying herself to sleep.

"I am starting to feel blame and guilt and it is only my two other kids that keep me strong enough. I feel the system sucking me dry and there is not a damn thing I can do about it. I have reached the point of resignation and don't feel I have any strength, financial or emotional, left."

Another, the second wife of a man who had just turned 50, said when she met her husband he was "what I can only describe as deeply depressed and definitely in distress over the mother of his three children driving away with all three kids to go to another relationship. He could not understand the reasons for her leaving with no explanation and moving straight into her new relationship. There was no discussion, no children's feelings taken into account, and no father's feelings mattered. The only thing that woman was focused on was establishing a relationship with another man and completely isolating the children's father in the process.

"After the court hearing to divvy up the money he was forced to sell the family home, a commercial fishing vessel and was left with a meagre sum to continue his life with. She went on to use the money to assist her new partner in paying off his debts, secured a new home, bought a new car, and had two incomes, hers and the new partner. My husband on the other hand arrived on my doorstep with an old Holden station wagon and a bag of clothes. He was camping in a tent where he could. Time passed and access visits did not happen.

"I have encouraged him to take the mother to court for deprivation of rights to see his children, total deliberate alienation strategies, openly giving negative and damaging information to the children and for compensation for the loss, grief and associated depression issues he has had to, and still struggles with today."

Another father wrote that he had two children he hadn't seen for six years. "I pay $380 a fortnight to the CSA, leaving me with a take home pay of about $700 per fortnight. I am casually employed and my income fluctuates. One payday I was left with $60 as, according to CSA I was still able to pay the full amount being just over the threshold. My ex-wife totally blocked all contact I had with my children for no reason and I have spent the last six years facing dead ends trying to recover my rights to no avail.

"I cannot afford solicitors, I'm frightened to earn more money. The CSA says I have a burgeoning debt of over $7000 – due to a period of unemployment some years ago.

"I have never actively avoided my payment responsibilities. Yet I have no rights, no kids and little prospects of financial improvement. I can honestly say if it wasn't for my partner I would have ended it by now. The CSA has told me that they are only concerned with collection and if I was serious about seeing my kids I would appoint a solicitor – WITH WHAT?"[184]

***

Then on June 20 came a march on Parliament House in Canberra in the name of family law and child support reform.[185] Most reform movements are made up of

---

184 Metherell, Mark, Many fathers to pay less child support", *The Sydney Morning Herald*, 14 June, 2006.

185 Angry fathers march on Canberra, *The Age*, 21 June, 2005.

a few activists and a silent, supportive majority. Nowhere was this more true than in the fatherhood movement, where their dispirited states, lack of resources and even embarrassment over their personal circumstances discouraged men from direct protest.

In the lead up to the protest Dads On The Air interviewed organisers Ken Parrington and Joseph Zammit.[186]

The group of approximately 100 protesting fathers chanted: "What do we want? 50/50" and carried banners reading: "CSA will happen to you – it's just a matter of time", "Family Court steals children from fathers" and "I want to support my kids, not my ex's lifestyle".

Only fundamental changes to family law could provide the changes that were needed, the fathers claimed. One protester, Maurice Mok, described the child support system as 'a modern-day holocaust'.

"The bias against men and fathers is the greatest bias of our time," he said.

Reform the Child Support Agency spokesman Ken Parrington said family law marginalised fathers, meaning many were unable to see their children. "The kids are suffering," he said. "They're used as weapons in the process. That needs to change. There's no accountability under the current system and in the proposed system, there is still no accountability for how the money's spent."

In material promoting the march the organising group said their key messages were that the Federal Government had failed to deliver on family law reform, children were being denied the love and affection of both parents following divorce due to a system that failed to recognise the overwhelming evidence that children are better off when both parents share equally in their upbringing. The group said proposed changes to family law did little to address current inequities and the federal government continued to pay mere lip-service to the concerns of the Australian public on issues such as joint residency for children, child support reform and male suicide.

Their press release read in part: "Parents, grandparents, new partners, relatives and supporters are coming to Canberra from all over Australia to support the march. We are uniting as citizens to show the government that the people of Australia have had enough of the adversarial family law system and the extortionate tactics of the Child Support Agency. People are coming from as far away as Adelaide, the Cooper Basin, Cairns, Brisbane, Melbourne and Sydney to send the government a message. This is a grassroots movement with no affiliations. The march will demonstrate to the government the impact that outdated policy is having on Australian families and the community as a whole.

---

186 Australia Protests For reform of the Family Court and Child Support System, Media Release, Reform Family Law and Child Support in Australia, 27 April, 2005.

"So many inquiries: So few results. How many inquiries are needed before we see family friendly outcomes."

***

Also highlighting some of the issues, in late June 2005 *The Age* ran an atmospheric piece on the counselling service Mensline, then three years old and established by the government in response to an obvious need. The high death rate amongst separated men was not disputed. Spokespeople for Mensline had been appearing on Dads On The Air since its inception. The service had only been able to answer a fraction of the 200,000 calls it had received since it opened in 2001.

The story began: "Tuesday, 5.55pm: The phone beeps, and counsellor John Evans picks up the receiver.

"I'm very down in the dumps," says the voice on the other end. "My wife left me two years ago and I'm still very lonely." He works long hours and goes to the pub most nights.

"It's the loneliness, the lack of joy," he tells John. "I can't see tomorrow, that's the difficult thing."

On every six-hour shift, the counsellors usually got two callers who mentioned suicide. With separated men nine times more likely to kill themselves than separated women, many men needed someone to talk to. Most had failed to see the signs leading to the break-up.

"Men will be angry with themselves, they haven't seen it coming, angry if they can't have access to the children," spokesman Terry Melvin said. "The one big thing that keeps coming through is the loss of the dream. Men's identity often comes from the role in the family, the home they've built, the job they've had. During a separation they can lose all of that and that's when the suicide calls come in."[187]

***

In late June 2005 the Howard government was embarrassed by revelations in the Fairfax press that they had wasted millions of taxpayer dollars on inquiries only to ignore them. It had not replied on time to a single public inquiry of the 62 it had ordered in the House of Representatives since December 1998. It had given no reply at all to almost half of them.

Politicians on committees in both houses had taken months – sometimes years – to travel the country, study submissions and hear from hundreds of witnesses. All for nothing.

---

187 Nader, Carol, Utter desperation on the line, *The Age*, 24 June, 2005.

Three days after the Fairfax revelations, and more than 18 months after the family law inquiry itself, the Minister for Family and Community Services, Kay Patterson, tabled her government's response. By the government's own rules this should have been completed inside three months.

"The Government has listened and responded comprehensively – instigating the most significant changes to the family law system in 30 years," a press release stated.

Patterson said the House of Representatives inquiry's report "Every Picture Tells a Story" attracted more than 2000 submissions. "There were many tears shed by the general public, witnesses, their families and even by the committee members. It has been an emotional experience for everyone."

The Government released an exposure draft of the shared parental responsibility bill to the House Standing Committee on Legal and Constitutional Affairs, with its report due two months hence.

The draft was available on line and submissions were invited. "The Government believes these changes will help separating parents sit down across the table and agree what is best for their children, rather than fighting in the courtroom," Attorney General Philip Ruddock said. "The changes to the law reflect the fact that parenting continues, even after a relationship ends."[188]

Ruddock also released an explanatory memorandum with the draft which stated that the aim of the amendments was to "bring about a cultural shift in how family separation is managed: away from litigation and towards cooperative parenting".

The government said some of the proposed changes included introducing a new presumption of joint parental responsibility, aimed at encouraging parents to consult together on decisions such as where a child goes to school or major health issues. It also aimed to make one of the primary factors when deciding the best interests of children their right to know both their parents and be protected from harm; required parents to attend dispute resolution and develop parenting plans before taking a parenting matter to court and recommended parents, advisers, mediators and the courts consider substantially equal sharing parenting time in appropriate cases to better recognise the interests of children in spending time with grandparents and other relatives.

It was proposed to amend the legislation to include a new object: "To ensure that children have the benefit of both their parents having a meaningful involvement in their lives, to the maximum extent consistent with the best interests

---

188 Grattan, Michelle, Ruddock promises tougher family law, *The Sydney Morning Herald*, June 22, 2005.

of the child" along with "a new principle to recognise that children need to be protected from physical or psychological harm, for example by witnessing family violence."

Clients applying to court for parenting orders were to first attempt to resolve their dispute using family dispute resolution services, such as mediation. The court would not be able to hear the application unless the applicant filed a certificate signed by a family dispute resolution practitioner.

There was no presumption that a child should spend equal time with each parent. However the court would be required to consider making an order that the child spend "substantial time" with each parent.

***

Other amendments included greater recognition of grandparents and other relatives, and an emphasis on consideration of Aboriginal and Torres Strait Islander culture and practices.

The draft exposure bill also suggested that a less adversarial, more inquisitorial process be implemented for children proceedings. The new regime would broadly reflect the Family Court's pilot Children's Cases Program. This included the court more actively managing the proceedings.

This style of proceeding left the running of the case and the determination of issues in the judges hands. They could be time consuming and more expensive than normal trials. DOTA had criticised them for handing far too much power to Family Court judges. But the court's own evaluations indicated they led to greater satisfaction amongst parents, less hostility between the parties and less anxious children.

As well, "proceedings were to be conducted without undue delay and with as little formality and legal technicality as possible."

Fat chance.

Once again the terminology was being altered. This time the terms "residence" and "contact" were to be removed and orders refer to who the child lives with and spends time or communicates with.

The release of the draft legislation for discussion attracted a vociferous response from the SPCA under the heading "Howard's Family Law Amendments a Cruel Failure".

Their press release read in part: "The Shared Parenting Council of Australia has rejected outright the proposed Family Law Amendments released by the Attorney General as failing fathers, failing children and failing the broader community."

The Council said the Howard government had ignored massive community support from men and women alike to stop the Family Court's present disastrous bias against fathers.

"For years now, every time John Howard has suggested he and his government support shared parenting and a child's fundamental right to an equal relationship with both parents he has received enormous support from the public and the media," Secretary of the Council Wayne Butler said.

"Yet when we finally see the legislation there is nothing in it to guarantee shared parenting outcomes as the norm for separating couples. The one million children of separated families in this country, the hundreds of thousands kids who rarely if ever see their dads, the millions of grandparents, second families and the parents themselves all deserve better."

***

Despite the Howard government's rhetoric supporting shared parenting, there was nothing in the legislation to guarantee that fathers, children, second families, grandparents and new partners would be treated any better, or that children would grow up maintaining a good relationship with both parents.

The Shared Parenting Council of Australia said the draft legislation had failed to address the fundamental problems in family law, a system which created chaos and bitterness while failing in its task of protecting children.

"The claim by the Attorney General that this is 'the most significant reform to Family Law ever' – simply does not stack up with the draft bill," Butler said.

"The Family Law Amendments fail to protect every child's fundamental right to an equal opportunity with both their parents - instead it reinforces the outdated and repressive regime that the mother's rights are superior in the Family Court and that father's are unable to provide primary care.

"Not only has there been a failure to recognise and amend the inequality of the current system, but the amendments themselves will make the family law act even more legalistic and incomprehensible. Even the most urgent cases will experience significant delays and costs due to the increased requirement to get legal advice."

Wayne Butler said the reforms as they stood would guarantee a windfall to the legal industry and continued distress to parents and children alike. Further Court delays were inevitable and increased conflict between separating parents would also be assured by these reforms.

"Australian parents and children will mourn this lost opportunity for meaningful change to a system which has been found by several government inquiries to be totally dysfunctional.

"We are at a complete loss as to why the Government will not respond. The public will continue to demand an adequate response from the government to the most pressing social justice issue facing Australia today.

"These proposed amendments are nothing more than smoke and mirrors and a cruel hoax to separated parents who took the Prime Minister at his word that he would fix this system once and for all."

***

The Fatherhood Foundation was also quick to criticise, calling the proposed family law amendments a betrayal of the children of Australia. Warwick Marsh, convener of a recent Fatherhood Forum at Parliament House, Canberra said the Howard government could take credit for the economic growth Australia was enjoying, but must also take credit for the growth in fatherlessness that was destroying the future of Australia's children.

"Shared parenting after divorce is the first stage of stemming the tide of fatherlessness in our nation," he said.

The Fatherhood Foundation had just released a document "Fathers in Families" at the Fatherhood Forum.[189] Marsh said It showed how fatherlessness was associated with many grave social problems including increased crime, poverty, drug abuse, physical and sexual child abuse, increased levels of teenage suicide and bad educational outcomes.

Marsh said fatherlessness costs Australia over 13 billion dollars per year, according to estimates by Dr Bruce Robinson from the University of Western Australia. An Office for the Status of Fathers, as recommended in the Fathers in Families document, would be the most cost effective investment the government could make. "Such an office could help reel in the out-of-control government bureaucracy that doesn't seem to understand the important contribution that fathers make to families," he said.

"Such an office could provide the necessary balance to ensure family law reform legislation is carried out correctly.

"If the government can show leadership in other areas of much-needed reform, why can't the present government reform the Family Law Court? The Senate majority, now held by the government, leaves no room for excuse regarding family law reform. The enshrining in Australian family law of Shared Parenting will show the families of Australia that the government actually cared.

"Common sense family law reform will encourage more men to marry. Stable marriages will encourage more men and women to have children. Only then can we begin to rebuild marriage as the bedrock institution of our nation. Strong

---

189 Fathers in Families, Available on the Dads4Kids website.

marriages build strong families. Strong families build a strong nation. The government must seize the opportunity for family law reform and lead the way."

***

Dads On The Air also put in a submission on the proposed Family Law Amendment Bill.

It read in part: "The Dads On The Air team is greatly disappointed in the proposed Family Law Amendment Bill, which we believe fails children, fathers, second families and the broader Australian community in its current form.

"While making an initial and vague pretence, the failure of this Bill to treat both parents as equally important in their children's lives means that the disaster of family law in Australia will continue unabated.

"The notion of 'shared responsibility' is so vague as to be not just meaningless but dangerous.

"We have had the Attorney General Phillip Ruddock on our program and not even he was able to explain what it means.

"What it means in reality is that fathers will continue to be ostracised from their children's lives and lawyers will continue to have a field day at the expense of separated families."

Our position could be summarised as follows: "The Government proposal to make equal shared parental responsibility the starting point under the Family Law Act just simply does not go far enough in ensuring joint custody or shared parenting arrangements are the norm post-separation.

"The government should immediately legislate for shared care and responsibility to ensure that joint custody outcomes are the norm post separation and that conflict between separating couples is eliminated as much as possible. This would truly be in the best interests of the children.

"As a result of this legislative failure an ever growing body of disaffected fathers, second families and others will continue to criticise and protest against the government.

"The legislation as it is now framed will do nothing to ensure shared parenting outcomes. As we all know, the Family Court of Australia has been historically opposed to shared parenting despite the community support for this common sense outcome. This legislation guarantees that the court will continue to do exactly as it pleases.

"Even on the vague notion of joint responsibility the Court finds itself under no real obligation: 'The presumption may be rebutted by evidence that satisfies the court that it would not be in the best interests of the child for the child's parents to have parental responsibility for the child jointly.

"As anyone who has been through the Court knows, what the court considers to be 'evidence' and what a lay person considers to be evidence are entirely different matters.

"The Family Court, in secret, will continue to destroy families and treat fathers as second class parents with complete impunity. This institution is not complying with its legislative obligations to act in the best interests of children. It is continuing to this day to perpetuate its sole custody model and continuing to treat fathers like dirt. We believe the culture of this institution is beyond repair and as such it should be abolished."

***

DOTA's submission claimed the laudable aim that "children have a right to spend time on a regular basis with, and communicate on a regular basis with both their parents and other people significant to their care, welfare and development" was undermined by other sections of the proposed legislation.

The proposal for instance that "parents should agree about the future parenting of their children" will be used to ensure that no shared parenting outcomes are achieved.

"Intact couples do not agree on many issues and it is ridiculous to impose this requirement on separating couples. Nor is the fact that separated couples do not agree on many issues a reason to deny a child the right to live with and be cared for by both parents. This requirement will be used as an excuse by lawyers and judges for fathers not to be given joint custody."

DOTA said the legislation's perhaps well intentioned pandering to the ideologically based domestic violence industry would also prove to be a disaster.

"While we can of course accept that children need to be protected from harm, the current hysteria over domestic violence and the epidemic of false allegations during litigation will ensure that rather than being protected they are more likely to be harmed.

"If there are accusations of violence then police and hospital records should be the only material relied on. Otherwise the centres will only be promoting yet more hysteria around the issue and perpetuating the use of false allegations in custody disputes. If there are genuine cases, then both parties should be sent to counselling and the matter reviewed after such counselling has occurred.

"A simple allegation should not be sufficient to deny a child contact with the other parent.

"In genuine cases the provision of counselling and other assistance in modifying behaviour should be resorted to in the first instance, rather than the blunt instrument of criminalising an individual on the basis of scant evidence or nothing but a potentially malicious or tactical allegation or expression of fear.

"Violence and assault, of which both genders can be guilty, are in genuine cases a matter for the police and for therapists.

"By writing this into the Family Law Act the government will ensure that the current rash of false and exaggerated allegations of domestic violence which have become a standard part of family law will further increase."

***

Dads On The Air also expressed concern over the rushed nature of the public consultation and the narrow range of views being sought. In Sydney the committee heard from the Law Society of NSW and Legal Aid, but was somehow incapable of finding a single father's group in a city of more than four million people.

The groups interviewed were all supporters of the status quo, from which they benefited.

Our editorial position, while unsubtle, reiterated: "A number of father's organisations, including ourselves, were not invited to give evidence; although we have all worked hard, and unlike the groups from which you are so willing to hear, without pay, to make submissions throughout the law reform process.

"This legislation does not in any way guarantee that fathers will be treated equally before the law and does nothing to properly encourage, far less guarantee, shared parenting outcomes after divorce.

"This legislation does nothing to guarantee that the conduct of the Family Court is exposed to public view. It does nothing to stop the corrupt use of shonky psychs that has characterised family law in this country for almost three decades. It does nothing to ensure that kids have a right to see and be cared for by their fathers. It will perpetuate the harassment and abuse of fathers by both the Family Court and the Child Support Agency.

"The reforms will fail unless joint custody is the mandatory starting point. Allowing the Family Court as the final arbiter of these disputes is wrong. Nor does requiring the court to act in the best interests of children mean anything at all. There wouldn't be a separated father in the country who believes the Family Court acts in the best interests of children.

"It is a fudging of the damage done by the family law industry to claim that 'for a range of reasons some parents lose contact with their child, either permanently or while issues are fought out in the courts.' The reason why most parents, usually fathers, lose contact with their beloved children is because the Family Court forbids them contact or refuses to enforce its own contact orders."

***

Throughout July and August of 2005 the Attorney General Philip Ruddock travelled the country promoting the family law changes. Under the headline "Ruddock Tours Australia Insulting Dads" DOTA claimed he was "peddling the bureaucratic lie that his government is implementing the most sweeping reforms to family law in 30 years. The government is doing nothing of the kind.

"By telling fathers that they are second class parents who do not deserve to be granted joint custody of their children after separation Ruddock has delivered an insult not just to fathers but hundreds of thousands of women as well, to grandparents, second partners, second wives, siblings and everyone who cares about dads, their children and the disaster that is being visited upon them by the extremist anti-male anti-father bias of the current system.

"In his tour of Sydney, Melbourne, Brisbane, Perth, Darwin and Adelaide, Ruddock has been confronted with furious fathers wherever he goes. What was meant to be a triumphal tour to champion reforms to family law turned rapidly into a fiasco. The government chose to take heed of the so-called experts and bureaucrats and ignored the voices of parents. They are now paying the price. What was meant to be an electoral plus has simply provoked more resentment. Media coverage has been lukewarm at best.

"The relationship centres the government is establishing as a so-called first port of call after separation will operate under the draconian secrecy provisions of the Family Law Act and will perpetuate the same anti-father bias and the same discrimination as the Family Court itself. No father can expect to be treated fairly in these Relationship Centres.

"Those tendering for the running of these centres, including Relationships Australia, have all put in submissions opposing shared parenting; and have therefore declared their bias up front. No father who wants to share the care of their children will be given a civil ear or encouraged to do so.

"In the process of touring the country, Ruddock has made nonsense claims that the Family Court is not biased against men. It is outrageous to make these claims in front of an audience of fathers and their families who know it to be a nonsense; and whose own children have been so savagely impacted by the serial bastardry of the Family Court."[190]

---

190 Ruddock tours Australia insulting Dads, Dads On The Air, 11 August, 2005.

Numerous individuals and groups were critical of the Family Law Amendment Bill. The flyer written by Sue Price from the Men's Right's Agency and handed out to audiences at the Ruddock meetings was headlined: "Proposed Family Law Changes will make little difference".

"Desperate parents have waited more than 18 months for the Government to respond to a report into family law and child support reform. The response released at the end of June is more than disappointing – it is deceptive and void of any understanding of what needs to be changed to achieve fairness and equity for parents and children in separating families. Now the draft Bill is being rushed through with interested parties given less than two weeks to respond and the Legal and Constitutional Affairs Committee less than six weeks to review the draft.

"The Committee has also been instructed not to re-open discussion on policy issues such as the rejection of the proposal of 50/50 custody in favour of the approach of sharing of parental responsibility. In other words the government has made up its mind and there WILL BE NO DEBATE OR DISCUSSION ALLOWED!

- Shared parental responsibility will not deliver shared and equal parenting.
- Shared parental responsibility does not imply more time with children.
- Shared parental responsibility is already included in the Family law Act and usually means Mum gets the kids and Dad pays the bills, with Dad being allowed just enough time with their children to ensure his interest in paying does not wane.
- 65 Family Relationship Centres, operating in the shadow of the law, will continue with the current bias against fathers unless the Family Law Act is changed to recognise that both parents have an equal right to share in their children's lives.
- A presumption against even shared parental responsibility if there are allegations of domestic violence and abuse presupposes the guilt of an accused party, thereby distorting the very basic tenet where a person is innocent until proven guilty.
- Ordering parents to go to a Family Relationship Centre will encourage more false allegations being used to avoid attendance.

"An 'Inquiry into Joint Custody 50/50', as announced by the Prime Minister in 2003 was bound to be rejected because of the seeming rigidity of the terminology. The mention of 50/50 allowed the opponents of shared and equal parenting to claim the proposal was too rigid and unworkable, because the assumption became that shared parenting was all about equally sharing the time with the children.

"This was never the case, but people such as the retired Chief Justice of the Family Court, Alastair Nicholson and others were able to make emotive statements ridiculing the proposal by using examples where the children spending equal time with each parent was clearly impractical and impossible logistically.

"Shared and equal parenting is about far more than just time – it is about being regarded as equally important and essential in the children's lives. It is about the joys and duties, responsibilities and rights to be regarded as equally as much a parent as the other. To be consulted, informed and have input into the children's lives and to spend time with the children as much as can be arranged up to 50 percent, but just because a parent is unable to spend 50 percent of the time with their children does not mean they should be regarded as any less of a parent, as happens now."

***

The Non-Custodial Parents Party's John Flanagan also produced a flyer to be handed out at the meetings: "The Attorney General has stated at the end of the terms of reference for the Committee of Inquiry into the new amendments that 'The Committee should not re-open discussions on policy issues such as the rejection of the proposal of 50:50 custody in favour of the approach of sharing of parental responsibility'.

"This summarises what is essentially wrong with the current proposed amendments. The amendments should not be simply about 'sharing parental responsibility'. We have always had this term in the Family Law Act and it has not worked. In the terms of reference, the Attorney General uses the term '50:50 custody'. The term that is more commonly and correctly used is 'a rebuttable presumption of 50:50 shared parenting'. It can be simply defined as: 'Both parents being consulted, informed and having input into their children's lives and to spend time with the children as much as can be arranged up to 50 per cent'.

"This concept does not exist in the Attorney General's amendments. Therefore we can only presume that the status quo will remain. That is, the custodial parent will continue to be responsible for the day-to-day care of the child. The non-custodial parent will continue to be responsible for the child support."

***

The normally quietly mannered and apolitical Tony Miller at Dads In Distress expressed his disgust at the lack of representation of fathers during the government's brief two week public consultation on the draft bill. He claimed the

Standing Committee on Legal and Constitutional Affairs was deliberately excluding fathers from the debate.

He was particularly incensed that his organisation had only been informed of a public meeting in Sydney, several hundred kilometres south of their headquarters in Coffs Harbour, the day before it was held. He said they had been swamped with emails protesting the situation.

"Where is the representation from men's groups you ask? Easy, they obviously didn't want you there. Dads in Distress was not invited to give evidence.

"NOTHING short of EQUAL time should be accepted. Every father's group in the country simply wants that. I would implore as many of you as possible to attend these hearings and have your say. I am disgusted that something as important as this, that concerns the future lives of our children, is dealt with so pitifully inadequately."

Miller quoted the chairman of the Legal and Constitutional Affairs Committee Peter Slipper announcing there would be two hearings in Melbourne and Sydney expressing a desire to hear "as many different viewpoints as possible within the short timeframe".

"Thanks Mr Slipper, two full days to hear us," Miller pronounced. "Some of us have been waiting patiently for over two years to see our children. The biggest reform to Family Law in 30 years and we get two full days in Melbourne and Sydney and you say the committee wants to hear as many different viewpoints as possible.

"Who's kidding who?

"You know I honestly believed this Government was fair dinkum in its reform process. I honestly believed the Bill put forward with some minor adjustments was excellent legislation. I honestly thought you were delivering dads back to their kids. But when you don't even want to hear from the very people this affects, your constituents, well you have lost me.

"The line has been drawn guys, You want war, you have got it."

**

Still more miserable stories kept appearing on the Dads In Distress website. Here's one: "Please help me! I live in Brisbane and up until 15 months ago, had regular fortnightly contact with my 5 year old daughter who then, lived on the Gold Coast. In March 2004, my ex-wife just up-and-left the Gold Coast and moved to Ballarat Victoria, taking my Daughter with her. There were no Contact Orders at this time.

"I have not seen my daughter since. There are the occasional phone calls but they are getting less and less. I am fast becoming just another voice on the phone. I cannot afford to go down there to visit, I pretty much can't do anything. Child support is killing me financially. I can't seem to get any answers from anyone about what I can do.

"I need to see my daughter, and she needs to see me and have her father as part of her life. We were very close before this happened. Please help me…"

And another: "I went to court today because the ex has breached the court orders 67 times we were in front of a Judicial Registrar. He would not hear the case today because we are part the way through a final hearing which the ex keeps putting off.

"Even though my solicitor pointed out to him it is a totally different case and has nothing to do with the final hearing he would not hear it. He has put it in for the same day as the final hearing in front of the same judge and told me that if I don't drop it, it will hold up my final hearing and the judge is retiring.

"Today was a waste of time as I had to pay for my solicitor and the ex got Legal Aid and she is the one breaking the law, how is that justice? I have spent nearly $40.000 in court and only have interim orders which are not worth the paper they are written on."

***

Amongst separated fathers, mobilised and alarmed at the turn of events, there was a considerable amount of rallying of the troops, urging of those who could to attend the meetings and lobbying of politicians as the committee examined the legislation. One father submitted: "A lot of men have these issues yet it seems that they are never addressed. I think people need to realise that ex wives/partners can be completely vindictive and hateful and stop fathers from seeing their children simply because they don't want them to."

To the Member for Hume Alby Schultz he wrote: "I ask that you please raise your concerns with your fellow members of parliament that men were simply not given the chance to be present. I miss my children and I want to see them and unfortunately until changes are made in Family Law, that is never going to happen. The changes can not be made if fathers are not given the right to speak."

Fuelling the debate, in Melbourne's high circulation *Herald Sun*, author of *Kangaroo Court* John Hirst wrote a moving piece of a man falsely accused of sexually abusing his four-year-old daughter, a story that could have been told many hundreds of times over. Hirst was a respected academic historian, co-editor of the *Oxford Companion to Australian History* and author of a number of books including *The Sentimental Nation: The making of the Australian Commonwealth*. He wielded a credibility most could only dream of.

The story began: "I am watching a man being tortured. The torture is mental and is being conducted officially in Melbourne." Hirst detailed the doctors and psychologists who had found no evidence to back up the mothers repeated claims, which were now progressing to a full trial in the Family Court.

"We have assumed, wrongly, that only in totalitarian regimes are courts of law perverted into instruments for harassing people on false charges. Every inquiry shows this man to be innocent, but the accusation against him does not go away. But surely the Family Court will clear him when all this evidence or lack of it comes to trial? Not necessarily.

"He could well be subjected for the future to supervised access only in order to satisfy the wife. He would then carry permanently the official stigma of being an abuser of his own child.

"The Family Court claims that it is always acting to secure the best interests of the child. In fact, by permitting these accusations to run unchecked the court is allowing the mother to poison a four-year-old girl against her father while subjecting him to continuous torment.

"The accusation never leaves his mind. So far he estimates that he has spent $40,000 on lawyers. If the father is destroyed mentally and materially, how is that in the best interests of the child?"

***

The individual responses to the Child Support Task Force continued to flood on to the Dads In Distress website. These were in turn widely distributed. With the latest rash of sad dad stories, often perplexing, moving and confounding all at once, the issue of suicide was once again a hot topic. While there had by now been years of talk about reform of family law and child support, nothing had actually eventuated. It was by no means clear anything ever would.

People had lost hope.

Barry Williams, President of the Lone Fathers Association, wrote on the Dads In Distress site: "Some forces within government wipe these issues aside as nonsense and untrue. They are covering up and hiding the fact that men are committing suicide in this country at five men a day. Many of these men take their lives because they are frustrated by the systems that treat them like criminals because their marriage or relationship breaks down, then they lose most of their property and assets, and are made to pay child support that is really not child support, but spousal maintenance.

"Then to rub the wounds even further they are denied contact to their loved children. The system does nothing to help them unless they have thousands of dollars to pursue it, then the guilty party escapes Scott free. The law has no teeth, especially where men are concerned.

"The government throws a few measly dollars to men's groups, compared to countless millions to women's groups. The money that is given for men's help go to the counselling services, yet these counselling services in most cases can't help the men, as its mostly not counselling that they need, rather they need help with their family law and child support problems at grass route level. They get this advice and help from Lone Fathers and Dads In Distress."

Barry Williams recounted an incident from a few days earlier, when he received a phone call from a granddad asking would I assist him. "He was crying the whole time he was talking to me about his grandson who was being so harassed by the CSA, that he was concerned his grandson was going to be yet another victim of suicide. Fortunately I was able to convince this young man that we were there to help him, and use all our resources to pursue his problems. How many more lives do we have to lose before the critics wake up and take note?"

***

At the end of the month Attorney General Philip Ruddock announced the location of the first 15 of the 65 Family Relationship Centres that were one of the centrepieces of the new family law system. Ruddock claimed the family relationship centres, to open in the middle of the following year, would become a source of support and assistance for families.

"The centres will become an integral part of their communities by becoming the first port of call when people need help to make their relationships stronger or when relationships end," he said. "We have located the first centres in areas with high numbers of families with young children and high numbers of divorced or separated families and blended families."

The Family Relationship Centres would be the front door for people seeking to strengthen family relationships, prevent separation and enable parents to resolve conflict after separation.

"We are not just changing the system, we are changing the culture of family breakdowns," Mr Ruddock said. "Separating parents will be encouraged to sit down and work out what is best for the children rather than fighting in the courtroom."[191]

DOTA once again expressed concern that the Centres would be staffed by groups such as Relationships Australia, declared opponents of shared parenting

---

191 Grattan, Michelle, Ruddock promises tougher family law", *The Sydney Morning Herald*, 22 June 22, 2005.

through their submissions to the inquiry. As such they would not encourage shared and cooperative parenting after separation and there are disturbing parallels with the counselling carried out by the various mediation centres of the Family Court.

A story in *The Age* in early August of 2005 by journalist John Elder was headlined "It's no kids' party as angry dads let rip". It brought smiles of recognition to many in the fatherhood movement because they had themselves witnessed similar scenes as Ruddock toured the country promoting the family law changes.[192]

The scene was the Frankston Arts Centre and the Attorney General Philip Ruddock was talking about the $400 million being spent on changing the Family Law system.

Elder reported that the first couple of questions were almost whispered with deference. Then a fellow named Simon Hunt stood up. He wondered "where are the concrete changes" that will allow fathers – who had been stripped of their rights by the Family Court – to see their children?

Simon went on for a very long time about the destructive influence of psychiatrists, the high rates of suicide and the power of unfounded allegations by vengeful former wives.

Simon was something of a loose cannon within the fatherhood movement. Colourful, unpredictable. Likeable to some, certainly not to all. He was unable to see his daughter through orders of court. He never gave up the fight and was never afraid to let everyone know what he thought about the people who had done this to him and his daughter. He had been a guest on DOTA. Some minutes into this tirade, one participant began pleading, "Simon, come on mate, let the Attorney General have a go."

Eventually Simon sat down. In reply, Ruddock stood to say, "I have no truck with unfounded allegations."

Elder recorded how his companion, Mary Lewis, who worked for a service connecting estranged fathers with their children, whispered in his ear: "Look at how Ruddock's taking the fight up to him ... the way he's standing."

"It was true: with his suit jacket undone, a hand on the hip, the Attorney General looked like John Wayne coolly staring down a bunch of gunslingers."

***

Ruddock had put on exactly the same performance when confronted by fathers at a similar function in Sydney.

A heavy sigh filled the room when a ponytailed man stood to say he had done

---

192 Elder, John, It's no kids' party as angry dads let rip, *The Age*, 20 August, 2005.

all the right things when his marriage broke down, he had agreed to accept the orders of the court – "and I never saw my children again".

A man up the back then made angry claims that a Family Law counsellor had abused his children. When he named the counsellor, more than a dozen women got to their feet and shuffled out of the hall. "Where are all the women going?" Elder asked.

His companion whispered in his ear, "They're leaving because to stay would be to collude with violence."

At the same time sandwiches, cordial and party pies were being set on tables down the back of the hall – "just as if at a children's party."

***

The following day came the sad news that Lionel Richards founder, coordinator. convener of the OzyDads Network, had passed away from a heart attack.

If you were an insomniac separated dad cruising the chatlines in the early hours of the morning for a bit of company, gossip, intrigue or advice, you would come across Lionel. He seemed always to be there, full of cheer, outrage, friendship. He had done much for other separated dads; and for the cause of family law and child support reform.

Lindsay Jackel, who ran the internet chat and news lines Manumit and Nuance and had been a key supporter of DOTA, said Lionel Richards was known across Australia and indeed thanks to the internet across the world for his tireless efforts on the part of separated fathers and separated families. He was the bloke who would ring you up when no one else cared, a notoriously manic night owl with a heart the size of the rock. Women devastated by the notorious bastardry of the Family Court and the Child Support Agency were amongst his staunchest fans.

Ian Windsor, a father from Canberra, summed up many people's feelings: "I am not ashamed to admit that I shed a tear for Lionel Richards yesterday when I read of his untimely death. Lionel was a humble but great man with a passion for changing Family Law to allow good fathers to continue their responsibility of raising their children after separation on an equal basis with the children's mothers.

"Lionel loved his children and was passionate about them and their welfare, and often spoke of them. He worked tirelessly for them; and for many separated parents and their children, both locally in the Fremantle, Armadale and Perth areas and thanks to the internet around Australia and the world. He loved people and enjoyed helping them.

"Ozydads Network was a home away from home. A small piece of Cyber World is dedicated to addressing the Anti-Father bias in the Family Law arena and support network filling the gaps between sparse to non-existent Father's Crisis facilities available.

"Lionel believed the Status of Fathers had sadly sunk to an all time low, largely due to a vicious attack by radical Gender Feminists who have hijacked the Women's movement to further their misandrist agenda.

"Lionel ran a number of chat lines which provided comfort to many people during the long night hours. They included not just Ozydads but others dedicated to various groups, including victims of Parental Alienation with the StopPAS e-group. He believed PAS is Emotional Child Abuse. There was also the FamilyRules Exchange.

"The OzyDads network supported the Child's Right to both Parents, endorsing 50/50 Shared Parenting as the default position in Family Law. Lionel Richards was also a founding member of the Shared Parenting Council of Australia.

"One among many crucial points he raised was the commonality of good fathers being wrongly accused of child abuse and domestic violence post separation when their behaviour during the marriage had never been in question. Sadly, very few legislators, judges, lawyers and other experts shared Lionel's passion for fatherhood. None recognised his expertise in child custody matters and the importance of separated fathers being fully involved in their children's lives."

Tony Miller said Lionel had shared his personal struggles at a DIDS meeting and those of the men he had been fortunate enough to meet and help along the way. "Dads in Distress everywhere send their sympathy to family and friends and we want you to know that Lionel has made a difference to our lives and that of our children's lives."

One woman wrote: "I want to thank you Lionel Richards for making my husband and I stronger, to believe in ourselves, that we have rights, that our children have rights and that together all of us in the groups can make a difference if we believe in what we are fighting for and believe in each other. I promise this, to keep up the fight and to help empower others going through the same things. I promise to help as many people as humanly possible to empower themselves and stand up for their children and their rights."[193]

***

Mid-August found Alby Schultz maintaining the rage against the Child Support Agency, confirming what most separated fathers already knew. "Over the last 12 months I have compiled 4,500 submissions from all round Australia on the body that I refer to as the national shame of Australia – that is, the Child Support Agency.

---

193 Stapleton, John, Chaos at the Crossroads, 5 December, 2010.

"Out of those 4,500 submissions I have, with the able assistance of a researcher, sifted through and compiled those submissions which carry detailed evidence of the way in which the Child Support Agency operates. Let me inform the House of a case relating to one of those submissions, which is the tip of the iceberg with regard to the problems associated with this government agency."

Schultz related the story of a 14-year-old runaway who ended up living with his aunt; who promptly applied for child support from the boy's biological parents.

"The rights of the parents are violated by the bizarre actions of the Child Support Agency approving the aunt's application for child support from the parents of this child. The CSA then advises the parents in writing that they have calculated the amount of child support the parents must pay the aunt.

"There are a number of questions that need to be asked about this particular Child Support Agency case. I can assure the minister of the Crown on my side of politics responsible for this agency in this parliament that they are going to be hearing a lot more about the illegal activity of the Child Support Agency."[194]

While father's groups were overlooked or had little time to present yet further submissions on the draft shared responsibility bill, the Family Court's submission claimed the Howard Government's family law reforms might encourage women to raise allegations of violence to stop former husbands gaining access to their children.

The court said the new legislation would place "great pressure" on mothers to "find something" to raise against their husbands, to stop them gaining greater access to the children.

"For example, in an ordinary case, of the kind that is often litigated, a father might seek more involvement with the child," it read. "If the father has a record of occasional fights in bars, the mother would be very likely to bring this up, even if it had only moderate relevance to the child's safety."

It said the new laws might also worsen relations between already warring spouses and lead to longer, more costly litigation. The submission said "an unintended consequence of the new law might be that the formula will encourage allegations of violence".

While fractionally less demented in tone under the new Chief Justice Diana Bryant than under the previous incumbent, the Family Court was still playing an active role in an ideological war. The court said 30 percent of cases included allegations of abuse or violence, and few of those people would "want to sit down with the other party and talk about violence/abuse issues".

---

194 Alby Schultz, Hansard, Child Support Agency, 16 August, 2005.

Chief Justice Diana Bryant said while many people resolved their disputes without going to court there remained a question over whether the Family Relationship Centres would divert others.

"There would be an unquantifiable number of applicants who do not want to go down the path of attending a Family Relationship Centre for any number of reasons and who will try to find something to give them an exemption," she said. "The other party's drug abuse, alcohol abuse or mental illness are some examples that spring to mind."

***

In mid August 2005 the Standing Committee on Legal and Constitutional Affairs handed up its report after being given just two months to consider the Government's draft legislation.

Divorced fathers would get more say in their children's lives and mothers would be pressured to back up claims of violence under the inquiry's recommendations. The committee largely endorsed the Government's proposals. Controversially, it recommended the definition of family violence in the legislation be changed to include the word "reasonable" in regards to fears about domestic violence, abuse or harm, following repeated allegations from fathers' groups that mothers often fabricated violence claims in order to minimise fathers contact with their children.

Penalties would apply for those making false accusations of domestic violence or sexual abuse.

That there could be such controversy over the word "reasonable" pretty well exemplified the fevered insanities of the debate. The disagreements between men's and women's groups over the proposed family law amendments ran purely along gender lines. Women's groups warned that the insertion of the word "reasonable" would put women and children in danger, while father's groups approved the move, saying it would stop men being deprived of access to their children through false allegations of violence.

The National Council of Single Mothers put out a press release stating the annual domestic violence death toll in Australia was 76 adults and 23 children in the 2002-03 financial year, but proposed family law amendments sought to make it harder for mothers and children to achieve safety from violent ex-partners and fathers.

Convener of the Council Elspeth McInnes urged Mr Ruddock not to accept the recommendations. She claimed existing laws already failed to stop almost 100 domestic murders a year. "Anything which diminishes the current protections is enabling a continuing growth of the death rate," she said.

McInnes said the annual domestic violence homicide toll of nearly 100 adults and children should be recognised. "It's time the war on terror included the terror of domestic violence," she said.

McInnes said the Shared Parental Responsibility Bill prioritised fathers rights groups propaganda that mothers falsely allege violence and abuse, despite national and international research confirming that violence was prevalent, severe and under- reported in family breakdown disputes. She said family law should have a safety-first approach when family violence was raised as an issue instead of creating new tests and fines for victims of violence.

"It's no secret that the Family Court sends children to see their violent fathers or that women get beaten by their partners. That's backed by reams of research. There is also no benefit to a woman to say she's been abused because if she can't prove it and the court thinks she's made up a false allegation, the court will punish her by granting custody to the father."

She claimed the proposed family law changes would give men who used violence and aggression greater control over mothers and force mothers to risk financial penalties and loss of care of their children to raise the issue of safety.

***

The latest official figures available for Australia from the National Homicide Monitoring Program showed that for the year 2006-2007 there were 260 homicide incidents. Of the victims, 185 were male and 81 were female. Of the offenders, 242 were male and 54 were female. Rates of intimate-partner homicide remained constant in 2006–07, with 22 percent of homicides occurring in this context. Of intimate-partner homicide, 23 males and 42 females were victims.

Forty three percent of homicides between intimates in 2006–07 had a domestic violence history with the police in some form prior to the homicide incident. Twenty seven children under the age of 15 years were killed in 2006–07, the overwhelming majority by a parent (84%). Of these 24 percent of perpetrators were the biological father. The majority of perpetrators were mothers. A further 24 percent of perpetrators were live in boyfriends or new partners.

Of the 14 offenders who committed suicide following the 2006–07 homicide incidents, four involved child victims. In all four cases, the offender was the custodial parent of the victim, two mothers and two fathers.

Then Shadow Attorney General and staunch feminist Nicola Roxon concurred with McInnes. In her dissenting report on the Committee's findings she wrote: "I believe there is substantial risk that the Bill prioritises meaningful relationships with parents over safety of children."

She said the Committee relied only on anecdotal evidence presented in submissions to the inquiry, not expert advice. "I do not accept that false allegations are made in a large number of cases," she said.

Roxon said the changes were a "one-way street" giving more rights to non-resident parents and more responsibilities to resident parents. Changes to the act could discourage people from reporting incidents of domestic violence because they were frightened of being penalised if the claims were not proved.

It was "borderline irresponsible" to recommend changes without knowing what impact it would have on violence, Roxon claimed.

On her one rather brief appearance 16 minute appearance on Dads On The Air Roxon emphasised the issue of relationship violence. She appeared decidedly uncomfortable throughout the interview, although we always tried to make our guests feel comfortable, whether we personally agreed with them or not.

***

Lone Fathers Association president Barry Williams applauded the committee for the gutsy change, saying existing violence laws were ridiculous and were used as a tool.

Committee chairman Peter Slipper said the move would crack down on false allegations of abuse, removing an assumption of guilt until innocence is proved.

Nationals MP Kay Hull said she had significant concerns about over-reporting of domestic violence and the inability of some parents to disprove allegations to regain access to their children. She said children had a right to be protected from untrue claims of abuse that affected who had custody of them as well as from abuse.

Men's groups argued that violence is often alleged but rarely proven in the Family Court and that women were using the allegations to prevent men from seeing their children. The child support formula also added an incentive to make false claims.

Two days later and Tony Miller at Dads In Distress was once again despairing of any progress. "Monday we have one of our guys in Newcastle court. Sixty Seven breaches of contact are on the table. Sixty Seven breaches of court orders. We are watching to see if what the Attorney General has been promising is filtering down to the courts. The fairness we have all been talking about. Because I have to tell you, we haven't seen it yet. It's been promised, any judge in the system today who doesn't see the writing on the wall is blind and shouldn't be there.

"We are looking for that fairness. We want to see our kids. We want to see that the Family Court is going to recognise the children's right to a relationship with their father and vice versa. Enough is enough. How pathetic that we have a dad in court where mum has breached the orders 67 times and nothing is done.

"Wake up. This has got to stop. Those orders need to be enforced if you want us to believe you are genuinely trying to reform the Family Court System."

***

Women's groups said children would lose the right to "one home, one carer, one neighbourhood" and instead would be shuffled between residences according to a parenting timetable.

Men's groups said the legislation would encourage more women to make false allegations of violence to avoid the presumption of shared parenting.

"We had high hopes for the law," Sue Price said. "But now I think the whole thing has been a waste of time. We wanted a guarantee that men would have frequent contact with their children after divorce. We didn't get that."

Attorney General Philip Ruddock said the new Relationship Centres would be "friendly, family places, like the local library, or medical centre".

Women's groups regarded this as fantasy. They said it's simply impossible for many women to attend face-to-face meetings with their former partners and that to force them to do so, without the protection provided by security guards at court, was a recipe for disaster.

Ruddock said the presumption of shared parenting would not apply in cases where violence had been alleged. Also, couples who claimed violence in the relationship would not have to attend the Family Relationship Centres. They could go straight to the Family Court.

Sue Price said the exceptions would make the new legislation worse for men: "As soon as the reforms go through, you'll see every woman in Australia claiming she's been beaten. We already know that women lie about abuse to get custody of their children, so now we'll have more women saying they've been attacked when it might have been a tap on the shoulder, so the presumption of shared parenting won't apply."

Weary of the arguments Ruddock said: "We want to create a new culture. We're going to change family law to emphasise that what we're concerned about is the rights of the children. People often focus on the difficulties in their relationships and children come second. But children do have a right to know both their parents."

***

Meanwhile new research showed the culture of fathering had changed. Professor Michael Bittman of the sociology department at the University of New England said in interviews with sociologists, men "will now say fathering is something that involves being there for a child, not just providing for a child. They regard it as terribly important. Even 10 years back, if there was something like a speech day at school, fathers would think it was important for their partner to turn up. Now they think it's important they turn up as well."

In contrast, an Australian Institute of Family Studies report released at the same time found that one in four children whose parents were separated had little or no contact with their non-resident parent. Twenty six per cent of children from broken families waited more than 12 months for contact with their non-resident parent, usually the father.

The report showed shared parenting remained the least common arrangement. While the number of children being jointly cared for had increased slightly since 1997, only six per cent were in shared parenting arrangements.

The report defined shared parenting as cases where children are in the care of either parent for at least 30 percent of nights a year.

About 88 percent of children lived with their mother after separation, the report's author Bruce Smyth, another periodic guest on Dads On The Air, said. About one in three children whose parents are separated saw their non-resident parent each weekend or every second weekend, the report, based on 2004 Australian Bureau of Statistics data, also found. Sixteen per cent had daytime-only contact, ten per cent saw their non-resident parent only during school holidays and seven percent saw their non-resident parent once every three to six months.[195]

Other data showed that in families where the non-resident parent had little or no contact with the child, 40 percent of resident mothers said there was not enough contact. About three-quarters of non-resident fathers in that group thought they did not spend enough time with their children.

The report said contact every other weekend provided resident parents with little respite, could interfere with a child's social activities and create resentment, particularly among older children.

The new research found "emerging evidence that a regime of every-other-weekend father-child contact" may diminish his importance to his children. Smyth said while recent debates had focused on the time fathers spent with children, the type of time children spent with non-resident parents was critical.

It needed to involve routine activities, he said. "If a child saw their father only on a Saturday, they might not have the everyday experiences needed to build a close relationship. Divorced fathers are often denied an opportunity to

---

195 Smyth, Bruce, Parent-child contact and post-separation parenting arrangements, Australian Institute of Family Studies, 2004.

have 'mundane' contact with their children, doing ordinary things, such as just tucking them into bed, or sitting down to peel potatoes".

Smyth said overnight visits often took place on Fridays and Saturdays, "when dads might feel they have to take the children out. It might be better if these visits happened on a weeknight, so the father can have the experience of making the child's lunch, and taking them to school, waking up and having breakfast with them."

Smyth said the "apparent obsession" with fathers for 50/50 shared parenting might reflect a desire for "time to develop more closeness with a child" by just "hanging out, talking about things".

"There are a lot of children in Australia who only see their fathers twice a month," he said. "So their dads become these good-time dads or Disneyland Dads, who feel like they have to do something, to show the kids a good time."

Smyth said non-custodial fathers often felt that the time allocated to them was "stilted, shallow, artificial and brief". He said custody arrangements should allow both parents to experience "fluid, meaningful time, with each parent".

***

Amazingly, around the same time the Family Court began talking to men's rights groups in an effort to become more "father-friendly". The court was also making staff who dealt with families undergo training to help them better understand the male perspective in divorce.

The initiatives were introduced by the court's new Chief Justice, Diana Bryant, who at the time was considered by men's groups to be more sympathetic to their concerns than former chief justice Alastair Nicholson.

Sue Price, who attended a meeting in Brisbane, said: "We were a bit taken aback when we were asked because the Family Court has pretty much ignored the way men feel."

The meeting was attended by representatives of the court, the Child Support Agency, Relationships Australia, Catholic welfare agency Centacare and men's groups. "We got out the butcher's paper and the whiteboards and we really talked about how we could make the system work better for men," Price said.

"We discussed the fairness of the court decisions, and why the court seemed to regard fathers as the lesser parents. We asked why fathers should be made to feel like criminals. It was extremely productive."

Price said Justice Bryant did not attend the meeting "but we spoke before she took over the court last year and I have the greatest respect for her. It's obvious that she wants to cooperate with men's groups and make the court more men-friendly."

Andrew Chudleigh, who was a consultant and adviser to the Family Court on men's issues, said the forums were "a way to pull all these players – the Government, the court, and the men's groups – together, so they could voice their concerns."

Terry Melvin of Mensline, who attended the first meeting in Sydney in June, said: "The Family Court comes in for quite a bit of criticism from men's groups and we thought that this was a way to build a connection. It was the first toe in the water, to start to build those links."

***

The Court was not the only institution showing a rare flash of humility. The Child Support Agency admitted it had been "insensitive" in dealing with feuding couples but promised a radical change in its treatment of divorced parents. Agency General Manager Matt Miller said he wanted people to have a positive experience with the Agency. Staff would be retrained to make sure they avoided upsetting clients.

"From the CSA perspective, we realise we need to take it to a new level, particularly being more caring with our parent client group," he said. "A lot of parents had difficult cases that the agency had failed to handle in a caring and sensitive way. They're very complex. It takes time to talk through those things, so we'll do more face-to-face on those complex cases.

"Sometimes your frontline people can take a less than caring attitude. That's where a lot of our energies are going to go next year, so in 12 months I would hope we've clearly been delivering a lot more caring and customer-centred service."

The Child Support changes were approved by cabinet in mid-October 2005, taking into account the incomes of both parents and the time they care for the children.

The government said legislation would be hastily drawn up in an attempt to have the new system in place by the start of the 2006-07 financial year. The Treasury had already been asked to cost the changes as part of the budget process. But the Government's hopes of getting the new payment scheme under way as soon as possible would be complicated by a shake-up of the Family Tax Benefit.

As part of the changes, almost all of the benefit would be paid to the custodial parent – usually the mother – to offset any reduction in child support payments.

President of the Sole Parents Union Kathleen Swinbourne, said there was no requirement that people would spend the money they saved on child support on their children. "Children will miss out," she said. "Single-parent families are the ones living in the most poverty and this will make it worse."

The president of the Lone Fathers Association Barry Williams supported a change in the way payments were calculated but was concerned that fathers would lose money as a result of higher payments for older children and changes to the Family Tax Benefit.

***

Sydney talk back king Alan Jones weighed in: "One of the issues that imposes great emotional toll on many Australian families is the issue of family break up. Who wins custody of the children and, when push turns to shove, who pays what. There has been long term resentment by the non-custodial parent that the system in place disadvantages that person enormously.

"Too often we hear that the parent with custody takes the children, often with another partner, to where the non-custodial parent could never afford to go, let alone afford to return the children for a custody break. Then, of course, payments are currently made by the non-custodial parent as a percentage of taxable income. It often leaves that parent with nothing to live on and therefore, no capacity to fashion any sort of future.

"What is more, too often, the custodial parent teams up with someone else and an income which surely ought to be considered in determining what a non-custodial parent should pay."

He paid tribute to Kay Patterson, Minister for Family and Community Services, as "a very caring person. She has done a hell of a job in bringing new and more sensible proposals to the Cabinet table."

"There has to be a better way of resolving differences than the current system whereby often, based on acrimony, one parent either doesn't see the children or can't afford to see the children. And the non-custodial parent, man or woman, fights for the rest of his or her life to make a fresh start because of ludicrous demands of the Family Court, which is biased in favour of the parent winning custody and seems to care little about the parent who is left behind.

"If Kay Patterson can resolve all of that, she will have made an important contribution to the lives of many."

***

Also in mid-October, and mirroring DOTA's own doubts about the proposed network of relationship centres, Bettina Arndt wrote in the *Herald Sun*: "Warning, Mr Howard. There's a red light flashing. Your vital new Family Law initiative looks set to derail. There's a very real risk the cool $189 million you were proposing to spend on Family Relationship Centres will be money wasted. The sure sign that something is going astray is the relaxed state of our family lawyers. They don't see the FRCs as any threat to their business. And they should.

"These centres were designed to satisfy parliamentarians seeking reform to the way our Family Court system handles divorces involving children. The parliamentary committee on child custody concluded the current adversarial system was a disaster for children."

The Government had not been convinced of the Hull Committee's proposal for a tribunal system and instead backed Professor Parkinson's idea of requiring parents to resolve their issues using child-centred mediation at family relationship centres.

Arndt wrote: "The whole idea was these centres would be the end point, the place where parents actually sorted out their business, not a mere road bump on the way to lawyers and the Family Court. That message has simply gone missing from the reams of waffle being produced by the Attorney General's department about the FRCs. The lawyers have sniffed the wind and are now seeing the FRC at worst as a minor inconvenience or perhaps even as a source of increased business."

The latest information sheets from the department did not suggest the centres were the place where decisions about children must be made – rather than lawyers' offices and the Family Court.

"The centres were supposed to be staffed by people skilled to perform the tortuously difficult child-focused mediation that helps warring parents concentrate on children's needs," Arndt wrote. "This type of mediation is different from the lawyer-led horse-trading offered by some mediation and dispute resolution services. It offers something new – an approach that has been shown to work even with extremely hostile parents who have spent years fighting over their children in the Family Court."

Surprise, surprise, Ruddocks's lawyer-filled department was ducking the issue because they didn't want to frighten the horses.

"The AG's department is playing to its legal constituency – one very good reason implementation of the FRCs should be handed over to the Department of Family and Community Services, which better understands the sensitive work that is at the heart of this great new plan."

Arndt also dismissed the department's proposal for families with a history of violence to be referred straight to the court. "That's a joke, considering the hash the court makes of many of these cases. Child-focused mediation is a far better option even in violent families."

DOTA had always been sceptical of the Relationship Centres and believed they would have been much more effective if they could have been shared parenting centres designed purely to assist separating couples into shared parenting arrangements. It was not to be.

DOTA would later interview Arti Sharma from the Centre for Independent Studies on her essay "Family Relationship Centres: Why We Don't Need Them". She claimed trials of a similar program undertaken in Britain led to the scheme being abandoned but the Australian government decided against a trial period.

"The proposal to establish Family Relationship Centres should be scrapped. They are an example of symbolic politics; in reality they will be no improvement at all. Family Relationship Centres represent the incorporation of private, voluntary and community services into intrusive bureaucracy. They will be costly to run, and if they fail, it will be a costly failure. They needlessly duplicate the voluntary and publicly-funded community sector relationship services.

"The danger is that this will end up destroying the community sector's independence, wasting taxpayers' money, and hindering rather than helping couples who need assistance with the divorce process."

***

Finally, the family law reform legislation was tabled in Parliament on December 8, 2005.

Still insisting on calling them the most significant reforms to the family law system in 30 years Attorney General Philip Ruddock's press release said Family Law Amendment (Shared Parental Responsibility) Bill 2005 reflected the Government's determination to ensure the right of children to grow up with the love and support of both of their parents.

"The Bill will move the focus from the rights of parents to the best interests of children," Ruddock said. "These initiatives represent a generational change in family law and aim to bring about a cultural shift in how family separation is managed: away from litigation and towards cooperative parenting.

"The legislative changes reinforce improvements already underway with the rollout of 65 new Family Relationship Centres and increased funding to expand services to support family relationships."

As foreshadowed, the Bill inserted a presumption, or starting point, of equal shared parental responsibility. This meant that both parents had an equal role in making decisions about major long term issues involving their children such as the choice of school. It also required the court to consider whether children spending equal time with both parents was practical and in the best interests of the child. If it was not appropriate, the court must consider substantial and significant time, including day to day routine, not just weekends or holidays.

The Bill gave the court power to impose costs against those who make false allegations of violence or abuse.

Ruddock said under the legislation the Family Court must consider an arrangement for "substantial and significant time" with both parents if equal time is not appropriate. "This means more than just weekends and holidays, it means doing the day-to-day things with children – tucking them into bed, picking them up after school, helping them with homework," he said. "It also means a mix of nights and days with children."

***

The next day the Shared Parenting Council congratulated the Howard government for tackling the "archaic" family law legislation.

The Association declared the introduction of the Shared Parental Responsibility was a landmark turning point for children of separated and divorced families.

"Today the light of democracy beamed out across this land as the Government took decisive action to strengthen children's right to an opportunity for equal or substantially equal relationships with both their parents", Ed Dabrowski, Federal Director of the Shared Parenting Council of Australia, said. "This is the greatest achievement in the support of human rights this country has experienced in recent history.

"It is the mark of a civilised society that values its families and parents and children. We have witnessed today and over the many years of this reform process, great statesmanship and leadership by our government which has shown the greatest respect and sensitivity for vulnerable children of divorce who deserve the love and protection of both their mother and father.

"Through its reform agenda and legislation introduced today, we have witnessed this Government do more to support the rights of children to the love and nurture of their parents than any other Australian Government in any other period in living memory. The legislation clearly protects children from violence and abuse with a range of new measures.

"The Bill coupled with the other three key pillars of reform through the Child Support legislation reforms, the creation of the Family Relationship Centres and the changes being implemented by the Family Court themselves to facilitate a new way of doing business, are sure to become a world setting precedent that other countries will rush to adopt.

"This is not a father's rights or mother's rights issue. This is about arresting the devastating outcomes for children that have resulted from over 30 years of failed Family Law policies."

The Association said the current legislation did not work in many cases and children were being deprived and alienated from good mums and dads.

"Many more children will have the physical stability of two homes and continuation of their local friends and school, with the emotional stability that comes from the security of knowing that two parents love them and that after separation or divorce, they will continue to preserve and develop lasting relationships with both of their parents", said Dabrowski.

"Never in the history of legislative change have we seen such a program of well thought out reforms that will give hope to the children of separating parents in Australia who simply want love, comfort and time with both parents."[196]

***

Former Chief Justice Alastair Nicholson hit the airwaves, talking down the changes. "The court has always been compelled to consider a situation that's in the best interests of the child," he claimed. He described joint custody as a "mathematical division" of time, "but the real problem is that it presumes that that is an ideal situation, whereas in most cases it's not for all sorts of reasons. I think that's more or less an attempt to, if you like, pander to the strong pressure that's been put on the Government by various militant fathers' groups.

"I think the downside of it is not so much from the effect on the court, but from the effect on people negotiating, they may think they're bound to start at a 50-50 division of time. And again, I don't think that's in the child's interest."

Reflecting the disconnect between legislation, public perception, and court practice, Stuart Fowler, a Sydney barrister who had practised family law for 45 years, told ABC radio that the only impact he saw from the legislation was a change in perception on the part of his clients, a change not reflected in the way the Family Court would proceed into the future.

"I think there's going to be a clear change in the way in which lawyers talk to their clients, because the public expectation has been, I think, raised in a way which doesn't reflect the legislation. What really needs to be done in our society is to educate parents to the view that what they do affects their children, that their children are not objects of ownership but they are little people who have their own bundle of rights which are very, very important."

---

196 Stapleton, John, Chaos at the Crossroads: Family Law Reform in Australia, 2010.

In an approving editorial *The Age* newspaper recalled its previous opposition to joint custody as unrealistic and potentially dangerous. "Importantly, the proposed bill does not create a presumption of equal division of time between parents. Instead it builds on the existing law by insisting on equal shared parenting responsibility in important decisions about the children of the marriage. *The Age* considers the reforms proposed are sensible and more likely to lead to just results than the current arrangements. It is also a much less prescriptive arrangement than Mr Howard originally suggested…"

Some writers, such as *Sydney Morning Herald* journalist Paola Totaro, reiterated their support for shared care.

"Divorce is traumatic and a profound disappointment and sadness for everyone involved," she wrote. "But its impact does not have to be the bitter, warlike legacy that custodial battles so often bring.

"In any dispute, it makes sense to begin mediating plans for a resolution from the middle position. When it comes to custody, the middle position – the starting point – is half the time with mum and half the time with dad: 50-50.

"What could be more simple? Or more fair?"

Totaro said she had brought up her children up for more than eight years now under shared custody arrangements.

"When it first went to court, it was the lawyers – who had worked in the Family Court for years and years – who urged us to drop the plan.

"Men don't win," they said. "Don't get your hopes up," they warned. "Judges don't often come down in favour of fathers," was the lugubrious refrain. I would never have believed it if I had not lived it. But our judges endorsed it. And our children won. They have two homes, two sets of parents, several grandparents - all who love them. Asked the question, they're unanimous: "Half and half, we love them both."

Totaro said a civilised family law framework must be flexible and allow for adjustments, one way or another. "OK, so mum and dad do not love each other any more. But in many cases not only will they continue to love their children but will want to play significant, equal roles in their lives."

Totaro said for some parents a 50-50 arrangement may be more difficult geographically or logistically.

"But if you start from a 50-50 situation you can work towards more time with mum – or with dad – depending on what works best for all of you, with the children in the first place. To start from the premise that mum is always the best parent is simply insulting to all the men who perform the role with passion – and all the women partnered with men who take being a father seriously. It is also intellectually primitive, sexist and profoundly unfair.

"As an educated, relatively affluent and civilised society, it is incumbent on us to… adapt and shape our behaviour to provide optimum experiences for our children."

***

Not all voices were so optimistic and many were sceptical that the Family Court would change its practices.

Sue Price wrote that the general opinion from fathers in the early days of the inquiry had been positive. "Women's groups who claimed rampant domestic violence or child abuse were for the first time challenged and asked to provide statistical evidence; fathers who could not see their children or had been tossed around in the legal system with no result were able to tell their story; second wives disclosed the uncertainly filling their lives as a direct result of unfair and often catastrophic dealings with the Child Support Agency and grandparents told of their devastation in not being able to see their grandchildren.

"In fact most fathers' groups were patting themselves on the back, us included, delighted with the impressions gained from the Committee members that fathers would at last be acknowledged as being essential in their children's lives.

"The publication of the Committee's report in December 2003, Every Picture Tells a Story told those of us with a little knowledge of past family law history that the recommendations apart from the proposal to instigate another tier of quasi-judicial activity in the form of Family Tribunals signified no change.

"The principle of shared parental responsibility, previously guardianship, had already been included in the Family Law Act since the 1995 reforms. Understandably, the general public embraced the proposals believing shared and equal parenting would become the norm."

The Government made little attempt to correct the impression created by the use of the terminology 'shared parental responsibility' until the first draft of the legislation appeared in June 2005, wherein it was particularly stated that shared parental responsibility described as Joint parental responsibility "does not involve or imply the child spending an equal amount of time, or a substantial amount of time, with each parent.

"Under the current legal situation 'parental responsibility' shared between the parents could cynically be interpreted as Mum gets the kids, Dad get the bills," Price wrote.

"Those who attended the hearings had trouble reconciling the visible reactions of many on the Committee with the final outcome in the Report.

"No person who sat through the hearings and listened to the desperate plight of separated fathers and their families could sign off on the most significant inquiry in 30 years without recommending shared and equal parenting. Not some gobbledygook wording of shared parental responsibility which at best could be described as confusing or at worst a deliberate attempt by the Government to deceive fathers into believing this would deliver equal rights and equal parenting time, which they were in no hurry to clarify."

***

Solicitor and former Family Court Judge associate, Waleed Aly wrote an opinion piece for the *Sydney Morning Herald* headlined: Shared parenting more a mirage than a breakthrough.

Aly wrote that the changes might not be the victory for father's groups they had first appeared. While pronouncements by Attorney General Philip Ruddock, describing the significance of recent amendments may be music to the ears of fathers' rights groups which had run "an incessant, and often intimidatory" campaign against the Family Law Act.

"It sounds like a significant win for fathers' groups, but there are good reasons to suspect it will be little more than a mirage. For all the promise of a new, shared parenting future, the key discretion remains with the courts. Shared living arrangements will be ordered only if reasonably practicable and the court considers it satisfies the paramount consideration: the child's best interests.

"Discretion is an inevitable feature of this area of the law. Family law courts are faced with infinitely varied and complex scenarios that continue to surprise even the most experienced judges. Rigidity in the face of so much variety would lead to injustice. But historically, judges have been reluctant to use this discretion to order equally shared residence. Reported cases where a court has ordered such an arrangement are rare exceptions – often with good reason.

"As long as judges have a discretion to be exercised in the best interests of the child – and not the parents – it is difficult to envisage how this judicial aversion to shared living arrangements will change. Certainly, judges will be required to consider them, but this is easily satisfied by raising the possibility and explaining why it should be dismissed because it is not in the child's best interests. Given the problems associated with shared residence, it is unlikely to become a common order."

Aly wrote that because of the way the Bill had been described in the media, there was a real risk it would come as a shock to the fathers' rights groups when changes to parenting were limited.

"Right now, expectations will be dizzyingly high. The fall is likely to be painful."

***

Reflecting the views of many family law reform advocates, *The Illawarra Mercury* editorialised that while the Bill tabled in parliament by Ruddock was being touted as helping to change the culture of family law, "In fact, there will be no change. It is simply an exercise in word-play. The words 'consideration of equal time' are now proposed to be added to the Family Law Act.

"A Family Court judge will at least have to consider if both parents can have equal contact with their kids after separation. The Labor Government made similar changes to the Family Law Act in 1995. The Family Court then subsequently chose to interpret the legislation in such a way as to make these changes ineffective. Less than two per cent of court orders continued to be made for equal time, shared parenting.

"Using words like 'equal time' is certainly a good start. However when linked to 'consideration', this change effectively means nothing has changed. The desired outcome of any change to family law amendments is the introduction of a rebuttable presumption of equal time, shared parenting. Our politicians have not been game enough to include this outcome in the current round of changes."

Correct.

***

In a lengthy feature, the *Newcastle Herald*'s Jim Keller said fathers believed the odds had been stacked against them. "Fathers don't win custody cases, mothers lose them," said Carl Boyd, a prominent family law solicitor in Newcastle.

"Ninety four percent of all contested applications are settled by consent. Dads figure they can't win them."

The average waiting period in Newcastle was 25 months from the date of filing an application for residence of children to the final hearing. "Because of the lengthy delay, people throw in the towel. Careers go ahead, life goes on," Boyd said.

During the wait for a final Family Court order, the court almost always sticks with the "status quo" which usually meant the mother retained custody of the children, giving the father access on alternate weekends and half of the school holidays.

"I think it must be absolutely bewildering, and there must be a lot of pain out there," said clinical psychologist Dr Tony Nicholas. "Like all things in life, when things are resolved amicably with children and property, then things are fine. But where this goes awry, where things become acrid, caustic, it's absolutely horrible."

Experts agreed that men were caught in a time warp: they were expected to be major wage earners for the family and at the same time live up to modern day parenting expectations by taking on increased family responsibilities.

"They are in the middle of a changing culture," says David Nagle, principal psychologist at Calm Solutions in Newcastle. "They have to be nurturing, they have to be the provider. They can be in a no-win situation."

***

More optimistic about the legislative moves were family law solicitor Andrew Hale and student specialising in family law Barry Apelbaum. The pair wrote in *The Age* that the laws could help bring about significant social transformation. Since the introduction of the Family Law Act in 1975, a generation of children have grown up living with mums while visiting their dads on weekends. Fathers have been shut out of a parenthood involving routine activities with their children and transformed into 'Disneyland Dads'.

The authors wrote: "The new Bill comes on the back of a need for more shared parenting. For fathers, the outlook after separation is grim. Dads In Distress points out that young separated Australian men are ten times more likely to die by suicide than through a car accident. The Family Law Reform Association NSW reiterated that at least half of the suicides of separated fathers are related to their harsh treatment by the family law and child support schemes.

"By far the strongest reason to encourage more shared parenting is because of the detriment caused to children by the absence of their fathers. Sadly, children report the loss of daily contact with one of their parents as the worst part of their parents' separation. Psychologically, children living with just one parent are significantly more likely to have emotional or behavioural problems, and account for more teenagers requiring psychiatric hospitalisation.

"Children without their fathers tend to have lower self-esteem, and are more likely to drop out of school, suffer depression, feel different from other children at school, be involved in accidents, and to attempt and commit suicide. When children have 'no father', they are more likely to develop criminal, delinquent, and violent behaviour. Daughters with absent fathers are more likely to have difficulties with other men in their lives, to fall pregnant out of wedlock, and – ironically – to divorce. Sons are described as less masculine, and more dependent."

One of the main furphies floated by the Family Court and opponents to shared parenting was that conflict needed to be absent for shared parenting to work. Hale and Apelbaum wrote: "To insist on an absence of conflict, may encourage it. If a father wants shared parenting, and the mother does not and believes the court's fallback order will be prime residence to her, she may promote conflict and be uncooperative, to provide evidence for the court to reject shared parenting."

The authors concluded that ultimately it was hoped that the Shared Parenting Bill, if passed, would mark a cultural change in the way family law treats fathers. "When children wish it, and their separated parents are emotionally and physically able to provide for them, and geographically proximate, shared equal time between households is practical and desirable. The arrangement is obviously fair, and encourages cooperation for the benefit of the children. It would be a proud achievement if more children could continue to have a loving relationship with both their father and mother."

***

In Melbourne's *Herald Sun* columnist Bettina Arndt wrote that Nicholson never knew when to keep his mouth shut.

"His term as Chief Justice of the Family Court was a public relations disaster as a result of his inflammatory comments, his dismissal of critics of the court as 'sinister', 'dysfunctional' and 'irrational', and his ill-informed contributions to public debate," she wrote. "Whatever the issue – Aborigines, refugees, homosexual rights, economic rationalism – there was Alastair.

"His latest attempt to make headlines really takes the cake. Mr Nicholson took the opportunity of a speech at a conference on homelessness to announce the Federal Government's changes to the child support scheme would mean that 'children will be thrown on to the streets'.

"The notion that the new child support scheme will plunge more children into homelessness is absurd but, sure enough, Alastair made the news."

There's a name for former public figures who keep trying to interfere in the contemporary narrative: relevance deprivation syndrome. Nicholson had a very bad dose of it.

Arndt, herself a Liberal Party loyalist keen to paint Howard in a positive light, said there was broad bipartisan support for the just announced overhaul of the scheme.

"Politicians are all too aware that the current scheme was widely perceived as unfair: much of their time in their electorates is taken up by complaints about the system.

"The expert taskforce sought to come up with a new formula that was fair to both parents, enabled both to afford to care for their children and reduced conflict between them over contact.

"In June 2003 Prime Minister John Howard declared family law was not working well because too many children were growing up without contact with their fathers. The various men's groups around the country hoped that finally they had an influential friend.

"Last week, after three years of deliberations, the Government's amendments to family law quietly passed through the Senate. For some changes there was bipartisan support; to carry others the Government's new majority in the upper house had to be called on.

"The men's groups are disappointed, claiming the changes do not go far enough. Whenever men's groups demand fathers should have more time with their children after divorce, women's groups complain children will be exposed to more violence."

***

Academic historian and author of *Kangaroo Court* John Hirst wrote that the Government attempted to solve this dilemma in gender politics by declaring that there shall be two prime considerations in divorce settlements: children should have meaningful contact with both parents and children must be protected from physical and psychological harm.

Where these principles conflicted, the court would have to decide.

"Meaningful contact is not to mean seeing the children every second weekend, which is the standard allowance to fathers at present. It may mean equal time where that is feasible but at least it must include a mix of weekends and weekdays so the parent can be involved in the child's regular routine and parent and child can be together for significant events in both their lives.

"This seems like a great advance, but men's groups are worried because these stipulations are recommendations only: in every case the settlement has to be determined according to the best interests of the child. And who decides that?"

Hirst said men's groups were right to be suspicious about the Family Court. The last great change to the law in 1995 was designed to promote the involvement of both parents in the lives of their children and had entirely backfired, leading to a decrease in shared parenting arrangements.

***

For an extended period of time after the passing of what as far as Dads On The Air was concerned were sadly watered down shared parenting laws, there was a quizzical silence.

No one was quite sure what impact the laws were having. Statistics were sparse or nonexistent. Anecdotal evidence was contradictory.

The editorial line of Dads On The Air had always been that the laws were not strong enough, could be too easily wound back, gave far too much discretion to the Family Court and failed to encourage and educate the public to embrace the benefits of shared parenting.

At the time Dads On The Air expressed bitter disappointment at the failure of the government to fully embrace cooperative parenting after divorce and to expose and reform the many destructive dysfunctions within the family law and child support systems.

In March 2006, with the legislation finally becoming law, Dads On The Air editorialised in a show titled Two Steps Forward One Step Back: "The mooted reaction from mainstream and alternative media and the sceptical response from a number of family law reform advocates demonstrates how far the debate has travelled and how underwhelming or confused is the outcome.

"The underwhelmed response showed the Howard government had simply equivocated or sat on the fence for too long."

SIXTEEN
THE TWILIGHT ZONE

Dads On The Air began the year with a program titled: 2006: What You Can Expect, featuring interviews with Geoffrey Greene and Wayne Butler from the Shared Parenting Council of Australia.

In characteristically blunt tones we declared: "The Family Court of Australia has been an unconscionable disgrace for the entire ten years the Howard government has been in power. Many people believe this Marxist feminist relic from the 1970s should have been abolished years ago."

With the so-called Shared Parenting legislation yet to pass into law, considerable jockeying and debate continued over its exact form. Debate over the proposed national network of 65 Family Relationship Centres was also intense.

President of the SPCA Matilda Bawden said she feared Anti Family Forces were hijacking New Family Relationship Centres. She also labelled the Federal Attorney General Phillip Ruddock's new Family Law Amendment (Shared Parental Responsibility) Bill as a betrayal of the trust and hopes placed by Australian families in the Federal Government and the Liberal Party.

"Non custodial parents have wrongly been led to believe that, unlike many since the 1995 Duncan amendments under the Keating Labor government, these reforms would be meaningful and convincing."

Bawden's comments come in response to complaints by non-custodial parent groups that they have been frozen out by the Attorney General's Department from fair and proper representation on the Community Services and Health Industry Services Committee Steering Committee, which was determining the professional make up of the Relationship Centres.

"There is almost no father-friendly representation on this Committee and certainly NO evidence to show it is even sympathetic to genuine shared parenting or joint residency outcomes or ideals. The Committee is saturated with representatives of organisations which are on the record as being opposed to shared parenting."

In February 2006 the legislation was being watered down still further. Attorney General Philip Ruddock announced that parents seeking equal custody of their children through the courts will have to prove they have had a "meaningful relationship" with and fulfilled their obligations towards their children under further changes to the Family Law Act.

How insulting were these people!!

***

Also in February of 2006 author Michael Green, writing in the journal Online Opinion under the heading The Myths About Shared Parenting, said on the face of it sensible proposals promoting cooperative parenting after separation and establishing relationship centres might be expected to meet with universal acceptance.

"Not so. There has been a chorus of dissent from significant interest groups and individuals.

"Why all the big noise? After all, the government was not merely responding to noisy fathers' groups, as some have claimed. A Federal Joint Select Committee, the Family Law Council, the Australian Law Reform Commission and others, over the past ten years, have pointed to serious deficiencies in the Family Law Act and its processes.

"Both mothers and fathers – individually and in consort with parenting groups – have responded vigorously to invitations for submissions to a number of inquiries."

Green noted that in 2003 the government commissioned an inter-party committee which found unanimous support for far-reaching reform of the system.

"The government responded, a draft Bill was produced, and this was subjected to further public scrutiny by way of another inter-party committee. Out of this process the current Family Law Amendment Bill is now before the parliament.

"Given all of the above, one would expect that the reforms would attract overwhelming support. That this is not the case bears close examination."

Green said there was a chorus of complaints from fathers and fathers' groups. However, they were by no means the only voices of dissent. For instance, the Australian Institute of Family Studies presented a report which revealed that 42 percent of the fathers surveyed wanted more contact with their children, and 50 percent had no contact at all.

***

Two Australian reports in 1992 showed similarly disturbing results. In one, only 48 percent had overnight contact with their children. In the other, the Family Law Council found that half of the children surveyed saw their fathers less than six times per year or not at all.

Research both in Australia and overseas demonstrated loss and maladjustment in children who lost contact with their absent parents.

Green argued that groups arguing equal or shared parenting was not in the best interests of children were ignoring the most relevant research.

"Separation and divorce are all about change and it is impossible to shield children from it. What is important is to engineer the necessary changes in parenting that look after them emotionally, intellectually and financially. The stability that children hunger for is not geographical stability, but the stability of meaningful relationships with the people most dear to them, their mothers and fathers, grandparents, relatives and friends, schools and communities. Shared parenting can deliver this."

Green also dismissed the objection that compulsory mediation may force separated parents, especially women, to negotiate with abusive former partners, and to agree to parenting arrangements that are not safe for them or their children

"This is not true and has never been true. Such mischievous nonsense shields deeper currents."

He said opposition to reform from lawyers could only be motivated by professional and financial insecurity.

"The brayings of feminist groups are rooted in a similar anxiety for self-preservation and in the feminist myth. Their support for the present system reveals a concern about power and money: if mothers share the parenting of children, it follows inevitably that they will have to share control of the family and of the resources that come with it, i.e. the home and financial support."

Green said the new system of family law and practice, so soundly based on reliable research and the aspirations of right-thinking men and women, would, if funded and supported by community education, bring enormous benefits to mothers, fathers and children.

Green concluded: "Radical feminism has done a disservice to women. It has sought to portray them as poor, suffering creatures that need protection from men and from paternalistic institutions. They are unable to speak confidently for themselves, to make their own choices, and are easily led into negotiations where their will and interests are overborne. Such thinking is a grave insult to the majority of women."

In the same year Green's book, written in conjunction with psychologist Jill Burrett, *Shared Parenting* was published. The authors wrote that sole custody regimes had "seriously disadvantaged children, and that fathers should be more engaged with their children than they have been. This requires real time, just like most mothers have always known – and given.

"For a very long time, gender stereotypes, 'the system' and other complex prejudices have discouraged some fathers and caused others to participate little in parenting, especially after separating.

"We don't think fortnightly weekend parenting is meaningful shared parenting. We think that shared parenting means having real chunks of time engaged with your children for a flexible 35-50 percent or more of their available time.

"Sole-mother 'custody', with mother doing all the parenting and father merely paying the bills and popping into the kids' lives from time to time, isn't really good enough for children – and often not for mothers – in either separated or 'intact' family situations."

***

Warnings in February 2006 by Minister for Human Services Joe Hockey that changes to child support might have to wait until after the next election met with a predictably hostile response.

Hockey said he was concerned that parents could accrue debts and be shocked by changes to their payments if the system was rushed. Any excuse for inaction from the Liberals, who were scared of the negative consequences of the many taxpayer funded women's advocacy groups unafraid to push their own barrows and with the ready ear of the media.

"It is impossible to implement Parkinson by July 1 this year, because we have not yet even got legislation. And my advice is that we would be struggling to do it by July 1, 2007," Mr Hockey said.

"The CSA needs a reasonable level of surgery and significant additional resources to be able to begin implementation of Parkinson."

The plan would see non-custodial parents on the dole pay $6 a week if they see their child one night a week, while fathers with low-wage jobs will pay $20 a week for each child – up from a flat $5 weekly.

Other changes would make it easier for men to support a second family after separation. Divorced fathers would be able to quarantine earnings from overtime or second jobs from their maintenance assessment, but only if the extra pay was earned after the separation.

The Child Support Agency was requesting $300 million to ensure it is capable of implementing Professor Parkinson's reforms.

Only 40 out of 750,000 CSA clients would not have their income changed under the Parkinson model and an estimated 60 percent of fathers would be financially better off under the changes, it was claimed.

The Government proposed to spend more than $1 billion compensating divorced parents, mainly single mothers, who could lose up to $50 a week under changes.

Lone Fathers Association national president Barry Williams warned that the Liberals would face a backlash at the polls if they did not implement the reforms sooner. "I have called Joe Hockey's office and told them that they will lose a lot of seats out there because men are sick of being treated like this. We were promised reform two years ago and the Parkinson report has been down for nearly 12 months. This is ludicrous".

Hockey warned the Child Support Agency was not ready to implement such radical change, despite promises by former minister for Community Services Kay Patterson that the reforms would be introduced as soon as possible.

Liberal backbencher Alby Schultz told the party room that while men waited for reform, they were committing suicide at increasing rates: "I can only deduce by the comments made by Minister Hockey that we've stood by and allowed a hoax to be perpetrated on people about the implementation of the Parkinson report, and to say it can't be implemented until the next federal election is outrageous."

***

In another piece of mischief Shadow Attorney General Nicola Roxon released a package of amendments to "further improve" the Family Law Amendment (Shared Parental Responsibility) Bill.

"We urge the Government to accept these amendments, which are in the best interests of Australian children," she declared.

Labor proposed several changes that would allegedly make safety a priority, including a "clear exemption from face-to-face mediation in violent relationships and proper screening for violent cases; protection from coercion and intimidation when making parenting plans and removing disincentives to raise concerns about violence".

In addition to amendments concerning family violence, Labor proposed a legislative framework to ensure that Family Relationship Centres met the challenges they would face - including proper accreditation standards, quality control and thorough training in how to recognise and handle family violence. In other words, DOTA commented, to make sure they all thought alike.

"Family law should not be about a tug-of-war between mums or dads, or a brawl between Liberal and Labor," Roxon said. "Family law is for the protection of children and we should always put them first. Children need love, care and security and we should shape our concerns around them. These amendments will be good for Australian children and we urge the Government to support them."

Ruddock fought back, accusing Labor of being "all over the shop" on the issue of family law. "The Government's reforms do protect children from the risk of violence or abuse by making it a primary factor to be considered in child custody cases, along with the right of children to know both their parents," he said. "The Government has a broader vision to protect children from exposure to violence and from growing up with conflict when parents separate. Court should always be the last resort, not the first."

He accused Labor of rejecting the prioritisation of a child's right to know both parents, removing the provision allowing cost orders against persons who made false accusations of family violence and removing the requirement for parents who go to court to first make a genuine effort to resolve their issues in mediation.

Sensitive to the propaganda by Labor and women's groups that their legislation could expose vulnerable women and children to violence and abuse, by the end of the month Ruddock released his so-called Family Law Violence Strategy.

"The Australian Government is taking steps to improve the handling of family violence and child abuse allegations in the family law system," he said. "I am concerned about false allegations of violence or abuse. I am also concerned about false denials.

"Family violence and child abuse have traumatic and long-lasting consequences. I want a better family law system where these cases are dealt with quickly, fairly and properly.

"Cases should not drag on while family members remain exposed to the risk of violence. Allegations should not hang out there indefinitely without an effective process to establish the facts."

***

Ruddock announced the Government would fund the Australian Institute of Family Studies to conduct independent research on how allegations of family violence and child abuse were raised and addressed in the family law system. The Government would also ask the Family Law Council – the Government's advisory body – to examine strategies to make sure Commonwealth and State and Territory laws and agencies can work together better in these cases.

He said the government would work with the courts to improve court processes for cases where family violence and child abuse allegations are raised; and ensure the family law reforms and proper screening at the new Family Relationship Centres helped people experiencing violence or abuse to access appropriate support and services.

By late March 2006, with the shared parental responsibility legislation having passed through yet another committee, this time the Senate Legal and Constitutional Committee, and the Bill about to become law, there was a spate of last minute jockeying by father's groups in an attempt to rescue the legislation.

On 24 March 2006 Steve Fielding of the Family First Party said he would table an urgently needed amendment to include a 'presumption of equal parenting time', as a starting point for child custody arrangements.

"In almost 98 percent of cases, a child will effectively lose one of their parents after a Family Court decision, creating a stolen generation of children," Senator Fielding said.

"Only 2.5 percent of Family Court orders allow children to have equal time with both parents, after a relationship breakdown. Shared parenting is the best outcome, because children can continue to have a real father and mother. For this to work, the parent has to want to exercise their responsibility and be with their child.

"It is not our purpose to force parents to exercise shared parenting. But Family First would hope that all parents would want to."

Fathers4Equality put out a supportive release. "Only a matter of two and a half years ago, Prime Minister John Howard was considered by many as the patron saint in waiting for long suffering non-custodial fathers and children of separated families, having promised Australia 'genuine' change to the universally condemned one size fits all Family Law system," spokesman Ash Patil said.

He said the Liberal coalition had won the last election partly because of blue collar traditional Labor voters believing Howard would do something about reforming family law and child support.

"But all the promise and all the hopes have since disappeared with the realisation that the proposed Family Law Amendment Bill, to be debated in the Senate this week, a Bill that had been sold to fathers as the law that would finally make Shared Residence the 'norm' in Australia, was simply re-packaged legislation that has an international track record of failing fathers, failing children, and failing separated families.

"The Prime Minister will no longer be able to take father's votes for granted. Whether it succeeds or fails, the Family First amendment to the Family Law Bill will have a resounding impact, and not simply on the families going through separation, but in the minds of every parent and grand-parent come election time."

***

As debate progressed in the Senate, the last obstacle before it became law, the Lone Fathers Association of Australia put out a release saying the bill should be renamed the Equal Parenting Bill.

"The starting point for this Bill should be a recognition that it is a natural and paramount right of children affected by marriage and relationship breakdowns to be able to spend equal parenting time with both parents," National President Barry Williams said.

"It is of the utmost importance that the words should be entrenched in law, and read as meaning that in separated and divorced families the children have a paramount right to equal parenting time with both parents, and that both parents have a paramount right to equal parenting time with their children.

"For too long now, we have witnessed children being prevented from exercising these natural rights – which is an infringement on their rights as spelt out in the UN charter of the rights of the child. Every day in our courts and on the say-so of one parent these rights are denied to the children. This immediately places the courts and the parent in conflict with the rights of the child."

Tony Miller from Dads In Distress also put out a release which read in part: "Until this Government wakes up to the reality that men in this country, certainly dads, are being led to the slaughter in the Family Courts of this land and that dads and their children simply want a fair go, we are going nowhere.

"I spent a week in Canberra recently with some of the movers and shakers of the fatherhood movement lobbying politicians to consider our plight. I came away mystified whether any of these politicians were actually dads. Because to be honest, I couldn't understand that if they were, how could they think any other way.

"We are not asking for anything special, we are not asking to be considered in any other way, but as fathers. And as fathers we should be able to hold our heads up, we should be allowed to continue a relationship with our children regardless of divorce or separation.

"For most of us we realise it's too bloody late. Especially as it seems the new legislation may not be retrospective, which in effect will block anyone with existing orders reapplying. I guess they are worried about the stampede back to courts to gain some fairness.

"At the end of the day, I'm a dad, who simply wants to spend as much time with his kids as is humanly possible. I simply want and so do my children, a fairer playing field. I want to be a part of their life. And they want to be a part of mine. Just because I am divorced from their mother doesn't mean I'm divorced from them."

***

Minor party of the left, the Democrats, which had been beating the domestic violence card for all it was worth, also had their amendments voted down, including to omit the provision that implemented costs orders for false allegations of violence – "as this provision is likely to further deter legitimate reporting of domestic violence".

"Our attempts to ameliorate the new definition of family violence in the bill, which now requires an 'objective' assessment of whether or not the victim's fear is reasonable, were also rejected," Democrat spokeswoman Senator Natasha Stott Despoja said. "The new definition flies in the face of a known fact about domestic violence, that often only the victim knows the signs that are likely to lead to violence.

"Laws change lives, and the Family Law Amendment (Shared Parental Responsibility) Bill 2006 is likely to have disastrous consequences for the safety of vulnerable family members, especially women and children, where there is a history of family violence."

With so much focus on the alleged violence of men DOTA repeated the findings of the 2005 Personal Safety Australia survey conducted by the Australian Bureau of Statistics. It found that in the previous 12 months almost twice as many men as women (808,300) were victims of all types of violence; twice as many men as women (485,400) were victims of physical assault; nearly a third of sexual assault victims were men; 864,300 men were harassed and 110,700 men were stalked.

The same study found that men were almost as likely as women to experience physical violence within the home (half from females, half from males) and were just as likely as women to experience physical violence from perpetrators who were known to them.

Finally, in the early hours of 31 March, 2006, the Family Law Amendment (Shared Parental Responsibility Bill 2005) was passed into law during an extended late night session of the Senate. There were accusations that the debate was guillotined and the legislation rushed through, literally in the dead of night.

The entire operation reeked of subterfuge.

That same day the Attorney General Philip Ruddock announced that "the most significant changes to the Family Law Act in more than 30 years" had passed through the Senate. Because of Senate amendments, the legislation had to return to the House of Representatives when Parliament resumed in May, with the majority of the reforms to take effect from July 1, 2006.

"The law will take the view that parenting is a responsibility which should be shared and, in most cases, parents will need to consult and agree on major issues affecting their children," said Mr Ruddock. "Where both parents share responsibility, consideration will also be given to the children spending equal or at least substantial time with both parents - providing that this is practical and not contrary to the best interests of the child."

Ruddock said that as a result of an amendment by the Government in the Senate, once the new laws commence they will apply to people who are already in the court system seeking parenting orders and to all new applications for parenting orders.

"This Bill along with the massive expansion of support services and the planned roll-out of new Family Relationship Centres later this year demonstrates the Government's commitment to changing the culture around family separation," Mr Ruddock said.

After the passing of the Bill a congratulatory media release from The Shared Parenting Council described the enactment as a major milestone for children and families.

"The ground has shifted significantly in favour of children's right to know and experience a meaningful relationship with both parents after separation or divorce," Ed Dabrowski, Federal Director of the Shared Parenting Council of Australia, said.

"The Parliament has exercised its will decisively today with the passing of this Bill. It is a considerable body of legislation and the second time in a decade that the Parliament had instructed the Family Court to change direction and commence expediting shared parenting outcomes for parents.

"The Family Court dare not flaunt these decisive measures to make shared parenting the normal outcome in disputed cases. The Family Court is now fully responsible for implementing the will of Parliament and the community expectation is that they will do so without fail.

"For 30 years the Family Court has created a generation of divorce orphans growing up without knowing one parent. The culture of Family law had created a generation of fatherless children and childless fathers. This blight on our nation stops right now, with the enactment of these laws.

"Democrat, Labor and Greens amendments to the Bill which would have significantly weakened the rights of children to be nurtured, loved and protected by both parents, thankfully faltered. Common sense and concern for families has won the day, but it was disappointing, that despite being fully educated in the benefits to children of shared parenting, that ideologies and party politics were put above the best interests of children by these opposition parties."

***

The Shared Parenting Council of Australia said the new law required monitoring of the Family Courts' performance in making shared parenting orders and community groups around Australia expected the Court to reach a high benchmark in this regard. "The first year is vital to the Court's survival", said Mr Dabrowski. "It must comply with the law and will of Parliament if it is to retain the responsibilities entrusted to it by the community and legislators. The Family Court is on probation and we intend to hold the Court fully responsible and accountable for its performance.

"Although parenting groups were disappointed that the Family First Party amendment for a presumption of equal time parenting had been lost, nevertheless, this highly supported reform would be the next logical outcome if the Family Court failed to deliver shared parenting outcomes according to the spirit of the new laws and the clear intentions of the Australian Parliament."

Prominent activist Wayne Butler agreed that the Bill was the most significant re-write of the Family Law Act in living memory. "This is a fabulous result for families. The court now must consider maximising the sharing of time so that children retain family life and their precious primary bonds with both mum and dad."

Barry Williams, President of the Lone Fathers Association of Australia said it was disappointing to see the display of gender politics in Senate time by the opposition parties and to witness the rhetoric aimed against the parental involvement of fathers.

"We support the new laws and will work with the Shared Parenting Council of Australia to further educate the community and the divorce industry insiders about the life-giving benefits of shared parenting," he said. "We firmly believe that these new laws, properly carried out by the Family Court, have the potential to save many lives and reduce the suffering and misery of children and many forgotten fathers. This is a day for fathers and the whole community to celebrate and look forward to better outcomes for families."

***

Other groups were not so positive.

Warwick Marsh, founder of the Fatherhood Foundation observed that at midnight on 30th March 2006 "the fatally flawed family law reform was passed by the Senate".

"Whilst the reform bill is a step in the right direction, and contains some good ideas, the fundamental problem has not been fixed," Marsh said.

"The problem is the gender bias against the male of the species that is embedded in the culture of the Family Law Court and its many agencies. This gender bias is expressed in the many submissions that have been put in by these government agencies and counselling services against the 'rebuttable presumption of equal parenting time' as a starting point in family law reform.

"The current one-size fits all policy of sole custody will continue to predominate and children will continue to be robbed of one of their parents in over 95 percent of cases. Ninety percent of the time, this will be the father. Children need a mother and a father for their proper development.

"Mothers and fathers contribute uniquely and importantly to a child's development. What part of the word equality does the Family Law Court establishment and the government not understand?

"Children need equal access to both their mother and father. The children of Australia need justice, not more broken promises. How much longer must our children wait?"

***

Fathers4Equality, in a joint press release with the Non Custodial Parents Party, declared that the feeble Family Law Act 2005 would fail children.

"This flawed legislation fails to protect children from being the pawns in family break-ups," the release declared. "This is a victory for the lawyers and others who profit from family break-up. This new Act does nothing but move the deckchairs on the sinking Titanic. It still leaves far too wide discretion for the lawyers and judges and does little to replace the 'winner-takes-all' culture of the Family Court.

"Years of work has gone into this legislation and parenting groups are outraged that nothing has been fixed! Both parents are equally important for a child's development. Children who miss out on either of their parents suffer. This legislation fails since it does not require the Court to maximise the time children can spend with both their natural parents in the absence of abuse.

"We are considering demanding a referendum on the issue. In Massachusetts the US referenda have won a resounding 85 percent of votes in favour of a strongly worded presumption of equal time after divorce. In Australia, various polls hosted by major media outlets have weighed-in with around 90 percent of Australians supporting it."

"Sharing is good," James Adams, a spokesman for Fathers4Equality, said. "Single parent households suffer from all kinds of social, emotional and economic hardship. Too often they can't hold everything together. Tragically, that's when children suffer. The present law forces mothers to be single mums and forces loving dads out of their children's lives and onto the scrap-heap.

"The Family Court's bias forces children to live in single parent households. This is based on discredited theories from the 1970's as the basis for deciding what is best for children. This results in a one-size fits all solution, where the kids lose a parent. This failed approach needs to be overturned.

"The research is overwhelming. Study after study shows that children in shared care, who have both their natural parents do better at school, have fewer behavioural problems, are less likely to take drugs or get pregnant as teenagers. Children need both natural parents!

"The livelihoods of many lawyers, CSA workers and others depend on all the pain and conflict caused by taking kids away from their fathers. The new act leaves the profiteers making decisions about our children. It's like putting Dracula in charge of the Blood Bank.

"They didn't want anything changed. And sadly, nothing has changed!"

***

Senator Steve Fielding of the Family First Party told the ABC the changes had not gone far enough to ensure children spend equal time with separated parents. The Senator's amendment to give parents split time with their children was voted down and he said an opportunity had now been lost.

"We had a real opportunity here of addressing a real concern and looking at children losing, effectively, one of their parents," he said. "I really believe we haven't gone far enough and I think you'll find in two or three years time, once there's a review done, you'll see that not a lot has changed."

On 3 April 2006 historian John Hirst wrote in *The Australian* that divorcing dads still faced an uphill struggle.

"In June 2003 Prime Minister John Howard declared family law was not working well because too many children were –growing up without contact with their fathers. The various men's groups around the country hoped that finally they had an influential friend.

"Last week, after three years of deliberations, the Government's amendments to family law quietly passed through the Senate. For some changes there was bipartisan support; to carry others the Government's new majority in the upper house had to be called on. The men's groups are disappointed, claiming the changes do not go far enough.

"Whenever men's groups demand fathers should have more time with their children after divorce, women's groups complain children will be exposed to more violence."

Hirst wrote that the Government attempted to solve this dilemma in gender politics by declaring that there shall be two prime considerations in divorce settlements: children should have meaningful contact with both parents and children must be protected from physical and psychological harm. Where these principles conflict, the court would decide.

"Meaningful contact is not to mean seeing the children every second weekend, which is the standard allowance to fathers at present. It may mean equal time where that is feasible but at least it must include a mix of weekends and weekdays so the parent can be involved in the child's regular routine and parent and child can be together for significant events in both their lives.

"This seems like a great advance, but men's groups are worried because these stipulations are recommendations only: in every case the settlement has to be determined according to the best interests of the child. And who decides that?"

Hirst said men's groups were right to be suspicious about the Family Court. The last great change to the law in 1995 was designed to promote the involvement of both parents in the lives of their children.[197]

***

For an extended period of time after the passing of as far as DOTA was concerned sadly watered down shared parenting laws, there was a quizzical silence. No one was quite sure what impact the laws were having. Statistics were sparse or nonexistent. Anecdotal evidence was contradictory.

The editorial line of Dads On The Air had always been that the laws as they passed were not strong enough, could be too easily wound back, allowed far too much discretion to the Family Court and failed to encourage and educate the public to embrace the benefits of shared parenting.

While the war might have been lost, DOTA continued to maintain the rage. In April 2006 we ran a show titled Why Shared Parenting Should Be Implemented.

That was followed by a show featuring Tanya Bollin, the spokeswoman for America's National Association of Non-Custodial Mothers.

We wrote: "Anyone who thinks that fathers and their children are the only

---

[197] Hirst, John, Divorcing dads still face an uphill struggle, *The Australian*, 3 April, 2006.

ones that suffer under the present sole-custody model adopted by family courts as supposedly being in the best interests of children should listen to this fascinating and moving interview. There are now an estimated three million non-custodial mothers in America and they are becoming an increasingly strong voice in the widespread demands for change."

In an angry enough show in May 2006 titled "The Death of 50/50, The Death Of Reason?" we declared: "The Howard government, idiotically rejected the hugely popular idea of rebuttable joint custody or shared parenting as the starting point for separating couples; instead whitewashing the troubled family law industry and the hated Child Support Agency with the incompetent bureaucrat written reports Every Picture Tells A Story and The Best interests of Children respectively."

We once again interviewed Senator Fielding, who we declared was one of the only politicians in the country to behave with any true integrity in the long running debate over family law and child support reform.

The Family First Party was Christian based and promoted family values. Unlike those in the main Catholic, Anglican and Uniting faiths Fielding had been consistently critical over a long period of the behaviour of the Family Court; and a staunch supporter of shared parenting as the only sensible outcome after divorce.

***

On 10 May 2006 Attorney General Phillip Ruddock announced that "the most significant family law changes in 30 years" had passed through parliament.

This followed the announcement in the previous night's Federal Budget of an additional investment of $45.8 million in family support services, building on the $397 million over four years pledged the previous year.

Ruddock reiterated that the new system was designed to keep families out of the courts and deliver practical, co-operative outcomes for separating families.

"The Government has delivered on its promise to Australian families," he said. "These significant legislative changes, combined with the biggest ever investment in the family law system, will encourage a co-operative approach to the difficult issues surrounding family breakdown.

"The new laws reflect the Government's belief that two factors are of primary importance in addressing the interests of children in family breakdowns – the right of the child to have a meaningful relationship with both parents, and the protection of the child from harm."

Passage of the reforms was confirmed when the House of Representatives accepted the Government's amendments to the Family Law Amendment (Shared Parental Responsibility) Bill in the Senate.

Then in June the government launched a $25 million public information campaign aimed at helping explain to Australian families a raft of new services and changes to the family law which would take effect from 1 July, 2006.

The information campaign initially featured national print and localised advertising as the first 15 new Family Relationship Centres began offering families a range of services, as well as promoting the new telephone Advice Line and website.

The government reiterated that the reforms promoted the right of children to know both their parents and to be protected from harm. They also recognised parenting as a responsibility that should be shared equally.

Also in June, Ruddock appeared on Dads On The Air, again spruiking "the most significant changes…"

Dads On The Air remained sceptical. There had been too many committees, too much prevarication, too much uncertainty. We had seen too much.

***

Unconvinced that the legislation would make any real difference on the ground, DOTA declared the war over and the fight lost. On air we reiterated: "The liars, the lawyers, the bureaucrats and the social engineers have won the day".

With the family law changes about to come into effect in July 2006, there remained some media interest. In Western Australia the national broadcaster the ABC profiled Ed Dabrowski, who had been a frequent guest on DOTA and for several years a major figure fighting for family law reform.

The ABC recorded that Dabrowski came home from work one day to find that his wife and children had gone to Perth. Divorce followed the separation. Now he had shared custody of his children and had started a suicide prevention group for men, Dads in Distress, in Bunbury.

The journey was difficult. "It's a terrible thing to be without children," said Ed. "My children were gone."

His children were also missing their father, he discovered.

Dabrowski said the biggest hurdle to overcome to maintain his relationship with the children was the Family Court and its adversarial processes. "The chances are that fathers will get only weekend contact – basically becoming a stranger in their children's lives."

Dabrowski was optimistic the new Bill coming into effect the following month would make a big difference. The courts will consider "equal time parenting" as a first option, he said. If that's not practicable, they'll look at substantial time. "It will come to be known as a substantial time order," Ed believes.

The usual once a fortnight visits will still happen on the weekend in addition to evenings during the week. It's about looking innovatively at what times dad can get to the kids.

Dabrowski said children and families, not just dads, have had a win with the new legislation.

"The system was so lopsided. We didn't have a culture of shared parenting in Australia. Even the language to talk about the concept didn't really exist till recently. The best outcome for children is to have two loving and involved parents."

***

Ed started Dads in Distress locally because he said five men kill themselves every day in Australia. And the statistics show that 80 per cent of those men are going through the trauma of a relationship breakdown.

"The big part of that is not getting access to their children. There's a lot of hopelessness that creeps into men's daily lives because they don't have the warmth of children around them. Certainly, I felt like the world was on top of me."

Dads in Distress welcomed the incoming legislative changes to family law. Their public statement declared: "We look forward to a fairer and more equitable solution to the current Family Law Crisis. Our greatest concern is whether these changes are going to be taken seriously by our Family Law Practitioners who ultimately are the ones who play this out in the courtrooms.

"To date the feedback from family law practitioners to which we have spoken is 'same old, same old', just different speak. We have voiced these concerns to the Attorney General's Department. There needs to be education programs re the legislation to these practitioners put in place.

"The other major concern is that the reality hasn't hit home yet with the majority of dads that the new legislation is not retrospective. Most dads who have been given lousy orders in the past believe that once the new legislation comes in they will be able to take their cases back to court and apply for either 50/50 or a better deal than they now have.

"This will not be the case and it will come as a big shock to the majority of dads out there. To apply there apparently needs to be a 'change of circumstance'. Just what that change of circumstance is is unclear."

***

Once again the punitive nightmare that was child support was in the news. Human Services Minister Joe Hockey announced that 120 officers would be employed specifically to watch suspect parents and gather video data on their lifestyles.

"If people are claiming to have no money or are not paying what they are required to pay, yet are living lavish lifestyles, then certain questions need to be answered and we'll make sure those questions are answered," Mr Hockey said.

The Government would use the evidence to prosecute the parents.

"It can be used to take the individual to court and to lift the veil from which they seek to hide," Hockey said.

He claimed there were between 40,000 and 70,000 fathers reporting no income but not claiming any welfare payments and that the spies were needed to ensure "deadbeat dads" did not "rip off their own children, their own flesh and blood".

In parliament Alby Schultz MP asked: "Are we going to fit these people out with grey uniforms and jackboots, which would be appropriate for the actions that the Minister says they are going to take out in the public arena? I have grave reservations and concerns about this initiative.

"I would have thought that there were other areas of the Child Support Agency that needed to be cleaned up with a great deal of vigour than putting 120 people out into the community specifically to watch 'suspect parents' and to gather video data on their lifestyles. That is not what this government is all about and what this government purports to be all about. It is an undemocratic process. Quite frankly, I think the Minister has bowed to the pressure of people within the CSA."

***

The new laws came into effect on 1 July, 2006.

Solicitors were reportedly being inundated with calls from fathers who thought they would be granted joint custody. Many were devastated to discover the law did not guarantee equal access and that earlier court orders were not covered by the act.

"I've spoken to many family practitioners around the country and the word I get from them is it's a joke," said Tony Miller, founder of Dads in Distress. "Most guys that ring us don't understand that it's not retrospective. They're saying, 'I've had bum orders for years – as soon as this law comes through I can rush back to court and get 50-50 custody'. That's not going to happen and they're in for a big shock."

Family lawyer Stephen Winspear had already taken dozens of calls from fathers who thought the changes would lead to joint custody. "There's quite a strong perception that it's going to be 50-50; it's very misleading," he said. "All the publicity is about sharing but in fact the actual presumption is equal shared parental responsibility and the emphasis is on responsibility, which doesn't say anything about time."

The *Herald Sun* paid tribute to one of the law's unsung heroes: "In the past few weeks a revolution has taken place in the family-law system, designed to improve the lives of divorced children by letting dads remain part of their lives. Sadly, the man responsible for this family-law revolution didn't live to see it.

"John Perrin didn't look like a powerful man. At first glance, John Howard's social issues adviser seemed plucked straight from the set of Yes, Prime Minister.

"With a grey suit, thinning hair, glasses and a trim moustache, this formal, mild-mannered man was the very model of the silent bureaucrat.

"But Perrin, who died in late May at 53 from cancer, was a mighty influential political operator, who changed the social map of Australia."

The *Herald Sun* said Perrin had long been determined to fix the family law system, a system which he knew to be a festering sore of discontent in the community. Inquiry after inquiry had shown that there was bias against fathers in both the Family Court and the Child Support system.

"For years, Perrin talked and listened – prodding the experts for new ideas. A plan for a revamp of the system gradually emerged. This month would have been a great one for Perrin."

Despite DOTA's doubts about their operation, the Family Relationship Centres were set for a surprisingly positive start.

***

Staunch feminist Adele Horin at *The Sydney Morning Herald* reported that families had flocked to the new centres. She began: "The father was bereft because his wife and children had left him. When he turned up at the Family Relationship Centre in Penrith it took staff only a short time to realise he was suicidal.

"He had considered throwing himself onto railway tracks. The staff called an ambulance that sped him to the mental health unit of a nearby hospital.

"Business has been surprisingly brisk in the four weeks since the Federal Government's 15 Family Relationship Centres opened, the managers report.

"From distressed and suicidal fathers to grandparents estranged from their grandchildren, the casualties of unhappy family life have flocked through the doors seeking help – hundreds of them."

Manager of the Penrith centre Stephen Hackett said: "We always knew we would become busy; I just wasn't expecting to be busy on the first day – but we were."

The story was similar at the Caringbah centre. "We were swamped, absolutely swamped," Karen Morris, the director of services, said.

Other coverage of the Relationships Centres was largely positive. In mid August Ann Hollands of Relationships Australia told the ABC: "I think that that initiative is going to capture a lot of people who otherwise are unknowingly might have ended up on that sort of adversarial pathway and then found that things got out of hand. Not because they wanted it to, but because they didn't know that there was another and a better way.

"Quite a number of people who otherwise we don't know where they would have gone for help, such as grandparents coming in who have lost contact with their grandchildren because there's been a separation or a divorce in the family or recently separated fathers who are depressed or even suicidal are coming in for help and for information about how they might be able to have more access to their children."

***

The first clear sign that the Family Court was once again not going to accept direction from Parliament came in October 2006 at a family law conference in Perth.

In an editorial piece titled Consequence Dads On The Air noted: "The changes were not accepted with good heart by the court; and this reluctance to accept reform was no more clearly evidenced than at their great tribal gathering, the National Family Law Conference.

"The retiring Justice Richard Chisholm, who had done much to set the tone of the court, showed how little regret for past practice was in play when he declared of the reforms: 'The ultimate goal has to remain the same: to do what's best for kids. So, we might see a lot of change in the way a case is presented, but the outcome should be the same as under old system.'"

On the final day of the conference, the Hon Richard Chisholm started the morning session with a song about the Family Law Act amendments. He sang with gusto to the tune of "On Top of Old Smokey" (better known as the "I Lost My Poor Meatball" song):

"It seems rather blokey the men won the fights
But now they all tell us
It's about children's rights
We struggle to read it,
We mutter and moan,
By the time that we've read it,
The kids have left home

I studied one section, got it into my head,
But it only told me what another section said..."

The ditty caused considerable offence; and indeed it is impossible to imagine a Family Court judge singing a song that ridiculed mothers without causing a media storm. As it happened, the ditty was applauded by conference attendees.

***

Chisholm went on to tell the conference it was the job of the court and practitioners to apply the law and not be guessing what the government wanted: "We know quite a bit of what the government intended, but then we have the legislation."

No truer words, of course, as critics had pointed out.

Male litigants who had appeared before Chisholm were often critical and at one point Dads On The Air contemplated offering a $100 reward for anyone who could find a father happy with a Chisholm judgement; but in such a litigious environment thought better of it.

A professional lifetime in the shrouds of importance and the peculiar psychopathology of the court did not lend to humility. The power play between the various branches of government was never more clearly displayed.

Chisholm cautioned practitioners to be careful about making the intention of government and the law the same thing. "At times of crises there's a lot to be said about orthodoxy; it's our job to administer the law."

Chisholm said the recent epidemic of obesity seemed to have extended to the Family Law Act before discussing what he saw as problematic parts of the provision setting out what constituted the best interests of the child.

"The ultimate goal has to remain the same: to do what's best for kids," Chisholm said. "So, we might see a lot of change in the way a case is presented, but the outcome should be the same as under the old system."

***

In turn head of the Family Court of Australia Chief Justice Diana Bryant sternly lectured the government on political interference.

"It is useful when considering the implementation of legislation to remind ourselves of the independence of the Court from the Executive and the Parliament," she declared. "In doing so I do not suggest for a moment that the Court is not required to implement the law in a real and substantive way and in a manner in which the Parliament intended it to operate. That I hope is gainsaid. But it is useful to consider what that independence means, because the Court has a separate and distinct role from that of the Parliament and the Government."

Bryant said that in the Family Court's 30 years of "service" since commencing operations on 5 January 1976 there had been 69 Acts of the Commonwealth Parliament of Australia which amended the Family Law Act 1975.

"Amongst the most recent, and possibly most significant to the principles which guide the resolution of parenting disputes and the means by which disputes are resolved, has been the Family Law Amendment (Shared Parental Responsibility) Act 2006."

Chief Justice Bryant said in 2004 the government had also published its framework statement for the reform of the Family Law System. In that statement the government identified four primary areas for reform: A greater emphasis on shared parental responsibility; the establishment of a network of Family Relationship Centres; the creation of a combined 'Family Law Registry' for the Family Court of Australia and the Federal Magistrates Court; and a less adversarial approach to children's cases.

Bryant said it was too early for any discernible trends in decision making or jurisprudence after the new Shared Parental Responsibility had passed into law.

***

At the end of October 2006 the Full Court would hear some appeals arising from interim hearings and the question of whether Cowling in its present form survived the amendments.

The Cowling case was essentially the "status quo" argument, regularly used to deny children contact with their fathers after they often ended in the mother's sole care in the weeks or months immediately following separation.

Dads On The Air later editorialised that sadly the appeals showed the weakness of the original legislation.

Bryant went on to say: "The Government's aim is to try to bring about social change, by designing a system which it is hoped will change outcomes over a period of time for a large number of the community, both those who do not seek the assistance of the court and those who do. The Court has an entirely different role.

"Its role is to resolve the disputes that come before it and where they proceed to a hearing, to determine each individual case according to the circumstances of that particular case, in the context of the Family Law Act, and in the best interests of the children in that family. Of course, the Court does not apply the law, much of which is about value judgments, in isolation. It does so in a social context.

"Much of the criticism of the Court in the past has been, in my view, because of a failure to comprehend that the discretionary nature of the considerations of what is in the best interests of an individual child in an individual family, requires making judgments about that child in that family, not all children in all families. But courts are an integral part of the arms of government.

"The hardest and most unpopular of decisions that have to be made are, and will continue to be made by the courts. Of course, the government should expect that the court will apply the law in accordance with and the spirit of the intention of government.

"But it is important to make these points at this time because the more successful the government's initiatives are in keeping the majority of separating couples out of court, then the more difficult the cases that will end up in litigation in the courts. That is already the case and will be even more so in the future."

***

Bryant went on to discuss the establishment of the network of Family Relationship Centres.

Like DOTA, Her Honour was not fully convinced: "To the extent that it is anticipated the Family Relationship Centres will help more separating families put aside their differences and reach agreement in the children's interests, the Government is to be applauded.

"Whether it is achievable in greater numbers remains to be seen but I am optimistic that attitudes can be changed with the right education, support and encouragement. Let me, however, add a word of caution.

"Any genuine change of this kind in my view will inevitably take years to be fully realised. In my own experience in practice, it took about ten years after the passing of the Family Law Act for the general community to accept that no-fault divorce was appropriate.

"Genuine reform takes time and it would be difficult indeed if these initiatives which promise much were to be seen as failures because they were evaluated in too short a time frame. Commitment is required to let the winds of change blow for sufficiently long to have a lasting impact on the climate."

Bryant also called on the government to define the future of the Family Court and whether its future lay as an appeals court.

"Whatever the government plans for the future of the Family Court is unquestionably its prerogative. But it is time for an indication by the government of what is the longer term plan for the Court and if there is none, to conceive a blueprint. The failure to do so is bad for morale within the court and could affect recruitment of potential judges."

The court's pilot program had not convinced critics who claimed the less adversarial trials gave too much power to judges and relied too heavily on poor quality family reports.

But Bryant was enthusiastic: "One of the most radical, and exciting departures from previous practice has been the development of the Less Adversarial Approach within the Family Court of Australia.

"The government put to one side a tribunal model, recommended in Every Picture Tells a Story partly on the basis that the Court would continue to embrace a less adversarial means of resolving parenting disputes.

"The nature of Less Adversarial Trial has meant a change in the manner in which hearings are conducted by Judges. All of the Judges of the Court have received training in what are essentially different communication skills and I thank all of them for their embracing of a new way of hearing cases. It is a significant change and will require ongoing support."

Bryant said an exploratory study of impacts on parenting capacity and child well being released earlier in the year showed greater satisfaction with post-court living arrangements, including for the children; significantly less difficulty in managing conflict; significantly less damage to the parenting relationship post-court and to the parent child relationship, and greater contentment and emotional stability in children after court.

***

In a subsequent evaluation of the reforms the Australian Institute of Family Studies showed this style of trial was not being used in the Federal Magistrate's Court and was only being used in a minority of cases in the Family Court. The model included limits on the size and number of affidavits and roles for family consultants that were based on pre-trial family assessments and involvement throughout the proceedings where necessary.

While family consultants and most judges believed the Family Court's less adversarial model was an improvement, particularly in the area of child focus, lawyers' views were divided, with many expressing hesitancy in endorsing the changes. Concerns include a lack of resources in the Family Court, leading to delays, more protracted and drawn-out processes, and inconsistencies in judicial approaches to case management.

Bryant also committed her court to the collection of statistics on case outcomes. "Oscar Wilde is quoted as stating that 'The only thing worse than being talked about is not being talked about.' Well, to those who have ever found themselves frustrated by media or political comment which trades on a gross generalisation or on the testimony of a dissatisfied litigant, you may well agree that it is far worse again to be spoken of inaccurately.

"The dissemination of statistics will enable the Court to address claims regarding the orders that it makes, including any suggestion of bias towards one parent or the other.

"There are many reasons why it is essential that the Court use its best endeavours to address inaccurate comments and misapprehensions as to the role of the Court and the nature of its objectivity. It is likely to compound the confusion of a litigant if they lack confidence in the Court because they have been exposed to misleading information.

"Criticism can further lead to a general lessening of confidence in the law, the erosion of the rule of law."

***

In November of 2006 the long awaited changes to Australia's child support system passed through parliament. The laws, as recommended by the Child Support Task Force, introduced a new formula for calculating liabilities. For the first time, the incomes of both custodial and non-custodial parents would be given equal weight. The new formula took into account the added costs of caring for teenagers and gave non-resident parents a discount on their payments if they looked after their children at least one night a week.

Dads In Distress and fathers groups in general were supportive of the changes. "We've been after a more transparent and equitable arrangement and now we've got that," Tony Miller said. "A reasonable and balanced expectation of support will help fathers meet their commitments to support the raising of their children, something the members of our group have been asking for years.

"Five men a day commit suicide in this country many because of the burden previously placed upon them by an unreasonable and unworkable child support system. These changes will go some way in helping those fathers already devastated by separation from their children to cope with the often heavy burden of supporting them financially and emotionally from outside the family.

"The changes to the Family Law Act introduced earlier this year made it easier legally for fathers to continue the relationship with their children post separation, these changes will make it easier for them to do so financially."

***

Figures from the Child Support Agency showed that more men were applying to become the primary carer of their children after their relationships ended, and one in five single-parent families were now headed by fathers. In June 1997 only 7.5 percent of people receiving child support payments were men. But figures released by the Federal Government showed that by the end of 2006, 21 percent of applications were from men, a jump being attributed to changing social attitudes.

"What we're seeing through our dealings with parents is dads wanting to play a greater role in their children's lives," said the CSA'S David Mole. "The trend is a welcome development. We're more flexible now with working part-time and the types of jobs people take up which might allow them to be the primary carer for children. That's reflected in more of a balance in caring arrangements with both parents playing a greater role."

Researcher Dr Bruce Smyth said: "You're getting an early read on the signs dads are becoming more involved."

The figures also showed that non-custodial parents who paid child support to the custodial parent were spending more time with their children. Nearly 10 per cent now look after their children for at least 30 percent of the time, while only 4.4 per cent did so in 1999.

The then Minister for Human Services Chris Ellison said the figures were a bright spot amid the difficulties of failing relationships.

"While no one wants relationships to fail, many families in Australia manage to go forward positively with their lives after separation and increasingly children are benefitting from more contact with both parents," he said.

***

In December of 2006 the Family Court and the country's longest serving judge Kemeri Murray, who had joined the court in 1972, delivered a broadside at the law reforms during her retirement ceremony in Adelaide.

She told the 200-strong crowd she was concerned that staff at the Relationship Centres were not obliged by law to tell separating couples that any parenting agreements they entered into were not legally recognised. She said she was most concerned that clients were not told they did not have to attend the compulsory mediation sessions if they were victims of domestic violence.

"And if some women, particularly the women, don't know about their rights to say 'look I'm not coming to a conciliation centre, I'm not going to agree to a particular plan which gives equal time with each parent because I'm frightened of domestic violence'," she said. "If the woman doesn't know that, that's not good enough."

Justice Murray said it was vital that separating couples were aware of their legal entitlements.

"I worry about that because, of course, I don't know that it's the workers' duties at the centres to tell parties their legal rights," she said. "The fact is I think there should be an obligation on them. They should be able to tell parties that come if you want to enter into a parenting plan, fine, but it's not binding."

***

In the same month Bryant came out strongly defending the Court against the frequently alleged bias. On the day before Christmas, the single most emotional and distressing time of the year for separated fathers who would not be seeing their children as a result of the Court's decisions, Bryant was quoted in *The Age* newspaper in Melbourne: "One of the things that frustrates me most is people saying that the court is biased – or that there is a systemic bias against fathers."

The timing of the claims showed an extraordinary insensitivity. The last thing a separated dad wants to hear if he's not seeing his kids on Christmas Day is that some heartless overpaid out-of-touch judicial officer believes it's all in their children's best interests.

Reporter Liz Porter wrote that, stung by criticism that it is biased, the Family Court was hitting back by keeping detailed records of its parenting orders.

Bryant said the court had already started documenting the number of shared parental responsibility arrangements and the number of orders where a mother or father was given sole responsibility for children.

Reasons for the exclusion of one parent were also being recorded, with the categories including "family violence", "mental illness", "substance abuse", "distance" and "entrenched conflict".

What Bryant neglected to say was that the court was being obliged to keep these statistics by the Attorney General's Department.

"With the parliamentary inquiry recently there was a lot of discussion about what the court was and wasn't doing," Justice Bryant said."There were a lot of people saying the court was biased. But nobody pulled out a judgement and said 'the result was wrong'. It was all about impressions and rhetoric and the court itself wasn't really able to respond well to that because we don't have the data."

***

While the shared parental responsibility legislation was now law, there was no let up from those beating the domestic violence drum.

Kowtowing to the feminist constituency within his own party, NSW Premier Morris Iemma called for changes to the co-parenting laws for separated parents.

He said it appeared the new laws were not working because they ended up, in some cases, having a "perverse" effect on women and children who had escaped abusive relationships.

"I would say that, certainly, the Federal authorities ought to heed the message of those victims who are now recounting how a black and white application of a 50:50 co- parenting rule, without taking into account circumstances, has the perverse effect of making life worse for the woman and for the child.

"Rather than making it better, it is actually increasing the harassment and the intimidation and prevents the mother and the child from rebuilding their lives."

lemma made the comments to an audience of domestic violence support groups after announcing an extra $28 million four-year package to improve support services for victims.

***

But there were other voices. In an interview which attracted attention around the world Dads On The Air interviewed Erin Pizzey, who founded the first women's refuge in 1971.

Picking up the story in the *Herald Sun*, columnist Bettina Arndt recorded how Pizzey became disenchanted when the refuge movement was hijacked by women promoting anti-male agendas.

"Since then, she has been fighting a mighty battle to expose the truth about family violence: namely that girls and boys, who are exposed to violence in early childhood, can grow up to repeat what they have learnt.

"She's written books and articles exposing the anti-male myths being propagated about domestic violence, documenting research that shows domestic violence is often reciprocal, with men and women locked into destructive behaviour.

"As she explained in her radio interview with Dads on the Air this week it made her unpopular with British feminists who had turned domestic violence into a million dollar industry. She received death threats and was heckled while speaking publicly in the UK and US. Yet, she continues to speak out about the failure to recognise that women can be equally complicit in such violence. It's not in our interests, she says, for women to be continually taught they are victims."

Pizzey took a swipe at Australia's Violence Against Women campaigns, which showed a parade of violent men. There was never a hint that men are sometimes victims.

"It's a terrible lie," said Pizzey.

***

In the same month the Australian Institute of Family Studies produced a report Allegations of Family Violence and Child Abuse in Family Law Children's Proceedings. It examined 399 cases and found most involved allegations of violence, often from both sides. In these circumstances, where unsubstantiated allegations fly in both directions, it's just too hard for judges to see the wood for the trees, suggested the AIFS researchers.

They found it was rare for judgments to deny contact on the basis of such allegations.

The report was critical of Australian research on violence in Family Court matters. The report showed much of the research relied on small, carefully selected samples to draw misleading conclusions about male violence.

The AIFS report said this blinkered research "rarely concedes the possibility that at least some of the violence may be situational, one-off, reciprocated, or even at times initiated by women."

With heightened attention on the Family Court and its alleged mistreatment of fathers in early 2007, the rare story of a mother jailed in a custody dispute was of particular significance.

In March, writing in Sydney's *Daily Telegraph*, Janet Fife-Yeomans recorded that a mother-of-two was behind bars for defying court orders. The woman, 31, was given a choice by the Federal Magistrates' Court: let the father see his children or go to jail.

Magistrate Michael Jarrett adjourned the case for 15 minutes but when he returned to the bench, the woman, already on a good behaviour bond for refusing access to her ex- partner, remained unrepentant. Mr Jarrett took the rare step of jailing her for four months.

The woman was sent to Grafton Jail and her children, a girl aged six and a boy aged eight, were with their father, 41, who was granted full custody.

The father's solicitor, Steven Tester, said the magistrate had no choice. "No one wanted to see the mother go to jail. The point of these kinds of cases is that there are laws in place and they apply to everyone. Compliance is not optional."

It was the culmination of six years and 22 Family Court and Federal Magistrates' Court hearings since the couple split when the woman was a few weeks pregnant with their second child.

Her claim that her children would be in danger from their father, who had a number of criminal convictions, was rejected by the court.

***

In May, the Full Bench of the Family Court, made up of three judges, halved the mother's four-month sentence and released her from jail immediately.

Still unrepentant, the mother declared she would do it all again.

She said her children were "extremely confused" after the court ordered the father to return the children to their mother the day after she got out of jail.

The Family Court restricted the father's access to six hours a month.

In their judgement the Family Court said the woman should never have been jailed.

Tony Miller of Dads In Distress commented: "Dad now receives six lousy hours a month and this is justice? What is the message we are now sending mothers who contravene orders? Simple, keep doing it and you will get away with it."

Barry Williams at Lone Fathers declared that being an election year it was vital, particularly should there be a change of government, that the changes made to family law and child support systems by the current government were maintained.

"This can only be achieved by people speaking up and to the people, the politicians, that make the law," he said. "Many of the changes made over the past few years have been as a direct result of participation by Ministers, Federal Members and persons affected by the family breakdown coming together."

***

With both sides of politics in election mode, in October columnist Bettina Arndt questioned in the *Canberra Times*: "Is Kevin Rudd interested in men? The answer, sadly, seems to be no. Rudd, unlike John Howard, rarely talks about issues affecting many of his own gender, such as family law, child support, fatherless families, boys' education.

"Indeed, this potential prime minister seems content to hand over the running on most social issues to female colleagues renowned for their anti-male bias. For anyone keen to ensure men and boys receive a fair go, the prospect of a Labor government is all bad news.

"As a prime minister, Howard has been most unusual in his passion for social issues, suggesting it isn't in our society's interest to encourage more fatherless families."

Arndt said Howard had picked up on community discontent about children losing contact with fathers after divorce and set up a bipartisan committee to look into the "rebuttable presumption of joint custody". But Labor's Jennie George and Jennie Macklin dug in and the committee was forced to water down its recommendations.

"Yet resulting changes to the Family Law Act have done much to ensure children's rights to contact with both parents. Labor reluctantly supported the legislation, with Rudd expressing great concern about the changes.

"He deferred to his then shadow Attorney general, Nicola Roxon, to spell out these concerns, who played up the fear that children would be forced to spend time with dangerous dads. She had previously dismissed the custody inquiry as dog-whistle politics to men's groups aggrieved by the Family Court.

"Labor's disdain for such groups is consistently demonstrated as Labor shadow ministers refuse to meet even the most respected of these organisations, despite strenuous efforts by a sprinkling of Labor backbenchers to encourage their party to take interest."

Arndt concluded that one main reason former Prime Minister Paul Keating lost power was the perception that Labor governed for some rather than for all. "The 750,000 non-resident parents in Australia should be wary that their interests have no place on a Labor agenda."

SEVENTEEN
MAKE NO MISTAKE ABOUT IT

COME 2007, and the fatherhood movement in Australia was still very much alive.

Not long before the Howard government lost power at the end of 2007 I was asked to give a speech to the Lone Fathers Conference at Parliament in Canberra which was titled: "The Family Law Reforms: Are They Working?"

DOTA's musical talent, Peter van de Voorde and Ian Purdie, had both brought their guitars and opened with a song to the tune of "Killing Me Softly" they had penned on the drive down from Sydney:

> Ruining my life with his reforms
> Wrecking my kids with his laws
> Killing me softly with his lies
> Taking my kids my whole life
> Giving it all to my ex-wife
> Killing me softly with his reforms
> I heard he was a good man
> I heard he had a plan
> So I voted for him
> Fell for his cruel scam
> Now I am left with nothing
> Kids and money gone
> Ruining my life with his reforms
> Wrecking my kids with his laws
> Killing me softly with his reforms.

The speech was greeted with enthusiasm by many of the fathers present at the well attended conference, and something akin to horror by the organisers, who were close to the incumbent government and concerned about what would happen with fatherhood issues if Labor came to power.

This, in part, is what I said:

Have Howard's family law and child support reforms been a success?

Absolutely not.

To understand why an air of decay and deceit has adhered to a dying Howard government, you need look no further than the Howard government's treatment of separated dads and their families.

It is a case study of how this government has dealt with social issues, with the electorate; and yes, with their once staunch supporters.

And why they are now on the nose from coast to coast.

By flirting with the separated father vote and then discarding it, by holding in front of grieving and distressed men who have had their children arbitrarily ripped off them the possibility that they could get to see their kids again, by promising and promoting family law reform and then failing to deliver, John Howard and his government have committed emotional abuse on a massive scale.

Hundreds of kids will have their relationships with their fathers destroyed this week by a multi-billion dollar bureaucratic and judicial juggernaut which makes its living off ripping kids away from their dads and creating that social artifice – the single mother as a modern day, noble hero.

Just like every other week in the 11 years the Howard government has been in power.

Hundreds of thousands of the nation's children have suffered the dreadful abuse of being denied a proper relationship with their fathers while a gutless Howard government has looked on, too afraid they might lose a few women's votes if they stood up for dads.

The Howard government has badly badly misread the politics around separated dads and their families.

For every woman who's supposedly advantaged by the blatant bias of the court, other women; grandparents, aunts, friends, are hurt by the outdated and draconian implementation of the court's sole custody regime. They would have won a damn sight more votes if they had stood up for what people once believed they stood for – fair treatment.

For every single mother out there – for some bizarre reason regarded in most cases as heroic for bloody mindedly and selfishly and often purely for financial reasons refusing to let their kids have a proper relationship with their dads – and those figures have gone up under the Howard government – there's a desperate dad who would love to be able to care for his kids.

It is often estimated there are about a million votes in the separated dad lobby; not that the small, unfashionable, atomised and marginally or minutely funded fathers groups are all that large or influential but the issues that concern them and the so-called "silent majority" they represent most certainly are.

I bet about now, with the polls indicating that the government faces annihilation at the coming election, Howard wishes he had a million votes in his pocket, I bet about now he's wishing he hadn't double crossed the dads; their kids, their grandparents and all those people in separated and blended families whose views, experiences and presentations to government he has ignored.

***

Dads would have died in the ditch for Johnny Howard in September 2003 when he publicly stated he was drawn to shared parenting and would be initiating a wide ranging inquiry into child custody. He brought great hope to hundreds of thousands of desperately sad separated parents who thought that for the first time ever we had a Prime Minister who understood their heart ache and was going to do something about the country's most despised, dysfunctional, discredited and destructive institutions, the Family Court and the Child Support Agency.

To illustrate just how far the Howard government has fallen in moral stature and in public standing, it's worth remembering back to the immediate aftermath of that 2003 announcement; the positive front page headlines around the country, the way talk back radio ran hot in support with call after call detailing the devastation being felt by separated parents. Television, too, ran numerous positive stories praising Howard for his vision and his government for its enlightened courage in finally fronting up to the desperately overdue need to reform family law. Separated parents happily and cooperatively caring for their kids after separation filled our screens.

In short, Howard won strong support from within the nation's media, widespread and excellent coverage and kudos for his government and praise for having the gumption to take on the entrenched interests of the judiciary and an out of touch and out of date bureaucracy.

It's a long time now since Howard has seen wall to wall positive front page headlines. He thrashes around trying to reignite that sense of coherence and excitement, desperately trying to solve his political problems with arbitrary National Water Plans, Climate Change announcements on YouTube, dolloping out yet more money on co-payments for superannuation, ramping up concern over national security. None of it works.

What did work, but is working no longer; was the government's flirtation with shared parenting or joint custody of children.

At the time of the original announcements Howard was almost universally acclaimed for his bold vision in fixing a terrible social problem curdling people's lives, destroying people's faith in the judiciary and the political process, damaging children and eating away at the social fabric.

Some of the toughest women journalists in the country, including Madonna King in Brisbane and Paola Totaro in Sydney, wrote moving opinion pieces in favour of joint custody, relaying their own experiences and the experiences of friends in dealing with separation and how they had to learn to behave with maturity for the sake of their children.

Which makes the government's actions even more puzzling: why did they backtrack; why did they double cross the dads when they had so much community and media support for change??

***

While many people will tell pollsters they are concerned about global warming or funding for public hospitals and schools, there are very few actual vote-changing issues. Make no mistake about it, your children are a vote changing issue.

If a politician comes along and tells a grieving, heart broken dad who has had his children arbitrarily ripped from him by an arrogant and uncaring judge and told it is in their best interests that he only see them occasionally, if at all, if a politician tells that father he will get his children back for him, he's going to vote for that person, no matter what party they come from. No matter what their policies on other issues are.

If a politician tells a deeply upset and distressed grandmother who can't get to see her beloved grandkids that his or her government is going to tackle the grotesque unfairness of family law, that is more than enough to sway that grandmother's vote.

In effect, that's what Howard did. By expressing support for the notion of joint custody aka shared parenting, he won the hearts and minds of separated dads around the country, and staunch support from many of the women in those fathers' lives, mothers, sisters, work colleagues, and of course lovers, the so-called second wives brigade.

Fast forward to 2007; and the end of the story is very sad indeed.

By flirting with the separated father vote and then discarding it, by holding in front of grieving and distressed men who have had their children ripped off them the possibility they could get to see their kids again, by promising and promoting family law reform and then failing to deliver, John Howard and his government have committed emotional abuse on a massive scale.

Despite all the evidence justifying reform of family law and child support; Howard failed to act; instead blinding people with smoke and mirrors. He has wasted hundreds of millions of dollars setting up so-called Relationship Centres, staffed without exception by the very same type of people who made the mess in the first place; by opponents of shared parenting, that is by opponents of the fair and equal treatment of fathers and opponents of letting children have good, strong, equal relationships with both parents.

These centres, peddled as the solution to taking the heat out of family law, instantly turned into yet another bureaucratic layer that separated parents have to negotiate.

***

Just the other day a story came to us of a father, recently separated and desperate to see his kids, who couldn't get any sense out of his local centre whatsoever. Privacy legislation, he was told, forbade them from telling him whether or not his ex-wife had agreed to his request for mediation.

Meanwhile, the "status quo" arguments used so devastatingly by lawyers against fathers was settling in; and he was rapidly becoming just another bloke who barely if ever gets to see his kids. Next thing in his life was going to be the loss of most if not all of his assets; the court can and often enough does make orders for 90 percent of the couple's assets to go to the wife, and then the loss of much of his income through child support.

A separated father in this country with four kids on a not particularly flash income can end up paying 84.5 cents in the dollar in tax, child support and the medicare levy. Separated fathers who've been to see John Howard report back that he treats them with courtesy, and has expressed astonishment at the high levels of taxation and child support they are paying.

But Howard's done nothing to abolish this modern day slavery; instead his government routinely and proudly announces yet more crackdowns on separated fathers, blocking them from leaving the country, hunting them down wherever they may be with the almost Gestapo style tacts of the despised Child Support Agency.

For some ludicrous reason bashing up on separated dads is seen as a vote winner.

The situation of fathers post separation has deteriorated disgracefully over the last 11 years and the only government member with enough common decency, courage and old-fashioned gumption to speak out on the issue has been maverik Liberal MP Alby Schultz.

Howard's failure to take appropriate action to fix the Family Court and the Child Support Agency, these hated and discredited relics from the 70s and 80s, and his failure to remedy the overweening bias of the family law units of Legal Aid has been a disgrace.

***

With the community, the media and significant elements of the legal profession uniting in their support for change, Prime Minister John Howard was presented with an historic opportunity to fix this rotten situation.

Prime Minister Howard's abject failure to act to remedy the rampant anti-male anti-father bias in his government's bureaucracies and in the courts means he has failed millions of the nation's children, both the present generation and many generations to come.

The Attorney General Phillip Ruddock, who has been a guest on Dads On The Air on a number of occasions and is speaking at this conference, went around the country, no doubt at great expense, telling everyone that his government had passed the most significant reforms to family law in 30 years.

With all due respect, as the lawyers like to say, the Howard government did nothing of the kind.

A little light housekeeping? asked the last tax-payer funded family law junket aka conference in Perth. That's how much respect the profession had for the reforms.

And I'm here to tell you: there hasn't even been any light housekeeping, as recent judgements on appeal have clearly demonstrated.

One of the saddest sights for those of us who have followed family law in Australia was the intense "tea leaf" reading of judgements and appeals by fathers after the legislation was introduced. Any judgement which showed even the slightest indication that the Court might at last be acting fairly towards fathers and their children was pored over intensely on the many internet chat lines and forums which have sprung up in recent years.

Time and again, without fail, fathers' advocates have found themselves bitterly disappointed. Even the government's own favourite academic, family law insider Patrick Parkinson, has admitted that the appeal judgements are all over the place and failing to fulfil the intent of the legislation; which allegedly was to improve children's relationships with their fathers post separation.

One classic example of a case being touted as a sign that common sense was finally starting to filter into family law and the judges and magistrates were finally starting to see reason was that of a Lismore mother of two young children, a boy aged eight and a girl aged six, who was jailed for four months by the Federal Magistrates Court after she repeatedly flouted orders to let the children see their father.

Jailed by Federal Magistrate Michael Jarrett, an event so rare it made judicial history, the mother's case quickly ended up before the Full Bench of the Family Court. Most people have to wait at least a year for such a hearing.

The woman was promptly released and awarded full custody of her children. She declared she would do it all again.

Steven Tester, the father's solicitor, said the children had "a ball" living with their dad.

Court orders now restrict the father's access to six hours a month. I bet you right now that's one sad dad.

Make no mistake about it; denying kids a relationship with their dad is child abuse, pure and simple.

Make no mistake about it, that judgement illustrates what many of us already knew: Family Court orders aren't worth the paper they're written on. And they amply demonstrate what many of us have said from the outset, the government's so-called family law reforms are completely useless.

If a vengeful, abusive and vindictive mother wants to deny her children a relationship with their father the courts, the state, even the police, will back her to the hilt.

***

Another example highlighting the current system's failure is a recent case presided over by Justice Le Poer Trench in Sydney on the 15th of May 2007.

In it, the Judge criticises the current adversarial system of Family Law, and sums up what all those that have been there already know, "This case illustrates to me the very worst of impacts on a family of the adversarial system."

There were a combined 140 pages of affidavits, 428 paragraphs, 201 pages of annexures and 102 exhibits. With this exercise in futility, the lawyers were able to plunder $220,000 from the family wealth in order for the parents to obtain some sort of "Shared Parenting arrangement".

The question has to be asked: "Who has a spare $220,000 laying around to hand over to the lawyers in order to achieve an outcome which, as has been shown by recent outcomes, can so easily be reversed on appeal by the Full Bench?????"

The fact that the Parliament as a whole has so little insight into this human tragedy playing out in the Australian community is alarming. The Parliament's combined ignorance of the ramifications of their failure to properly legislate for relief of the plight of the nations' fathers and their children is a sad reflection of a lack of moral courage, intellect and common decency needed to eradicate this continued systemic attack on the basic human rights of the nations' children and their fathers.

We as a nation have a duty of care to protect the rights of our children. If we continue to get this wrong, if we continue to pretend that our current path of destroying father/child relationships is acceptable, if we continue to shy away from a presumption of a shared parenting outcome, as a starting point, then we are failing our duty of care and history will see this failure as being one of the great moral evils of our time.

The Family Court has always been a law unto itself; disdainful of its critics, contemptuous of the general social values of the community and paying little heed of or respect towards parliament. Anyone with half a brain should have been able to see that it was never going to change its spots, that introducing some ridiculously vague notion called shared responsibility while leaving the judge's discretion as paramount would do nothing to alter this secretive and unaccountable court's conduct, its championing of single mothers and its clear belief that fathers have little or no value in a child's life.

Dads on the Air declared at the time this weak, watered down "shared responsibility" legislation was passed through parliament that "the liars, the lawyers, the bureaucrats and the social engineers have won the day".

Everything that has happened since confirms that view.

***

All John Howard had to do was play a straight bat. All he had to do was treat the citizens of this country fairly and equally, regardless of their gender. All he had to do was make sure our courts and bureaucracies complied with the latest sociological research, which backs up what commonsense has already told us, that kids do best when they have a mum and dad in their lives.

Flirting with the separated dad vote – and don't forget this includes aunts, uncles and grandparents – was one of the worst things the Howard government has ever done. It constituted emotional abuse on a massive scale.

Before we trace the history of how we got here, it is necessary to understand how abject the Howard government's failings in this area, let's not forget, this legislation was passed through literally in the middle of the night; well after midnight.

While the Democrats Natasha Stott Despoja, one of the earliest self-avowed feminists to flounce and pronounce across Australia's political landscape, showed not the slightest sympathy for separated blokes, she was right about one thing when she warned during that long and disgraceful session of the senate which saw this legislation passed so thoughtlessly into law – that the nation would one day regret having rushed through, so rapidly, with so little oversight and with so little thought, such important life altering legislation.

While it's impossible to say that the legislation was passed "secretly"; it may as well have been. It was passed in the dead of night well after the deadlines of every major media outlet, print, radio and television.

***

Before we move on; it is worth pointing out that an ever revolving door of politicians taking brief responsibility for the Child Support Agency have been on to Dads On The Air, including Ross Cameron, remember him? And Larry Anthony, remember him? Not one of them could tell us how many of their clients were dying; despite every father's group in the country making the claim that there was a direct link between the bureaucratic abuses of the Agency and the high death rate of separated fathers. And what is worse: from what we can tell not one of them, after being asked the question, bothered to investigate the issue.

Indeed, we recently had yet another politician briefly responsible for the Agency, Joe Hockey, declaring that he and his government would pursue separated fathers who owed child support to the grave. As we put up on our website: News flash Joe, you and your government are already doing it.

At that time last year, it almost seems historical so much has happened, there was no more disgusting sight in public life than the sight of a cherubic Joe Hockey, with his well fed belly, his massive income and his intact family; boasting about how he was going to pursue dads unfortunate enough to have become divorced, "to the grave".

All he had to do was follow the advice of his own government's chief legal adviser, The Australian Law Reform Commission.

The Commission, in 1999, delivered its massive Managing Justice - a compilation of inquiries and reports into the Federal justice system which included the most extensive study of the Family Court of Australia ever conducted, including interviewing more than 3,000 clients.

The Commission found overwhelming disquiet within the legal profession and within the community over the operations of family law in this country and recommended an external review – that is a Royal Commission or something similar.

Put simply: the Family Court is regarded as a disaster zone by much of the legal profession. Every lawyer out there knows how utterly arbitrary its decision making processes are and how farcical its notions of evidence.

Indeed the Family "Court" is not a court as understood by the general population, hearing evidence, balancing claims, treating the constituents who come before it with respect.

But playing fair, doing the right thing by the nation's children, was the last thing Howard and his government did.

The Howard government's role throughout the family law inquiry was pernicious and duplicitous.

Will anyone ever forget those remarkably offensive comments by the then so-called "Sex Discrimination" Commissioner Pru Goward, who at one of the public hearings declared that fathers would need an auto-cue to remember the names of their children.

You don't get much more disgusting or much more offensive than that.

Why should Australian men pay taxes to support the magnificent wage of a Sex Discrimination Commissioner who both in public and behind the scenes waged a campaign against shared parenting – that is against allowing children to have a decent level of contact with their fathers; or to allow the fathers to care for their much loved kids.

***

The chickens, as some headlines have suggested, are coming home to roost for the Howard government.

It did its level best not to appear to be reacting to, or even paying the slightest bit of attention, to the various fathers groups around the country.

The public inquiry; which unveiled so much poignant material and provided more than enough evidence to shut down the present system and to introduce joint custody as the norm; was instead overwhelmed by taxpayer funded domestic violence advocates peddling the outdated 70s notion of women as victims and men as abusive members of the patriarchy.

To these angry hate filled and taxpayer fuelled advocates there's no such thing as a good man or a good father. By blocking up the schedule with these people and downgrading the unfunded lobby groups and streams of individuals who wanted to have a say, the family law inquiry cheerfully distorted both the information publicly available and the final results.

What was produced was that ridiculously bad report Every Picture Tells A Story; while the politicians all congratulated each other in parliament over the report with high-flying words and Kay Hull and her group were proud to announce that they had reached bipartisan agreement, even the most cursory reading of this report showed what a pathetic effort it was.

Written by a Family and Community Services bureaucrat who was then promptly moved from her position so that she didn't have to take responsibility for the rotten outcome; Every Picture Tells A Story was exactly like a Family Court judgement: it bore no relationship to the evidence and no relationship to reality.

***

In DOTA's submission we warned to no avail that scandals would continue to emerge about the Family Court, bringing discredit to the government of the day and to the legal profession.

Such has well proved to be the case; and yet the monolithic arrogance and disregard both of its political custodians and of the court itself continues unabated and unchanged.

And indeed scandals do continue to rock the court. Remember the recent front page headlines of the court ordering a Tasmanian boy into the household of his stripper mother and her boyfriend — a porn addict who had collected hundreds of thousands of pornographic images, including of prepubescent girls.

The court decreed that the boy was fine because the man's obsession was with young girls, not boys.

The frantic grandmothers; desperate to protect their young grandson and give the kid a decent home and a decent start in life, went to the media.

Their reward. A judge of the court castigated the couple for daring to take the case to the media; thereby endangering "the best interests of the child". You have to be joking!!!

But what is sadder still: the only thing unusual about this case was that the media actually wrote about it.

While their traditional working class supporters have been ravaged by the impacts of the Family Court and the Child Support Agency, there has been not one whisper of concern or discontent with the outrageous conduct of these institutions from the Labor Party itself.

While Howard's duplicitous two-faced double crossing of fathers has been shameful to behold, don't think for one minute incoming Prime Minister Kevin Rudd will be any better.

An unholy alliance of elite opinion; of bureaucrats, lawyers, politicians and so-called "experts", with the complicity of the Liberal National Party coalition and full cooperation of the Labor Party, took the family law reform process hostage. Much of this was done under the guise of that great motherhood issue, domestic violence.

Instead of listening to the people, the schedulers of the public inquiry jammed it full of taxpayer funded advocates; all of whom were keen to paint men as violent patriarchal brutes and women as their hapless, defenceless victims in urgent need of protection by the state.

Indeed the Howard government was embarrassed by the support it originally got from men's groups and peddled rapidly away from them.

Treasurer Peter Costello declared to anyone who would listen that he wanted Australia to be the best country in the world for women. Not for men, not for children, not for the community as a whole, for women; and women alone. As if men were a mere appendage, here to service the nobler sex.

The government, thinking it was onto a winning issue which would make it look good as a protector of women, ignored all the warnings that writing domestic violence into family law legislation was inappropriate and would escalate the volume of false allegations – anecdotally reported to have jumped by some 50 percent.

Violence is a crime; it's a matter for the police. It's not a matter for ideologues in a secretive and unaccountable tribunal like the Family Court to use as an excuse for the perpetration of anti-father ideologies and the denial of children a right to know, to have a relationship with and to be cared for by their dads.

Tens upon tens of thousands of fathers who have lost contact with their children as a result of false allegations of sexual misconduct or violence can attest to the fact that the court is not a court of fact; that what it regards as evidence bears no relationship to reality and that the court's evidentiary bar for these sorts of claims is ludicrously low.

Just as in the British Family Courts, even more secretive than our own, where fathers have been jailed for waving at their children, so too fathers in Australia are denied contact with their children on completely spurious grounds. One father, a successful businessman, lost his case because the judge accused him of having a "controlling intelligence". Another father was jailed when he defied court orders and sent his kids a Christmas card.

It is hard to believe that these sorts of abuses are going on in a country like Australia. But the issue has hit a tipping point. Most Australians by now have met or know separated dads; as lovers, sons, brothers, friends, even as just that lonely bloke over the road who looks so sad after his kids go back to his former wife on Sunday afternoon. Or as that work colleague suddenly in tears at his desk. And word is well and truly out that they've been dudded.

***

Absolute power corrupts absolutely. There is a very strange pathology within the court; protected by the some of the most draconian secrecy legislation in the country; protected by the fact that Australia ranks 35th in the world in terms of press freedom and protected, too, by the currents and fashions in academe and in journalism which has in the past few decades seen the pack mentality of extremist feminism dominate the entire public debate.

A father who speaks out about the injustices perpetrated against him and his children is dismissed as little more than an embarrassing joke; an unreconstructed Neanderthal, a member of the great unwashed who has not grasped the nobler visions of the educated liberal class. He is immediately classed as a defender of domestic violence, an abuser of women who wants to keep them subjugated, chained to the kitchen sink. For 99.99 percent of them, nothing, of course, could be further from the truth.

Most of these men have daughters who they want to see have careers, working partners they are enormously proud of and mothers they bend over backwards to protect and support. Yet when these same blokes speak about injustices being perpetrated against parents by fundamentally misguided and biased ideologues they are dismissed as somehow anti-woman.

What they are is anti-injustice.

And let's not forget the Violence Against Women: Australia Says No campaign.

This utterly dishonest campaign, costing tens of millions of dollars; hundreds of millions if you include all the associated programs, has reached into the country's lounge rooms and into people's lives. No bloke in this country can even go to the urinals at the movies these days without being assaulted with domestic violence propaganda, finding themselves staring at a picture of some limpid male who, as many commentators have observed, looks like he'd rather kiss you than hit you.

This government knew perfectly well that there is no evidence from anywhere in the world that these types of campaigns decrease interpersonal violence.

They knew perfectly well that far from resolving a community issue the deliberate promotion of public hysteria over domestic violence was likely to increase the rate of false and puerile allegations or simply have the opposite to the intended effect.

Equality is equality. You don't get progress and you don't get social justice by advancing the interests of one gender over the other. When you do, all you get is backlash from the great unwashed who have been ignored. That, in the end, is what this country will face as a result of the perfidy of John Howard and his government.

So sceptical were Dads On The Air of the watered down "reforms" that we asked the Attorney General Phillip Ruddock when he came on to our program last year what would he do if the Family Court remained the anti-father cesspit that it is today.

Somewhat taken aback by the question, he responded that yes, he had seen some terrible judgements by the court and if it did not reform itself the government would revisit the issue and change the legislation.

Well it's now perfectly clear that the court has no intention of changing its ways, has no intention of reforming its style of custody orders, is impervious to outside criticism and is an unfit organisation to be making decisions over the future of our children.

So will the government be revisiting the legislation?

Unfortunately, it's all too late.

The government is likely to be thrashed in the polls, and a Labor government will not confront its ideological anti-nuclear family cronies in the bureaucracy and the judiciary. Prime Minister John Howard missed a once in a generation opportunity to fix this poisonous system and blew it. Millions of parents, and millions of children, now and into the future, will suffer as a consequence.

EIGHTEEN
WORST CASE SCENARIO

The Conservatives lost the 2007 election and Labor wasted no time setting out dismantling the changes to Family Law.

On 3 December 2007 Kevin Rudd was sworn in as Prime Minister of Australia.

Labor was back in power in Australia federally after more than a decade in the wilderness. The reactionary forces in the family law industry now had the ear of government. They wasted little time.

The incoming Labor government moved quickly to appease its academic, bureaucratic and feminist constituencies by announcing an overhaul of the new family law reforms – ostensibly to protect the safety of women and children.

To the dismay of every father's group in the country in July 2008 the Attorney General Robert McClelland appointed former Family Court judge Richard Chisholm to head yet another inquiry into family law, this time focusing on issues of family violence.

The former Family Court judge's hostility to the shared parenting laws, his espousing of radical feminist analyses of family life and the patriarchy, his close relationship to the former Chief Justice Alastair Nicholson and his antipathy towards separated fathers were well known.

This was the same Chisholm who at the 12th National Family Law Conference had started his talk about the Family Law Act amendments by singing, to the tune of On Top of Old Smokey: "It seems rather blokey the men won the fights, but now they all tell us it's about children's' rights…"

Chisholm had previously declared the new legislation should make no difference to outcomes because of the court's continuing obligation to act in the best interests of children. Chisholm's appointment by the Rudd government was compared by family law reformers to putting a fox in charge of the chicken coop.

It was a classic government strategy, to appoint a supposedly independent figure whose biases concurred with their own in order to produce a report to their liking. There was nothing independent about Chisholm.

Co-author of the book *Shared Parenting* Michael Green QC, who had never been consulted by the so-called experts running the Labor government's review of the legislation, put out a statement: "The worst is happening: the appointment of Richard Chisholm to review the legislation will inevitably see regressive change to the shared parenting provisions.

"The Labor Party has always listened to the feminists and their social policy is heavily influenced by them.

"Now is the time to start writing to your federal members and the Attorney General. Remind them that we can harness over a million votes at the next election. The future of over a million children is at stake."

***

With the appointment of Chisholm, Nicholson finally had his revenge.

When it became patently obvious that the Australian Institute of Family Studies meticulous research on the impacts of the new laws would find that they were popular with the public and had not increased levels of conflict, the Rudd government and the apparatchiks in the Attorney General's Department launched a blizzard of counter-balancing reports.

The Institute had been established under the same legislation as the Family Court as the appropriate body to research its social impacts.

One of the newly commissioned reports only interviewed disgruntled women in domestic violence refuges, who were, naturally enough, of the view that shared parenting did not work.

When Chisholm's review of Family Courts and Violence was delivered he described the laws as "a tangle of legal technicality" which had taken the focus off the best interests of the child and were both confusing and troublesome.

He advocated abandoning the push towards shared parenting.

Chisholm's report said many people wrongly believed the changes to family law meant that separated fathers were automatically entitled to 50-50 custody of their kids.

He wrote: "The presumption of equal parental responsibility has been wrongly taken to mean that there was also a presumption favouring children spending equal time with each parent."

The retired judge argued that the provision emphasising the importance of a child's relationship with both parents should be dropped and judges required only to consider what was in the best interest of the child.

Professor Chisholm recommended family violence be presumed in all parenting cases presented to the Court and recommended every case automatically be assessed for risk of violence. He also suggested the court should receive additional funding to do the job.

Once more displaying zero neutrality, Chief Justice Bryant, issued a statement welcoming Chisholm's findings. Dads On The Air suggested that her pronouncements on the "problematic" nature of the laws and the adequacy or otherwise of the violence provisions inappropriately distorted the debate. Her position as Chief Justice should have ensured her public neutrality. She was neither a politician nor a community spokeswoman, and should have stayed right out of it.

Former Chief Justice Alastair Nicholson also declared the Chisholm recommendations were "absolutely the way I would have gone". He said changes to the Family Law Act to emphasise family violence were long overdue and the Howard government's changes to the Family Law Act had not been thought through.

"The fault lies with the legislation," Nicholson said. "I have great sympathy for the judges trying to interpret it. Absolutely, yes, it must be up to judges and magistrates to decide what is best for each child in each case.

"There was too much sound and fury and not enough proper analysis," Nicholson declared.

***

The Howard government had been scrupulous in ensuring that in such a contentious field the passing of legislation was bipartisan. The courtesy was not returned.

The painfully slow reform process of Howard, fond of hiving off contentious issues into committees, had frustrated many lobbyists. There was nothing slow about Labor's moves to turn back the clock.

The new definition of domestic violence was extremely broad. It contained a long list of matters including "behaviour that torments, intimidates, or harasses a family member. That effect could be caused by repeated derogatory taunts or racial taunts, or intentionally causing death or injury to an animal or damaging property."

Family violence would also include unreasonably controlling, dominating or deceiving a family member. This could be brought about by denying a family member financial autonomy or preventing a family member from making or keeping connections with family, friends or culture.

Threatening to commit suicide with the intention of tormenting or intimidating a family member would also be deemed family violence.

If you're not happy in a relationship, just leave. How hard is it? Why drag all this personal baggage through courts full of money grubbing lawyers and fraudulent expert witnesses. The only answer to that was: money. The same reason the lawyers were in the game. And the way the Australian system worked, to receive parenting payments after separation you needed a court order. Bang. Everybody makes money; except the loser, normally the male, whose life is frequently destroyed.

As part of Labor's proposed changes lawyers and those working in the family law system would also be required to report wider categories of abuse to child welfare authorities.

Neglect and psychological harm through exposure to family violence would join assault, sexual assault and sexual exploitation as matters that trigger mandatory reporting.

"The proposed legislative changes will not undermine the effectiveness of the Family Law Act in promoting a child's right to a meaningful relationship with both parents where there are no safety concerns," then Attorney General Robert McClelland claimed.

The broad definition of domestic violence was aimed squarely at men. In a secretive, biased and discretionary jurisdiction with extremely low standards of proof, a reputation for dishonesty and no investigative capacity of its own, where hearsay and opinion count as evidence, it is hard to see how accusations of attempting to control or dominate another family member could be proved or disproved.

The new definitions of domestic violence were so broad as to include much common human behaviour of which both genders are or certainly can be guilty.

In reality, despite all the fire and brimstone of feminist advocates and for all the smoke and haze surrounding family law, Labor Prime Minister Kevin Rudd, while making all the appropriate noises, refused to repeal the modest changes to the Family Law Act introduced by his predecessor. There's a million votes in it, he declared.

***

First cab off the rank was a report published in the journal Australian Family Lawyer which claimed that where parents cannot cooperate and remain hostile towards each other, shared-parenting arrangements could result in a higher-than-normal rate of clinical anxiety in the children.

The report was written by Jennifer McIntosh, a child psychologist and associate professor of psychology at La Trobe University with a long and close association with the Family Court across a number of projects. She was also on the Editorial Board of the Family Court Review and the Journal of Family Studies. Co-author was former Family Court judge Richard Chisholm, whose hostility to shared parenting was well established. The research was partly funded by the Family Court.

Critics saw such clearly partisan appointments as advocacy research at its worst conducted by parties who had benefited enormously from the status quo.

The report Cautionary Notes on the Shared Care of Children in Conflicted Parental Separation was based on two samples of high conflict parents already in the court system. It recommended mediators and Family Court judges screen warring couples to ensure that their level of conflict did not make them unsuitable for shared care.

McIntosh told *The Age* newspaper that to be successful, shared parenting must involve parents living close to each other and getting along well enough to have a working arrangement.

"They must each feel confident that the other is a competent parent, be financially comfortable, have family-friendly work practices and keep the child out of their disagreements," she said. "These conditions do not exist for many parents who have arrangements adjudicated by a court.

"We have a very high percentage of very high conflict families sharing the care of their children and this goes against all the good research. This is not a good situation – developmentally – for children to be in.

"Shared care puts children more frequently in the pathway of animosity and acrimony between their parents, witnessing derogatory exchanges, for example. The core issue is that shared care can inadvertently rob children of security in their relationships with both parents."

McIntosh, who was intensely disliked within the fathers and family reform groups, said the legislative and social environment had created a "shared-care frenzy", with parents entering arrangements ill-advised and ill-prepared. She claimed living in substantially shared care, being unhappy with those arrangements, and having parents in conflict were associated with poor mental health.

"One of the other realities of shared care is that it's less stable," she said. "It very often breaks down. Older children vote with their feet and say, 'I don't want to do this any more'. My concern is for the little kids who can't vote and have to live in these conditions of sharing their time between two enemies."

She said the new law "tried to do good things. It tried to say that relationships with fathers are important, and they are. My data show that too. But, inadvertently, these changes seem to be creating new difficulties."

***

In a rejoinder to the McIntosh piece, Professor Patrick Parkinson said her work needed to be put into perspective. She did not record that there had been a massive growth in equal time arrangements. She used a different definition of shared care – five days or more a fortnight.

Nor did she point out that many of the shared parenting arrangements she used in her study had been imposed by the court only on an interim basis.

"Many such arrangements will break down, and that experience can help the parents to develop more workable arrangements for the future," Parkinson said. "Children also suffer significantly from ongoing litigation, and a temporary agreement that is not at all optimal for the child might be a lesser evil than going to trial. Conflict tends to diminish. Parents can be very raw and angry in the aftermath of separation.

"As time passes, most parents manage to rebuild their lives and move on.

"McIntosh's study reports on relatively short time frames. To assess what is happening, we need to follow families in shared parenting arrangements over a longer period of time and to measure children's adjustment, as she plans to do.

"There are good reasons why the law changed. It wasn't just pressure from fathers' groups. Research – in Australia and overseas – shows that many children want more time with the non-resident parent. The international research also shows that children benefit from the active involvement of both parents where both parents are competent in the parental role, committed to it and can manage to work together without high conflict."

***

In another rejoinder to the McIntosh/Chisholm piece, the joint authors of *Shared Parenting*, mediator Michael Green and psychologist Jill Burrett wrote in a piece called The Problem With Caution: "Well publicised voices have been raised to question the wisdom and benefits of the shared parenting provisions of the amended Family Law Act. Some have pointed to suggestions of harm for children.

"Generally these affirmations have not been supported by research nor clinical data, and have been made without reference to contrasting studies and the experience of practitioners in the field.

"It is emerging that there is a minority resistance movement against the shared parenting provisions of the amended Family Law Act. This resistance appears to be located in at least three quarters, and as with similar phenomena in other areas of human activity, it captures a voice and audience which exceeds its value and rationale.

"The first is the small, strongly conservative section of the family law "industry", highly paid lawyers who tend to promote lengthy adversarial proceedings rather than effective negotiation.

"Secondly, there are women's groups, inspired by radical feminists, who see the shift in parenting patterns as a means to remove power and money from women and hand it to men.

"Thirdly, and most worrying of all, are complaints from several academics, who are using data from early research on parenting patterns following the amendments to voice concern about the wisdom of shared parenting. Unlike the US which has a large number of highly respected academics, researchers and clinicians strongly supportive of shared parenting, such a powerful voice is not apparent in Australia."

***

If there was ever any doubt by April 2008 it was becoming even clearer where Labor's sympathies lay. Kathleen Swinbourne of the Lone Parents Union was selected to participate in the much touted talkfest the 2020 Summit, which was bringing together 1,000 of the country's purportedly brightest minds. As had former Family Court Chief Justice Alastair Nicholson. But not a single member of the fatherhood movement.

DOTA editorialised: "The government has put together a list that reads more like an Australian left wing feminists' who's who than a genuine list of people who could contribute to the debate on families. Believe it or not, they have the audacity to use the word 'social inclusion' while ignoring every single figure in the fatherhood movement from coast to coast.

"John Howard blew a rare historical confluence of public and professional opinion when he baulked at introducing proper shared parenting and opted for a meaningless notion of shared responsibility for separating families.

"Now, with the left in power from coast to coast and alternative and progressive views from the fatherhood movement ignored by the reactionary elements within the massive family law industry, we are all paying the consequences for his timidity.

"The Liberal government had, for reasons known only to themselves, bent over backwards to ensure the shared parenting reforms were bipartisan. In effect this meant that a supposedly conservative party with traditional family values was allowing its social policies to be dictated by the left of the Labor Party. The legislation was significantly watered down to ensure both parties were behind it, perhaps to ensure that the accusation they were overly influenced by father's groups did not stick. The then Labor Opposition, seeing no votes for them in the issue, went along for the ride.

"In government the Labor Party did not return the favour, shamelessly pandering to their feminist, single mother and welfare constituencies."

***

Also In January 2008, demonstrating the depth of disenchantment that remained despite years of talk of reform, DOTA's own Peter van de Voorde penned "A Societal Cancer", which was widely distributed and popped up on websites around the world.

It read in part: "The Family Justice System has become a societal cancer, a place to be avoided at all cost. Like any cancer, if left unchecked, it will continue to grow, gaining momentum and eventually destroying its host victims and subsequently the culture which supports and feeds this malignant growth.

"It has removed parental rights and replaced them with parental responsibilities. However without rights, parents are denied their human right and duty to responsibly protect and share the love and care of their own biological children.

"We are now looking at a 35 year old cancer that has been allowed to grow unchecked and is by far the most dangerous place for men, women and children, to come into contact with, in the event of relationship breakdown.

"It has become a law unto itself, a dictatorship within a democracy. Secret and seemingly untouchable, it has been allowed to grow into a multi billion dollar industry, with many poisonous tentacles which have gradually and unnoticeably crept into many of our institutions and bureaucracies.

"These in turn have each spawned their own agencies and pseudo expert organisations and bodies, who play host to a variety of so called professional expert specialist advisers, who keep feeding the cancer with a continuous supply of misinformation and dodgy statistical data, which flows into the system, thereby guaranteeing malignant growth.

"All of this is made possible because society has unsuspectingly and unquestionably accepted the misleading 'Best Interest of the Child' principle."

His words turned out to be amazingly prophetic.

***

As September and Father's Day 2008 rolled around, in the typical tin-eared and abusive fashion of their feminist bureaucrats, the government used it as a chance to flog the issue of child support.

Others, such as *The Star* newspaper in Newcastle, suggested more kindly that: "This Sunday, while showing your father just how much he means to you, spare a thought for the separated dads who won't get to see their children. For the 558,000 men in Australia who are denied regular access to their children, Father's Day is a dark and painful time when the grief can become overwhelming.

"Figures from the Australian Bureau of Statistics show that 87 percent of the one million children with separated parents live with their mother. On average, 77 mothers and fathers separate every day and 52 out of those 77 fathers will be denied the access to their children they want to see."

A Family Court of Australia spokesperson could not confirm any statistics but said there was no "philosophical bias against fathers" in the court system, and that the courts only focus was on the "best interests of the child".

***

The war of research studies and the dispute over shared parenting would continue apace throughout the first years of the Labor government. Critics rightly claimed that most of the studies were "advocacy research" done by researchers with a clear bias against shared parenting who found what they wanted to find.

In October 2008 the *Herald Sun* reported under the headline "Break-up kids hurt by family court" that children of separated parents were being forced to have contact with violent fathers against their will.

Some of the parents had allegedly threatened to kill or burn former partners, while others stalked, abused and harassed them.

The research, published in the *Journal of Family Studies*, said such behaviour was excused or ignored by judges who were determined to ensure separated fathers continue to have a presence in their children's lives.

The small study of 20 cases of contested contact of children involving allegations of domestic violence reportedly showed judges ignored the wishes of vulnerable children, and blamed mothers for failing to support access by violent fathers, feminist researchers Amanda Shea Hart and Dale Bagshaw claimed.

The pair wrote that in nearly half of the cases the child was a direct witness to the violence. While in no cases was the child physically harmed there was "little visible consideration of the potential or current effects of domestic violence on the children".

They said notions of the "idealised post-separation family" took precedence over the special needs of the children in the cases they analysed from a five-year period.

The 33 children involved in the cases, aged between two and 16 at the time of the final hearings, had a range of problems, including violence, anti-social behaviour and emotional fragility. Some expressed a "wish to die".

The researchers also found that in all of the cases judges expressed concerns about the effect of the absence of the fathers on their children's lives, despite the presence of domestic violence. In 13 of the cases the allegedly violent husbands were described as "loving fathers".

Hart and Bagshaw said an emphasis on shared care or father contact had made life difficult for children and mothers in cases where the break-up was caused by domestic violence perpetrated by fathers.

"There can be concerning outcomes for children who are required to spend time with their violent fathers," they said. "The safety and psychological needs of these children must be recognised and understood for their best interests to be served."

***

In contrast, the following month Adele Horin at *The Sydney Morning Herald*, no friend of fathers in her many columns over many years, wrote that with soaring numbers of separated and divorced parents sharing the care of their children more or less equally, the first major Australian study into the revolution showed it was not causing the big problems its detractors had feared.

But nor was the 50-50 split better for children than more conventional arrangements, as supporters of equal time had claimed.

The study of 5,000 parents on the Child Support Agency register indicated it made no difference to children's wellbeing whether they saw the non-resident parent half the time or every second weekend. What counted was how well parents got on.

"It's not the arrangement that matters but the quality of the parental relationship," said demography researcher at the Australian National University Bruce Smyth. The study allegedly showed the children who do less well are those in near-equal share arrangements where the non-resident parent saw them for two to three nights a week.

Smyth said near-equal care arrangements may be an unhappy compromise between conflicted parents. The "new high water mark" in parenting after separation is a 50-50 arrangement. "Unequal shared care may be the new soil to which conflicted couples move. Unequal care looks to be a proxy for conflict. In some cases, unequal shared care may represent an unhappy compromise. Parents who had an equal share of care were probably more likely to get along better and to have an egalitarian approach to parenting."

With ANU colleague Bryan Rodgers, Smyth examined differences in reported wellbeing and conflict among three groups of separated and divorced parents and their children: those with 50-50 care, those with 30-70 or 40-60 splits, and those with the "standard" pattern, usually alternate weekends with the non-resident parent.

The study showed the main beneficiaries of the 50-50 arrangement were the parents, who were happier in themselves and happier with their child-care regime than parents in the other two groups.

Happy parents don't make happy kids? Not in the eyes of academics.

Professor Rodgers said, "The bottom line is that the move to shared care is not going to make things worse for kids. But the presumption it will lead to better development of the children is looking very flimsy."

However, he said, a lot of parents wanted a more equal arrangement and other research had shown this included many mothers with sole care, as well as many children. Since the 2006 amendments to the Family Law Act put more focus on joint parenting time, the number of parents opting for more balanced care arrangements had soared.

New data from the Child Support Agency showed that in the year to June, 17 percent of new cases were non-standard child-care arrangements – with the non-resident parent having the children more than two nights a week. This was a dramatic leap from the seven percent of all cases in 2002 managed by the Child Support Agency, 12 percent now had shared care, compared with seven percent five years before. Children were deemed to be in shared care when they spend 30 to 70 percent of time with each parent.

Some arrangements were short-lived. The study showed that about one in 10 parents with sole care of the children had tried a more balanced arrangement at some point but ended it for practical reasons. These included distance, work commitments or the fact that the children did not like constantly moving between houses or were unsettled.

***

Next step on the way back came with the Rudd government's announcement that Federal Magistrates Court, created by the former government primarily as a faster, simpler, cheaper and thereby fairer alternative to the Family Court, would be dismantled.

The Federal Magistrates Court had grown rapidly into the largest federal court since it was founded in 2000, and by then was handling 79 percent of all family law applications.

Attorney General Robert McClelland released a report by consultant Des Semple, to his critics a bureaucratic insider and apologist for the system, which recommended the Federal Magistrate's family law division become part of the Family Court and its general division should fold into the Federal Court.

The Semple report praised the court's "service culture" but said it created friction and resentment with the Family Court, particularly over resources.

McClelland said "no change is not an option" and the creation of the court – the principal judicial reform of the Howard government – was a mistake.

The Attorney General said he wanted the "faster, cheaper and less formal" practices of the Federal Magistrates Court to become part of family law culture, and described Mr Semple's model as "a reverse takeover".

Up to 36 of the 59 magistrates would be transferred to a general division of the Family Court.

Former Attorney General Philip Ruddock said he feared the Family Court culture would adversely affect the way the magistrates undertook their functions, leading to increased costs and delays. "I think the culture of the magistrates has been to produce very timely outcomes for litigants," he said.

McClelland said "getting our family law system right is a significant access-to-justice issue. If we do it well then kids can be substantially shielded from the trauma of divorce. Family law is still horrifically expensive. It still takes too long and it is unfortunately more fragmented than it needs to be.

"I think the former government experienced frustration in reforming the Family Court and rather than focusing on reforming the court effectively, gave up and created an entirely separate court."

***

By November of 2008, a year into his government's first term, the Attorney General Robert McClelland was declaring that the controversial and "distressing" equal-time parenting laws for divorced couples could be overhauled.

Robert McClelland said some shared-parenting orders following relationship breakdowns were "clearly not appropriate and were causing extreme distress for children and their parents".

McClelland made the remarks during a Women's Legal Service family law forum in Brisbane.

"I assure you that I appreciate the seriousness of all I am hearing and that we will be mindful of these views when it comes to formulating new policies and making possible amendments to legislation."

He confirmed that the Australian Institute of Family Studies had begun a "comprehensive empirical assessment" of how families were faring under the shared parenting regime.

The propaganda war was escalating.

On 25 November 2008 *Sydney Morning Herald* journalist Ruth Pollard wrote: "Children are handed over to violent fathers and women are exposed to further harm in family mediation sessions because of flawed amendments to the Family

Law Act. Too often these changes place parenting rights over the safety of children, experts warn.

"The changes, made by the Howard government two years ago, have forced women with current apprehended violence orders against their partners into mediation where further threats of abuse occur, the *Herald* has learned.

"And the presence of domestic violence or child abuse made little difference to whether fathers were given overnight access to their children, research from the Australian Institute of Family Studies found, prompting calls for urgent reforms to the system and better training for magistrates and mediators."

Betty Green, convener of the NSW Domestic Violence Coalition said: "It is having horrendous consequences for women who are desperately trying to keep their children safe and yet the family law court is handing over children to violent men who are not necessarily interested in parenting these children."

Green called on the Federal Government to implement urgent changes to the act so the safety of children was privileged over a parent's right to contact.

"The idea of shared parenting is fine in those relationships where prior to that there was some kind of joint responsibility in raising children, but in domestic violence relationships that is not what happens," she said.

"You get a crazy situation where from a state perspective child protection agencies may be involved, where if a mother were to provide contact for the abuser that would be grounds to lose her children because she was exposing them to violence.

"On the other hand, you have a family law court in the federal system that puts that order to one side, and says, 'Here is a father and he must have access rights to his children'."

***

Attorney General McClelland said the Government was aware of concerns over the way shared parenting provisions in the Act had been applied in cases where domestic violence was present.

"That is why the Government is implementing new accreditation standards that will require all professionals – from mediator to judge – to be able to identify and respond to evidence of domestic violence," he said in a statement. "My department is currently consulting with key stakeholders to find better ways to address family violence in the family law system. The Institute of Family Studies is also conducting a detailed examination of the impact of the shared parenting presumption."

Karen Mifsud, a solicitor in the Women's Legal Resource Centre Domestic

Violence Advocacy Service, said they had clients reporting that they did not want to go to mediation because they felt intimidated or scared but felt they had no option as they needed to get some sort of arrangement for children in place.

The Shared Parenting Council of Australia, concerned at the direction of the public debate, shot back that claims changes to the Family Law Act were compelling courts to hand children over to violent fathers was false and scurrilous. "These claims are an insult to judges and magistrates who apply the law and deal daily with serious relationship issues," their press release declared.

"There are precise safeguards in the Act to exclude shared parenting and joint parental responsibility in cases where there are real issues of violence, conflict or abuse. The allegation that women are being 'forced' into mediation with violent ex-partners is particularly mischievous. The Act does nothing of the kind, and mediators and community agencies have screening strategies to identify cases in which mediation is inappropriate.

"Reducing mothers to victim status is a favoured strategy of radical feminists opposed to men and does nothing for the protection and welfare of women and children."

The SPCA urged the Attorney General to reject the arguments of biased advocates more concerned with advancing their own agendas than with the real interests of children.

Wayne Butler, Executive Secretary of the SPCA, said recent judgements showed clearly it was a complete nonsense to suggest the Family Law Act had in any way softened the approach of the judicial officers to cases of family violence and alleged violence.

The SPCA suggested the Attorney General consult widely with the judges, magistrates, lawyers, mediators and counsellors who dealt with separated families in and outside the courts. "Reports that have come to our attention speak favourably of the application of the shared parenting legislation and the new collaborative approach to sound parenting post divorce," Butler said.

"We strongly suggest that nothing less than five years would provide adequate time, experience and material for a full and careful review of the effects of the reformed Family Law legislation."

***

At the end of January 2009 the entire debate took a sickening lurch.

It was meant to be her first day of school. Darcey Iris Freeman was just a couple of days off turning five. Her father had promised to get her and her older brother to their primary school on time.

No one knows what made Arthur Phillip Freeman apparently change his mind. Not his lawyers, who could not believe what happened. Not the police, who could get no sense out of him. Not the forensic psychiatrist who concluded he was not fit to plead.

Freeman had taken all three of his children to a beach house overnight to escape Melbourne's summer heat. Coming back to town, the traffic across the West Gate bridge was slow.

But what police say happened in front of horrified witnesses happened fast – so fast, police would claim later, that there was no chance for anyone to stop it.

Just after 9am Freeman's white Toyota Land Cruiser, driving towards the city, slowed in the left lane. Then stopped.

Witnesses told police they saw Freeman get out of the car and walk to the rear passenger door. His two sons Benjamin, 6, and Jack, 2, were in the back seat. But it was Darcey whom he leaned over and unbuckled.

He allegedly lifted her up and carried her to the edge of the bridge near its highest point. Witnesses later told police the child seemed limp and did not protest.

Freeman walked to the edge of the bridge, lifted his daughter over the railing – and let go.

Darcey fell past the railings, past the pylons, 58 metres into the waters below. Her father got back into his car and drove off. Motorists called police.

Water Police dragged the little girl from the water in a critical condition with internal injuries. A massive police hunt swung into action.

At about 10.30am police were called to the Family Court building. Security staff had phoned police after observing a man in the foyer crying and shaking uncontrollably. He looked, one said later, like "he'd had enough".

His two sons were clinging to him. He begged security guards, "Can you take my kids for me?"

He was having trouble talking. It was his older son who gave the guards his parents' names. When police arrived, Freeman was arrested and handcuffed. He offered no resistance. Family friends were called to the court to collect the children. Mother Peta Freeman rushed to the hospital to be with her daughter, who died at 1.35 pm.

Reportedly while in police custody Freeman was unable to speak, shaking and weeping, apparently in deep shock. He was charged with murder. A doctor found him unfit for interview and was concerned he was suicidal.

Zelma Rudstein, whose law firm Rudstein Kron Lawyers had acted for Freeman, described him as a "devoted and loving father".

"It's devastating and unexpected. We are just trying to come to grips with it," she said. "It's very tragic and certainly not anything anyone could have predicted would happen. He was very committed to his children."

Freeman and his wife Peta separated in March 2007. He had reportedly recently returned from overseas and had been looking forward to sharing the care of his children after having previously been in such an arrangement. Instead he had found himself facing days of proceedings in the Family Court to establish a contact regime.

The case got worldwide media coverage and disturbed almost everyone who heard it.

***

Federal Attorney General Robert McClelland ordered a review of the case. But Justice Diana Bryant said the court orders were made by consent.

Chief Justice Bryant claimed the Family Court was not responsible for the Darcy Freeman incident, despite his having just been subjected to days of gruelling cross examination in the court and having shown up in its precincts straight after the incident with his two surviving children.

There had been no murder trial. There was no coroner's report. But as DOTA pointed out, that didn't stop her absolving herself and her court of any fault.

"The parties did not present to the judicial officer concerned as part of their case that this child was at risk of harm in the father's care," Bryant said. "The issues for determination were how much time the father should have with the child. Nothing was raised before the court about violence."

Justice Bryant said the Family Court would cooperate with a review of the case but would not explain any of its decisions.

"Everybody naturally wants to say 'well what was the last involvement' and if the last involvement was an order of the court, then people naturally want to say 'well it was the court's fault'," Bryant said. "But that is not necessarily the case, I mean it isn't the case. There are so many factors that cause people to be distressed."

Justice Bryant said relationship breakdowns caused incredible stress, including having to deal with money and children's issues and attending court if agreement could not be reached. "All of those things are stresses. And all of those things add to the ways in which people cope with breakdowns. Some people cope with it all right, some people don't. Some people are predisposed to mental illness, some aren't."

***

The women's lobby groups and the feminist bureaucrats so diametrically opposed to shared care took full advantage of the tragedy.

There is no doubt the prolonged and extreme stress and distress associated with custody battles makes people behave in strange ways. Many separated men display symptoms of post-traumatic stress disorder, obsessive, compulsive, difficult to deal with. Both men and women have killed their children in custody battles.

A woman had jumped from exactly the same bridge with her child strapped to her not long before. As a number of observers noted, the press made no fuss of that, no government determined used the tragedy to push through their agenda or alter legislation.

A few years before, in NSW, a woman was sent home from the Newcastle registry after learning she was about to lose custody of her children. She drove out into a forest with them and set the car alight. No one talked of changing the laws because of her actions.

I sometimes wonder how these well paid, self-confident, self-assured, self-righteous legal figures would behave if they had been subjected to months of extreme stress prior to a trial over the custody of their own children, then had been repeatedly humiliated for days on end in the witness box, been ridiculed from the bench, had their assets and income stripped, been offered not a shred of sympathy but instead painted as violent and abusive figures, all for the personal gain of the partner they had once so deeply loved. Would they be so quick to condemn, so quick to defend the indefensible?

Dads On The Air labelled our next show Insane Levels Of Stress.

Our editorial read in part: "While vigilantes have called for the man's blood, others have called for compassion and understanding. Disgracefully, some feminist commentators have attempted to use the incident in their ideological campaign against the commonsense notion of shared parenting.

"While making no direct comment on the case itself – the father has now been charged with murder – we do look at the insane levels of stress that fathers are put under by our reviled family law system.

"The situation has been made worse by the previous conservative government's failure to fully reform the jurisdiction.

"Their half-baked reforms requiring the Family Court to at least examine the concept of equal time parenting has not resulted in any significant reform of the court's conduct. Many fathers are now expecting but not getting shared parenting after separation; many leave the court utterly heartbroken and with little contact with their children.

"Fathers regularly lose everything: the assets they have worked all their lives to build, much of their income, much if not all of their social network and worst of all, their beloved children."

***

While the Freeman case had little or nothing to do with shared parenting, Attorney General McClelland seized on it to justify a review of the shared parenting legislation.

In March, just to prove that nothing had really changed, a Melbourne father of three was jailed for sending a birthday card to his daughter.

The man "Mick" – who could not be identified for legal reasons – was locked up in a suburban police station for seven nights and spent another in the tough Melbourne Custody Centre.

Mick claimed he was a victim of Family Court bias.

"I was jailed for nine days and eight nights for sending my 11-year-old daughter a birthday card," he said. "Apparently I broke an intervention order. It's ludicrous and it breaks your heart."

The 51-year-old was estranged from his wife and claims she has brought a series of intervention orders against him, banning him from contact with his children, without any evidence.

"Until my wife divorced me I was a legally unimpeachable citizen – now I'm being treated like a criminal just because I want some contact with my kids," he said. "And that contact was ended arbitrarily without even a hearing or the presentation of evidence.

"In a court of law, if you are accused of something you are supposed to have the ability to cross examine your accusers and call witnesses. In the secret chambers of the Family Court you are not guaranteed that at all."

Mick said the experience cost him $20,000: "It's a plundering and looting exercise on the part of lawyers involved in this and there are no juries or scrutiny by media to keep them accountable."

***

Also in March 2009, in a string of stories questioning the wisdom of the Shared Parental Responsibility Bill, Caroline Overington at *The Australian* reported that a mother had lost custody of her two children because of her anti-dad stance.

Two children, a girl, aged nine, and a boy, aged seven, who had been in the care of their mother since separation in 2005 were sent from Hobart in Tasmania to live with their father in Melbourne. The Family Court heard the mother encouraged them to have "negative" feelings about their dad.

The two children allegedly had been struggling with "change overs", saying things such as "I don't want to go" and "I don't have to go" when their father arrived in Tasmania from Melbourne to collect them.

The court found the mother did not discourage them from saying these things, and did not encourage a positive relationship between the children and their father. The children told counsellors they were angry their father had left their mother, and lived with his new girlfriend in Melbourne.

Family Court judge Robert Benjamin said the children "clearly wanted" to stay with their mother, who had been their primary carer since birth, and acknowledged the "disruption to the children's family unit and their stability if they were to move to Melbourne to live with their father".

But he said he had concerns that the denigration of the father would continue into the future."Sadly, this is a case where the children may be at unacceptable risk of psychological harm if they remain with the mother."

The orders allowed the mother to see the children during school holidays and on Mother's Day. She was also entitled to a phone call "each Sunday between 6.30pm and 7.30pm".

"These children are being slowly indoctrinated into believing that their father is cruel and unkind and likely to hurt them, when this is not the case," the psychologist said.

***

Reaction to the story split along gender lines,

Solo Mums Australian convenor Elspeth McInnes said Justice Benjamin had not taken into account psychological damage to the children, who had lived solely with their mother since 2005. "From the child development perspective, it seems extraordinary," she said. "It seems the judge is saying that mothers must make their children happy to see their fathers, or else they will be punished. I don't think such punishment has any regard to the children's wellbeing."

Wayne Butler of the Shared Parenting Council said the Family Court had undergone a radical change in direction since the Howard government's changes to the Family Law Act came into effect, and the emphasis was now firmly on fathers having relationships with their children after separation and divorce. He said the law was quite clear "that children are entitled to a relationship with their dad, and it's good to see the Family Court coming around to that".

Mr Butler said the changes to the Act meant fathers were getting better outcomes than they had previously. "You're better off now with a judge than you were before, and you're better off than you would be, if you just accept what your former partner gives you," he said.

Patricia Merkin, who advocated on behalf of women in Family Court disputes, said the changes were "nothing less than a social engineering experiment to respond to the so-called bias against fathers".

Attorney General Robert McClelland admitted more may need to be done to stop custodial parents denying access to the children.

He said the Australian Institute of Family Studies was conducting an evaluation of the way the new shared care rules are working. It would particularly look at whether the desire to reduce child support obligations was behind the actions of parents seeking shared care, the standard insulting piece of denigration emanating from women's groups against fathers who wanted to see more of their kids.

***

Also in March 2009 the Family Court issued its first statistical analysis of its orders. It revealed that fathers who want custody of their children had more success in the Court than by trying to strike a deal with their ex-partners.

In a break with conventional wisdom, fathers were twice as likely to get majority custody of their children if they took their fight to the court.

The Court warned that the majority of cases were dealt with by the Federal Magistrates Court and they only dealt with the most difficult cases. But their review showed fathers were given majority custody in 17 percent of litigated cases, but only in eight percent of those settled by consent, or early agreement, with the mothers.

The review of the shared parental responsibility reforms of 2006 showed that in 14 percent of litigated cases, the father received between 30 and 45 percent of custody. This figure fell to 11 percent for early agreements.

The review also showed that if fathers were given less than 30 per cent custody, abuse and violence were the main alleged reasons. And about one in 12 court cases end with an order that a child should spend time with their grandparents.

Only 15 percent of the litigated cases and 19 per cent of the consent agreements ended in orders for 50-50 care between the parents.

Although mothers continue to be awarded the bulk of custody there was significant change in favour of fathers. In 1997 just 2.6 percent of divorced parents shared the care of their children.

The biggest group was mothers who were awarded the majority of time with their children – they represented 60 per cent of the litigated cases and 68 per cent of consent cases.

The survey assessed 1,448 of the 6,992 litigated cases in 2007-08, and 2719 of 10,575 cases settled by consent or early agreement.

The biggest group of men, one third, were those awarded less than 30 per cent custody.

Alleged abuse and family violence was the main reason in 29 per cent of these matters, followed by entrenched conflict.

Of the nine percent of cases in which women were awarded less than 30 per cent custody, mental health was the dominant factor in 31 percent of cases followed by distance and financial barriers, abuse and family violence.

Substance abuse was cited as a main reason for the Family Court making sub-30 per cent orders. In six percent of litigated cases, the father was ordered to spend no time with their child. The same order applied to only one percent of women.

The information was posted on the Family Court's website and marked a breakthrough in the court's transparency and public accountability.

"The aim was to encourage parents to consider, where appropriate, reaching an agreement regarding parenting arrangements in the first instance themselves rather than having the court as a first option," the report recorded. "Given this, it is to be expected that there might be a higher number of shared care or substantial sharing of time cases negotiated outside the courts."

Lone Fathers Association spokesman Barry Williams said in 2005 mothers were awarded custody 83 percent of the time. "There has been significant improvement," he said.

**

A national campaign by women's groups to highlight the alleged dangers children faced under the family law culminated in early May 2009 in a number of small rallies around the country. The Safer Family Law campaign was led by author and activist Barbara Biggs. The campaign included 14 videos on YouTube that used actors to portray parents unable to tell their stories. Another video used young actors to tell the stories of two children sent on court-ordered access visits to abusive parents; 10 professionals appeared in the videos; and three journalists spoke about the problems of the court's secrecy provisions.

There came a spate of stories about fearful women and abusive men, with single mother's groups exploiting their sympathisers and fellow travellers in the mainstream media.

An online petition calling on the Federal Government to amend the law to better protect children garnered several thousand names. It called on Australia to follow New Zealand where the onus had shifted to allegedly violent parents having to prove they were safe before custody or access was considered.

"I've had 2000 emails, some of them harrowing Family Court stories of how children were taken from mothers who were trying to protect them," Biggs said.

She said many mothers were in a bind – either lacking corroborating evidence of the violence or sexual abuse, or liable to be labeled "alienating, hysterical or neurotic" if they took their children to psychologists or sexual assault counselors.

It was the first many fathers had heard of Barbara Biggs. It wouldn't be the last.

***

Family Court Chief Justice Diana Bryant told *The Sydney Morning Herald* provisions in the Act on family violence were not ineffective. She said in every case in which violence is alleged the court must weigh up the benefit to the child of having a meaningful relationship with both parents and the need to protect the child. Neither principle was more important. "It is a matter of the evidence and facts in each case."

As well, the standard of evidence required to prove allegations of violence was less than in other jurisdictions. Hearsay and opinion were allowed. "Even so, the violence must be proven to some extent, and at least to the extent that the court can find that there is an unacceptable risk to the child," she said. "Courts are not entirely evidence-free zones."

Oh right!!! Sure about that?? Anyone, including much of the broader legal profession, knew perfectly well that the Family Court was an almost entirely evidence free zone, their decisions based on the prejudices or ideological dispositions of its own judicial officers, in concert with compliant if not patently corrupt family report writers.

Adele Horin reported that Chief Justice Bryant had written to the Attorney General Robert McClelland suggesting "urgent consideration" be given to repealing parts of the Act because of "strong" misunderstanding in the community.

Of particular concern to the Chief Justice was a section dealing with the awarding of costs against the party who maliciously raised untrue allegations of violence or made untrue denials.

She said it was widely and wrongly interpreted in the community to mean that costs would be awarded against the party if they could not prove the act complained of actually occurred.

Because of concerns about this section, people were "rarely" filing the form required under the Act to bring allegations of family violence to the attention of the court. Repeating a feminist trope, the judge said. "I understand the reason is that parties are concerned that they will be ordered to pay costs if they do not prove the allegations of violence. Basically, this section is only relevant in cases where a person makes a malicious allegation that is found to be untrue and applies with equal force to false denials."

She also wanted the Attorney General to review the sections of the Act that had promoted the view parties will be considered "unfriendly" if they raise allegations of violence.

One section, for example, required the court to consider the "willingness of each child's parents to facilitate and encourage a close and continuing relationship between the child and the other parent".

"It may be the myth that raising allegations of violence will result in a mother being branded unfriendly arises because of these sections," Bryant said. "I do not fully understand how some of these shibboleths have come about. However, the fact they have is concerning and, in my view, makes it essential for the Attorney General to have a close look at whether there should be some amendments to overcome these problems."

Once again Australia was blessed with an activist judge who might have done her office more credit if she had stayed well out of the political arena. Policy formation wasn't her job.

Interesting that at taxpayer's expense the story should be leaked to probably the most sympathetic journalist in the country, Adele Horin at that Bible of the chattering classes *The Sydney Morning Herald*.

It was impossible to imagine any other Chief Justice in any other jurisdiction running a public commentary on the legislation and the need or otherwise for change, but this was family law.

It was a very long way from the days when Diana Bryant appeared happy to come on to Dads On The Air – and appeared to be promoting shared parenting as a rational alternative after divorce.

Now we had a Chief Justice who appeared to want to turn the clock back.

With so much taxpayer funded fear mongering and so much misinformation being spread by so many different government funded groups, Bryant's words were condemned within the fatherhood movement as inflammatory and inappropriate. Not a word, not one word, of concern was ever expressed for the thousands of broken hearted men whose relationships with their children had been destroyed by false allegations.

The Palace of Lies had not altered its ways. Nor had the lawyers routinely pushing stories they knew not to be true.

***

As part of my work at Dads On The Air, I have personally met some of the men falsely accused. At one stage the former head of the Australian Family Law Reform Association Max King determinedly, with a great deal of documentation, tried to demonstrate to me the process by which so many men were falsely accused of sexually molesting their children, based on no evidence at all.

One psychiatrist or family report writer might raise a sliver of doubt; subsequent report writers amplify it. Often there was no evidence whatsoever at the base of the allegation. Often enough the report writers had never even met the father, basing their reports solely on the mother's word or on previous reports by writers who had also never met the father or interviewed the children.

There were ample examples of hysteria and false allegations destroying lives. They were difficult to report, sad beyond reach, these cases which defied belief, if only they hadn't been true.

One day, when I was on holiday with my kids in the country beyond the Blue Mountains where he lived, Max travelled out to see me with boxes of documents. He had with him a man who lost contact with his children because it was alleged he had put his daughter on his shoulders in a play park in a suggestive manner.

Sad man, nothing but sad.

In the secretive atmosphere of the Family Court of old, the one we were told acted in the best interests of children, these allegations had been allowed to thrive. Max told me of how at the meetings of the Association they would sometimes ask the room: how many of you have been accused of molesting your children? Sometimes most of the men in the room would put up their hands.

***

Bryant's statements provoked a rapid response.

The Shared Parenting Council of Australia put out a media release titled Family Law Court 'Soft' on Justice:

It read: "Recent media reports that the Chief Justice of the Family Court, Diana Bryant has called upon the Attorney General to give urgent consideration to repealing one of the most fundamental protections in the recent Family Law Act amendments is almost without precedent and a recipe for wholesale failure in the integrity and operation of the Family Court System.

"The Chief Justice's call to repeal amendments to the Family Law Act in relation to awarding of costs against the party that maliciously raises untrue allegations of violence or makes untrue denials, will re-open the floodgates to increased perjury, false allegations and flies in the face of findings by two parliamentary enquiries, and natural justice – with an end result diametrically opposed to a child's best interest", Ed Dabrowski, Federal Director of the Shared Parenting Council said.

"Without any supporting evidence, that there is in fact any harm at all being created by these reasonable and well accepted amendments in the 2006 legislation, the Chief Justice has engaged in a media campaign to undo one of the fundamental protections available to any litigant, anywhere in any other law jurisdiction in the world.

"It is even more curious that notwithstanding that these amendments had been foreshadowed since 2003 and enacted in 2006, the Chief Justice herself has only just released guidelines for judges, The Family Violence Best Practice Principles, to guide the judiciary in this regard.

"It would appear that any deficiency in the lodging of 'Notification of Abuse' forms should rest with a failure to educate lawyers and those members of Family Relationship Centres. If such education is required, then the education of practitioners in the correct use of these forms should be enacted, not the wholesale repeal of this fundamental protection in law", Dabrowski said.

"Surely, the Chief Justice couldn't be condoning the re-establishment of a 'penalty free' process for one parent to make false and malicious allegations against the other – this defies every process of law in the Westminster system. If any amendment would be required, it should be to ensure that perjury is punished by criminal sanction, not the repealing of research based amendments made just some three years ago."

The Shared Parenting Council maintained that such a retrograde step would encourage a wholesale rise in mischievous allegations made in Court and to Child Protective Services. It would increase the frequency and severity of false statements including false allegations of abuse and violence against parents and grandparents who were simply seeking to continue parenting and maintain contact with their children and grandchildren after separation and divorce.

***

In an adversarial system allegations are routinely reported to the courts in case documents and it is for a Judicial Officer to determine the basis of these allegations.

According to Ed Dabrowski from the SPCA, "the Family Court had proven reluctant to sanction or fine parents in apparent defiance of the new laws, yet had shown no hesitation in segregating accused parents from their children and making no-contact orders on hearing untested allegations or removing one parent when entrenched conflict was a case factor".

The Shared Parenting Council of Australia received many complaints from parents where the Court's 'cautionary' approach to allegations resulted in impaired or total loss of contact without the allegations ever being proved or even investigated.

Dabrowski lamented that "legally unimpeachable parents were being treated like criminals and easily lose their children, without due process, at the discretion of judges. Diana Bryant is in effect saying that the most hostile parent ought to have the power to veto the other parent's involvement, no matter what.

"She is advocating the law change to grant permission for one of the litigants to come in with fabricated or at best flimsy allegations which would veto the child's best interest, to veto shared parenting, a remedy that fosters the best interests of children and is otherwise encouraged by the law.

"The new legislation in 2006 was designed specifically to ensure that children did not lose all contact with one parent and to ensure both parents understood their responsibilities in parenting after separation. Any watering down of the section relating to a "willingness of each child's parents to facilitate and encourage a close and continuing relationship between the child and the other parent" will be vigorously opposed."

***

The group Fathers4Equality also put out a release, with the heading: "Lying in the Family Court is CHILD ABUSE".

"A case of poor judgement" the release called Bryant's comments, saying she had launched an extraordinary attack on Australia's internationally regarded 2006 Family Law amendments.

According to Ash Patil, President of the group, said: "These provisions in the family law act were specifically implemented to reduce the epidemic of false allegations and parental alienation that permeate every corridor of the Family Law Courts, to the clear detriment of the innocent children caught in the cross-fire. But Bryant wants them removed, and fails to explain how the innocent victims of maliciously false allegations would be protected without them."

Another spokesman, James Adams, said the provisions were agreed to by a bi-partisan parliamentary committee that went around Australia canvassing the views of all Australians.

"What is more astonishing it seems is that unlike the parliamentary committee that recommended these laws in the first place, the Chief Justice has not consulted widely before making such an extraordinary intervention," he said. "In fact she has not consulted with any fathers' groups at all. Rightly or wrongly, Bryant will now be perceived to have compromised views on this issue, denying her the opportunity to have played a unifying force in the process of family law reform in this country, much like the wasted opportunities of her predecessor.

"These provisions have been specifically implemented to reduce the disturbingly common practices by some separated parents in making contrived and sinister allegations in Court against the other parent, and to otherwise engage in concerted efforts to destroy the relationship between the child and the other parent.

"This is done knowing full well the children will be irrevocably harmed in the process, both psychologically and emotionally. Yet it goes on and will continue to go on given human nature, unless we have laws to help it stop.

"Finally this committee was so appalled at the extent of institutional abuse in the Family Court that it recommended measures to protect innocent children and parents who were victims of contrived allegations and parental alienation by spiteful ex-partners. But Bryant wants to override the will of the Australian people and the will of Parliament and to completely remove all disincentives against lying in the Family Court.

"A request to the Attorney General to implement an educational campaign about these provisions would go a long way in addressing any existing misconceptions, and would be a more measured and effective approach to the issue at hand."

The group concluded: "In reference to a recent campaign that has promoted a less than accurate reflection of these new laws, we would ask the Chief Justice to consider making a public statement to the effect, as is the case, that no evidence exists of any escalation of child abuse as a result of the new amendments.

"This would be an important statement from the Chief Justice in the interests of an informed community discussion on this matter, and would help ensure that the debate is discussed in terms of facts, not innuendo."[198]

---

198 Media Release: ...Because Lying in the Family Court is Child Abuse, Says Fathers4Equality" published by PRWeb on 7 May, 2009.

NINETEEN
THE BLESSED BARABARA BIGGS

In May 2009 Dads On The Air was asked to speak at a forum organised by a group known as The Fellowship of the Round Table on the subject: "Family law – is the man the loser?"

I found myself sitting next to the poster girl of the anti-shared movement in Australia, Barbara Biggs. She was a former prostitute turned property developer and all round colourful character who had authored a number of books about her life. Her first book, *In Moral Danger*, explored her life up to the age of 22. It recorded her alleged abuse at the hands of a prominent criminal barrister beginning at the age of 14, and subsequent suicide attempts and a period in a psychiatric hospital. Her fifth book, *Sex and Money: How to Get More*, was released in 2006. One of her first acts at the event was to assemble her books for sale.

Biggs had seized on family law as a cause for reasons none of us could understand.

Her claims that the shared parenting laws were forcing children into abusive relationships with their fathers were hotly disputed, but unfortunately received ready play in the national media.

Guests on the program had previously criticised her campaign as hysterical, just the latest incarnation of extreme male bashing. But the Safer Family Law Campaign, as Biggs' quest became known, attracted considerable attention.

The event took place in the Jubilee Room at parliament house. Kathleen Swinbourne from the Lone Parents union was originally scheduled to speak at the forum, and we had been relatively unconcerned by this. She was not an impressive public speaker.

Barbara Biggs, on the other hand, was a different kettle of fish. I had always said I would bet money on Swinbourne not appearing at the forum for the simple reason that these people always avoided debating on open ground if they could. I was proven right. She cancelled on the day, throwing the organisers into a spin.

They ended up flying Barbara Biggs up from Melbourne. This was the first time I had met her.

"Are you nervous?" she asked as we stood next to each other making a cup of tea, after I had confessed to hating public speaking. "No, no," I said, not entirely truthfully but not wishing to show vulnerability. When you're vulnerable people attack.

Cleverly, she insisted with the organisers that she go last, ensuring that her claims could not be challenged. After earnest speeches from family lawyer Mark Youssef, who provided statistics on the slow rate of adoption of shared parenting, and myself, who back grounded the debate, it was Dads On The Air's turn.

In my role as Program Director I gave the following speech.

***

I would like to thank the organisers Forum Of The Round Table and everyone else who has helped to put on this event. For those of you who don't know, Dads On The Air is a community radio program run out of 2GLF in Liverpool in western Sydney which by dint of pure perseverance has become the longest running fathers show in the world.

Our topic today, "Is the man the loser in family law?", is shorthand for a much broader debate on whether the style of custody order most common in the Family Court, and most family courts around the Western world, that is sole-mother custody, is really the best for our kids. And whether or not the almost universal anti-father bias in our public institutions in child support, child protection and legal aid is producing the best outcomes.

There isn't much doubt family law is biased against men – unless you want to discount the voices of hundreds of thousands of fathers here and around the world.

Dads On The Air would not exist if family law was not biased against fathers. It was the collective outrage of a group of heartbroken men which meant when the opportunity came up back in 2000, we started a dads show. We've gone on to attract a talented team with journalistic, entertainment and internet experience. The first few years must have been a bit of a strain on the audience, with long spiels against the impacts of family law and elaborate deconstructions of domestic violence or anti-father ideologies.

Dads On The Air was born not just out of a sense of injustice, but out of frustration with the mainstream media's failure to take men's issues seriously, often confusing social affairs reporting with feminist causes.

We have been proud to provide an outlet for a number of groups including the Shared Parenting Council of Australia, the Men's Rights Agency, the Fatherhood Foundation, Fathers4Equality, Fairness In Child Support, Lone Fathers and Dads In Distress, mostly sad dads who want to see more of their kids.

The single most barbaric thing any civilisation can do to its citizenry is the removal of children, yet this happens every day. They're told it is in their children's best interests. Separated fathers often show signs of post traumatic stress disorder, repetitive, obsessive, fragile, fighting injustices they have no hope of solving. We've broadcast their voices, taxi drivers, teachers, firemen, policemen. It does the country no good to have such a large body of disaffected people.

Recent guests such as Professor Stephen Baskerville, author of *Taken Into Custody*, argue the long march through the institutions is almost complete and the divorce regime comprises the most totalitarian institutions ever to arise in the western democracies. Families have been systematically portrayed as dangerous places for women and children.

***

Men have been systematically propagandised as violent, abusive patriarchs or historical relics. Separated men have been ridiculed as nothing but aggrieved litigants. The divorce industry is a serious perpetrator of human and constitutional rights violations. No political party and no politicians question it. No journalists investigate it in any depth.

It is common, perhaps even fashionable in family law circles, to blame the litigants for their own problems. The fact they are silly enough to get bound up in complex and expensive family litigation is sniffed at. But unfortunately separated parents have to have family law orders in order to gain payments through Centrelink or that much reviled institution, the Child Support Agency.

Nothing sends a shiver up a politician's spine more than the sight of a separated dad clutching a large file of legal documents making a beeline for him or her at a public function. For these things are insoluble. Their grief and their sense of aggrievement cannot be assuaged by a few rote letters to department heads. Family law creates an enormous well of pain. How can this politician help this poor bastard, who has just been through the worst time of his life, who has lost his children, his home, much of his assets and income, his dignity, his social position, his sense of self worth?

The issues which affect men are not being addressed. One simple example: On the Dads On The Air website we have a counter which estimates the number of clients of the Child Support Agency who die every day. We estimate the figure at around 12 a day, probably an underestimate. Every fathers group in the country has linked family law and child support with the high death rate amongst separated men. Where are the inquiries, the concern?

We covered the family law process in Australia begun by the previous Howard government closer than any other media outlet. There was ample evidence during the family law inquiry, including most powerfully from many grandparents, of the pain the present system creates. We interviewed many people who hoped the well of misery would be resolved. It is deeply unfortunate in our view that the previous Howard government baulked at true reform of family law, despite widespread public support, and even those modest reforms keeping father's in children's lives could now be wound back. But at least now a detailed record of the hopes and frustrations of so many people is actually on line, documented, undeniable. Available for future researchers.

I often wonder how younger generations of fathers, those you now see walking their kids to school or in shopping malls with their children climbing all over them, will deal with all this. Surely there are enough cautionary warnings to suggest further reform is needed so broken hearted dads and children unnecessarily deprived of their fathers becomes a thing of the past.

All is not lost. But governments are wise to listen to the voices of the people over those of their own tax payer funded academic, bureaucratic and judicial elites. I hope when the history of all of all this is written Dads On The Air will be seen as having had a civilising influence on the debate, making available voices and points of view which may otherwise have been ignored. Men are the losers under the present family law regime, but so are we all. Thank you.

***

Also on behalf of Dads On The Air, Peter van de Voorde gave an impassioned speech on the harm being done to parents and children by the nation's family law and child support systems.

"Family law – is the man the loser? Well of course he is! Because the only winners in family law are those involved with the administering of family law, which has now ballooned into a multi-billion dollar industry.

"Unfortunately contrary to community perceptions, in the jurisdiction of family law, equality and justice are missing in action and I see the real losers more as being the many millions of responsible non custodial parents around the globe, who have been forcibly removed from their biological children against their will, by this industry.

"So as to the question of 'is the man the loser' I would have to say a resounding yes, but qualify that, by saying he is not alone, because equally so, are responsible non-custodial mothers and I hasten to add that the greatest losers of all, are those who do not have a voice of their own, and rely on us to speak for them, in the hope they can somehow escape the nightmare they are forced to live, and I speak of course of the children.

"What drives noncustodial parents like myself is grief, pain and absolute outrage," he said. "It saddens me greatly to witness the continuing lack of community awareness because these are human rights violations. Denying its citizens their fundamental human rights, are the policies of a morally failed state which is universally regarded as unacceptable.

"But you see, historically we've been here before many times, and sooner or later, the tide's going to turn. It took many years for the world to recognise the injustices perpetrated against Indigenous populations, slavery, apartheid, black civil rights and so on. These injustices were also ignored for many decades due to community ignorance.

"Unfortunately we're repeating the same injustices under another name against a different group, and once again witness this same community's ignorance.

"Saying SORRY to one deserving dispossessed group, while at the same time completely ignoring the dispossession taking place right under our noses, smacks of hypocrisy.

"According to the latest Australian Bureau of Statistics figure there are now almost 700,000 Australian children who no longer have any meaningful contact with their non-custodial parents. When you add the estimated 1.5 million extended family members such as grandparents, uncles, aunts and cousins who are also denied their ties of kinship with those much loved members of their families, you find that more than 2.6 million of the nation's citizens are already affected.

"Incredibly both parents and children have been forced to go cap in hand to this immoral State institution, for more than 30 years now, only to walk away with bloodied noses.

"Without parenting rights and stripped of their children and family wealth, which has left them financially and emotionally destitute, many parents are forced to walk away in utter despair or risk facing a jail term. Then to add insult to injury, they are offensively labelled 'deadbeat' parents, and are mercilessly persecuted by heartless child support agencies.

"This has to stop!! It's madness!! How much longer do we think we can continue to keep on removing up to a quarter of the nation's children from the ties of kinship with half of their families, before it starts to tear apart the very fabric of our society?

"No society can withstand a sustained attack on the biological bonds of its citizens and escape the inevitable disastrous consequences. Yet we stand idly by and allow a dictatorial family law industry to continue to impose its perverted will on our society."

***

Barbara Biggs, who had already spread her books for sale up the back of the Forum, then rose to speak.

She immediately made a play out of the fact that she was the only woman on the panel. Out the window went any reasoned discussion. It was fascinating to watch.

As Biggs spoke, hostility within the audience mounted.

"Codswallop" shouted the normally reserved Wayne Butler, founder of the Family Law Web Guide and one of the Shared Parenting Council's leading lights. Biggs promptly put him back in his box. After her speech, almost all the questions from the audience were directed at her.

In a sense it was a relief.

Dads On The Air recorded the evening and spread the results over the next two weeks of shows.[199]

There was considerable debate within Dads On The Air over whether we should broadcast Barbara Biggs speech and the answers she gave to questions from the floor.

Several people warned me against it, but as the Program Director it was my call. My thinking was that everyone knew what we thought; but most people hadn't had the opportunity to hear Barbara Biggs. All most people knew of her was that she kept popping up in newspapers criticising men and characterising them as abusers. I decided to run her in full and title the program The Barbara Biggs Show.

As far as I am concerned, "let them hang themselves" is a potent strategy. By exposing her extreme male bashing views to the light surely people would see how deranged the so-called "safer family law" campaign really was.

Noting that Barbara Biggs had become the figurehead for the anti-shared-parenting movement, our flyer for the show read: "Family law reformers around the country have been alarmed at the scurrilous campaign, including a number of demonstrations outside family courts and other locations, to return family law to the dark ages when more than half of all children entering the Family Court

---

199 The Barbara Biggs Show, Dads On The Air, 39 June, 2009.

arena rarely if ever saw their fathers again and almost no fathers were ever given any substantial time with their children.

"The campaign is being conducted under the guise of preventing domestic violence against women and sexual abuse against children. Biggs claims that the shared parenting laws have forced children to spend time with abusive parents, but her target is clearly fathers. One simple point reformers make is that child abuse is committed by both genders and is a crime, it is a police matter, but Biggs only focuses on sexual abuse of children ignoring homicide, infanticide, neglect, emotional and physical abuse where women make up the majority of perpetrators.

"Most sexual abuse of children occurs at the hands of other siblings, stepparents, mother's boyfriends or de factos and other relatives. Fathers are the least likely to sexually abuse their children. For the vast majority of family law cases, the research is clear: children benefit from a continued relationship with both parents after separation.

"Barbara Biggs has made a career out of her colourful life, including alleging she was sold as a sex slave by her grandmother at 14 as well doing stints as a prostitute, mental health patient and property developer. Her books include: *In Moral Danger, The Journey Home, The Accidental Renovator* and *Money and Sex: How To Get More*. Whether Biggs is a dangerous hysteric promoting irrational hatred against men or a true champion of the nation's abused children, you can decide for yourself.

"Surprisingly Barbara Biggs said at the forum the Child Support Agency should be abolished as it caused more trouble than it was worth. Most fathers would agree! As well, interesting for a feminist advocate, she claimed that about 30 percent of all child sexual abuse cases were perpetrated by women. At last we saw a leading feminist figure admitting that abuse was perpetrated by both genders."

***

Ms Biggs claimed that she wanted to work with fathers and fathers groups in her campaign for safer family law. But within 24 hours the most virulent of the anti-father websites, Anonymoms, with which Biggs appeared closely linked, was frothing at the mouth that men would dare speak at parliament house.

They invited readers to click on a link to the song Who Let The Dogs Out?

Very funny. We gently suggest that if you really wanted to work with fathers, the first step might be not to call them dogs.

Many of her critics were concerned about the anti-male tone which permeated Ms Bigg's work and the hatred displayed in her campaigning. Here is a sample from *In Moral Danger*: 'I am still staring guys back but I can't help buying into what I know is in their heads about me. I am trying to assert myself on behalf of women but when I see the look in their eyes and the whole thing fucks with my head. The more I have to look away the worse I feel.

"Then I start noticing how guys sit on the bus with their legs wide apart like they own the place when we women are all squished up being polite making room for other passengers. The more I hate guys for taking up so much space in the world the more I hate myself for being such a worm about not meeting their eyes in the street."

***

The Safer Family Law campaign, with Biggs as one of its front women, kicked off in May 2009.

The *Sunday Herald Sun* observed: "For both sides, the battle is emotional and personal and could easily descend into acrimony. And, as in all emotional exchanges, sometimes fact, myth and assumption become blurred in the haze of propaganda and spin."

Chief Justice Bryant, back in the fray, told the newspaper there was a "tension" between what the Family Law Act described as "the benefit to the child of having a meaningful relationship with both of the child's parents" and "the need to protect the child from physical or psychological harm from being subjected to or exposed to abuse, neglect or family violence".

This tension had to be determined by judges on evidence – not populist public campaigns.

"Protection of children should need no debate," she said. "We live in a society where we regard the protection of children as being vitally important and we want our courts and other institutions to support that position."

But she realised theory and reality differed sometimes: "It is a controversial topic that usually breaks down on gender lines."

As an example of the protests Barbara Biggs had been organising, in June 2009 a group of "blood-stained" and bandaged mothers paraded outside NSW Parliament House in Sydney, calling on the Family Court to stop ordering children to see abusive parents. With arms in fake slings, artificially bruised faces and broken dolls in prams, about 30 mums took part in the "Bandage Parade" hoping to highlight the danger of giving unsupervised custody of children to abusive parents after separation.

"He Can't Bash Mum and Be A Good Dad Kids Deserve Safe Parents" read one of their largest placards. Why the group was demonstrating outside a state parliament over federal legislation is anybody's guess.

"We have a systemic failure when more than 15,000 Australian children are ordered into ongoing contact with parents the court itself has deemed violent and abusive," Barbara Biggs claimed to reporters in her role as spokeswoman for the National Council for Children Post-Separation. "This has happened because of hastily written shared parenting laws and the Family Court turning a blind eye to abuse when it comes to its duty of care for Australian children."

Ms Biggs said the marches would continue until the end of the year, when family law was expected to be reviewed. She said parents were being forced to conceal claims that their child was being abused, for fear of losing custody of their children.

"If you can't prove abuse beyond reasonable doubt, then you have to pay the court costs and risk losing custody of the child because you are deemed a dangerous parent for poisoning your child against the father or mother. You have to make a choice – agree to some custody with an abusive ex-partner or risk losing custody. What do you do?

"We are a group who care about the physical, emotional and psychological wellbeing of our children and until that is part of family law – not the parents' right to access their children – we will continue to have problems."

***

Amazingly it appeared the Labor government had the appetite to overthrow the modest bipartisan reforms of the Howard government it had in the end so readily agreed to and which despite their weaknesses had in fact encouraged fathers to be involved in their children's lives after divorce, as early statistics from both the Family Court and the Child Support Agency had demonstrated.

Fathers groups dismissed Ms Biggs claims as dangerous, hysterical and wildly inaccurate and pointed out they could equally parade any number of fathers before the cameras who have spent months if not years fighting desperately to rescue their children from terrible situations.

DOTA editorialised: "The Family Court, with no investigative capabilities beyond its own coterie of suspect experts, is the last place for genuine cases of abuse to be handled.

"Meanwhile, the collateral damage of these vicious campaigns could be the destruction of thousands upon thousands of children's relationships with their falsely accused fathers. Wherever you stand, whatever you think, the coming months will no doubt be chaotic as the campaign against fathers escalates."

To counterbalance the Biggs poison, the following week we called the show The Case For Shared Parenting, and interviewed amongst others Maurice Vellacott, the

Canadian MP who was introducing shared parenting legislation into the Canadian Parliament. We subsequently interviewed an Australian father who was jailed for a month for inadvertently playing golf next to a sporting field where his son, unbeknown to him, was playing soccer.

Our editorial read: "With moves clearly afoot to wind back the modest reforms of the previous government on shared parenting legislation designed to encourage a relationship between both parents and children after separation, we take a look at the very strong case for shared parenting as the norm post-separation, with advocates arguing it works best for both children and parents - as well as saving the government a great deal of money by encouraging single parents to get off welfare and into work. The main obstruction to the commonsense notion of shared parenting comes from government bureaucrats and the family law industry itself."

Canadian Member of Parliament Maurice Vellacott had just introduced a bill promoting shared parenting. A poll he commissioned, conducted by Nanos Research, showed that 78 percent of Canadians supported equal shared parenting, with a high of 86 percent support in the province of Quebec. Slightly more women than men support equal shared parenting.

Surveys in Australia had shown similar high levels of support. But instead there was a ceaseless tide of anti-male anti-father anti-nuclear family propaganda to fight against.

***

In June of 2009 Caroline Overington at *The Australian* reported on a paper by retired Family Court judge Richard Chisholm rebuking the public impression that the care of children was now expected to be shared after divorce. He stated that the shared parenting laws introduced by the Howard government in 2006 did not guarantee divorced fathers the right to a 50-50 split with their children because "such an arrangement is not always in the best interests of the children".[200]

As if, Dads On The Air sighed loudly on radio, the Family Court had ever acted in the best interests of children.

Already it seemed that the golden era, when *The Sydney Morning Herald* trumpeted shared parenting on its front page as a bold and necessary reform, was a millennium ago. Political, media and community support for change had been widespread in those seemingly far off days.

---

200 Overington, Caroline, Lives torn asunder, *The Australian*, 8 June, 2009.

Dispelling the myth which had arisen in the public imagination that family law was now fairer and the manifest difficulties of the past had been resolved, Chisholm reiterated that the legislation only required the Family Court to consider whether equal time with both parents suited a particular child.

The report followed on from a previous story reporting that fathers expecting 50-50 time splits with their children were overwhelming staff at the Family Relationship Centres, where all separating parents were now expected to go before approaching the Family Court.

Staff at the centres said a "pub law" belief about a father's right to a 50-50 time split had taken hold in the community.

But Chisholm said the shared parenting laws, introduced in 2006 and now under review, never guaranteed anybody a 50-50 time split. In a paper titled Shared Care and Children's Best Interests presented at a Legal Aid NSW family law conference, Professor Chisholm said there was "a lot of evidence to support the idea that children will generally benefit if they experience a loving and involved relationship with both parents after separation.

"There is also evidence that children care a lot about their parents and generally want to remain closely involved with both of them."

Professor Chisholm reiterated that the Howard government amendment "envisaged the non-resident parent participating in various aspects of the child's life, for example being involved in the child's daily routine".

"But the provisions about equal time did not reflect what most expert researchers believed was important for children. What seems to matter most to children, and what seems most important for their healthy development, has more to do with what happens when they are with each parent, and in particular whether they feel loved and cared for.

"The idea of equal time makes a lot of sense in terms of adult entitlement.

"As far as I can tell, it does not reflect what research scholars believe is important for children's development."

He urged academics to do more research into the benefits of shared parenting, particularly in cases where parents are in conflict. He said: "We need to know much more about the nature of conflict, the extent to which children are being exposed to it, and the extent to which parents and the courts might be treating the legislation as requiring some form of shared parenting, even when it is damaging to the children."

The Australian Institute of Family Studies had been commissioned to do a review of the Howard government amendments. If the review recommended changes, Professor Chisholm said, "I hope the focus will be on how it impacts on families, rather than how it impacts on voters and lobby groups".

Throughout the first half of 2009 the Rudd Labor government stuck to the official line that they were awaiting a report from the Australian Institute of Family Studies, sometimes referred to at DOTA as the Institute of Feminist Studies because of its historical biases.

While there was concern amongst family law reformers, there were no sustained protests. Most separated fathers were simply getting on with their own lives. There was none of the momentum that had built up in the lead-up to the passing of the shared parenting legislation in 2006. The general public thought the problem had been solved.

By July fears were increasing that change was afoot. At a public forum Sue Price from the Men's Rights Agency confronted the Attorney General Robert McClelland over the issue and was told she could make a submission to the Institute of Family Studies if she wished. But a phone call to Moloney revealed they were not interested in public submissions.

Incensed, she put out a press release which stated in part: "The Attorney General says he will be guided by the report from AIFS which, disturbingly, is only taking submissions from a select and 'anointed' group of organisations – rather than the broader community.

"Over the years the judiciary has overwhelmingly supported maternal preference, and the now discredited 'tender years doctrine', losing sight of the need to assess the suitability of each parent and the benefits to be gained by a child still having both parents in their life.

"The Australian Institute of Family Studies will not, according to researcher Lawrie Moloney, be extending an invitation to men's and fathers' groups to contribute to the research. The rights of hundreds-of-thousands of men, not to mention their children, have been cruelly struck down."[201]

It appeared clear the mandarins were back in control; and the stitch up was in process.

But as the December deadline approached the government, at least on the face of it, became concerned the AIFS report might be too neutral. In our interviews with Moloney he had always been very reserved and rigidly academic when queried on his own support for family law reform. He would stick to the evidence.

***

Caroline Overington at *The Australian* reported in a front page story on July 24 that the Attorney General had pledged to make changes to the Howard

---

201 Important Policy Review Slams the Door, Media Release, Men's Rights Agency, 19 August, 2010.

government's "contentious" shared parenting laws – and to the entire family law system – to ensure the safety of children after divorce."

On the face of it exploiting private tragedy, Attorney General Robert McClelland once again cited the sad story of Darcey Freeman as a reason for the review. "There will always be differing perspectives about how our family law system should function. That's especially true for those individuals and groups directly affected by the laws and processes."

But he said the Rudd government's priority was the safety and wellbeing of children, which may not always mean equal, or a lot of, time with both parents.

"If it becomes clear that current laws and practices may jeopardise the safety of families and children, we must work together to address these shortcomings. It is paramount that our family law system is capable of identifying and responding to violence."

Overington claimed the decision to intervene came after "an avalanche of complaints about the way the family law system is working, particularly in relation to the custody of children."

The avalanche came from taxpayer funded groups representing the interests of single mothers.

She went on to record that several prominent women from Kevin Rudd's front bench, including Minister for the Status of Women Tanya Plibersek and Health Minister Nicola Roxon, were concerned about the way family law was operating, fearing the laws requiring the Family Court to presume the best interests of a child were served by a meaningful relationship with both parents after divorce were forcing children into damaging shared parenting arrangements.

It was, hook line and sinker, the story feminist lobby groups wanted McClelland to tell.

Overington copped considerable criticism and claims of bias from fathers groups amidst allegations she was misusing her privileged position as a journalist on the national newspaper to run a campaign against shared parenting. In a five day period mid-2009 stories included "Family Law experts slate shared-parenting", "Flaws in John Howard's parenting law", "Agony of children at divorce has clout" and "Parent law ties women to men".

Talk of a complaint to the Australian Press Council did not proceed but there was barely a single father's group or father's representative who did not complain that their comments were either misreported or taken out of context.

***

Whatever her failings may or may not have been, Overington remained abreast of the news and had a clear eye for controversy. It was a point the men's lobby groups, inexperienced in the ways of the media and passionate if not occasionally obsessive about their cause, failed to appreciate.

The story on McClelland's moves was followed by another headlined: "Divorced dads fear rollback of parent laws."[202]

Now it was time for at least some of the other side of the story.

Overington opened with the salvo: "The shared parenting laws that have given divorced fathers more time with their children will be rolled back because of the power of left-wing feminist women in Kevin Rudd's cabinet."

She quoted Sue Price lamenting that "15 years of progress in getting fathers and children to spend time together is about to be undone. I met with the Attorney General Robert McClelland a few weeks ago, and it was clear to me that these laws are being rolled back.

"The Rudd government say they are reviewing the law, but basically the law will change because in the Labor government there are a number of women who are well and truly indoctrinated in a 1970s feminist movement background, and they do not value the role of men in society.

"Tanya Plibersek pushes domestic violence based on incorrect data. Nicola Roxon dances a merry dance around men. The fact is that children are at far greater risk from their mothers. Mothers kill more children than fathers, and that's a fact."

***

The Australian government deliberately stopped collecting or at least publishing gender breakdowns of child killers because the results did not fit their agenda.

The definitive word on this oft raised subject fell to Greg Andresen at One In Three, under questioning during a 2020 Inquiry into Family, Domestic and Sexual Violence, when the organisation claimed in their submission that women were a significant family violence risk to children.[203]

Andresen said: "The 2015 Children's Rights Report, by the National Children's Commissioner, found that children comprised the second-most-frequent group of victims of family and domestic homicides, after intimate partner homicides. They were quoting data from the Australian Institute of Criminology's National Homicide Monitoring Program.

"For the 10 years between 2002 and 2012, over half—52 per cent—of all family violence child murders were perpetrated by women. In the most recent

---

202 Overington, Caroline, Divorced dads fear rollback of parent laws, *The Australian*, 7 August, 2010.

203 One in Three's appearance before the Inquiry into family, domestic and sexual violence, Hansard, available under Submissions on the One in Three Website, 1 December, 2020.

biennial reporting period of the National Homicide Monitoring Program, which is 2014 to 2016, mothers killed 20 children, while fathers killed 13 children, and four children were killed by mothers' new male partners.

"In 1997, the Australian Institute of Health and Welfare made a decision not to publish any more data indicating the gender of child abuse perpetrators. No such data has been published since. That's about a 23-year gap, where no data has been published on the gender of child abuse perpetrators.

"That action was taken just one year after the figures were first published, in 1996, which showed that 1,138 women and 968 men were perpetrators of child abuse. A more recent FOI request to all states and territories to obtain more data – and only the WA government complied – found that mothers, once again, made up the vast majority of reported child abusers in WA in 2007 and 2008.

"I think that data provides ample evidence that women are a significant family violence risk to children, and it's on that basis that we make that claim."

***

On the other hand Ed Dabrowski, of the Shared Parenting Council, was dismayed, saying: "Vocal minority groups, mostly women, have latched on to a few cases and are now saying the shared parenting laws are leading to situations that are loaded with domestic violence.

"That is not the case, and if there is to be a review, it ought to be a public review. They should have a full inquiry and let's see what the public, including fathers, think about going back to the old days."

NSW Acting Attorney General Verity Firth entered the fray, saying there "seems to have been considerable problems" with the new shared parenting law in reconciling a child's right to a "meaningful relationship" with both parents "and the protection of the child from exposure to violence".

Ms Firth said there was some evidence that a "very strong pro-contact culture had arisen even where the safety of children couldn't be guaranteed".

Jen Jewel Brown, of the National Council for Children Post-Separation, a single mother's lobby group, also welcomed the review, saying the new Family Law Act was working as a "wrecking ball for many damaged children and their parents, in particular, as they try to re-establish themselves after the breakdown of abusive relationships".

She said mothers had grown reluctant to raise allegations of violence in the Family Court because they feared being "accused of raising false allegations or not promoting a meaningful relationship with the other parent", which can mean they lose custody or face the entire bill for court costs.

The chairman of the Family Law Council, John Wade, known for his hostility to shared parenting, said there was an "appetite for change" and "a feeling that we need to look at it again, and see whether it's working", but any changes were "bound to be controversial because it's the area of law that most Australians have contact with, either themselves or through their relatives."

Without any public consultation, and zero consultation with father's or family law reform groups, it was clear the appetite for change was coming solely from the mandarins and certain government funded women's groups. There could have been no clearer example of the gulf between the mandarins and the masses, who by and large appeared to still strongly support shared parenting.

***

There were many impassioned and furious responses to the government's moves to wind back the legislation.

Dads On The Air's own Peter van de Voorde, for example, wrote: "Why are we so surprised that the current crop of legislators have turned out no different than the last lot? Have we forgotten that it was the whole of Parliament who voted for the watered down, ineffective changes to the destructive Family Laws, which have continued to plague our society for the past 35 years? Now they are looking at rolling them back!

"The suggestion has been made that we all write letters to our politicians, but 'Hello', we have been doing that for the past 35 years and it has proved a useless exercise, which has brought about no effective change."

Van de Voorde went on to state that the Parliament and its attendant bureaucracies were stacked to the rafters with those driving their own personal agendas regarding what was best for the nation's parents and their children. The wishes of the vast majority of the general public had been ignored while at the same time voices of reason and logic had been ignored or ridiculed.

"If anyone should be in doubt about the direction of this back to the future Australian Government, one needs to look no further, then the appointment by our current Attorney General of former Family Court judge Richard Chisholm to review family law processes.

"This relic of the disgraced Nicholson era, who happily sang songs at a Family Law convention, making fun of the despair of the nation's responsible fathers and their children, who were being forcibly separated by him and his cronies, is now going to advise our Government on what is in the best Interests of our children.

"These destructive relics of a bygone era are firmly in the camp of the anti-shared parenting lobby."

Failure Family Law Reform Australia

***

Late in July, The Australian's legal affairs writer Michael Pelly reported the Family Court Chief Justice Diana Bryant's description of the shared parenting laws as "problematic" and the expectations of fathers as "a concern".

By this stage the government had embarked on three different inquiries into family violence and family law. Three inquiries: yet not one of them invited the contributions of fathers or even the general public.

The Chief Justice also repeated her claims that punitive costs orders for those who raise false allegations of violence have been counterproductive and that women feared being branded "unfriendly".

There was not a single word of concern about the thousands, tens of thousands of men whose lives had been turned to mud by false allegations.

Pelly wrote that her principal issue of concern was "the perception of the reforms, which created a presumption that the best interests of the child were served by a meaningful relationship with both parents after divorce.

"However, at the time of the 2006 reforms, it was sold to the public as an 'equal time' provision rather than a starting point that could be altered due to the circumstances of the case."

Chief Justice Diana Bryant Chief Justice Bryant told the newspaper: "It is problematic in that it is creating problems in the community because people do not understand the Act. It's not seen as a concern inside the court, but the expectations of the parties are a problem.

"It may have led to misunderstandings and may dissuade women from raising issues of violence and abuse. There is also concern that they might be branded 'unfriendly' if they raise allegations of violence and that they don't pursue them because of that."

This was backed by senior family lawyers who said the fathers in particular came to them with firm expectations.

DOTA editorialised that on the face of it this represented bias on the part of a woman who, with her handsome government salary, was meant to be representing everyone neutrally.

"We have these terrible expressions, which say there shall be a presumption of joint responsibility," said Stephen Winspear of the Victorian Law Institute. "That is not joint time but as soon as it says the word 'joint' people jump on it and think they have got all these rights. You have to be careful; language is dangerous."

The editor of *Australian Family Lawyer*, Ian Kennedy, agreed: "The sausage is fine. It's the sizzle that is causing the problem."

The head of the family law section of the Law Council, Geoff Sinclair, drew attention to section 117AB of the Family Law Act which deals with costs orders where false allegations are made.

"It should not be there," said Mr Sinclair. "It may stop people raising issues they are legitimately concerned about."

***

The Australian Law Reform Commission had by this stage joined The Australian Institute of Family Studies and former Family Court judge Richard Chisholm in conducting an inquiry into the shared parenting laws and family violence at the behest of the Rudd government.

The Commission had been formally asked to develop a national legal framework to tackle family violence.

In our weekly flyer we wrote: "Arrogantly, the government is not even pretending to consult dads. One report is by the Australian Institute of Family Studies. The next is by the Law Council of Australia, whose feminist stances are also well known. And finally retired Family Court judge Richard Chisholm is conducting another review. His hostility to shared parenting is equally well known and he is perceived in the separated dads community as displaying the worst characteristics of the old style of Family Court, which almost invariably treated fathers with contempt.

"A better choice than Chisholm would have been Michael Green QC, co-author of the book *Shared Parenting*. That this government is prepared to overthrow the popular reforms to our despised family law system and return the country to the dark ages when the majority of fathers entering the court rarely if ever saw their children again defies belief. The government's kowtowing to the wild exaggerations of the taxpayer funded domestic violence industry and the peddling of hysterical hatred against men has sickened many."

DOTA editorialised that the Family Court was directly involved in the campaign against the reforms, which it had never welcomed. Always a law unto itself, the Court had brooked no criticism of its operations.

The reforms encouraging it to treat fathers with some measure of dignity after its long history of treating them dismissively had been imposed upon the Family Court by the legislature for the simple reason that there had been overwhelming disquiet in the community over its conduct. The reforms did not sit well within the Court itself. They were only ever adopted reluctantly and the Court appeared to do all it could to circumvent them.

The slow rate of adoption of shared parenting despite the widespread support for such an option from the public was ample evidence of this. It continued a long history of refusing to accept responsibility for its own poor reputation and doing its best to ignore the will of Parliament.

***

As evidence of the Family Court's direct involvement in and even manipulation of the campaign to turn back the shared parenting laws, under the headline "Court lets children and mother hide from father" *The Age* newspaper ran a story in late July 2009 which the Family Court had specifically alerted them to. It was a case where the Court had granted a woman and her two young children permission "to go into hiding and change their identity to escape her 'violent, abusive and controlling' former partner."

The newspaper reported the court's use of people's private tragedies for propaganda purposes without question.

Carol Nader wrote that the Family Court had upheld the woman's complaints that she and her children had endured a history of domestic violence and said the family could move from their home in Tasmania to anywhere in Australia without telling the father of their new location.

"The father had sought shared parental responsibility, where the children would live with their mother but he would spend time with them on alternate weekends, one evening a week during school term, and for half of school holidays and special occasions. But last week, a Family Court judge ordered him to not go within 500 metres of the woman or his children.

The Age reported: "The mother claimed the father had threatened to kill her. But he denied virtually all the allegations of violence, and said they had been made to exclude him from the children's lives."

No evidence was offered to prove that the father was indeed "violent, abusive and controlling" and it was perfectly feasible no such evidence existed beyond the claims of the mother.

Were there any police or medical reports at all to back up the claims? If the case was similar to so many others, the only "evidence" to back up the woman's claims may have been a psychiatric report from one of the Court's controversial and from a father's perspective often complained about family report writers.

We will probably never know the truth about this case, as we will never know the truth about so many others. The thousands upon thousands of trials where fathers had been denied a relationship with their children based solely on false allegations and the word of the mother made fathers and their representative groups naturally sceptical.

One can't help wondering, if the man really was such a bastard, why did this woman not just have a relationship with him, but have two of his children?

***

DOTA editorialised: "If in the perhaps unlikely circumstance the father genuinely did suffer from anger or violence issues, surely the state had a responsibility to see that he was sent into treatment. Rather than damaging the children by denying them a relationship with him – and no doubt as a consequence with their paternal grandparents as well. Instead we had the Family Court manipulating the media coverage of family law by using a father's sad personal circumstances for propaganda purposes."

The judge said: "In this case the father has been violent, abusive and controlling. This is one of those exceptional cases where spending time with a parent may do more overall harm to the children than good."

Just like that, without a trace of conscience, these children were made fatherless. Quite possibly, in a secretive and unaccountable court remarkably resistant to change, without a trace of evidence either.

How many fathers could the court have equally bowled up to the media who were now seeing and maintaining a relationship with their children when under the previous regime they would be lucky to see them once or twice a year? How many examples of fathers who had fought long and hard to protect their children against the overwhelming bias of the court and the country's child protection agencies could the men's groups have bowled up? If only they had been asked. If only the secrecy provisions of the legislation allowed open debate and reporting.

TWENTY
SWINGS AND
ROUNDABOUTS

For those concerned about family law in Australia, the year 2010 got off to a lively start with the simultaneous release of three separate reports on shared parenting commissioned by the government of Kevin Rudd, the left now in the ascendent after years on the Opposition benches.

The reviews were conducted by the Australian Institute of Family studies, the Family Law Council and former Family Court judge Richard Chisholm. These would be followed later in the year by yet more reports, most falling into the category of feminist advocacy research, relying on small or self-selecting samples or written with a clear agenda in mind.

Governments fund what they want to find and find what they fund for, never more true than in this arena. Neutral professional inquiry and a genuine search for the truth never has anything to do with it.

The Australian Law Reform Commission was also busy through much of the year, releasing mid-year a discussion paper Family Violence – Improving Legal Frameworks followed in November by their final report Family Violence – A National Legal Response.

The Labor Party turned directly to the established industry and made only limited attempts to consult the views of the public or of lobby groups. By this time most lobby groups had come to the conclusion their views were ignored and only sought to give credence to the government's claim they had consulted widely. They had not. To have consulted more widely would have meant they did not get the answers they sought.

The blizzard of reports was presaged by another piece of classic Family Court behaviour. A mother found by the Family Court to be violent, untruthful, lacking moral values and responsible for the psychological and emotional abuse of her children had been awarded full custody. The father, deemed "principled" and with "much to offer his children", was effectively banned from seeing his daughters.

As DOTA had always maintained, violent, drunken, abusive and drug addicted women were given custody of their children every day of the week. It was simply a lie to claim the court was acting in the best interests of children.

The *Herald Sun* in its report predicted the case would spark renewed debate about family law and the issue of shared parenting.

The father, who could not be named for legal reasons, was described by a Family Court judge as no threat to his daughters, a successful parent who was "courteous" and "intelligent".

The same judge found the mother abandoned her first daughter at two and spurned the child's subsequent attempts at reconciliation and had displayed "dreadful", "cruel" and "malicious" behaviour.

The comments from readers were also fairly classic: Ron O for example declared: "Best solution – sack ALL Family Court judges. None of them have a clue. They give a whole new meaning to the word incompetence. They are NOT acting in the interests of the children – they are acting in the interests of their own inflated egos."

S. Kelvin declared: "This is what feminism has led to throughout the western world: women with no character and men with no rights. Decent people are getting sick of the double standards."

***

Of the first three 2010 reports by far the most comprehensive and scientific was the AIFS report, whose authors included Professor Lawrie Moloney, an occasional DOTA guest, and a team of other researchers from the AIFS.

It showed that for most parents and their children reforms had been well received and were working well. The new network of Family Relationship Centres, in particular, were helping to deflect parents from going to court to fight over the children and most people felt they were treated fairly.

The report took three years to complete and was based on the experiences of 28,000 Australians, including 10,000 parents affected by the reforms, as well as grandparents and lawyers. The evaluation was claimed to be the largest examination of the family law and service system ever undertaken.

The philosophy of shared parental responsibility was overwhelmingly supported by parents, legal professionals and family relationship service providers.

"There's more use of family relationship services, a decline in court filings and some evidence of a shift away from people going straight to court to resolve post-separation relationship difficulties," said Australian Institute of Family Studies Director Professor Alan Hayes.

The report showed relationship services clients provided favourable assessments of the services they attended. Pre-separation services were regarded very highly by clients. At the post-separation level, over 70% of family relationship and family dispute clients said that the service treated everyone fairly and over half said that the services provided them with the help they needed. This represented a high level of satisfaction given the cases often involve strong emotions, high levels of conflict often lacked easy solutions.

The substantial increase in the use of relationship-oriented services, both pre- and post-separation, suggested a cultural shift in the way in which problems that affect family relationships were being dealt with.

The report found a 22 per cent drop in the number of cases going to court.

Professor Hayes said that overall, the reform goal of getting separated parents to work things out for themselves was being achieved, with most separated parents resolving their parenting arrangements within one year and without the use of the legal system.

"This is evidenced in a reduction in child-related parenting matters reaching court, with a fall in applications for court orders and a greater proportion of parents reporting they were able to resolve their issues themselves, supported by the new family relationship services," he said.

Of those surveyed the AIFS found that 80 percent said they supported shared parenting and 70 percent of couples who were in a shared parenting arrangements said they were working well.

"More than a million Australian children currently live in separated families," Professor Hayes said. "The way in which separated couples resolve parenting arrangements, make decisions about their children and conduct their relationships all have significant and lasting impacts on their children's lives for better or worse depending on how well they manage post-separation parenting."

***

The Australian Institute of Family Studies found there was confusion about the new laws, leading to disillusionment, especially amongst fathers, causing anger and time-wasting. The wording of the Act had led many fathers into wrongly believing that equal shared parental responsibility allowed for equal shared care – or 50/50 time. They believed shared care was a right providing they were not violent. In fact, judges only had to consider granting shared care.

The AIFS noted the confusion could make it more difficult for parents, relationship services professionals, lawyers and the courts to get parents to focus on the best interests of the child.

Lawyers in particular indicated that the 2006 reforms promoted a focus on parents' rights rather than children's needs and that the family law system didn't do enough to support arrangements suitable for a child's particular level of development.

More positively, the AIFS Evaluation observed that the changes had encouraged more creativity in making arrangements that involved fathers in children's everyday routines, as well as special activities.

Although only a minority of children had shared care time, the proportion of children with these arrangements had increased. This was part of a longer term trend in Australia and internationally.

The majority of parents with shared care-time arrangements thought the arrangements were working well for both parents and children. On average, parents with shared care time had better quality inter-parental relationships.

The AIFS recorded that generally, shared care time did not appear to have a negative impact on the wellbeing of children.

The exception was where mothers had safety concerns. Irrespective of care-time arrangements, safety concerns – real or not – had a negative impact on children's wellbeing. The impact of mothers' safety concerns on children's wellbeing was exacerbated where they experienced shared care-time arrangements.

"The message out of this evaluation is clear – ongoing conflict between separated parents leads to worse outcomes for children," Professor Hayes said.

The AIFS Evaluation did detect room for improvement in dealing with issues of family violence. More than half the lawyers working in the jurisdiction felt the system did not deal adequately with the issue.

This could well reflect the ideologies of those lawyers attracted to the jurisdiction. Given the low socio-economic status, high unemployment levels, poor educational attainments and dysfunctional lives of the largely welfare and drug or alcohol dependent clients who took up so much of the Court's time, there would probably always be issues of violence amongst at least some of its client groups.

***

Significantly, the AIFS found: "There is no evidence to suggest that family violence and highly conflictual inter-parental relationships are any greater in children with shared care time than for children with other care time arrangements."

Despite the quality of the AIFS's extensive analysis, this finding was subsequently ignored by the government, by women's groups and by the family law and domestic violence industries.

"The evaluation provides clear evidence that while there have been some positive developments, the family law system has some way to go in effectively responding to family violence and child abuse, mental health and substance misuse," Professor Hayes said.

"Where there were safety concerns reported by parents, these were linked to poorer outcomes for their children in all types of care relationships, but for those in shared care time, it was even worse. This is a small but extremely significant minority.

"But it's worth remembering that while the evaluation found that for an important minority equal care time was a serious concern, for children where there's no violence or abuse, equal care time was found to work well."

Key findings from the evaluation included:
- 71 percent of fathers and 73 percent of mothers say they've sorted out their care arrangements
- 39 percent of parents who used family dispute resolution reported reaching an agreement
- 78 percent of Family Relationship Centre staff and 86 per cent of family dispute resolution staff say that family dispute resolution is inappropriate due to family violence for up to a quarter of parents they see
- 16 percent of children are in shared care-time arrangements (i.e., where 35-65 percent of time is spent with both parents)
- More fathers than mothers proposed equal time arrangements when going to court - 10 percent of mothers and 27 percent of fathers
- A majority of separated parents, just over 60 percent, were in friendly or cooperative relationships
- Just under one fifth of separated parents reported their relationship to be full of conflict or fearful, with mothers twice as likely as fathers to report a fearful relationship
- 26 percent of mothers and 17 percent of fathers reported their partner had physically hurt them before or during separation.

In his Family Courts Violence Review that old lion of the Family Court of Australia Richard Chisholm was entirely less positive. He said the laws were "a tangle of legal technicality" which had taken the focus off the best interests of the child and were both confusing and troublesome.

He advocated abandoning the push towards shared parenting. His report said many people wrongly believed the changes to family law meant that separated fathers were automatically entitled to 50-50 custody of their kids. Chisholm wrote: "The presumption of equal parental responsibility has been wrongly taken to mean that there was also a presumption favouring children spending equal time with each parent."

***

Many within the Australian fatherhood movement believed the Family Court had long thrived on false claims of child sexual abuse and inflated claims over domestic violence and its secretive nature and adversarial style of determination simply encouraged this. The claims almost invariably first appeared during custody disputes and were often used as the justification for the removal of children from their fathers. These views were neither sought nor provided by any of the inquiries looking at the issue.

While not mentioned in any of the inquiries, the One In Three campaign by Men's Health Australia was beginning to play a significant part in raising doubt about the government's exaggerations and the domestic violence industry's excesses. The organisation began systematically taking issue with official distortion of statistics.

Their campaign led to stories such as that in the *Herald Sun* in September of 2010: "The issues of child protection and domestic violence have been hijacked by politically motivated feminist cliques, according to a coalition of men's groups."

The paper reported the claim came after an ombudsman's report found bureaucrats guilty of "unreasonable and wrong administrative action" after failing to correct false and misleading information that promoted the idea men were overwhelmingly responsible for domestic violence.

The ombudsman found that South Australia's Office for Women presented erroneous statistics, such as that 95 percent of domestic violence involved a male perpetrator and a female victim. On the contrary, raw data show that, overall, at least one in three victims were male.

Men's Health Australia spokesman Greg Andresen said the SA Ombudsman's report should make the Gillard Government think twice about rolling back the shared parenting reforms introduced to family law by the Howard government – which effectively guaranteed fathers some level of access to their children in the event of marital breakdown.

"The picture seems to be emerging of offices of women around the country – who advise state and federal ministers – having taken deeply feminist lines on domestic abuse and child protection," Andresen said. "These bureaucrats have a strong feminist perspective – and that's probably appropriate for people concerned with women's issues.

"But the problem is that when governments roll out programs relating to children, what gets rolled out is a program for women, not one that has equal regard for men and women. The conventional wisdom among these people is that the only perpetrators of domestic violence are men and the only perpetrators of violence against children are men. There is a wealth of research that shows that men are almost as likely to suffer domestic violence or abuse."

***

Tony Miller from DIDS declared AVOs and false allegations were often the first tool used by warring parties in the early days of divorce or separation to secure custody of children or to exclude contact or punish one parent for the failure of the relationship.

"Once an AVO has been issued, most often against the male, it makes it extremely difficult and complex when it comes to obtaining time with their children. In the past the AVO system has been abused and the concern now is with the new reforms to the Family Law System that AVOs will be used to circumvent any chance of dispute resolution through the new Family Relationship Centres and force people back into the court system."

Miller said he had once been one of those sad dads denied contact with their children peering through the wire fence surrounding his son's school. "I was spotted and asked to move on," he recalled. "I explained who I was and that I just wanted to catch a glimpse of my little boy who I hadn't seen for many years. I was taken to the principal's office and after explaining the circumstances was told that I was listed to have no contact. It was many years ago but I remember it as yesterday.

"After breaking down in front of him, the principal took pity on me and let me peer through the blinds of his office. He had to point him out to me because I, his father, couldn't recognise my own son. I left quietly, humbly thanking him for his kindness and in tears.

"My boy grew up not knowing his dad and now I am still peering through the fence unable to break through, only now it's not wire, it's heroin addiction.

"Whilst our children need protection against any form of violence we must be ever vigilant of the use of our children as pawns between warring parents and come to terms with the reality that fatherlessness is destroying Australian society today."

In a father free zone, the Family Law Council's report titled "Improving responses to family violence in the family law system: An advice on the intersection of family violence and family law issues" was released concurrently with the AIFS and Chisholm reports.

The report demonstrated why the previous government had tended to work around the Council rather than with it.

"Improving Responses To Family Violence" opened with the claim that the pattern of family violence which became visible in the family law system was only the tip of the iceberg of family violence, alcoholism, drug addiction and mental illness entrenched in Australia.

The report repeated the myths of the domestic violence industry that one in three Australian women experienced physical violence and one in five experience sexual violence over their lifetime, figures which could only be obtained by the widest definition of domestic violence. The possibility there could be male victims of domestic violence received not a mention.

***

The Council urged the government to address the concerns of women that if they could not prove their claims of domestic violence they would be labelled an "unfriendly parent". It also recommended that the definition of "family violence" in the Family Law Act be widened to include behaviour by a person towards a family member which was physically or sexually abusive; emotionally or psychologically abusive; economically abusive or was threatening, coercive, or in any other way controlled or dominated a family member or caused them to feel fear for the safety or their well being or behaviour that caused a child to hear or witness, or otherwise be exposed to the effects of such behaviour.

The Council also recommended the clearing up of public confusion between the 2006 shared responsibility reforms and provision of equal time joint custody.

Rick O'Brien, the deputy chairman of the Law Council's family law section, said: "A law that cannot be understood by the people affected by it – or, worse still, lends itself to being actively misunderstood – is a bad law," he said. A significant proportion of the community thinks the 2006 reforms mandate equal shared time. They do not. Shared care is only an arrangement judges must consider, though consider it they must after going through various other steps."

The left, and their buddies in the entirely tax payer funded family law industry, were back in town.

Shadow Attorney General George Brandis disagreed with the moves to wind back shared parenting and dismissed Chisholm's report as taking "a fairly tendentious view of the operation of the 2006 reform". He said the Howard government's 2006 laws adequately protected children and the proposed expansion of the definition of violence would weaken the definition of genuine violence.

Brandis referred to the Institute of Family Studies findings that in general the

2006 reforms had worked well and there was no evidence to suggest children were being exposed to any greater level of family violence. "So there seems to be something of a difference of emphasis, if not a conflict, between Professor Chisholm and Australian Institute of Family Studies."

Senator Brandis said the reports did not justify a change in direction for family law. "They should not be used by the Government as a pretext or an excuse to walk away from the principle that every child has a right to a meaningful relationship with both parents on the occasion of family breakdown, while always maintaining, as has never been in doubt, the paramount interests of the child as the first consideration.

"The Opposition's position is that we do not believe that the shared parenting arrangements should be walked away from. We are not persuaded that there is sufficient evidence or, indeed, any persuasive evidence that the 2006 legislation has not worked in a satisfactory fashion."

Nor was it good policy to define domestic violence so broadly that almost any conduct could constitute violence. "If the Act does that then what it is in fact doing is watering down the concept of violence," he said.

***

On the other hand, Shayne Neumann, head of Labor's Social Affairs Caucus Committee and a former family lawyer, said the shared responsibility laws had gone too far and had hurt women and children. He claimed the Howard Government got it wrong on shared parenting in 2006, moving without any social research and in a knee jerk reaction to the urgings of a vocal minority of men's groups. He seems to forget that the changes were introduced with bipartisan support.

"By elevating the rights of parents above the need to protect children, the Howard Government fettered judicial discretion and created a legislative pathway fixated on shared parenting," he said. "Children were exposed to violence. The definitions in the past were too narrow and pandering to the men's rights groups. Howard listened to extremists. What Howard was doing for political expediency was listening to the Hansonite voices of the men's rights groups."

Low politics at best, that was all this was. Amazing, truly amazing, the contempt these politicians displayed to their fellow Australians. In reality these supposedly evil men's rights groups were nothing but groups of sad dads who missed their kids and in many cases had had their lives destroyed by an uncompromising and brutally cruel system which did not value them one jot. Hang yourself in the back shed. We truly don't care. That was the message the government was giving these men.

The Attorney General said it was clear from the Chisholm report and the other reviews that women had become reluctant to raise allegations of violence, in part because the court could now punish them by hitting them with the entire bill for proceedings if the allegations were not proved. In other words women, based purely on their gender, should be given the freedom to lie. God forbid if you were a man caught out lying in The Palace of Lies.

McClelland agreed that this "misunderstanding needed to be addressed" but "the question is whether you need legislation to get that information out". He said the government would be looking at the "lighter touch" approach of public education, before diving into the "deeper waters of legislative change".

For the first time McClelland acknowledged that there had been some positive developments from the 2006 changes, chiefly that fathers no longer assumed that they had to accept an 80/20 time split with their children after divorce.

"We've moved past that, but we are now in a situation where the misconception (that each parent is entitled to a 50-50 time split) has taken hold. Our task now is to clarify that. The focus has to be on the best interests of the children, and not the rights of parents."

***

In an election year family law posed a peculiar conundrum for the Rudd government, bringing its feminist and working class constituencies into conflict at a time when polls showed they could not afford to lose votes. Kevin Rudd knew perfectly well there was a million votes in it and he had to tread carefully.

With the Chisholm report and others the Labor government had rigged or arranged enough enquiries to satisfy its feminist supporters with a plethora of recommendations to rewrite the legislation to emphasise domestic violence and the safety of mother and child above any other consideration.

At the same time the Labor government, recognising the popularity of shared parenting in the community, could not afford to alienate its many backers amongst working and middle class fathers, mothers and families supportive of the family law changes.

After the considerable amount of original fanfare and high flying words about protecting the vulnerable from violence as being of paramount concern when the Chisholm inquiry was first announced, an election year was no time to relive the emotional debates over family law of the Howard years.

Perhaps to minimise their impact, all three commissioned reports on shared parenting and violence were released simultaneously and without public fanfare. McClelland emphasised the importance of the AIFS Evaluation and downplayed in particular the contentious recommendations of the Chisholm inquiry, which would have seen family law issues played out in parliament for the remainder of the year.

Brisbane based journalist Madonna King wrote that the Rudd Government, in an election year, now had to decide whether to address the recommendations to change family law yet again, this time to emphasise issues of family violence, and thereby raise the ire of one set of parents, particularly fathers, or let it slide, with the promise of something less than legislation, and increase the frustration of another set of parents, often mothers.

"Either way, the Prime Minister and his team will face a sustained lobby effort that began this week, with a campaign by fathers' groups to fight any suggestion shared-care provisions be wound back.

"The problem is that the law is only one of the pillars of a system that just isn't working. Listen to talkback, and hear the hurt and pain as individual parents tell their story about custody battles, false allegations of violence, real violence that is not acted upon, lengthy delays in hearings, and family wars that know no bounds.

"And both sides of this debate have strong ammunition, which is at the crux of the problem now faced by Kevin Rudd."

***

King retold the story of Dionne Fehring who blamed the emphasis on shared parenting for the deaths of her two young children. Her former partner suffocated her 17-month-old daughter Jessie and baby son Patrick, who was only 12 weeks old, with plastic bags, before killing himself – on the day he was due to hand the children back to her after the Family Court had reversed custody after hearing her accusations of domestic violence.

King said Fehring believed shared parenting couldn't always work, and the assumption that has existed since the 2006 law changes, that 50/50 custody is a right, needed to be wound back.

"You wonder, after hearing the pain in her voice, how shared parenting, and the assumption of shared custody, can be prescribed in law," King wrote.

But on the other hand fathers' groups were signalling a nationwide campaign if the laws were changed.

"There are two sides to every argument," King wrote. "Take the case of the father who…sought custody of his three-year-old son, against his mother's wishes.

"She shopped around at doctors, lodging numerous allegations against the father, who persisted in his attempts to be part of his son's life. He just wanted to be there for his son. He wanted to know him; to be part of his life.

"Eventually, the father was awarded custody. And the mother, two weeks before handover, killed herself and the child."

King concluded: "With tens of thousands of Australian children in shared-care arrangements, it's not an issue the Rudd Government can fudge."

***

The Men's Rights Agency issued a press release declaring the Labor governments moves to roll back shared parenting would cost them votes. Sue Price said a recent survey of nearly 500 people showed the issue was a vote changer.

"The swing against Labor is being almost exclusively fuelled by the expected rollback of shared parenting arrangements gained under the Howard Government," Sue Price said.

"Nearly 60 percent said they would have voted Labor in the coming election if they had not known about the reviews to family law."

The following month Chief Justice Diana Bryant was playing her part in the moral panic of the day by calling for a radical change to the law to provide more protection to family members "at risk of violence".

While critics did not see her role as appropriate, she appeared determined to play her part in the campaign to roll back shared parenting.

The Chief Justice said she wanted more information from confidential mediation sessions between separating couples to be given to family law courts if there was believed to be a risk to a child or a parent's safety. She presented her concerns to the Attorney General.

She argued that the types of information provided would include evidence of violence or mental health and drug and alcohol issues. Judges would use the information to help with decisions about parental access and where children live.

Under existing law, any information that emerged in a mediation session was confidential.

She said there might be cases where risk factors could be missed if full information was not given to the court in the early stages of a case: "You might have a mediator who has formed a view that mental health issues are a serious problem. They can't provide that information.

"All of the information that is conveyed to mediators in family relationship centres is privileged. They might have quite a lot of information about family violence from their screening tool which can't be shared with courts. So when people come to court they just start off fresh with an application.

"I do think we ought to look at whether we can get something more from those organisations. Something more that informs the courts when an application is filed to alert them to issues that need to be dealt with as a matter of urgency."

***

With so much institutional propaganda, there were few voices publicly defending shared parenting or raising questions about the negative consequences of exaggerating fears over domestic violence.

One exception was Alby Schultz, the member for Hume whose percentage of the vote in his rural electorate of Hume, already high, had increased since he began speaking out on issues around family law and child support.

"The release of these reports should not be used by the Rudd Labor Government as a pretext or an excuse to walk away from the principle that every child has a right to a meaningful relationship with both parents on the occasion of family breakdown, while always maintaining, as has never been in doubt, the paramount interests of the child as the first consideration," he said.

Echoing a common story heard by Dads On The Air, Schultz said he believed many instances of family conflict could be averted by a shake up of the Child Support Agency.

"The overwhelming similarity in cases that are brought to my attention is that even though a separated couple have entered into a shared parenting agreement, there is no recognition of this fact by the CSA in calculating the maintenance that is to be paid by the paying parent.

"Is it not surprising then, why a father continually questions where his maintenance is going when it is plainly obvious that it is not being spent on what it is intended for and why, in some sensitive cases, the father becomes so disillusioned and distressed by the continual aggressive tactics employed by the CSA with respect to the collection of his child maintenance, that a tragedy sometimes occurs.

"I dare say that if the paying parent was able to direct and observe through CSA administration, a certain percentage of their payment go into a trust account specifically designed to ensure child maintenance is used for the daily and future care of the child, these extreme cases may reduce."

***

Lone Father's president Barry Williams condemned the Chisholm report, saying it was plain wrong and shared parenting was the way to go.

Tony Miller from Dads in Distress said parenting laws were being "rolled back to the Dark Ages".

"We've fought hard in the last 10 years to ensure fathers and children get a fair go," he said. "Since shared parenting came in, we are most definitely seeing a fairer deal in the court system than we did in the past. If it's going to be changed and rolled back to the dark ages that would just astound us. All we're after is to make sure dads get to see kids as often as they can. Any change to that and we would be absolutely horrified."

On the other hand the Family Court's campaign against the intent of the legislation continued apace. Again in February, the Full Bench of the Family Court clarified what it meant by "shared care" and "substantial and significant time" for children after divorce – and it wasn't a 50/50 time split between parents.

The Court posted an appeal decision to their website in a case known as Whisler and Whisler (2010).

The judgement demonstrated that fathers who won "shared parental responsibility" of their children could find they still saw them only on alternate weekends, for two hours after school on Wednesdays, and half the school holidays.

Mr Whisler had been the "house-husband" and stay-at-home dad for two years before separating. He appealed against a decision by a Federal Magistrate to scrap a "week about" arrangement for his children, aged six and four, and replace it with one in which the children lived mainly with their mother and saw their father on alternate weekends, for 2 1/2 hours on Wednesday nights, half the school holidays and on special occasions such as Fathers' Day.

Mr Whisler complained that the orders did not amount to the children having "substantial and significant time" with him.

The Family Court thought otherwise.

"These orders are clearly for substantial and significant time between father and children," the decision read. The Court said this was in part because he could see his children for two and a half hours on Wednesdays.

"That doesn't sound like the spirit of the new law at all," Michael Green QC of the Shared Parenting Council said of the decision. "There's no way in the world that that is shared parenting."

Just as it had done with the 1995 reforms, the Court ignored the will of parliament and subverted legislative reform.

The legislators should have known, in all likelihood they did know, that this would happen.

The decision also vindicated DOTA's editorial stance that the Family Court would not change direction unless it absolutely had to. The 2006 laws had not been bold enough in the first instance, leaving too much discretion to Family Court judges. The parliament's purported desire to lessen the pain and acrimony common amongst separated parents and to promote cooperative parenting after separation was simply too easily ignored.

***

In a brief respite to the wave of anti-father and anti-shared parenting propaganda, in May *The Age* ran a tribute story to shared care by Jo Case, editor of *The Big Issue*.

She told the story of missing her son so badly she climbed into his bed and started crying. Then she dragged herself off to the bathroom and looked at herself in the mirror. "Come on, I told myself sternly, looking deep into my own slitted red eyes. He's not dead, he's just at his father's. Like he is every other week of his life. You'll see him soon. The next thought, the one that really sobered me up, was, What if his father rang you right now and asked you to take him for the week? How would you get your work done and your deadlines met?"

Case said the most common reaction from harried mothers when they discovered she shared the care of her son on a week about basis was: "You're so lucky. You get the best of both worlds."

The second reaction was, "I could never do that. I'd just go insane with missing them. That's so good of you." Case said this also came from fellow mothers, but these were the types who disinfected their kids' toys when they dropped on the floor and no longer accepted lunch or dinner invitations because their children needed routine.

The third reaction was, "Wow. Really? That is great. Good on you." This came from separated fathers who were only allowed access to their children for one weekend a fortnight.

"They tend to beam at me like I am a saint," she wrote.

"Sometimes I wish I had never been so 'reasonable', and suspect myself of having been so depressed when I left my son's father that I accepted shared custody out of exhaustion rather than fairness. But, when all my guilt-tinged analysis has been exhausted, one fact remains. Shared custody, despite its effects on me or my former partner, is the best thing for my son. He has two parents who want him, who care about him, and who are intimately involved in his everyday life."

***

In mid-June of 2010 Tony Miller from Dads In Distress, was awarded a medal of the Order of Australia for his contribution to the welfare of men through his role as the group's founder.

Miller started the group after his own personal breakdown. "My life was a mess, I was suicidal and I couldn't find someone to talk to who I thought would understand what I was going through," he recounted. "I realise now it was a completely selfish act on my part but I wrote a letter to *The Advocate* in Coffs Harbour and almost immediately other men contacted me with similar stories of isolation, anger and confusion."

Dads in Distress was formed in 2000, the same year as Dads On The Air.

Although a decade had passed, Miller told his local paper not enough had changed.

"People are still going back and forth to the Family Court, there are still battles over the contravention of court orders and sadly men in crisis are still taking their own lives," Miller said.

Dads On The Air ran a tribute to Dads In Distress, with our editorial reading in part: "For Australian men, who have reached the end of their emotional ability to cope with the ravages of a Family Justice system which has removed their children, property and savings, Dads In Distress, now ten years old, provides a safe and supportive haven for them to regain their emotional strength and sense of self-worth."

It was unfortunate that the need for an organisation like DIDS remained so strong. Miller left the organisation in 2010 for internal political reasons and when last heard of was homeless and sleeping in his car.

For the cast of characters that now made up Dads On The Air, monitoring the issue of family law and child support reform in Australia had become like watching a back to the future movie in slow motion.

It was a time to reflect.

After all those years, the resistance of the Family Court and its flanking bureaucracies to reform in the face of widespread public and professional odium remained nothing short of astonishing.

As of 2010 the Court was the same institution that a decade or more before both the public and the legal profession were so widely disenchanted with. It used many of the same suspect family report writers as it did back then. It had the same excruciatingly complex and distressing processes which imposed extreme, prolonged and unfair pressure on litigants. It had the same leisurely pace, the same extensive delays and the same style of judgements.

***

While the Family Court made great claims for its new less-adversarial, supposedly more child centred style of trials, with the legislation mandating that such methods be implemented, as of 2010 there remained a need for a broader and more independent confirmation of their success, including published interviews with parents.

The court's own evaluation was positive, but in the AIFS evaluation of the reforms lawyers had expressed a number of concerns, including increased delays and costs. One lawyer said: "There is simply not the resources for matters to be dealt with in a proper and timely fashion. The delay is prejudicial to all involved".

Several participants in the AIFS evaluation made mention of the need to prepare or "coach" clients prior to trial and to think carefully about the evidence that was to be presented. This required clients to engage more resources and therefore money in preparing for the first part of the court process.

Lawyers said the Less Adversarial Trial Scheme required more preparation and more court events, and consumed more judicial resources.

"Participants noted that, along with the obvious financial costs that multiple appearances entail, clients also face an emotional cost, as the reforms have resulted in multiple court events that heighten conflict and have a negative impact on children."

The AIFS's examination of the trials as part of its evaluation of the 2006 reforms did not examine the views of parents.

The expressed view at Dads On The Air was that, If possible, these styles of trials inappropriately handed even more power to the Court's judges and the Court's contentious family report writers.

Contentious being a polite way to describe their truly shocking practices.

Despite Dads On The Air's scepticism and at times strident criticism of the "little steps" reforms finally passed into law by the Howard government in 2006 they did in fact bring about some significant and positive changes.

As a result of the 2003 inquiry and the extensive community debate and media coverage it generated, shared parenting was by 2010 far more widely accepted and supported as the best outcome for both parents and children post-separation. Surveys confirmed the popularity of the laws.

Despite DOTA's belief that the legislation was not strong enough to deliver shared parenting outcomes, statistics released by both the Family Court and the Child Support Agency demonstrated an increase, albeit from a low base. Perhaps it was not just a matter of legislation. Perhaps it was an idea whose time had come, the necessary revolution.

The government's Family Characteristics Surveys of 1997 showed low levels of shared care – in just three percent of divorced families.

The Family Characteristics Survey of 2006-07 conducted 12 months after the legislative changes found the level of shared parenting had risen to eight percent.

DOTA's view was it should be at 90 percent, but at least there was progress.

***

The Family Court's first release of statistics following the reforms also showed progress, with fathers being granted primary care in 17 percent of decided cases; equal parenting time in 15 percent of these cases; and shared parenting of around five days per fortnight in 14 percent. In consent cases, fathers were granted primary care in 8 percent of cases; equal parenting in 19 percent of cases; and shared parenting in 14 percent of cases.

An Australian Institute of Family Studies Evaluation showed the majority of parents in shared parenting situations were happy, believing the arrangement worked well for themselves and their children.

But more parents were reaching their own arrangements in terms of both custody and child support, leading to less acrimony and more workable solutions.

DOTA had been more than doubtful the Family Relationship Centres would succeed, fearful they would turn into yet another secretive and counter-productive layer of bureaucracy staffed by hostile man haters, determinedly opposed to shared parenting outcomes and determined to take the woman's side no matter what.

In their early days inconsistent stories emerged from clients having both positive and negative experiences.

But the AIFS Evaluation of the 2006 Reforms suggested they had been a success. A clear majority of parents who tried to resolve their differences in the centres said they "worked well".

"A significant proportion of separated parents are able to sort out their post-separation arrangements with minimal engagement with the formal system," the report recorded.

Considering the frustrating, expensive and lengthy nightmare litigants still faced if they were determined to resolve their issues in the Court, that was a major achievement.

But the Australian community was still throwing up many heart breaking stories of lives needlessly mangled through the process of separation and divorce. There remained many complaints of the family law and child support systems themselves contributing to animosity and dysfunction between separated parents, with predictably negative results on parents and children alike.

Dads On The Air suggested that the back to the future moves of the Labor government and its reliance on a narrow range of elite opinion, the fact that the Parliament as a whole had so little insight into and so little will to act on the human tragedy playing out in the Australian community remained alarming. The Parliament's combined ignorance of the ramifications of their failure to properly legislate for relief of the plight of the nations' fathers and their children, and indeed for non-custodial mothers, was a sad reflection of an inability to value the voices of ordinary people

If implemented more boldly, the shared parenting reforms would ultimately have benefited not just non-custodial parents and their children, but single mothers. Laws requiring both genders to be treated equally in achieving the best outcomes for children could have been heralded nationally as a proud sign of an increasingly civilised and equitable society.

With government research indicating single mothers remained on welfare for an average of 12 years each, the reforms would have helped break the often intergenerational cycle of welfare dependency and unemployment characteristic of single parents. As a result it would have provided many of these mothers – and their children – with richer and more fulfilling life experiences as they returned to the workforce.

Perhaps, too, with a bit of realism and spirit of cooperation in place, they would have prevented or mitigated the whirl of hysteria that was now being deliberately promoted around issues of family law and domestic violence.

***

Dads On The Air editorialised: "We, as a nation, have a duty to protect the rights of our children. If we continue to get this wrong, if we continue to pretend that our current path of destroying father child relationships is acceptable in the name of ideologically driven hysteria over alleged male brutality, if we continue to shy away from a presumption of a shared parenting outcomes as a starting point for separating parents, then we are failing in one of our most fundamental duties to future generations.

"While there have been some improvements, history may well see this larger failure, this continuing abuse of children, as one of the great moral evils of our time.

"The moral panic or mass hysteria, being promoted by opponents of shared parenting over the issue of domestic violence will ultimately prove counterproductive, causing more harm than good, sowing distrust, doubt and dislike between the genders.

"The industry's exaggerated hyperbole has already contributed over the years to many false or grossly exaggerated claims amongst separating couples. And to many innocent fathers being denied contact with their children. The claims, usually made at the height of a custody battle for the single purpose of embarrassing, humiliating, and denigrating the children's fathers, acquiring advantage in the dispute over property and assets, and procuring a knockout blow in the fight over their offspring and the welfare funds that come with them, has lead parents to inadvertently harming their own offspring.

"While its proponents cast themselves as champions and protectors of children, many of the actions of the family violence brigade are misguided. Both men and women inhabit this earth, and to paint half the human race as violent abusers in such a reckless manner does great harm to society as a whole. Like all ideologically based mass movements, it will ultimately founder on a lack of truth – which is that there have always been high conflict and low conflict couples and always will be, that most people are of good will but a small percentage of both men and women are abusive.

"The expansion of the definition of domestic violence to include much of what is perfectly ordinary if not always praiseworthy human behaviour – such as emotional or financial manipulation – will create a legislative quagmire which will diminish the standing of the Family Court still further.

"Passing laws which criminalise the behaviour of such large numbers represents a dramatic expansion of the role of the state in people's private lives and will prove counterproductive. But given the shibboleths involved, the intimidating high moral ground advocates occupy, most people's unquestioning wish to do the right thing, the sympathy and chivalry the alleged victim group of women and children elicits and the astonishing amount of government money poured into the arena, moving forward to a saner era may prove difficult.

"The astonishing number of groups, academics and lawyers making a living from the hundreds of millions of government dollars being poured into domestic violence programs ensures that the arena becomes self perpetuating and difficult to reform, or even to question.

"It also ensures that the misuse of domestic violence allegations in custody disputes would continue. The truth will not come out before many people have been needlessly harmed."

***

Dads On The Air was virtually the only media outlet in Australia to consistently raise doubts about the operation of the domestic violence industry. We regularly pointed out studies in Australia and around the world that showed domestic violence was not the gendered crime feminist advocates claimed it to be.

We also pointed out the hypocrisy of failing to show concern for male victims, despite for example the Personal Safety Survey by the Australian Bureau of Statistics showing men were twice as likely as women to be the victim of violence, either from other men or from their intimate partners.

Our editorial position had always been that, perhaps with the best of intentions, the industry's self-serving promotion of what had descended into public hysteria over domestic violence, was ultimately counterproductive. The failure of all this government inspired activity to decrease the level of intimate partner violence in the community is testament to this.

The propaganda and heightened fears now being whipped up by various interest groups around issues of family violence and family law have simply validated Dads On The Air's position. Alternative views are never sought. The marginalisation of father's and men's voices is plain for all to see.

We wrote and broadcast our views: "The Family Court of Australia is in large degree today all too much like the institution it was when Dads On The Air began broadcasting in 2000. It remains impervious to criticism, overly legalistic, out of touch with mainstream Australian society and continues to push its own out-dated agendas onto the public.

"While there had been hope for positive change after the retirement of Nicholson, the new Chief Justice Diana Bryant has not proved to be the great reforming broom some might have dreamt about. However she was something of a relief after the long reign of her predecessor, if only because she did not feel compelled to comment on every major social issue of the day from asylum seekers to the smacking of children.

"Bryant however has not hesitated to use her position as head of the Court to directly interfere in the debate over the shared parenting provisions in the 2006 legislation and to play a part in their potential rollback."

***

The 2006 family law reforms of the Howard government, while not introducing a rebuttable presumption of joint custody, were for a period, more successful than Dads On The Air had expected. While much about the divorce regime remained as bad or worse than ever; a cultural shift took place in the community as a result of the heightened awareness of the problems. Many fathers now expected to share the care of their children after separation. Many separating couples also seemed to expect the same thing. An amicable divorce became almost a fashion accessory.

Whatever the lettering of the law, through the prolonged debate many separating couples had come to expect and accept that they would both share the care of their children after separation.

Dads On The Air editorialised: "While the levels of shared care are nowhere near where they might have been with bolder and more visionary legislative reform and expansive public education campaigns, and the lives of children and parents alike are still being badly impacted by the very institutions meant to assist them, more children were getting to see both parents after separation.

"To a fair degree the Howard reforms did promote cultural change and encouraged shared parenting outcomes. Rightly or wrongly, whether technically it was written into the legislation or not, separated fathers expected and in many cases believed they had the right to substantially care for their kids on an equal footing with their ex-wives or partners. In many instances starting from a different point ensured more positive outcomes.

"While insufficient, the legislative changes also appeared to have engendered some improvement in the institutional treatment of separated fathers."

***

Dads On The Air's editorial position had always been, perhaps from the comfortable position of pundits, that the Howard government reforms were too little too late, were not nearly as effective as they should be, left far too much power into the hands of secretive, unaccountable and ideologically driven judges and could be too easily rolled back.

We had always maintained that the government should have made the legislation bolder, stronger and more definitive, to assure the public that both parents would be treated equally after divorce and that the government expected both parents to care for their children in the tough love spirit of "you both made them you can both look after them".

We supported the campaign for a rebuttable notion of joint custody aka shared parenting because it was the only solution we could see to the wasteland of unhappy lives that the Family Court's sole custody model had created.

But while they were nowhere near as forthright as DOTA would have liked, by 2010, as a result of the reforms, anecdotally public opprobrium of the court appeared to have diminished substantially. The offices of parliamentarians were no longer clogged with unhappy litigants. Results for the Child Support Agency were more mixed.

While DOTA criticised the reforms for not going far enough in encouraging cooperative parenting after divorce or separation, claiming they failed to tackle many of the endemic problems in family law and were too easily wound back, the public impression was that the system's problems and its anti-father bias had been fixed.

In its various speculations on the subject DOTA maintained that one should never underestimate the power of fashion in changing entrenched social attitudes. The middle and upper classes, already financially secure, were waking up to the destructive impacts and spectacular waste of money involved in prolonged Family Court disputes. One of the tricks in expanding the benefits of cooperative parenting is to spread this cultural shift towards shared parenting, already becoming established amongst affluent sections of the community, further down the income scale.

***

The Howard era from 1994 to 2007 saw the percentage of single parent households as a percentage of all parents increased by a couple of points to around 22 per cent. For just over 60 percent of one parent families, government payments were their largest source of income.

At the end of 2010, a decade after Dads On The Air first began broadcasting two steps forward and one step back had become more like a hundred yard dash into a nightmare combining the worst elements of the past with a more sophisticated totalitarianism, a higher level of state control and penetration into private lives than Australia had yet seen.

During 13 years of a "conservative" supposedly pro-family Liberal government headed by John Howard hundreds of thousands of fathers and their children had their relationship with each other mangled by the established divorce industry.

According to the Australian Bureau of Statistics, in 2006, towards the end of Howard's reign, 87 percent of one-parent families with children under 15 years were headed by mothers. The proportion headed by fathers had changed little, from 12 percent in 1997 to 13 percent in 2006.

The style of custody order favoured by The Family Court of Australia had created great personal suffering on the part of disenfranchised fathers but also had significant social consequences.

As well, during the Howard era thousands upon thousands of separated fathers were driven to despair and suicide as the Child Support Agency plundered whatever remained of their assets and income and subjected them to routine and often incessant institutional harassment.

After many years of fumbling around the issue with indecisive inquiries the conservatives finally moved in its last term of government to establish the vague notion of "shared responsibility" into law. For many fathers it was far too little, far too late. The Family Court made it's reluctance to embrace the reforms very clear.

It was open on the evidence before it for the 2003 parliamentary committee investigating child custody to recommend a rebuttable presumption of joint custody. It failed to do so and the ramifications of that mistake continue to the present day.

Whether or not it's true it certainly looked like there was a good deal of political interference behind the execrable Every Picture Tells A Story. Howard could have found a way to introduce stronger shared parenting provisions but baulked, in his final term, at more profound reform of the divorce industry and its government institutions. Perhaps as some of his followers said, he was a true conservative in every sense, making change only slowly.

But this was a man who could take decisive and radical action when it suited. Howard took the country to war in Iraq, against the wishes of much of the population, in a single decisive move for the sole reason that he saw it as expedient to support America as an ally. The same man's incremental moves to reform family law and child support moved through so many committees and so many inquiries over so many years, and was so watered down in the process, that the original media support and public acclaim his bold expressions of interest in joint custody generated died away.

Ironically, despite the number of commissioned reports designed to give the Labor government justification in winding back Howard's modest shared parental responsibility reforms, when it came to the steeple gate the new government also baulked. At least, that is, prior to the 2010 election. Then Prime Minister Kevin Rudd reportedly had little appetite for moving against the nation's separated dads in the run up to a difficult campaign.

Many of those separated fathers were union members, the bulwark of the Labor Party, and senior parliamentarians with close links were reported to have warned against the move.

***

The notion of shared parenting, as others have noted, was popular in the pub.

But by June of 2010 Australia was blessed with its first woman Prime Minister Julia Gillard. While many of her pronouncements after ousting Kevin Rudd in a palace coup were decidedly mainstream, she owed much to feminist supporters and political groups such as Emily's List and was justifiably proud of her achievements. While the bandwagon was already on a roll, she made no effort to reign in her Attorney General or the Party and its sympathisers' assault on the shared parenting legislation.

The year also saw the Labor government moving to essentially destroy another Howard initiative, the Federal Magistrate's Court, by bringing it under the umbrella of the Family Court. As a simpler, faster and less expensive court in closer contact with litigants the Magistracy had been more inclined to embrace the spirit of the reforms. Its family arm was to be folded into the Family Court as a kind of lower tier of the "superior" court. Opposition Legal Affairs spokesman George Brandis had described the plan as a shambles.

The media's treatment of father's issues had not improved significantly, although a number of separated men now working in the media have at times helped to add some realism. At least for a time after the 2006 legislative reforms a broader range of father's advocates were likely to be quoted, although that impact faded over time.

The tone and substance of debates over family issues, in particular shared parenting and in the latter days family violence and family law, was still largely set by feminist columnists and sympathetic journalists.

A number of newspapers including *The Age* and *The Sydney Morning Herald*, the dominant broadsheets in Australia's two largest cities, still felt free to run feminist advocacy without the provision of any countervailing views.

***

Mirroring the outside world, male editors and chiefs of staff from intact families showed little understanding of the issues and zero empathy with their separated colleagues, believing they must have brought it on themselves. Acting as champions of women during your working day was a simple piece of almost animal psychology guaranteeing the big man goes home to a smooth bed and a calm home life.

Unfortunately, while it had the opportunity, the Howard government did not reform or repeal Section 121 of the Family Law Act, the secrecy provisions forbidding the naming or identifying of litigants. They continue to effectively protect the court and its operations from proper journalistic inquiry and to engender an environment where wild accusations can be made with impunity. Nothing has changed there.

The problems at the Child Support Agency, impacting so heavily on separated parents and undeniably implicated in the despair and suicide rates of separated parents, remain under-reported.

Fatherhood advocates claimed the problems with the Agency were as bad or worse than ever.

Sue Price at Men's Rights told DOTA it was becoming apparent from whistleblowers that the CSA was making decisions contrary to court orders; such as those on legal and actual residency.

"They have an ability to determine whether the child is legal according to court orders or actual care, depending on their determination of the child's living circumstances," Price said. "A person can spend $200,000 on getting residency with their children, a parent disobeys them and the CSA will take the mother's word on what the actual care is, thereby financially rewarding her for defying the court.

"The CSA are in effect thumbing their nose at the court orders. The Labor Government has given the CSA legislative approval to make such decisions in the latest round of amendments.

"Just how effective CSA is when one takes into account a death rate amongst their clientele which is two and a half times that of the normal population; the questionability of the CSA's performance in reducing debt levels, only achieved to any significant degree in 2003-04, when the CSA staff 4 percent pay rise was in the balance, (a whistleblower suggested the debt level was artificially reduced by removing missing payers who had been given a default income) and the financial viability of the cost of collection compared to the claw back savings afforded to the taxpayer in family tax benefits.

"Strangely the cost of collection was removed from the CSA published Facts & Figures data after 2004. It is now a mammoth proposition to troll through Annual expenditure figures of the CSA, Family and Community Services and the Attorney General's department to calculate the cost of collecting each dollar of child support."

These moves coincided with researcher Richard Cruickshank's exposes of the Agency's costs.

***

The Howard Government had an opportunity to fix the appalling mess which is the Australian Child Support Agency. They failed because most politicians do not understand the CSA legislation nor the attitude of those driving CSA doctrine of debt collection and punitive action against fathers, who have been deliberately demonised as criminals and falsely accused of trying to avoid responsibility for their children. And the Parkinson report they relied on to fix the mess did not take seriously the voluminous complaints coming from its clients.

It appeared the Labor government had listened to none of the numerous complaints emanating from the Child Support Agency's clients. During the election campaign in August 2010 Prime Minister Julia Gillard announced her government would hit so-called "deadbeat dads" by strengthening the regime on the use of default income in child support assessments with a "new, more accurate default income arrangement".

She claimed that some parents had failed to lodge tax returns for more than seven years and a new default income of two-thirds of male total average incomes would be applied where tax returns were not filed within two years.

The default would be $39,000 per annum. She said there had been a 325 per cent increase in the use of default incomes where it was lower than the person's taxable income. As well, if no tax return was filed their last known income, as long as it wasn't lower than the default income, would be indexed to wages growth and then used to calculate child support.

In other words, the Labor government was giving Child Support officers even more power to invent father's incomes and drive many of them into lifelong debt. Gillard accepted no responsibility for the mess the Agency continued to create in the lives of separated parents. There were no plans afoot to institute a long overdue investigation into the Agency's social outcomes or its implication in the high unemployment rates amongst separated men or its associated death toll.

***

For a number of days in August 2010 Australia was in a kind of no-man's land after elections delivered a hung parliament. But even as the jostling went on to determine which side of politics would govern, the anti-father forces kept on shipping out their anti-shared parenting propaganda.

Feminist academic Belinda Fehlberg, law professor at Melbourne university specialising in family law noted that there had been almost no mention of family law reform during the election campaign. But, she said, the Howard government's changes to the Family Law Act continue to damage a significant minority of children.

She cited a case recently before the Full Court of Family Court of Australia, known as "Collu & Rinaldo" which involved a four-year-old child who had been travelling a month about between his father in Sydney and his mother in Dubai for 14 months, while the case awaited court hearing.

Fehlberg claimed such arrangements may suit parents, but this case – and the research – showed the psychological damage that can result from constant disruption and lack of stability for such young children.

Fehlberg cited the Australian Institute of Family Studies and the Chisholm Inquiry, saying the demonstrated shared parenting time was not working well for a significant minority of Australian children.

"They showed that fathers have been encouraged to seek shared care and more mothers now feel pressured into it. They also showed that shared care is now used by a substantial minority of parents with significant problems such as high parental conflict, substance abuse and or mental health issues. It is being agreed to by parents and, even more often, ordered by courts in cases where it seems not to be in children's best interests, partly due to community and professional misunderstandings about what the law says."

She wrote that since the spate of reports at the beginning of the year, three further reports examining the shared parenting bill, also commissioned and paid for by the federal Attorney General's Department and released in July, also raised questions.

***

The gravy train of advocacy research that had been characteristic of the entire family law arena for decades remained well in place. The neutrality, even their bona fides, at least as far as family law reform advocates were concerned, remained highly questionable.

Family Court favourite, clinical child psychologist Dr Jennifer McIntosh, looked at the allegedly negative impact of shared care arrangements on children under the age of four.

Her report claimed that children under four who spent substantial time away from the "primary carer" were doing less well than other children on a range of developmental measures, with higher levels of anxiety, aggression and eating disturbances.

Another report by social work professors and feminist advocates Dale Bagshaw, Thea Brown, Elspeth McInness and colleagues was a massive two volume document titled Family Violence and Family Law in Australia: The Experiences and Views of Children and Adults who separated Post-1995 and Post-2006.

This piece of advocacy research was also amply funded by the Attorney General's Department, the services of three universities and a number of women's and domestic violence services.

Blind in their gendered assault on fathers and the commonsense notion of shared parenting, the Attorney General's department had never thought to either employ neutral researchers or to at least make some show of achieving balance through university based organisations such as the Men's Health and Information Research Centre. All done without shame and against the abiding interests of Australian taxpayers.

The authoritative sounding Family Violence and Family Law in Australia relied on responses to on-line questionnaires and phone-ins organised through various women's and domestic violence services.

Many of the women were involved in or were survivors of custody battles.

The researchers declared "A consistency of responses suggested the strong reliability of the data". Give it a rest. This self-selecting group would automatically attract people with grievances, barrows to push, the mentally ill who believed their own fabrications and deluded activists more than capable of manufacturing stories.

And lo and behold their responses were all much the same. They were extremely unlikely to admit to having falsified or exaggerated their claims, indeed on average they claimed to have lived with domestic violence for 10 years. In Australia today, with women more than capable of standing up for themselves, that seems extremely unlikely. But why ruin the story of the noble victim? The just over a hundred children involved in the phone-ins and questionnaires were quite possibly encouraged to participate or tutored by their parents.

The authors claimed their research demonstrated that the family law system did a poor job of supporting and assisting victims of family violence. Which, of course, was exactly what they wanted to find.

The ideological advocacy for what was being paraded as a plausible piece of scholarship defied belief: "One complication is what is defined and accepted as family violence by clients, as victims do not conceptualise their experiences as being family violence in many circumstances and certainly not in legal terms that meet court definitions."

The tone was set in the acknowledgements when they thanked the "courageous children, women and men" who filled out the questionnaires and responded to phone-ins. Courage is saving someone else's life at risk to your own, not filling out a questionnaire.

The authors alleged that: "Their constant complaint was that, instead of receiving sympathy and support from the service providers, they received disbelief and disregard in relation to their experiences of family violence and their concerns for their children's safety."

The claims were often disbelieved for the simple reason that they were often not true, made in the context of an adversarial system which specifically encouraged parents to make claims against each other for personal gain and without consequence. In many cases there existed no proof, no photographs, no police reports, no doctors or hospital reports, no disturbed neighbours. A raised voice or a raised eyebrow is not domestic violence.

The report went on: "Adult victims were frequently advised by lawyers and others not to report family violence for fear of losing their children, even when the violence could be substantiated, and when they did report violence they were often not believed, or were accused of trying to alienate the child from the other parent. Women complained that the perpetrators (who were more often than not men) falsely denied that family violence occurred and this was not investigated. Women also feared for their children's safety when they were in their violent father's care.

"Male and female respondents were also extremely concerned that allegations and denials of child abuse were rarely investigated by the state child protection agencies when they were reported. For some women, their fear as a result of the violence and the threats of retaliation from their male partners was so great that they reported they could not use any services relevant for separating couples."

***

In life you find what you choose to seek. In research you find what you choose to fund. Yet another report, from the Social Policy Research Centre at the University of NSW, found that shared care was experienced differently by mothers and fathers and was most problematic when mothers had serious concerns about their children's safety or there was high parental conflict.

The report concluded that factors such as the level of parental cooperation and conflict were more important than the structure of parenting arrangements.

"In other words, shared care of itself is not necessarily better for children than other care arrangements. Given this, there seems to be no justification for our current legislative approach, which encourages parents in this direction."

During the election the political party most clearly in favour of rolling back the shared parenting provisions was the Greens, who at the beginning of the year had used the Chisholm report as justification for their position.

The article concluded that the incoming government "should act on consistent evidence showing us that a significant number of children are being damaged by our shared parenting laws. What we need are laws that require us to determine children's best interests on a case-by-case basis without preconceived ideas, and laws that require us to take family violence seriously at every step along the way."

That a feminist academic could quote a former Family Court judge as justification for junking shared parenting laws showed just how closed the circuit of logic had become. No light of reason, no reasoned truth, need enter here.

***

The Family Court's traditional style of custody orders was once again being paraded as being in the best interests of children. Feminist columnist Adele Horin, writing in *The Sydney Morning Herald*, continued her decades long hostility to fathers as parents on the paper's opinion pages, this time under the headline "Next government must confront the dangers in family law reforms".

She wrote: "In an election degraded by bipartisan fear-mongering on asylum seekers and climate change, we can be grateful the hot-button issue of family law remained safely off limits.

"Who gets the kids after parents separate, for how long, and in what circumstances is an issue that is far from settled, despite the changes in the Family Law Act the Howard government introduced in 2006 with Labor's support."

She noted that awaiting the incoming Attorney general was $7 million worth of freshly minted, government-commissioned research on the effect of the changes, specifically the impact of shared care arrangements where children spend equal or near-equal time with both parents.

"So sensitive is the subject that a senior officer in the Attorney General's Department remarked to a researcher this year: We have to slow this down; we know it's worth one million votes."

Any suggestion of rolling back the 2006 reforms risked reigniting emotive campaigns by men's groups that considered the changes a victory for fathers' rights.

Horin accused the Labor Attorney General, Robert McClelland of having done his best to bury the reports, including the two volume tome on violence and family law. She said the reports were slipped onto the departmental website without any official publicity, simultaneously and late in the afternoon, ensuring reduced media coverage.

Horin also claimed that with lawyers and mediators required by the law to raise the possibility of shared care "unrealistic expectations and fears have been raised. And, without doubt, many people have been led to believe they have no choice but to agree to equal time, and that not to do so may count against them should they end up in court. Some of these agreements, based on misinformation, may not be in the children's best interest."

Horin, whose regular depositions against fathers on the pages of *The Sydney Morning Herald* had made her a reviled figure among family law reformers, concluded it was a relief that the issue of family law and custody arrangements did not become politicised in the election: "The new government can make a considered decision about how to make a good system better. It should heed the voices of respected legal experts and researchers. Doing nothing is the coward's way out."

Garbage in, garbage out. No need to listen to the voices of the people themselves.

As was the norm, *The Sydney Morning Herald* once again failed to run any countering views.

***

After the Labor party succeeded in brokering its way back into power during those dramatic days following the August 2010 election, little time was wasted before pursuing the feminist inspired alarm over family law. Prior to the election that very same party had done its best to avoid the topic altogether. Democracy is a wonderful thing.

In early November of 2010 the Attorney General Robert McClelland flagged his "concern" that the existing laws did not adequately deal with family violence concerns. He said he wanted to change the law to make it clear safety concerns outweighed the need for a child to have a meaningful relationship with both parents.

"We're effectively switching the two around so that in considering their discretion, the courts will be required to have regard to, first and foremost, the welfare of the best interests of the child," he said.

He said the changes would not affect cases where there were no safety risks. Right. Senior figure in the Family Court and a significant shaper of its culture, Justice Richard Chisholm, had already declared that every case coming before the court should be viewed through the lens of domestic violence.

Adopting the Law Council's proposals, McClelland proposed to expand the definition of family violence to include emotional and financial manipulation.

The definition of domestic violence, as his critics observed, was being expanded to include almost any human behaviour at all, as long as it was committed by a male.

Can anyone in Australia, male or female, honestly claim to have never been emotionally or financially manipulative at some stage of their life?

***

On 11 November 2010 McClelland released a draft bill proposing amendments to the Family Law Act to allegedly "provide better protections for children and families at risk of violence".

Public submissions were invited. However the government deliberately attempted to minimise controversy and the contributions from the unfunded fathers and family law reform sector by having a tight period of consultation spread across the festive season and a closing date of 14 January, when much of the country was still on holidays. A very tired trick used by any government was determined to introduce controversial legislation and didn't give a fig what the public thought.

The Labor Government led by Julia Gillard and ably assisted by Attorney General Robert McClelland appeared determined to press on with its lunacy in not just pandering to but leading the way for the worst excesses of the domestic violence industry, along with its academic and bureaucratic cheer squads.

McClelland also claimed the Chisholm report demonstrated "that the family law system has some way to go in effectively responding to issues relating to family violence."

It did nothing of the kind. It demonstrated the entrenched biases of the ancient regime and the ideological proclivities of the left, now back in the driving seat. The fact the Labor Party's intentions on family law, fundamental to the interests of so many Australians, was not mentioned once during the election campaign demonstrated the government's deliberate hoodwinking of the public, a sleight of hand and a shameful level of dishonesty.

The draft Family Violence Bill sought to amend the Family Law Act in areas including prioritising the safety of children; changing the meaning of "family violence" and "abuse" to "better capture harmful behaviour" and strengthening the obligations of lawyers, family dispute resolution practitioners, family consultants and family counsellors.

It also aimed to ensure that courts had better access to evidence of family violence and abuse and made it easier for state and territory child protection authorities to participate in family law proceedings.

Another recommendation in the draft bill was the deletion of the "friendly" parent provision, which obliged judges to have regard to whether a parent encouraged the child's relationship with the other parent. McClelland claimed some parents were afraid to raise claims of violence in case they were considered "unfriendly" parents.

As well, parents would no longer have cost orders made against them for making false allegations or statements. McClelland claimed this provision deterred parents from raising truthful claims in case the court did not believe them.

***

At the same time as the government released the draft exposure Family Violence Bill 2010 and invited public submissions, it also released a consultation paper. With a short reporting period and no effort to specifically consult with the community, certainly not to garner or examine dissenting voices outside the self referencing pack mentality of the family law and domestic violence industries themselves, the chances of the government paying any heed at all to submissions that disagreed with their agenda was zero.

They certainly had no intention of consulting father's groups, despite the obvious impact on them. To respond to and critique this level of detailed information and a fairly complex Bill was beyond the resources of most of the unfunded family law reform groups.

The seeming armada of generously funded reports virtually all complied with the government's agenda, which was to accord as closely as it could with the stance of women's groups, feminist advocates and domestic violence services against shared parenting. It was nothing short of a snow job.

The Australian Law Reform Commission released concurrently in November its voluminous two volume report Family Violence - A National Legal Response, designed to provide the government with a legal framework on which to proceed. It recommended that the discriminatory words "Domestic violence is predominantly perpetrated by men against women and children" be inserted in front of all relevant state and federal legislation, including the Family Law Act.

It was a deliberate attempt to prejudice Family Court judges against fathers, despite the body of evidence demonstrating both genders could be equally guilty of domestic violence.

The ALRC made 187 recommendations. The consultation paper earlier in the year had run to more than 1,000 pages. The summary of the final report alone ran to 76 pages. It was introduced by Attorney General Robert McClelland noting "the scale of violence affecting Australian women and their children". No mention of men except as perpetrators.

The Family Violence Team, the Child Protection Team, the Sexual Assault team and the Over-arching Issues Team who produced the report were almost all women lawyers. There were 236 consultations nationwide. God knows how much this all cost.

Time and again the report repeated the ideologically driven claims that family violence was "predominantly committed by men; it can occur in all sectors of society; it can involve exploitation of power imbalances; its incidence is under-reported."

Under their recommendations a man could be excluded from his own home on the basis of an accusation.

Here's a small sample of the recommendations: "That a person is not to be regarded as having consented to a sexual act just because the person did not say or do anything to indicate that she or he did not consent; or the person did not protest or physically resist; or the person did not sustain physical injury.

"State and territory legislation dealing with sexual offences, criminal procedure or evidence, should contain guiding principles to which courts should have regard when interpreting provisions relating to sexual offences. At a minimum, these guiding principles should refer to the high incidence of sexual violence within society; sexual offences are significantly under-reported; a significant number of sexual offences are committed against women, children and other vulnerable persons and sexual offences often occur in circumstances where there are unlikely to be any physical signs of an offence having occurred."

It wasn't enough for yet another feminist academic, Annie Cousins, who writing in *The Australian* noted that the ALRC'S recommendations "included behaviour that many would not consider to be violence but, in the context of a family situation, would probably make a lot of sense to victims. It includes stalking, economic abuse, emotional abuse, deprivation of liberty, and causing damage to property and injury to animals. In other words, it recognises that violent men use a range of behaviours to control partners. A victim of family violence is a product of all her experiences of emotional, physical, economic or sexual abuse and this makes her vulnerable to delays, indifference, and bureaucratic and legal difficulties."

***

The Law Council, that old Labor favourite, also announced its support of the Family Violence Bill.

The Council said that having taken a number of steps over the years to raise awareness of family violence it had been working closely with the government and other agencies to explore innovative and practical ways to address the issue.

Chair of the Council's Family Law Section Geoff Sinclair said: "The current provision makes it more difficult for genuine victims of violence to present their case without fear of costs orders being made against them if they are not believed."

In their submission to the 2006 Senate Inquiry the Council had argued that the insertion of the word "reasonable" in regards to the fear of violence would only ferment dispute between the parties and distract them from the real issue of children's welfare by focusing on arguments about whether statements were, or were not, false. They claimed the word "reasonable" would encourage parties to litigate rather than focus on resolving their dispute.

Sue Price at the Men's Rights Agency said the government was trying to destroy shared parenting. "It's the first move in rolling back shared parenting, which is very foolish, and ultimately all the blame will be placed on men," she said. "That's the established agenda. Statistics say that more biological mothers kill their children than biological fathers and more mothers abuse and neglect their children."

Sole Parents Union president Kathleen Swinbourne said the changes did not go far enough. "Broadening out the definition of violence doesn't make it easier to prove in the Family Court," she said. "And the other issue is that children need to be protected from a lot more than violence."

In Australia the blizzards of domestic violence propaganda peaked on November

25, so-called White Ribbon Day. With the majority of domestic violence allegations made in the context of custody battles, the White Ribbon Foundation's work promoting public misconceptions and moral panic had done nothing to restore sanity to family law debates.

***

There were some signs of countering views but with the media rarely reporting the views of father's groups except perhaps as an afterthought and with the poorly resourced groups having little power and zero leverage with government, the organisations which channelled the voices of many members of the Australian public were largely invisible.

However Men's Health Australia continued to raise concerns over government abuse of domestic violence data.

In November they condemned the misuse of public funds by the White Ribbon Foundation with a formal complaint to the Minister for the Status of Women Kate Ellis.

Men's Health Australia pointed out the many errors in their documentation including that men were less likely than women to experience violence within family and other relationships, that the impact of violence on men's overall health was not known and that there was no evidence male victims were less likely to report domestic violence than were female victims.

"Rigorous research by the Australian Bureau of Statistics, the Australian Institute of Health and Welfare, and the South Australian Department of Human Services has clearly debunked these dangerous myths," said Greg Andresen from Men's Health Australia.

"This is not the first time the White Ribbon Foundation has been caught using incorrect and misleading statistics. We now know that Australian men and women are equally likely to be physically assaulted by persons known to them; that the contribution of violence to the burden of disease in men is approximately 2.5 times higher than in women; and that women are almost three times as likely as men to report being a victim of domestic violence to the police."

Other demonstrably false errors in their documentation included claims that domestic violence was the leading cause of death for women aged between 15 and 44 and that men were less likely to suffer injury during a domestic incident, when the opposite was true, perhaps because of the more likely use of weapons against them.

Men's Health Australia went on to say that abuse of men took many of the same forms as abuse of women – physical violence, intimidation and threats;

sexual, emotional, psychological, verbal and financial abuse; property damage, harming pets, and social isolation. Men, more so than women, can also experience legal and administrative abuse – the use of institutions to inflict further abuse on a victim, for example, taking out false restraining orders or not allowing the victim access to his children.

One man described his experience of this sort of abuse thus: "My wife would not let me see the kids. She accused me of sexually molesting my daughter. I was devastated. I didn't see my kids for ages. After a Court hearing which lasted ten days, the judge found that my ex-wife herself had molested my daughter in an effort to generate evidence against me.

"Despite this, she was still allowed custody. And the Court and the child welfare agency refused to take any action against her."

Andresen concluded that there were many misunderstandings about male victims of family violence. "Some argue that men aren't affected as badly as women. Others argue that female violence is usually carried out in self-defence. Yet others assert that women's violence isn't part of an overall pattern of control and domination. An extensive review of Australian and international research finds little evidence to support these claims.

"As well as the effects of violence on men, their children can suffer the same impacts as do children of female victims. These include witnessing family violence by their parents or step-parents, experiencing direct violence and abuse themselves, and suffering a range of negative impacts on their behavioural, cognitive and emotional functioning and social development. Neglecting violence against men means neglecting these children."

**

The then prestigious site Online Opinion, the focus for many of the country's most sophisticated cultural and political debates, was the only media outlet in the country to run a full spread of views on domestic violence and the moves to use it to abolish any semblance of shared parenting; all amply fleshed out on their active forums.

Debate at Online Opinion was lively after one of the anti-shared parenting movement's most prominent leaders Elspeth McInnes penned her support under the headline "Safety first in family law is long overdue". She once again told the sad story of Darcey Freeman, the little girl thrown from a bridge, ignoring the fact that statistically mothers murdered the majority of the two dozen or more children killed by adults each year in Australia and that for propaganda purposes father's could equally tell lurid and appalling stories against mothers if they wanted to be so tasteless.

The McInnes article was little more than a dressed up hate campaign under the guise of exposing the difficulties which mothers and children faced leaving violent and abusive men. She wrote: "Many are advised by state child protection workers that they will have their children taken into care if they stay living in a domestically violent relationship. Once they leave, the current family law system normally ensures that the children will have time in the care of the violent or abusive parent. The task of Family Relationship Centre workers and legal system professionals has been to get mothers to co-operate in handing their children into the care of abusive parents."

McInnes quoted her own feminist advocacy research with other feminist oriented academics, all funded by the government and duly promoted on the Attorney General's website. If men paid much of the country's taxes, that was where their usefulness ended. They certainly weren't afforded the courtesy of neutrality in gender related research.

***

In contrast to most Australian media outlets, Online Opinion ran the counter view. If only some of the nation's hard copy publications could have done the same. Perhaps then the tidal wave of fear mongering and empire building over so- called "family violence" would have been more muted, the middle aged band of powerful and amply funded advocates less certain of their unflinching belief that all men were violent bastards, or as Gloria Steinem's claimed, "the patriarchy requires violence or the subliminal threat of violence in order to maintain itself."

Author Roger A. Smith, who trained as a lawyer and spent many years living in Asia, noted in his article Gender Based Approaches Missing The Mark that the gender-centric message gives the impression that domestic violence and partner abuse is only committed by men.

"The best evidence suggests that this is far from the truth. Nearly all rigorous peer-reviewed academic population-based studies published in academic journals around the world have found that at least one-third, and often one half or more, of the victims of domestic violence are men.

"If we are serious about tackling family violence, we must not ignore these findings. Tackling two-thirds or one-half of the problem, while ignoring the other third to half, is doing a disservice to Australian families. We need to found the solutions to domestic violence firmly on the evidence base."

He observed that the gender based DV campaigns of "break the silence" enforced silence on male victims – the very thing they claimed to be against.

"The fact that this message is so insistent and that specialist services are largely withheld from male victims of domestic violence means that this group must usually suffer in appalling silence that has lasting health consequences on them, their children and families.

"The incessant message that men are perpetrators and women are victims means that men who do have the courage to come forward and make claims of this nature will often be treated as 'less than a man' or liars or both. Where are they to turn? Domestic violence policy should not become a weapon for inflicting domestic violence by making this class of victim voiceless."

Smith went on to say that like the famous line in the 2008 film Frost/Nixon that "if the president does it, it's not illegal", so it sometimes seems that if a woman does it, it's not domestic violence. This is how far the ideology has taken us in some instances. But implied impunity for any group in society only makes the situation worse and will increase the rates of domestic violence and family dysfunction.

"The irony of gender-based campaigns that mandate discriminatory legal regimes is that they can only be achieved by also discarding the principles of English common law and twentieth century international human rights law. The erosion of these principles becomes collateral damage, or in economists' jargon, a 'negative externality' in the quest to advance a particular cultural agenda.

"We would certainly never tolerate a law against terrorism that states that a crime of this nature is predominately committed by Muslims. Even anti-hooning laws could never state that these offences are predominantly committed by young males – even if this is statistically correct – because it would erode the ability of the justice system to fairly and effectively deal with offenders of whatever socio-demographic background.

"Unfortunately, however, these same human rights norms are not respected when it comes to domestic violence. Recently enacted domestic violence acts in several states are prefaced by the words: Domestic violence is predominantly perpetrated by men against women and children."

Smith condemned the Australian Law Reform Commission's recommendation earlier in the month that these discriminatory words be extended to include the Family Law Act.

"Racial, or in this case gender-profiling, of offenders is controversial in law enforcement procedures, but to upgrade it into legislation is nothing short of extraordinary. It creates an obvious bias in the minds of judges and magistrates that a particular class of defendants is more likely to be guilty by reason of his gender or race than would be the case if he were of a different gender or race (and likewise the other gender or race more likely to be innocent).

"In the case of the Family Law Act, its only possible application would be to prejudice fathers in parenting disputes since the Court would be required to assume that fathers are more likely to be abusive toward their children than mothers. To suggest that courts are somehow able to discard such bias in determining individual cases, while maintaining the general rule as to which groups are most likely to commit certain offences, is naïve and stupid. And if the bias is to somehow be withheld in the determination of individual cases, then why legislatively prescribe it in the first place?

"The intent to breach international human rights provisions on discrimination – in particular, Articles 2, 4, 23 (4) and 26 of the International Covenant on Civil and Political Rights, and Articles 2, 7, and 16 (1) of the Universal Declaration of Human Rights – is so brazen as to be almost beyond belief. But we need to remind ourselves that we are entering into a world where ideology reigns.

"Assuming the ALRC recommendation is adopted, which seems likely, we have to accept that for the foreseeable future at least our country will be a place where justice is blind, but apparently not gender-blind."

Smith went on to say that laws of this type represented arguably the first time in the history of our system of law, or of any civilised system of law, where statute prescribed the socio-demographic characteristics of the persons who predominantly committed a particular crime. Even the criminal codes of Apartheid-era South Africa did not prescribe which race or ethnic group was prone to committing a particular offence.

He concluded: "By seeming to institutionalise discrimination, the ALRC could very well weaken public confidence and support for anti-violence measures and weaken confidence in the legal system itself. The victims of violence, whether male or female, deserve better than this.

"Family violence law and policy is not an arena to argue which group in society is more abusive than the other. We are never going to reduce violence with a one-sided ideological approach. The challenge now for practitioners, activists, police and legislators is to move beyond the gender blame game. Most of all, innocent children caught up in their parents' messes require us to put inclusion before ideology, safety before sexism and protection before parochialism."

In an earlier call to "end sexism in domestic violence policy" Smith wrote: "The State and Territory-based laws and the attitudes of the mostly middle-aged women who run domestic violence services in Australia are still, in many respects, stuck in a 1970's time warp. It is time to remind these mostly fair-minded older sisters in charge of DV services from which men are excluded of the non-discriminatory ideals for which they once fought.

"There are no longer any excuses. It's time for Western feminists to move into the 21st century and embrace the ideals of equality that they themselves once advocated. Because at the end of the day, we are really only asking for a simple acknowledgement – 'yes', women do commit domestic violence and 'no' it is not acceptable."

***

There could be only one result from defining domestic or family violence so broadly, in such a gendered way and couched in such a manner as to target only men as perpetrators and include much ordinary human behaviour – a return to the days when many fathers entering the Family Court of Australia were denied any or given only minimal contact with their children on entirely spurious grounds. The resultant personal pain created a large body of disaffected men as well as grandparents and other extended family members, did the community as a whole great harm, brought the judiciary into disrepute and impacted badly on the children involved.

The Australian government was moving in the opposite direction to much enlightened opinion in the Western world. By 2010, while reactionary forces continued to promote sole-mother custody, it was being recognised or at least debated across US, Canadian, Scandinavian and European jurisdictions that shared parenting was the obvious way out of the morass of individual pain, social consequence and gendered roles created by sole mother custody and the marginalisation of fathers.

And there, in 2010, the matter lay. After more than 20 years of ferment, community agitation, government inquiry, thousands of submissions and countless stories of suffering and distress, when it came to the country's most controversial institution, the Family Court of Australia, the Labor Party and the feminist bureaucracies were back in the driver's seat.

The Family Court's indifference to the suffering of its clients and its resistance to reform remained as appalling as ever. As for the "evil sister", the wretched tyranny of the hated Child Support Agency continued on its path, a disgrace to the Australian Public Service and a potent reminder of the insanity which had gripped public policy in Australia.

TWENTY-ONE
THE GILLARD CHAPTER

ULTIMATELY FAUX reforms to family law introduced by the Howard government made no difference to the judgements being made in the court, and no difference to the reality on the ground.

In a paper titled Family Characteristics and Transitions, the Australian Bureau of Statistics recorded that six years after the laws came into effect little had changed, or the situation had worsened: "The pattern of regular contact that children had with their natural parent living elsewhere remained relatively stable over time, with just under half having contact at least once per fortnight (43 percent in 2006-07, 48 percent in 2009-10 and 45 percent in 2012-13).[204]

The proportion of children who rarely had contact with their natural parent living elsewhere (less than once per year or never) remained relatively stable over time as well (28 percent in 2006-07, 24 percent in 2009-10 and 26 percent in 2012-13).

The laws which had been dishonestly peddled to the public as the greatest reforms to family law in 30 years had, on the ground, achieved nothing.

***

Julia Gillard became Australia's 27th Prime Minister on the 24th of June, 2010.

As the saying goes, the evil that men do lives after them.

Or in this case, the evil that women do.

To put it simply: Gillard introduced domestic violence into family law and removed any penalty for perjury. Thereby creating chaos in many thousands of people's lives.

---

[204] Family Characteristics and Transitions, Australia, Australian Bureau of Statistics, 2013.

Working class men may have once been the foundation of the Labor Party, but by the 2000s they were reduced to a bit part, constantly maligned and ridiculed, and the subject of some of the most vicious laws found anywhere in the world.

The Family Law Legislation Amendment (Family Violence and Other Measures) Act 2011 in Australia, introduced on 24 March 2011 and effective from 7 June 2012, purportedly aimed to address criticisms regarding the handling of family violence and child abuse within the family law system. In reality it was a sop to her feminist constituency, and part of her own long march to eradicate the so-called patriarchy.

Once again the same nasty processes. The self glorification of the political announcement. The same false claims that the aim was to make family law quicker, safer and fairer. The same lies that this was all in the best interests of children. The same appointments of industry insiders. The same insults claiming that fathers were a danger to women and children.

The same conferences. The same reports. The same faux inquiry. The draft legislation. The snow job from compliant journalists in the mainstream media.

Once again there were very few voices brave enough to speak up against the industry tidal wave.

After the Labor party succeeded in brokering its way back into power during those dramatic days following the August 2010 election, little time was wasted before pursuing the feminist inspired alarm over family law. Prior to the election that very same party had done its best to avoid the topic altogether. Democracy is a wonderful thing.

In early November of 2010 the Attorney General Robert McClelland flagged his "concern" that the existing laws did not adequately deal with family violence concerns. He said he wanted to change the law to make it clear safety concerns outweighed the need for a child to have a meaningful relationship with both parents.

"We're effectively switching the two around so that in considering their discretion, the courts will be required to have regard to, first and foremost, the welfare of the best interests of the child," he said.[205]

He said the changes would not affect cases where there were no safety risks. Right. Senior figure in the Family Court and a significant shaper of its culture, Justice Richard Chisholm, had already declared that every case coming before the court should be viewed through the lens of domestic violence.

Adopting the Law Council's proposals, McClelland proposed to expand the definition of family violence to include emotional and financial manipulation.

---

205 McClelland flags family law changes, *The Australian*, 2 November, 2010.

The definition of domestic violence, as his critics observed, was being expanded to include almost any human behaviour at all, as long as it was committed by a male.

Can anyone in Australia, male or female, honestly claim to have never been emotionally or financially manipulative at some stage of their life?

***

The sides were lined up. The *Sydney Morning Herald*, which had long since abandoned neutrality to become one-eyed feminist advocates, began its piece The kids are not all right by two female academics from the notoriously left-leaning University of Technology Sydney with lurid descriptions of children damaged in an adversarial system.[206]

The paper noted that the Family Violence and Other Measures Bill 2011 expanded the definition of family violence beyond violent behaviour. It will also take in threatening or other behaviour that coerces or controls' and causes children – or former partners – to be fearful.

The definition of child abuse would also be changed to include psychological damage caused by exposure to family violence. This includes a child seeing or hearing violence, or being present when police or paramedics attend an incident involving the assault of one family member by another.

The point of all this being that child protection concerns, such as abuse and neglect, are dealt with by state and territory systems authorised to intervene when children are at risk of harm in their family's care. But it is the federal family law system that determines which parent has custody.

The Family Court has no investigative capacity of its own.

Therefore, in this dark realm, an accusation becomes enough for a father to lose his children, his property, his assets, everything he has ever worked for.

***

Warwick Marsh began his piece in the journal Online Opinion titled Fathers Day present from Hell citing the all too familiar case of a father whose former partner was routinely flouting Family Court orders for him to see his kids: "This man is on his fourth set of court orders, but even these are regularly flouted by the mother with impunity. The father and his new partner are at their wits end because this has been going on for 10 years and they no longer know what to do.

---

[206] The Kids are not all right, Petrie, Andrea and Griffin, Michelle, *The Sydney Morning Herald*, 17 August, 2011.

"The poor grandmother has been watching the proposed Gillard government's rollback of shared parenting and was wondering if she will ever see her grandson again. She said to me, 'It's no wonder fathers commit suicide because they love their children but the courts are against them, legal aid is against them and now the government is against them'. Sadly I could do little but agree with her.

"The Gillard Government has declared a war on fatherhood and wants to give a diabolical Fathers Day gift to the men of Australia which will bring even more fatherlessness to Australian children."

The Bill removed all the so-called friendly parent provisions which encouraged mediation and cooperation between parents post separation.

Marsh cited a string of studies to demonstrate that fatherlessness was directly linked to an increase in violence society wide, demonstrating that legislation purportedly being introduced to make women and children safer would do the exact opposite.

But evidence, who needed it?

Marsh wrote: "Prime Minister Julia Gillard's Green Labor Government is about to enact changes to the Family Law Act that will demonise dads in the court system and deprive even more children of their biological birthright to a father and a mother. This rollback of shared parenting is being brought in under the guise of 'reducing family violence.

"The new changes will make Family Violence mean anything you want it to mean. It's called Orwellian doublespeak. In other words if any man was to raise his voice at his wife he could be charged with family violence and put in gaol."[207]

***

Oddly enough, perhaps, some of the most outspoken opponents of the legislation were women themselves. One of those was Jewell Drury, who ran a Facebook page Advocate for Justice with more than 9,000 followers.

She wrote: "Julia Gillard, the legacy you left on Australia as Prime Minister, will ALWAYS be remembered. You knew exactly what you were doing when you introduced the Family Law Amendment Bill 2011.

"Never before in Australian parliamentary history, had there been major changes to family law, enacted without bipartisan agreement, removing any possible penalties for perjury and false accusations in the Family Court.

"These laws state that no proof or evidence is needed, when making an allegation of Domestic Violence. A mere statement saying I'm in fear is enough to put

---

[207] Marsh, Warwick, Fathers Day present from hell, Online Opinion, 2 September, 2011.

a domestic violence order on a man that will ruin his life, his career and alienate him from his children.

"These laws now assure that a lie told in the Family Court will no longer have any penalty attached to it. In other words you can make as many false accusations as you like and you will never have costs awarded against you.

"Perjury should be completely unacceptable in any court. Truth should never be traded for lies.

"Julia, you have outdone yourself in your silent war on men. We, the women of Australia, are the mothers of sons. We are the grandmothers of grandsons. We are the sisters of brothers and friends of mates. The damage you have done to Australian men and their families IS your legacy."

***

Interestingly the Australian Institute of Family Studies submission showed data demonstrating that the percentage cases involving allegations of violence and child abuse doubled between 2009-10 and 2012-2014 from 8.2 percent to 17.0 percent. Blame for much of this was sheeted home to Australia's first woman Prime Minister Julia Gillard and the legislation she pushed through.

Orders for shared parental responsibility dropped from 51 percent to 40 percent, while orders for shared care time were less frequent to a statistically significant extent and orders for children to spend a majority of their time with mothers were also more frequent to a statistically significant extent.

As family law reform advocate John Flanagan submitted, the changes to the credence of domestic violence allegations was "despite the fact that many of these allegations are not true and are not required to be substantiated. These allegations are often merely made to obtain an advantage under the Family Law Act and also to obtain an advantage with other issues such as property settlements and child support."

Fatherless children. That's a shameful legacy. Not that Gillard, another lawyer turned politician, didn't do very well after her turn at making Australia's family law system worse.

After she herself became the victim of an internal coup, she went on to become a multi-millionaire, with her lucrative gigs including becoming Chair of the Big Pharma behemoth the Wellcome Trust and the wealthy Brookings Institute, where she was a Senior Fellow.

To add insult to injury, after leaving office Julia Gillard became chair of Beyond Blue, an organisation aimed at reducing suicide rates. Men committed suicide at four times the rate of women. And Beyond Blue was now headed by a woman who had never or very rarely ever said a positive word about men, or fathers, except, curiously, her own father, and who had contributed significantly to the diabolical disaster that was Australian family law.

***

Sue Price of the Men's Rights Agency said the consequences of the 2011 changes introducing violence into the Family Law Act were disastrous.

"Some research conducted by academics is tainted by the denial that women can be just as abusive and violent as men to their ex partners. The questions to uncover such abuse often remain unasked and unanswered and there is an overwhelming suggestion that children are assumed to be safe with their mother. Sadly this is not always the case."

Ms Price said there was ample research, both in Australian and internationally, to suggest that in fact children were more at risk from their mothers.

She referred to research from the Australian Institute of Criminology's National Homicide Monitoring program, the Child abuse and neglect statistics from the National Child Protection Clearinghouse, and from the lobby group One in Three.

"A well orchestrated campaign has been used to make the claim children are at risk from violent fathers and their mothers are subjected to domestic violence," she said. "Thirty years of propaganda about domestic violence has influenced the publication of accurate statistics. The figures do not support the allegations and false claims made by the many domestic violence women's groups in pursuit of the demonisation of men."

At the same time, in the 2010 budget, $50 million was cut from the Family Relationships Centres.

"We're going backwards, it's worse than it ever was," said Price. "The 2011 changes rolled back any advantage the 2006 changes might have given, and made the entire arena for separating a minefield, and encouraged still further false allegations of domestic violence.

"Meanwhile, thousands of children are left without any contact with one of their parents, usually the father."

***

Retiring Family Court Justice David Collier said allegations of child sexual abuse allegations were being increasingly invented by mothers to stop fathers from seeing their children.

"If a husband and wife really get down to it in this day and age, dirt flies," he said. "The worst are those mothers who direct false allegations of abuse against former partners. It's a horrible weapon. They are difficult to disprove. The allegation lingers there."[208]

A judge from the Magellan project, which dealt with serious allegations within the Family Court, concurred, suggesting many of the accusations were false.

"I have a sense that in the overwhelming majority of cases abuse is not confirmed," one judge said. "And probably in not many cases is there found to be an unacceptable risk. I don't have the stats, so it's probably silly of me to quote stats, but I'm talking of probably upwards of 70 or 80 percent where the relationship with the father was restored. Which, in itself, is a worry if that is true. Why are so few being confirmed? Is it mum – usually – using it as a weapon to get dad out of the kid's life?"[209]

***

To soar across the years, in 2015 the Australian edition of the *Huffington Post* published a piece by Independent Victorian Senator John Madigan who told the story of the devastation being wrecked by Australia's family law and child support systems, while devoid of empathy fat cats looked on.

The piece was headlined The Family Court Is Broken, And So Are The Parents: "At a recent meeting in a converted warehouse in inner-Sydney 30 or so people – both men and women – told stories of devastation and heartbreaking loss. In this modern age, the sense of inhumanity and crisis beggars belief. Can this be happening in Australia in 2015? Why is this allowed?

"Over the last month I have attended similar meetings at community halls in the outer-Melbourne suburbs of Bayswater, Frankston and Geelong.

"People frequently cry at these meetings. They fall apart. They tell stories that seem Orwellian and grotesque.

"In this modern age, the sense of inhumanity and crisis beggars belief. Can this be happening in Australia in 2015? Why is this allowed?"

And yet the same messages resonate and repeat.

"I am a mother and I have done nothing wrong."

"I am a father and I have done nothing wrong."

"I am a grandparent and I have done nothing wrong."

"It has now been more than a decade since a review of Australia's Family Law system produced the report Every Picture Tells A Story. The inquiry attracted 1,716 submissions – at the time a record.

---

208 Alexander, Harriet, False Abuse Claims are the new Court weapon, retiring judge says, Family Law News, 5 July, 2013.

209 Higgins, D.J., Cooperation and Coordination: An Evaluation of the Family Court of Australia's Magellan case-management model, Australian Institute of Family Studies, 2007.

"But now, 12 years later, Family Court practitioners – lawyers, psychologists, social workers and police – along with thousands of Australian parents agree on one thing – the system is broken."[210]

In other words, all that talk of reform was nothing but a monumental failure.

And the only people in the country who would disagree with those words were the beneficiaries of the status quo, the bureaucrats gorging themselves at the trough of this insanity, the lawyers making a handsome living off it all, the judicial personnel on their handsome salaries and far removed from those impacted by their decisions, and the politicians afraid of the bad publicity from the hundreds of advocacy groups around the country if they dared to speak up.

Not a word from those most affected, not a word of concern about the boys growing up being taught there is something wrong with their gender, not a word about the countless fathers damaged by false allegations, not a word for the police who find their profession being degraded and misused in family court battles.

Why would young men join the military of a country which has such blatant contempt for them? Why, indeed, do men pay taxes at all for a system so intrinsically hostile to them?

***

But there were two sides to this story.

As Senator Madigan recorded: "Allegations about violence, alcohol and drug taking can be made in the Family Court without the need for proof, nor incurring any penalties if found to be untrue. Those who have been through the system say unfounded allegations are a weapon that can be used without restraint or liability by one partner to win financial support and custody of children."

Madigan went on to say that the community groups Dads In Distress and Mothers In Distress aimed to keep people off the edge, quite literally.

He said: "The Family Court recognises that separation and divorce contribute to three-fold and four-fold increases in suicide rates for men and women respectively.

"The first advice we give people is don't breach your intervention or apprehended violence order," a senior DIDS counsellor told me. "That elevates the matter into the criminal sphere."

But sometimes a non-breach can be the most difficult thing in the world.

"I was in a pub," a father said in a group meeting. "I'd had a few beers. I picked up the phone and called my ex. I had tears in my eyes and I said please can you let me see the kids. That was a breach."

---

210 Maddigan, John, The Family Court Is Broken, And So Are The Parents, The Huffington Post Australia, 13 April, 2015.

Madigan wrote: "The Family Court must be put back on the political and public agenda. It is disappointing to many that the most recent Federal Government pronouncements about the Family Court consist of raising fees for applicants. This is not a question about men or women. This is not about a gender war."

***

Also in 2015, Wayne Butler, executive director of the Shared Parenting Council of Australia, wrote that parties can pretty much do and say what they like in a family court matter and get away with it. And the drawn-out nature of the process was life-destroying.

"Looking back at changes after the implementation of the Family Law Amendment (Shared Parental Responsibility) Bill 2005 and the more recent 2010 changes in the Family Law Amendment (Family Violence) Bill 2010 it is very clear to practitioners that we have again reached a crisis point in the family law system.

"The family law system is simply crumbling. There are many clients in the family law system waiting for in excess of two years and some three years and more, trying to deal with obstacles in the system preventing them from seeing their children.

"At the same time they face denial of contact time with their children, they further have to deal with complex issues such as re-establishing accommodation. Many parents find that working is almost impossible with the huge impost placed on them by a legal system that is laboriously slow, exhibits no urgency to reach resolution, but consumes all their available time, energy and finances

"In some cases we are aware of parents losing employment directly due to the time they have had to be involved in court and related appearances.

"When separating couples are arguing about contact and financial arrangements the system that they enter is a system that results in extraordinary delays and in many cases, a complete annihilation of one parent's relationship with their children.

"The ability of one parent to withhold contact on baseless false allegations is out of control. False allegations about violence, false allegations about alcohol, false allegations about drug taking and the previous section s119AB which allowed for penalties was removed by Labor. Penalties are usually never made, the time lines to return documents are never adhered to, and parties can pretty much do what they like in a family court matter (and get away with it).

"The whole system is either in, or very near, a complete meltdown. It needs to be exposed to a full inquiry similar to that which was carried out by Kay Hull and the courageous Ken Ticehurst in 2003, when he and fellow backbenchers lobbied Prime Minister John Howard to launch the HORISP (House of Representatives Inquiry into Shared Parenting) This inquiry was the catalyst which 'kicked off' some urgently needed reform measures.

"Whatever the options might be for reducing gridlock in the family court and child support systems, they need to be explored and implemented urgently. It is simply not good enough to allow this broken system to keep churning along in a state of complete disrepair."

A decade before Dads On The Air had condemned the mealy mouthed changes introduced by the Howard government as too easily ignored by the court, too easily overturned, and would ultimately lead to more inquiries, more desperation and more suffering.

And so it came to pass.

***

In March of 2019, in a piece titled "Another family law review, another shrug. Why conduct time-consuming inquiries if they go nowhere?", published in the academic journal *The Conversation*, leading family law academic Patrick Parkinson, who had also been a guest on Dads On The Air back in the day, expressed his pure frustration at the groundhog day nature of it all.[211]

Once resident at Sydney University, Parkinson had followed many of the country's denizens in moving to the warmer, sunnier climes of the north, and was now Professor of Law at Queensland University. DOTA had once been somewhat critical of the professor for not being strong enough in his critique of the malpractice inside the Family Court and the Child Support Agency. Never mind. His piece offered a good summary of the intervening years.

"Another month, another report on the family law system: and a disappointing government response on one of our most pressing domestic issues.

"Two weeks ago, the Joint Select Committee on Australia's Family Law System published its major report on ways to reform the overstretched, beleaguered legal system overseeing parenting and property disputes when relationships break down.

"Meanwhile, another substantial report from the Australian Law Reform Commission (ALRC) in April 2019 has all but been forgotten.

---

211 Parkinson, Patrick, Another family law review, another shrug. Why conduct time-consuming inquiries if they go nowhere?", *The Conversation*, 31 March, 2019.

"Launched with great fanfare in 2017 by then-Attorney General George Brandis, the inquiry was billed as the first comprehensive review of the Family Law Act since its commencement in 1976 – a rather bold claim, given the plethora of inquiries and reports on almost every aspect of family law in the intervening years."

The ALRC review was headed by feminist academic and favourite of the Family Court, Helen Rhoades, Professor of Law at Melbourne University and former chair of the Family Law Council, in other words, an industry insider.

Yet again we saw the quixotic picture of a supposedly conservative pro-family government handing over family law inquiries to staunch ancien régime feminists and determinedly ignoring the litigants being churned through the system at great cost to themselves and the society at large. Two-faced doesn't even begin to describe the level of deceit.

***

Back in 2017 One Nation Senator Pauline Hanson managed to upset the then Attorney General George Brandis by declaring that "no one within the government was interested in dealing with family law until I returned to Parliament and hounded both the Attorney General and Prime Minister."

Senator Brandis said "it would be a stretch to say that we are having this review because Senator Hanson urged it upon us. It is something I have wanted to do for quite some time, going back to before Senator Hanson was a member of Parliament."

Brandis claimed the first comprehensive review of family law in nearly half a century would examine how to make the system faster and less adversarial.

As Parkinson noted, the Australian Law Reform Commission's terms of reference were so broad as to be utterly unmanageable. They included such things as: the appropriate, early and cost-effective resolution of all family law disputes, how to determine the best interests of children and listen to their views, issues concerning family violence, child abuse, drug or alcohol addiction and serious mental illness, whether the adversarial court system is the best way to deal with family law issue, the desirability of finality in the resolution of family disputes, the need to ensure compliance with family law orders and the benefits of the engagement of appropriately skilled professionals in the family law system.

The government must have known, or at least the politicians must have known, even as they were pouring this garbage into the public square, that the entire multi-million dollar enterprise was a waste of public funds and would lead precisely nowhere.

Or as Parkinson put it: "The list went on and on. Any one of these topics alone was worthy of a reference to a law reform body. Most of these issues had already been extensively explored in reports by parliamentary committees, previous ALRC inquiries and the many carefully considered reports of the Family Law Council, a statutory body that was put into hibernation by the Turnbull government."

The extensive list of participants in the inquiry, all of whom were no doubt paid handsomely, read like an industry roll call, including our old friend Richard Chisholm, former Family Court judge and a staunch opponent of shared parenting, Ms Sandra Elhelw-Wright, Women's Chair, Federation of Ethnic Communities' Councils of Australia; Policy Officer, Ms Louise Glanville, Managing Director, Victoria Legal Aid, Magistrate Anne Goldsbrough, Magistrates' Court of Victoria, Commissioner Megan Mitchell, National Children's Commissioner, Justice Jillian Williams, Family Court of Australia. On and on and on it went.

There was, of course, no one representing the litigants, one might refer to them as survivors, of the family law jurisdiction, no one examining the impacts on individuals, much less fathers, no one examining the suicide levels directly associated with family breakdown and the institutions overseeing this debacle.

Recommendations included: "The Australian Government, together with state and territory governments, should consider expanding the information sharing platform as part of the National Domestic Violence Order Scheme to include family court orders and orders made under state and territory child protection legislation."

As if the Palace of Lies was a reliable source of information which they should be sharing with anyone.

"The Family Law Act 1975 (Cth) should be amended to provide that in determining what arrangements promote the best interests of an Aboriginal or Torres Strait Islander child, a court must consider the child's opportunities to connect with, and maintain the child's connection to, the child's family, community, culture, and country."

Never mind everybody else!!

And: "Section 65DAA of the Family Law Act 1975 (Cth), which requires the courts to consider, in certain circumstances, the possibility of the child spending equal time, or substantial and significant time with each parent, should be repealed."

What could anyone do at this point but sigh?

Quietly, in March of 2019, nearly two years after the report was published, the Morrison government released its response. Some recommendations were accepted, some simply noted, and others agreed to in principle or in part.

Another report disappeared into the ether, the taxpayers funding this circus none the wiser. On the ground nothing changed.

***

No one can say anything about all of this without being hit by an orchestrated campaign of outrage. Government funded outrage. Brandis made sure he had all bases covered.

Concurrently, way back in early 2017, as if to emphasise the duplicity of it all, Brandis launched a Parliamentary inquiry into a better family law system to support and protect those affected by family violence, another flood of millions of dollars of taxpayer funds into the hands of the industry.

As the official announcement went: "On 16 March 2017 a Committee of the Australian Parliament adopted an inquiry into how Australia's federal family law system can better support and protect people affected by family violence. The Committee aims to make recommendations that will improve the system for all participants. The Committee wants to ensure that its findings are informed by those with personal experience at the intersection of family violence and the family law system."[212]

Unlike the ALRC inquiry, this one would report promptly. It found that the family law system's approach to family violence was frequently and in many ways failing to support and protect families affected by family violence.

Committee Chair, Sarah Henderson, another former lawyer turned Liberal Party politician, said: "It is clear that the family law system is not providing adequate support to and protection of families experiencing family violence. In many cases, the safety of families, particularly children, is being compromised.

"Our inquiry was underpinned by the strong message that 'your voice matters.' We have listened to thousands of everyday Australians affected by family violence who have with courage told us about their experiences with the family law system. The Committee thanks all those who took the time to tell us their stories. We appreciate that this would not have been easy.

"We are confident that the reforms we have suggested in this report will help families, confronting the turmoil and trauma of family violence, better navigate the family law system and receive the justice they deserve."

The inquiry made 33 recommendations including: the earliest possible determination of family violence allegations to enable the courts to make informed

---

[212] Parliament of Australia, House of Representatives Standing Committee on Social Policy and Legal Affairs, Inquiry into a better family law system to support and protect those affected by family violence, 16 March, 2017.

decisions about parenting and property matters; the removal of the presumption of equal shared parental responsibility in the Family Law Act; the incorporation of a child safety service within the courts and the introduction of multi-disciplinary panels to interview children in child abuse cases and legislative amendments enabling express consideration of family violence in property settlements when assessing both parties' contributions, as well as early resolution of small claim property matters and superannuation splitting orders.

In practice, out there in the real world of squabbling couples and daily life, all this meant was: make the claim, get the lot.

What exact percentage of claims of violence, that is the male as the perpetrator, were either false or exaggerated? In the Palace of Lies, when these types of allegations almost invariably arose at the time of separation and almost invariably used to gain advantage in court cases, it was impossible to tell. But a lot. Claims by males that they were the subject of violence were almost always dismissed. This was a one way street.

Why, if there truly was violence, would anyone have stayed in the relationship in the first place and only raised the allegations when there was an advantage in doing so?

But common sense and rationality lay nowhere near any of this.

***

Amidst the wall of submissions from the domestic violence industry, which prospered on the notion that men were invariably the perpetrators and women the victims, there were a few of the old family law reform guard trying to point out the bleeding obvious, that the entire system thrived on lies.

In their submission the Lone Fathers Association declared: "We believe that in respect to all allegations of family violence that before a finding is made it is critical that the evidence is tested beyond reasonable doubt and not on the test of probability.

Many criminal cases, following allegations of family violence of assault are made, are dismissed after trial in a criminal Court jurisdiction.

However in the same case the assumption of family violence continues in the hearing of the family matter in the Family Court or Federal Circuit Jurisdiction.

The Lone Fathers Association of Australia proposes that allegations of domestic violence involving an assault should be a criminal matter and require proof beyond reasonable doubt."

The Non-Custodial Parents Party suggested that the 2012 amendments under the Julia Gillard government had led to many children not being able to have contact with both parents after either separation or divorce.

"This is despite the fact that many of these allegations are not true and are not required to be substantiated. These allegations are often merely made to obtain an advantage and also to obtain an advantage with other issues such as property settlements and child support."

The group made a number of suggestions, concluding that it is hoped that many of the currently false allegations of family violence would then become less prevalent.

Nothing could be more abusive than falsely accusing a person and then proceeding to rob them of their property, their assets, their income and contact with their children. It happens all the time. And in this hyperbolic realm, the perpetrators are almost always the mothers. No one benefits but lawyers. Not the women themselves, not the fathers, not the children, not the extended family. And not the country as a whole.

The Attorney General overseeing all this, George Brandis, another former lawyer turned Liberal Party high flyer, like so many of the other political bit players in this saga, went on to a plum posting. In Brandis's case, he was appointed as High Commissioner to the United Kingdom, with all the pomp and circumstance that entailed.

As the *Sydney Morning Herald* reported of his tenure: "Invitations to Australia House parties became the hottest ticket in town, as Brandis threw bash after bash for Britain's elite and the expat community from satirist Barry Humphries to Prince Charles."

Meanwhile the victims of the system he failed to reform wondered how they were going to make it through the night; while the inquiries he populated with industry hacks and the reviews he only launched out of political opportunism gathered dust. And the lawyers and judicial officers who so greatly benefited from his failure to expose the dishonesty, corruption and malpractice rampant throughout the family law system just got richer.

TWENTY-TWO
PAULINE HANSON
GETS SNOWED

Senator Pauline Hanson has had a long history of stepping on time bombs since she gave up working in a fish and chip shop and became a politician way back in 1994.

For those who might be reading this outside Australia, or who haven't paid much attention to Australian politics, perhaps a word of explanation.

Pauline Hanson, the founder of populist rural based party One Nation, was controversial almost from the beginning of her political career, much ridiculed by Australia's intelligentsia, left leaning media and other politicians for her anti-woke beliefs, long before anyone had even heard the word "woke". More in touch with voters than most Australian politicians, she was popular in farming districts, had a significant male following and had long complained about the harm the Family Court was doing to her constituents.

Whether it was mass immigration, multiculturalism, climate change, renewable energy, gay marriage or bureaucratic waste, Hanson had been igniting fires for more than a quarter of a century.

But stepping on the toes of the family law, child support and domestic violence industries provoked a conflagration which was spectacular even by her standards.

The spark was an interview Senator Hanson did with the national broadcaster the ABC.

The subject was false claims of domestic violence.

"There are people out there who are nothing but liars and who will use that in the court system," Hanson told the ABC. "I am hearing too many cases where parents are using domestic violence to stop the other parent from seeing their children; perjury is in our system but they are not charged with perjury.

"These people need to move on with their lives. Get over the hate, the pain of a breakup, it's about working together to find the answers to all this."[213]

The leftwing *Guardian Australia* went ballistic: "Pauline Hanson sparks fury with claim domestic violence victims are lying to family court," read the headline. And the strapline: "Citing prominent grievance among men's rights groups, One Nation leader says she has personal experience to back up the claim."[214]

Strangely for an article which put the words "Men's Rights Groups" into its headlines, it did not bother to quote a single one. Apart from their extreme bias, that was because by this time there basically weren't any.

Faced with a multi-billion dollar taxpayer funded industry, most of the amorphous scattering of groups which had coalesced under the banner of the Shared Parenting Council of Australia had disappeared; the unfunded personnel burnt out. The few that remained had neither the ear of the government nor the media. The fearsomely named Men's Rights Agency was in reality a woman in her 70s. At that time, prior to his passing, the founder of Lone Fathers Australia, Barry Williams, was in failing health. Perhaps the most active of them, Dads in Distress, was essentially apolitical.

But nothing stopped the stalwarts of the domestic violence industry. *Guardian Australia* reported: "A controversial new inquiry into the family court system being pushed by Pauline Hanson will go ahead, despite anger from anti-domestic violence campaigners and opposition from Labor and the Greens.

"Prime minister Scott Morrison has said the new parliamentary inquiry will not take sides, but women's groups are concerned it will become a platform for men's rights activists who believe the court system is biased against fathers.

"While Labor and the Greens have said they will vote against the inquiry, the government has the support of enough crossbench senators for it to go ahead with the support of One Nation and Centre Alliance.

"Hanson's support for the inquiry has sparked furore among anti-domestic violence campaigners after she claimed women were lying about abuse to gain advantage in family courts."[215]

***

Australia's leftwing media lived in an altered universe. The claim that some women lied to gain advantage in family court proceedings was demonstrably

---

213 Pauline Hanson says women fabricate domestic violence allegations, ABC, 19 September, 2019.

214 Pauline Hanson sparks fury with claim domestic violence victims are lying to family court, *The Guardian*, 18 September, 2019.

215 Ibid.

true, as well as being a belief held by millions of Australians, and by no means all of them men. In an adversarial system, and at times of personal crisis, people can hardly be blamed for reaching for whatever tools they can find to better their own position.

In her speech to Parliament on 30 July 2019 Pauline Hanson said: "I am so pleased that this matter of public importance is here to be debated on the floor of parliament, and it is One Nation that is driving this matter of family law reform in Australia. When I was first elected in 1996 it was the most important issue that came across my desk. Here I find myself elected again in 2016, and nothing has changed. If anything, it is worse."

Hanson said Australia's failed family law system was a contributing factor in the high rate of male suicide: "These people are often dying lonely, depressed and frustrated and are left broke by today's dangerously hurtful family law system.

"These are the non-custodial parents, predominantly male, who cannot see their children. And I do not take away from the females, the women, at all, because there are a lot of women out there who are not custodial parents of their children. But it is predominantly males who are the non-custodial parents.

"Just imagine how difficult it is being a bloke, or a woman, on their own in a court environment, pleading their innocence in DVOs and other family law matters. There are many reasons why I have advocated a royal commission into family law. The pathetic domestic violence orders are just one of them, and I'm tired of the vexatious complaints that are lodged with the police because the non-custodial parent wants, in one instance, simply to speak to their kids over the phone or on Facebook. That warrants a domestic violence order against that person, just because they want to speak on the phone to their kids – pleading, begging! This is nothing but spiteful and inconsiderate.

"I know this feeling because, for years, my own son faced these destructive allegations in an attempt to stop him having access to his young son. My ex-daughter-in-law claimed to police that my son was outside her home in Townsville, which led to a DVO being taken out against him. That was despite him being sick and on the Gold Coast, some 1,000 kilometres away. He was forced to defend himself, at enormous expense, and was dragged through the courts. She also falsely alleged – a soul-crushing claim – that my son had sexually abused his boy. Again, the false claim was designed to stop him having any connection with his son. No charges were brought against my son."[216]

---

216 Matters of Public Importance, Pauline Hanson, Hansard, Senate, Parliament House of Australia, 30 July, 2019.

John Stapleton

***

At the same parliamentary hearing Queensland Senator Malcolm Roberts, one of the most direct, common sense politicians and amongst only a very few in the entire parliament to have the intestinal fortitude to stand up to the bureaucratic agendas which had proved so destructive to Australian society.

He recorded: "One Nation is deeply concerned about the large number of avoidable deaths through suicide and homicide that are directly related to the broken system of family law that currently is a blight on the Australian legal system.

"Men on the tail end of broken relationships are at the end of their tether when they have limited or no access to their children as the result of the confusion, excessive costs and long delays that are a feature of the family law system in most of Australia. Many of these men are not able to cope and become further victims of this oppressive system by taking their own lives as a final solution to the unbearable processes of marital breakdown and the forced tribulations of dealing with the family law court.

"There are multiple issues raised in this matter for discussion, ranging from the financial dramas of property settlements and child support, custody, guardianship to issues related to access to any children of the relationship. It is this latter issue that often leads to the most grief for fathers when the courts seem to take an often biased view of the father's needs and accept often unsubstantiated allegations aimed at limiting the father's access to his children.

"The current system is broken, and it needs to be fixed. The current practices of the Family Court have resulted in lengthy delays, dragging out an already flawed process. It can take up to 18 months or beyond to get to trial in the Family Court, and even longer to receive a decision of the court. Damaged relationships are being destroyed by the time and expense of resolving disputes in the Family Court. Domestic violence orders, sought often through the state systems, are given out in many instances on the basis of fabricated complaints made for the specific purpose of being used as a weapon to deny fathers access to their kids. Money-grubbing lawyers acting for women do this for leverage against fathers in divorce proceedings, either for revenge or to get more money in the property split.

"Dollar costs in the Family Court to get to trial average out at $110,000.

"Suicide is a terrible cause of death of men and women in Australia, but it is mostly men. Of 1,966 coroner-certified suicides in 2017, where psychosocial factors contribute, 1,465 were of men and 501 of women. Suicide is the leading cause of death of people under the age of 45, with the number of men committing suicide three times that of females. There were 420 persons who suicided as a direct connection with disruption of family by separation or divorce. This is too many people who have taken their own lives because of the broken family law system that could not relieve their pain. These numbers are shameful. They relate to real people who should be still alive, whose needs for help were not met. The system needs to be fixed.

"In 2018 there were 375 reported homicides in Australia. Of these 375 murders, 140 related to domestic violence breakdowns; 75 women were killed as a result of family breakdown. However, 65 deaths were of males. Where are the protections that should have prevented these terrible deaths – children left without a parent?"[217]

***

Pauline Hanson was widely ridiculed by various spokespeople for personalising her push for family law reform. Except the story she told could be endlessly repeated around the country with a thousand different variations, but always the same result: endless expense, a fatherless child.

The Senator continued: "These are just a few small examples of the efforts some spiteful, inconsiderate parents will go to in order to prevent the non-custodial parent seeing their kids. When the tables were turned in my own son's family law case, and the court revealed the perjury by my ex-daughter-in-law, there was no punishment. There is no deterrent whatsoever.

"When the court reporter, whose evidence is taken very seriously by the court, suggested my son be given custody of his boy, his ex-wife was inconsolable to the point where they stopped proceedings and adjourned the case for another three months. Isn't it funny what happens when the shoe's on the other foot?

"Here was this spiteful partner who thought she could prevent the father from having anything to do with their child until he was a teenager – a child who is now five years old, and she has been stopping him from seeing his son since the child was 15 months old. Isn't it exceptional that, when the mother faced the same outcome she wanted to inflict on my son, she couldn't handle the thought?

"Family law deaths are not acceptable and have reached epidemic proportions.

"How do you think the men feel about the reality of not being able to see their kids? This is what leaves them depressed, frustrated and unable to focus on a bright future. It's what leads to the thoughts of suicide – being ripped away from their own child's lives. We encourage men to be a part of every element of their

---

217 Matters of Public Importance, Malcolm Roberts, Hansard, Senate, Parliament House of Australia, 30 July, 2019.

children's lives. We don't think twice about the dad being in the birthing suite of the hospital. We actively encourage men to take paternity leave.

"Family law is slowly killing good people, and I for one will move heaven and hell to get through to the lazy minds and do-nothing attitudes of many of you in this parliament when it comes to family law matters."[218]

***

In announcing the inquiry two decades after his predecessor John Howard had announced similar inquiries, Prime Minister Scott Morrison said the review would look at whether the current system, which was intended to support parents and children during the end of a relationship, was fit for purpose.

"We want to ensure families can resolve issues as quickly and fairly as possible, so everyone can move on with their lives," the Prime Minister said. "This inquiry will allow the Parliament to hear directly from families and listen to them as they give their accounts of how the family law system has been impacting them and how it interacts with the child support system.

"This is a serious issue that has been raised by Members and Senators across the Parliament and I look forward to the Parliament working together through this Committee to bring forward recommendations that look at how the system can be improved."

Morrison told reporters: "There are blokes who are victims, there are women who are victims, and most tragically there are children who are victims. It's just an awful human mess.

"The reason to do a joint select committee is to be able to truly listen to the stories and evidence it can bring forward in a sensible, apartisan way."[219]

The *Australian Financial Review* reported that after demanding the government call a royal commission into the Family Court in exchange for One Nation's support on personal income tax cuts in June, Mr Morrison agreed to Senator Hanson's request to help lead the probe with former Liberal minister Kevin Andrews.

Opposition Leader Anthony Albanese opposed the inquiry amidst questions about the deal between One Nation leader Pauline Hanson and Prime Minister Scott Morrison.

The Labor leader held an emergency shadow cabinet meeting over the One Nation leader's role as deputy chair of the probe, and said: "I say to the Prime

---

218 Maiden, Samantha, Pauline Hanson uses parliamentary privilege to accuse son's ex of false sexual abuse claims, *The New Daily*, 18 September, 2019.

219 Scott Morrison announces inquiry into family law system, *The Australian*, 17 September, 2019.

Minister, we can't support an inquiry in which he has unilaterally, along with Pauline Hanson, done a deal."

Mr Albanese accused Mr Morrison of acting unilaterally to make a deal with One Nation, failing to follow through on a promise to consult Labor.[220]

***

The ever broadening definition of the term domestic violence and the ever burgeoning army of lobby groups vested in creating a moral panic made for a febrile atmosphere at best, while the mainstream media's refusal to cover the consequences as they stayed in their politically correct lanes constituted an abandonment of their responsibilities to the public and the broader Australian society.

Right on the heels of Pauline Hanson's speech, away went the industry, every last one of them beneficiaries of substantial amounts of public funding.

The most prominent of them was former Chief Justice of the Family Court Diana Bryant, who had retired two years earlier and left the jurisdiction in just as parlours a state as she found it. This was the same activist feminist judge who some two decades earlier had been appointed by conservative Prime Minister John Howard at the same time he had been flirting with the separated dad vote, a remarkable piece of duplicity in and of itself.

Bryant was quick into the fray: "When Prime Minister Scott Morrison announced another review into family law on Tuesday, he was concerned to assure the community that there would be no agenda.

"On Wednesday, senator Pauline Hanson went out of her way to prove otherwise – and ruin the credibility of the review before it was even under way."

Bryant said the PM's announcement was "initially met in some quarters by dismay, Women's groups in particular cited government inaction after numerous inquiries have highlighted risks to women and children.

"Notwithstanding the opposition of the women's groups, whose concerns certainly have validity, there is merit in a genuine independent inquiry. Crucial to wide support for the inquiry, and ultimately its recommendations, is the appointment of a well-respected chair and committee members.

"Crucial also is the belief by the community that the committee will conduct the inquiry with fairness and integrity.

"Senator Hanson has put the government in a difficult position."[221]

---

220 Tom McIlroy, Some women lie about domestic violence: Hanson, *Australian Financial Review*, 19 September, 2019.

221 Bryant, Diana, Hanson mocks PM on family law inquiry, Australian Financial Review, 19 September, 2019.

Vociferous domestic violence campaigner Rosie Batty, who Bryant quoted to back her case, was also quick to join the pile on. She claimed publicly that Pauline Hanson's obvious agenda made her an unsuitable choice to co-chair the inquiry.

"It is completely unacceptable for us to have another inquiry. We have had multiple inquiries about the failings of the family law court system. I have campaigned also for changes," Batty said. "There has been a Law Reform Commission inquiry with 60 recommendations presented to the government earlier this year – not one recommendation has been acknowledged or enforced.

"I would call on Labor, the Greens and the Prime Minister to block this unnecessary inquiry," she said. "We know the failings, we need to start investing in this court system that is broken, overwhelmed and failing. It is continuing to put families, particularly children, in danger."[222]

***

The pile on didn't end there, of course.

Labor's shadow minister for women Julie Collins said the government should condemn Hanson's remarks. "Pauline Hanson's comments this morning regarding domestic violence are completely inappropriate and deeply disrespectful to survivors of domestic violence," she said.

Greens senator Rachel Siewert said the party would oppose the "toxic" family law inquiry, saying it was a political "stitch-up" between One Nation and the Coalition. "I'm deeply concerned about what I hear about the direction this inquiry would head, the best interest of the child must be at the centre of decision making in the family law system and what I hear from One Nation is men's rights, not what is best for the child," Siewert said.

Queensland's Women's Legal Services chief executive, Angela Lynch, said another inquiry was not needed. "The greatest impediment to women leaving domestic violence in this country is the family law system," she said. "Women and children who are affected by domestic violence turn to the family law system for safety, and at the moment it isn't a system that is responsive to their needs."

***

So many inquiries. So damn many of them. By the nation veered towards the 50th anniversary of the Family Law Act in 2025 there had been so many inquiries into family law any lay person could be forgiven for getting confused and frustrated over this endless march to nowhere.

---

222 Martin, Sarah, Pauline Hanson sparks fury with claim domestic violence victims are lying to family court, *The Guardian*, 18 September, 2019.

Back to the future it really was.

Law Society of NSW Journal LSJ noted in one of the few thoughtful pieces published at the time: "A multitude of inquiries have sought answers to Australia's family law woes. The most recent was completed in April, when the Australian Law Reform Commission (ALRC) handed down a 574-page report with 60 recommendations. In the course of its investigation, the ALRC considered the findings of at least 13 other inquiries that investigated family law, as well as 31 reports exposing systemic issues on topics ranging from surrogacy to child support.

"Thirty-eight of them have been handed down in the last 20 years.

"Most tell a familiar story: Australia's family courts are drowning under enormous caseloads. The system is overwhelmed and under-resourced. The intense stress arising from long delays and burgeoning costs is a symptom of a system failing to serve those who need it most.

"The circle of inquiry shows no sign of resolving any time soon."[223]

As the Journal noted, in fact, the government was yet to even respond to the findings of the Australian Law Reform Commission report announced by the Attorney General back in 2017 and which had already been formally tabled in Parliament.

***

The Joint Select Committee on Australia's Family Law System was appointed by resolution of the Senate on 18 September 2019 and resolution of the House of Representatives on 19 September 2019.

The committee was originally due to present its final report on or before 7 October 2020. On 31 August 2020, both Houses of Parliament agreed to extend the reporting date to 25 February 2021.

The committee tabled its first interim report on 7 October 2020.

The committee tabled its second interim report on 15 and 16 March 2021. The second interim report detailed the committee's views and recommendations on the family law system. This concluded the committee's inquiry into the family law system.

The Parliament agreed to extend the presentation of the final report until 29 October 2021 and subsequently until 16 December 2021. The committee intended to report on the committee's views and recommendations on the child support system and its interaction with the family law system.

---

223 Schwarz, Kirrily, 'Awful human mess': inside our family law system, LSJ Online, 4 November, 2019.

The committee tabled its third interim report on 22 November 2021. The third interim report outlined the committee's views and recommendations regarding the child support system.

The committee also tabled its final report on 22 November 2021 with some further recommendations on the family law system.

However the 2022 Australian federal election was held on Saturday 21 May 2022. The report disappeared. The multi-million dollar report had taken more than two years from the date of the appointment of the Committee to the date of tabling of the report. One can only suspect that there was a political agenda behind the inquiry. Was the then Prime Minister Scott Morrison just after Pauline Hanson's and the One Nation vote? Many commentators thought so.

***

The position of all the various parties was by now well known. Once again, it was largely a case of the profession and the government talking to each other and to themselves. There was none of the heat and passionate representations from outraged litigants and broken hearted family members that was witnessed in the Howard inquiry two decades previously. Nobody wanted an outpouring of grief. Everyone had learnt their lesson about allowing the messy voices of people damaged by the system to leak into the public domain.

Most of the Committee's hearings were held in Canberra but there were also hearings in Townsville, Rockhampton and Brisbane in Queensland and Sydney in New South Wales.

Taxpayer funded bodies making representations to the Committee included a number of industry heavyweights: National Council of Single Mothers and their Children, Child Support Australia, Australian Institute of Family Studies, the Department of Social Services, the Attorney General's Department, No to Violence, National Legal Aid, Victoria Legal Aid, Australian Women Against Violence Alliance, National Legal Aid, the National Foundation for Women, Law Council of Australia, Women's Legal Services Australia, Rape and Domestic Violence Services Australia, the Australian Bar Association and the Australia's National Research Organisation for Women's Safety, to name a few.

Outnumbered representatives of fathers, largely survivors from the turn of the millennium, included Lone Fathers Association Australia, the Non-Custodial Parents Party (Equal Parenting) and Men's Rights.

John Flanagan at the Non-Custodial Parents Party noted: "We have made submissions to many family law, child support and related inquiries over the years. This is to outline the cause of the problem and to show how the system can be fixed in order to prevent this problem from recurring.

"We believe that you should also recommend the reversal of some of the negative effects of the changes made by the Family Law Amendment (Family Violence and Other Measures) Act 2011. This includes the removal of the effects of the domestic violence provisions contained therein and the reinstatement of the previous perjury provisions.

"As a result of these changes, the issue of family violence is increasingly being used to wrongly undermine legitimate attempts at children being able to have contact with both parents after either separation or divorce.

"We do not condone family violence. However the result of this particular amendment has significantly undermined legitimate attempts at children being able to have contact with both parents after either separation or divorce; when this should not be the case.

"This is despite the fact that many of these allegations are not true and are not required to be substantiated. These allegations are often merely made to obtain an advantage ... with other issues such as property settlements and superannuation splitting; child support payments and Centrelink payments."[224]

Longtime activist Andrew Thompson told the committee he had been left with nothing but the clothes on his back after family separation, an all too familiar circumstance for many Australian men.

"May I give you a reality scenario: "A wife has been having an affair with another man. She wants to leave her husband so she decides to ring the police and says she feels threatened by her husband. The accusations are totally false but the husband is unaware of the situation."

One day while watching the cricket there is a knock on the door: It is the police asking him to come down to the station. His wife allegedly feels threatened.

"He is asked to sign an Apprehended Violence Order. He is told it is only a formality.

"He is then released but informed that he is not permitted to go within 500 metres of the matrimonial home. He now has nowhere to live. He is unable to access his children.

"You all wonder why we have the highest suicide rates of men per capita in the Western world.

"In the Lone Fathers submission founder Barry Williams suggested that travelling around the country we hear the view that the whole Family Law System and Family Court System is broken beyond repair, a system that costs them not only most of their income, and property but in many cases their blood. The cost of

---

[224] Submission, Non Custodial Parents Party, Joint Select Committee on Australia's Family Law System, 23 September, 2019.

litigation, reports and the cost of transcripts are outrageous. All members agree that there was a good feeling of satisfaction and support for the 2006 rebuttable presumption of shared responsibility and shared care laws that saw more shared equal time outcomes than ever before in the history of Australia Family law.

"Our members report that there were more happy and contented children who had a relationship with both parents, Grandparents and extended Families. However, they see a terrible decline since 2011, where the system has broken down completely in every avenue.

"Much of this has occurred through the discrimination and, as we believe, the criminal amendment to the 2010 Family Violence Bill that accepts a person is guilty on accusation alone. This is a smack in the face to the Australian law presumption that one is innocent until proven guilty. The Government of the day and indeed, the Senate was made aware that this Bill was a bill that borders on discrimination and indeed, would wreak havoc on many lives as it was written with no consequences for perjury."[225]

In the flood of submissions from legal and women's groups such voices were given zero credence. And on the ground nothing changed.

***

In 2023 the Government finally released a response to the Hanson Inquiry.[226]

It noted that the final report and the second interim report of the Joint Select Committee into Australia's Family Law System, initiated in 2019, considered several pilot programs aimed at identifying and managing family violence risk, and achieving more equitable and affordable settlement of property disputes.

"The Government will closely consider the evaluations of these pilot programs.

"Further measures in the 2022-23 Budget that relate to the recommendations of the Committee include: $169.4 million for 500 frontline service and community workers to support women and children experiencing family, domestic and sexual violence', $12.6 million over five years from 2022-23 to support a nationally coordinated approach to education and training on family, domestic and sexual violence for community frontline workers, health professionals, and the justice sector, and funding for the Attorney General's Department to undertake a national review of family and domestic violence order frameworks."

Most of the recommendations from the Committee were simply "noted".

---

225 Thompson, Andrew. Submission Joint Select Committee on Australia's Family Law System, 25 September, 2019.

226 Government response, The Joint Select Committee on Australia's Family Law System, 23 January, 2023. Available on the Parliament of Australia website.

Here's a sample: "Recommendation Three: The committee recommends that if the Family Law Amendment (Federal Family Violence Orders) Bill 2021 is passed, the Australian Government continues to consult closely with the Federal Circuit and Family Court of Australia to ensure that it has sufficient resources to implement and enforce Federal Family Violence Orders."

Government response: Noted.

There was nothing in all this that even acknowledged the many problems being inflicted upon separated fathers and their families, nothing even remotely helpful.

The original purpose of the Inquiry, to expose the malpractices and injustices within the system, was entirely lost.

Pauline Hanson was snowed.

TWENTY-THREE
ENOUGH IS ENOUGH

Even by the very low standards of the Australian Parliament and the nation's family law jurisdiction in particular it was hard to believe what happened in the months preceding the 50th anniversary of the passing of the Family Law Act (1975).

The extreme anti-male anti-father Marxist inspired feminism of the 1970s had metastasised through the nation's institutions. What happens at the end of The Long March? Something like this. Australia went from a larrikin culture to ultra-woke, and became the laughing stock of the world.

The appointment of a so-called Minister for Men's Behaviour Change in the state of Victoria in May of 2024 epitomised what had happened in this increasingly sad country, plundered by overseas corporations, betrayed by its own politicians, and ideologically corrupted.

Victorian Premier Jacinta Allan, who took over from the despised Dictator Dan, the Premier Daniel Andrews who had imposed on his fellow Victorians the longest and most extreme Covid lockdowns in the world, announced that state Member of Parliament Tim Richardson would serve as the inaugural Parliamentary Secretary for Men's Behaviour Change – the first position of its kind in the country.[227]

Richardson said he would focus on the influence the internet and social media had on male attitudes towards women, and on building respectful relationships. It would not be "easy work, but it is important," he added.

"We must make Victoria a safer place for women and children and work to end the tragedy of deaths of Victorian women at the hands of men. This role gives me

---

[227] Milienos, Antoinette, Victorian Premier Jacinta Allan creates social media backlash by creating new role of Parliamentary Secretary for Men's Behaviour Change, *Daily Mail*, 29 May, 2024.

some semblance of hope that the focus is shifting away from this being a women's problem to solve and instead is a men's issue that we can take leadership for. But it also requires the Parliamentary Secretary to consult and collaborate on solutions with those working on the ground, with men, to understand their attitudes, the drivers of their actions and work to change their behaviours."

Within hours of announcing the position, Richardson took to X, writing: "Some pretty hectic reactions here to an important role and Australian first. It will be about modelling positive role models for boys and men and ensuring we break away from gender based stereotypes and building respectful relationships. As boys and men we need to lead this."

***

Media coverage couched the initiative in heavy domestic violence rhetoric, never mind that Australian men were twice as likely as women to die a violent death or that despite decades of programs and millions of dollars of advertising campaigns the multi-billion dollar DV industry always claimed, year on escalating year, that the situation was deteriorating and more government funding, more education programs, more women's refuges, more advocacy groups were desperately needed. And never mind that the homicide rate in Australia had been declining for years. Or that the definition of domestic violence was now so broad as to include much normal human behaviour.

Never mind the many, many thousands of falsely accused men who have had their lives destroyed by the industry. The very men whose taxes were being used to perpetuate this insanity.

Never mind that pouring billions into a public service blackhole only to make relations between the genders worse was a true example of profligate waste. The only certainty being that year on year the claims that there was an epidemic of domestic violence would increase, along with the demands for yet more public money.

How was any of this deliberately engineered moral panic helping anyone?

As always in the blizzard of rhetoric and ideologically driven propaganda surrounding Australia's government engendered gender wars, truth was irrelevant.

Very very few Australian commentators had the nerve to stand up to this tidal wave of virtue signalling.

One exception was Terry Barnes writing in *The Spectator*: "When it comes to identity politics and the state government's obsession with progressive causes – to the point of being extremist – Victoria is very much Australia's place to be.

"To assume, as Allan has, that all men are toxic perpetrators-in-waiting is an insult to the overwhelming majority of men who deplore family violence of any sort.

"Allan has put Victoria on the international map with one of the most bizarre pieces of identity politics yet seen from a western government. To assume, as Allan has, that all men are toxic perpetrators-in-waiting is both lazy feminist and identity politics, and an insult to the overwhelming majority of men who deplore family violence of any sort as utterly repugnant, and who strive to be kind and loving husbands, partners and fathers.

"Instead of leading serious and respectful community conversations about relationship violence, and how best to confront and combat it, Allan is instead playing gesture politics with an untrue and judgmental generalisation about men in Australian society. This is an absurd clickbait gimmick that collectively has made her, her government, and the state of Victoria an international laughing stock."[228]

***

In case anyone thought common sense had any chance of leaking into any of this, Australian Prime Minister Anthony Albanese also announced in May a rapid review into the prevention of domestic violence after calling the problem a "national crisis".

"We recognise that governments need to act, but we also recognise that this is an issue for the whole of society. Women should not be responsible for ending violence against women."[229]

The review featured a roll call of feminist advocates, including Anne Summers, author and journalist who had a formative role in the Women's Liberation Movement in Australia, including the establishment of Australia's first refuge for women. Her counterparts in Britain and Canada, Erin Pizzey and Anne Cools respectively, who established the first women's refuge their own countries, had both came out saying there were numbers of violent women in those early refuges and they had never meant the refuge movement to become part of the extremist anti-male rhetoric of the hard-left feminism which became the dominant narrative. No such luck with Australia's Anne Summers.

---

228 Barnes, Terry, Victoria's absurd new minister for men's behaviour, *The Spectator Australia*, 29 May, 2024.

229 Anthony Albanese tells rally gendered violence is a problem of our entire society, ABC, 27 April, 2024.

The Panel was to be co-convened by Australia's Domestic, Family and Sexual Violence Commissioner, Ms Micaela Cronin and the Executive Director of the Commonwealth Office for Women, Ms Padma Raman. The Panel included Jess Hill, "journalist, author and educator globally renown for ground-breaking work on gendered-violence"; Elena Campbell, Associate Director of Research, Advocacy and Policy at RMIT's Centre for Innovative Justice; and Dr Leigh Gassner, Assistant Commissioner at Victoria Police "who has managed significant cultural and organisational change processes, including undertaking a previous review of policing responses into violence against women".

One might be forgiven for thinking that if the government was genuinely concerned about decreasing interpersonal violence they might have included a broader range of views, and a few representatives from genuine community groups servicing men and fathers. The very few men included in this pile-on were feminist apologists who knew what side their bread was buttered on. Otherwise they would never have got the job.

The Minister for Women Katy Gallagher said: "This review will provide important advice to the Commonwealth, and all governments through National Cabinet, on more effective, targeted ways to prevent violence, including to stop women being killed. We know this is a crisis and this violence must stop."[230]

Minister for Social Services Amanda Rishworth said: "Violence against women and children is a national shame. One life lost to intimate partner homicide is one too many.

"In order to reach our shared goal of ending violence against women and children in one generation we must have a considered focus on perpetrator intervention and prevention activities."

***

Building on all this, later in the year, in September, at an announcement by the Prime Minister Anthony Albanese of an additional $4.7 billion dollars in domestic violence funding, the questions of a male reporter were dismissed in favour of female reporters.[231]

The announcement followed a meeting between the Prime Minister and chief ministers of the states and territories to discuss what he repeatedly labelled a "national crisis", and reassert his government's commitment to end family, domestic and sexual violence "in a generation".

---

230 Working to end violence against women with rapid review into prevention approaches, Joint Media Release, Australian Government, 28 May, 2024.

231 'We must act': Where the extra $4.7 billion in gender-based violence funding is going, SBS, 6 September, 2024.

The package included $3.9 billion over five years for "frontline" legal services. Domestic violence allegations almost invariably occur at the time of separation and are routinely weaponised. Rich pickings. All parts of the "legal assistance" sector would get "funding support", including women's legal services, Aboriginal and Torres Strait Islander legal services, family violence prevention legal services, legal aid, and community legal centres.

Pouring yet more billions down the gullets of conscience free lawyers operating in an entirely dysfunctional arena was only going to pour petrol on an already inflamed situation. And here, in front of our eyes, in real time, we could watch yet another government program fail, while the public service expanded its remit and the increasing totalitarianism of Australian society grew ever worse.

It constituted blatantly one-sided funding of the family law jurisdiction.

The aim of "eliminating domestic violence in a generation" was eerily reminiscent of another Labor Prime Minister, Bob Hawke, who back in the 1980s claimed he would eliminate child poverty, birthing the despised Child Support Agency, creating one of the Australian Public Service's most labyrinthine, expensive and despised bureaucracies.

Albanese's reputation was in tatters, his political enemies inside and outside his own party were circling, housing and cost of living crises beset the country, and there had been a serious loss of faith in government in the post-Covid era. Just like his predecessor Bob Hawke, Albanese had to reach for something. It was all about politics. It had nothing to do with the welfare of the population.

The National Cabinet, that is the Prime Minister and state and territory leaders, also committed to developing a "new national family and domestic violence risk assessment framework", enhancing the sharing of "warning flags" on perpetrators across jurisdictions and strengthening the system to prevent violence from escalating. Profiling in other words.

***

The Commonwealth also announced it would fund the establishment of national standards for men's behaviour change and audit key government systems to identify areas where they were being weaponised by perpetrators. Whatever that meant in the real world.

We're talking billions of dollars here. None of which would make the situation any better.

Arrayed against hundreds of women's groups there was one group that had been attempting for years to introduce sanity into the domestic violence arena, not just its routine abuse of domestic violence data but its highly selective use of so-called "experts" and their streams of advocacy research and reports.

That group was One In Three, founded by a former contributor and organiser with Dads On The Air Greg Andresen, who was still going all these years later.

Ever polite, truly a gentleman in the old sense, he had persistently, with occasional success, written to governments and domestic violence advocates suggesting they correct their many inaccuracies.

The point of this being that the government, before promulgating moral panic around violence to women for their own political purposes, knew perfectly well there was another extremely well credentialed and well documented side to the story.

Instead of using billions of dollars of public money to push a seriously outdated gender war, if they had used that money to decrease interpersonal violence, including its precursors such as financial and housing stress as well as substance and alcohol abuse, then it might have had the whole of the society onboard.

Instead, we had all the old hatreds, exemplified by Clementine Ford's "Kill All Men" extremist rhetoric.

As the group's website noted: "One in Three is a diverse group of male and female professionals – academics, researchers, social workers, psychologists, counsellors, lawyers, health promotion workers, trainers and survivor/advocates.

"We aim to raise public awareness of the existence and needs of male victims of family violence and abuse; to work with government and non-government services alike to provide assistance to everyone affected by family violence; and to reduce the incidence and impacts of family violence on Australian men, women and children.

"We believe our society has the capacity to support all victims of family violence, whether male or female, young or old, gay or straight, rich or poor, wherever they live."

Anyone with their ear to the ground can hear multiple stories of men whose lives have been seriously damaged as they're maliciously dragged through the court system on false allegations made by women attempting to gain the upper hand in a family court case. Indeed, the legal system encourages them to do so. Not to mention there is also a financial motive.

***

At yet another inquiry, this one the 2020 Federal Inquiry into family, domestic and sexual violence, social worker with One In Three, Andrew Humphreys, wrote of his experience helping both a young woman and a young man through the thicket of a domestic violence aftermath. The woman had plenty of resources she could access. Different story for the bloke.

"After previous assaults, I counselled him that, when this occurs, he should leave his home, photograph his injuries, seek medical attention and go to the police. He did this, and his partner was charged and an interim AVO was put in place. Despite this, the alleged perpetrator retained custody of their child and then denied him access, in breach of Family Court orders.

"When the matter progressed to court, the perpetrator said that she was the victim, that my client had assaulted her and that he had, in fact, held her over a balcony by her ankles. This was despite the court having before it medical evidence that, due to a spinal tumour and a fracture, my client cannot lift anything heavier than a pound of butter. The perpetrator was acquitted, and my client is yet to see his child again. When I raised the possibility of perjury with the police, I was told that people lie in court all the time.

"There's been no formal support for my client. The various helplines, if they believe the man, have no services to refer to."[232]

That story could be told a thousand times over with a thousand different variations. But we've all heard them. We all know they're true. Everyone but the government's gender warriors pursuing their agendas at our expense.

***

After a long and troubled period of conservative government spanning across three Prime Ministers, the left finally regained control of the government in May, 2022. They failed to fulfil their promises, such as cheaper electricity, but moved quickly to implement a range of policies they had not broached with the electorate, including a dramatic increase in mass immigration and a radical rewrite of family law.

Of all the many things that the most leftwing government in Australian history, Anthony Albanese's Labor Government, did not bother to tell the Australian public prior to the 2022 election was that they intended to take Australia's utterly dysfunctional family law system even further backwards, to the dark ages when many fathers entering the Family Court rarely if ever saw their children again.

The government had no public mandate whatsoever to implement the family law changes it was now proceeding with.

Another flurry of announcements. Another whirl of self-aggrandising speeches from politicians, another round of claims of simpler, safer, fairer. Another round of comments from pontificating family law "experts".

---

[232] Humphreys, Andrew, One in Three's appearance before the Inquiry into family, domestic and sexual violence, Hansard, 1 December, 2020.

All in "the best interests of the child".

Another splattering of submissions from unfunded fathers and family law advocates, another tsunami of submissions from the taxpayer funded industry.

The innocuously named Family Law Amendment Bill (2023) was first presented to the House of Representatives on 29 March 2023.

There was a smattering of media coverage, but nothing like the halcyon days of the early 2000s, when hope, and feelings, were running high.

The warnings came as Family Law expert Patrick Parkinson, always pretty conservative in his public pronouncements, branded the changes "staggering" and said they would result in higher rates of litigation with disputes becoming harder to resolve. He warned the government's proposed changes would have damaging consequences for parents, children, courts and social cohesion.

In his submission to the review, Professor Parkinson said the changes stripped "almost every reference" to the importance of both parents in a child's lives and repealed all provisions about how this idea should translate into parenting arrangements after separation. He said the legal system was likely to become "unsettled" by the changes causing litigation to increase and making disputes harder to resolve.

"These are staggering deletions and I doubt very much that the Albanese government wants to send the damaging message to the community that these deletions involve," he wrote. "The proposals represent a fundamental change to the values that are expressed to underlie the family law system."

Labor's proposed changes were welcomed by domestic violence advocates, who repeatedly argued the presumption of equal shared responsibility provision was often used by violent perpetrators to control the family and children.

Professor Parkinson said this argument was not based on evidence and that the family law system should be designed to serve the population as a whole.

"This is not a position supported by any research evidence, and were that view to be accepted, the whole family law system would need to be designed for the sole purpose of dealing with the most violent of men, who, it is assumed, will continue with that violence when parents are living apart," he said.[233]

***

Twenty years on from the original fatherhood movement of the early 2020s Australia was a very different place.

---

[233] Parkinson, Patrick. Family law reform 'not good for kids', *The Australian*, 2020.

The legacy media was tamer and more controlled, all by design, heavily manipulated and infiltrated by government operatives and far more obsequious towards government agendas than ever before – in large part due to their reliance on government advertising and the parlous financial state into which they had descended as the digital age transformed the media landscape.

Across its limited bipolar spectrum of left and right Australia's mainstream media outlets had become little less than government propaganda units aimed at controlling, deceiving and subjugating the very people they pretended to serve.

Elected in 2022, the Albanese government proved itself time and time again to be not the least bit interested in the views of the general public, and the process of government inquiry had become so degraded as to be more or less pointless. They knew what they wanted to implement and didn't give a flying fig what the citizenry thought. Post Covid, it had become essentially communistic, enormously bureaucratic, and totalitarian in its determination to reach into the corners of everybody's lives.

Australia had some of the world's highest electricity, housing and petrol costs, not to mention alcohol and tobacco, slowest and most expensive internet, most insane immigration system and consequently one of the most fractured societies on Earth. Not to mention ramping costs of living and extreme housing stress in one of the most heavily taxed and over regulated societies anywhere on the planet. Australia was a basket case woven by the nation's hapless political class.

***

The Albanese government had spent the previous 18 months obsessing about a Referendum on an Indigenous Voice to Parliament, an extremely ill conceived project which deeply divided the nation and resulted in a crushing defeat for the government.

Not content with dividing the nation on the grounds of race, Prime Minister Anthony Albanese and his ageing feminist cohorts in the Attorney General's Department were determined to reignite the Gender Wars of the previous century, making the lives of separated dads, and therefore their children, even worse than they already were.

Shockingly bad legislation, The Family Law Amendment Bill 2023, whistled through both houses of Parliament and was passed into law in October of 2023.

Twenty years on, after the initial fatherhood movement galvanised so many people, some of the same commentators and activists were still in play, including social commentator Bettina Arndt. Now publishing freely on her Substack page, she wrote: "Chances are most people reading this wouldn't even know the Family

Law bill had passed. Men across Australia wouldn't have a clue that their rights as parents are now far more precarious, their chances of being a proper father after divorce severely reduced. The likelihood that fathers will end up as victims of false allegations is also much increased."

The Bill removed the Objects Section of the Act which stated that family court decisions should encourage the participation of both parents in their children's lives. The aim of involving both parents was first introduced some 20 years ago by the conservatives after massive public backlash over the extremism of Australia's family law, the well acknowledged fact that the highest rates of suicide in the country were directly related to mistreatment of fathers during family law and child support matters, and the desperate concerns not just of fathers but mothers, sisters, daughters, grandparents over the extreme damage the court system was inflicting on the nation's children, the phrase "the best interests of the child" being the greatest lie of all.

The Australian Attorney General's Department claimed their Family Law Amendment Bill 2023 was a "landmark" which would "ensure the best interests of children are at the centre of all parenting decisions".

So there, straight up, we have a pack of bureaucrats saying Australia's parents didn't have the best interests of their children at heart, and they knew better. Some kids are dragged up rather than brought up. Different parents and different ethnic and socio-economic groups have very different styles. It's not, or should not be, a matter for a bunch of out of touch and unaccountable middle class bureaucrats to decide.

One thing we know for sure: the state makes a very bad parent. Studies have consistently shown that children are better off in intact families or when both parents are involved, never mind whether those parents are saints or not, fundamentalist Christians or hippies out on a commune.

"The best interests of the child" is a legal fiction which in the hands of lawyers can mean virtually anything, and in Australia's antiquated and corrupted family law system means sole mother custody, contempt for fathers and the perpetuation of the blizzard of false allegations which led to the Family Court of Australia routinely being called as "The Palace Of Lies", a moniker still relevant after all these decades.

***

Bettina Arndt summed it all up in a piece Winner Takes All: "According to bright new world of Family Law being promised by the Albanese government, the following will no longer be deemed important in making decisions about children's care: Ensuring children benefit from meaningful involvement with both parents, Children's right to know and be cared for by both parents, Children's right to spend regular time with both parents and other significant people like grandparents, Parents jointly sharing duties and responsibilities for the kids' care and development, Parents agreeing about future parenting of children.

"All gone. All the language that provided the scaffolding that enabled children to have divorced dads remain part of their lives is being ripped out of the legislation.

Now the new family law will be all about safety. That's hardly a surprise. Feminists have been using the violence card to undermine father's contact with their children since the 2006 laws were first introduced, with constant claims about violent dads putting children at risk, and legal efforts to beef up safety considerations working very effectively to shut fathers out of children's lives.

"It's another superb victory for the feminists, one more achievement for their mighty domestic violence juggernaut, which already works a treat stacking the family law system to favour women. Currently all it takes is one vague claim that violence could occur, requiring zero supportive evidence, to set in train a sequence of events starting with Dad being removed from the home."[234]

***

Australia, already known as the least democratic of Western democracies, saw only a very few politicians stand up in Parliament and question the passage of this anti-father anti-family legislation.

One of those, one of the only politicians with the integrity and courage to have stood up to the bureaucratic blitzkrieg of the Soviet era in Australia, aka the Covid era, was Senator Malcolm Roberts of Queensland. He said: "The Family Law Act has been called the slaughterhouse of the nation. It has been killing people in this country, killing families and killing kids, since 1975 when it was introduced by the Labor Party following UN policy. That is a fact.

"There have been 48 years of the slaughterhouse of the nation thanks to Lionel Murphy and the Labor Party. Now they are introducing bills to make it even more complex. They won't allow scrutiny of that complexity. What are they hiding?

"Instead of consulting properly in the first place, the government has chosen to put forward poor legislation and just ram it through. The Labor Party need to start doing what Anthony Albanese promised as opposition leader and start

---

234 Arndt, Bettina, Winner Takes All, Bettina Arndt Substack page, 8 February, 2023.

listening and consulting, not walking with their ears closed and ramming through legislation.

"What they are hiding is a multi billion dollar gravy train for their mates, their fellow travellers, their academic bum chums and for the legal fraternity.

"And the widespread societal wreckage their extremely sexist anti-male rhetoric causes."[235]

***

All rationality, all reason had fled the building.

The government didn't even front with the Attorney General Michael Dreyfus, who just like the Prime Minister was Missing in Action during this whole sorry affair.

Instead a singularly uninformed and entirely unimpressive Assistant Education Minister Anthony Chisholm, bamboozled by the Opposition questions thrown at him and flanked by departmental bureaucrats providing the answers, could only resort to that ultimate legal and bureaucratic lie, "The best Interest of the Child".

It was one of the most dismal displays in Australian parliamentary history. Which, of course, in a floundering democracy, takes some doing.

Some participants put in a valiant effort at sanity. Liberal National Senator for Queensland Paul Scarr, another lawyer turned politician, wanted to know why various sections of the Act were being removed: "Objects and principles that are currently in the act that are going to be removed include ensuring that children have the benefit of both of their parents having a meaningful involvement in their lives to the maximum extent consistent with the child's best interest, that children have the right to be know and be cared for by both of their parents, that children have a right to spend time and communicate with both their parents and also grandparents and other relatives on a regular basis.

"Parents jointly share duties and responsibilities concerning the care, welfare and development of the children. The parents should agree about the future parenting of their children. When I look at those objectives, they don't seem particularly controversial to me. I would have thought they reflect a lot of the views of many Australians."

The Chair responded: "It was a very long question, unfortunately…"

And the response from a spokeswoman for the Family Law Section of the Law Council was that they did not share the concerns that the Bill represented a retrograde change for parents: "It's important that we have legislation that allows

---

[235] Malcolm Roberts, Hansard, Australian Parliament, 18 October, 2023.

them to make their negotiations freely and with confidence, because the legislation is simple and they can understand it."

***

Since the early 2000s, those naive days of optimism, billions of dollars had been spent ever since on the lucrative government funding industry of demonising men and lionising women. While other countries had moved on, the now totally outmoded "all men are rapists" style of feminism originating in the academic halls of the 1960s and 1970s remained alive and well in Australia, nurtured by cravenly weak politicians ever scared of the powerful women's lobby and frightened of the accusation of being influenced by fathers groups.

Senator Pauline Hanson, who had been deputy chair of yet another inquiry, The Joint Select Committee on Australia's Family Law System appointed in 2019, was one of the few Australian politicians actually taking note of the dire impacts on her constituents of Australia's utterly dysfunctional family law and child support systems when 2023 rolled around.

"The demonisation of Australian men is unjustified and needs to stop," she said. "Men are already over represented in homelessness, in jobs with high risk to safety, as victims of violent crimes and, tragically, in suicides. Many of these studies are associated with unfair and unjust family law outcomes from a system biased against fathers. The removal of shared parental responsibility carries a strong risk of even more unjust outcomes.

"There was clear evidence presented to the Joint Select Committee that many mothers made unfounded or deliberately false allegations of violence against fathers. Ninety per cent of parents alleging child sexual abuse in contested hearings from 2012 until 2019 were mothers. In 90 percent of these hearings, the judge found no risk of sexual harm to the child or children – 90 percent.

"In 25 percent of these cases, the allegations were found to be deliberately misleading. In another 46 percent of these cases, the allegations were mistaken.

"In 88 percent of these cases, the allegations were not believed by the judge. In 62 percent of these cases, the judge awarded shared parental responsibility or sole responsibility to the parent against whom the allegations were made. In 66 percent of these cases, orders were made increasing parenting time with the parent against whom the allegations were made."[236]

***

---

[236] Pauline Hanson, Hansard, Parliament of Australia, 16 October, 2023.

Senator Hanson said her statements were confirmed by a former Family Court judge, Justice David Collier, who claimed allegations of child sexual abuse were being increasingly invented by mothers to stop fathers from seeing their children.

He said: "I'm satisfied that a number of people who have appeared before me have known that it is one of the ways of completely shutting husbands out of the child's life."

Hanson said: "Families experiencing the system, both now and in the future, have my profound sympathies, because the chance of genuine reform has been squandered.

"You're going to keep people going through the court system. Lawyers are going to make a lot of money out of this. I feel sorry for the children. You're not considering the children at all. You're a selfish bunch."

Leading campaigners for fathers all expressed bitter disappointment.

Bettina Arndt, who still wrote regularly for the mainstream press and now also had a Substack page, said the draconian bill saw the Greens joining forces with Labor to enshrine women's absolute power to use false allegations to destroy men's relationships with their children.

She wrote: "Proposed family law changes could see more strained custody battles, with dads likely to lose out. It's a brilliant ploy, which feminists have been systematically cementing in place. Soon their ship will come in.

"This new Act will mean Australia will return to the grim days of mostly sole mother custody. This is the most significant social change in recent history, impacting millions of families across the country. Current estimates suggest there will be more than 300,000 family breakups involving children in the next decade.

"It is just astonishing that this is all passing unchallenged, indeed almost unnoticed. Australia has become one of the world leaders when it comes to men suffering false allegations.

"A new YouGov survey, involving 9432 people across eight countries, found Australia was the worst country, after India, when people were asked if they had been falsely accused of abuse.

"What's going on here? The answer is simple. It's the feminist capture of our family law system.

"The YouGov survey showed false accusations in Australia are more likely to be made as part of a child custody dispute than anywhere else in the world – they are 41 per cent of such allegations in this country."

***

After all these years Sue Price at Men's Rights, now 78, recently bereaved and in a wheelchair, was still dealing with an endless stream of confused, distressed and heartbroken men, who would find her number on her website.

"It's a very sad day," she said. "The whole of the shared parenting concept has now been removed. We are back to the 1990s principles where mothers are considered to be the sole carers of children, with fathers playing just a visitor's role, when allowed.

"This is a backward step for Australia . We are possibly the only country in the world to reverse the shared parenting principles where it is considered vital for children to have the benefit of care and love of both their parents.

"In virtually all cases, the best interests of the child are best served by having both parents around.

"The inquiry into this bill was headed by a woman married to another woman. I couldn't care less what she does in her own life. But it seems quite obvious to me that she has no interest in understanding a father's role in their children's lives.

"According to the Australian Bureau of Statistics one woman in Australia dies every six days in a domestic homicide, while one man loses his life every eight days. Do we really accept that difference of two days to ignore the violence of women or instigated against the man by another willing to do her bidding. Are their lives not just as important."

Warwick Marsh, also still soldiering on at Dads4Kids said the Labor Party's Family Law Amendment Bill 2023 created a day of mourning for Australian children.

"The team at Dads4Kids believes this bill will in fact harm our children and is against their best interests and therefore unjust."

Marsh said if you were a father with an intact family, you might well say that this is not your problem. He would answer with the famous quote from civil rights campaigner Martin Luther King: "Injustice anywhere is a threat to justice everywhere. We are caught in an inescapable network of mutuality, tied in a single garment of destiny."

The prophet Isaiah said these timeless words in 700 BC: "Injustice is everywhere; justice seems far away. Truth is chased out of court; honesty is shoved aside."

Marsh went on to say: "There are over 870,000 children who will go to sleep tonight in Australia without their biological father in the home. Many of these children cry themselves to sleep, whilst others bury the pain through damaging addictions and/or behaviours. For many, the pain comes out in unexplained and damaging behaviours as they grow to adulthood.

"Children have a biological birthright of equal access to their mother and their father in the event of separation. The bill passed last Thursday will deprive them further of that biological birthright.

"Simply put, we must make a stand for our nation's children. We have to stand against the spread of fatherlessness."

***

Former Attorney General Michaelia Cash, who led the Opposition's position on the Bill, began strongly: "At the outset of this debate, I said that there are very few things in the Commonwealth Attorney General's portfolio that have a more direct impact on Australians than family law.

"Every year, thousands of Australians will find themselves going through the pain and sadness of separation, and, in a small proportion of those cases, disputes will be decided by a judge in Australia's family law courts. As a nation, we should aim for a system that resolves those disputes as quickly and cleanly as possible.

"Regardless of the circumstances, if children are involved, we should at all times prioritise their best interests.

"We do not agree with the solutions adopted in many places in this bill. It is not a bill that has been worked through over many years. It is not even a bill that has been subject to proper scrutiny. There are actually more schedules in the bill than there have been hours of committee inquiry. It is embarrassing.

"Even with the small amount of scrutiny that we have been able to give, it has become increasingly clear that the government consistently puts its ideological agenda over the best interest of Australian families."

It fell to Bettina Arndt, the only mainstream journalist in the country following the story in any depth, to pick up the story.

"What a moment of triumph," she wrote in a piece titled Parliament Votes for More Fatherless Children. "Powerful Liberal Senator Michaela Cash was glorious to watch, fervently questioning the treacherous betrayal of fathers by Labor. She reduced the unfortunate government minister defending the Family Law bill to stuttering gibberish. He was unable to put forward one coherent argument as to why this government is removing the key protections for children's rights to be cared for by both parents after divorce.

"But then they sold us out. When it came to a vote, the bill went through, with the Greens, Pocock and Jacqui Lambie's group, all happily supporting Labor. And get this…. almost all the Opposition Senators abstained! Sat on the sidelines and ducked their heads. AND MICHAELA CASH ACTUALLY VOTED FOR THE BILL!

"Asked why she would do that, Cash's office came up with mumbo jumbo about the Opposition's amendments having been rejected by the Senate. The word is that they don't see this as a hill to die on. They aren't prepared to take flak for being labelled as soft on domestic violence by voting against the bill.

"No question that is what would happen", Bettina Arndt wrote. "Look at this press release from the Women's Legal Services Australia, congratulating Attorney General Dreyfus on the bill, which was circulated within minutes of the vote going through.

"We strongly support reform of the Family Law Act to make the law clearer and fairer, including the removal of the presumption of equal shared parental responsibility to improve safety," the statement read. "When violence and abuse are factors, courts will be able to deal with them more easily and reduce the number of children and mothers forced into dangerous situations. Removing this dangerous provision will give the courts the freedom to focus on safety and the genuine best interests of children and families."

Bettina Arndt declared that this was how the bill was packaged and sold to the public, with the media narrative superbly controlled.

"There's been barely a breach in the keeping-children-safe mantra and absolutely no media coverage of the exposure of Labor's lies about the bill. Chances are most people reading this wouldn't even know the Family Law bill had passed.

"Men across Australia wouldn't have a clue that their rights as parents are now far more precarious, their chances of being a proper father after divorce severely reduced. The likelihood that fathers will end up as victims of false allegations is also much increased.

"Where was the press gallery this week, as the flaws in this critical bill were being so thoroughly exposed? Well, clearly none of the young ladies now crowding into Canberra's elite press circles had any interest in the story. As if these ideologues would have any interest in protecting the rights of fathers, let alone considering the true best interests of children."[237]

There were actually four Liberal senators who voted for the Family Law Amendment Bill 2023. Senior Liberal Senators Askew, Cash, Henderson and Rushton voted with Labor and the Greens for the Family Law Amendment Bill 2023. This was on 19 October 2023. The other Liberal senators and National senators and Senator Jacqui Lambie then just did not turn up and thereby by their absence abstained from voting.

Labor and the Greens members of the House of Representatives voted for the Bill. Similarly all the Liberal and National members of the House of Representatives just did not turn up and thereby abstained from voting on 19 October 2023.

Critics called it a day of national shame. Emboldened by the acquiescence of the conservatives, with the most leftwing government in Australian history now in power, the left was determined to push on with yet more legislation.

---

237 Arndt, Bettina, Parliament votes for more fatherless children, Substack, 21 October, 2023.

Just as there were very few politicians prepared to stand up against the tide, commentators in the nation's media who stood up were equally rare.

One of the few was Angela Shanahan, the Catholic mother of nine children, wife of senior political analyst Dennis Shanahan. In November of 2023 she wrote: "For two days this week the lawns of Parliament House have been strewn with 2500 empty shoes, one for each of the men and boys who die in Australia each year through suicide.

"According to the Australian Institute of Health and Welfare our male suicide rate is overall three to four times higher than the female rate, and mainly involves men in mid-life. These are the major predictive facts about suicide: being male; being divorced, widowed or separated; living alone; being unemployed."

Instead, as Shanahan wrote, the government was concentrating all preventive efforts on domestic violence against women, always seen as "gendered" violence; in other words, men being violent towards women.

"According to the Australian Bureau of Statistics there are 47 male deaths from suicide per week. Meanwhile, there are 71 females who die from fatal domestic violence per year, that equals 1.36 per week. So male suicides, which are 35 times as numerous as deaths from DV, should also be everyone's issue. But where is the advertising campaign? Where is the support?"

What of the pathologies that plague all of us, and our whole society? Why is something that involves two people presented as one-dimensional: man bad perpetrator, woman good victim? The DV lobby does not allow presentation of this problem in any other way, because allowing any nuance might question the simplistic assumptions that underlie the narrow, prismatic feminist ideology that governs all current social legislation, especially in family law.

"Male suicide, though complex, is often triggered, in the words of the AIHW research, by a recent stressful life event, especially divorce or final separation from a long-term partner. That has been cited by all research into Australian male suicide as the overwhelming reason behind the rise in middle-life suicide, especially where children are involved.

"Divorce is not just a single event; it causes a cascading series of problems, and men in contested divorce cases often find themselves in a maze of legal and financial dead ends, with a mounting psychological toll of usually concealed trauma."

Like many conservatives, Shanahan pointed back to the inquiries of the Howard era as showing "the level of false accusations was outrageous". She slammed the Family Law Amendment Bill 2023 as being anything but reform: "It is a regression to the past. It is a disastrous change, which will cause more false accusations of violence and more harm to fathers of children and, consequently, more male suicides."[238]

***

On May 6, 2024, Attorney General Michael Dreyfus issued a press release headlined "Landmark Family Law Act reforms come into effect".[239]

That would be the same Attorney General who did not bother to front parliament as the Bill was passed the previous October.

He stated: "Today the Albanese Government's significant reforms to the Family Law Act come into effect, making Australia's family law system simpler, safer and easier for separating families and their children.

"The changes will make what is an often-confusing and overly complex system easier to navigate for families going through a challenging period of their lives.

"These two pieces of legislation recognise the need for a simpler and safer family law system, and improved information sharing to address family safety risks. Significantly, it is now law that the resolution of parenting disputes should always be based solely on what is in the best interests of the child.

"Australians need a family law system that is simple, accessible and that puts the safety of children at the heart of every decision.

"The Family Law Amendment Act 2023 aims to assist courts and parents to resolve parenting disputes safely, efficiently and with a clear focus on the best interests of the children involved.

"The reforms remove the presumption of equal shared parental responsibility, which has often been misunderstood as meaning parents have a right to equal shared time. This has allowed some parents to be coerced into agreeing to equal time arrangements that are unsafe. This change makes it clear that all decisions about parenting arrangements should be based on what arrangements best meet the needs of the individual child.

"The changes will ensure the courts have access to a holistic picture of family safety risk in order to prioritise the safety of children and families, particularly in circumstances where there is risk of child abuse, neglect or family violence.

"The Government recognises the significant impact family violence and safety concerns can have on children and families and thanks those who have shared their experiences throughout the development of these laws.

---

238 Shanahan, Angela, Empty Shoes on Parliament House Lawns Highlight Male Suicide, *The Australian*, 16 November, 2023.

239 Attorney General's Department, Press Release, Landmark Family Law Act reforms come into effect, 6 May, 2024.

"The Government also acknowledges the important contributions of stakeholders whose perspectives have been invaluable to the development of these reforms and will be critical to their effective implementation."

Stakeholders being the flotilla of taxpayer funded entities allegedly serving the interests of women and children.

That was by no means the end of the matter.

TWENTY-FOUR
AT THE END
OF THE LONG MARCH

As if all this wasn't toxic enough, along came Coercive Control, an extremely nasty piece of legislation which in the hands of lawyers could mean virtually anything at all, and certainly compassed a broad spectrum of human behaviour, both male and female.

It was yet another far left piece of legal insanity eagerly embraced by Australia's virtue signalling politicians and peddled by machine bureaucrats, half a century on from when the country embraced the Marxist feminist style family courts pioneered in other parts of the Western world. Self-evidently, in the hands of lawyers, coercive control can cover a multitude of sins.

On 1 July 2024, coercive control became a criminal offence in NSW, that is when a person uses abusive behaviours towards a current or former intimate partner with the intention to coerce or control them. If found guilty, alleged perpetrators can face up to seven years in jail.

In Queensland, with its reputation as having the most extreme anti-male laws in the country, coercive control is due to become a criminal offence from 26 May 2025, fittingly half a century on from the enactment of the Family Law Act which progressively enabled more and more extreme legislation to become the Australian norm. The offence, which includes patterns of behaviour which may have humiliated a current or former intimate partner, a family member or a carer, carries a penalty of up to 14 years imprisonment.

"Partner won't pay for a new kitchen? That's coercive control."

"Keeps asking for sex? That's coercive control."

"Get that male sent to jail with new coercive control."

So Bettina Arndt began her piece on the latest legislative fad. She was once again the only mainstream journalist highlighting the insanity of it all. Describing coercive control as "massive chicanery" she wrote: "After decades of watching our justice system systematically tilted to favour women, it's hard not to be blasé about each new feminist power grab. But this one leaves you reeling."[240]

***

In a piece titled Coercive Control Con Job: The latest weapon aimed at destroying men, Arndt recorded its origins.

"Let's start with the man who made the whole thing up. Oh yes, coercive control was only invented in 2007, not that long ago. It was proposed not by an eminent criminologist or similar expert but rather a feminist academic working in women's studies.

"Evan Stark's reason for concocting coercive control is most revealing. In his book, *Coercive Control: The Entrapment of Women in Personal Life*, Stark argued the domestic violence industry was running into problems because of mounting evidence that men and women are equally violent.

"So, he decided to come up with something new. He took ideas that had been floating around in the domestic violence industry about patterns of 'patriarchal terrorism' and invented a brand-new form of domestic 'violence' he called 'coercive control' which he claimed men started to use to control their relationships after society moved on from the systematic, widespread 'wife torture' of the past, due to women's liberation eroding men's sex-based patriarchal privilege. How's that for barking mad ideological claptrap?

"Proposing new laws for coercive control proved a brilliant career move – Evan Stark quickly became the pinup boy for the feminist movement, travelling from country to country promoting this inventive means of targeting men.

"Even though everyone knows that both men and women use controlling behaviours, Stark declared that people should 'take on faith' that 'the pattern of intimidation, isolation, and control is unique to men's abuse of women.'

"But the real power in Stark's idea is that he was promoting this as a new criminal offence, which makes these laws a far more effective weapon to use against men than the old violence protections orders used for domestic violence. On the basis of the flimsiest evidence describing behaviours that can't even be properly defined, and that victims may not even see as a problem, men would be sent to prison.

"Within a decade, Stark's ideas were incorporated into new laws criminalising coercive control across the UK, and he was playing a key role in pushing for similar laws in Canada, New Zealand, and here, in Queensland and NSW."

---

240 Arndt, Bettina, Coercive Control Con Job, Substack, 16 March, 2023.

***

Then came the Family Law Amendment Bill 2024. This one was also going to make family law simpler and fairer. You are free to roll your eyes. Essentially it broadened or "clarified" issues of domestic violence to include the distribution of property. Put in crude terms it meant: make an accusation of domestic violence and you get the lot. It further increased the motivation to make false allegations, it further empowered the stripping of fathers of property and income, and it increased the dangers of any father establishing a family or entering a relationship.

Emboldened by pushing through the egregious Family Law Amendment Bill 2023 the Labor Party launched another fuselage. The Bill amended six Commonwealth Acts, including the Evidence Act.

The same lies: fairer, simpler, safer. The same submissions from the same industry stalwarts. The same faux inquiry inviting public submissions, when 99 percent of the public had no idea what the government was up to. The same draft exposure bill steamrolled through Parliament.

The Labor Party was determined to push through a yet further raft of changes in their determination to appease the ever growing industry around separation and divorce, so much of it driven by leftwing public service ideologues determined to abolish the nuclear family as some kind of high minded march to a utopian future.

The Explanatory Memorandum alone ran to 153 pages.

Point One declared: "These amendments will make the family law system safer and simpler for separating couples to navigate, and ensure the property and financial aspects of relationship breakdown are resolved safely and fairly."

Not a good sign to start with a lie.

The next 150 plus pages were essentially impenetrable to any lay person, and probably to most lawyers.

For critics reform fatigue had set in long ago.

***

One of the very few voices in Parliament to raise any doubt about this particular tranche of legislation was Shadow Attorney General Paul Fletcher, a Liberal Party blue blood and yet another lawyer turned politician. He advocated caution. It was all very lawyerly.

At a second reading of the Bill he told Parliament: "We have seen how cynical the government has been in this area in the past. We saw how last year the government was preparing to ram through a surprise amendment. We saw Labor was prepared to drastically undermine and rewrite what it means to make decisions in the best interest of the child. We saw how Labor sought to repeal a requirement that a court consider the benefits of a meaningful relationship with the child's parent and other significant people in the child's life where it would be safe to do so.

"Labor said the courts just needed to consider the 'benefits' of a relationship; they described the change as 'minor'. On this side of the House we take a more cautious approach. We are not satisfied that removing the requirement that a relationship be meaningful is a minor change."

Fletcher concluded: "The appropriate way forward is to look at these measures carefully so that we understand their impact on families before committing them to law. We will continue to be sensible, cautious, sensitive and pragmatic in these areas. I thank the House."

That's about as vigorous as the opposition got.

***

The left had long since seized the high moral ground on this one. Anyone seeking courage or fortitude, common sense or decency from the conservatives had already been severely disappointed. Neither side of Australia's LibLab UniParty ever bothered to listen to cries of pain and outrage and confusion from litigants. Mere litigants. That would be the parents being destroyed in an abomination of a system.

Not that the Family Court had ever paid much attention to reality or the truth of any matter, but this was reinforced in a new section 102NL of the Family Law Amendment Act 2024, which proposed that the rules of evidence were not to apply unless the court decided to do so.

As family law reform advocate John Flanagan put it: "This proposed legislation, if passed by Parliament, will no doubt create further litigation. This is simply due to the need for greater testing of unproven evidence. This will no doubt then result in increased costs, further delays and even more impact on the participants."

Virtually all custody cases are decided on scant or non-existent evidence. The posturings and pronouncements of the court's infamously suspect family report writers cannot be seriously regarded as evidence.

Flanagan described the standard process where sole custody of children is obtained after family separation, in child-related matters, using family violence issues: One parent, normally the mother, makes an application for a family violence order. This is made at the local police station. It can be by either phone or in person. Very often this application is based on unfounded and unsubstantiated allegations.

The police with their limited resources will usually not investigate the allegations. However an interim family violence order is still issued. When the matter does come to court, the police prosecutor will pressure the alleged offender to accept a family violence order "without admission". The alleged offender is told if the order is accepted "without admission", then the problem will go away.

A family violence order is then issued by the magistrate.

Even if the family violence order is not accepted and is contested, the family violence order is normally made by the court at a later date.

Once the family violence order has been made, this order will then be used as evidence of family violence in later court proceedings. Full custody is obtained and the other parent is given supervised access because of perceived safety issues.

It does not matter that the order was based on unfounded and unsubstantiated accusations, in the first instance. The orders are still classed as evidence of family violence.

As Flanagan concluded: "I have no doubt that a similar procedure will be used to obtain the evidence of family violence that will be used in property matters."

***

The Family Law Amendment Bill 2024 was pushed through the Australian Parliament in late November with 27 other bills, all on the same day. [241] There was almost no discussion at all, and most of the public would have no idea what the Bill contained. The government notice said the Bill would "enable the court to control and manage the conduct of property and other non-child-related proceedings, including to address family violence and ensure appropriate evidence is before the court; codify the duty of disclosure relevant to financial information; amend the arbitration regime for court-ordered or privately arranged family law arbitrations; provide a regulatory framework for Children's Contact services…"

In the explanatory memorandum the government noted: "This Bill will amend the Family Law Act to clearly signal that the family law courts will consider the economic effects of family violence in property and spousal maintenance proceedings under the Family Law Act.

"These amendments send a strong message to the community that property settlement outcomes should recognise the effect of family violence on individuals, and on the wealth and welfare of the family, where this is relevant. The

---

241 From the RBA to Social Media: what did and didn't pass in the Guillotine Senate Sitting, SBS News, 28 November, 2024.

amendments make clear to the family law courts, and parties negotiating outside of court, that the economic consequences of family violence can be considered when resolving the property and financial aspects of relationship breakdown."

All without public discussion or support.

So, a father gets tossed out of his home on the basis of an allegation alone. And if in the prolonged court washup he was dreaming of a 50/50 property split, he can dream again.

***

In this upside down world, lies are almost always rewarded. The situation on the ground, the so-called "lived experience", almost always gets worse.

Who, by this stage, could possibly be surprised?

Certainly not social commentator Bettina Arndt, who around the same time published a story titled Whistleblower Police: Reluctant Enforcers for Feminist Domestic Violence Regime.

"The feminists have it all sewn up. All it took was very effective bullying of politicians to have draconian legislation pushed through various state parliaments resulting in unproven domestic violence accusations flooding our criminal law system.

"My focus is on the reluctant enforcers required to do the dirty work for this evil regime – namely our co-opted police officers. I receive regular emails from these long-suffering people, many of whom are appalled at finding themselves having to enforce such unjust laws.

"The stories they told me were shocking, even to a seasoned commentator like me.

"Take, for example, Paul's experience at a recent police training course where they were presented with an example of a woman smashing up the windscreen of her partner's car. Surely this was evidence of a violent, potentially dangerous woman? Oh no. The instructors informed the police officers that they were to assume it was the man who was behind the violence. 'He must have done something to drive her to that point.'

"At another training course unrelated to domestic violence, it was announced that there would be a further three days' training at the end of the course, all about DV. A wag at the back of the room called out, 'It's the man!' and the whole room dissolved in hysterics.

"Everyone knows the point of all this training is to make sure police go into every investigation with only one focus: it must be the man. It's become a joke because the ideological spin is so ridiculously heavy-handed."

The tranches of changes to the Family Law Act under Labor beginning in 2022 were a dream come true for the feminist activists encrusted into Australia's Public Service, most particularly in the Attorney General's Department.

Just as the anti-woke agenda was gripping the world, upturning governments and bureaucracies, and just as the anti-male "toxic masculinity" rhetoric of traditional feminism became unfashionable, Australia, that upside down world, went in exactly the opposite direction, introducing some of the most extremist anti-father legislation to be found anywhere on Earth.

The amendments were shoved through parliament without any proper public consultation, without bipartisan support, and without listening to the individuals damaged by Australia's dire family law and child support systems. And without any proper analysis of the dire social consequences.

There is no underestimating the incompetence of Australia's political class.

On the 50th anniversary of the Family Law Act it is almost impossible to believe that this jurisdiction was established with good will. That the Family Court was to be a caring court, helpful court with simple procedures. That joint custody and cooperation after divorce were to be established as the norm.

Across 50 years the Family Law Act of 1975 has grown steadily more complex, way beyond the capacity of any lay person or any self-represented litigant to understand or negotiate, while at the same time it has become steadily more extreme in its intent to demonise men, abolish the patriarchy and destroy the traditional concept of fatherhood.

Notions of the importance of fathers in their children's lives and the idea that fathers should have a say in the family law that impoverishes them and their children so drastically have been washed away.

The failure to reform the family law jurisdiction and to remedy the many injustices being perpetrated under its enveloping framework truly has truly been a failure of democracy itself. For nobody in the public, and none of the millions of people so negatively impacted, voted to have this travesty visited upon them.

At the end of the Long March Through The Institutions lies a travesty, a graveyard of human decency, a triumph of bureaucratic insanity, and a heartless abuse of the nation's citizenry.

It is a city of the dead full of the gravestones of people who have fought the good fight. For this is what defeat looks like. Many fought the good fight and all were defeated. It is a devastation of the human spirit

Thousands of hours of volunteer work, literally thousands of submissions and thousands of representations and protestations by individuals and family law reform groups to politicians and to all the various inquiries, all have been ignored.

***

The violence card has been played, and it won the game. A Royal Flush. As Dads On The Air said so long ago, the liars, the lawyers, the bureaucrats and the social engineers have won the day.

Fifty years of ferment, debate, inquiries, bureaucratic obfuscation and the expenditure of millions upon millions of dollars, all that effort from so many people, the thousands of hours that volunteers hoped would succeed in family law reform. All of it was for nothing.

The many hundreds of unpaid hours we all poured into Dads On The Air at the cusp of the millennium, all of it came up against an unbeatable machine, a wave of taxpayer funded propaganda, Marx inspired male bashing, deliberately promoted moral panic, mission bent bureaucracies as the government continued on its harmful, family destroying ways.

Having won the ear of government, having won the day on simplistic ideological notions of destroying the patriarchy, the traditional family and toxic masculinity, Australia's social justice are left in their own self-contradictory quagmires at the End of the Long March.

They're not happier, they're not more fulfilled, their souls are more derelict, the society is more troubled, faith in government is approaching zero, and cap in hand, we approach the revolution.

For at the core of any revolution is a large body of underemployed, underappreciated males.

The Marxist feminist derived ideology which has driven the Family Law Act, the Family Court and the Child Support Agency enmeshed with the education system has inexorably led to a totalitarian outcome. Step by terrible step.

In a totalitarian society, traditional family structures face significant erosion as the state seeks to supplant familial loyalty with loyalty to the regime through indoctrination and policies that prioritise state needs over family bonds.

Personal and familial privacy is frequently invaded. State control over marriage, reproduction, and child-rearing practices transforms the family from a natural social unit into an instrument for state propaganda and control.

The abuses the Australian government has meted out to the citizenry over the past 50 years defies belief. What is morally indefensible is the failure to act on the part of those who were in a position to do so, those who held the political power and could have actually wrought positive change to this wretched jurisdiction.

Abandon all hope, ye who enter here.

John Stapleton

***

Totalitarianism is a political system where the state holds total authority over all aspects of public and private life, exerting control through a single political party or ideology, and often employing surveillance, propaganda, and suppression of dissent to enforce compliance. It aims to completely subsume individual rights and freedoms to the collective will or state power, typically eliminating any form of opposition or alternate sources of power, such as that which lies within the traditional family structure.

In a totalitarian society, children's minds are often subjected to intense indoctrination, where education and propaganda are used to instil loyalty to the state and its ideology, often suppressing critical thinking and individual identity in favour of conformity. Children are systematically isolated from alternative viewpoints, with their development focused on service to the state rather than personal growth or family values.

This can lead to a generation that, while unified in its adherence to the regime, may lack the ability to think independently or question authority, potentially suffering from fear, paranoia, a fragmented sense of self, without natural affection.

The vicious abuses meted out by the family law industry and the encouragement of false or highly exaggerated claims of violence in order to remove a father from his home, his children, his assets, his superannuation and a lot more is in itself an extreme form of violence.

The moral stain of what the Australian state has done, and continues to do, heard in the culture as a ripple of disturbed kids and sad dads and damaged family members rarely surfaces onto the public record, rarely making it into the nation's media or into the government reports churned out by bureaucrats intent on protecting the family law industry.

Many of the major players in the fathers' rights movement which flourished in the early 2000s in Australia have gone, including the umbrella organisation the Shared Parenting Council of Australia and the very active Lone Fathers Association of Australia. Their websites, which contained a good deal of history, have also been closed down. A casual observer would have no idea that there had ever even been an Australian movement exposing the many injustices perpetrated by the nation's family law and child support systems, almost as if they have been deliberately scrubbed from the internet. The situation is reminiscent of that famous observation, he who controls the present controls the past.

This book is just a small effort to try and set the record straight. Here at the end of the Long March. In my view it is now demonstrably true: Australia has the worst family law system in the Western world.

POSTSCRIPT

I couldn't face writing this book at home. If nothing else, for the sake of my blood pressure. It was too complex, too emotionally telling, and the multiple injustices and government sleights of hand over so many years simply too outrageous. So I drove 800 kilometres north to sit at the dining room table of Sue Price, who I had known at this stage for some 25 years.

She and her husband Reg had set up the unfashionably named Men's Rights Agency some 40 years before after noticing how badly some of their employees in their tyre business were impacted by the rigours of the Family Court.

She is now 79 years old, in a wheelchair after an accident in the home, and recently bereaved after Reg, the love of her life, passed away. To add to things, her beloved doberman also passed away not so long ago.

The Men's Rights Agency is essentially in retirement. It maintains a website, but doesn't advertise or promote itself.

Nonetheless, the phone rings constantly. Confused, damaged and heartbroken fathers bewildered by the ferocity of the court and child protection systems stigmatising them ring up scandalised by the way they have been treated.

She takes these calls, mostly men who ring up nervously before spilling their story, but also sometimes women, friends, mothers, sisters, concerned about the welfare of a male in their lives and equally outraged by their mistreatment.

While the Australian government is spending upwards of $60 billion on the National Disability Insurance Scheme, and billions of dollars on women's advocacy groups, no money, or virtually no money, goes to addressing men's concerns.

Sue is Unpaid. Not a shred of public money comes her way. Yet community groups, some of them government funded, send clients her way. She listens to them, quite likely the first time they've even had a sympathetic ear. Assures them they are not alone and assures them that the treatment they have endured is by no means unusual. Tries to put some steel into their shattered spines and offers some common sense advice.

As I assemble this book, I can't help but overhear some of the people calling in. Often enough I hear the phrase: "I've been stitched up." No doubt they have.

***

Here's a sampling of some of the stories passing across Sue's desk.

One Queensland farmer whose wife decided she wanted to become a professional and live in town. He paid for her university degree. She pressured him to sell the farm for the property settlement. Unfortunately the young adult son, when he saw his future disappear, took a gun and shot himself in the head. He lost his farm. He lost his son. The father was destroyed. He rang for advice on how to find a solicitor after the woman continued to push for the property development.

Another, a young man with a three year old toddler, the mother didn't want him to have any contact at all. He took it into court. He was successful. The mother was denied contact and had to hand the little one over to dad. The day before she was due to hand over the child she gassed herself and the child. So instead of the child arriving on Sunday morning, the police were standing on the doorstep telling him he had lost his son.

He arranged a funeral for his son, and the mother's family decided they were going to continue to sue him over a property development. And then said they would drop the lawsuit if he exhumed the boy's body and interned it with the mother. He was devastated, of course.

In another case, the father was trying to get every service to act. The mother was off with some new boyfriend. They finally found her with the boyfriend, the boy was in a box, with cigarette burns all over him. He went back down south. That was a horrific story.

Another, Sue recalls, had his twin boys on a holiday. They were so unhappy. They didn't want to go back to mum. They were about 12-years-old. He worked into the workshops, saw one of the boys hanging from a beam. If Dad hadn't walked in at that specific moment, the kid would have died.

One father writes that it doesn't matter how much evidence he provides about his former partner's violent conduct, "a simple lie from her which I have factual evidence proving it wrong is believed".

"Cheating, lying, manipulation and gaslighting with facts and evidence is not enough but her statement is enough. So let's all understand men are by default the perpetrators for family violence no matter what the facts, children or witnesses say."

Another father, Sue recalls, with a Russian wife, was charged with breach of an Domestic Violence Order. He worked as a flying instructor and was accused of flying over her house while he was instructing a client how to fly an ultralight. The student was flying. In a country town, the woman recognised the plane. He spent two months in jail. His appeals failed. He closed his business, lost his house, packed up and moved to the Philippines. He couldn't bear to stay in Australia any longer. His son now lives with him.

Another father rings up three years after he separated: "My ex-wife has decided to levy false family violence accusations towards me, forcing mediation and making me unable to see my children except through supervised visits that she knows I cannot afford.

"This crap seemingly out of the blue. I'm not violent or threatening, I have no record of violent history at all either personally or legally. I've recently become unemployed due to a knee injury and rehabilitation for such. I'm living in shared accommodation, desperate for work. It's been a month since I've seen or heard from them, I used to see them five times a week on facetime and whenever I was allowed to see them in person.

"I'm worried I'm just being manipulated by money and the legal system now just as I was during our whole relationship and I just want to see my kids. I want nothing to do with the mother and have only ever been thankful and polite to her. I just don't get why I'm copping this."

Another: The mother died when the child was young and she had lived with the father for the previous eight years. He made a complaint to the school about her child not being protected from bullying. He believes the teacher then got upset and vengefully reported him to Child Safety. They investigated and took his daughter off him. In the process they determined that the child was Aboriginal, yet there was aboriginality whatsoever in the family. His daughter kept telling welfare officers she just wanted to go back home. As Sue recalls, the child was ultimately returned. Just another tortuous stuff up."

Another. The child had a mental health issue, probably ADHD. He wouldn't do his seat belt up and nobody was able to provide a solution for the father, who then got accused of not taking proper care of the child and Child Services got involved, leading to endless drama.

Another father has been trying to prove his innocence in the Magistrates Court against a domestic violence order. The problem he has is that he cannot get a hearing. He has had over 15 adjournments. The same problem is apparent for many fathers trying to prosecute an order against the ex partner. The Courts will not allow these claims to proceed.

One man, once professionally successful and with millions in assets, says he has been driven to the brink. While now on Centrelink Payments, Child Support was still basing his calculations on an income of $160,000 a year. He was plunging yet further and further into debt. "I have lost almost everything including my home, my children, my job, my health, most of my 35 years of super and yet the other parent is being rewarded for bad behaviour and lies. Child Support has been ruthless and non-evidenced based."

Another father reports: I am deeply concerned about the well-being and legal rights of my three children, which are currently being violated due to a grave miscarriage of justice within our family court system. Since March 2018, judicial officers have disregarded family law and human rights conventions, leading to my children's lives being turned upside down. They've been subjected to emotional, mental, and physical abuse, contrary to their expressed wishes and needs, all under the guise of judicial orders that lack legal grounding or evidential support.

All the cases are messy. And in every last case the authorities have made the situation worse.

It's a ceaseless tide, this Marxist inspired carnage, this destruction of the so-called patriarchy, that is, men – fathers, lovers, brothers and sons.

Anyone who thinks the system is working for the betterment of the society as a whole needs their head read. Apologists for this level of bastardry and dysfunction are all government funded, to the tune of billions of dollars annually.

They should all have their funding cut. Then you might see a bit of reality and human decency creeping back into the system. You wouldn't find a single one of the public servants who have helped perpetuate this fiasco taking calls at all hours, listening to the human side of the carnage they have propagated, the damage and heartbreak they have inflicted on so many individuals. And on Australia as a whole.

ACKNOWLEDGEMENTS

This book has many fathers; and quite a significant number of mothers. Many people contributed directly or indirectly to this book, either through their initial work with Dads On The Air in the early 2000s, or through their continued advocacy in the years that followed.

In particular I would like to thank Sue Price of the Men's Rights Agency, a tireless campaigner for gender equality. While now in her late 70s, she's the one who to this day fields a steady stream of calls from fathers pouring out their disbelief over the rampant dishonesty of family report writers, child protection officers and many of the other characters and institutions circling family law.

She made her home available for the writing of this book, bought ink and paper, hunted down pieces of information as a de facto researcher, and provided encouragement.

Rick Torning aka Uncle Buck was one of the co-founders of Dads On The Air, and the man who originally invited me to join Dads On The Air. As such, this book would never have happened without him.

Rod Hardwick, originally of Dads Australia and one of the co-founders of DOTA, was also vital in the development of the project.

David Hardidge read the final manuscript and was extremely helpful with the footnoting and research.

Ian Purdie, who also poured hundreds of volunteer hours into Dads On The Air as a co-presenter, panel operator and music programmer. As a musician he brought a great deal of energy and passion to the program, providing a non-academic breath of fresh hair into an arena crowded with the betrayals of the credentialed class, academic poseurs and privileged, sanctimonious, intellectually shallow bureaucrats.

Peter van de Voorde, who we called Rockin' Pop, poured many hundreds of hours into Dads On The Air as a co-presenter, administrator, researcher and music programmer. We played much of his album *Our Stolen Children* as musical interludes. His book *Children of the State: Stolen for Profit* was a significant contribution to literature of the fatherhood movement.

Lindsay Jackel, provided information and news sourcing and website support. His online journal Nuance provided a constant provider of the latest news and academic studies since the show began in 2000.

Greg Andresen, researcher and co-presenter, did an excellent job creating a new and more modern web site and lent considerable credibility to the program through his rigorous academic work and in his role with Men's Health Australia.

Warwick Marsh from the Fatherhood Foundation and later Fathers4Kids was a significant supporter of the program and later was helpful in promoting this book.

John Flanagan from the Non-Custodial Parents Party and the Fairness in Child Support did countless hundreds of hours attempting to reform the system, and was a significant contributor to the program and to this book.

Phil York from Dads In Distress was also an invaluable addition to the show, and thereby, indirectly, to the successful publication of this project.

Geoffrey Greene, President of the Shared Parenting Council of Australia, was also a major supporter of Dads On The Air and thanks to his political connections saw many of the major players of the day come on the program. Both he and some of the people he brought us in touch with are quoted extensively.

One of the founding legends of the fatherhood movement, the recently deceased Barry Williams from the Lone Fathers Association, was a major supporter of the program and is also referred to in this book.

Tony Miller from Dads In Distress was also a frequent guest on the program and thereby contributed to this publication.

President of the Shared Parenting Council of Australia Ed Dabrowski was also a frequent contributor to DOTA and thereby to this book.

Barrister and author of *Fathers After Divorce* Michael Green was an important early supporter of the program and is referenced.

Other supporters and contributors included Yuri Joakimidis from the Joint Parenting Association, Mark Bourne from the Richard Hillman Foundation and James Adams from Fathers4Equality.

It was telling that amongst academics who have come on the show, the University of Western Sydney was the only dedicated men's study unit, the Men's Health and Information Resource Centre. John MacDonald and Michael Woods, both supporters of the program and thereby to this narrative, lent academic credibility to the enterprise.

All of these people have worked hard to expose one of the greatest injustices in Australian society and deserve to be recognised for their contribution.

Others include the politician Ken Ticehurst, Alison Pearce from Second Wives, Lionel Richards, a friend to many during the long nights, Malcolm Matthias of

Fathers for Equity, Ray Lenton, who contributed a great deal to DOTA over a number of years, and Ibid for Phil York of Dads In Distress.

And my apologies to anyone I've inadvertently overlooked in the rush to complete this text.

ABOUT THE AUTHOR

John Stapleton was born in the Australian town of Bangalow on the New South Wales north coast on 21 June 1952. The first money he ever made out of writing was in 1974 when he was co-winner of a short story competition held by what was then Australia's leading cultural celebration, the Adelaide Arts Festival.

He graduated from Macquarie University in 1975 with a double major in philosophy and anthropology and did post-graduate work with the Sociology Department at Flinders University.

As a freelance journalist in the 1970s and 1980s, while alternating between living in Sydney and London, his articles and fiction appeared in a wide range of magazines, newspapers and anthologies, including *The Australian Financial Review* and the now defunct *Bulletin*.

After a period as a casual, John Stapleton worked on *The Sydney Morning Herald* as a staff news reporter between 1986 and 1994. The paper was then listed as one of the Top 20 newspapers in the world.

He worked for the national newspaper *The Australian* from 1994 until the end of 2009.

His books include: *Thailand: Deadly Destination*, *Terror in Australia: Workers' Paradise Lost*, *Hideout in the Apocalypse*, *Dark Dark Policing*, *Unfolding Catastrophe: Australia* and *Australia Breaks Apart*.

As a news reporter, Stapleton encountered and wrote literally thousands of stories about everyone from street alcoholics to Australian Prime Ministers; from the staple flood, drought, fire and natural disasters of the Australian bush to scenes of urban dysfunction.

In 2000 he joined a small group of separated dads at 2GLF in western Sydney and helped to found Dads On The Air, now the world's longest running fathers radio program. Over the next nine years he spent many hundreds of hours keeping the then struggling program alive.

He currently edits *A Sense of Place Magazine*.

He is the proud father of two professionally successful adult children who, as he likes to say, have done very well despite their parents.

www.ingramcontent.com/pod-product-compliance
Lightning Source LLC
Chambersburg PA
CBHW061732070526
44585CB00024B/2643